THE JEWISH PEOPLE'S ALMANAC

OTHER BOOKS BY DAVID C. GROSS

PRIDE OF OUR PEOPLE

1,001 QUESTIONS AND ANSWERS ABOUT JUDAISM

A DICTIONARY OF THE JEWISH RELIGION (ED.),
with Ben Isaacson

LOVE POEMS FROM THE HEBREW (ED.)

SHALOM CALENDAR FOR YOUNG PEOPLE

EDITED AND TRANSLATED BY DAVID C. GROSS

ONE HUNDRED CHILDREN
by Lena Kuchler-Silberman

THE HUNTER
by Tuviah Friedman

THE
JEWISH PEOPLE'S
ALMANAC

David C. Gross

HIPPOCRENE BOOKS
New York

For Esther

Revised edition, 1994.

Hippocrene paperback edition, 1988.

Copyright © 1981 by David C. Gross

For information, address
Hippocrene Books, Inc.
171 Madison Avenue
New York, NY 10016

Library of Congress Cataloging in Publication Data
Main entry under title:

The Jewish people's almanac

   Includes index.
   1. Jews—Miscellanea.   2. Judaism—Miscellanea.
I. Gross, David C., 1923–
DS102.4.J43   909'.04924
ISBN 0-87052-583-2

Printed in the United States of America.

Contributors

Beth Zion Abrahams	BZA	Michael Checinski	MC
Herbert H. Adise	HHA	Shneor Z. Cheshin	SZC
Morris Adler	MAd	Arthur A. Chiel	AAC
Herbert Agar	HA	Chaim Chissin	CCh
Gershon Ahituv	GA	David Civval	DC
William Aiken	WA	Ida G. Cowen	IGC
Marc D. Angel	MDA	Abraham Cronbach	ACr
Rachel Arad	RA		
Marcus Arkin	MA	Lucy S. Davidowicz	LSD
C. C. Aronsfeld	CCA	S. Dagoni	SD
Martin Ashery	MAs	Rachel Dalven	RD
		Sammy Davis, Jr.	SDa
Yomtov Ludwig Bato	YLB		
Jacob Beller	JB	Andy Edelstein	AE
Nathan C. Belth	NCB	David Max Eichhorn	DME
David Ben-Gurion	DB-G	Albert Einstein	AEi
Joseph Israel Benjamin II	JIB	Isaac Ben Eliakim	IBE
Rahel Yanait Ben-Zvi	RYB-Z	Lili Eylon	LE
Lena Pearlstein Berkman	LPB	Harry A. Ezratty	HAE
Ted Berkman	TB		
Obadiah Yareh da		Abraham J. Feldman	AJF
Bertinoro	OYDB	Trude B. Feldman	TBF
Henry V. Besso	HVB	Norman Fendell	NF
Lisa Palmieri-Billig	LP-B	Charles Fenyvesi	CF
Patricia Blake	PB	Walter J. Fischel	WJF
Kurt Kaiser-Blueth	KK-B	A. J. Fischer	AJFi
Bernard Blumenkranz	BB	Abraham H. Foxman	AHF
Louis Brandt	LB	Solomon B. Freehof	SBF
S. Braum	SB		
E. M. Broner	EMB	Ben Gallob	BG
Leah Bronner	LBro	Moshe Geller	MG
Reuben S. Brookes	RSB	Daniel Gerson	DG
		Eli Ginzberg	EG
Abraham Carmel	AC	Samuel Glasner	SGl
Saul Carson	SC	Philip Goodman	PG
Gloria Charnes	GC	Benjamin L. Gordon	BLG

Solomon Grayzel	SGr	Franz Landzberger	FL
Martin Greenfield	MGr	Sam Lazar	SL
Alice M. Greenwald	AMG	Ruth P. Lehmann	RPL
David C. Gross	DCG	Arthur Lelyveld	AL
Kurt R. Grossman	KRG	Diane Lerner	DL
Max Grunewald	MGru	Elenore Lester	EL
Martin Gumpert	MGu	Meyer Levin	ML
		Gabriel Levenson	GL
A. M. Haberman	AMH	Henry W. Levy	HWL
Devora and Menahem		Dulcy Liebler	DLi
Hacohen	D-MH	Seymour B. Liebman	SBL
Stuart Hanau	SH	Ezekiel Lifschutz	ELi
Hugh Harris	HH	Oscar M. Lifschutz	OML
Ben Hecht	BH	Inez Marks Lowdermilk	IML
Leo Heiman	LH	Zivia Lubetkin	ZL
Sondra Henry	SHe		
Nat Hentoff	NH	Jacob R. Marcus	JRM
Joseph J. Hertz	JJH	Edward Trueblood Martin	ETM
Richard C. Hertz	RCH	Amichai Mazar	AM
Shmuel Himelstein	SHi	R. Meinertzhagen	RM
Martin Hoffman	MH	Adina Michaeli	AMi
Edith Lynn Hornick	ELH		
		Joseph Nedava	JN
Lynne Ianniello	LI	Matthew Nesvisky	MN
Rudolph Iltis	RI	Isaac Neuman	INe
		Aryeh Newman	AN
Immanuel Jacobovits	IJ		
Louis Jacobs	LJ	Geoffrey Paul	GP
Monty Jacobs	MJ	W. Gunther Plaut	WGP
Joseph A. Joel	JAJ	Tiberio Porges	TP
Robert St. John	RSJ	Bernard Postal	BP
		Harold Preece	HP
Benzion C. Kaganoff	BCK		
Jacqueline Kahanoff	JK	Elias H. Rabinowitz	EHR
Shabtai Kaplan	SK	Louis I. Rabinowitz	LIR
Abraham I. Katsh	AIK	Yanetz Rammgal	YR
John F. Kennedy	JFK	Ch. W. Reines	CWR
Ralph Kolodny	RK	Harold Reinhart	HR
Bertram W. Korn	BWK	Ernest Renan	ER
Meyer Kramer	MK	Harold U. Ribalow	HUR
James Kraus	JKr	Louis Richman	LR

Cecil Roth	CR	Sefton D. Temkin	SDT
Burton S. Rudman	BSR	Saul I. Teplitz	SIT
Benjamin Rush	BR	Edward L. Tepper	ELT
		Marvin Tokayer	MT
Edward T. Sandrow	ETS	Leo Tolstoy	LT
Hayyim Schauss	HS	Harry S. Truman	HST
Barry D. Schwartz	BDS	Mark Twain	MTw
Charles and Bertie G.		David Twersky	DT
Schwartz	C-BGS		
Ruth Seligman	RS	Elijah de Veah	EDV
Hyman Shapiro	HSh		
Lynn Sharon	LS	Allen A. Warsen	AAW
		Gideon Weigert	GW
Abba Hillel Silver	AHS	Reska Gertl Weiss	RGW
Baruch Silverstein	BSi	Martin M. Weitz	MMW
Isaac Bashevis Singer	IBS	Frederick E. Werbell	FEW
K. Jason Sitewell	KJS	Eliezer Whartman	EW
Philip Slomovitz	PS	Maxwell Whiteman	MW
Walter Sneader	WS	Otto Wolfgang	OW
Elsa A. Solender	EAS	Rochelle S. Wolk	RSW
Elijah Ben Solomon	EBS		
Herman Spector	HSp	Yehuda Yaari	YY
Irving Spiegel	IS	Richard Yaffe	RY
Samuel Spiegler	SS	Sam Yurman	SY
Bea Stadtler	BSt		
Ezra Stiles	ES	Leon M. Zeldis	LMZ
Samuel S. Strouse	SSS	Sybil Zimmerman	SZ
David M. Szonyi	DMS		
Emily Taitz	ET		
Paul Tentler	PT		

ACKNOWLEDGMENTS

Part I: America: Sweet Land of Liberty
"So Who Really Discovered America?" *Jewish Digest*, April 1966. "Jewish Influence on the Framing of the Constitution," *Pioneer Woman*, April 1976. "America: 1791," *Pioneer Woman*, December 1974. "The Oldest Synagogue in America," *Judaica Post*, May–June 1979. "A Gentile's Reaction to a Jewish Wedding in Philadelphia in 1787," *Publications, American Jewish Historical Society* (vol. 42, part 2). "When George Washington Slept in a Jewish Home," *The Light* [Temple Israel, Great Neck, N.Y.], November 1979. "Voyage to America: Eleven Weeks on a 'Sail Ship'" (original title: "A Tragic Voyage"), *American Jewish Archives*, April 1979. "Jewish Names on the Map of the U.S.," *Jewish Digest*, June 1957. "The Synagogue with a Secret Tunnel," *The Light*, Spring 1979. "When Ulysses S. Grant Ordered the Expulsion of All Jews," *The Light* [Temple Israel, Great Neck, N.Y.], Spring 1979. "Harvard's President, in the 1920s, Insisted on Need to Restrict Jewish Student Body," *A Promise to Keep: A Narrative Encounter with Anti-Semitism*, by Nathan C. Belth. Times Books, 1979. "How the First Jewish Chaplain Got into the U.S. Army," Jewish Telegraphic Agency Features, 1961. "When American Jews Refused to Be Second-class Citizens." *Jewish Digest*, December 1961. "Trial by Prejudice: The Leo Frank Case," *ADL Bulletin*, March 1963. "A Sukkah: Courtesy of U.S. Army Engineers" (original title: "Sukkah in Bavaria"), *Sukkot and Simhat Torah Anthology*, Jewish Publication Society, 1973; originally published in *Jewish Life*, October 1958. "It Couldn't Have Happened in Russia," *Jewish Digest*, August 1961. "Father Coughlin and the Jews," *Journal of Jewish Communal Service;* reprinted in *Jewish Digest*, March 1978. "When the Shofar Blew on Capitol Hill." Yeshiva University news release, 1966. "The Sonneborn Institute: An Incredible Chapter in American Jewish History," *Congress Monthly*, February 1978. "The Last Synagogue in Harlem," *Jewish Week*, June 24, 1979. "Jews in the American Economy," *Jewish Life in America: Historical Perspectives*, published by the American Jewish Committee, 1978. "Ten-Gallon Hats with a Yiddish Accent," Jewish Telegraphic Agency Features, 1979.

Part II: Laws, Customs, Practices—and Superstitions
"Law and Order in Ancient 'Torah Israel,'" *Jewish Digest*, October 1961. "How to Make Kosher Steam," *Journal of Jewish Communal Service*, 1978. "Pendant or Amulet?" *Women's League Outlook*, Spring 1979. "Why Jews *Shokel* at Prayer," *Jewish Digest*, July 1966. "Heirloom of History: Origin of the Menorah," *National Jewish Monthly*, September 1956. "The Oath in Judaism," *Tears and Laughter in an Israeli Courtroom*, Jewish Publication Society © 1959. "The Debate Over Machine-made Matzot," *The Passover Anthology*, Jewish Publication Society © 1961. "Floggings Before Yom Kippur," *Pioneer Woman*, September 1976. "The Origin of the *Mezuzah* and Its Decorations," *Hebrew Union College Annual*, vol. 31. "Origins of the Ancient Rite of Circumcision," *The Light* [Temple Israel, Great Neck, N.Y.], September 1975. "Please Forgive Me!" *Messenger* [Temple Emanu-El, Brooklyn, N.Y.], undated. "Some Enduring Jewish Superstitions and Customs," *Jewish Recorder* [Birmingham, England], September 1962. "The Ninth Day of Av: A Black Day for the Jews," World Zionist Organization [Jerusalem] Press Service, 1979. "How the Haggadah Came to Be." Jewish Telegraphic Agency Features, 1962. "A Burial That Saves Lives: Incident in Morocco," *L'Arche* [Paris], undated. "Demons and Spirits in Jewish Tradition," *Hebrew Medical Journal*, 1964. "In Yemen, *Shofar* Was Blown When Worshipers Marched Around Synagogue on Simhat Torah" and "Why Bukharan Jews Used to Remain Indoors on Hoshanah Rabbah," *One People: The Story of the Eastern Jews*, Sabra Books, 1969.

Part III: Turning Back the Clock: A Look into History
"When *Etrogim* Pelted the High Priest," *Jewish Digest*, October 1979. "Jewish Life Two

Millennia Ago," *The Lifetime of a Jew*, Union of American Hebrew Congregations ©
1950 (original title: "In the First Centuries c.e."). "How Jews Made a Living in the
Early Roman Empire," *Jewish Affairs* [Johannesburg], September 1961. "What Hap-
pened to King Solomon's Treasure?" *Jewish Digest*, August 1962. "Jewish Fund-raising
Three Thousand Years Ago," Jewish Theological Seminary press release. "Early Medical Knowledge Among the Ancient Hebrews," *Hebrew Medical Journal*, 1957. *"Kiddush
Hashem* in a Castle in York," *The Light* [Temple Israel, Great Neck, N.Y.], Fall 1976.
"Benjamin of Tudela's Fantastic Twelfth-Century Book," *Jewish Digest*, May 1963.
"Jewish Buccaneers and the Spanish Main," *National Jewish Monthly*, July–August
1962. "When Spain Expelled the Jews in 1492," *The Jew in the Medieval World*, Union
of American Hebrew Congregations. "Sabbath Among the Arabian Jews in the Fif-
teenth Century," *Miscellany of Hebrew Literature*, London, 1872. "Witness to a
Pogrom," *Middle Eastern Diary, 1917–1956*, London, Cresset Press, 1959. "Jews Have
Had Their Share of False Messiahs," *Jewish Week*, December 10, 1978. "The Jew Who
Was King of Poland for a Day," *Jewish Digest*, October 1961. "How the Marranos
Settled in Amsterdam," *Jewish Digest*, October 1960. "The Foiled Assassin: One Jew
Tried and Failed to Kill Hitler in 1938," *Jewish Week*, August 7, 1977. "Napoleon:
Champion of Jewish Rights," *Revista Familiar Israelia del Uruguay* [Montevideo]; trans-
lated by Annabelle Sinai, *Jewish Digest*, September 1956. "When Palestine Was in
Ashes," *Pioneer Woman*, April 1976.

Part IV: The Bible: The Jew's Contribution to Civilization
"The Eternal Book," *Congress Bulletin* [Montreal], November 1963. "Bibletown: What
It Was Like," pamphlet of UAHC Commission on Information About Judaism. "Economics in the Bible," *Aspects of Jewish Economic History*, Jewish Publication Society
© 1975. "The Making of the Bible," *Bulletin* [Temple Beth El, Detroit], undated. "The
Bible and Talmud Understood and Regulated Laws of Ecology," Jewish National Fund
press release. "Exodus from Egypt," *The Light* [Temple Israel, Great Neck, N.Y.],
Spring 1975. "The Eternal Language of the Prophets," *Concepts, Critiques and Comments: Wide and Varied*, edited by Bern Dibner and Murray Rubien, privately printed,
1976. "In Biblical Days, Farmers Were Protected from Becoming Landless Serfs," *Aspects of Jewish Economic History*, Jewish Publication Society © 1975. "Jewish Law Is
Being Transformed from 'Messianic' to 'Operative,'" Jewish National Fund press
release. "Second Only to the Bible," *The World of the Talmud*. Bnai Brith Hillel Foundation series.

Part V: Holidays, Festivals, Weddings: Now and Then
"Shavuoth Services in Newport, R.I., May 28, 1773," *The Literary Diary of Ezra Stiles*,
Scribner, 1901. "Civil War Seder." *Jewish Messenger*, March 30, 1866. "Holy Days in
the Holy City," *Pioneer Woman*, September 1977. "Hanukkah in a Monastery," *American Judaism*, Winter 1963–64. "The Purim Mysteries," *Purim Anthology*, Jewish Publication Society © 1949. "The Dancing Jews of Brooklyn," *The Reporter*, September
1959. "A New Suit for Rosh Hashanah," *Jewish Week*, September 6, 1976. "Fasting on
Yom Kippur Saved a Soldier's Life," *Jewish Digest*, September 1977. "Samaritan Passover: Ancient Rites on Mount Gerizim," *Hadassah* magazine, May 1964. "Holy Days in
Faraway Places," *Pioneer Woman*, September 1976. "Shavuoth at the Tomb of the
Prophet Nahum," *Eight Years in Asia and Africa from 1846 to 1855* (originally published in Hanover, 1859; reprinted in *The Shavuoth Anthology*, Jewish Publication Soci-
ety, 1974). "A Passover Seder in a Women's Prison," *Jewish Week*, April 15, 1979.
"Jews from Eight Countries Celebrated Seder in Communist China," *Jewish Week*, June
11, 1978. "Merrymakers at Jewish Weddings," *YIVO Annual of Social Science*, 1952.
"Bikkurim in Kibbutz Matzuba," *Shavuoth Sheaves*, JNF Youth Department, 1965.
"Pistol-Shooting Wedding in the Caucasus," *Jewish Encyclopedia*, 1905.

Part VI: Israel: "Land of Milk and Honey"—and Challenges Galore!
"Truman Had to Wait for Jewish State's Name Before Announcing Recognition," *Jew-
ish Week*, May 17, 1978. "A Happy Man in an Israeli Village," *Pioneer Woman*,
January 1978. "My Faith in Israel's Future," address at Zionist Organization of America

convention, September 1959. "Why an Arab Farmer Brought a Bar Mitzvah Present," *Jewish Week*, July 31, 1977. "Memoirs of a Bilu Pioneer," *A Palestine Diary*, Herzl Press © 1976. "The Jewish Legion: A Turning Point in Modern Jewish History," *Pioneer Woman*, June 1977. "You Felt As a Partner in the Act of Creation," *Sound the Great Trumpet*, Whittier Books, 1955; reprinted in *Eyewitnesses to Jewish History*, UAHC © 1973. "Operation Magic Carpet," *I Flew Them Home*, Herzl Press. "Tel Aviv: 99 Percent of Its Citizens Are Jewish," World Zionist Organization Press Service, July 1979. "Egypt and Israel Were Once Military Allies," *Jewish Week*, April 1, 1979. "Bees in the Land of Milk and Honey," Features from Jerusalem, Israel Consulate-General, N.Y. "The Menu of Israel," World Zionist Organization [Jerusalem] Features. "The Rabbi Who Loves Soccer—Even on the Sabbath," *Israel* magazine [Tel Aviv], 1978. "Israel and the Single Girl," *Pioneer Woman*, September 1977. "A 'University to Evoke the Respect of Cultured Mankind,' " World Zionist Organization Press Service. "Time Stands Still in Safad," Jewish Telegraphic Agency Features, 1978. "Baseball Comes to Israel," *Hadassah* magazine, October 1979. "Israel's 'Mother of the Sons' Was Singled Out at White House Peace Ceremony," *Jewish Week*, April 8, 1979. "Israel's Wild Wheat," *Rehovot* [Weizmann Institute of Science], 1977.

Part VII: People: Whatever They Were, They Were Originals.
"Hernando Alonso, Conquistador: The First Jew on the North American Continent," *Journal of Inter-American Studies* [Univ. of Miami], April 1963. "When Dickens Apologized for the Character Fagin," *Ajax* [Cardiff, Wales], September 1964; reprinted in *Jewish Digest*, December 1964. "Harpo Marx and the Doorman," *1001 Afternoons in New York*, by Ben Hecht © 1941 by Viking Press, Inc.; © renewed 1969 by Rose Hecht; reprinted by permission of Viking Penguin Inc. "The Jew Who Saved the Chinese Revolution," *Jewish Digest*, September 1965. "A Yiddish-Speaking FBI Agent," *American Judaism*, Spring 1964. "The Rabbinical Sherlock Holmes," *Inside Detective*, April 1964. "The Incredible Saly Mayer" *The Saving Remnant*, by Herbert Agar © 1961 by Herbert Agar; reprinted by permission of Viking Penguin Inc. "Maimonides' Day," Story of the Jews of Spain, UAHC, 1974. "Humanity Was His Heir," *Jewish Digest*, February 1962. "The End of the House of Herzl," *Zionist Quarterly*; reprinted in *Jewish Digest*, May 1960. "My Favorite Hero: Commodore Uriah P. Levy," Message of Israel radio broadcast, 1959. "Albert Einstein, Jew," *Women's American ORT Reporter*, March–April 1979. "The Husid from New Hampshire," *Jewish Week*, January 9, 1977. "Israel's Musical Ambassador to the World," *Jewish Week*, August 12, 1979. "The Man Behind 'Hatikvah.' " *Detroit Jewish News*, undated. "First General in Army of Israel Since Judah Maccabee," *Hadassah* magazine, April 1962. "Reb Nachman Remained Silent for Forty Years," *Jewish Week*, June 12, 1977. "He Gave New Life to Two Hundred Victims of the Holocaust," *Jewish Week*, September 4, 1977. "The Rabbi Who Outlawed Polygamy Among Jews," *Jewish Affairs* [Johannesburg], June 1961. "Holocaust Survivor Behind the Wheel of a New York Taxicab," *Jewish Week*, March 12, 1978. "The Colonial Jewish Peddler," *Jewish Digest*, November 1964.

Part VIII: Holocaust: Amidst Darkness Some Rays of Light
"Miracle in Lyons," *Jewish Week*, March 25, 1979. "The Physicians of Warsaw," *Pioneer Woman*, June 1978; originally published in *American Scholar*, Summer 1949. "The Tattooed People," *Shdemot* [Tel Aviv], Spring 1975. "When Spain Rescued Jews from Hitler," *Jewish Digest*, May 1962. "How the Warsaw Ghetto Revolt Began," official transcript of the trial of Adolf Eichmann in Jerusalem, released by Israeli Government, 1963. "The German Who Personally Saved the Lives of Over 1,000 Jews," *Coronet*, September 1959; reprinted in *Jewish Digest*, January 1960. "I Was Buried Alive," *Jewish Affairs* [Johannesburg], 1959. "The Synagogue with 1,564 Sifrei Torah," *Jewish Digest*, February 1966; originally published in *Common Ground* [London], Winter, 1964. "The Strangest Encounter of My Life," *Israelitische Wochenblatt* [Zurich]. "A Visit to Ness Amim," *Pioneer Woman*, May 1976. "A German Officer Saved Us from the Nazis," *Jewish Digest*, March 1962. "The Blue Rug," *Jewish Digest*, May 1965. "How Rumkowski Died: A Holocaust Memoir," *Commentary*, May 1979. "A Polish Jew

Thanks the Polish Pope," Anti-Defamation League press release, 1979. "Vengeance or Justice? An Israeli Sailor Kills His Parents' Nazi Murderer," *Jewish Week*, January 8, 1978. "A Rabbi Saved Priests Who Earlier Had Saved Jews," *Jewish Digest*, January 1963. "Between Rosh Hashanah and Yom Kippur the Danes Saved Their Jews," *Jewish Week*, September 23, 1979. "Is Swedish Savior of 40,000 Jews Languishing in Siberia?" *Jewish Week*, April 15, 1979.

Part IX: The Precepts of the Jewish Way of Life
"Resurrection: A Jewish View," *Faith Through Reason*, Schocken Books—Women's League for Conservative Judaism. "The Least Difficult Way of Being Truly Human," address at 45th annual General Assembly, Council of Jewish Federations, Philadelphia. "A Jewish View on Homosexuality," *What Does Judaism Say About . . . ?* © Keter Publishing House, Jerusalem, 1973. "Rearing a Family Is the First of Judaism's 613 Mitzvot," *Authorized Daily Prayer Book*, Bloch Publishing Co., 1952. "What Is a Jew?" Reprinted from Tolstoy's collected works in *Jewish Digest*, October 1955. "Israel, Greece and Rome," from the collected works of Ernest Renan, 1887. "Even from Their Graves Fathers Sought to Impart Jewish Ethics," *The Light* [Temple Israel, Great Neck, N.Y.], June 1975. "Jewish Roots of Western Culture," *Pioneer Woman*, June 1978. "Chief Rabbi Kook Allowed Yom Kippur Desecration," Jewish National Fund press release, 1979. "Sexual Decency," *Where Judaism Differed*, Macmillan, 1956. " 'The Pill' and Jewish Law," *Jewish Law Faces Modern Problems*, Yeshiva University Studies in Torah Judaism series, 1965. "What Does Judaism Say About Astrology?" *What Does Judaism Say About . . . ?* © Keter Publishing House, Jerusalem, 1973.

Part X: Off the Beaten Track: Wandering Jews, Now and Then
"The Most Southerly Jewish Congregation on Earth," Jewish Telegraphic Agency Features, 1977. "The Jews of Jannina: An Ancient Community in Greece," *Sephardic Home News* [Brooklyn, N.Y.]. "How Should Jews Behave on the Moon?" *Jewish Digest*, February 1960. "Czechoslovakia's Jewish Treasures," *Jewish Spectator*, May 1963. "Adventurer Extraordinary: In Search of the Lost Ten Tribes," *Jewish Digest*, May 1963. "The Last Chinese Jew Is Hiding Out on Taiwan," *Jewish Week*, May 28, 1979. "The Jewish Slaves of Malta," translated by Annabelle Sinai, *Israelitische Wochenblatt* [Zurich], October 30, 1964. "Life and Death of the Jews of St. Eustatius," *Jewish Digest*, August 1962. "Mexico's Indian Jews," *Jewish Digest*, March 1961. "The Port of the Smiling Jews," *The Lookout* [Seaman's Institute], July 1959. "The Good Samaritans: Somehow They Have Survived," *Present Tense*, Summer 1979. "Incident in North Africa," *Pioneer Woman*, March 1976. "The Japanese Planned a Jewish State—in Manchuria," *Jewish Week*, May 20, 1979. "When a Jewish Kingdom Ruled Southern Russia," *Judaica Post* [Detroit], January–February 1962. "In Rome Jews Still Live in Ancient Ghetto," *Hadassah* magazine, vol. 59, no. 2. "The Proud Jews of Finland," *Women's League Outlook*, vol. 46, no. 4. "Are the American Indians a 'Lost' Tribe of Israel?" *Michigan Jewish History* [Detroit], undated; reprinted in *Jewish Digest*, July 1961.

Part XI: Women in Judaism and Jewish Women of Special Interest
"Jewish Women in Colonial Days," *Pioneer Woman*, September 1975. "Golfing with Golda and Ben-Gurion." Reprinted courtesy of Golf Digest Magazine. From the April 1977 issue. Copyright © 1981, Golf Digest/Tennis, Inc. "Jewish Women in Remote Corners of the World," *Pioneer Woman*, May 1976. "The Lady Physicist Who Dug Her Own Grave," *Jewish Week*, October 10, 1977. "A Sister's Daring Rescued Young Boy from Czarist Conscription," *Jewish Week*, October 22, 1978. "The Middle Ages: A Time of Growth and Education for Jewish Women" and "The *Agunah* and the Devoted Sister," *Written Out of History: A Hidden Legacy of Jewish Women Revealed through Their Writings and Letters*, Henry and Taitz © 1978, Bloch Publishing Co. "Life on a Fence," *ADL Bulletin*, 1960. "A Wedding in Cochin," *American Mizrachi Woman*, June 1979. "How a Mother Superior Defied the Church and Saved the Jews," *Jewish Digest*, December 1962. "The Bride Was Fourteen: Sephardic Weddings of Yesterday," translated by Annabelle Sinai, *Le Judaïsme Sephardi* [London], undated; reprinted in

Jewish Digest, May 1956. "Aftermath of the Holocaust: One Sister Married to Catholic, Another an Observant, Committed Jew," *Jewish Week*, September 30, 1979.

Part XII: On Learning, Language, and Literature
"There's More Hebrew in English Than You Realize," *Jewish Spectator*, November 1970. "A Forgotten Heritage: A Language Called Ladino," World Zionist Organization Press Service, September 1978. "Books for the People of the Book," *Israel Argosy*, Youth and Hechalutz Dept., World Zionist Organization, 1954. "How 'Kibbutz' Got Its Name," *Jewish Digest*, April 1979. "The Case of the Hidden Talmud," *Jewish Week*, July 24, 1977. "Hebrew Literary Treasures in the U.S.S.R.," *Jewish Digest*, August 1963. "Operation Parchment," *Congress Weekly*, 1955. "Four-letter Words in Jewish Literature," translated by Mirra Ginsburg, *Jewish Heritage*, Summer 1965. "Yeshivah of the Air," *Baltimore Jewish Times*, June 29, 1979. "Isolated from Mainstream of Jewry, Kurdistan Jews Produced Unique Literature," *Jewish Book Annual*, 1973–74. "Does More Education Mean Less Anti-Semitism?" *Science Looks at Anti-Semitism*, American Jewish Committee pamphlet, 1961.

Part XIII: Choosing Judaism: Converts and Penitents
"Why I Became a Jew," *Ebony* [Chicago] © Trude B. Feldman. "A Pool Hall Yeshiva," *Israel Digest*, 1978. "The Making and Unmaking of a Jewish Moonie," *National Jewish Monthly*, December 1978. "From Italian Playboy to Committed Jew." *Jewish Week*, October 2, 1977. "From Priest to Orthodox Jew," *Jewish Digest*, November 1961. "Some of the Best Jews Are Proselytes," *Jewish Week*, May 13, 1979. "The Western Wall: A Catalyst for Returnees," *Jewish Week*, September 3, 1979. "From Ashram to Yeshiva: Getting Your Head Together," *Present Tense*, Spring 1979. "With a Tallis I Can Die," *Reporter*, January 1961. "A Sefer Torah Bequeathed to a Nurse in Nebraska," *Jewish Week*, March 18, 1979. "Study Torah—and Get Free Karate Lesson," *Jewish Week*, February 3, 1979.

Part XIV: Some Points of Interest Around the World
"The Secret Jews of Iran," *Jewish Week*, October 14, 1979. "The Little Tailors' Synagogue," *Hadassah* magazine, March 1979. "Visiting Spanish Jewry," *Jerusalem Post*, 1978. "Journey to the Kingdom of Morocco," *National Jewish Monthly*, July–August 1978. "Jews in the Emerald Isle," *Jewish Chronicle* [London], April 4, 1979. "Jews in the Land of the Incas," *Jewish Frontier*, vol. 45, no. 1; reprinted in *Jewish Digest*, June 1978. "Jews in China: A Flourishing Community in the Twelfth Century," *Jewish Week*, December 24, 1978. "An Oriental Jewish Mystery: Case of the Nagasaki Cemetery," *United Synagogue Review*, April 1966; reprinted in *Jewish Digest*, August 1966. "The Hidden Synagogue of the Azores," *Jewish Chronicle* [Pittsburgh], 1966; reprinted in *Jewish Digest*, August 1966. "Jews in the Frozen North," translated by Annabelle Sinai, *Allgemeine Wochenzeitung* [Düsseldorf]; reprinted in *Jewish Digest*, December 1956.

Part XV: Mishmash: A Little of This and a Little of That
"A Christian Diplomat Offers Unique Interpretation of *Kashruth*," *Jewish Week*, June 10, 1979. "Jewish First Names Through the Ages," *Commentary*, 1955. "How the Mezuzah Got in the Church Compound," *Jewish Digest*, April 1965. "King Hezekiah's Tunnel: A Mystery to This Day," *Jewish National Fund Yearbook*, 1979. "Origins of Some Jewish Philanthropic Practices," Commission of Information About Judaism, UAHC–CCAR, 1965. "Tracking Down the Yarmulke," *Hebrew Union College Annual*, 1955. "The Torah That Was Rescued by a Chandelier," *Jewish Week*, August 5, 1979. "New York Once Had a Hebrew Daily," *Jewish Week*, July 1, 1979. "When Jews Quarrel," *Congress Monthly*, 1956. "The Dinghy Comes Home," *Jewish Affairs* [Johannesburg]. "The Mizrah: Compass of the Heart," *Hadassah* magazine, October 1979. "The Case of the Stolen Torah," *Tears and Laughter in an Israeli Courtroom*, Jewish Publication Society © 1959. "Jew, Go Home!" *Gazette-Telegraph* [Colorado Springs, Col.]; reprinted in *Jewish Digest*, June 1960. "The Rabbi and the Wafer," *Jewish Digest*, May 1965. "The Great Sturgeon Controversy," *The Responsa Literature*, Jewish Publication Society © 1955.

Preface

Judaism is a people's religion. It is distinct from other traditions in that it insists that every man, woman, and child personally participate in every aspect of life. The Bible teaches that the entire Jewish people is to be a holy people, in which each of its members assumes responsibility for one another. That is what makes this book a "people's almanac," a record of human events around the world and throughout history. Here are those special individuals, famous and obscure, who have illuminated the Jews' history, contributed to their culture, helped to weave the rich, often exciting, sometimes tragic fabric of experience called Judaism.

This volume is not designed to give the reader a basic knowledge of Jewish religion, history, or culture. For that one must study the classic works and apply oneself, for Jewish studies encompass thirty centuries of the wisdom and insight of the sages. There *is* something unique about the Jews, for what people has endured for so long, espousing such noble ideals and, despite pogroms, inquisitions, and crematoria, has managed to retain its humanity, its hope, its humor and, above all, its faith? To know and understand Judaism and the Jewish people is practically a lifelong pursuit, and the more one knows, it is said, the more one knows how little one knows!

The purpose of THE JEWISH PEOPLE'S ALMANAC is to introduce its readers to a panoply of little-known data about the Jewish people . . . information that is amusing, moving, or surprising, and that will, it is hoped, reinforce their commitment to the Jewish people's traditional reverence and love of life.

Contents

I America, Sweet Land of Liberty

So Who Really Discovered America? — 2
Jewish Influence on the Framing of the Constitution. — 3
America: 1791. — 5
The Oldest Synagogue in America. — 7
A Gentile's Reaction to a Jewish Wedding in Philadelphia
  in 1787. — 12
When George Washington Slept in a Jewish Home. — 13
Voyage to America: Eleven Weeks on a "Sail Ship." — 14
Jewish Names on the Map of the United States. — 16
The Synagogue with a Secret Tunnel. — 19
When Ulysses S. Grant Ordered the Expulsion of All Jews. — 21
Harvard's President, in the 1920s, Insisted on Need to
  Restrict Jewish Student Body. — 23
How the First Jewish Chaplain Got into the U. S. Army. — 26
When American Jews Refused to Be Second-class Citizens. — 28
Trial by Prejudice: The Leo Frank Case. — 30
A *Sukkah*, Courtesy of U. S. Army Engineers. — 32
It Couldn't Have Happened in Russia! — 34
Father Coughlin and the Jews. — 38
When the Shofar Blew on Capitol Hill. — 42
The Sonneborn Institute: An Incredible Chapter in
  American Jewish History. — 45
The Last Synagogue in Harlem. — 50
Jews in the American Economy. — 52
A Home Town I'll Never Know. — 56

II Laws, Customs, Practices—and Superstitions

Law and Order in Ancient "Torah Israel." — 60
How to Make Kosher Steam. — 62
Pendant or Amulet? — 63

Why Jews *Shokel* at Prayer. 66

Heirloom of History: Origin of the Menorah. 67

The Oath in Judaism. 70

The Debate Over Machine-made *Matzot*. 73

Floggings Before Yom Kippur. 74

The Origin of the *Mezuzah* and Its Decorations. 76

Origins of the Ancient Rite of Circumcision. 80

"Please Forgive Me!": An Old World Custom. 83

Some Enduring Jewish Superstitions and Customs. 84

The Ninth Day of Av: A Black Day for the Jews. 86

How the Haggadah Came to Be. 87

A Burial That Saves Lives: Incident in Morocco. 89

Demons and Spirits in Jewish Tradition. 92

In Yemen, *Shofar* Was Blown When Worshipers Marched Around Synagogue on Simhat Torah. 94

Why Bukharan Jews Used to Remain Indoors on Hoshanah Rabbah. 95

III   Turning Back the Clock: A Look into History

When *Etrogim* Pelted the High Priest. 98

Jewish Life Two Millennia Ago: A Son Is Born and a Cedar Is Planted. 99

How Jews Made a Living in the Early Roman Empire. 104

What Happened to King Solomon's Treasure? 108

Jewish Fund-raising Three Thousand Years Ago. 110

Early Medical Knowledge Among the Ancient Hebrews. 112

Kiddush Hashem in a Castle in York. 116

Benjamin of Tudela's Fantastic Twelfth-Century Book. 119

Jewish Buccaneers and the Spanish Main. 122

When Spain Expelled the Jews in 1492. 123

Sabbath Among the Arabian Jews in the Fifteenth Century. 125

Witness to a Pogrom. 126

Jews Have Had Their Share of False Messiahs. 127

The Jew Who Was King of Poland for a Day. 129

How the Marranos Settled in Amsterdam. 130

The Foiled Assassin: One Jew Tried and Failed to Kill
   Hitler in 1938. 132
Napoleon: Champion of Jewish Rights. 134
When Palestine Was in Ashes: Mark Twain's Bleak
   Report. 135

IV   The Bible: The Jew's Contribution to Civilization

The Eternal Book. 138
Bibletown: What It Was Like. 140
Economics in the Bible: Hard Work, Individual Freedom,
   Enterprise Were Encouraged. 147
The Making of the Bible. 152
The Bible and Talmud Understood and Regulated Laws of
   Ecology. 154
Exodus from Egypt: The Floods *Did* Stand "Straight Like a
   Wall." 157
The Eternal Language of the Prophets. 160
In Biblical Days, Farmers Were Protected from Becoming
   Landless Serfs. 168
Jewish Law Is Being Transformed from "Messianic" to
   "Operative." 172
Second Only to the Bible: The Story of the Mishna and Its
   Compiler. 174

V   Holidays, Festivals, Weddings: Now and Then

Shavuoth Services in Newport, R.I., May 28, 1773. 180
Civil War Seder. 181
Holy Days in the Holy City. 182
Hanukkah in a Monastery. 184
The Purim Mysteries. 186
The Dancing Jews of Brooklyn: A Simhat Torah Tableau. 189
A New Suit for Rosh Hashanah. 192
Fasting on Yom Kippur Saved a Soldier's Life. 194
Samaritan Passover: Ancient Rites on Mount Gerizim. 195

Holy Days in Faraway Places.   199
Shavuoth at the Tomb of the Prophet Nahum.   202
A Passover Seder in a Women's Prison.   204
Jews from Eight Countries Celebrated Seder in Communist
    China.   206
Merrymakers at Jewish Weddings.   207
Bikkurim in Kibbutz Matzuba.   210
Pistol-Shooting Wedding in the Caucasus.   211

VI Israel: "Land of Milk and Honey"— and Challenges Galore!

Truman Had to Wait for Jewish State's Name Before
    Announcing Recognition.   214
A Happy Man in an Israeli Village.   217
My Faith in Israel's Future.   221
Why an Arab Farmer Brought a Bar Mitzvah Present.   222
Memoirs of a Bilu Pioneer En Route to Palestine from Russia
    in 1882.   224
The Jewish Legion: A Turning Point in Modern Jewish
    History.   233
"You Felt As a Partner in the Act of Creation."   238
Operation Magic Carpet: Bringing Yemenite Jews to
    Israel.   240
Tel Aviv: 99 Percent of Its Citizens Are Jewish.   242
Egypt and Israel Were Once Military Allies.   244
Bees in the Land of Milk and Honey.   246
The Menu of Israel.   248
The Rabbi Who Loves Soccer—Even on the Sabbath.   249
Israel and the Single Girl.   253
A "University to Evoke the Respect of Cultured Mankind."   255
Time Stands Still in Safad.   256
Baseball Comes to Israel.   258
Israel's "Mother of the Sons" Was Singled Out at White
    House Peace Ceremony.   261
Israel's Wild Wheat.   262

VII   People: Whatever They Were, They Were Originals

Hernando Alonso, Conquistador: The First Jew on the
  North American Continent.   266
When Dickens Apologized for the Character Fagin.   269
Harpo Marx and the Doorman.   272
The Jew Who Saved the Chinese Revolution.   273
A Yiddish-Speaking FBI Agent.   277
The Rabbinical Sherlock Holmes.   278
The Incredible Saly Mayer.   284
Maimonides' Day.   286
Humanity Was His Heir.   288
Why Luther Turned Anti-Semite.   290
The End of the House of Herzl.   291
My Favorite Hero: Commodore Uriah P. Levy.   295
Albert Einstein, Jew.   297
The Hasid from New Hampshire.   301
Israel's Musical Ambassador to the World.   303
The Man Behind "Hatikvah."   306
First General in Army of Israel Since Judah Maccabee.   310
Reb Nachman Remained Silent for Forty Years.   313
He Gave New Life to Two Hundred Victims of the
  Holocaust.   316
The Rabbi Who Outlawed Polygamy Among Jews.   318
Holocaust Survivor Behind the Wheel of a New York
  Taxicab.   320
The Colonial Jewish Peddler.   322

VIII   Holocaust: Amidst Darkness Some Rays of Light

Miracle in Lyons: Congregants Stared and Nazis Retreated.   328
The Physicians of Warsaw.   329
The Tattooed People.   333
When Spain Rescued Jews from Hitler.   334
How the Warsaw Ghetto Revolt Began.   336
The German Who Personally Saved the Lives of Over One
  Thousand Jews.   339

I Was Buried Alive and Dreamt of Potatoes. 342
The Synagogue with 1,564 Sifrei Torah. 346
The Strangest Encounter of My Life. 349
A Visit to Ness Amim: A Christian Colony in Galilee. 351
A German Officer Saved Us from the Nazis. 355
The Blue Rug. 360
How Rumkowski Died: A Holocaust Memoir. 361
A Polish Jew Thanks the Polish Pope. 365
Vengeance or Justice? An Israeli Sailor Kills His Parents'
Nazi Murderer. 367
A Rabbi Saved Priests Who Earlier Had Saved Jews. 369
Between Rosh Hashanah and Yom Kippur the Danes Saved
Their Jews. 373
Is Swedish Savior of Forty Thousand Jews Languishing
in Siberia? 374

IX   The Precepts of the Jewish Way of Life

Resurrection: A Jewish View. 378
The Least Difficult Way of Being Truly Human. 379
A Jewish View on Homosexuality. 380
Rearing a Family Is the First of Judaism's 613 *Mitzvot*. 382
What Is a Jew? 383
Israel, Greece, and Rome. 384
Even from Their Graves Fathers Sought to Impart
Jewish Ethics. 384
The Jewish Roots of Western Culture. 387
Chief Rabbi Kook Allowed Yom Kippur Desecration for
Sake of Land. 389
Sexual Decency. 391
"The Pill" and Jewish Law. 393
What Does Judaism Say About Astrology? 395

X   Off the Beaten Track: Wandering Jews, Now and Then

The Most Southerly Jewish Congregation on Earth. 398
The Jews of Jannina: An Ancient Community in Greece. 400

How Should Jews Behave on the Moon?   402
Czechoslovakia's Jewish Treasures.   405
Adventurer Extraordinary: In Search of the Lost Ten
    Tribes.   407
The Last Chinese Jew Is Hiding Out in Taiwan.   410
The Jewish Slaves of Malta.   411
Life and Death of the Jews of St. Eustatius.   413
Mexico's Indian Jews.   416
The Port of the Smiling Jews.   419
The Good Samaritans: Somehow They Have Survived.   422
Incident in North Africa.   426
The Japanese Planned a Jewish State—in Manchuria.   428
When a Jewish Kingdom Ruled Southern Russia.   430
In Rome Jews Still Live in Ancient Ghetto.   431
The Proud Jews of Finland.   434
Are the American Indians a "Lost" Tribe of Israel?   436

XI   Women in Judaism and Jewish Women
of Special Interest

Jewish Women in Colonial Days.   440
Golfing with Golda and Ben-Gurion.   442
Jewish Women in Remote Corners of the World.   446
The Lady Physicist Who Dug Her Own Grave.   451
A Sister's Daring Rescued Young Boy from Czarist
    Conscription.   452
The Middle Ages: A Time of Growth and Education for
    Jewish Women.   454
The *Agunah* and the Devoted Sister.   457
Life on a Fence.   459
A Wedding in Cochin.   462
How a Mother Superior Defied the Church and Saved the
    Jews.   465
The Bride Was Fourteen: Sephardic Weddings of Yesterday.   467
Remembering Mother's Day.   470

XII   On Learning, Language, and Literature

There's More Hebrew in English Than You Realize!   474
A Forgotten Heritage: A Language Called Ladino.   479
Books for the "People of the Book."   481
How "Kibbutz" Got Its Name.   488
The Case of the Hidden Talmud.   489
Hebrew Literary Treasures in the U.S.S.R.   491
"Operation Parchment": The Dead Sea Scrolls.   495
Four-letter Words in Jewish Literature.   498
"Yeshivah of the Air": Hams Study Judaism Nightly.   500
Isolated from Mainstream of Jewry, Kurdistan Jews
    Produced Unique Literature.   502
Does More Education Mean Less Anti-Semitism?   505

XIII   Choosing Judaism: Converts and Penitents

Why I Became a Jew.   508
"A Pool Hall Yeshiva."   512
The Making and Unmaking of a Jewish Moonie.   514
From Italian Playboy to Committed Jew.   518
From Priest to Orthodox Jew.   520
Some of the Best Jews Are Proselytes!   522
The Western Wall: A Catalyst for Returnees to Judaism. 524
From Ashram to Yeshiva: Getting Your Head Together.   526
"With a Tallis I Can Die."   531
A Sefer Torah Bequeathed to a Nurse in Nebraska Is Now
    in Use in Tiny Pennsylvania Congregation.   534
Study Torah—and Get Free Karate Lesson.   536

XIV   Some Points of Interest Around the World

The Secret Jews of Iran.   540
The Little Tailors' Synagogue.   541
Visiting Spanish Jewry: Site of Past Glories.   544
Journey to the Kingdom of Morocco.   546
Jews in the Emerald Isle.   549

Jews in the Land of the Incas. 551

Jews in China: A Flourishing Community—in the Twelfth
Century. 554

An Oriental Jewish Mystery: The Case of the Nagasaki
Cemetery. 556

The Hidden Synagogue of the Azores. 558

Jews in the Frozen North. 560

XV Mishmash: A Little of This and a Little of That

A Christian Diplomat Offers Unique Interpretation of
Kashruth. 564

Jewish First Names Through the Ages. 566

How the Mezuzah Got in the Church Compound. 571

King Hezekiah's Tunnel: A Mystery to This Day. 572

Origins of Some Jewish Philanthropic Practices. 574

Tracking Down the Yarmulke. 580

The Torah That Was Rescued by a Chandelier. 582

New York Once Had a Hebrew Daily. 584

When Jews Quarrel. 585

The Dinghy Comes Home. 587

The Mizrah: Compass of the Heart. 588

The Case of the Stolen Torah. 591

Jew, Go Home! 592

The Rabbi and the Wafer. 593

The Man Who Brought Hope and Love. 594

THE JEWISH PEOPLE'S ALMANAC

I
America,
Sweet Land of Liberty

So Who Really Discovered America?

It's open season now—this matter of just who really discovered America. Columbus held the stage for a fair number of years. More recently, Leif Ericson was put forward as a strong candidate for the honor.

Then, Dr. Jacob Friend of Atlanta tossed a bomb into the affray more recently. Adducing evidence from a seventeenth-century work by David Ben Solomon Gans (1541–1613), Dr. Friend informs the world that sailors of King Solomon and King Hiram of Tyre reached Peru some 2,800 years ago, making of Leif Ericson and Columbus later, interloping upstarts and *chutzpadigge* claimants to the coveted achievement of being the first to reach the Western Hemisphere.

Since this is open season, we bring forward yet another claim, though it is hardly of the first-to-touch-the-Western Hemisphere category. This one has rather to do with a possible first discovery of the west coast of what is modern Canada, more specifically British Columbia.

Bruce A. McKelvie, in his book *Pageant of B.C.* (Thomas Nelson & Sons Ltd., 1957), offers a number of fascinating nuggets that would point in the direction of oriental voyagers who came across the Pacific and made contact with Canada's west coast. McKelvie calls upon a Chinese historian of the early seventh century, Li Yan Tcheou, who reports that a band of Buddhist priests crossed the Pacific and coasted from Alaska south to Mexico. These priests sailed from China in 458, and one of them who returned to China recorded his tale in 499. That puts Ericson and Columbus down a couple of pegs but leaves King Solomon's sailors unsullied!

But here we come again to those remarkably peripatetic Hebrews. McKelvie suggests the possibility that "Jews from China were at one time located on the Coast [today British Columbia], and remained there long enough to leave the imprint of their culture upon the tribes they encountered." When did this take place? At some time in the thirteenth century, during the reign of the colorful Kublai Khan. How did Chinese Jews *farblondzhe* to Canada's West Coast? McKelvie sets forth "the theory—that when Kublai Khan made his ill-starred expedition against Japan—towards the end of the thirteenth century—his fleet was dispersed by storm and was blown out into the Pacific Ocean, and junks bearing the Jewish contingent of his troops made the great drift across and landed on the American coast—possibly in the vicinity of the Queen Charlotte Islands, or the Nass River."

McKelvie falls back for support of this Chinese-Jewish junkmen theory on the writings of a Catholic missionary to the Indians, Father Jean Marie LeJeune, an expert in Indian dialects and customs. LeJeune recorded that he had discovered Hebrew words in every Indian dialect west of the Canadian Rockies. McKelvie enumerates a large variety of Indian customs that bear striking parallel to biblical traditions. In short, the British Columbia chronicler proposes "that numerous distinctive habits and ways of Coast Indians suggest that long ago Jews from China —the most likely place—visited the littoral of the North Pacific."

So there you have it in this era of claims! King Solomon's boys got to Peru 2,800 years ago. Kublai Khan's Chinese Jews got to British Columbia 700 years ago. Now if we could prove that Columbus was a Jew . . . but we'll leave that to other *chachamim!* As for Ericson, his first name really was "Leib," and you can reach your own conclusions.

—A.A.C.

 ## Jewish Influence on the Framing of the Constitution

Had the Constitutional Convention been open to the public, more than one eminent Jew would have had no difficulty in mingling on terms of equality with many of the best-known delegates. To George Washington, who presided over the sessions, Jews were of course no strangers. During the Revolution he had on his personal staff Manuel Mordecai Noah of South Carolina, David Salisbury Franks of Philadelphia, and Major Benjamin Nones, a French volunteer.

He was also familiar with Philip Moses Russell, a surgeon's mate, who shared the hardships at Valley Forge, and with Private Asher Pollock of the 2nd Rhode Island Battalion. Colonel Franks was personally cleared by Washington of the suspicion of having been involved in Benedict Arnold's treason.

The Deshler-Morris House in the Germantown section of Philadelphia, the oldest "White House" still standing, was owned by Colonel Isaac Franks when Washington rented it on November 17, 1793, and made it his temporary home when the federal government fled the yellow fever epidemic in Philadelphia and took refuge in the suburb of Germantown.

Benjamin Franklin, the oldest member of the Constitutional Convention, numbered many Philadelphia Jews among his friends. Notwithstanding heavy-handed attempts to brand Franklin as an anti-Semite by attributing to him a mythical effort to prevail upon the convention to exclude Jews from the country, he was sufficiently friendly with them to be one of the contributors to the building fund for Philadelphia's first synagogue, Mikveh Israel. Samuel Keimer, an English printer who was one of Franklin's first employers, was a Jew.

Virtually all of the delegates knew Haym Salomon, who died two years before the convention met. Six of the delegates had long been dependent on his generosity for their own livelihoods or for the maintenance of the particular government function for which they were responsible.

Impoverished by the failure of the Virginia legislature to pay its delegates to the Continental Congress, James Madison, a future President, sought out Salomon. Madison's papers record his indebtedness to the Jewish financier, who refused both a note and interest.

On one occasion Madison wrote that the "kindness of our little friend in Front Street near the Coffee House, is a fund that will prevent me from extremities, but I never resort to it without great mortification, as he obstinately rejects all recompense. The price of money is so usurious that he thinks it ought to be extorted from none but those that aim at a profitable speculation. To a necessitous delegate he gratuitously spares a supply out of his private stock."

Salomon's generosity was well known to other delegates. Edmund Randolph, a Virginia colleague of Madison's, later Attorney General and Secretary of State; James Wilson and Thomas Mifflin of Pennsylvania; and Robert Morris, the "financier of the Revolution," all had good cause to be thankful to the Jewish broker of Philadelphia.

Like Madison, Wilson and Randolph, who played important roles at the convention, were for some time regular recipients of substantial aid from Salomon. Morris' desperate efforts to find the funds to pay for the Revolution might well have come to naught without Salomon's assistance.

Wilson, later governor of Pennsylvania, was also a close friend of Michael and Barnard Gratz, prominent traders and land speculators, with whom he had been in partnership in land deals after the Revolution. Wilson was also an associate of Aaron Lopez of Rhode Island in privateering ventures.

Thomas Jefferson, author of the Declaration of Independence, was in France as the United States ambassador while the Constitution was being hammered out, but he was the author of the celebrated Virginia Bill of Rights, which became law in 1786. Before he went abroad, Jefferson and the Jews of America had been no strangers to each other. David Franks and Isaac Franks frequently corresponded with him, the former having served as his diplomatic courier.

Jefferson also knew Haym Salomon, who is known to have helped Jefferson with occasional loans. Just when the debate over the Bill of Rights raged most fiercely, Jefferson returned from Europe to bring his influence to bear in favor of adding to the Constitution, through the first ten amendments, the fundamental rights that the original Constitution had omitted.

Apart from the Virginia delegates, the most distinguished Southern leader at the convention was Charles Pinckney of South Carolina. Pinckney, the man who was alleged to have taken down notes of Franklin's alleged anti-Semitic utterances at the convention, was the dearest friend of Francis Salvador, the first Jew to die fighting for the Revolution. Pinckney and Salvador served together in the first South Carolina legislature. They also fought side by side in many battles with Indians and Tories in the first year of the Revolution.

Salvador had been a comrade-in-arms of Hugh Williamson, a delegate from North Carolina. The latter owed his life to a heroic twenty-eight-mile ride by Salvador, who raced to warn him that the British fleet was nearing Charleston. Salvador also shared with Williamson command of an expedition against the Indians. John Rutledge, another delegate from South Carolina, thought so highly of Salvador that he appointed him to the commission established to prepare the South Carolina Provincial Congress of 1775.

Mordecai Sheftall, one of the most celebrated of Georgia patriots during the Revolution, was a close friend and business associate of Abraham Baldwin and William Few, Georgia's delegates to the convention. Sheftall had served with both during the Revolution.

During the convention, Jonas Phillips, the post-Revolutionary leader of the Philadelphia Jewish community, who had once served as the *shochet* of New York's Congregation Shearith Israel, the oldest existing synagogue in the New World, sent a letter to the delegates urging them not to include a religious test for public office in the federal Constitution they were drafting.

His plea was dated September 7, 1787, but because the convention's sessions were not open to the public, he did not know that two weeks earlier the delegates had adopted what is now Article VI, Clause 3 of the Constitution, declaring that no religious test was to be required of federal officials. Curiously, not until a new state constitution was adopted in 1790 was the religious test for Pennsylvania state officers eliminated.

On July 4, 1788, when Philadelphia staged a great parade to celebrate the ratification of the new Constitution by the requisite number of states, the Rev. Gershom Mendez Seixas, then the temporary religious leader of Philadelphia's Congregation Mikveh Israel (he had left New York during the years the British occupied it, taking with him Shearith Israel's Torahs), marched arm in arm with

Christian clergymen. When the parade ended and the marchers were invited to partake of refreshments, Seixas and other Jewish paraders found one table set aside with kosher edibles.

—B.P.

 ## America: 1791

When President Washington informed the nation on December 15, 1791, that enough states had ratified the first ten amendments to the Constitution to bring the Bill of Rights—the generic term by which these amendments are known—into force as the fundamental law of the land, American Jewry already had a history of 137 years behind it.

There had been Jews who shared the hardships of the pioneer colonists who took the first steps toward building the future America out of a wilderness. And there had been Jews among the patriots who took up arms for freedom and fought and died in the Revolution to win independence.

Though numerically insignificant in 1791, the Jews were already a deeply rooted element of the American people. Had a religious census been taken, it would have disclosed a Jewish population of 3,000 out of a total of somewhat less than 3,000,000. Newport, the largest Jewish center before the Revolution, had been overshadowed by Philadelphia, which in 1791 counted 1,000 Jewish inhabitants. New York had 750 Jews, and Newport claimed 500. Savannah, Georgia, and Charleston, South Carolina, each had about 200. The rest were scattered in other towns.

Small as these Jewish communities were, they already had the beginnings of communal life. There were synagogues in Newport, New York, Charleston, Philadelphia, Savannah, and Richmond, but no ordained rabbis. Moses Cohen in Charleston and Gershom Mendez Seixas in New York were *hazzanim*. Charleston and Newport boasted of Hebrew clubs. In every Jewish community there was a religious school in which secular subjects were taught, in addition to the strict tenets of Orthodox Judaism.

New York's pioneer synagogue had a ladies auxiliary, and in Charleston there was a Jewish benevolent and fraternal society. The vast system of philanthropy developed by American Jewry in the past century stems from this post-Revolutionary era. Those tiny Jewish communities were generous givers. In the absence of established charitable organizations, the synagogue elders boarded sick and aged Jews in their own homes, a method now widely used in child care. A similar plan was adopted for orphans.

Charitable and educational undertakings constantly depleted synagogue treasuries, which from their limited resources maintained an amazing variety of social services. Indigent Jews were frequently sent from one town to another until they were permanently settled and assured of a livelihood. A strong feeling of kinship and cooperation existed between the Jewish communities.

The commercial interdependence of Jewish traders and merchants in Savannah, Charleston, Philadelphia, Newport, and New York was effectively utilized to help distant and isolated co-religionists. Couriers for Jewish merchants always carried funds and messages for Jews in other towns.

Old congregational minute books reveal that as early as 1791 American Jews were no strangers to fund-raising campaigns. When a new synagogue was built, it received contributions not only from local donors but often from Jews in other towns. One synagogue received building fund support from London, Curaçao, and Barbados. Another was given books by the Jewish community in Jamaica. House-to-house solicitation of charitable funds was used with success even then. Individual Jews paid for single stones, parts of windows, decorations, and other sections of synagogues.

In those early days even the wealthiest Jews were Orthodox in belief and practice. The Jewish leadership struggled to maintain Jewish unity by an unbending Orthodoxy. Absentees from Sabbath services were fined. Even a minor desecration of the Sabbath, such as shaving, created angry criticism. Violators of the dietary laws were threatened with excommunication. Jewish holy days and festivals were scrupulously observed. Proselytes were not tolerated, and marriages between Jews and Christians were taboo. In matters of *kashruth* and religion, the word of the synagogue elders was law. They had the power to withhold or withdraw membership in the synagogue, almost the sole center of Jewish life, and few Jews braved such ostracism.

Although most Jews lived apart from their Gentile neighbors, Christian-Jewish relations were no problem. Some of the wealthy Jewish families found a ready welcome in Christian society. The Frankses, Sheftalls, Riveras, Lopezes, Touros, Gratzes, and Levys were no strangers to Christian social life. Masonry was an important point of contact between Jew and Gentile. The camaraderie engendered by the Revolution was still strong enough to prevent the emergence of serious racial or religious prejudice. The children of the Jewish patriots of 1776 found few, if any, obstacles of bigotry barring their way. Indeed, in time intermarriages between Jews and the most aristocratic families became fairly common.

Conversion made constant inroads into the Jewish population, so much so that today many blue-blooded American families find a Jewish ancestor in their pedigree as their claim to membership in the Sons and Daughters of the American Revolution.

Among the more prominent apostates were Judah Monis, a Hebrew instructor at Harvard; Isaac Miranda, who became a judge in Philadelphia; the Pinto brothers in New Haven; Moses Levy, who turned down an offer of appointment as U. S. Attorney General by President Jefferson; and David Emanuel, governor of Georgia. Intermarriage between the daughters of the well-to-do Jewish families and the landed gentry was not uncommon. The most famous of these united the Franks family and a scion of the aristocratic De Lanceys, whose name is preserved in Delancey Street on the Lower East Side. To counteract apostasy and intermarriage, strenuous efforts were made to strengthen the appeal of Judaism. One of the most notable of these was Isaac Pinto's translation of the Hebrew prayers into English.

Much has been written about the Jewish merchants, brokers, shipowners, Indian traders, land speculators, soldiers, and financiers who rendered great service to the American cause during the Revolution. But by 1791, American Jews numbered not only successful traders and merchants, but doctors, scientists, lawyers, patrons of the arts, scholars, and skilled craftsmen. Gilbert, Sully, Stuart, and Malbourne were among the prominent American portrait painters commissioned to paint the wealthy Jew of 1791 and his wife.

Some of these portraits, still extant, show that Jews dressed like their neighbors. Synagogue elders wore the same waistcoats, knee breeches, buckled shoes, and powdered wigs to be seen on the delegates to the Constitutional Convention. Jewish ladies of that time were as well groomed as their Christian sisters, and those who could afford it spared no expense in importing finery from Paris and London. The silver pieces produced by Myer Myers, the great Jewish silversmith, were to be found in Jewish as well as non-Jewish homes.

Jewish professional men were not unknown but not too numerous. Jewish physicians were practicing in Philadelphia, Savannah, and New York. The first graduating classes of Columbia University and the University of Pennsylvania numbered Jews among them. Some of the more prosperous Jews were generous supporters of educational institutions. Moses Franks was a liberal donor to Columbia. Israel Joseph and Moses Lindo gave substantial sums to Brown University. Aaron Lopez helped found Leicester Academy in Newport, and Abraham Hart and Jacob Rivera were patrons of Newport's first library. The Rev. Gershom Mendez Seixas was a trustee of Columbia University.

In 1791 there were only two states in which an observant Jew could hold public office. Although the Bill of Rights outlawed religious tests for officeholders under the federal government, it took years before Jews could legally be appointed or elected to public office in all states. Nevertheless, by 1791 there were a number of Jews in local public positions.

In short, the handful of Jews in the United States between 1787, when the Constitution was written, and 1791, when the Bill of Rights became law, had won a solid foothold in many spheres of American life and had laid the groundwork for Jewish participation in the future growth of the United States and for the emergence of the great Jewish community of today.

—B.P.

 ## The Oldest Synagogue in America

Each year during the month of September a ceremony takes place under the aegis of the American Jewish Historical Society and the Jewish Historical Society of New York, commemorating the arrival of the first Jews in New Amsterdam in 1654. Those twenty-three Jews had sailed from Recife, Brazil, when the Portuguese conquered the Dutch and took control of that area. Many of the Jews who had left Brazil at that time went to Holland, their place of origin. These twenty-three Jews, however, were victims of a great storm and were captured by pirates. A French ship rescued them from the hands of the outlaws and conducted them safely to what was then called New Amsterdam, known now as New York City.

This small group arrived several days before Rosh Hashanah. There was no synagogue, no facilities to accommodate Jewish religious needs. As they celebrated that New Year, they viewed themselves as a remnant of Israel in a distant land, and the congregation they founded was named Shearith Israel, the "remnant of Israel."

The Jews were not welcomed by Governor Peter Stuyvesant. Efforts were made to have the new arrivals expelled. Through their perseverance, as well as through the assistance of their coreligionists in Amsterdam, the Jews did win the right to remain.

Of Spanish and Portuguese origin, most of them belonged to families who had left Spain and Portugal to settle in Amsterdam. Therefore, the synagogue that they established followed the custom of Sephardi Jews of Amsterdam and has become popularly known as the Spanish and Portuguese Synagogue. In fact, all of the Jewish congregations in Colonial America were Spanish and Portuguese in custom. Ashkenazim who arrived in this country adapted themselves to the existing rite. It was even quite common for Ashkenazim to identify strongly with Sephardi modes.

The Jews of New Amsterdam had to fight for many basic rights. For a while, Jews had no right to own real estate. On November 29, 1655, Abraham de Lucena, Salvador D'Andrada, and Jacob Cohen Henriques entered a petition requesting the authorities to allow them permission to travel, reside, and trade in New Amsterdam like the other inhabitants of the city. This petition was denied. In March of 1656, these three men were joined by Joseph d'Acosta and David de Ferera in seeking for themselves, and in the name of the other Jews residing in the city, equal rights with all other citizens. Other efforts were made to win complete religious freedom, including the right to have a public place of worship. Through their tireless efforts, this small group of Jews and others who joined them in the following years won general recognition by the end of the seventeenth century.

Aside from winning basic freedoms, the early Jewish settlers helped lay the foundation for Jewish life in this country. Their synagogue not only provided them a place for worshiping God but also provided a communal center. It was awesome to recognize the outstanding sacrifices that were made by this remnant of Israel in order to provide Jewish education for their children, to provide kosher meat to the members of the community, to provide welfare for the needy. Shearith Israel was the only Jewish congregation in New York City from 1654 until 1825.

Since the Jewish community was quite small, they worshiped in rented quarters. Jewish religious services were held in a building that was openly recognized as a synagogue. In 1695, John Miller (chaplain in New York to the forces of King William and Queen Mary), marked "The Jews Synagogue" on his map on the south side of Beaver Street, between Broadway and Broad Street, immediately opposite New Street. Five years later, a real estate document of 1700 describes a lot on the north side of Mill Street as being bounded on the "east by the house and ground of John Haperdinck, now commonly known by the name of the Jews' synagogue." The site of the house of John Haperdinck that was rented for a synagogue would today bear the address of 18 South William Street.

The frame building on that site was rented for eight pounds a year and was used as the synagogue through the first three decades of the eighteenth century. In 1728 there was a burst of vigorous new life in the congregation. On October 28 the parnas of the congregation "called a Publick meeting of the whole Congregation in order to Subscribe for the purchasing of Land for the Building of a Sinagoga [sic] and for a Buring [sic] place which was then Efected [sic]."

For the price of a hundred pounds, one loaf of sugar, and a pound of Bohea tea, they bought on December 19, 1728, from Cornelius Clopper and Catherine, his wife, a lot of land on Mill Street immediately to the west of the rented house that was being used as a synagogue. That plot is today the site of 22 and parts of 20 and 24 South William Street.

The new synagogue, unlike the former rented wooden frame house, was a brick building with blue-faced bricks on the outside. In structure it followed the general architectural pattern of its sister Sephardi synagogue in London and its mother synagogue in Amsterdam. The Ark was at the east end of the building behind a railing of banisters. The men's seats ran east and west along the north and south sides of the synagogue, and the women's seats were set in a special gallery. There was a seat (*banco*) for the president (*parnas presidente*) and one for the vice-president (*parnas residente*) on the north and south side of the Ark, respectively. This general architectural form has not varied in each of the synagogues built by Shearith Israel during the last two centuries, although the dimensions of each newly built synagogue have progressively increased with the growth of the congregation.

The Ark with its sliding doors, a silk curtain behind them, was approached by three steps, with candlesticks in front of them and at their side. Three steps above the floor level, in the center of the building, was the reading desk (*shulhan, tebah*) covered with red tapestry fringed with silver lace. Near the corners of the building there hung from the roof four brass candelabras, each holding sixteen candles, and in' the center there was a fifth on which thirty-two candles were set. The candles for all these fixtures had to be made by the *shamash* from kosher wax. Hanging before the Ark was the perpetual lamp, which now is in the small synagogue of the congregation.

The severely simple little synagogue on Mill Street, the first structure designed and built to be a synagogue in continental North America, was consecrated on the seventh day of Passover, April 8, 1730. It was but thirty-five feet square, and even though it contained a women's gallery, it was only twenty-one feet in height. It was set back from the street in its own little courtyard. Six months later there was built in the yard in the rear of the synagogue the harvest booth (*sukkah, cabana*); an adjoining ritual bath (*mikveh*) was soon completed. One year later, a two-story wooden structure was erected immediately to the north of the synagogue for the school.

The pressure of immigration and the large size of families began to strain the accommodation that the synagogue offered. In 1817 it was decided to rebuild and enlarge the aging structure. The rebuilding was done thoroughly. A new structure was put up that was 35 by 58 feet, and 9 feet higher than the old one. It provided 167 seats for men and 133 (and eventually 137) seats for women. It ran east and west, not north and south as had the first Mill Street Synagogue. The new synagogue was built of brick and stone with a surface of Roman cement. The women's gallery was reached by a covered passageway from the upper story of the adjoining brick schoolhouse on the north.

Only fifteen years after that synagogue was consecrated, the struggle to maintain it on that site was abandoned. Its days were numbered from the beginning because of the movement of population from the progressively commercialized district of Mill Street to the residential districts a mile and more to the north. The last service was held in the second Mill Street Synagogue on April 13, 1833. The building had to be vacated at once as it was to be demolished. The congregation rented temporary quarters on the middle story of the New York Dispensary at the northwest corner of White and Centre streets.

The site chosen on March 31, 1833, for a new synagogue consisted of four lots on the west side of Crosby Street, covering numbers fifty-six to sixty-two, about two thirds of the way up the block between Broome and Spring streets. The third synagogue building built here was fifty-three feet in breadth and seventy-five feet in length.

The cornerstone for the new building carried history with it, for it was the same cornerstone used more than a hundred years earlier for the first Mill Street Synagogue. The general frame of the outwardly curving Ark of the Mill Street Synagogue was used in the new building. Other characteristic symbols and furnishings of the earlier synagogue were not discarded. The Crosby Street building was on the west side of the street. In order to meet the requirement of the Ark being placed in the east, the front of the structure, which was its eastern end, was built as a solid wall and the Ark rested against it. Then entrance to the building was set in the rear and approached from a high curved stoop from which a double flight of steps led up and down to the basement.

The illumination within the synagogue came at night from gas fixtures and by day from five windows on each side. Seating was provided by wooden benches, two of them still in use in the present small synagogue. The twelve-foot square mahogany enclosure for the reading desk in the center of the synagogue was approached by three steps. Its floor was covered with a Brussels carpet, and the seat facing the desk was upholstered with a haircloth cushion. The white reading desk had a red covering hung around the sides in festoons.

The Ark was approached by five steps covered with a bright hued Brussels carpet. The sliding doors of the Ark revealed a richly lined interior of crimson red silk hanging in festoons, with a red brocade drapery over the two outwardly carving tiers on which the scrolls of the Torah were set. Attached to the wall on either side of the Ark were the two white marble tablets commemorating the generosity of Abraham Touro and Washington Henricks; these are set up at the west end of the present synagogue.

The new building was consecrated on June 12, 1834—the first day of the festival of Shavuoth. This synagogue served the congregation for twenty-five years. Then, once more the relentless changing process affected Crosby Street. By the 1850s residents were moving away from the district, and parents were loath to have their children go to the synagogue unattended. The building was converted to a Minstrel Hall and subsequently to a theater. The congregation used temporary quarters at 894 Broadway, just south of Fourteenth Street.

In 1859 lots were acquired for a new house of worship on the north side of Nineteenth Street, west from Fifth Avenue. They covered seventy by ninety feet on Nineteenth Street and twenty-seven feet eight-and-a-half inches by one hundred feet on Fifth Avenue. Still holding onto the Sephardi custom of not placing a synagogue conspicuously on a main street, the congregation soon sold the corner lot with the stipulation that the purchaser not erect stables or other nuisances.

The laying of the cornerstone for the new building was set for Monday afternoon, July 11, 1859. Fifteen months later the building was completed at a total cost of $99,935.01. The ceremonies of consecration were set for Wednesday, September 12, 1860.

The style of this unusual building introduced into the United States the neobaroque, which was then current in Paris. The engaged columns and pilasters of the giant Ionic order surmounted by the Corinthian, the segmental pediment, and above all the massing of the effect on the central bay are all features highly characteristic of the seventeenth-century baroque. The building was facing south; the hall of worship, however, was properly oriented east. The columnar framework of the canopied Ark was a variation of the theme of the main exterior portal. In contrast to the Crosby Street building with its windowless Ark wall, we have here three windows above the Ark area, a motif that recurs in the present building.

The life of that building, thirty-seven years in all, was attended by a trail of difficulties from the very outset. There were problems resulting from design characteristics, maintenance and upkeep problems, heating problems, too many steps to climb, acoustical problems. In September 1866 a committee was appointed to seek an eligible site for the erection of a new synagogue.

The sale of the Nineteenth Street building presented many problems. Finally, in January 1895 the congregation purchased for $130,000 six lots of 100 feet on Eighth Avenue (Central Park West) and 150 feet to the west on the south side of

Seventieth Street, where the present synagogue stands. When the new building was ready, the Nineteenth Street building was torn down to avoid the possible repetition of the embarrassment experienced when the Crosby Street building was converted to a theater.

The first estimate of the cost of construction of the new building was in the neighborhood of one hundred thousand dollars. When the building was finished, it represented an expenditure of more than a quarter of a million dollars. The completed synagogue was dedicated on the evening of Lag b'Omer, Wednesday, May 19, 1897. The Renaissance Greek architecture of the building was something of an innovation at a time when the Moorish style, associated with monotheistic culture, was considered appropriate for a synagogue. Soon, however, it was copied in other synagogues.

The preacher's pulpit stands on the steps leading toward the Ark, as it did in the Crosby Street building. The balustraded choir gallery over the arch is lighted by the windows overlooking Central Park West, the window motif having been inspired by the Nineteenth Street synagogue. For the sake of proper orientation, the Ark is set up on what is actually the entrance side of the building. The reader's platform stands in the center, slightly more to the west, in conformance with Sephardic usage. The benches are set parallel to the lateral sides in the traditional way. The women's balcony runs on two sides. The weekday chapel furnished with the relics of the past adjoins the synagogue and may be entered also from Central Park West. There are subsidiary rooms on the main floor. A large assembly room and offices are in the basement.

Shearith Israel is unique in that its members have always represented diverse backgrounds. Sephardim and Ashkenazim have been involved in the congregation since the earliest years. Even today the synagogue's membership reflects the past three centuries of Jewish history in a real way. A number of families trace their origin to Jews who came here in Colonial days. There are also a number of families whose ancestors, stemming from Western and Eastern Europe, first became involved in Shearith Israel during the nineteenth century. During the late nineteenth and early twentieth centuries, Jewish immigrants from Russia as well as from the Levant arrived in New York. The sisterhood of the congregation operated settlement houses on the Lower East Side to help the Jewish immigrants adjust to American life. Shearith Israel warmly received Jews fleeing the terrors of the Holocaust and in recent years has also welcomed Jews from Arab lands.

The congregation has always been involved in all aspects of Jewish and civic life. Its members have been instrumental in fostering many important causes and institutions. The congregation founded or helped found such institutions as Mount Sinai Hospital, Montefiore Hospital, the Jewish Theological Seminary, and the Union of Orthodox Jewish Congregations of America and such projects as the Sephardic Studies Program at Yeshiva University. Members of the Shearith Israel community were among the founders of the New York Stock Exchange. The Henricks family developed the copper industry in America. Congregants served with distinction in every war of this country, going back to the American Revolution. Each year on Memorial Day a special service is held at the synagogue's Chatham Square Cemetery, at which time graves of individuals who served in the Revolution are marked with American flags.

Shearith Israel has a long history of support for the communities in the Holy Land. As early as Colonial days, the congregation received messengers with honor and contributed funds for the communities there.

—M.D.A.

A Gentile's Reaction to a Jewish Wedding in Philadelphia in 1787

Philadelphia, June 27, 1787

My dear Julia,

Being called a few days ago to attend in the family of Jonas Phillips, I was honored this morning with an invitation to attend the marriage of his daughter to a young man of the name of Levy from Virginia . . . I accepted with great pleasure. . . .

At 1 o'clock the company, consisting of thirty or forty men, assembled in Mr. Phillips's common parlor which was accommodated with benches . . . The ceremony began with prayers in the Hebrew language, chaunted [sic] by an old rabbi . . . followed by the whole company. As I did not understand a word except now and then an Amen or Hallelujah, my attention was directed to the haste with which they covered their heads with their hats as soon as the prayers began and to the freedom with which some of them conversed during . . . this part of their worship. As soon as these prayers were ended, . . . about twenty minutes, a small piece of parchment was produced, written in Hebrew, which contained a deed of settlement and which the groom subscribed in the presence of four witnesses. In this deed he conveyed a part of his fortune to his bride, by which she was provided for after his death . . . This was followed by the erection of a beautiful canopy of white and red silk . . . supported by four young men (by means of four poles) who put on white gloves for the purpose. As soon as this canopy was fixed, the bride, accompanied with . . . a long train of female relations, came downstairs. Her face was covered with a veil which reached halfways down her body. She was handsome at all times, but the occasion and dress rendered her . . . a most lovely and affecting object . . . I gazed with delight upon her. Innocence, modesty, fear, respect, and devotion appeared all at once in her countenance. She was led by her two bridesmaids under the canopy. Two young men led the bridegroom . . . directly opposite to her. The priest now began again to chaunt an Hebrew prayer, . . . followed by part of the company. After this he gave to the groom and bride a glass full of wine, from which they each sipped . . . Another prayer followed . . . after which he took a ring and directed the groom to place it upon the finger of his bride . . . as in the marriage service of the Church of England. This was followed by handing the wine to the father of the bride and then . . . to the bride and groom. The groom after sipping the wine took the glass . . . and threw it upon a large pewter dish which was suddenly placed at his feet. Upon its breaking into a number of small pieces, there was a general shout of joy and a declaration that the ceremony was over. The groom now saluted his bride, and kisses and congratulations became general . . . I asked the meaning . . . of the canopy and of the wine and breaking of the glass. I was told . . . that in Europe they generally marry in the open air and that the canopy was introduced to defend the bride and groom from the sun and the rain . . . Partaking of the same glass of wine was intended to denote the mutuality of their goods, and the breaking of the glass . . . to teach them the brittleness and uncertainty of human life and the certainty of death, and thereby to temper their present joys.

Mr. Phillips pressed me to stay and dine with the company, but business . . .

forbade it. I stayed, however, to eat some wedding cake and to drink a glass of wine . . . Upon going . . . upstairs to ask how Mrs. Phillips did, who had fainted downstairs under the pressure of the heat . . . I discovered the bride and groom supping a bowl of broth together. Mrs. Phillips apologized for them by telling me they had eaten nothing (agreeably to the custom prescribed by their religion) since the night before.

Upon my taking leave, Mrs. Phillips put a large piece of cake into my pocket for you, which she begged I would present to you with her best compliments . . .

During the whole of this new and curious scene . . . I was carried back to the ancient world and was led to contemplate the Passovers, the sacrifices, the jubilees, and other ceremonies of the Jewish Church. After this, I . . . anticipated the time foretold by the prophets when this once-beloved race of men shall again be restored to the divine favor and shall unite with Christians . . . in celebrating the praises of a common and universal Saviour . . .

Adieu. With love to your Mama, sisters, and brothers, and to our dear children, I am your affectionate husband,

B. Rush

P.S. . . . I have sent the wedding cake by Mr. Stockton.

—B.R.

 When George Washington Slept in a Jewish Home

A yellow fever epidemic was raging in Philadelphia, the capital of the new American nation, and there was concern for the President's health. Where could they take him so that he would be safe from contagion?

Someone had heard that Isaac Franks, the Jew and patriot, had a comfortable home outside of Philadelphia, in Germantown. The perfect place for the President! The entire presidential household was removed there and displaced the Franks family so completely that a bill was later sent to the capital in the sum of sixteen dollars for the rental of beds "while the President was occupying mine." A bill was also sent for the replacement of dishes and cups missing after the President's sojourn there.

Who was this man, Isaac Franks, the Jew and patriot? He was one of a large family named Franks. They were Sephardic Jews who had left Spain and settled in Hanover, Germany. By the 1700s the family was scattered throughout the world: some in England, some in Canada, and others in the colonies—mostly Philadelphia and New York.

One of the most famous men in the Franks family was a Tory who sided with the Crown during the Revolution. He was David Franks of Philadelphia, most probably Isaac's uncle. David was a trader and merchant, best known for his work in developing trade with the Western territories along with the Gratz brothers. Less well known is the fact that he was jailed by the Americans for his pro-Tory activities in Philadelphia and released only after the intervention of his brother, Moses. David Franks later was given the opportunity to escape to New York (then Tory territory) when the English were driven out of Philadelphia. Once the war was over, he left America for England and applied for compen-

sation for his losses while engaging in the protection of the Crown. It would seem
that the Crown put a much smaller price on his activities than did Mr. Franks.
They settled on him one tenth the amount that he asked, and he returned to
America a disappointed man.

David Franks was only one Tory in a large family of patriots and revolu-
tionaries, of which Isaac was one of the most outstanding members. Isaac was
born in New York and joined the New York volunteer regiment when he was seventeen. He fought in the Battle of Long Island and was later captured by the British. After several months, he managed to escape across the Hudson River in a
leaky boat and made his way to Philadelphia, a stronghold of the Revolution.
There he rejoined the Continental Army and ended his career as a major.

It was after the war, when Isaac was a successful merchant and businessman,
that his lodgings in Germantown were used by the President. He was, at that
time, one of the most prominent citizens of Philadelphia. The fact that he was
Jewish and belonged to the first Philadelphia congregation, Mikveh Israel, was
only incidental to President Washington. The President was known to be unbi-
ased, and a firm believer in equality, and he was more than happy to accept the
hospitality of his fellow patriot during the yellow fever epidemic.

The fact that George Washington slept in his bed and that his home was, for a
short time, the capital of the nation did not seem to help Isaac Franks too much
in his later years, however. After several business reverses he was left as penniless
as his Tory uncle and had to apply for a veterans pension from the American
government to support himself.

—E.T.

 Voyage to America: Eleven Weeks on a "Sail Ship"

*These reminiscences were written in 1931 by Lena Pearlstein Berkman, who was
then eighty-two years of age. This excerpt is from a larger memoir, a copy of
which is on deposit at the American Jewish Archives.*

When we first left Tresteny, Russia, my birthplace, it was in the fall of 1855, after
Sukkoth, near Hanukkah. We started out in a covered wagon bedded with straw
at the bottom, with feather beds and pillows. Mother tried all she could to make
us comfortable as, no doubt, all mothers do. Those that were with us were my
dear mother, then about thirty-four years of age; my oldest brother, Louis C.,
about eighteen; my uncle, Jacob, sixteen; my oldest sister, Fagah Etta, fourteen;
Miriam Rose, eleven; brother Samuel Wolff, nine; myself—Baile Leah, not quite
seven; sister Sarah Hyah, three; and my brother Louis's baby boy, not quite a
year old, who died in Berlin, Germany. Brother Louis was divorced from his wife,
and she refused to keep the child though she was given every assurance for its
support and hers. I cannot perceive how a young mother would part from her first
child or any of her children. My dear mother often remarked that she—my good,
pious mother—was punished for taking the child from its mother, but there was
no alternative left her. Even the grandparents on the mother's side refused to keep
the child. The weather was bitter cold. I well remember we got as far as the towns
of Stavicks and Gryeevy. We could go no farther and had to return back home
till after Pesach. Remember so well that Saturday night when we again left the

dear home, relatives, and friends, all that were near and dear. I also remember my dear mother would not let her mother know she was leaving that night. (The grief of parting was far too great to go through again.) So my dear old grandmother did not know we had left that night never to see each other again. My Uncle Jacob was her youngest son, just sixteen years of age. My dear old grandmother did not live very long after; she died heartbroken. I think she lived about two months after we left. I cannot remember where we went from the last towns, but recollect we were in Königsberg, Danzig, Berlin—all German towns. Also Liverpool, England, and London. I fail to remember where we sailed from, but think it was from Liverpool, England. We were to sail in a steamship with a captain, a very nice and good man, a German. But when we got to the pier, it was another —a sail ship, not Captain Witting of the steamship. We returned to our lodging place waiting for Captain Witting. My poor dear mother went to the wharf for several days, and each time it was the same, ill-fated ship that we were destined to take after finding out that Captain Witting had already sailed for the States. We were on the sail ship eleven weeks. My poor mother was sick nearly all the time. The ship was an English one. The only one that could speak German was the mate. My mother asked for some food that she could make a soup or gruel. So the mate and captain gave her a grain that was prepared for rats. Of course they did not mean to do harm, and yet they did not take the precaution they should. My mother saw that when they put some of the grain on their tongues, that showed a doubt they had. They should not have given it to cook without further proof.

My oldest sister, Fagah Etta, cooked the broth and while cooking must have undoubtedly tasted as to its seasoning that it had a quicker effect on her than on the others that had partaken of it. I noticed my mother bringing up the food she ate. I distinctly remember her telling me not to eat any of the food or the Irish potato that came out of the soup. Of course, I did just the opposite, went down and ate some of the potato that was on a pot cover and ate some. Evidently did not eat enough to hurt, as I did not get sick as the others did. My sister could not bring up any of the food though she was given emetics. It had no effects as to produce vomiting. She died that night lying next to me. I asked her to get me a drink of water. She got up, got me some water. I drank it. She again lay down and in about half an hour or so I again woke her to give me more water, but she failed to answer me. With that I, as young as I was (only six and a half years of age), woke my mother and told her, "Fagah is dead. Fagah is dead." I remember so well I repeated it twice. As soon as the officers found she was dead, they immediately took her from us, and my mother never saw her again though she begged and implored of them to let her dress her as becomes one of our kind, but all of her beseeching was in vain. The officers and crew threw her in the ocean. . . . That was sometime in August 1856. My younger (second) sister, Miriam Rose, who was eleven years old, died the next day about sunset. I remember so well every detail of her death, witnessed her dying and what she said before she died. Remember her telling my poor mother not to delay her death. Did she not see her grandfather waiting on her? And they must not tarry and keep them waiting and also so many distinguished people waiting to take her, and so on. I noticed [her] closing her eyes, and she was no more. A few minutes before she died, I saw my mother motion to those that were standing behind her to step back; as soon as they did, breath left my darling sister. My mother dressed her or rather wrapped her in a clean white sheet. Some of the men on board tied her on a board with a large rock on each end, put it on the railing of the ship, and shoved her overboard. I can see everything now as then after more than seventy-five years. The splash I shall never forget if I live to be a thousand years old. Years after when I would see my poor mother weeping, I would say to her, "Mother, why are you crying?" Her answer was, "My dear child, haven't I got lots to cry for?" My poor dear mother. My great and sore regret shall always be, as long as I live, that I was not good enough to my suffering mother as I should have been. . . . I've been praying and begging her forgiveness ever since she died. She was so good to everybody, and particularly to me, that I feel sure she has forgiven me. The Lord rest her soul in peace. Amen. I know she was received immediately after death by the good angels into heaven and feel sure her dear, good, pious ancestors were there to meet her.

—L.P.B.

 ## Jewish Names on the Map of the United States

"It's fourteen miles to Kaplan." . . . "Turn right at Levys!" . . . "Let's stop for lunch in Seligman!" . . . "That sign reads Aaronsburg." . . . "There's a detour at Cohen's Bluff." . . . "That new motel is just outside of Weiner."

This is familiar talk to everyone who has traveled anywhere in the United States by car, but who ever heard of those places? What map are they on?

You've lunched in Ypsilanti, detoured at Wenatchee, had a flat at Tuscaloosa, gassed up in Fiddletown, spent the night at Rising Sun, visited in Wantagh, turned off the turnpike at King of Prussia, and stretched your legs at Altadena. You've sped through hundreds of places with odd names, historic names, hard-to-pronounce names, but you've probably never seen—and perhaps never heard of—places bearing such common Jewish surnames as Cohen, Levy, Goldman, Edelstein, Altman, Strauss, and Goldstein.

But there are such places on the map, even though most Jewish tourists are unaware of them. That's because so many of the ninety-two towns, villages, hamlets, counties, mountains, lakes, and forests named for Jews are not along the main traveled highways.

This writer has located one or more geographical units named for Jews in thirty-four states. More than a third of these places are in the South. In Texas alone there are nine. Sixteen can be found in eight of the original thirteen colonies. The only states without at least one place named for a Jew are Delaware, Indiana, Kansas, Maine, Maryland, Massachusetts, Michigan, New Hampshire, North Dakota, Ohio, Rhode Island, Tennessee, Utah, and West Virginia.

The combined population of the 92 places named for Jews is 230,000. Most of them, however, have no Jewish residents. The two largest towns having Jewish patronymics are Levittown, New York, and Levittown, Pennsylvania, both founded by and named for the Levitt brothers, real estate developers, and both with substantial Jewish communities. The oldest place named for Jews is Aaronsburg, Pennsylvania, population 350. It was founded in 1779 by Aaron Levy, a Revolutionary patriot. It's on Route 45, a few miles from the geographic center of Pennsylvania.

America's heritage of place-names is linked to the story of the people who built the nation. Our place-names tell of men and women who struggled and hoped and dreamed, who succeeded and failed, who sought fortune and lost it, whose life blood was poured out to keep America free. Among the hundreds of thousands of names of cities, towns, villages, rivers, mountains, and lakes, only a few hundred recall names known to all Americans. The rest are little names, sometimes even unknown to those who live nearby. One by one these names came to stand on maps as the names rose on the tongues and in the memories of people of different times and origin and blood and language.

Wherever you go in the United States you'll probably not be too far from places whose Jewish namesakes contributed in some way to local, state or national history.

In Texas you'll find two of the three counties named for Jews. Castro County, in the panhandle, south of Amarillo, honors Henry de Castro, a French Jew who in 1842 signed a contract with President Sam Houston of the Republic of Texas to colonize the area west of the Medina River. The town of Castroville, on the west bank of the river, was founded by Castro in the 1840s. Kaufman County and its county seat, Kaufman, just east of Fort Worth, memorialize the services of David S. Kaufman, who was one of the first members of Congress from Texas after that state joined the Union.

The third county that bears a Jew's name is Levy County, on the Gulf Coast of Florida. Levy was the original name of David Levy Yulee, who helped draft the first constitution of Florida. Chosen Florida's first congressman-at-large in 1841, he was the first Jew elected to Congress. In 1845 he also became the first Jew to win a seat in the U. S. Senate. Levy Lake, a popular fishing spot in nearby Alachua County, is named for Moses Levy, Yulee's father, who settled in Florida before it became American territory.

If your summer route takes you through Colorado, New Mexico, and Arizona, you'll be in country with fifteen places named for Jews and another that was once so named. Near the Dallas Divide in the Colorado Rockies is Mears Peak, named for Otto Mears, a Lithuanian-born frontiersman, road builder, and colonizer, who helped settle the San Luis Valley in the 1870s. The abandoned mining town of Altman in the Cripple Creek area recalls Sam Altman, who ran a saw mill there during the gold boom of the 1890s. Just outside of Denver is Spivak, which gets its name from the late Dr. Charles Spivak, one of the founders of the Jewish Consumptive Relief Society, whose buildings occupy most of the town.

On U.S. 60–70, near Safford, Arizona, you pass Solomonsville, once the seat of Graham County. It stands where Isador Elkan Solomon opened a trading post in 1876. Seligman, on U.S. 66, at the point where Pacific time begins, is named for Jesse Seligman, New York banker and philanthropist, who financed the old Atlantic and Pacific Railroad. Nogales, on the border between Arizona and Mexico, was founded by Jacob Isaacson, and for years the place was known as Isaactown.

In northwest New Mexico is a tiny hamlet called Levy, which acquired its name from an early merchant who ran a commissary for the workers who built the first stretch of the Santa Fe Railroad to reach New Mexico. On the route of the Santa Fe is a crossroads hamlet known as Seligman. It is named for Bernard Seligman, who came to New Mexico in 1850. His son, Arthur, was governor of the state from 1930 to 1933.

You'll be within reach of many other places named for Jews if you vacation in the Ohio and Mississippi valley states. On the Mesabi Range iron ore country in Minnesota you'll run into the St. Louis County village of Sax, founded by Solomon Sax, a Lithuanian immigrant who opened that area to settlement in 1893. Just north of Madison, Wisconsin, is the oddly named town of Slinger, which is a contraction of Schlisingerville, founded in the 1840s by Solomon Weil Schlesinger.

Through Arkansas, Mississippi, and Louisiana the tourist will see road signs bearing the names of fifteen towns named for Jews. In Arkansas you'll pass through the rice-growing community of Goldman, named for J. D. Goldman; Levy, a suburb of Little Rock, which honors Max Levy, a Jewish businessman who lent the town's founder money to open a store; and Weiner, a spot on the St. Louis Southwestern Railroad, named for a railroad official. Mississippi signposts point to Kahnville, founded in the 1850s by Louis Kahn; Marks, established in the 1870s by Leopold Marks; and Mayersville, county seat of Issaquena County, named for David Mayer.

One of the largest rice-growing towns in the South is Kaplan, Louisiana, founded in 1901 by Abram Kaplan, who pioneered the rice industry in Vermilion parish. Marksville, seat of Avoyelles parish, memorializes Marc Eliche, an Alsatian Jew, who came there in 1820. Brandenburg, Kentucky, recalls Colonel Solomon Brandenburg, who fought in the War of 1812 and ran a tavern in Meade County. The once bustling but now virtually deserted Kentucky River town of Gratz is a reminder that the Gratz family of Philadelphia had mercantile interests that linked the east with the newly opened western country in the late eighteenth and early nineteenth centuries.

Whatever corner of the country you select for your vacation, you won't be too far from some place named for a Jew. If you're in Oregon, take a look at Roseberg, in Doublas County, named for Aaron Rose, who founded it in 1851. In King's Canyon National Park, California, you can climb Mount Reinstein and Goldstein Peak, memorials to early Jewish settlers. In Montana you can hike through the Bob Marshall Wilderness Area at the entrance to the Flathead National Forest. It's named for the great recreation and forestry leader, Robert Marshall, a son of Louis Marshall. In Idaho, remember Stein Mountain, in the Beaverhead Mountains, named for Henry Stein, prospector and sheepman; and the tiny hamlet of Alexander, which recalls Moses Alexander, governor of Idaho from 1915 to 1919. In Wyoming you'll see Hahn's Peak on the Wyoming-Colorado line, burial place of Joseph Hahn, pioneer prospector.

East or west, north or south, the Jews are on the map of the United States. There's Fleischmanns in New York, Gilman in Vermont, Manassas in Virginia, Mendes in Georgia, Gratz in Pennsylvania, Falkville in Alabama, Marcus in Washington, Seligman in Missouri, Edelstein in Illinois, Lehman Caves National Monument in Nevada, Cohen's Bluff and Levys in South Carolina, and many more.

When you find the places that go with the names, you'll stub your toes on some of the bits and pieces that add up to the exciting story that is American Jewish history.

—B.P.

The Synagogue with a Secret Tunnel

In the picturesque city of Newport, Rhode Island, stands an historic edifice, Touro Synagogue, which testifies to the early settlement of Jews in America. Adjacent to the synagogue, the Society of Friends of Touro Synagogue is constructing Patriots' Park, to prove to the world that both Christians and Jews can found a nation and live in harmony. The park will give recognition to American Jewish patriots who served our country before and during the War of Independence. It is envisaged that Patriots' Park will inspire in tourists, as Touro Synagogue has done in the past, feelings of regard and esteem for Colonial Jews who settled in America and who, with their fellow citizens of diverse faiths, succeeded in making this a great, dynamic, and progressive country.

Touro Synagogue is an unpretentious building, yet it is so typically colonial that it attracts the attention and the admiration of all passersby. Every year a growing number of tourists come to see this architectural gem of the colonial era. As they enter the building and listen with rapt attention to the story of the founding of the congregation, one can see the glow of pride sparkle in their eyes when they learn of the accomplishments of the small Jewish community in colonial Newport.

In the spring of 1658, fifteen Spanish-Portuguese Jewish families arrived in Newport. Historians do not agree on the point of origin of these early Jewish settlers. The view most widely held, however, is that they came from Curaçao, in the West Indies. The Jews, some of whom were Marranos, wanted to start a new life in a land where they could live as free men and women and practice the religion of their fathers without hindrance or fear. They believed this to be possible in the Colony of Rhode Island and the Providence plantations because of the assurance of freedom of religion and liberty of conscience promised by Governor Roger Williams to all who came within its borders. Roger Williams had said: "I desire not that liberty to myself which I would not freely and impartially weigh out to all the consciences of the world besides."

Such liberal sentiments appealed to those whose lives had been scarred by religious intolerance and persecution. The early Jewish settlers in Newport hoped to resurrect their broken lives in a hospitable climate of religious freedom, where they could become useful citizens in the New World and at the same time carry out the practices and traditions of Judaism.

For one hundred years the members of the congregation, few in number and modest in means, worshiped in private homes. But by 1759 the congregation had sufficiently increased to undertake the building of a synagogue, which would also incorporate religious instruction for the young. This was of great importance to the early settler, as was stated in a letter to Congregation Shearith Israel, in New York, written on March 21, 1759, and appealing for funds: "—it is our duty to instruct children in the path of virtuous religion and Divine Law." Shearith Israel sent a generous contribution, which amounted to about one tenth of the cost of the building. Contributions of money and ceremonial objects were received from congregations in London, Jamaica, Curaçao, and Surinam. The London congregation of Bevis Marks sent two charity boxes, which are affixed to the columns at the entrance to the synagogue. In 1769, Judah Jacobs of London sent as a gift the clock that is on the railing of the women's gallery.

A lot was purchased and the architect selected for the work was the renowned

Peter Harrison. With consummate skill, he applied his great talents to this assignment. Harrison succeeded in erecting a synagogue of outstanding beauty, and impressive dignity. Among his many other accomplishments are the Brick Market in Newport (ca. 1760) and design for the Christ Church in Cambridge, Massachusetts (1761).

The synagogue, built of brick imported from England, stands at an acute angle to the street. This is because of the desire to have the Holy Ark facing the east, toward Jerusalem. The interior architecture is of classic colonial style, incorporating some features of traditional Spanish-Portuguese synagogues. There is a similarity with the Sephardi synagogue that was erected in Amsterdam in 1675, particularly in the seating arrangement and in the imposing columns. The columns, which support the women's gallery and the ceiling, are twelve in number, symbolizing the twelve tribes of Israel. We are indebted to Dr. Ezra Stiles, a Congregational minister in Newport, who later became president of Yale University, for much of the early history of the Newport Jewish congregation. In his diary, Dr. Stiles wrote about the dedication of the synagogue on December 2, 1763, in these words:

In the afternoon was the dedication of the new Synagogue in the town. It began by a handsome procession in which were carried the Books of the Law to be deposited in the Ark. Several portions of Scripture and of their Service with a prayer for the Royal Family, were read and finely sung by the Priest and people. There were present many gentlemen and ladies. The order and decorum, the harmony, solemnity and music, together with a handsome assembly of people, in an edifice the most perfect of the Temple kind perhaps in America, and splendidly illuminated, could not but raise in the mind a faint idea of the majesty and grandeur of the ancient Jewish worship mentioned in Scripture.

An appeal for a Torah made by the early Jewish settlers in Newport to the Jewish congregation in Amsterdam was quickly answered. Stiles in his diary noted that in 1764 the Torah was over two hundred years old. This scroll, which is now over four hundred years old, is still well preserved.

Among the silver ornaments that embellish the scrolls are two sets of *rimmonim,* which are the work of Myer Myers, the famous pre-Revolutionary silver craftsman. Of the four silver breastplates that hang on the scrolls, one was made in Poland over two hundred years ago, one in Germany more than two hundred years ago, and one in America over approximately one hundred years ago. A fourth breastplate is a replica of an Italian antique.

Above the Ark is a beautiful painting of the captions of the Ten Commandments in Hebrew by Benjamin Howland, a clerk of the City of Newport, who was paid twelve dollars for his work in 1828.

During George Washington's visit to Newport in 1781, a town meeting was held in the synagogue. In 1790, Washington was the recipient of an address by Moses Seixas, warden of the synagogue. In reply, Washington sent the famous letter "To the Hebrew Congregation in Newport, Rhode Island," which since has become the classical expression of religious liberty in America.

A feature exciting the interest of all visitors to Touro Synagogue is the tunnel under the *bimah,* which extends to the courtyard outside. The original Jews who came to Newport were of Spanish-Portuguese origin, and during the Inquisition Jews were not allowed to worship in public. Very often, they would pray in cellars to avoid the attention of the inquisitors. But when they came to Newport, they were not afraid of their Christian neighbors. They were able to practice the tenets of their religion freely. Yet they wanted to preserve a symbol for their children, always to remember and value the freedom that they enjoyed in America, as opposed to the persecution to which their forebears were subjected.

In the early years of the nineteenth century, few Jews remained in Newport. The services were discontinued, and the synagogue had fallen into disrepair. However, in 1822, Abraham Touro, son of Reverend Isaac Touro, bequeathed money for the repair and upkeep of the beloved synagogue where his father had officiated. When his brother Judah died in 1854, among Judah's bequests were funds for the establishment of a Ministerial Fund at Touro Synagogue. Judah Touro, a great philanthropist, left over five hundred thousand dollars to charities, probably the largest amount left to charity in the United States up until 1854.

In 1946 Touro Synagogue was designated a national historic site by the United States Government. This does not mean that the government pays for its upkeep. The congregation members' dues and assessments support the upkeep of the synagogue and the Society of Friends of Touro Synagogue assumes responsibility for its maintenance as a shrine.

In 1954 a Restoration Committee was formed by the Society of Friends of Touro Synagogue to undertake the restoration, preservation, and the refurbishing of the historic edifice. About twenty coats of paint were removed from the interior wood work to determine the original color of the first coat of paint. Two centuries of grit and grime that had accumulated on the candelabra and candlesticks were removed, and the original brass luster was restored.

—M.Gr.

 When Ulysses S. Grant Ordered the Expulsion of All Jews

On December 17, 1862, as the North was scoring important victories in the Civil War, the most vicious anti-Jewish regulation in the history of the United States was issued by the headquarters of General Ulysses S. Grant. It read:

General Order No. 11

The Jews, as a class violating every regulation of trade established by the Treasury Department and also department orders, are hereby expelled from the department within twenty-four hours from the receipt of this order.

Post commanders will see that all of this class of people be furnished passes and required to leave, and any one returning after such notification will be arrested and held in confinement until an opportunity occurs of sending them out as prisoners, unless furnished with permit from headquarters.

No passes will be given these people to visit headquarters for the purpose of making personal application for trade permits.

Grant's command, which included parts of Tennessee, Mississippi, and Kentucky, was the scene of frantic commercial activity between the North and the South. Conflicting regulations created havoc as legal and illegal traders swarmed into the area. The idle northern mills needed cotton, and the South was desperately short of medical supplies. Legal traders, smugglers, and speculators bribed army personnel of all ranks to get the needed material, and they all reaped enormous profits. Although the commercial activity was authorized by the White

House and the Treasury Department, Grant vehemently opposed it and was determined to curtail, at the very least, the illegal trade.

Although there were Jews engaged in illegal trade, available records show that only a small number of the illicit traders were Jewish. According to W. E. Woodward, a Grant biographer, "most were Yankees and dyed-in-the-wool Protestants." Why then were the Jews singled out for expulsion? Though prejudice was the likely reason, economics and greed played an important role. If the Jewish trader were eliminated, the non-Jewish trader or speculator would gain even greater profits. As this trade was discussed in Grant's headquarters, Jews were continually referred to as smugglers and speculators. This, no doubt, influenced Grant, who did not have the time or temperament to differentiate between fact and fancy. In any case, when the order was issued, it effectively removed the Jewish competition.

The Jewish community reacted with shock and urgency. Even as the expulsion order was carried out, Jewish organizations were alerted by telegrams, and both individuals and delegations descended on Washington. These efforts were inspired by Cesar Kaskel, a determined and resourceful man, who had been expelled from Paducah, Kentucky, where there was no record of any illegal Jewish traders. He sent letters and telegrams to newspapers and Jewish leaders. He wrote to President Abraham Lincoln, and when he did not receive an answer, he decided to go to Washington and see the President personally. It was doubtful that his letter ever reached the President.

With the help of a congressman who was sympathetic to his cause, Kaskel was able to secure admission to see Lincoln. As Kaskel spoke to him and showed him documents to verify the expulsion order, it was obvious that Lincoln knew little if anything of the situation. The President was sympathetic, and after he was fully briefed, he engaged in a whimsical exchange with Kaskel. Lincoln said:

"And so the children of Israel were driven from the happy land of Canaan."

Kaskel replied: "Yes, and that is why we have come unto Father Abraham's bosom, asking protection."

"And this protection they shall have at once," said Lincoln emphatically.

The President instructed the General-in-Chief, Henry W. Halleck, to revoke the order immediately. Halleck telegraphed Grant's headquarters, and three days later, on January 7, 1863, the notorious General Order No. 11 was canceled.

The aftermath of the order produced a storm of controversy. There were meetings of protest in many large cities at which Grant's dismissal was demanded. Depending on their leanings, newspapers and politicians supported or attacked him. Some of Grant's supporters resorted to anti-Semitic rhetoric as they defended him by attacking Jews. When Grant became the presidential candidate of the Republican party, the Democrats used the order to berate him, and the Republicans either minimized it or blamed it on subordinates.

Though most Jews were openly distressed, there were others who came to his defense for various reasons. Some were afraid of anti-Semitic reactions to an attack on a war hero. Others, especially Republicans, supported him for political reasons. Simon Wolf, a prominent Jewish Republican, not only defended Grant but defended the order. He insisted that the order never hurt anyone. In a display of admiration for Grant, he even named his newborn baby after him.

Was Ulysses S. Grant a bigot? An examination of his career as both general and President presents conflicting evidence. Although there is little doubt that he was responsible for the order, as President he was decidedly friendly to Jews and Jewish causes. He appointed many Jews to public office, including Edward S. Solomon as governor of the Washington Territory and Joseph Seligman as Secretary of the Treasury. When a pogrom broke out in Rumania, Grant appointed a prominent Jewish leader, Benjamin Peixotto, to serve as consul in Bucharest and to bring pressure on the Rumanian Government to halt violent attacks on Jews.

During the Civil War, Grant never made an apology or gave any explanation for the order. In later years, however, when he was running for President, he claimed that "the order was sent without reflection." He further stated that "it never would have been issued if it had not been telegraphed the moment it was penned."

An interesting analysis is offered by historian Bertram W. Korn. He notes that "some persons are victims of unconscious prejudices . . . men sometimes assimilate stereotyped images, mythological concepts, bigoted ideas, from their environment, of which they are utterly unaware and which lie dormant in their unconscious mind until called forth by some severe experience." Then, according to Korn, Grant "became conscious of the prejudice and perhaps he was able, by virtue of that consciousness, to root it out from his spirit although he was too shamed to admit it."

—M.As.

Harvard's President, in the 1920s, Insisted on Need to Restrict Jewish Student Body

The emphasis of Jewish students (in the 1920s) was, as a matter of course, upon scholarship, intellectual pursuits, academic achievement. Coming largely from a lower economic stratum, they were not inclined to play—and were mostly incapable of playing—the social game. Their goal was the practical one of advancement through education. In that sense, their presence was a challenge to the student establishment.

Except in terms of this conflict in values and interests, this resistance to the "invader," there was no logical argument for quota restrictions. The colleges were expanding, and the qualifications for admission called for minimal academic credentials. A student could get into Harvard in the 1920s with a diploma from an acceptable high school and a not overly challenging entrance examination. Average intellect and application to his studies would carry him through.

The elitist colleges were not the only ones that played the restrictive game. Criticism of Jewish students took on a pejorative note whenever their numbers grew to a point where they began to be noticed. Always it struck at their social characteristics—often cruelly so—as if they were untrained creatures of a lower order. They didn't fit. Of recent alien origin, they should wait a generation or two before knocking at the door of the colleges, else they might pollute American civilization. The argument was an extension to the second generation of the one used to close the gates to their immigrant fathers.

Statistical data on college restrictions in the 1920s and earlier are hard to come by, but the operation of the informal college quota system was clear. It had its roots seemingly in the student body itself. At the elitist schools, Jewish students were barred by the honor societies, the eating clubs, and the fraternity houses. Even at publicly operated City College of New York in 1913, a fraternity dropped its affiliate because too many Jews had been "pledged." These incidents took place though they were rarely discussed. But a dean at New York University, explaining a sudden drop in the number of Jewish students in 1922, remarked that "whenever the student body is found to contain elements from any source in such proportions as to threaten our capacity for assimilating them, we . . . restore the balance."

Columbia University, a prestige school within New York City, finding its Jewish enrollment in 1929 stood at 40 percent, took steps to cut it to 22 percent within two years. Syracuse had its little internal battle in 1923, when about 15 percent of the student body was Jewish. Except for Harvard, the numbers of Jews at the Ivy League schools were minimal and the records vague, though the situation was quite clear. In 1930, Rutgers, still a prestige small college and many years from its transformation into a state university, limited its admissions to 33 Jewish students, to "equalize the proportion."

What emerges is an informal but determined system of bias, almost untouchable as long as it retained its surreptitious character but increasingly harmful to the ambitions and goals of larger and larger numbers of young Jews seeking to find their way into mainstream America. Suddenly, and in the most unexpected way in June 1922 it all came out in the open. The cover of secrecy, as the contemporary phrase has it, "was blown." College admissions quotas became a topic of public discussion; the subterfuges, subject to exposure; their reform, a matter of political agitation. At the center of the storm stood President A. Lawrence Lowell and Harvard University, probably the least culpable of all the elitist schools.

On June 1, 1922, Harvard abruptly issued an announcement stating that since "the great increase in the number of students at Harvard College" and because of a lack of enough classroom and dormitory space and related problems, "it is natural . . . there should be talk about the proportion of Jews at the college."

The very bluntness of the statement sent shock waves around the country. Lowell seemed determined to bring the whole subject out in the open. Whether it was candor, naïveté, prejudice, or sheer assurance of his patrician place that moved him, he was not going to pursue a quota policy of admissions—if it came to that—surreptitiously. Year by year, the proportion of Jews at the college had grown until it stood at 20 percent.

"To shut the eyes to an actual problem of this kind and ignore its existence," he said in his commencement address a few days later, "or to refuse to grapple with it courageously would be unworthy of a university."

And shortly afterward, Lowell expressed the thought to an alumnus that it would be to the benefit of Jews themselves if not so many of them came to Harvard.

A reading of the record reveals that it was probably neither excessive candor nor academic statesmanship nor a courageous decision not to play the game by the old rules that motivated Lowell. In a sense, his hand was pushed. The subject of quota restrictions had been under discussion among Jewish and Christian students and faculty for some months—discussions on an intellectual and controlled level. Soon, however, it began to appear in garbled form in Boston newspapers, and it was obvious to so practiced a hand as Lowell that the matter would become a political football at the State House.

The events of that week in June were so startling and the flavor of the discussions so significant in the context of the social conflict that it is valuable to replay the record here. On June 7, 1922, Alfred A. Benesch, a Cleveland lawyer, an officer of both B'nai B'rith and the Anti-Defamation League, having read Lowell's announcement, wrote to him in protest as a Jewish alumnus of Harvard and one of its substantial contributors.

Lowell replied, putting the onus on the increasing "anti-Semitic feeling among the students," which "grows in proportion to the increase in the number of Jews."

"If every college in the country would take a limited proportion of Jews," he proposed, "we should go a long way toward eliminating race feeling among the students and, as these students passed out into the world, eliminating it in the community."

Benesch rejected so drastic a solution on the grounds that, carried to its logical conclusion, "a complete prohibition against Jewish students in the colleges would solve the problem of anti-Semitism. Moreover, it might lead to the establishment of a distinctively Jewish university, a consummation most sincerely to be deplored."

He asked that Lowell convene a meeting of Jewish graduates and corporation members to discuss the matter, a proposal Lowell agreed to accept.

The New York *Times* was so impressed with their exchange of correspondence that it devoted a goodly portion of its first page of June 17 to reprinting it without comment.

Meanwhile, back on the Harvard campus, the drama was being played out by students, faculty, and administration. Once the news was out, Lowell quickly went up Beacon Hill to the State House to confer with the Speaker of the House when a member of the legislature offered a bill to investigate Harvard. Lowell failed to forestall the discussions, but the Speaker issued a press statement that "Harvard would remain as in the past, a great university for all the people. . . ." The other legislators remained unimpressed. It was proposed that Harvard's tax exemption be reviewed and that references to the university be stricken from the state constitution. The governor named a committee to investigate discrimination at the school, and the Boston City Council condemned the university's administration. Of course, this may have all been sheer political opportunism, but it indicated that ethnic and racial prejudice had become an emotional and sensitive matter in a state such as Massachusetts. The State House politicos and the Boston press fed upon each other's sensational responses to the "troubles" at Harvard, adding little to the verities. Lowell's statements, frank and open though they were, did not alleviate greatly the disquiet felt by Jews and others concerned with race discrimination at what was accepted at the nation's leading university.

The storm raised by the Harvard announcement, Lowell's commencement address, and the sudden public awareness of the discussions that had been going on at the university subsided with an announcement by the Harvard Board of Overseers that the matter had been placed in the hands of a faculty committee. No changes in admissions procedures would be made until the committee had completed its work.

Ten months later, the committee reported its findings. No doubt, it had taken cognizance of the strong feelings called forth by the possibility that Harvard might slip into the ways of racial bias practiced at other colleges. The concern of an active Jewish alumni and student body, the presence of distinguished Jewish scholars on the faculty, and an eminent Jewish leader, Judge Julian W. Mack, on the Board of Overseers unquestionably had their impact. Nor could public criticism of the university and indeed the position of liberal spirits associated with Harvard, such as Professor David Gordon Lyon, be readily put aside. More was expected of Harvard.

More was forthcoming. The committee found that a quota system would run counter to the Harvard tradition of "equal opportunity for all regardless of race and religion." Like Caesar's wife, Harvard had to be above suspicion so that "even so rational a method as a personal conference or an intelligence test, if now adopted . . . as a means of selection, would inevitably be regarded as a covert device to eliminate those deemed racially or socially undesirable. . . ."

On another facet of admissions policy, the committee did recommend that the university seek a wider regional representation for its student body. For an institution such as Harvard, there was merit to such a proposal, yet it had been used by other eastern schools—notably Columbia University in New York—to restrict the number of students from the heavily concentrated Jewish population in the East. With somewhat eased admissions standards for students from small cities and towns, there soon was a perceptible effect on enrollment of Jews. By 1931, the ratio of Jewish students dropped from 20 percent (when Lowell first voiced his views) to 10 percent. Lowell retired in 1933 to be succeeded by James Bryant Conant. In 1940, the proportion of Jewish students had risen again to 25 percent. Conant had redefined Harvard's mission:

> *The primary concern of American education . . . is not the development of the good life in young gentlemen born to the purple. . . . Our purpose is to cultivate in the largest possible number of our future citizens an appreciation of both the responsibilities and the benefits which come to them because they are Americans and free.*

The affair at Harvard is central to this narrative on several counts. It dramatized for Jews the critical importance of maintaining merit as the principal criterion for educational advancement, which in turn provided the pathway into the mainstream of American life. For the first time, too, Jews were able to grapple with the secretive—often denied—quota system of admissions practiced by colleges, universities, professional schools, and other institutions to a greater or lesser degree all through the nation. Nicholas Murray Butler could invoke a Jewish quota at Columbia simply by never acknowledging it; Lowell, as we have seen, because of his own character and that of Harvard, could not or would not follow a similar tactic. But elsewhere the secretive approach persisted, and the quota system became an emotion-laden issue for Jews. Not until after World War II did the educational establishment hit the sawdust trail—admitting its transgressions and taking steps to reform its procedures.

—N.C.B.

 ### How the First Jewish Chaplain Got into the U. S. Army

On Sunday, Sept. 8, 1861, Michael Mitchell Allen, thirty-year-old, Philadelphia-born cantor, returned to his tent in the encampment of "Cameron's Dragoons," a Union Army outfit known officially as the 65th Regiment of the 5th Pennsylvania Cavalry.

Allen opened his diary, and wrote:

> *Arose at 5½ A.M. Very cool and invigorating. Fast of Gedaliah. Did not fast, not feeling able to do so. Had service at 8 o'clock. Lectured on "Peace and Harmony." All the officers and companies were present under command of Lieut. Col. Becker, and they all in their uniform looked very well.*

Cameron's Dragoons was a regiment recruited and organized by Jews. Its commanding officer was Colonel Max Friedman, of Philadelphia. Most of the twelve hundred men and officers were Jews. It was named in honor of the Union's Secretary of War, Simon Cameron.

When the "Dragoons" went into encampment in Virginia, near Washington, they elected a chaplain to serve the entire regiment, non-Jews and Jews alike. The chaplain was Michael Mitchell Allen.

He tried to teach the soldiers a reasonable, ethical respect and reverence for the Deity and obedience to superiors, lectured on the evils of camp life, did not fear to mention such subjects as sex and desertion, and comported himself as a man of God setting an example to men of all religions.

Two weeks after Allen's "Fast of Gedaliah" entry in his diary, the encampment was visited by a YMCA worker. When he discovered that the chaplain was a Jew, he wrote to the very Secretary of War in whose honor the "Dragoons" were named. Secretary of War Cameron passed the matter on to George D. Ruggles, assistant adjutant general of the Army. Ruggles issued an order stating the following: "Any person mustered into service as a chaplain, who is not a regularly ordained clergyman of a Christian denomination, will be at once discharged without pay or allowance."

Allen, who knew such an order would come after the YMCA man's complaint, had already resigned by the time the Ruggles order came down through channels. His excuse: "Ill health."

The courageous young *hazzan* from Philadelphia knew he had no chance because, in fact, Congress had closed the doors to any Jewish chaplain in the Union Army.

When Abe Lincoln's Congress had passed the Volunteer Bill, for raising the Union Army, that measure included a clause on chaplains. But the clause requiring the naming of regimental chaplains stated clearly that such a chaplain must be a "regularly ordained minister of some Christian denomination."

In July 1861 President Lincoln pushed Congress to introduce new legislation that would permit non-Christians to be named chaplains. A year later, in July 1862, such a bill was signed into law, and Jewish chaplains have been serving in the armed services ever since.

As of the year 1980, there are eighty-seven full-time Jewish chaplains in the armed services of the United States of America. All have been trained and ordained as rabbis by the seminaries of the three American Jewish denominations—Reform, Conservative, and Orthodox.

The Jewish chaplains are under the supervision of the Commission on Jewish Chaplaincy of the National Jewish Welfare Board.

During World War II, 311 rabbis served as full-time chaplains in our armed services under the supervision of the JWB Commission on Jewish Chaplaincy.

In all, since the beginning of World War II, seven hundred American-trained, American-ordained rabbis have served as full-time chaplains in the U.S. armed services.

We take the Jewish chaplain for granted now. But it took a good deal of organized effort to reverse the congressional act of 1861 before Jews became eligible to serve as chaplains.

Legally, Allen was unfit because he was neither a Christian nor an ordained clergyman. Complicating his case was the fact that he had been commissioned an officer by his regiment and, thereby, subjected to military discipline.

Colonel Friedman—commander of Cameron's Dragoons—selected as his regimental chaplain a Dutch-born preacher at New York's Spanish-Portuguese Synagogue, Rabbi Arnold Fischel.

Being a civilian, Rabbi Fischel had to apply directly to the Secretary of War for his commission. He did. Cameron turned him down. A campaign was launched to amend the Volunteer Bill so that Jewish chaplains would be permitted to serve.

For the first time in its history, the Jewish community in the United States had an issue on which it could take a common stand. The Jew was a soldier; the Jew was a taxpayer; the Jew was officially a full citizen with full rights. But chaplaincy in the very armed services where Jews were fighting and dying—that was denied the American Jew by act of Congress.

The Jewish attitude on the issue was firm, forthright, and expressed both loudly and with good logic.

The Jewish press was voluble, but not all of it supported Rabbi Fischel as the individual who put himself out on a limb to make a test case.

Many Jewish leaders derided the newly formed Board of Delegates of American Israelites, insisting that the board was a narrow group, not representative of the entire Jewish community.

But the board went ahead. It formally appointed Rabbi Fischel as its lobbyist in Washington to work for revision of the Volunteer Bill.

Meanwhile, petitions flooded Washington. And not only Jews signed those petitions. In Baltimore alone, seven hundred Christians signed a petition to Congress circulated by a non-Jewish member of the Maryland legislature.

In Washington, Fischel presented his arguments for a change in the law to virtually every member of Lincoln's Cabinet. He was not given much encouragement. Finally, he reached Abraham Lincoln himself.

On December 13, 1861, a letter signed "Yours truly, A. Lincoln," was sent from the White House to "Rev. Dr. A. Fischel." The letter read:

> *I find there are several particulars in which the present law in regard to Chaplains is supposed to be deficient, all of which I now design presenting to the appropriate Committee of Congress. I shall try to have a law broad enough to cover what is desired by you in behalf of the Israelites.*

The President made good on his pledge. It took many more months, however, before the law was amended. Many Protestant clergymen opposed an amendment, and many members of both Houses of Congress were either lukewarm or hostile in their attitudes.

It was not until July 17, 1862, that the issue was resolved finally. Congress interpreted its older "Christian" clause to mean the following: "That no person shall be appointed a chaplain in the United States Army that is not a regular ordained minister of some religious denomination."

The back of officially sanctioned religious discrimination in the United States had been broken. Jews were eligible for appointment as chaplains if their qualifications as rabbis were otherwise in order.

—S.C.

 ## When American Jews Refused to Be
Second-class Citizens

Seventy years ago, the leading Jewish organizations of the United States were in the midst of a sustained and proud struggle to persuade the government of the United States to insist on the sanctity of American passports irrespective of the religious affiliation of the citizens who carried them. This historic effort involved the relations of the United States and czarist Russia; it lasted many years but reached its climax at the end of 1911 during the administration of President William Howard Taft.

In 1832, the United States and Russia had entered into a Treaty of Commerce and Navigation. The first clause of this treaty declared that the citizens of each country should "be at liberty to sojourn and reside in all parts whatsoever" of the territories of the other and should enjoy "the same security as natives of the country wherein they reside on condition of their submitting to the laws and ordinances there prevailing . . ." It was on the interpretation of this clause that the struggle concentrated.

The czarist government discriminated viciously against its Jewish subjects and allowed Russia to become the scene of violent anti-Jewish pogroms. Whatever feelings these events engendered in the hearts of American statesmen, the comity of nations allowed the United States to do little about them. When, however, the Russian government refused to honor the passports of American citizens or denied Americans residence rights because they were Jews, the government of the United States was in a position to assert that Russia was breaking its treaty obligation.*

As early as 1881, James G. Blaine, Secretary of State in the Garfield administration, had instructed the United States Minister to Russia that the United States could "make no new treaty with Russia, nor accept any construction of our existing treaty, which shall discriminate against any class of American citizens on account of their religious faith."

Unfortunately, this led to no practical results. Russian bureaucrats were masters of the art of evasion, and whenever they were cornered, they simply argued that the treaty of 1832 did not concede to American citizens of the Jewish faith any privileges that Russian Jews did not enjoy.

After the terrible pogrom at Kishinev in 1903, concern over Russian malpractices became sharper. But the State Department began to take a more complaisant attitude and in 1907 issued a circular stating that it would not issue passports to Jews who intended to go to Russia unless it had an assurance that the Russian government would consent to their admission. A protest from the American Jewish Committee brought about the withdrawal by the State Department of words that segregated Jews from the mass of American citizens, but the Russian government did not change its ways.

In a powerful address to the 1911 convention of the Union of American Hebrew Congregations, Louis Marshall urged that, since Russia had violated her obligation, the treaty be abrogated. The union and many other Jewish bodies adopted resolutions to this effect. Resolutions were forwarded to President Taft, but when he met a representative delegation of American Jews, the President showed himself adverse to taking action. Greatly disappointed by the President's attitude, the leading American Jewish organizations organized a vigorous campaign to secure the abrogation of the treaty.

Meetings of protest were held throughout the country. Delegations met with

* An identical problem now confronts American Jews in the case of the Arab states that refuse visas to American citizens who are Jewish, forbid them to disembark in some Arab League countries, prevent American Jewish GIs and civilian employees from serving at an American air base built in an Arab country with American funds and maintained by the United States, and blacklist many American companies who have American Jews among their officers, owners, directors, or personnel. The major American Jewish organizations have been pressing the State Department to stop bowing to Arab discrimination against American Jews and to uphold the sanctity of the American passport.—Ed.

senators and congressmen. Non-Jewish groups became interested in the question. Resolutions were adopted by many state legislatures, either asking that steps be taken to compel the Russian government to observe the treaty or urging that it be abrogated. The press echoed these sentiments.

The entire campaign was in the nature of a response to the unfavorable attitude of President Taft, who was concerned lest American trade interests suffer. Chagrined by Taft's immovability, Jacob H. Schiff said, "I feel personally a warm attachment for the President . . . but in this controversy we owe a duty to ourselves and to the American people which we must fulfill without fear or favor." This was the spirit that the leading American Jew of his day inspired in the community as a whole.

The campaign against the treaty was not the work of one group alone. It was a united effort by several major organizations fighting for the rights of Jews as American citizens, and it demonstrated that concerted action on the part of American Jewry could have some hope of success. One of the most strenuous fighters in this now forgotten struggle was Louis Marshall, whose papers and letters, preserved in the American Jewish Archives in Cincinnati, shed much light on this important episode.

Resolutions demanding that the treaty with Russia be brought to an end passed both Houses of Congress before the end of 1911. The treaty itself contained a period of notice, and after the requisite time had elapsed, the treaty lapsed in January 1913.

—S.D.T.

 Trial by Prejudice: The Leo Frank Case

Enraged mobs choked the area around the courthouse. Men with loaded rifles stood at the open windows of the courtroom: some aimed at the jury; some aimed at the judge. Over and over and louder and louder the men repeated the same chant: "Hang the Jew. Hang the Jew. Hang the Jew."

It could not have happened here. Yet it did happen in America, in Atlanta, Georgia, to be exact, in the year 1913, to a young American Jew named Leo Frank. The case, now famous in the annals of law, has been called a "trial by prejudice." It was one of the events that led to the founding of the Anti-Defamation League. It was an event that still gives an eighty-one-year-old man nightmares.

Herman A. Binder was a friend of Leo Frank. In 1909, as president of an Atlanta B'nai B'rith lodge—Gate City Lodge No. 144—he had inducted Leo into the organization.

"We were the same age and had the same interests," Binder said. "In 1910, when I introduced a resolution to a B'nai B'rith convention decrying the caricaturing of Jews in magazines, cartoons and vaudeville, and calling for counteraction, Leo agreed wholeheartedly with me. Such stereotyping was dangerous because it fanned the flames of hatred and could lead to violence. Three years later, poor Leo found out exactly how dangerous that could be."

Leo Frank was a Cornell University graduate. Slight of build, soft-spoken, he was intellectually predisposed. Frank had come to Atlanta to manage a pencil factory for a friend of the family. He became a part owner, was married to a local girl, and settled down to a quiet, unobtrusive life. In 1913 he was elected president of Gate City Lodge. The same year, on April 27, Leo Frank was arrested for the brutal rape and murder of Mary Phagan, a fourteen-year-old worker in his factory.

"They arrested Leo and a young Negro janitor named Jim Conley," Mr. Binder related. "Jim told one story after another as to where he had been at the time of the crime. Leo admitted having seen Mary—he had paid her wages and thought she had gone home."

There had been several rape cases in the community, all unsolved. The sheriff had been criticized for not doing his job. To restore his reputation, he needed a case and a conviction. The prosecuting attorney, Hugh Dorsey, was an ambitious man, anxious to advance himself politically. He, too, needed a case and a conviction.

"Now they had their case and two suspects," Mr. Binder said. "A Negro and a Jew—both hated."

Leo Frank was accused of rape and murder with no more evidence than his own admission that he had seen Mary Phagan the day of the murder. Jim Conley was accused of being an accessory to murder.

"The trial was a farce. Prosecuting attorney Dorsey had his case and didn't care how he won it. The mobs kept up their chants. I can still hear them screaming, 'Hang the Jew' through those open windows. And inside the courtroom, spectators were allowed to give free vent to their anti-Semitism. The jury were threatened with death unless they brought in a verdict of guilty; the judge was threatened with death if he didn't pass a sentence of hanging. No deputies tried to clear the windows or the courtroom. And sitting there, looking so small and forlorn, was my friend Leo. He was found guilty and sentenced to die. Conley was given one year in the chain gang."

Indignant editorials in newspapers throughout the country excoriated the persecution of Frank. The *Atlanta Journal* of March 11, 1914, denounced the court procedures and in two full columns pleaded for a new trial so that "the people of Georgia would not stand before the world convicted of murdering an innocent man by refusing him an impartial trial."

Prominent lawyers analyzed the testimony and pointed out that it indicated Conley's guilt rather than Frank's. Herman Binder traveled across the country asking B'nai B'rith lodges to issue protests. Congressmen, senators, and governors made appeals in Frank's behalf. The execution was delayed; the delay only brought further demonstrations.

"Jew money is trying to thwart justice," the anti-Semites said.

Thomas E. Watson, Georgia's top bigot and a friend of the prosecuting attorney Dorsey, jumped at the new chance to use his nationally circulated publications to preach anti-Semitism. In one of them, *Watson's Magazine*, the anti-Catholic, anti-Negro, anti-Jewish hatemonger called Leo Frank "a typical young Jewish man of business who lives for pleasure and runs after Gentile girls. Every student of sociology knows that the black man's lust for the white woman is not much fiercer than the lust of the licentious Jew for the Gentile."

Despite the noisy protests of Georgia's bigots, Governor John M. Slaton reduced the sentence to life imprisonment and, to protect Frank from a threatened lynching, ordered him moved to the "safer confines" of the fortresslike Milledgeville Prison.

Now rage was turned against Governor Slaton. He was denounced as "king of the Jews" and "traitor." Week after week Watson issued the most venomous attacks against Slaton, Frank, and the Jews. Watson's Georgia following, already considerable, increased.

Governor Slaton, his life threatened, his political career in jeopardy, refused to exchange his principles for mob rule. Leo Frank was to stay in Milledgeville Prison.

"I received letters from Leo," Mr. Binder said. "It was now 1915 and he still hoped to establish his innocence. He thanked me for my help and begged me to keep on trying."

But time was running out for Leo Frank. Frequently assaulted by both white and Negro prisoners as the Jewish Northerner, his throat was slashed by a convict cellmate.

"Leo was transferred to the prison hospital, and after about a week showed signs of recovering. Then one day—it was August 15, 1915—about thirty men came. They called themselves a Vigilance Committee. They marched into Milledgeville Prison as though it had no iron gates or armed guards. They pulled Leo out of his hospital bed and no one stopped them. They chained him to the back of a car and hauled him about fifty miles to the outskirts of Marietta. Then they took Leo's broken body and strung it up. They murdered Leo Frank . . ."

Herman Binder shook his head, still not fully believing what he knew was true.

What happened after the murder was just as hard to believe. Watson's publication kept up the tirade. "A Vigilance Committee redeems Georgia and carries out the sentence of the law on the Jew who raped and murdered the little Gentile girl, Mary Phagan . . . Let Jew libertines take notice . . ." it said the day after the lynching. Other articles used every trick by which anti-Jewish prejudice could be kept boiling. Frank was headlined as JEW PERVERT. The old canard of "Jewish ritual murder" was revived.

In New York and other cities, newspapers denounced the lynching in editorial expressions of horror.

"But Leo was dead," Mr. Binder said, "and no one in Georgia looked for his murderers."

And the others in the case? Governor Slaton's political life was indeed over. In 1917, the prosecuting attorney, Hugh Dorsey, was elected governor of Georgia. In 1919, Conley, the man many lawyers thought was guilty but who had received one year in the chain gang as an "accessory to murder," was sentenced to twenty years in the state penitentiary for attempted burglary in an Atlanta drugstore.

—L.I.

 ## A *Sukkah*, Courtesy of U. S. Army Engineers

"Chaplain," the voice on the telephone asked, "what in the Sam Hill is a *sukkah*? You sure you spelled it right?"

"Certainly," I answered the lieutenant from the engineering section. "It's spelled right."

"But it's not in the book, Chaplain. How about changing the nomenclature?"

Thus began my friendly encounter with the U. S. Army Engineers to build a *sukkah* for the Feast of Tabernacles in Munich, Germany. Now don't get me wrong. The army can build anything, but they have to know what they are building, and there are always a few technicalities to be complied with if you want to have it done right or at all. GIs call it red tape. But that's not true. It's a matter of getting the right idea to the right place in proper form—and, of course, with proper approval. The army will build a five-hundred-foot TV tower if you can prove you're entitled to it or build a bridge across the deepest gorge if you can assure them that you have to cross it. But when it comes to building a *sukkah*—that's another matter.

A few weeks before Rosh Hashanah I conferred with Chaplain Terry, my administrative chief, and laid out my plans for the High Holy Days and Sukkoth. He was enthusiastic about the entire program and told me to make sure to put my requisitions in on time. Thus I had gotten across the first hurdle when I cleared my program and the other chaplain concurred.

Then I called in my assistant, Sam Roth, and told him to type up a 447, which is the army way of putting in a work order. We dispatched it immediately to the Engineers for action. A few days later a German civilian called on the phone and asked for the chaplain. When I answered the phone, he asked, "Chaplain, *was ist das—sukkah?*" I explained to him the nature of the *sukkah* and gave him a brief idea as to its construction.

"Oh, *Sie wollen ein* chapel annex *haben,*" he answered. "This is *verboten. Kein* building. Military economy."

I again explained to him that this *sukkah* didn't have a roof and was only a temporary structure. He quickly answered that this would make no difference, but if I would hang on for a moment, he would check it with the boss. After waiting for a while I heard his voice again, and he told me that the boss might go along with me but added with a chuckle, "*Warum kein* roof? For the same money and approval *können Sie einen* roof *haben.*"

"But I don't want a roof," I answered heatedly. "I just want a *sukkah.*"

It was then that the lieutenant in charge of the engineering unit got on the phone and asked me what a *sukkah* was.

"Long ago when the children of Israel came out of Egypt and traveled in the desert, they lived in booths," I started to tell him. And after a few moments of scriptural history I conveyed to him the significance of the *sukkah.*

"We'll approve it, Chaplain," he answered, "and I'll send my representative out to see you."

We were still far from having a *sukkah* but were over the major hump. The next morning a representative came out to see me, and we visited the chapel grounds.

"How large do you want it?" he asked, as we surveyed our possible location. I gave him a rough idea as to our needs.

"Ah, come on, Chaplain," he said, "as long as we're building a *sukkah*, let's build a big one!" I tried to explain to him that I didn't want to overdo it, and every time I measured, he added on a couple of feet for good measure.

"Now, Chaplain," he said, "let's understand something. Maybe you were a little modest; let me give you a roof."

"But we don't want a roof," I said. "It would be contrary to Jewish law, and it wouldn't be a *sukkah* if it had one."

"It rains awful bad here in Bavaria, and I for one am well acquainted with the liquid sunshine we have been receiving."

"Don't worry," I told him. "It never rains on Jewish holidays."

With a mirthful look he assured me it would be accomplished according to our plans and religious directives.

Next I had to get permission from the supervisor of grounds in order to put up the structure. Then we called the fire department to get their concurrence. They assured us it would be approved if they could come in and fireproof the place before it was used. Then we called the utilities to get permission to put an electric extension line from the chapel into the *sukkah*. Permission was granted.

A few days later as I left my home across the street from the chapel, I witnessed a beautiful sight. There by the chapel was a huge army truck being unloaded by its crew. I went over to see what was going on and found to my extreme satisfaction that the U. S. Army Engineers were ready to tackle the problem—one deluxe *sukkah* for the Jewish chaplain. While the crew began to lay out materials, one of the German civilians assisting came over to me and whispered quietly, "*Ja*, I know *was ein sukkah ist*. Years ago there was one of your people who used to build a *sukkah* behind his house."

"Years ago?" I asked him.

He answered in a mournful tone, "It was before they took him away."

By midafternoon our *sukkah* was completed. It was a delight to behold. Several of the Jewish GIs came out and gave it their approving nods. We were happy, but we still had some problems to overcome. We needed the covering for the *sukkah*. Although we cover the top with foliage, it must allow those inside to peer through and see the stars. My delegation of Jewish boys went to see the forester of Perlacher Forest, the area in which we reside. When I explained to him what we needed, he not only gave us his immediate approval, but asked us if we would like to have a few trees planted around it. I told him that it wasn't necessary and thanked him profusely.

The Jewish Women's Club came down and decorated the *sukkah* with fruit, candy, tinsel, the bright autumn foliage, and the aromatic pine cones. Army folding tables and chairs were brought in. Sam Roth stood high on a ladder and hung up strings of bright red apples handed to him by my wife, Miriam, Frieda Kolieb, and Mrs. Cill Reitler, who also filled little paper bags with sweets, nuts, and surprise gifts for the children.

Then we ran into a most hilarious situation. The schoolchildren on their homeward way stopped to take notice. They asked if they could have a *sukkah*, too. The children of our neighbors wanted to know if they could have a party in it after the Jewish children were through. Our neighbors arrived to congratulate us. I arranged with the Christian chaplain to take the Sunday school children into the *sukkah*. The Sunday sightseers came by in droves. One commented that at last the army had begun to build a chapel annex.

But little did they know that out here in southern Bavaria, across the street from Stadleheim Prison of Nazi infamy—on the edge of a forest, a *sukkah* was filled with joyous sons and daughters of Israel who were commemorating the Feast of Tabernacles. The walls hid from our sight the tyranny and terror that once lived here. They now encompassed the merry throng and hid from sight the dread reminders of the past. We looked upward in song through the roof and saw the stars.

—O.M.L.

 ## It Couldn't Have Happened in Russia!

I lived through the infamous pogrom at Kishinev in 1903. I saw the slaughter with my own eyes. I experienced czarist tyranny and its disdain for individual human beings, firsthand. This is why what happened to me on my arrival in America fourteen years later possessed in its bright contrast the quality of a democratic miracle.

Now that I have been a citizen of the United States for almost forty years I still marvel at it. I shall never take for granted the wonder of American egalitarianism and the greater wonder that I was one day able to joke about it in retrospect with the distinguished gentleman who was the principal figure in the incident. But by then I was already an established businessman, living in Cleveland, the home city of this man who had so casually helped me in my immigrant plight.

I was born in Kishinev, and I was ten years old at the time of the government-inspired massacre in which scores of Jews died—my townspeople and relatives and friends. I remember it was a Sunday and the last day of the Passover. A group of friends had dropped into our home for *Kiddush*—that sanctification of wine, with the partylike tea and goodies following it, which is a feature of every Jewish festival.

Our holiday mood was suddenly pierced by the sound of breaking glass, pounding footsteps, and cries of terror. With the swiftness of a planned military maneuver, the mob had invaded the Jewish quarter and was striking at the unprepared innocents, smashing, pillaging, and killing. My father and his friends quickly saw what was happening, pulled down the shutters and barricaded doors and windows. It was a precarious and temporary safety. During the night a friendly police official brought warning: "Today there will be another slaughter."

At dawn we made our way through deserted streets to a fortresslike hotel, where a relative lived behind the greater security of iron-grill doors, and we took refuge with him. Twenty-four hours later, word came that the fury had passed. We returned home. Seared into my mind to this day is the sight of dazed survivors cleaning up the debris, loading dead bodies onto mortuary carts. Two years later when the mob pounced again, the Jewish community was ready—a Jewish self-defense corps had been organized, which gave as much as it received.

But that this same Russian autocracy that had drowned my people in humiliation and blood should demand my service in its army was an irony whose sharpness did not amuse me. My family had moved to Odessa and a slightly greater degree of physical security in 1906, but this did not increase my ambition to be a soldier of the Czar when the war broke out in 1914. For a while, I was able to keep moving in connection with my job for a textile manufacturing firm—from Odessa to Warsaw and as far east again as fabled Samarkand. In 1916 it became apparent that I could no longer escape seizure for Russian military service. I determined to take the risk of escaping Russia once and for all. It was not to be easy.

I had no permit to leave, and the way out lay through Harbin, a four-thousand-mile journey through Asia and across the bleak route of the Trans-Siberian railroad. Buying my railroad tickets from station to station to escape detection, I began my trek. From Kharkov to Harbin took ten days by rail. Then finally to Japan and an open door to freedom. I sailed for America.

On New Year's Day, 1917, the ship *Korea Maru*, on which I was a passenger, touched at Honolulu, and one week later I gratefully walked down the plank in San Francisco into the *goldeneh medina*—the "golden country" of the United States.

I had no one to whom to turn and only the smattering of English I had picked up in Japan. New York beckoned because there I might find a distant relative and some *landsleit*—people who had also come from Kishinev and might offer me some guidance. They did—I got a job in Philadelphia—enough to provide me with shelter and food. But no sooner did my journey end than the army was seeking me again. This time it was the army of the blessed land that had given me haven, and I had no objection to serving. But—I felt—give a bewildered immigrant a few moments to catch his breath, to get oriented among the strange customs of his new land, to learn a little English. Mentally and emotionally, I was still a captive of my past experiences, and often I was tortured by bad dreams in which I relived the tragedies and persecutions I had witnessed in Russia.

I registered, and then I learned that the draft boards—stretching the letter of the law—were calling even aliens and those who had just gotten their first papers. My "greenness," the strain of my recent experiences, my feeling of awkwardness in a new land with a strange language—all of this was now further confused by the well-meant pressure of my Philadelphia and fellow workers that I try to get a deferment. I determined to seek the counsel of others.

Thus began an adventure in which I was passed from hand to hand, up to the moment of revelation.

"Go to see Ossip Dymov," I was told. "He's a great novelist and playwright and he should be able to advise you."

And so I was off to New York and then out to the very end of the elevated railway that terminated near the Bronx Zoo to walk a mile into the East Bronx countryside to see Mr. Dymov.

"Go to see Yitschak Horwitz," Mr. Dymov told me. "He's a big writer for the daily Yiddish paper *Der Tog* [*The Day*], and he can help you."

Back into the city and down to East Broadway to see Mr. Horwitz I patiently went.

"I'll give you a note that will get you in to see our Washington correspondent, Reuben Fink," said Horwitz.

And so the following weekend, I was off to Washington.

This merry-go-round did not seem too strange to me. In Russia, in order to get in to see even a minor government bureaucrat, one had to go through a chain of connivances, and "connections," even bribes—and then take one's chances. So, I would play out my string.

In Washington I made my way to Mr. Fink's apartment. "He's away for the weekend," the maid told me. "Try his office on Pennsylvania Avenue tomorrow morning."

The office building on Pennsylvania Avenue was impressive, and what seemed to a "greenhorn" to be a huge and expensively furnished reception room was even more impressive. I gave my name and my request to the pretty but haughty receptionist and I sat down to wait for Mr. Fink. I sat and I sat. I waited from nine o'clock until noon, and there was no sign that Mr. Fink or anyone else was aware of my existence.

A little later in the afternoon, a young man who had passed in and out of the reception room several times walked in again, and this time he took notice of me. I remember him as a handsome, well-groomed fellow in his thirties, with black hair and black-rimmed eyeglasses.

"You've been waiting quite a while," he said to me with what seemed to be a pleasant demonstration of interest.

In my broken English, I acknowledged his concern and told him that I was waiting for Mr. Reuben Fink.

"What do you want of Mr. Fink?" he asked.

I told him.

"It'll take you days to get to see Mr. Fink, and then it'll be a week or ten days before he'll be able to do anything for you," my unknown counselor said. "Will you do what I tell you?"

I had little choice. He led me to the window. "Do you see that large building there? Go over to that building and ask for Mr. Baker. He'll take care of you."

I thanked him and left to carry out his advice. Timidly, I went through the main entrance of the building he had pointed out and found myself in a lobby with tall columns overwhelming me with its magnificence. In the center of the lobby there was a semicircle of desks, and behind each desk alternately around the semicircle was a soldier or a sailor, receiving the visitors.

I walked to the first desk vacant and said that I had come to see Mr. Baker. I was given a register to sign and told to have a seat.

Not two minutes had elapsed when a soldier walked over to me with a slip of paper in his hand. "Mr. Brandt?" he said. "Follow me, please."

He took me to an elevator, and we went up several floors. Then he ushered me out and led me along a long, high-ceilinged corridor and through a door into a large room in which there were chairs along one wall and a desk at which a young woman was seated. The soldier gave his slip to the young woman and beckoned me into a chair.

The young woman used her telephone and then in but a minute or two stood up and said, "Follow me, please, Mr. Brandt."

I was led into another large office with big windows overlooking official Washington and one long desk—but no one there. The young woman asked me to be seated. This time I must have waited five minutes when a man walked in. He was middle-aged, about five feet five inches tall, wearing glasses, and dressed in a light summer suit.

I stood up.

"Sit down, Mr. Brandt," he said to me, and then in a friendly, easy tone he asked, "What can I do for you?"

I told him my story.

"When did you arrive in this country?"

"I'm here six weeks," I said.

The man's kindliness made it easy for me to respond, despite my halting English. We talked.

Finally he said, "Don't worry. Give your registration card to the young lady at the desk outside, and she'll take care of it. Goodbye, Mr. Brandt." He stood up. I stood up. We shook hands.

Bewildered and reluctant to part with the registration card, which the law required me to carry, I went through the door to the outer office to the young lady as I had been instructed. She took my card, made a copy of it, put a mark in its upper right-hand corner and said, "There! You have been given a deferment."

Hesitantly, I asked, "Could you please tell me—who was that gentleman I just spoke to?"

"You don't know?" Her raised eyebrows registered amazement. "That," she said, "was Mr. Newton D. Baker, the Secretary of War."

The soldier was waiting to lead me out. Shakily, I followed. And—thanks to the advice of the strange young man (was he a practical joker or a good Samaritan?) —I left the huge pile of the Army and Navy Building, my head spinning and my knees unsteady, to enter my adopted country a second time—but with a new understanding and a glow of affection that has kept warm my love for America to this day.

—L.B. and A.L.

Father Coughlin and the Jews

For me, the individual whose activities had particular salience for American Jews in the 1930s was Father Charles E. Coughlin,* who founded and led the National Union for Social Justice. It was this popular radio priest who, after beginning by attacking "international bankers" early in the decade, ended by leading a nation-wide political attack on "atheistic and communistic" Jews, giving new respect-ability to the bizarre allegations contained in the Protocols of the Elders of Zion. Coughlin's weekly paper, *Social Justice,* is now gathering dust in bound volumes in the stacks. Recently, however, I scanned many of its columns. As one who had read them when they originally appeared on newsstands and library reading racks, I found myself contending with many of the same feelings with which I had to wrestle almost forty years ago. A sampling of the contents of even a few of these columns may provide my younger fellow Jews with a sense of what the thirties felt like for the American Jew as a Jew. Perhaps they will then understand better why, for many of us, our emotional clocks are fixed at that time, shaping our con-sciousness as a community and as individuals to this day.

Interviewing Father Coughlin in the 1960s, Sheldon Marcus (*Father Coughlin,* Little, Brown and Company) was bemused by the fact that "this lonely, solitary figure was once the most hated and the most feared American of his time. He was Christ; he was Hitler; he was savior; he was destroyer; he was patriot; he was demagogue . . ."

The *Detroit Free Press* by 1938 was referring to his regular radio program as Father Coughlin's weekly attack on the Jews. (By his own estimate this program was heard by seventeen million at least.) "There was always a great fear among us about Father Coughlin because of his tremendous following . . . we were afraid," Philip Slomovitz remembered in 1970.

Indeed there was good reason to be worried. Hadley Cantril and Gordon All-port (*The Psychology of Radio,* Harper & Brothers), two of the most eminent so-cial psychologists of that era, attested to the awesome power Coughlin was achiev-ing through his radio programs:

> *Were it not for Father Coughlin's feat in creating exclusively on the basis of radio appeal an immensely significant political crowd, one could scarcely believe that the radio had such potentialities for crowding. In the case of Huey Long, of Mussolini, of Hitler, the leaders were well-known in advance, and the listeners had ready-made attitudes toward these leaders that needed only to be intensified and directed through vocal appeal. But in Father Coughlin's case the attitudes required creation as well as shaping.*

What made for the fear of which Slomovitz speaks was not so much the extent of anti-Semitism—after all, widespread anti-Jewish sentiment was nothing new in America—but rather the fact that it had become part of the creed of a political movement.

Yet time in some cases softens perceptions.

By 1965, Charles Tull (*Father Coughlin and the New Deal,* Syracuse Univer-sity Press) was reminding us that ". . . 'fascist' was the scare word of the 1930s . . . Except for his occasional references to a corporate state there is little reason

* He died in 1979.

to charge Coughlin with fascist sympathies." Andrew Greeley (*The Catholic Experience*, Doubleday & Co., Inc.), writing two years after Tull, admits that "it is possible to see Coughlin as a fascist and quite easy to think of him as an anti-Semite." He suggests, despite this, that:

> *It may be more charitable, however, to see him as a sincere and well-meaning social reformer without much scholarly or intellectual understanding of economic problems and social problems whose head was turned by the immense popularity of his radio broadcasts. Disillusioned by the New Deal's failure to take him seriously he turned more and more against it and his anger and frustration carried him down the path that ended in the worst sort of demagoguery.*

How easy it is in retrospect to explain away the anti-Semitic activity of former political leaders like Coughlin. At the time, however, particularly from 1938 on, those Jews who listened to Coughlin's broadcasts and who read what he and his supporters wrote were neither in the position nor the mood to accept explanations of why he was behaving in this manner. All that most of them knew was the sound of his rich baritone on the radio every Sunday, mouthing theories that by direction or innuendo held Jews to be responsible for the twin evils of atheistic communism and unfettered capitalism and their attendant miseries while all the while the horrors of Nazism were being visited on Europe's Jews, as Hitler devoured central Europe piecemeal.

From 1936 into early 1938 the Jewish readers of *Social Justice* would simply have been left uneasy by vague, contradictory signals in its columns. The Jewish question was referred to sparingly. For weeks it was not mentioned. A few references to Jews were negative but in the nature of supposedly helpful criticisms, and some were actually positive in tone.

Early in 1938, the reader of *Social Justice* received strong intimations of what was to come on the Jewish question. The material contained in the volumes for this particular year is perhaps most evocative of feeling for those of us who were growing into adulthood at the time. This was a watershed year, the year of *Kristallnacht*—the destruction of Germany's synagogues—the year of the Anschluss and Jewish flight from Austria, the last twelve months of peace in Europe.

As horror began to engulf Jews overseas, one read nothing of this in *Social Justice*. What one did read in the lead article for March 28, 1938, was the need of the American workingman to defend himself against the most important Jew of all, Bernard Baruch.

Clearly, if he sought compassion for his people now being bloodied in the streets of Europe, the Jewish reader would not find it in the pages of *Social Justice*. On the contrary, he discovered there that the Jews were only getting what they deserved. After all, hadn't they not only created bolshevism, or so the litany went, but also seized control of the finances of the world through the capitalist wing of their secret polity? Revealing their designs in the May 16 issue of that year, Ben Marcin set about describing the manner in which the Sassoons, the "Oriental" branch of this conspiracy, had "captured the rich and progressive civilization of India" during the nineteenth century. Two weeks later it was explained how the Sassoons had arranged to intermarry with the Rothschilds, who dominated Europe. The next month there followed a thunderous attack on these Jewish bankers in an article entitled "Punch and Judy Banking."

If he did not feel himself overwhelmed by incredulity, the Jewish reader might at this point have been intrigued, wondering how *Social Justice* and Father Coughlin would now finally demonstrate the existence of unbreakable ties and

unity of purpose between the two sets of "bad" Jews to whom they constantly referred, the usurious Jewish capitalists and their brothers, the Jewish Communists.
Beginning in July 1938, the answer was laid out in full detail. Jewish Communists
and Jewish bankers are united partners in an organized conspiracy. Their
nefarious plans are revealed in a document known as the *Protocols of the Elders
of Zion.*

Published in Russia in 1903 and circulated throughout the world by the anti-
Semitic organizations in every Western country, the Protocols purported to be the
minutes of a meeting of three hundred leaders of world Jewry who were plotting
the takeover of Christian civilization. The modern Jewish reader would find both
the language of the Protocols and the intention behind their fabrication ludicrous.
He dismisses them at his peril, however; during recent years they are said to have
been widely disseminated in Arab countries, and one does not have to take too
dark a view of human nature or history to expect that they will surface here
again someday.

The American Jew who read the Protocols in 1938 could not afford to laugh at
them. Week after week, throughout the summer and fall, Father Coughlin in his
column, as well as on the air, commented on selected segments of the Protocols.
Yet he generously excused most Jews for what the Protocols contained, noting in
his first article on the subject that:

> *Everyone who mentions the Protocols is listed immediately as a Jew-baiter.
> That is very poor logic. Although the Protocols are supposed to represent an
> account of a meeting held by certain so-called Jewish leaders, it is fair to say
> that the vast masses of Jewry know little or nothing about them. It is likewise
> fair to assert that the vast mass of Jews entertain no organized thought
> against Gentiles or Christians.*

Wallace Stegner, in his essay "The Radio Priest and His Flock" (*The Aspirin
Age*), wrote that Coughlin's voice, "without doubt one of the great speaking
voices of the twentieth century," would have to be heard to understand fully why,
as he commented on the Protocols, millions responded with such fervor to his
"manly . . . intimacy" and "ingratiating charm."

But the Jewish reader of the 1930s may very well have encountered the Protocols before. What was new and important was Father Coughlin's commentary, for
his major point was that it is evident that what is now taking place is in accord
with the plans the Protocols reveal:

> *Read again this plan explained in the Sixth Protocol to destroy civilization.
> No wonder the author of this document foresaw many years ago how to cre-
> ate want in the midst of plenty and how to agitate the thoughtless masses to
> the point of revolution.*
>
> *We shall raise the rate of wages which, however, will not bring any advan-
> tage to the workers for, at the same time, we shall produce a rise in prices,
> of the first necessaries of life, alleging that it arises from the decline of agri-
> culture and cattle-breeding.*
>
> *This has been accomplished under the regency of the New Deal.*
>
> *We shall further undermine artfully and deeply sources of production by
> accustoming the workers to anarchy and to drunkenness.*
>
> *This has been accomplished through the agency of the C.I.O. which for
> many months has been under the influence and leadership of communistic
> philosophy with its needless and unauthorized strikes and its destruction of
> property; with its clubbing of officers and its seizure of government in vari-
> ous states . . .*

One misreads the mind of the times if one believes that all of this was dismissed by everyone, at least everyone of any intelligence, as balderdash. For various reasons, rather than assess the more outrageous of Coughlin's pronouncements, of which the number was now steadily mounting, some of his readers and listeners chose to fasten on those few of his ideas that at least could be given a coating of respectability. Ignoring his more bizarre distortions, they continued to see him as essentially a defender of the faith against communism. Particularly isolating in its effects for Jews was the tendency on the part of other readers, who, while dismissing the Protocols as obviously fraudulent, cautioned the Jews that they were setting themselves up for persecution by the kinds of positions that a number of them were taking on ideological issues throughout the world. The editors of one diocesan newspaper quoted by George Seldes were typical of this group. They wrote, "We feel it our duty to again expose the forgery of the Protocols. We also feel it our duty to inform the mass of the Jewish people of the dangerous paths charted by their alleged leaders."

The views reflected in *Social Justice* appeared to enjoy the support of at least a substantial minority of the American public. The beliefs of this segment of society included, at worst, a large element of virulent anti-Semitism and, at best, devotion to the idea that no more Jews should be included in American life. This last, which took the form of strong opposition to Jewish immigration, was encouraged openly by the Coughlinites. "Who Comes First, Aliens or Americans," read one column heading in the January 23, 1939, issue of *Social Justice*. Among its highlights were the following:

> *Every foreigner at work in this country means an American out of work.*
> *Every additional foreigner admitted means that another American may be*
> *deprived of his just opportunity to work . . .*
> *Of the total immigration of last year 19,736 were Jews.*
> *Jewish refugees are rapidly using up the quotas permitted under immigration laws from Central Europe.*

This type of antirefugee propaganda had a telling effect on American immigration policy. The Wagner-Rogers bill, for instance, which would have admitted 20,000 refugee children over a two-year period beginning in 1939 was, as Irving Howe describes it in *World of Our Fathers*, killed through asphyxiating amendments. It never reached the floor of either house of Congress. A Gallup poll found only 26 percent of the population approving of the proposal to rescue these youngsters. Several factors are said by Howe to account for this frightening and saddening response. Among them, "People feared that refugees would compete for scarce jobs. Anti-Semitism fanned by demagogues like Father Coughlin played its part."

Columns such as that cited above worked more than idle mischief. They helped to make it certain that children who could otherwise have lived would never escape the death trap of Europe. Individual Jews may have reacted to Coughlinite propaganda with inner serenity and disdain for its promulgators or, at the other extreme, by redoubling their efforts to conceal their Jewish identity. All, however, whether courageous or craven or even if they somehow managed to avoid thinking about the matter overly much, shared a sense of bewilderment over the strength of this onslaught and the depth of hatred it revealed. Furthermore, Coughlin's columns and broadcasts subtly exploited internal differences among Jews. The left among us was teased by the idea that, were it not for those terrible Jewish supercapitalists, we could be part of a genuine American populist movement. The right and center could wonder whether, if it weren't for those Jewish radicals, we could remain undisturbed alongside other patriotic Americans. Each, in this sense, could be perceived by the other as thwarting the respective aspirations.

Coughlinism could also trigger off a host of self-defeating emotions and self-criticism. Some of the most committed Jews among us felt emotionally vulnerable whenever charges of economic parasitism were leveled against our people. As Hayyim Greenberg, foremost among America's Labor Zionist thinkers, cautioned his readers in 1942, not only was the Tolstoyan idea of the special virtue of manual labor responsible for the attitude of self-condemnation among some Jewish intellectuals; Zionism itself bore its share of responsibility.

In the past, Zionist leaders, himself included, Greenberg noted, had not hesitated, on occasion, to declare from the platform that "to be a good Zionist one must first be somewhat of an anti-Semite." The return to *Eretz Israel*, so this line of thinking went, "required physical work above all and the normalization of the economic structure of the Jewish people. Whosoever does not engage in so-called 'productive' manual labor, is to be held a sinner against mankind." Greenberg went on to point out that "when addressing the non-Jewish world we become exceedingly apologetic and talk of extenuating circumstances to explain our supposedly incriminating economic position . . . We admit expressly or by implication that we constitute a useless and unlovely element in the economic set-up of every country."

Greenberg actually felt it necessary to remind the sophisticated and dedicated Zionists for whom he was writing that "the present economic structure of the Jews may not be ideal, but there is nothing evil or parasitic about work which is not manual . . . Any work which satisfies human needs or is socially useful is productive work." Anti-Jewish attacks such as Coughlin's had taken their toll; too frequently they turned us inward in masochistic self-examination instead of outward against those who would denigrate us.

This, then, is the silhouette of the "bad old dream" that fleetingly haunts American Jewry in its middle years, reminding us of something we hope is no longer there. Certainly we can reassure ourselves that the acceptance of Jews into the mainstream of American intellectual, economic, and political life is incomparably greater than it was when *Social Justice* was being hawked from street corners, newspaper kiosks, and church steps. There is no denying that times have changed.

—R.K.

 # When the Shofar Blew on Capitol Hill

With my *kittel* over my arm flowing in the brisk morning breeze, I walked up New Jersey Avenue with Congressman Herbert Tenzer toward the Capitol Building. September 27, 1965, the first day of Rosh Hashanah, 5726, was truly a *Yom ha-Zikaron* (a Day of Remembrance). This was the first time that a Jewish religious service was being held in the United States Capitol Building.

As we entered the building of the House of Representatives, I followed my ebullient host, Mr. Herbert Tenzer, to our destination, the Congressional Meditation Room. This small vestibule, a nondenominational, dimly lit room, situated behind the famed rotunda, had been set aside to serve as our sanctuary. Through the efforts of John McCormack, the Speaker of the House; his chief assistant, William

"Fishbait" Miller; and Congressman Tenzer and his staff, this room had been converted into a makeshift, but beautiful house of worship.

Our little synagogue included an ark, made from a discarded bookcase; two large, lovely golden *menorahs;* an "altar" draped with purple velvet curtains, the beautiful "Tenzer Torah Crown," which was perched on the windowsill overlooking the altar; a reader's table; a special mahogany lectern; two bouquets of flowers; a special table for *talleitim, machzorim,* and *yarmulkes;* and twenty-five leather-backed seats. We even had an informal *mechitzah* of several large plants placed between the men's and women's sections, which was voluntarily respected and used by the women present.

When we arrived at 8:45 A.M., it was heartening to find several of my "congregants" already assembled. The services were scheduled to start at 9:00 A.M.; they had to be concluded by 12:00 noon owing to a scheduled roll call vote. Therefore, it was essential that we keep to our planned schedule. We recited the *P'sukei D'zimrah* prayers. However, when we reached the *Hamelech* prayer, which commences the morning services, we had achieved our required *minyan,* the first successful congressional quorum-call of the day. With Congressmen Tenzer and Multer serving as *gabboim* and hosts, Mike Bromley, Mr. Tenzer's aide, serving as sexton, and two guards outside the closed door to restrict entrance to invited guests only, the service started.

Conscious of the intimacy of the congregation, I started the "Hamelech" prayer on a low note. By the time I reached the *Shir Ha-Maalot* prayer I was in full voice. As I executed the traditional High Holiday liturgical chants, my numerically small congregation joined in frequently in tunes vaguely familiar to them. I emphasized a few "major" prayers while using straight *nusach* for the other prayers. I did not omit any prayers yet was able to keep to our time limitations.

Mr. Tenzer kept the assemblage informed periodically of the page in the Machzor being covered by the prayers as they were recited. I had placed paper clips in his machzor on the pages where I felt announcements were necessary, and in this way our efforts were effectively coordinated.

The Torah Service was brief since we limited ourselves to one general *Me Sheberach* blessing. Aryeh Maidenbaum, a young family friend of the Tenzers, read the Torah capably. He and his bride of three weeks, had accompanied me from New York. Despite the aid of a transliterated Torah-blessings card, many of my distinguished congregants had to struggle through the recitation of the blessings when called to the Torah.

The invitations that were extended specifically indicated that Reform and Conservative *machzorim* would be available for all those who chose to use them but I noticed that all the worshipers were using the Orthodox *machzorim.* Several of the people had started the service with these other *machzorim* but had quickly switched when they found that they could readily follow the service in the Orthodox *machzor*.

Instead of the usual sermon, Congressman Multer read a special message from President Johnson, and Congressman Tenzer read the Prayer to our Government. They were flanked by Senator Ribicoff and Congressman Friedel, each holding one of the Torah scrolls. The *shofar*-sounding ceremony seemed to outweigh much of the rest of the services in its effect on those assembled.

Upon returning the Torah scrolls after the *shofar* sounding, I noticed that an additional member of my congregation had slipped into the services and was standing solemnly in the back row. As I approached him on my excursion around the room, his face appeared vaguely familiar. At first glance he looked like a typical old, *shul-Yid*, but soon I recognized this distinguished visitor, the Speaker of the House, John W. McCormack. With his white *yarmulke* perched on his equally white mane of hair, he solemnly kissed the Torah as I passed with the *tallith* he had donned. He remained for about a half hour and displayed a great deal of respect for our humble services.

Upon the conclusion of the services a spontaneous series of highly complimentary short speeches were made, concerning the services, the participants, and the joint efforts of Congressman Tenzer and Yeshiva University in making the arrangements. Senator Ribicoff spoke in behalf of the Senate; Congressman Multer, in behalf of the House; Congressman Halpern, in behalf of the Republican minority; and Congressman Tenzer, in behalf of all the others. He also announced that the Speaker had asked for reports from all the congressmen to be placed in the *Congressional Record* and the National Archives. Thus, we had truly written and participated in a "page from American history." We were all invited to a Tenzer-sponsored *Kiddush* in the Speaker's private dining room in the Capitol Building.

Although most of my congressional congregants had to go to the House chamber for the initial attendance roll call, I headed for the Speaker's dining room. Although somewhat conspicuous because of my white *yarmulke* and large *tallith* bag, I confidently strode through the rotunda and the crowded corridors, with two Tenzer aides at my side and several reporters trailing behind. In a few moments my legislative *baalebatim* returned from the roll call and listened to my recitation of the *Kiddush* for wine. I passed around the *Kiddush* cup, and each person was able to partake of the wine in this manner.

Carl, the Speaker's personal butler, who served the *Kiddush* and lunch, once worked for a kosher caterer and had learned many of the traditional food customs. He refused to open the closet, where the kosher wine had been put, until I arrived, since he had been taught that only a *mashgiach* (he pronounced it "mosquito") should be allowed to handle the wine.

We partook of gefilte fish, cake, honey *tagelach*, and similar snacks. The *Kiddush* ended when we heard a buzz signal for a quorum call. This signal was arranged by "Fishbait" Miller, who was subsequently given the unofficial title of honorary sexton of the Congressional Synagogue.

A holiday meal, mainly the kosher frozen-food meals that we brought with us from New York, was served in the Speaker's dining room. Emanuel Celler joined our group for lunch, making the total ten, the first day.

Congressman Multer, obviously inspired by the spirit of Rosh Hashanah that had been engendered by our services, initiated the day's debate in the House with the traditional greeting, *"L'shona tovah tikosevoo."*

The procedures and successes of the first day were basically repeated the second day, except for the publicity aspect, which seemed to die down. Special guests at the services included the chaplain of the House, and Congressman Bingham, a Gentile congressman from the Bronx. Although most of the fanfare was absent, the spirit and morale of the worshipers remained at a high pitch.

—H.Sh.

 ## The Sonneborn Institute:
An Incredible Chapter in American Jewish History

As the fighting in Europe drew to a close during World War II, the Jewish Agency girded for stiffer resistance against Britain, confident that one way or another she would ultimately be forced out of Palestine. In anticipation of this eventuality and the likelihood that war with the Arab states would follow, the Jewish Agency moved to mobilize Palestinian Jewry and to flood Palestine with illegal immigrants.

In March 1945, at a secret meeting in Paris between Ben-Gurion, chairman of the agency executive, and the high command of Mossad, Haganah's committee for illegal immigration, two Haganah subgroups were created, Bricha and Rehesh. Bricha was made responsible for manning an escape route for smuggling concentration camp survivors to Palestine in defiance of the British blockade. Rehesh was set up as an underground task force to procure arms and military equipment for Haganah however and wherever it could.

Early in June, Ben-Gurion slipped into New York quietly, grimly determined to raise the immense sums needed for both operations. Nettled by what he regarded as a lack of vision and courage manifested by the leaders of the Zionist Organization of America in whom he had confided, he turned for help to Henry Montor and Rudolf Sonneborn. Montor was then executive vice-president of the United Jewish Appeal and had previously been executive director of the United Israel Appeal. Sonneborn, a wealthy industrialist and chairman of the finance committee of the United Jewish Appeal, had been involved in Zionist affairs since 1918, and he was the youngest member of the American Zionist Commission that had accompanied Chaim Weizmann to Palestine. Montor was not specially close to Ben-Gurion but was widely known in Palestine as "the fund raiser." He knew intimately all the leading Jews in the United States, to most of whom Ben-Gurion was still only a name.

Sprawled on a divan in a bleak suite of the Hotel Fourteen on East Sixtieth Street, Ben-Gurion, on June 25, divulged to Montor what he had in mind. He asked Montor to bring together quietly for a private briefing a small but reliable group of men so committed to Palestine that they would be ready to undertake a major assignment upon whose success the future of Jewish Palestine might depend. Montor agreed and, in consultation with Sonneborn, quickly rounded up sixteen prominent Jewish bankers, business tycoons, and industrialists. All of the invitees were contacted by telephone to avoid putting anything in writing. No one was told more than the date, time, and place and the urgent need for his presence at an off-the-record conference with a highly placed personage from Palestine. Not even the wives of those invited knew what it was all about until much later.

It was a blisteringly hot Sunday that July 1, when the sixteen men gathered in Sonneborn's duplex bachelor apartment on West Fifty-seventh Street. The time was 9:30 A.M. Ben-Gurion, in an open shirt, was perspiring heavily as Montor and Sonneborn introduced eacn man. Ben-Gurion, in turn, presented the three key advisers he had brought along: Eliezer Kaplan, treasurer of the Jewish Agency; Dr. Yaacov Dori, a trained engineer and Haganah chief of staff; and Reuven Shiloah, chief of Haganah intelligence and later minister to Washington. Also on hand was Meyer Weisgal, confidant of Chaim Weizmann.

There were no "assembly atmosphere" and no formal agenda, Montor recalled. Sonneborn acted as chairman. Everyone sat where he was when each man spoke, but the room was charged with an electric air of excitement even though the real purpose of the gathering was still vague. What the assembled leaders heard from Ben-Gurion in a long speech "seemed at the time remote from reality and tempered by visionary hopes," Sonneborn said some years later. Yet everything Ben-Gurion predicted in a remarkably frank analysis of the Jewish position turned out to be unerringly accurate: The Labour party would win the upcoming parliamentary elections in England, but this would not alter British policy in Palestine; England would yield the Mandate before too long, and the Jews would then seize the opportunity to create an independent state; the British would interfere, the Arabs would resist through widespread attacks on the Jewish community, and open warfare would ensue; the Yishuv had at best two years to prepare its defenses and to increase its manpower by massive illegal immigration from the DP camps; the youth of Palestine, if they had tanks, heavy artillery, planes, and guns, would defeat the Arabs.

To arm the Yishuv,* Ben-Gurion proposed the immediate expansion of its tiny munitions industry and the stockpiling in Europe for later use in Palestine of the heavy stuff that could not be brought in while England retained control of the country. Dori pointed out that once the Japanese were defeated, immense quantities of surplus arms-making machinery and military hardware would become available in the United States at bargain prices. Kaplan spelled out the potential cost of such purchases, and Shiloah sketched the methods by which arms could be obtained and smuggled into Palestine.

Having taken his rapt listeners into his confidence, Ben-Gurion invited them to create an American arm of Haganah. He merely hinted at what they would be asked to do and gave them no clues as to who would do the asking. All he told them was to be ready to move, discreetly and boldly, when called upon, and to bring into their circle other like-minded men and women throughout the country. No one in the room made any formal pledge or promise, but neither did anyone demur. All sensed they had become part of something historic, and implicitly they agreed to make themselves available without reservations for the mission Ben-Gurion had outlined. The all-day meeting adjourned with a final word of warning not to divulge the names of Ben-Gurion, Shiloah, Dori, and Kaplan as having been present.

Anyone who claims "to have total recall of that meeting is pretending to information he does not have," Montor says, "because no notes of any kind were taken." Since there was no official record of what took place in Sonneborn's apartment, "some people not present have had their reputations enhanced by recording themselves as among the participants," Montor told the authors.

Montor's list of the participants on July 1, made available for the first time for this article, contains the following names, besides his own: Sonneborn, Ben-Gurion, Kaplan, Dori, Shiloah, and Weisgal: Shepard Broad, Miami, Florida; Abe Berkowitz, Montgomery, Alabama; Julius Fligelman, Los Angeles, California; Max Livingston, New Haven, Connecticut; Dr. Jacob C. Shohan and Joel

* The Jewish Community of Palestine.

Gross, Newark, New Jersey; Charles Gutwirth and Jacques Torczyner, New York, New York; Ezra Shapiro, Cleveland, Ohio; Harold J. Goldenberg, Minneapolis, Minnesota; William S. Cohen, St. Louis, Missouri; Charles J. Rosenbloom, Pittsburgh, Pennsylvania; William H. Sylk, Philadelphia, Pennsylvania; James L. Permutt, Birmingham, Alabama; Martin Abelove, Utica, New York, and Albert Schiff, Columbus, Ohio.

Out of the July 1 meeting was born the nameless, nationwide secret movement that became the American section of Haganah. Its operations began in the early fall of 1945 after Britain's Foreign Secretary Bevin confirmed Ben-Gurion's prediction that the new Labour Government would not budge from the 1939 White Paper. One morning in September, Sonneborn received a mysterious telephone call from an Englishman, who said: "I'm trying to locate the Sonneborn Institute. Perhaps you can help me." Unwittingly, the caller had coined a cover name. Sonneborn gave no sign of recognition but agreed to meet for lunch. The man was Sir Simon Marks, one of Weizmann's young associates in 1917, who handed Sonneborn a terse, four-word message from David Ben-Gurion: "The time has come."

The next day the Sonneborn Institute opened headquarters in an unmarked office at 250 West Fifty-seventh Street. Similar unidentified branches were established in major cities, all financed by the original group of sixteen. Each of them coopted trustworthy associates, who recruited collaborators of their own. Within a fortnight the entire country was covered by a network of volunteer committees whose secret parlor meetings gave their activities a conspiratorial character. The movement had no officers, directors, or letterhead. Its unofficial leader was Sonneborn, who presided at meetings of the high command every Thursday at 12:30 P.M. In a private dining room of the Hotel McAlpin, visitors from Palestine brought confidential instructions, and institute leaders from around the country reported on how things were going.

The institute's first assignment was a private fund-raising effort that raised more than one million dollars for the purchase and shipment of machinery, tool dies, and blueprints for the Yishuv's munitions industry. Armed with specifications, a cadre of Haganah experts, headed by General Dori and Chaim Slavin, director of the hidden defense factories, fanned out over the country. For months they scoured scrap metal yards, used machinery lots, army and navy stores, surplus ammunition dumps, and government offices disposing of World War II materiel, snatching up whatever was available. The Sonneborn Institute paid the bills and set up the intricate channels through which the stuff reached its destination. Every crate got by the British customs inspectors, and some of the contents were still in use during the Six-Day War in 1967.

A second undertaking involved the Sonneborn Institute in helping Haganah locate, buy and transport guns, used planes, ammunition, and explosives. This was not yet illegal, but it was carried out in secret because British security agents were doing all they could to thwart it. The actual arms smuggling was done by a tightly knit group of Haganah agents who arrived in New York in 1947. They included Zev Shind, father of the Israeli Merchant Marine; Hy Issacher, builder of the El Al Israel Airlines; Shlomo Shamir, organizer of the Israeli Navy; Yehuda Arazi and his twin brother, Tuvia, and Teddy Kollek, later mayor of Jerusalem. Kollek was the coordinator of fund raising and also in charge of the main purchasing center in the Hotel Empire at Broadway and Sixty-third Street. He found the Irish stevedores on New York's waterfront helpful allies in getting arms out of the country because of their traditional dislike of the British. Haganah's New York base was next door to the Copacabana, in the same hotel where Ben-Gurion had met Montor. Several suites and rooms in the inconspicuous hotel were reserved for Haganah emissaries under a variety of aliases. The location was extremely handy because of its proximity to Jewish Agency headquarters, then on East Sixty-sixth Street.

In the Hotel Fourteen, Yehuda Arazi, chief organizer of the arms procurement program, recruited his most important American agent, Adolph (Al) Schwimmer. A World War II ferry command pilot, Schwimmer became known to Haganah while serving as a TWA flight engineer. With Ray Salk and William Sosnov, he bought and reconditioned scrapped transport planes from surplus U.S. war stocks and set up a cover organization, Schwimmer Aviation Co., to enlist mechanics, pilots, and gunners. Planes were flown to an operations base at Burbank, California, where Bill Gerson and Al Auerback, U. S. Air Force veterans, and an unnamed retired U. S. Marine Air Force major supervised their overhauling. Eleanor Rudnick, owner of a fleet of crop-dusting planes, made her private airport south of Los Angeles available for testing and crew training by Leo Gardner, son of a rabbi and a World War II U.S. pilot, and Sam Lewis, a flying buff.

In Honolulu, Schwimmer contacted a dealer with a large supply of spare engine parts and surplus arms. Machine guns flown in from Hawaii in crates labeled "Engines" narrowly escaped a search by FBI agents at Burbank. Schwimmer and Arazi enlisted Hank Greenspun, a New York-born Nevada newspaper publisher and World War II combat officer, for his brief but fantastic career as a gunrunner. Before Greenspun was through, he plundered a naval depot in Hawaii, acquired an airport and two airlines in Panama, and posed successfully as a confidential agent of Chiang Kai-shek in Mexico. When he was arrested, he pleaded guilty to violation of the neutrality act in order to spare Haganah embarrassment. His exploits cost him his citizenship and a fine of $10,000, but he was later pardoned. Others, too, risked reputations in the desperate effort to arm Haganah. Some Jewish manufacturers slipped nonexplosive war materiel into cartons of export goods that eventually turned up in Haganah warehouses.

Social workers and rabbis were among the active participants in the collection of "pots and pans," a euphemism for guns, trucks, small arms, and drill presses that reached Haganah piecemeal from collection points in New York, Florida, and California. Haganah war materiel was often stored temporarily in the basements of public buildings, synagogues, Jewish community centers and Hillel Foundations, labeled "Czechoslovak crockery." Teamster union locals cooperated in trucking heavy items to ports.

One fund-raising pitch that added forty used army trucks to Haganah's arsenal was made before a crowd of crapshooters in the cellar of a midwestern city hall. Escorted to the game by one of the city's leading criminal lawyers, a Sonneborn Institute agent, the social worker who made the appeal was told he could have everything in the next ten pots. From time to time high school and college students were arrested on charges of illegal possession of pistols and rifles that they were caching for Haganah in loft buildings, factories, and private homes. One of these, Joseph Untermeyer, son of the poet, Louis Untermeyer, was acquitted after a passionate defense by Paul O'Dwyer. The former presidential yacht, USS *Mayflower*, which had been acquired for Haganah, was loading guns in Panama when the Panamanian Government withdrew its registry at the request of the U. S. Embassy.

Directly or indirectly, virtually every Jewish organization was linked to the Sonneborn Institute and its many auxiliaries, but few talked about it. Worshipers in Congregation Sons of Israel, Woodmere, Long Island, on Friday night, May 14, heard their rabbi, Irving Miller, describe for the first time what the Jews of Woodmere, Lawrence, Hewlett, and Cedarhurst had been doing for many months to procure arms and war materiel for Haganah. Without mentioning names, he revealed the existence of a shortwave radio transmitter aboard a Jewish-owned yacht anchored in Hewlett Harbor. It had been part of the communications network through which Haganah arms buyers in the United States received their orders from Paris and Tel Aviv. Aboard that same yacht, Moshe Sharett, the Jewish Agency's chief negotiator at the United Nations, often met with friendly delegations.

More than one Jewish radio amateur was admonished by the FCC for sending and receiving messages on behalf of Haganah in technical violation of the international treaty governing radio communication. British intelligence and Arab spokesmen repeatedly complained about such infractions. One American ham operator who had been cooperating with Haganah was the first to give Tel Aviv the news that Truman had recognized Israel. At 10:28 P.M. on May 14, 1948, this amateur contacted Station ZC61A in Tel Aviv and talked to Joseph Baer. He was the engineer who had patched together an underground Haganah transmitter from bits and pieces left after the British dismantled the official government station. The American reached Baer several times between 10:35 P.M. and 11:25 P.M. EDT (3:35 A.M. and 5:25 A.M., Tel Aviv time, May 15). He also managed to raise the ZC6XY operator in the U.S. consulate in Jerusalem.

A second major clandestine project of the Sonneborn Institute provided ships and crews for the Bricha agents smuggling refugees out of Europe via tiny ports in France, Italy, and the Balkans. It began with the purchase of a pair of corvettes from the Canadian Government. Manned almost entirely by former American Merchant Marine seamen and GIs and outfitted with surplus U. S. Navy equipment, the two 925-ton vessels delivered 5,200 Jews to Palestine before being captured by the British. One unloaded its first "cargo" on the high seas onto small craft and made a second round trip before being caught.

All told, the Sonneborn organization bought eighteen ships that carried over 75,000 Jews to Palestine illegally. One of its purchases was the *Exodus 1947*, for whose dedication in Baltimore Harbor in 1947 some of the Institute leaders made a rare public appearance. Other groups made noisy claims to the credit, but the Institute could not deny them without risking exposure. Doggedly and anonymously, it continued this phase of its work without recognition or the desire for it.

When private fund raising for Haganah was discontinued at the beginning of 1947 because it was producing only a small part of what was needed, the Sonneborn Institute switched to public activity. At the end of 1947, Eliezer Kaplan, Jewish Agency treasurer, had returned to Tel Aviv from the United States with a depressing report on the prospects of substantial funds for arms. Ben-Gurion wanted to leave for the United States at once with Kaplan, but he was overruled, and Mrs. Golda Meir took on the assignment.

In an emotion-drenched speech before the general assembly of the Council of Jewish Federations and Welfare Funds in Chicago, late in January 1948, she described the dangers the Yishuv faced unless it were adequately armed. She asked for an immediate twenty-five to thirty million dollars—five times what Kaplan had said was possible—to enable Rehesh to buy what its purchasing missions had already taken options on. Her listeners—the key leaders in organized Jewish fund raising—gasped but quickly provided the cash through bank loans secured by future contributions to local fund-raising campaigns. In this way over twenty-eight million dollars became available to Haganah in the next four months through the 1948 campaign of the United Jewish Appeal, on whose behalf the federations outside New York raised the bulk of their money.

When the chief of the Rehesh mission in Paris cabled he could buy tanks if he had ten million dollars, he was instructed to close the deal. Similar good news went to Prague, where negotiations were under way for planes and heavy guns. On Mrs. Meir's return to Palestine, Ben-Gurion said, "Some day, when history will be written, it will be said that there was a Jewish woman who got the money which made the state possible."

On February 16, 1948, Sonneborn wrote to his collaborators that "certain confidential activities" carried out for two and a half years were ended with the "successful accomplishment" of the mission. That same day he assumed the open leadership of the newly incorporated "Materials for Palestine," which collected immense quantities of noncontraband goods through a campaign for cash or gifts in kind. Thousands of volunteers engaged in fund-raising projects for the new organization, which provided the Yishuv with ambulances, medical supplies, hospital equipment, blood plasma, clothing, and shoes and made available to Haganah heavy trucks, jeeps, barbed wire, steel sheeting, rubber tires, tents, field glasses, mess kits, cable wire, burlap bags for making sandbags, compasses, and field telephones.

After May 14, "Materials for Palestine" became "Materials for Israel," which was succeeded by the Israel Purchasing Mission in the United States.

—B.P. and H.W.L.

 ## The Last Synagogue in Harlem

"It's a strange phenomenon. Somehow, there's always a *minyan*."

Jacob Mazo, rabbi of the last congregation of white Jews in Harlem, sighed as he looked across at his tiny flock.

"It's a miracle, almost," he said. "If someone cardinal to the minyan were, God forbid, to die, the whole place would fall apart."

None of the worshipers at Congregation Tikvath Israel of Harlem, on East 112th Street between Lexington and Third Avenues, remembers when the congregation was founded. Professor Jeffrey Gurock of Yeshiva University, who has written extensively about Harlem Jewry, believes that the sanctuary in the twenty-five-foot-wide, five-story, tenementlike building was built around 1910, when Harlem's Jewish population of 100,000 made it the second largest Jewish community in the United States, after Manhattan's Lower East Side.

At that time, large synagogues lined Lenox Avenue and 116th Street. Businessmen, office workers, storekeepers, garment workers, and manual laborers who had escaped the crowded Lower East Side filled Harlem's synagogues. They came to the Institutional Synagogue to hear the inspiring oratory of Rabbi Herbert S. Goldstein, who was among the first English-speaking rabbis in New York, and to hear the sweet voice of Cantor Joseph Rosenblatt, who was paid the astonishing sum of $2,400 per year by Congregation Ohab Zedek of Harlem. Many of Harlem's Jews were prosperous. Their thriving synagogues sponsored speakers, dances, social clubs, and youth groups.

Harry Rosenthal, eighty-six, a resident of the Hebrew Home for the Aged in Riverdale, remembers his Harlem neighborhood as "100 percent Jewish."

Harlem's Jewish population grew to 178,000 during World War I, and families doubled up to share apartments. But housing construction was curtailed during the war, and Harlem was bursting at its seams.

At the war's end, construction began along the new subway lines. Jewish Harlemites moved to newer apartment buildings in Washington Heights, along the Grand Concourse and White Plains Road, and across the East River to Bay Ridge, Bensonhurst, Flatbush, Astoria, Jackson Heights, and Long Island City. Blacks replaced the Jews, and by 1930, fewer than twenty-five thousand Jews lived in Harlem. Synagogues sold their buildings to church groups (who still occupy them today) and followed what one rabbi called the "drift of our congregants" to the new neighborhoods.

A few Jews, and Congregation Tikvath Israel, remained.

Services are held at Tikvath Israel on Saturdays, Sundays, and holidays. The synagogue pews can seat about two hundred persons on the main floor and perhaps one hundred more in the now closed women's gallery. Though the harsh fluorescent lighting hides the beautiful carvings in the wood of the Holy Ark, it cannot hide the paint peeling from the cracked walls and ceiling. Water leaks through the walls onto the pitted, bare wood floor. The benches are covered with boxes of unused prayer books and Bibles; a congregation with about twenty-five members does not need many prayer books or Bibles. The scene is reminiscent of photographs of rundown *shtetl* synagogues in Eastern Europe.

On a recent Sunday morning, while nine men prayed at the front of the synagogue, Becky Shapiro, elderly daughter of the former sexton of Tikvath Israel, set up breakfast for the worshipers in the rear. She has been caring for the synagogue since 1936. "God pays my wages," she says. She does most of the cleaning herself and hires neighborhood women to help her with the heavy work. She manages to keep the main floor relatively clean, but the upper four stories are, she claims, inaccessible and "a mess."

After the services ended, the nine men drifted to the back of the synagogue for a breakfast of Italian bread, cream cheese, and sardines. The half-filled quart bottle of whiskey is about two years old, according to Jacob Grodnick, the unofficial president of Tikvath Israel. The members do not drink much.

Much of the conversation revolves around real estate and the produce business. Some of the members have stayed in Harlem because they own the apartment houses in which they live.

Sixty-nine-year-old Meyer Grossman is a bachelor who used to own a hardware store in Harlem. He lives alone in one apartment of the house he owns near the synagogue. He says he has few problems with his tenants: "Some pay the rent; some don't pay." He takes some meals at a senior citizens center and spends much of his time caring for his four dogs and analyzing the racing charts.

Rubin Kugler, an elderly man with bright blue eyes, has lived with his wife for over fifty years in the rooming house they own in East Harlem. He has few problems in this rough, predominantly Hispanic neighborhood because, he feels, "the people here respect us."

Larry, a fifty-year-old Hispanic with an earring in his left ear, quickly agreed. Born in Spain of Gypsy heritage, he occasionally accompanies Meyer Grossman to the synagogue. He had sat quietly during the services, wearing a skullcap and a prayer shawl. "I sympathize with the Jewish people; they're the people of Christ," he added.

Other people have stayed in the neighborhood to be near their business in and around the Park Avenue Market, the *Marketa*.

Jacob Grodnick explained that contributions from Jewish merchants who worked in the market had kept the congregation financially secure until the market fire of July 1977, when many of the merchants gave up their businesses. The synagogue's financial position is precarious now. Tikvath Israel charges dues, but not all the members can pay.

"Our biggest contributor is also our oldest member, a ninety-two-year-old man," Grodnick said.

One of those who works around the market is seventy-five-year-old Sam Spiegel, who owns a wholesale produce business on East 105th Street and lives with his daughter on East 107th Street. He drives his truck to the Hunt's Point Market each morning at 2:30 A.M. to buy merchandise. "All I'm still good for is driving the truck," Spiegel says. An assistant helps him load and unload the produce.

Another man, known to the members as Peewee, is younger than the others. He appears to be no more than fifty years old. Peewee owns a dairy and delicatessen in the market and is active in its merchants' association. For these reasons, he says, "I have to live in this area."

The members are reluctant to talk about the future of their community. Sam Davis, the unofficial cantor and philosopher of the congregation, has two important reasons for staying in his five-room apartment on East Ninety-eighth Street, on the fringes of Harlem. Davis walks to Tikvath Israel, rather than to a closer congregation in the East Nineties, so that the minyan at Tikvath Israel can continue. In addition, he and his wife are often hosts to Orthodox Jews, who, forbidden to travel on the Sabbath, want to be able to visit relatives hospitalized at nearby Mount Sinai Hospital over the weekend.

Grodnick moved out of the neighborhood seven years ago, but he continues to attend services at Tikvath Israel. "We don't know how long the synagogue is going to live," he says.

"Nobody knows what will be," Spiegel says.

When the others had all left, Miss Shapiro agreed. "If we knew what was gonna be in the end, we would have started out in the beginning. This place is our cemetery. This is the last synagogue in Harlem. It has to be remembered."

—S.H.

 Jews in the American Economy

How did it happen that the American economy did so well for the Jews?

Other ethnic groups fared well in the United States, although some, like the blacks, did so belatedly and slowly. The critical question is how it happened that, within four to five generations, the descendants of largely impoverished immigrants from Eastern Europe, without knowledge of English or the ways of the West, were able to create the largest, most affluent, and secure community in the recorded history of the Jewish people.

Settling In

In 1880, the Jewish population in the United States numbered 250,000. Today it stands at just under six million. It is estimated that eight out of ten Jews in the United States are of East European origin. The large inflow started in the eighties and continued right up to World War I. These thirty-to-thirty-five years can be looked upon as the era of "Getting Established." The Jews who came intended to stay. Most of them did remain—only one in fourteen left. This is a sharp contrast with other immigrants, about one in three of whom sooner or later returned to their country of origin. Many Southern Europeans, especially Italians, came with the idea of working hard for some thirty years, saving their money, and returning home to set up business. The East European Jews sank their roots in their country of adoption. They saw their future and, more importantly, their children's future in the United States.

They came to stay in a country that had jobs for them, not always good jobs, but jobs. There were exceptions, of course—the major depression in the mid-nineties; recurrent seasonal unemployment in the clothing industry, where so many Jews had obtained employment; and periodic strikes that, when they lasted for any length of time, brought severe hardships to the workers and their families.

Certain demographic, family, and personal characteristics also contributed to speeding the assimilation of the newly arrived masses of East European Jewry. They had a smaller than average number of children than their neighbors in the Old World, and this continued to be true after they arrived in the New World. With fewer children to support, they could make their limited family resources stretch further. Moreover, the Jewish family was not only intensely child-centered but also had a strong sense of family obligation; successful relatives were willing to help the younger generation of both sexes stay in school or acquire a skill.

The final characteristic of this period of getting established relates to the fact that the Jews settled in large urban centers, which offered better than average public educational opportunities. There is a lot of nonsense bruited about concerning how smart the Jews are. Jews are probably better educated than other segments of the population because of their strong, centuries-old traditions stressing the importance of learning.

Moving Up

The second stage in Jewish immigration and economic progress divides into two distinct periods—from 1915 to 1929, followed by the depression years up to 1940. First, the children of blue-collar workers did not remain blue-collar workers. The sons of painters, clothing workers, mechanics moved into white-collar occupations. Not all of them by any means, but a high proportion of the total. We forget that even among the third and fourth generation there remains a distinct minority of Jews in blue-collar jobs.

Next, since many Jews came to the United States with some background in trade and commerce, significant numbers found it relatively easy to get started in business and, by working hard and accumulating modest savings, to speculate in real estate and in stocks during the prosperous 1920s, when everything was booming.

The extent to which the Jews are overrepresented in business is indicated by the fact that if one looks at a later generation of Jewish youngsters entering college in the 1960s, one finds that businessmen are almost twice as likely to be fathers of the Jewish freshmen than of the non-Jewish entrants (55 versus 20 percent).

The depression wiped out many Jews: some became despondent to the point of suicide. The depression years also helped to illuminate some of the important relations between education and occupational mobility. A considerably higher than average number of Jewish youth were college graduates, and when the private job market went into rapid decline, many succeeded in entering public employment as schoolteachers, as local and state civil servants, and as federal employees after Roosevelt went to Washington.

But employment dragged badly throughout the thirties. The country never got below 10 percent unemployment throughout the entire decade. Many young Jews prolonged their stay at the university and even pursued training in physics, engineering, and mathematics, fields they had eschewed earlier. This turned out to be a lucky move for Jews, since when the war economy got under way in 1940–41, there was a high demand for people trained in the hard sciences.

Making It

This brings me to my third period, "Making It." During the three and a half decades from World War II to 1976, the American economy escaped a serious depression. We had recurrent recessions and suffered severe post-World War II setbacks. (But we escaped any major period of economic hardship.) As a result, it was a propitious time for people to begin to make it, and many Jews did.

Favorable demographic trends assisted the upward mobility of Jews further. Any good Jewish student could gain admission to medical school. The explanation lay in the shrinkage of the total student pool. The much reduced birth rates of the depression years were being reflected in a much reduced number of applicants.

The democratization resulting from the war, reinforced by demographic trends and rapid economic growth, helped to reduce religious discrimination in the executive suite. It was reported that only after the war did the great Mellon empire, headquartered in Pittsburgh, allow Catholics into senior management. All non-Protestants were benefited, and among these the Jews were well positioned to move to levels formerly closed to them.

The postwar era saw a rapid expansion and absorption of scientific, professional, and technical manpower. Large governmental contracts for R & D, the explosive growth of the university system, and the expansion of science-based industry, such as computers, set the stage. The high proportion of Jews attending college created a jumping-off base for them to move rapidly into these expanding areas. Since 1970 the figures reveal that with one out of six in the nation's labor force classified as belonging to this highest occupational category, the proportion of Jews is about one out of three.

An important consideration is the contribution that many wives made to improving the income of their family. American Jews, following the national pattern, encouraged their daughters to seek a higher education; and as the barriers against working married women were lowered, increasing numbers pursued careers in teaching, social work, and business.

Five strands run through this story from 1880 to 1976. First, Jews had the good fortune to be in the right place at the right time. They came to New York, and those who moved on settled in other large East Coast and Middle Western cities—Boston, Philadelphia, Baltimore, Chicago—at a time when these large cities were in their heyday. In 1930 Jews accounted for one out of every three persons in New York City.

Jews had a second advantage owing to the value they place upon education, including higher education, which, as we have seen, yielded large rewards, especially after 1940. In fact the breakthrough of the Jews into the executive suite is closely linked to their antecedent breakthrough into the higher technical ranks of large corporations.

Third, the shift of the economy from agriculture and manufacturing to services was a positive development as far as the Jews were concerned. They had acquired considerable experience in trade and commerce, which stood them in good stead as these fields expanded.

Fourth, the lowering of the barriers against religious minorities proved a major boon. In my undergraduate days at Columbia in the late twenties, the number of Jews on the faculty could have been counted on one hand. My class had a 10 percent quota for Jewish students, not for New York City but for the entire school. The Graduate School of Business at Columbia, established in 1916, had no tenured Jewish professor until I achieved that rank at the end of World War II—thirty years later until the first appointment! Today an informed count suggests that about half of the tenured faculty is Jewish.

To supplement the above: a few years ago the deans of the major law schools on the East Coast—Harvard, Yale, Columbia—were Jewish. Jews have been elected president of such Ivy League institutions as Dartmouth, Brown, Pennsylvania. Professor Seymour Lipset's analysis in the early seventies revealed that Jews accounted for over 20 percent of all faculty members at elite institutions of higher education.

The fifth and final strand that should be identified as contributing to the rapid economic gains of the Jews relates to the significant growth in the not-for-profit sector, that is, in government and nonprofit employment. It is estimated that one out of every three, or possibly as many as two out of every five, jobs are in this sector. And it has been relatively easier for minorities—Jews, blacks, women—to obtain jobs and pursue careers in the public rather than the private arena, especially since the 1930s.

It would be a serious error to see American Jews as a wholly distinctive group with experiences that have no counterpart among other ethnic and racial groups. That would be as false a postulate as the alternative, which argues, for instance, that there is nothing distinctive about the way in which Jews climbed up the job and income ladder. Among the many interesting phenomena that have been little studied is the ethnic replacement cycle. I am struck with the increasing replacement in New York City of Jews by Italians in dentistry as the Jews move in larger numbers into medicine.

Although the future is always uncertain, it is worthwhile to speculate about the likely decline in the relative incomes of scientists, professionals, and technical personnel, an arena where Jews have done very well till now. In the future the American economy may pay off a little less handsomely for educated manpower now that so many more Americans are becoming educated. It does not follow that every physician at the end of his residency will be able to earn $50,000 and at the end of a decade of practice over $100,000.

There is the probability that fourth- and fifth-generation Jewish youngsters may be less hungry, less competitive, less inner-directed. The people who try the hardest seldom start at the top. When I think back to the Columbia troubles of 1968, there were almost as many Jewish youngsters working strenuously to unmake American society as there were Jewish youngsters out to make it for themselves.

Another point worth stressing is the shift in the locus of economic expansion from the usual area of Jewish concentration. Let us consider the following figures. Approximately 60 percent of all the Jews in the United States are on the East Coast, in contrast to less than 20 percent of the total population. The South, with about a third of the nation's population, accounts for only one-sixth of the Jewish population. Only in the West is there an approximate balance: 18 percent of the nation's population, 13 percent of the Jewish population.

To sharpen the focus: Jews account for 0.6 percent of the total population of Texas, 6 percent of New Jersey's population, and 12 percent of New York State's. That means that proportionately there are twenty times more Jews in New York State than in Texas, and we are told that the Northeast is in decline and Texas is still on its way up. I do believe that the Jewish population is poorly distributed to take full advantage of the next cycle of the country's expansion. Jews, both as individuals and as members of a distinctive community, have been adversely affected by the rapid transformation of neighborhoods where they earlier had made large private and communal investments. I will only mention the Bronx and Brooklyn, although similar instances are found in all large northern cities with substantial Jewish populations.

The final point relates to the characteristics of some of the new Jewish immigrants and their descendants. Orthodox, frequently ultra-Orthodox, they keep themselves at arm's length from the economy and society. They discourage their children from attending college. And they look askance at married women working out of the home. In fact, their women, with four, five, or six children, couldn't find the time to work for pay if they wanted to. These new immigrants may not require public assistance, but they have positioned themselves in a manner that is likely to keep most of them in the lower range of the income distribution. They do so because they have values more important than "making it."

What does the future look like, then, for American Jews, postulating as I do that the economy will not seriously falter and that the Club of Rome is wrong in its dire predictions of a world of scarcity?

• The relative rate of progress of Jews will be slower, among other reasons because other ethnic and racial groups are likely to move faster.

• The retardation in the rate of growth of Jewish economic well-being may be speeded if a significant proportion of young Jews opt out of the competitive race, as they are likely to do.

• But all of the foregoing factors added together are still likely to leave Jews at, or close to the top of, the economic heap as the United States enters the twenty-first century.

—E.G.

 A Home Town I'll Never Know

A horrible pogrom took place some eight decades ago in my parents' home town, Proskurov, in the Ukraine. In the wake of the Bolshevik revolution, the Ukrainian nationalists and the anti-Communist White Russians were fighting the revolutionists. Almost as a diversion, these traditional anti-Semites butchered every Jew they could find in peaceful Proskurov. Thousands were killed or maimed; those who could fled.

My newly-married parents, natives of the small city, crossed the border into Poland without papers. The Jewish aid agency, HIAS, helped them proceed westward, to the port city of Antwerp, from where ships sailed regularly to the western world. My parents spoke no Polish or Flemish; they certainly had very little money, and yet they managed. In Antwerp they gravitated to the Jewish community. A Jewish family, rooted in Belgium, took them in, rented them a room, and advised them to open a *haimishe* eating place for the many immigrants then living in Antwerp. My parents' landlord became their friend and advanced the money to set up the little restaurant.

Mother had always been a good cook, so she cooked, while my father did everything else in their new enterprise. Meanwhile they were undecided where to proceed. Mother had sisters in Palestine and in Argentina, who wrote that they should come and join them. Father had parents, brothers and a sister in America. After a while the letters from Palestine and Argentina changed in tone. They said "it's hard to make a living here, if you can get into America, go."

Father's brother somehow managed to obtain a visa for him. He wrote to my father that a brief separation from his young wife would make sense—he would learn a vocation in America, learn English, find an apartment, and then send for his wife. The young couple decided on America; they were separated for nearly a year, during which I was born, and my mother's new friends helped her run the business and take care of me.

America's immigration laws at the time were rigid. My parents were listed as being on the Russian quota, and I—born in Antwerp—was on the Belgian quota. My mother and I had to remain in Belgium until I was nearly four before we were allowed to enter America.

I still remember our little cold-water apartment, where a coal stove provided a modicum of heat in the winter, and was our only source of cooking through the year. But it was a beginning.

How the world has changed since the pogroms in Proskurov! In those years there had been some five million Jews living in Russia. Today, maybe there are a million and a half—millions immigrated to America, huge numbers were massacred during the Nazi era, very large numbers intermarried and were permanently lost to the Jewish people, and in recent years nearly a million were permitted to emigrate, mostly to the United States and Israel.

More than once I wondered: What if my parents had not fled their home town? Would I have grown up only to be massacred by Nazis? What if my parents had immigrated to Palestine or Argentina, how different my life would have been.

My children have asked me if I ever felt a desire to visit Proskurov, and my answer has always been a firm no. I explain that a home town from which my parents had to flee for their lives holds no attraction or interest for me. Besides, the town's name has been changed to honor Bogdan Chmelnitzky, a 17th century mass murderer of Jews of that period.

It is not a place I care to visit.

—D.C.G.

II
Laws, Customs, Practices
—and Superstitions

Law and Order in Ancient "Torah Israel"

Despite the fact that rabbinical law—the *Halakhah*—is still officially recognized in Israel in many instances of civil law, such as marriage and divorce, Israel today has emerged from its childhood as a modern, secular state. It would be interesting, therefore, to compare it with the Jewish state of the biblical period.

When the Children of Israel entered the Promised Land, Canaan was a monarchy. The Jews themselves were ruled by a form of tribal law. It was in a later period in order to cope with outside difficulties that the need for unified political leadership arose, was intensified in the period of the Judges, and finally became a reality under the rule of King Saul. True monarchy, however, was achieved only under David and Solomon. During King Solomon's reign *Eretz Yisrael* emerged as a unified state body, encompassing both the Jewish and the non-Jewish population.

On the other hand, it must be stressed that even then the rule of the monarch was not absolute. Solomon's son, Rehoboam, had to secure the approval of the elders prior to his ascension to the throne. The voice of the prophets, too, was heard when a new king was chosen. Among other, special qualities, a royal candidate had to be tall and well built. The king had the power over the army and government. He had private land holdings and could dispose of property owned by the state that provided the support for the court household. State property was acquired through purchases or by confiscation of land from private individuals as a punitive measure. Other income came from head and property taxes.

Three thousand years ago, the rule of brute force and the most despotic form of subjugation of individual rights were the accepted form of government throughout the then known world. It was against this background that the Jewish state achieved an almost modern form of government with a complete separation of the legislative and the executive branches.

The king's rights and duties were stipulated in the Torah* and the Halakhah.† The king was allotted a high income but not more than necessary to cover the large expenses arising from his elevated position and the upkeep of the court. He was required to copy the Torah in his own hand and to carry it on him at all times. He named the high priest and at times performed the functions of a priest himself.

The building of the Temple by King Solomon stresses the close bonds existing between the head of the state and its religion. All orders and decrees point to the fact that the Jewish state was a theocracy rather than a monarchy.

Following the Babylonian exile, political leadership was exercised by the high priest. Later in history, under the Hasmoneans, the balance of power again shifted, again gradually, until the king emerged as absolute ruler. The first symptoms of disintegration made their appearance at this time, and history notes this phenomena.

The king was the supreme military commander. He led his armies into battle. Before undertaking an aggressive campaign (*milchemet r'shut*), however, the au-

* TORAH: The Five Books of Moses, or Pentateuch.
† HALAKHAH, Jewish religious law.

thorization of the Sanhedrin‡ had to be secured. A defensive war (*milcheme mitzva*) was left entirely to the king's own judgment.

The old Jewish state had a standing army since its establishment as a monarchy. Saul reportedly had a guard of three thousand warriors. The first units were foot soldiers—spear-throwers, archers, slingers; only their chiefs were mounted. King Solomon introduced battle chariots and cavalry. The king was the supreme military authority but was advised by his commanders in charge. The largest unit was a "thousand"; there were also units of fifty and one hundred men. Not all ablebodied men were taken as soldiers. Exempt from military service were, among others, men recently married or engaged to be married and such who by nature were fearful and timid.

On their campaigns the soldiers were accompanied by priests who, specially anointed for this task, inspired them with speeches and the reading of portions of the Torah dealing with the law of war. According to historic reports, Jews often showed themselves as great strategic masters and were less barbaric than their contemporaries. The vanquished enemy was shown mercy on many occasions. This appears in an order to spare cities that surrendered and to prevent the cutting down of fruit trees. On the other hand, the soldier was expected to demonstrate bravery, and fear was considered equal to treason (Maimonides in *Hilchot Melachim*).

The act of dispensing justice was always considered to be of divine nature. "The justice of the Lord," the Torah says. The judges are, therefore, instruments of God and speak justice in His name. The prophets also raised their voices demanding fair, nonpartisan jurisdiction and condemned the use of force and arbitrary decisions.

In the Talmudic era there was a well-organized judicial system in addition to the traditional councils of the elders. Each village with less than 120 inhabitants had a council of three judges, the *Beth Din shel Shlosha*, dealing with civil law and minor criminal offenses. In a larger town 23 judges composed the "Small Sanhedrin," which had the power to pronounce the death penalty. The seat of the "Great Sanhedrin" was in Jerusalem. It dealt with matters of war and peace, accusations of false prophecy, and incitation to idol worship as well as all cases not terminated by the lower courts. The Sanhedrin was the supreme court and the highest governing council at the same time, combining the powers of the legislative branch with those of a law enforcement agency. It met in the Temple hall and was presided over by a *Nasi*. To reach the verdict of "not guilty," a simple majority was required; two additional votes were needed for verdict of "guilty." The hearings took place in public and were conducted according to strict procedure—such as presentation of witnesses, establishment of proof, and the like.

Another class of officials, dedicated to protect law and order, were the *shotrim*, or the police force. Maimonides describes them as follows: "*Shotrim* are officials who precede the judges and carry staffs and straps; they walk through markets and streets, enter the shop of the merchants, indicate prices, measures and weights and punish those who act against it." The *shotrim* also enforced the rulings of the judges as well as ordinances dealing with the payment of wages, public health, and protection of animals and laws dealing with human freedom and dignity, decency in public, and the protection of life and property.

There was also a large staff of public service officials, called the *sarim*. These were the civil servants of the king in the preexilic period. The highest ranking minister was the *maskir*, who controlled the court administration, whereas the

‡ SANHEDRIN, supreme religious and judicial body during the Temple period.

nagid was in charge of the palace household. The official scribe, or *sofer,* handled the correspondence with foreign powers and officials in the provinces. The provinces were headed by prefects, called *netzivim,* and there were, of course, tax collectors. The temple and synagogue administration alone counted about fifteen categories of officials.

The education of children always received special attention. The establishment of schools dates from the postbiblical era. Prior to that the father was responsible for the education of his children. An adult education program also existed under the supervision of priests and Levites. Jerusalem had 480 schools, and Rabbi Shimon Ben Gamliel relates that in his father's house alone one thousand children were taught.

In general, the Jewish child started school in his fifth year. The schedule called for five hours of study; there were homework, prizes and awards, and even punishment. In addition to religious matters, the students were instructed in science, music, singing, and physical exercises, especially swimming. Languages must have been taught to some extent, for many Jews spoke the languages of the neighboring countries.

Israel was largely a land of farmers. In addition to agricultural produce and farm animals, wine, oil, and fruit were the main products. Oil production was quite sizable, and shipments went out to many lands by way of Phoenicia. Among the first trades developed were metal and textile work, as well as baking, carpentry, and bricklaying. Commerce, prior to the Babylonian exile, was negligible. Inland trading did exist, but commerce with foreign countries was mostly in the hands of the Phoenicians, although King Solomon recognized the importance of maritime trading. Several centuries later, Simon the Maccabean developed the foreign trade and Joppa—today's Jaffa—began taking shape as a Jewish seaport.

Judaism teaches the importance of cleanliness, not as a religious precept alone but as a matter of health protection. A sanitation service developed early, and the streets of Israel were swept daily. Certain installations that could be damaging to public health had to be at a certain distance from the city.

Public baths (*mikvaot*) were numerous and considered so important that for centuries the building of a *mikveh* received priority even over a synagogue if there were not sufficient funds for both.

A certain measure of meat inspection also existed before it was offered to the public for sale.

The ancient Israel of the Bible thus emerges before our eyes as a sternly but humanely governed state, headed by a king but controlled by its religious leaders: a theocracy. This does not imply that it was ruled by a caste of priests. Rather, the explanation lies in the basic idea of being chosen to love God and to live according to His precepts. This idea was ever present in the minds of the individual Jews and continuously preached by the prophets. It is, therefore, not surprising that it found its reflection in the public life of the People of the Book.

—M.G.

 ## How to Make Kosher Steam

Kosher steam? Well, in a manner of speaking, that is what some Israeli engineers have achieved. One of them is Dov Zioni. He works at the Institute for Science and Halakhah, in Jerusalem. The institute's purpose is to adapt contemporary technology to the prescriptive and proscriptive laws of the Halakhah, the system of religious law.

Whatever steam there was in those ancient times was a waste by-product of boiling water. But today steam is purposely made to—among many other things that will not concern us here—keep food hot after cooking and before serving in hospitals, restaurants, and other places. Problem: if kosher foods on the same steam table include both *fleishig* (meat) and *milchig* (dairy), the steam passing over them impairs the *kashruth* of both by contact.

So—how do the Halakhah and engineering ingenuity combine to make steam *parve*—that is, neither meat nor dairy? Quite simply: According to the Halakhah, only something that is food can contaminate food—that is, make it *tref*. And how does one determine what is and what is not food? It is not food, says a maxim in the Halakhah, if dogs won't eat it.

Dov Zioni now had something to work with. By a process of experimentation, he found that pine oil is offensive to the canine palate. Since the dog won't eat it, it isn't food. But what does all that have to do with steam? Steam, condensed, is water. Dogs drink water. Ah, but when water to which pine oil has been added is used to make steam and is then condensed, it is spurned even by thirsty dogs. Therefore, such steam is not food. Thus, kosher steam.

Of course, this is only one—and a minor one, at that—of the devices that the institute has developed for enjoying the benefits of modern science without sinning. The kindling of fire is forbidden on the Sabbath. Devout Orthodox Jews construe this as forbidding the turning on of lights—or even using the telephone because at some remote location it may cause a light to appear on a switchboard —or riding in an elevator because the motor might produce a spark. And they may not ask others to do things for them, for causing others to sin is even more sinful than sinning.

But extinguishing fire is not forbidden (unless it be deemed work, which is). So the institute's resourceful scientists have designed for doctors an otoscope—that little flashlight with which the doctor looks into the ear—that lights up (don't ask us how; miraculously, for all we know)—when the current is turned *off*.

—S.S.

 ## Pendant or Amulet?

Adding my favorite silver pendant to my costume and carrying a bag, I set off one Thursday for Jerusalem's open air marketplace, Machaneh Yehudah. Gradually, I accumulated my provisions for Shabbat, savoring the smells, the sights, and the sounds of the bustling market as I meandered through its crowded, colorful streets—some bearing names of fruits, others named for trees, some with no names at all.

Suddenly a man in oriental robe, taking his ease on the ground next to a wall, jumped up and addressed me. How happy he was to see me wearing a *kamayah* (an amulet), for, said he, "It's better than a *mezuzah;* surely no evil can befall you. Only good can come your way from now on."

A heartwarming Machaneh Yehudah moment when this Persian Jew, overlooking all scruples against talking to a strange woman, gave expression to his ardent belief in the efficacy of the *kamayah* I was wearing! Up to that moment, it had

been for me only a favorite triangular, incised silver pendant, which had captivated me the previous year in Iran's fascinating city, Isfahan.

This faith in the power of an amulet to protect its wearer against misfortune and illness; to counter the evil eye and the potent influence of demons, witches, and evil spirits; to protect people's possessions, is an old tradition bound up in the folklore of most peoples, including the Jews.

Sometimes the amulet with its magical power was in the form of an object—herbs, the eaglestone worn to prevent miscarriage, a coral necklace worn by a child to protect him or her against the evil eye, a red thread placed by a horse's forehead to guard it against the evil eye.

But most frequently the amulet was in the form of an inscription on paper, parchment, or silver in triangular, square, or rectangular shape, to be worn as part of the clothing or as an ornament. Women and children usually wore the amulet on a necklace; men placed it on their arms.

As the verses were chosen from the Holy Writings, which were held to be divinely inspired, the amulet inscription itself was believed to have the power of the Holy Writings. Psalm 91 was often used as an amulet inscription:

> *I will say of the Lord, who is my refuge and my fortress,*
> *My God, in whom I trust,*
> *That He will deliver thee from the snare of the fowler,*
> *And from the noisome pestilence,*
> *He will cover thee with His pinions,*
> *And under His wings shalt thou take refuge,*
> *His truth is a shield and buckler.*
> *Thou shalt not be afraid of the terror by night,*
> *Nor of the arrow that flieth by day;*
> *Of the pestilence that walketh in darkness,*
> *Nor of the destruction that wasteth at noonday.*
> *A thousand may fall at thy side.*
> *And ten thousand at thy right hand;*
> *It shall not come nigh thee.*
> *For thou hast made the Lord Who is my refuge,*
> *Even the Most High thy habitation.*
> *There shall no evil befall thee,*
> *Neither shall any plague come nigh thy tent.*
> *For He will give His angels charge over thee,*
> *To keep thee in all thy ways.*

The use of amulets was general among the masses and accepted by many rabbis throughout the ages. In the Mishnah, the traditional Law, transmitted orally and compiled in the third century, the rabbis discussed whether or not one might wear an amulet on Shabbat. The decision reached was that if the amulet's inscription had been prepared by an expert or by a qualified person, it could be worn on Shabbat for the sake of the protection it afforded. But if the amulet had not been prepared by such a qualified person, then it was to be considered a burden, and as such it must not be worn on Shabbat.

The Gemara, the Talmudic commentary on the Mishnah, edited in the fifth century, gives instructions for noting a person's name in the inscription of the amulet.

Moses Maimonides, in the twelfth century, spoke out against the use of amulets. But in the following century, Moses Ben Nahman Gerondi, the Spanish Talmudist and physician known as Nahmanides, permitted the wearing of a metal disk with the image of a lion as a remedy against a cough. (This is the same Nahmanides who was called upon in 1263 by King James of Aragon to represent Judaism in public debate with the apostate Pablo Christiani. Their four-day-long verbal controversy, held in the presence of king, court, and ecclesiastical dignitaries, ended in victory for Nahmanides.)

Following the Inquisition and the explusion of Jews from Spain in 1492, the mystic belief in amulets spread from that country, where it had been very strong, to Eastern Europe.

The Shulhan Arukh, the last great codification of Jewish law, compiled in the sixteenth century, also contains an examination of the question of amulets. On the permissibility of wearing an amulet on Shabbat, the conclusion was, as earlier, that it depended on the maker of the amulet. The Shulhan Arukh spells out his competency. A qualified person is one who had made one amulet known to have cured three different people or one who had made three amulets, each of which had cured one person.

Another question raised in the Shulhan Arukh is whether it is legal, on Shabbat, to carry out amulets (containing verses from Holy Writ) from a burning house. On this question there is divided opinion. It is agreed, in another situation, that an illness may be treated with a *kamayah*, even if such an amulet contains the name of God.

Coming closer to modern times, there is the case of Jonathan Eybeschütz, an eighteenth-century rabbi in Metz, later chief rabbi of the united communities of Hamburg, Altona, and Wandsbek, who prepared some amulets to aid pregnant women and sick children and others to cure epilepsy and nosebleed. Statistics of the local *Hevrah Kaddisha* (community burial society) supported this rabbi's statement that since he had acted as the local rabbi, scarcely one Jewish woman had died in childbirth, whereas in the year preceding his coming there had been a veritable epidemic of such deaths.

Other rabbis declared him a heretic, unfit to hold rabbinical office. Charges were brought against him in a civil court. In all the strife and allegations made in this litigation, the accusation against Rabbi Eybeschütz was not that he had written amulets but rather that he had invoked the name of the false messiah, Shabbetai Tzevi, in some of them.

As the wrangling continued, the sixty-five-year-old Rabbi Eybeschütz appealed to a much younger man to examine the entire question of amulets. This was the highly regarded Talmudist, then thirty-five years old, Elijah, the *gaon* of Vilna. Rationalist though he was, the Vilna *gaon* stated he was in full sympathy with Rabbi Eybeschütz.

Since the nineteenth century, the *Magen David*, the six-pointed shield of David, has become a symbol of Judaism, part of the flag of Israel. Formerly, however, the *Magen David* was placed on amulets, with appropriate inscriptions. It has also been accepted for its magical role by such other peoples as the Japanese and Hindus.

On a visit to a Jewish community in Asia, I heard of yet another item in religious use that is believed to hold magical powers. This is the *afikomen*, the piece of *matzah* eaten as dessert during the Pesach Seder. In Afghanistan, the afikomen is not consumed in its entirety at the Seder table. Part is preserved and placed in the synagogue near the Ark of the Law, to remain for a full year. Part of the afikomen may also be kept in the home, for it is believed to have the power to bring good health and well-being. It also accompanies one when taking a sea journey, for the afikomen is assumed to have the power to calm a stormy sea.

—I.G.C.

 ## Why Jews *Shokel* at Prayer

An anonymous nineteenth-century English writer wrote:

> *When a Yuder's at prayers, his most fervent devotion,*
> *He calls to your mind the perpetual motion;*
> *He rolls about like a ship in a storm on the ocean,*
> *(Unless you have seen him you can't form a notion)* . . .

What do we actually know about the habit identified as *shokeling*? Let us, without however discussing the merits or otherwise of the habit, adduce but a very few of the classical references to it.

The Gemara (Berakhot 31a), describing Rabbi Akiva's mode of worship when alone, says that a "man would leave him in one corner and find him later in another, on account of his many genuflections and prostrations." To have acted thus in public would have proved inconvenient to the congregation. Rabbi Akiva, in worshiping as he did, may well have derived his inspiration from the interpretation of Psalm 35:10: "All my bones shall say: Lord, who is like unto Thee?" For how better can one pray to God than by bringing all one's physique into the act of worship? Moreover, this selfsame verse was also found acceptable as a source by the fourteenth-century Spanish liturgical writer, Abudarham.

The Zohar (Pinhas) asks the question: "How is it that of all the people of the world, only the Jews sway to and fro when they study the Torah—a habit which seems to come natural to them and they are unable to keep still?" The Zohar goes on to explain that the souls of Israel have been hewn from the holy lamp, and once this lamp has been kindled by the Torah, the light upon it never ceases, like the ever-flickering flame of a wick. Similarly, when a Jew has said a word of Torah, a light is kindled, and he can no longer keep still, swaying to and fro like the flame of a wick.

Two writers in the Middle Ages also concerned themselves with this question: the Spanish Jewish-Arabic poet Samuel ha-Nagid (993–1056), who satirized the custom in a description of a school in which he speaks of "teacher and pupils shaking their heads like stripped trees in the desert," and Judah ha-Levi (1075–1141), poet and philosopher, who discusses seriously in his *Kuzari* why Jews sway to and fro when they "read Hebrew." Coming near to the mystical explanation of the Zohar, he states that people say that it is in order to generate natural warmth or indeed because natural warmth has been generated. Not content, however, with abstract reasoning, he suggests a more practical reason, which, if correct, would obviate the reason for *shokeling* today, and indeed since 1475, when modern printing began. Writing in the time of large manuscript codices, Hebrew scholars found that as many as ten or more people would share one book while squatting on the floor in oriental fashion and that, while some leaned forward to catch a glimpse of the text, others leaned back, with the result that a rhythmic movement to and fro, forward and backward, eventually developed.

In spite of some ridicule and even opposition, also from non-Jewish sources, as, for example, from Muhammad, who warned his followers not to behave like the Jews, the custom of *shokeling* eventually became so deeply entrenched in Jewish life as to be regarded as a religious obligation. In fact, Judah he-Hassid (b. 1217) in his *Sefer Hassidim* specifically states, quoting the verse from the Psalms, that it is necessary to shake the whole body during a time of prayer, a view that was however not adopted by all later authorities.

—R.P.L.

 ## Heirloom of History: Origin of the Menorah

The *menorah* is older than Hanukkah, and precedes most of the festivals of Israel. It is older than any synagogue in the world and any of the temples that crowned Mt. Zion. It was one with the Ark and Decalogue in desert days. It was wrought finely of pure gold and stood firmly on a solid tabret before the lustrous and wondrous curtain of the holy of holies. Each branch was adorned with a flower, two knobs, two flowers, and a final knob nearest the stem.

In the Temple of Solomon at Jerusalem, ten candlesticks graced the golden table and formed a row of five sentries of light on either side of the original *menorah*. These were lost in the mists of history when taken by the Babylonians under Nebuzaradan, Nebuchadnezzar's captain, in 586 B.C.E.

Later *menorahs* were probably modeled after mosaic patterns. The synagogue, in time, replaced the central sanctuary, even as the prayer book replaced the cult of sacrifice and as the rabbis displaced the priests. The Torah and the *menorah* survived this transition even as they revived the spirit of Israel with light and learning.

As the Torah came into high centrality after the liberation by Ezra and Nehemiah from Samaritan as well as Babylonian influences during the Persian pe-

riod, so the *menorah* received high priority after the liberation from Greek and Syrian tyranny by the Maccabean revolt during the Greek period in Jewish history.

The *menorah* grew in stature. It was more than a sacred heirloom of history. It became history. It became the silent, sacred witness whereby the light of Jehovah was greater than the might of Jupiter.

Menorahs were not always of gold. When Antiochus shattered the gold *menorah* in the Temple, according to one tradition, it was replaced by the Maccabees in wood, then silver, and finally in gold again. This suggests our search for values in the presence of the *menorah:* wood for the individual, silver for Israel, gold for the aspirations of mankind.

The Arch of Titus, in a significant area of the Roman Forum, only a stone's throw from the Colosseum (built largely by Jewish slaves) and a shadow's length from the greater and younger Arch of Constantine, is one authentic arrow that points to the life of Jerusalem even in the midst of Rome. Somehow both these ancient and modern capitals, one of conscience and the other of culture, are related, if not united, in history.

Since we no longer have access to the *menorah* of the Herodian Temple, which was purloined from Jerusalem by Vespasian and his legions in 70 c.e. and then lost in Rome, possibly during the reign of Maximus, about 455 c.e., we find the Arch of Titus one source for the dimensions of the *menorah*.

In size, according to Talmudic descriptions, it stood at about 72 inches in height, 32 inches from base to first branches, 4 inches in thickness for branches, and was created of beaten gold as specified in biblical literature. In shape, it comprised floral knobs, suggestive of vine, tree, and bush, with three cups, three knobs, and three flowers for the central shaft, which stood 20 inches above the others.

The cups are said to have resembled Alexandrian drinking vessels, the knobs patterned after apples from Keraze near Capernaum, and the flowers imitated those grown in Amudim in the area of the Sea of Galilee.

A most interesting feature of this *menorah* was that the *ner tamid* (eternal light) and *menorah* were one. For the western lamp in this *menorah* of the Temple of Herod was aglow all day and night. It was called *Ner Elohim*—light divine —and the wicks of the other six faced toward it. Miracles were associated with this perpetual light, as with the cruse of oil for Hanukkah. Its cup had no more oil than the other, legend insists, but it burned brighter and longer than the rest. One curious legend relates that this "miracle" ceased forty years before the loss of the Temple in 70 c.e.

The *menorah* is as a sevenfold benediction to history. Its seven branches bespeak the great continents that are one land mass underneath the sea. Its seven cups are suggestive of seven days of light, culminating in a Sabbath that borrows light from each of the seven days. Its seven lights illuminate great words from Psalms, such as "The law is a lamp unto my feet" and "Who covereth himself with light! . . ."

The eventide of *Kiddush,* the sundown shadow of *Havdalah,* the candleglow of *Yahrzeit,* and the *ner tamid* of both the memories of yesteryear and hopes of the morrow commingle in an elemental silence in tribute to the *menorah* as sacred symbol supreme.

Patterned after the ancient Silva plant, the *menorah* is Israel's oldest and most honored symbol, far more than the *Magen David* or other designs. An ancient synagogue in Capernaum, recently uncovered, has the *menorah* in mosaic. It is found on coins of the Maccabees and of King Antigonus (40 B.C.E.), rings, tombstones, murals, vaults, and oil lamps.

The Temple courtyard itself in Jerusalem was graced with improvised *menorahs*, attended by priests on ladders to make the ascent to our hilltops of history not as a journey but as a pilgrimage. Israelites who came from even the distant villages on the great festivals found a highway of light with priests as lamplighters, and Levites sounded *shofar* calls, blew forth trumpets, and sang rhapsodic hallelujahs.

Hanukkah became a festival of light in 165 B.C.E., when the delayed *Hag* or *Sukkoth,* denied to the Maccabean hosts for years, became a "double festival" for all Israel. The word conquered the sword when the legend of the cruse of oil took spiritual precedence over Maccabean prowess of arms. The festival of Hanukkah was more than a recovery of Jerusalem and a rededication of the Temple. It was Israel's dual victory over idolatry and immorality and also the world's first and foremost struggle for religious liberty. Hearken to the voice of Judah the Maccabee when on the eve of battle he charges his warriors:

> *O, my fellow soldiers, no other time remains more opportune than the present for courage and contempt of dangers; for if you now fight manfully, you may recover your liberty, which is a thing in itself agreeable to all men; so it proves to be to us much more desirable, by its affording us the liberty of worshiping God. Since therefore, you are in such circumstances at present you must either recover that liberty, and so regain a happy and blessed way of living, which is that according to our laws, and customs of our country, or to submit to the most opprobrious suffering; nor will seed of your nation remain if you be beat in this battle. Fight therefore manfully; and suppose that you must die, though you do not fight, but believe that besides such glorious rewards of those of the liberty of your country, of your laws, of your religion, you shall then obtain everlasting glory. Prepare yourselves, therefore, and put yourselves into such an agreeable posture, that you may be ready to fight with the enemy as soon as it is day.*

The opera *The Maccabees* by Anton Rubinstein, as well as the oratorio *Judas Maccabaeus* by Georg Frideric Handel, and all their parallels do for the ear what the *menorah* does for the eye—and make the challenge of Judah the very echo of "Hear O Israel."

Historically, *menorahs* have appeared in over two hundred variable designs, including eggshells, potato shells, and colorful materials in metals and plastics. A stone *menorah* was even unearthed at Hammat near Tiberias in the Sea of Galilee area.

Double *menorahs* were in many mosaics uncovered in recent years. Some were fashioned in gilt glass of synagogues in ancient Israel, and some appeared on materials found in the Jewish as well as Christian catacombs of Rome. Josephus, who knew Rome as well as Jerusalem, describes two *menorahs,* one on either side of the Ark in the Temple.

We in America are as the base and body of the *menorah* today, whereas Israel is as the set of tapers ignited for our day, yet with borrowed light from the past. Together we form an unbroken bridge of light and hope to show a way of light for a world in half-darkness.

—M.M.W.

The Oath in Judaism

The oath is an ancient legal institution that is found among most peoples and religions. Its primary purpose is to bring the swearer into a closer contact with those divine or mystic powers in whose omnipotence he or she believes, so that they may guarantee the fulfillment of the promise made or the punishment of the person who violates it.

In ancient times the oath served chiefly as an instrument for guaranteeing the fulfillment of a covenant, such as that between Isaac and Abimelech or between Jacob and Laban; or to assure the carrying out of some special request, such as Eliezer's promise to Abraham to bring a wife for Isaac from Aram-naharaim, and the oath taken by the Israelites to bring Joseph's bones to their eternal rest in the land of Canaan.

In a less solemn form, the oath was used in common speech to add a certain seriousness and weight to statements, such as "as Pharaoh liveth, surely ye are spies" (Genesis 42:16) or the oath of Joab to David after the death of Absalom: "For I swear by the Lord, if thou go not forth, there will not tarry a man with thee this night" (2 Samuel 19:8).

In courtroom usage the oath has become a means for securing the revelation of truth. As one expert on jurisprudence explained, experience has shown that in most instances witnesses who have taken an oath seem to feel compelled by some outside power to tell the truth.

The oath is thus a religious rite that has become universally accepted, and before a witness can testify in court, he or she is in almost every case required to give some assurance that he or she will tell the truth. This assurance usually takes the form of an oath or a solemn declaration in the forms prescribed by the law.

The oath itself is accompanied by certain ceremonies that are intended to envelop the witness in a supernatural atmosphere that will induce him or her to live up to this oath. In our courts (in Israel) it is the custom to place three holy books on the witness stand, one for each of the major religions: The Holy Scriptures in Hebrew, for Jews; the Old and New Testaments in English, for Christians; the Koran in Arabic, for Moslems.

The witness places his or her hand on the book that is holy to him or her or holds it in one hand—if a Jew, he or she also covers the head—raises the other hand with the palm turned outward, and repeats the customary phrase: "I swear that the testimony I am about to give will be the truth, the whole truth, and nothing but the truth, so help me God."

The reason for placing the hand on the book is that it brings the witness into direct physical contact with what is holiest to him or her; the custom of raising the other hand is thought to have its origin in the oath sworn by Abraham before the king of Sodom—"I have lifted up my hand unto the Lord, God Most High, Maker of heaven and earth" (Genesis 14:22).

Another theory traces the raising of the hand to an Anglo-Saxon tradition: according to the old English law, not everyone was admissible as a witness: among those disqualified was anyone who had been convicted of a crime. Criminals were branded with the letter "F" (for "felony") on the palm of the right hand. The witness, therefore, had to raise his or her right hand to demonstrate to the court that he or she was not so marked and was eligible to give evidence.

One of the perplexing problems that faced the courts during the long process of evolving courtroom procedure was that of the atheist who admits to no religious beliefs whatever, as well as the adherents of sects that do not acknowledge an omnipotent God but worship various other divinities.

For a long time the accepted position was that such an individual was, in fact, not eligible to be a witness, unless he or she consented to take an oath in the name of God. Support for this view was found in the Bible—for example, in Deuteronomy 6:13-14: "Thou shalt fear the Lord thy God; and Him shalt thou serve, and by His name shalt thou swear. Ye shall not go after other gods of the people that are round about you." Again, in Psalm 36, there is the reference to the wicked one who does not fear God: "The words of his mouth are iniquity and deceit . . . he abhorreth not evil"; and in Psalm 115: "But our God is in the heavens . . . their idols are silver and gold, the work of men's hands . . ."

But there was a minority opinion that insisted on every man's right to take an oath in accordance with his own conscience and not to be compelled to swear by something he does not believe; this argument, too, drew its support from the Bible; for example, in the covenant between Laban and Jacob, Laban swore by the gods of Nahor, while Jacob swore by the fear of his father, Isaac.

Eventually, the more liberal interpretation prevailed, and it became accepted that it was proper to permit each person to take an oath according to the customs of his or her own people and religion or in any other form that the person would consider binding upon his or her conscience.

In the courts of ancient Israel, witnesses were not required to take oaths; instead, they were "taken into the court and were admonished" (Sanhedrin 29a).

What form did this "admonishment" take? In civil cases, they were told that "because of false witnesses the rains are withheld, and even though the sky may be overcast with clouds and the winds blow, the rain will not fall." Another version went as follows: "As a maul, and a sword, and a sharp arrow, so is a man that beareth false witness against his neighbor" (Proverbs 25:18).

In criminal cases the witnesses were told: "Know ye that a criminal case is not like a monetary case; in monetary matters, a man may pay for damages and thereby atone for his sin—but in a matter of criminal violence, his life and the life of his descendants is forfeit forever" (Sanhedrin 37a).

The parties to a dispute, however, were required to take an oath. The form of the oath differed in different periods. Thus, in the Scriptures we find the raising of the hand toward heaven, as well as placing the hand under the thigh of the person who administered the oath.

In the Talmudic era the court would warn the swearer as to the solemnity of the oath and the severity of punishment for false testimony. The swearer was also required to hold some sacred object while swearing, such as a Torah scroll or phylacteries. In documents of the Middle Ages we find the following references to oaths: "She swore by the Ten Commandments"; "I swore by the oath of the Torah"; "It was sworn before us while holding a Torah"; and so on.

To this day, there remains a deep-seated opposition on the part of many Jews—outspoken freethinkers as well as the most pious—to taking an oath. The Orthodox and the nonbeliever alike will use every subterfuge in order to avoid it.

An argument frequently heard is this: "This is the first time in my life that I have even been inside a court" or "I have never yet taken an oath; why should I start now?" This argument, however, does not suffice to free the witness from the obligation to take an oath. He or she has to convince the court either that he or she really has no religious beliefs, or that taking an oath is indeed a violation of his or her religious principles.

One Orthodox Jew, a respected businessman, was asked to take an oath. Astonished, he said to me, "Why, in Barclay's Bank they trust me with thousands on my signature alone and here, for a few pitiful pennies, I am to take a solemn oath?"

Another devout Jew refused to be sworn. When I attempted to explain to him that he was expected to attest only to what was true, he began a long exegesis of the commandment "Thou shalt not take the name of the Lord thy God in vain" and proved that it referred even to truthful oaths.

This was a learned man, who was able to cite the sayings of the sages to support his argument. But the same opposition to swearing prevails among the less educated, the simple people who cannot explain their motives logically. When one seeks to understand this attitude, one begins to unearth a still fermenting folklore that originated far back in the life of our people and has taken root there, in the background of the national consciousness, for hundreds of years.

Thus one workingman refused to take an oath because—he said—it is written in the holy books that hundreds of cities were destroyed for the sin of swearing. When asked to name at least one of these cities, he replied resentfully, "Was I called here to take an examination?"

An old woman explained her refusal to take an oath thus: "Even Judah, the righteous, who swore a truthful oath [that he would bring back Benjamin to his father Jacob] could find no repose in the grave until Moses interceded for him." When asked to cite her source, she answered simply, "That is what I was taught."

Another old woman, when told to take an oath, smiled at me with a motherly smile and said, "If you only knew who I am and who my parents were, you would believe me without an oath."

One venerable Jewish woman said quite simply, "*Nu,* I ask you—would I, a woman of eighty, come to court to tell lies? Do you think I have nothing better to do at my age?"

The fear of taking an oath is especially strong among the Oriental Jews. Once an Eastern Jew was called to appear as a witness, and before I had the time to instruct him to take an oath, he quickly said to me, "Your Honor, my wife said: 'Tell the judge that we are Bukharans, not Ashkenazim [European Jews], and with us Bukharans oaths are not like potatoes.'" In other words, an oath is not a cheap commodity to be treated lightly.

Another Oriental Jew, a tailor, when told that he must swear to tell the truth, pleaded piteously, his voice trembling: "Your Honor, I have only one son. Maybe I'll say one word too little or one word too much, and it won't be the whole truth. I can't take chances with the life of my only son."

A young man who appeared in court as a plaintiff, when asked to take an oath, pulled out of his pocket a document signed by the defendant in which the following condition had been explicitly stated: "Should a dispute arise between the parties to this contract, they mutually agree that they will not require each other to take an oath in court."

When asked whether he was an Orthodox Jew, the young man replied in the negative, but added: "My father was a rabbi in Czechoslovakia; he left us no material legacy, but before his death he made us promise that we would neither take oaths nor be the cause of others taking oaths. I honor this last request made by my father, and whenever I sign a contract, I include a clause to that effect."

It seems to me that this fear of taking an oath has become so deeply imbedded in the consciousness, if not indeed in the subconscious, of most Jews, largely because of the fearful ceremonial that used to surround the oath in the Jewish courts of old, especially in the post-Talmudic era. In one of the Responsa of the Gaonic period we find this description of the ritual:

> It was customary for the cantor to hold a Torah in his arms, or the disputants would stand before an open Ark containing the sacred scrolls; a bier covered with a shroud would be brought in, as well as inflated skin-bottles and burning candles and Shofarot; then the students would enter, blow out the candles and break the bottles and say to the accused: "Ploni ben Ploni! if you owe money to the plaintiff and falsely deny it on oath, may all the curses in this book follow you!" Then they would sound the Shofarot and all the congregation would answer: "Amen."

No wonder that such a ceremony frightened most litigants into telling the absolute truth. The ritual has disappeared from our modern courts, but the fear of the false oath has penetrated deep into the soul of Israel.

It is not unusual for a plaintiff to withdraw his or her charge rather than take an oath or for both parties to settle their dispute by a compromise so as to avoid being sworn in court.

Once, in a civil case, the defendant was about to take an oath to the effect that he owed the plaintiff nothing; before he had placed his hand on the Bible, the plaintiff called out, in a voice trembling with excitement, his face ashen: "Your Honor, a Jew is about to take a false oath, may God forgive us! I withdraw my complaint. I forgive him everything. I will not, God forbid, be the cause of another Jew's swearing to a falsehood!"

—S.Z.C.

The Debate Over Machine-made *Matzot*

In the 1850s the first *matzah*-baking machine was invented in Austria, beginning the heated controversy that raged for half a century. Dr. Solomon B. Freehof has given us a full account of this dispute, which he calls "one of the most acrimonious discussions in the history of the responsa literature." However, this should not be surprising as this was, indeed, a radical innovation for the fulfillment of a duty whose execution had long ago been elaborately defined to the minutest detail.

The newly invented machine kneaded the dough and rolled it through two metal rollers, from which it came out thin, perforated, and round. It was then placed in an oven. As the corners of the dough, cut to make the *matzot* round, were reused, it was feared that the time elapsing until these pieces of dough were used again might allow them to become leavened. A later machine was developed that produced square matzot so that there would be no leftovers. Other subsequent improvements in the machinery speeded up the entire process of production, leading to a general acceptance of the modern method. Meanwhile, many distinguished rabbis raised their voices in protest against the new machine, whereas others, equally respected, permitted its use.

Solomon Kluger of Brody, in a letter to Rabbi Hayyim Nathan and Rabbi Leibush Horowitz of Cracow, Galicia, where the machine was already in use, prohibited the eating of the machine-made *matzot,* especially for the *matzot mitzvah.* This letter and similar pronouncements by other rabbis were published under the title: *Moda'ah le-Bet Yisrael* ("Announcement to the House of Israel," Breslau, 1859). In rebuttal, Rabbi Joseph Saul Nathanson published this pamphlet: *Bittul Moda'ah* ("Annulment of the Announcement," Lemberg, 1859).

One of Kluger's most telling arguments was that the opportunity given to the poor to earn money for their Passover needs by working in *matzah* bakeries would be denied to them, as the use of machinery required fewer manual workers. He and his adherents also argued that *matzah shemurah* particularly, must be made with the intention of fulfilling the precept that requires the understanding of a mature adult. They also claimed that there was a suspicion that the pieces of dough left in the wheels of the machine, which were difficult to clean, would become leavened.

In the forefront of the rabbis who permitted the use of machinery was Joseph Saul Nathanson of Lemberg. These rabbis refuted the arguments of the opposition seriatim. If concern need be expressed about the displacement of the hand-bakers, the same solicitude should be shown to scribes whose replacement by the printing press had been universally accepted. They also held that these *matzot* are baked with the intent to comply with the law, as it is necessary for an adult to start the machine. They had no fear that dough would be left in the machines as they are cleaned well and often. Furthermore, they contended that the machine speeds the process and is more efficient than the men and women who worked in the bakery day and night. The views of Nathanson and those who sided with him have been accepted by most Jews.

—P.G.

 ## Floggings Before Yom Kippur

On a Rosh Hashanah morning, to walk through Tel Aviv's Florentine Quarter, colorful with the mixture of seventy different communities, is to hear a medley of liturgical incantation that has, no doubt, never yet been captured in any prayer book. And when members of this richly heterogeneous community march in procession to cast their sins away at the Tel Aviv seafront (in the *tashlikh* ceremony), one views a cross section of Israel's ingathered nations, united by the common bond of religious fervor.

They are all there in their colorful native costumes: the *Hasidim* in black fur hats, sidecurls bouncing as they walk, white socks peeping out from shiny trousers and black shoes—their long caftans reaching to their ankles; the Bukharans with long, flowing robes of different colors and high capes and elaborately embroidered square hats that sit up proudly on dark, curly heads; the Yemenites, dark, thin, delicate in brilliant colors embroidered on mantles and tunics. Each chants in his or her own dialect; each is part of a small bright cluster of swaying worship.

The Florentine Quarter starts High Holiday observances on the first of Elul and ends the holiday season on *Motzei* Simhat Torah with an all-night street festival, which has become a national event.

The community's spiritual head, Rabbi Yizhak Yedida Frankel, known as the *rav hashechunot* (rabbi of the communities) and called "Abba" by his parishioners, organizes the celebration.

Their custom and folklore happily untampered with, the residents of the neighborhood, in Tel Aviv's oldest area, celebrate the festivals as they did in their countries of origin with unique interpretations of the law handed down by centuries of worshipers.

Thirty days before Rosh Hashanah they have already inaugurated recitation of *slichot* (prayers for forgiveness, which precede the High Holidays). This takes place in the early hours of the morning, between three and five. The neighborhood has even grown accustomed to being awakened in its sleep several times a night, night after night throughout the month of Elul, by the blowing of the *shofar*, which accompanies each mention of the divine attributes (*eser midot*).

Ashkenazi Jews recite the *yizkor* (memorial prayer) as part of the Yom Kippur service. Members of the oriental community have a separate session for this service.

The 80,000 residents of the Florentine Quarter come from all corners of the globe. Their twenty-seven synagogues are crowded into this already congested area. Of these, seven are of Bukharan origin.

The members of this community are ardent penitents. In an old dwelling on one side street of the Florentine Quarter, one may even find an elderly patriarch dispensing *malkot* (floggings) on *erev* Yom Kippur to those who wish to absolve themselves of their sins this way. His clients are not just neighborhood sinners or those who keep the commandments to the letter. They are of different origins and come a long way, driving up in taxis or modern sedans, humbly waiting their turn to receive blows from the patriarch's wide leather belt.

According to one story, it was almost time to get ready for the *Kol Nidre* service one year, when the rabbi had wearily fulfilled his obligation to his last caller. But he himself had not received his corporal punishment. He quickly looked outside for someone to perform this ritual on him and found only a lorry driver. Bending over, the rabbi motioned him to take the strap to his back. The overwhelmed driver begged off, beseeching, "Is a poor ignorant fellow like myself worthy of raising a hand to his holiness? The rabbi is deserving of a whipping from the Lord Himself."

Immediately after Yom Kippur, the neighborhood, like every other in Israel, is feverishly building *sukkoth* (booths). There are no prefabs here; and, with all hands helping, in no time there is a small hut, with a roof of *schach*, leaves and branches placed so sparsely as to allow the stars to shine through. Prayers, pictures from home, and decorations line the walls. Flags and seven different kinds of agricultural product are hung as decoration.

But it is the *Simhat* Torah celebration that calls for the greatest merriment. It is "so that our people may be the host and not the guests," explains Rabbi Frankel. A handsome man with a long black beard, Rabbi Frankel came to the quarter from Poland forty years ago and since then has served the community as a kind of chief rabbi; justice of the peace; interpreter of the law; enforcer of order; and mediator of ethnic, civil, or personal conflicts. Much of the credit for the inner rhythm and harmony that prevail in this colorful community is due to Rabbi Frankel's personality in resolving differences.

As soon as the first stars appear to indicate the holiday is out, the quarter becomes alive. Leading the festivities are elders of the Bukharan community, who start the evening streaming out of their synagogues in their square, gold, and red brocade skullcaps with Scrolls of the Torah in their arms. Followed by a band of musicians and escorted by a police guard on horseback, they proceed, stopping at each of the synagogues along the way from which worshipers pour out singing and dancing to the music of stringed instruments and drums. While the men dance with the Torah, the women clap hands and beat tambourines. Children carrying flags fill the streets. The singing and dancing continue far into the night.

At the center of the main thoroughfare in which thousands of people gather, a beautifully decorated balcony serves as an entertainment platform. It is here that celebrities and special guests sit to watch the holiday-making below.

When this celebration is over, usually past midnight, the High Holiday season, after a full month of festivities, is officially at an end.

—D.L.

The Origin of the *Mezuzah* and Its Decorations

The use of the *mezuzah* rests upon the twice expressed command (Deuteronomy 6:4–9; 11:13–21) that the essentials of the Jewish faith be written upon the doorposts of the house and upon the gates. That command might have been taken figuratively like the admonition to the young man who is told, regarding the parental commandments that he is to obey:

> *Bind them continually upon thy heart, Tie them about thy neck (Proverbs 6:21).*

Those commands of Deuteronomy, however, were—we know not when—construed literally, perhaps because of a related Hebrew phenomenon that they suggested. The first Temple had, on each side of its portal, a bronze pillar that obviously carried an inscription. One of these pillars was named Boaz: the other, Jachin (1 Kings 7:21). The significance of these names has been debated. Yet there can be no doubt that they were names of exalted religious import; at the entrance of the Temple, all comers were to be impressed with the omnipotence of

God. That which stood at the entrance of the Temple was extended to the private dwelling in the form of the *mezuzah.*

Still, it is not entirely clear how the Deuteronomic command was to be understood in detail. "Doorposts," in the plural, could apply only to the two posts flanking the abode's entrance. Ever intent upon a strict interpretation of their ordinances, the Jews became inclined to attach a *mezuzah* to every door in the house, no matter how many rooms. Rabbi Meir of Rothenburg had twenty-four *mezuzot* in his domicile.

"Gates," in ancient times, must have meant the gates of the city. The city, already at an early period, had a surrounding wall and gates leading through the wall. With advancing urbanization, the *mezuzah* may have become attached to other gates, for example, the gates of courthouses. From the obligation to have a *mezuzah*, religious edifices were exempt; the edifice itself made those entering aware of the divine presence (Ber. 47a). In the Second Temple, only the Nicanor Gate bore a *mezuzah*, for the reasons that, behind it, lay "the cell of the counselors" (*Yom 11a*).

How the *mezuzah* was originally attached to doorposts and gates, we are not entirely clear. Was the inscription written directly on the building, or was it attached separately, as in later usage? The ancient Egyptians are reported to have had, at the entrance of the home, the inscription of some sacred adage. It has been surmised that this custom may have been borrowed by the Israelites. In Palmyra, Syria, there has been found a door lintel of the third Christian century with the Jewish creed of Deuteronomy 6:4–9 in Hebrew letters.

The grandeur of that portal suggests a synagogue, but the synagogue, as we have heard, did not require a *mezuzah*. That portal may have belonged to some large secular edifice, possibly one of the above-mentioned courthouses. All this warrants the surmise that the text of the *mezuzah*, perhaps in an abbreviated form, stood inscribed directly on the door or on the gate. Owing to the complications of the procedure, as well as to the subsequent expansion of the text, the requisite words would stand on a piece of parchment.

Such a strip of parchment would come rolled up in such a way that the inscription was on the inside, the empty side lying outward. Thus was the inscription protected. The writings of non-Jews were on scrolls likewise. The difference was that the Jews have, down to the present, clung to scrolls for such of their sacred literature as was read aloud in the synagogue, whereas the non-Jews have, since the second century of the present era, substituted the codex, the type of book in common use today.

How was the roll attached? Originally the method seems to have been to place the roll in a cavity scooped in the doorpost. To us, such a thing seems strange—boring a hole in a post as a place for storing. But we have a visible demonstration of this usage. E. L. Sukenik published an account of a stone that was once part of a synagogue in Palestinian Caesarea. Engraved on this stone are the Greek words: "O God help! The donation of the people in the time of Marutha." (Marutha was probably the head of the synagogue.) The stone shows a perfectly circular concavity in which, according to Sukenik, there was kept "a candelabrum or something similar."

My surmise is that there was kept not "a candelabrum or something similar," but rather the Books of Moses on a number of scrolls or perhaps one scroll containing the entire Pentateuch. At the time when the synagogue was not yet equipped with a fixed cabinet for the Torah, the Torah would, after the service, be carried outside the synagogue and, as in our case, placed in the concavity.

Similarly, a small niche in the doorpost of the house may have admitted the *mezuzah*.

The tractate *Mezuzah* (II, 10) also mentions the practice of enclosing the *mezuzah* in a "hull." There is nothing unusual about this custom. The scroll of the Torah was likewise protected either with a mantle or, as in the Orient, by enclosure in a chest of wood or metal. That the incasement of the *mezuzah* was, in the Talmudic period, an innovation is indicated by the fact that it was a matter of debate. Rabbi Meir (second century of the present era) favored it; Rabbi Judah (third century) objected. That was, nevertheless, the usage that came to prevail. The result was the tendency to give the container artistic embellishment. Originally, however, the container was completely plain—a botanical reed or a closed receptacle of wood or metal.

The ordinance of the *mezuzah* was regarded as a constant admonition to be mindful of God and His laws. But, as early as Talmudic times, there came to be associated with the *mezuzah* the intent of safeguarding the inhabitants of the house by barring the entrance against evil spirits. During the Middle Ages, with their mystic tendencies, this conception came to be held with growing intensity.

The increasing perils of Jewish life and hostile surroundings likewise generated a deepening concern for protection. What could be more likely than making the *mezuzah* an expression of this solicitude? This was achieved by placing on the hitherto blank side of the roll the word *"Shaddai,"* the Almighty, a word often inscribed on amulets. This was further accomplished by adding certain touches to the text written on the inner side. For example, to various lines of the text were added the names of certain angels; in the Bible there is imputed to the angels the role "to keep thee in all thy ways" (Psalm 91:11). Five-pointed or six-pointed figures would stand sketched in the *mezuzah's* margins; the six-pointed star was deemed especially potent.

Maimonides sanctions nothing more than the word *"Shaddai"* on the side that is otherwise blank. This has remained, whereas the addenda on the text side have completely disappeared.

As a result of this development, what happened on the container? In its oldest form, the container had no opening; the newer form is supplied with a round or rectangular orifice through which peers the word *"Shaddai."*

Conflicts were generated by the exposure of the divine name. The name was regarded not as a mere piece of writing; it often happens in religion that a word gets to be imbued with a divine potency. A word can be honored; but, were it to look upon something unseemly, that word would be desecrated. Moses of Coucy, a French rabbi of the thirteenth century, points the way out of this difficulty: "If the *mezuzah* is intended for a room occupied by small children, I cover the opening of the *mezuzah* with a little wax." The Shulhan Arukh lays down the rule: "In a place where there is filth, it is well to keep the *mezuzah* covered." In the Ture Zahab, a commentary on the Shulhan Arukh, David b. Samuel Halevy (ca. 1586–1667), discussing that passage, observes that the covering of the divine name applies, by extension, to the bedchamber of the wedded. A singular procedure! But we must recall that, in Eastern Europe, the sacred pictures of the Christian house-altar receive a covering when something unseemly is to take place in their presence.

Instead of covering with wax—hardly an ideal solution—there sometimes came into use the device of placing, over the orifice through which the divine name appears, a kind of doorlet, the wings of which could, as occasion demanded, be closed or opened.

Originally the container of the *mezuzah* stood on the doorpost in a vertical position as recommended in the Shulhan Arukh, *Yore De'ah* 289,6. Others preferred it horizontal. Isserlein, in his commentary on the passage, urges the sloping position as a compromise between the two.

So much for the development of the *mezuzah* into its present form. What about its beautification? Concerning phylacteries, based upon the same biblical verses as the *mezuzah*, we hear about case overlays of gold. This is reported in the *Mishnah*, a source dating from the third century of our era. About further adornment, nothing is reported for almost a millennium and a half. From the seventeenth century, not any earlier, there have been preserved silver and golden receptacles in which phylacteries were kept when not in use.

Was it likewise with the *mezuzah?* As regards the inscribed parchment, artistic attempts are discernible from an early date. The Talmud (Menahot 31b) quotes a remark of Rabbi Johanan bar Nappaha (died 279): "A *mezuzah* is permitted if it is written with two or three or even one word (to the line), provided the writing does not form a tent or a tail." This obviously refers to an ornamental style of writing familiar to the Romans, who would write out poems in such a way that the lines, by their varying lengths, formed the shape of some object such as an altar, a double ax, a shepherd's flute, or a Cupid's wing.

Poems thus shaped were called *carmina figurata.* This, like many other Roman practices, evoked Jewish imitation. The Jews would, here and there, write out the text of the *mezuzah* in like manner. Why the form of an animal's tail is to be avoided needs no explanation. As for the tent, the word *kubbah*, though it means a vaulted tent, also means a place of prostitution. On a *mezuzah*, this would, as a matter of course, not be allowed. The practice of fashioning various figures out of letters persisted in Jewish writing for a long time.

When this playful kind of writing disappeared from the *mezuzah*, we do not know. That selfsame passage, Menahot 31b, mentions writing in a column, in the manner of the Torah. Such writing had to be done with utmost care. One's *mezuzah* was not to be written by oneself. One purchased it from a professional scribe, who saw to it that the inscription was not something printed but that it was handwritten on parchment and that every *mezuzah* had twenty-two lines, and every corresponding line the same number of words, thus making a regularized structure. The *Mishnah* (Menahot III, 7) asserts that the lack of the malformation of a single letter would render the *mezuzah* unusable. The manifestation of religious zeal through punctilious penmanship is a Jewish characteristic.

The oldest ornamental *mezuzah* existent is to be found in the Jewish Museum in London. It has been explained as a product of the late fifteenth or the early sixteenth century. But that dating is incorrect. Beginning with the palmetto at the lower end and ascending to the garlands spreading over the lions, everything shows the neoclassical taste dominating the latter part of the eighteenth century.

Barring the golden phylactery cases of antiquity, our oldest ornamented phylactery cases are known to date from the seventeenth century. The ornamented *mezuzot* were not yet in existence in the fifteenth century or the early sixteenth century. In some quarters there was hesitancy on this score as late as the 1700s. In his *Cérémonies et coutumes religieuses,* which appeared in 1723–43, Bernard Picart supplies the picture of a *mezuzah* in Holland. The container has the form of a staff with a number of bulgings. There is no other ornamentation. The container lacks even the little window exposing the divine name, owing to the scruple, no doubt, to avoid everything that might give the *mezuzah* the character of an amulet. In his *Hebrew Ritual of the Jewish Community in England* (London, 1819), Levy Alexander furnishes the illustration of a *mezuzah* that is totally plain.

The actual home of *mezuzah* decoration appears to have been Eastern Europe —countries such as Poland, Russia, or Bohemia, though there is no evidence that even here such existed prior to the seventeenth century. In the woody Carpathians, the woodcarving of the *Mezuzah* became popular as a specimen of a folk art continuing to this day. Though generally avoided, the human figure is sometimes employed, especially when showing a religious thought. One shows Moses with the Tablets of the Law, the Law on which the *mezuzah* is founded.

In other areas of Russia, the *mezuzah* is beautified by means of silver. In the artistic use of silver, the Jews of Eastern Europe, unlike those of Western Europe, showed skill. The artistic adornment of the *mezuzah* was the work of the Jews themselves. I know of only one *mezuzah* that was produced by a non-Jew—a *mezuzah* of the early nineteenth century with the trademark of the Breslau goldsmith Gottlieb Freitag. This *mezuzah* is preserved in the Jewish Museum of New York City.

Another *mezuzah* shows a crown—the *Kether Torah*—and beneath it, the Tablets of the Law. Then follows the tiny window with the shutter, which, to our surprise, carries the inscription "*Shaddai*," thus displaying what, in other instances, is concealed. Beneath this is a long-necked bird, the significance of which I do not know.

—F.L.

 # Origins of the Ancient Rite of Circumcision

Circumcision, a practice ingrained in the culture of the Jewish people, has its origins deep in the prepatriarchal past. Uncovering these origins requires consideration of anthropological and archaeological as well as biblical evidence, evidence that in itself is still viewed by many scholars as contradictory.

For Jews, circumcision has evolved from a primitive blood rite to the operation as it is known among Jews today. What began as a prenuptial initiatory ritual, took on, particularly by the final Second Temple period, a moral and spiritual meaning, marking an important milestone in the life of every Jewish male. Today it is still a sign of the Jew's commitment to a moral ethic, a sign of his covenant with God.

But circumcision was not confined to the Jewish people. Among the aboriginal tribes of central Australia, boys to be circumcised are laid on a platform formed of the living bodies of their tribesmen so that the blood that is spilled does not fall upon the ground.

In Nicaragua, the practice is reported of natives drawing blood from the flesh of the male organ, dipping corn into this blood and sowing the corn in the ground, in "the womb of Earth Mother." In Mexico, a similar practice was found by Cortez, according to the report of Garcia de Palacio (1576), but the blood drawn was offered at the altar. An analogous rite was also reported among the Aztecs and among the Mayas of Yucatan.

In each instance, blood, the most sacred of fluids, is offered to a god to ensure fertility, fertility of the crop, fertility of the tribe. The biblical injunction to circumcision echoes the fertility rite, the fertility of a people as pronounced by God's covenant with Abraham in Genesis 17. ". . . As for Me this is My Covenant with you: You shall be the father of a host of nations . . . I will cause you to be exceedingly fertile, and make nations of you, and kings shall stem from you. And I will maintain the Covenant between Myself and you and your offspring to follow through the ages, as an everlasting pact to be God to you and to your offspring to follow . . ."

And in return, God demands of Abraham, "For your part, you must keep My Covenant, you and your offspring to follow, through the ages. And this shall be the Covenant . . . every male among you shall be circumcised. You shall circumcise the flesh of your foreskin . . . At the age of eight days every male among you, through the ages, shall be circumcised, even household slaves . . ."

God demands a sign, a visible sign of membership in the covenant community, from Abraham and his "offspring to follow, through the ages."

The importance of blood in this rite is noted in the Shulhan Arukh (*Yore De'ah* 263:4) with regard to the child born already circumcised, that is, without a foreskin. The ceremony of "shedding the blood of the Covenant" (*hattafat dam berit*) must be performed. This is done by puncturing the skin of the glans with a scalpel or needle and allowing a drop of blood to exude.

The sacred importance of blood and the association of blood and circumcision with fertility indicate that circumcision probably originated as a blood rite. The evolution of this simple practice to one calling for actual removal of skin may well have been instituted as a lasting sign to the tribe of the initiatory ceremony, a "Sign of the Covenant."

As a portion of grain is offered at the altar in hope of a bounteous crop or as an animal is bled or sacrificed for promise of an increased herd or flock, so the blood of the reproductive organ is offered for promise of fertility.

This practice has been known at one time or another to most of the cultures of the world. The only peoples unacquainted with it are the Indo-Germanics, the Mongols, and those of the Finno-Ugric language group. It is known in parts of the Balkans; Asia Minor; Persia; part of India; parts of North, Central, and South America; New Guinea; the Malay Archipelago; practically the whole of North Africa; and throughout the Muhammadan world. Neither is the presence of the rite in North Africa altogether Muhammadan in inspiration, as it occurs quite as frequently among the tribes of the east and west coasts, which have not been in contact with Islam.

Among the uncircumcised were the Philistines, a people who came from a totally different cultural background than Israel's other neighbors. In 1 Samuel 18:25, "And Saul said: Thus shall ye say to David: The king desireth not any dowry, but a hundred foreskins of the Philistines to be avenged of the king's enemies." Neither did the Hivites of Shechem (Horites of central Palestine) follow the practice, as is evidenced by the Dinah story of Genesis 34. The Hivites were a foreign element in Canaan, with a political regime that differed from those of the other inhabitants of the area.

Also among the uncircumcised, according to Ezekiel in 32:19–32, were Elam (Persia) and Meshech and Tubal (northern tribes, originally from beyond the Caucasus). Neither was the rite in practice in Mesopotamia, and so the patriarchs themselves, as indicated by the covenant passage, were introduced to circumcision only after their arrival in Canaan.

The age at which circumcision is performed varies. Wherever the operation is performed as a traditional rite, it is done either before or at puberty and sometimes, as among some Arabian peoples, immediately before marriage. Among the ancient Egyptians, boys were generally circumcised at twelve years (that is, puberty) although some sources indicate age as early as six years. Generally, among the Egyptians, the rite signified admission of the boy into the rank of priesthood as a *web* (the Egyptian word for "pure" or "holy"). Among the Ethiopians, Jews, Muslims, and a few other peoples, the operation is currently performed shortly after birth.

In Exodus, however, as Moses was returning to Egypt with his Midianite wife Zipporah and their son, Gershom, chapter 4:24 relates, At a night encampment on the way, the Lord encountered him and sought to kill him. "So Zipporah took a flint and cut off her son's foreskin and cast it at his feet, saying, 'You are truly a bridegroom of blood to me.' When He let him alone, she added, 'A bridegroom of blood because of circumcision.'"

Moses obviously had never been circumcised, and this ritual circumcision by Zipporah's touching to his leg the blood of their son's circumcision, indicates the prenuptial association of the rite. The fact that the Arabic *hatana* signifies both "to marry" (compare the Hebrew *hatan* for bridegroom) and "to circumcise" indicates an original connection between the rite and the marriage ceremony. Gershom also had not yet been circumcised at this time, and some biblical scholars suggest that this neglect was possibly associated with the marriage of Moses to a Midianite woman.

Furthermore, in Joshua, after the Children of Israel had spent some years of wandering in the desert following their Exodus from Egypt, chapter 5:3–7 relates,

> *And Joshua made him knives of flint and circumcised the children of Israel at Gibeath-ha-araloth. And this is the cause why Joshua did circumcise: all the people that came forth out of Egypt, that were males, even all the men of war, died in the wilderness by the way, after they came forth out of Egypt. For all the people that came out were circumcised, but all the people that were born in the wilderness by the way as they came forth out of the land of Egypt, had not been circumcised. For the children of Israel walked forty years in the wilderness, till all the nations, even the men of war that came forth out of Egypt, were consumed . . . And he raised up their children in their stead; them did Joshua circumcise; for they were uncircumcised, because they had not been circumcised by the way.*

There are scholars who feel that the Exodus and Joshua passages of the Bible suggest that the rite had been forsaken among the Hebrews during their sojourn in Egypt and reintroduced only after their reentrance into Canaan. However, the Joshua passage clearly states "the people that came out were circumcised." Furthermore, the covenant passage in Genesis was a P-contribution to the Bible (priestly school of writers) and was probably set down at the time of the late monarchy or even in the postexilic period, that is, as late as the end of the sixth century B.C.E. The author or authors, therefore, were referring to the custom as they knew it and not necessarily as it existed in the time of Abraham, over a thousand years earlier.

At one time it was only Egyptian priests who were circumcised, and it was only later that royalty practiced the rite.

The various apparent contradictions fall into place, therefore, if one assumes, as is fairly evident, that the Hebrew practice of circumcision before the settlement was at thirteen years of age. Moses, assuming the biblical story of his origin is true, would not have been circumcised when he was found by Pharaoh's daughter, and, since circumcision was not at the time practiced in the Egyptian royal house, he was never circumcised. Furthermore, Moses' firstborn, Gershom, had not yet been circumcised, only because he had not yet turned thirteen before leaving Midian.

The Joshua passage is also noncontradictory, except possibly in the matter of the duration of the wandering, that is, forty years. The number "forty," however, is a magic number in the Bible and may not be literal, for example, the forty days and forty nights of the flood, Moses' "forty days and forty nights on Sinai," and Moses' men returning "from spying out the land at the end of forty days."

After the settlement, the rite among the Israelites of Palestine was transferred to the eighth day after birth. This may have been done to fix the time of the rite at an age when its severity would be less felt or perhaps merely to differentiate further the Jews from their neighbors, the Canaanites, who still circumcised at thirteen years.

Whatever the age, the rite became an ingrained part of the Jewish culture, although, unlike Christian baptism, circumcision is not a sacrament that is needed to give the Jew his religious character as a Jew. An uncircumcised Jew is a full Jew by birth of a Jewish mother, according to the Shulhan Arukh (*Yore De'ah* 264:1). Nevertheless, the Shulhan Arukh (YD 260:1) tells us that it is a Jewish father's duty to have his son circumcised.

—B.S.R.

 ## "Please Forgive Me!": An Old World Custom

In the synagogues of the East European *shtetl,* a most unusual custom was observed on the eve of Yom Kippur. Prior to the chanting of *Kol Nidre,* each congregant was expected to approach his fellow-worshipers and ask their forgiveness. Each worshiper would move from person to person and whisper quietly to his neighbor: "Please forgive me—*Zeit mir mochel."* The person to whom it was addressed would listen attentively to the declaration and would reply in a most serious vein: "I am forgiving you—*Ich bin dir mochel."* Immediately after this reply, the respondent would change his inflection, assume the role of pleader and address the identical plea of forgiveness to the person whom he had just forgiven. The entire house of worship became, for a substantial period of time, a beehive of whispering couples. Even the respected and universally admired rabbi would join in this exchange of pleas and responses. Bitter enemies also used to approach each other on this sacred day. If two antagonists refused to draw near, a neutral party of mutual acquaintance would intervene and bodily force one or the other to take the initiative. By the time the cantor began to chant the traditional Kol Nidre, all rifts may not have been healed, but sharp antagonisms had been assuaged, and lesser conflicts ended. When order and silence returned to the house of worship, all sins may not have been forgiven, but many a pain had been relieved, and many a burden had been lifted.

With some modifications, the same custom was also observed during funeral services. When a member of the East European *shtetl* passed away, all residents were expected to participate in the mourning rites. When a person was prevented from attending the special services, he felt duty-bound to join in the funeral procession as it weaved its way through the city streets and to walk behind the coffin for at least a few blocks. Participation in the funeral rites required more than passive attendance. Some time during the long journey to the cemetery, each participant would reverently draw near the coffin, gently touch its rough boards, and whisper a prayerful request to the deceased. In a subdued and penitential voice, he would address the departed by his first name and say: *"Reb Yitschok, zeit mir mochel—Revered Isaac, please forgive me."* Huddling close to the simple wooden box and tremblingly clasping its horizontal panels, each mourner followed up the general plea with a detailed description of the wrongs and irritations that he may have caused the deceased during his lifetime. The absence of any known wrongful acts did not absolve one from making this declaration. At the conclusion of the confessional monologue, the speaker addressing the silent coffin, said: "If you will forgive me, I will forgive you." With these words, he would devoutly take a few steps backwards and join the ranks of the marching mourners.

Such customs reveal a sensitivity of soul rarely found in the folklore of ancient or modern society. Above everything else, however, they constitute dramatic illustrations of the Jewish emphasis upon cultivation of the faculty of asking and granting forgiveness.

—B.Si.

 # Some Enduring Jewish Superstitions and Customs

In common with other peoples, the Jews have their superstitious beliefs, many of which already existed in biblical times. A number of these beliefs had an idolatrous character, which disappeared with the establishment of monotheism, but some of the superstitions remained. The biblical prohibition of certain of these pagan practices proves that they existed (Deuteronomy 18:9; Exodus 22:18).

Jews share with their non-Jewish neighbors the belief in "luck." Although from earliest times Judaism has endeavored to fight against many foreign cults and superstitions, it never entirely succeeded. In the Talmud and the Kabbalah numerous statements show a belief in the efficacy of astrology, in the cult of the stars, in the existence and power of demons and spirits. Yet all such beliefs bear a religious tinge, and the monotheistic trend is apparent.

Astrology is condemned in the Mosaic code and by the prophets, but this belief that human destiny depends upon and is subject to the influence of the stars and the changing planetary system pervaded Judaism. Originating in Babylon, astrology attempted to discover in the stars an occult influence on man and his affairs, and this had an effect on many Jewish scholars. This was due to the fact that at one time astrology was regarded as identical with astronomy. During the Babylonian exile (ca. 586 B.C.E.) the Jews not only adopted the names of the Babylonian-Assyrian months, but they also followed the Assyrian astronomers and astrologers who took a great interest in the zodiac, the imaginary zone in the heavens containing twelve constellations or signs within which the sun traverses annually. These signs, which mostly represent symbols of animals and their divisions, are first mentioned in the *Sefer Yetzirah* (Book of Creation), a mystic Kabbalistic work first published in the Middle Ages but certainly known as far back as the sixth century.

These constellations were also called *mazzalot*, hence the word *Mazzal* (luck) and the commonly used *Mazzal tov* (may your star be good)—good luck to you.

In the passage in Exodus 30:12, we are told that "when you take the sum of the children of Israel, according their number, then shall they give every man a ransom to the Lord, when you number them; that there be no plague among them, when you number them." This passage had been connected with 2 Samuel 24, where we find that a pestilence befell Israel on account of David's having numbered the people. As a result of these two biblical passages, a strange superstition started among Jews, that it is unlucky to number or count a group of people. Thus, when it was necessary to ascertain how many people were present in a room or around a table, a method grew up to count so, usually in Yiddish: "*Nisht eins, nisht tzvay, nisht dry,*" and so on (not one, not two, not three, and so on). A sort of counting and not counting, as it were. It has now become a custom in many communities to count the number of men present for a *minyan* in that way. The idea thus became current among Jews that counting individuals was sure to be followed by some misfortune.

There are a number of customs or superstitions that have taken root in the Jewish mind and are part of Jewish life. Many people observe these without, in some cases, knowing why they do so and without knowing whether they are actual law or just custom. Sometimes they are astonished to find that what they and perhaps their parents believed to be law started as custom. The rabbis stated that if a custom, a *minhag*, took root in a community, it became stronger than law; it could override and cancel the law and become, in fact, law itself. Thus, certain prayers and forms of service have, as a result of frequent usage and repetition, become so well established that they have subsequently been made into laws. The rabbis said: "Custom always precedes law" (Soferim XIV, 18), when it comes to the recital of the *yizkor* (memorial) prayer on festivals.

All sorts of practices have grown up. In some synagogues it seems to be the custom for those who have both parents living to leave the synagogue till after the memorial prayer has been recited, returning to their seats later. Others don't leave the synagogue but remain during the recital of *yizkor*, preferring not to participate in the recital of prayers. There is no law that states that those having parents should leave during that part of the service.

The custom of changing one's seat on the first visit to the synagogue after a bereavement arose no doubt as a way of pointing out mourners to the congregation. There seems to have been a superstition at one time to change one's seat owing to the belief that the Angel of Death might be hovering over the seat of the mourner.

Belief in the magic of the evil eye is to be found in the folklore of all nations of antiquity and even in our own day. The Jewish conception differs in that the evil eye is never attributed to God as being jealous of His creatures.

It is still the custom for many to say, "*Kayn ein horrah*" (without an evil eye) to avert some misfortune befalling someone we hold dear. This superstition, which was a universal one, found its way into Jewish folklore and is often referred to in the Talmud. Yet to many minds it held the place of a prayer to God to preserve and protect from harm one's dear ones, and the phrase was seldom off the lips of both pious and not-so-pious Eastern European Jewry.

A custom often taken to be law is the practice among Ashkenazic Jews that forbids the naming of a newly born child after a living relative. Some Sephardic Jews do this quite freely, but with Ashkenazic Jews this custom is as binding as law. The superstition seems to have been that it was unsafe to name a child after a living person for fear that it might rob the living of his full life. We are thus left with the custom, which to most Jews is as binding as law.

—R.S.B.

The Ninth Day of Av: A Black Day for the Jews

Most people are probably familiar with the biblical account of the twelve spies sent by Moses to investigate the conditions in Canaan, and how their negative report resulted in the Jews being punished by having to wander in the desert for forty years.

Less familiar is the Midrashic comment on the whole episode. The Midrash relates that the spies returned on the ninth day of the month of Av, and when the people heard their report, they all began weeping and wailing. At that time, the Midrash relates, God told them: "On this ninth day of Av you have mourned without any cause. In future generations I will give you cause to indeed mourn on this day."

And historically, we know that both the First and the Second Temples fell on the same day, the ninth of Av. Both of our exiles, the short one of seventy years and the long one lasting close to two thousand years, followed those ninth days of Av.

But these were not the only calamities that befell us on that fateful date. Let us examine a few examples of events that affected us on the ninth of Av. Some of them are better known than others, but they share a common characteristic—all were sources of mourning for the Jewish people.

In 1492, the Golden Age of Spain, with all its great Jewish scholars and statesmen, its glory and splendor, suddenly came to an abrupt end. With one stroke of his pen, King Ferdinand gave all the Jews of Spain the option of converting or leaving the country. Literally hundreds of thousands of Jews fled, many falling prey to brigands or being drowned in the small boats they were forced to use to leave the country at the last moment.

The well-established Spanish Jews who fled were in almost all cases reduced to abject poverty in their new countries of residence. When was the day when the decree came into effect? The ninth of Av, 1492.

Moving up about one hundred and fifty years, we come to the Chmielnicki massacres by the Cossacks. In 1648, the Cossacks overran the Jewish community of Constantine and killed three thousand men, women, and children. The date was the ninth of Av, 1648.

And now we come to modern times. World War I broke out on August 1, 1914. That was to be "the war to end all wars." Before it had run its course, millions lay dead, and a whole generation of young men in countries throughout the world vanished. August 1, 1914 happened to be the ninth day of Av that year.

Of course, when we come to World War II, we cannot single out any day as being a day in which the Jews were slaughtered, for the gas chambers worked 365 days a year, year after year, each day devouring thousands of our brothers. We can, however, see that crucial events in the Holocaust were also somehow linked to that day. The decree to establish the Warsaw ghetto, for instance, was adopted on the ninth day of Av in 1941. It was there that a half-million Jews were herded together before being ultimately shipped to their deaths.

And exactly one year later, on the ninth of Av, 1942, the "relocation," as the Germans called it, "to the East," was begun within the Warsaw ghetto. That was the day, as an anonymous writer noted in his diary within the ghetto, that was "the blackest day in the history of the Jews in modern times." That was when the

Jews were first herded into the *Umschlagplatz* for deportation. It was the day that the "policemen" went about methodically from house to house, using their truncheons to force the frightened people into the station marked for death. It was the day that the "policemen" separated husbands from wives, parents from children, and brothers from sisters.

As the same writer notes: "The cries and calls of anguish reached up to the very heavens, as the 'policemen' herded the people onto the railroad carriages, as if they were 'sheep for the slaughter.'" That was the night that echoed over and over to the sound of shots, as Jews fell in their hundreds throughout the ghetto. That same night the SS visited the head of the Judenrat and demanded that he "deliver" ten thousand Jews by the next morning. That night, the head of the Judenrat committed suicide.

It fell on the ninth day of Av in 1942.

Even the State of Israel has not been spared its own ninth of Av tragedy. In all its years of operation, El Al has only lost a single airplane, and that happened when the plane accidently wandered into Bulgarian airspace and was shot down. The date: the ninth of Av, 1955.

Given all the memories that the ninth day of Av brings to mind, it is not surprising that in Israel the day is observed as part of the national heritage. The whole country seems to be cloaked in mourning. Over a hundred thousand people find their way to the Western Wall, the symbol of our past, to recite Lamentations. The radio and TV programs are all related to the events of the day. If there is any music at all, it is that of a dirge. Somber poems and tales replace the rock and disco melodies on the light channels. The whole nation seems to bow its head in mourning symbolically.

The ninth of Av is indeed our national day of mourning, not only for the First and Second Temples, which were destroyed thousands of years ago, but for all the tragedies of Jewish life throughout all the ages.

—S.Hi.

 ## How the Haggadah Came to Be

The biblical basis of the observance of Passover is in the Book of Exodus, where two commandments are listed.

One instructs the Jewish father to "tell thy son in that day, saying: It is because of that which the Lord did for me when I came forth out of Egypt." The other passage deals with the eating of the Paschal Lamb, the lamb that the Children of Israel sacrificed just before they began their great journey to freedom. This passage specifies the requirement of the eating of the Paschal Lamb and suggests that the children will ask what the ceremony means and adds that the parents are to explain it.

No one is certain when the celebration of Passover began, but what is certain is that it was very different from the present ritual. The original form probably consisted of the eating of the Paschal Lamb as ordained and the narration of the story of the flight from Egypt by the head of the family. There was no formal text —the *Haggadah* was yet to come—and the head of the house presumably decided how he would tell the Exodus story and what he would put into it.

Presently there developed a desire for a more uniform procedure for the Passover meal, particularly during the period of the Second Temple in ancient Israel, roughly from the sixth century B.C.E. to the first century of our era. At that time, the daily, Sabbath, and festival prayers were beginning to assume a standard form.

The first step toward a standarized ritual came from a chapter in the *Mishnah* that provides for the four cups of the Passover benediction and gives the form for the four questions. The form of the questions in the *Mishnah* indicates that the entire ceremony was performed at the end of the Passover meal.

Rabbi Gamaliel specified that the symbols of the Paschal feast—the lamb, the unleavened bread, and the bitter herbs—were to be mentioned in the ritual. To this was added a thanksgiving for liberation from the Pharaoh and the reciting of the Hallel Psalms, numbers 113 to 118.

By the time the *Mishnah* was completed in about the year 200 C.E., the narration, or Haggadah, had reached a fairly fixed form. Considerable latitude was still permitted, however, for expanding the narrative. Learned men would expand and expound on the wonders of the Exodus until the daybreak after the Seder.

Modifications and enlargements of the *Haggadah* were made as the centuries passed. A particularly favored source of such changes was the *Mishnah*, from which was added the description of the four types of children who ask what the Passover rites mean. Some of the songs at the end of the narration were not added until the sixteenth century. At about that time, the fixed text emerged.

Some time in the Middle Ages, the procedure was changed; a large part of the questions, answers, and explanations of the meanings of the symbolic objects was recited before the meal. This change has been followed to this day and explains why the structure of the *Haggadah*, with its opening questions and answers, has lost its original meaning.

The various groupings within Jewry have differing customs relating to various parts of the ceremony. Among Ashkenazic Jews during the Middle Ages, for example, and among some groups of observant Jews at the present time, the master of the house and other participants in the Seder dip their fingers in the cups of wine at each mention of each of the ten plagues visited upon the Egyptians before the Exodus. They also spill a little of the wine into a plate.

The origin and meaning of this custom is not known. It has been explained as symbolic of the idea that the cup of joy is rarely completely full. Another explanation is that this is a reminder that Jews should avoid gloating over the misfortunes of others, even of their oppressors.

The *Haggadah* was a book for home use and was, therefore, promptly translated into various languages of Jewish residence.

After centuries of relative fixity of content, a number of adaptations of the *Haggadah* appeared in the United States and Germany, generally under Reform Jewish auspices. (There is a Reconstructionist *Haggadah* and also a simple *Haggadah* for very young children.) These were basically abridgements, eliminating many of the passages dealing with miracles, the Talmudic debates, and the discussion of the ten plagues. All modern *Haggadahs*, as a rule, retain the four questions, the explanations of the symbols, and the concluding songs. The prayers are usually abridged, and the vernacular translation is included.

Another abridgement, wholly unofficial and unauthorized, has taken place in the twentieth century American Jewish home under the pressure of the cult of the child. The *Haggadah* was designed by the sages to attract and hold the attention of children, particularly through the device of the reciting of the four questions by the child, as well as through the search for the *afikoman*. However, even a modest inquiry into the conduct of the Seder in the typical American Jewish home, particularly in suburbia, will reveal that the frequently harassed head of the house must trim the recital if he is to hold the attention of his children at all.

Despite the impact of child-centered harassment of parents, Passover is being ever more widely celebrated in the American Jewish community. The sages who over the centuries contributed to the final form of the Seder ceremony might be surprised at what changes life in America has brought about, but there is no doubt they would recognize it as part of the continuity of Jewish experience through the ages.

—B.G.

 ## A Burial That Saves Lives: Incident in Morocco

Religion plays an enormous role among the Jews in Morocco. It is the live, throbbing center of the family and the community. The holidays take on a special importance in the lives of Moroccan Jews; not only the major holidays, but all holidays are scrupulously observed according to the age-old Sephardic tradition. And since social life evolves exclusively around the synagogue and the home, it is enriched by many rites and customs that break up the monotony of the months stretching between the principal holidays.

One of the most colorful customs is the *Genizah,* held throughout North African communities every four or five years. In complete contrast to the somber character these burial rites have in the Ashkenazic countries, where they are carried out by the rabbi and a few worshipers, this ceremony becomes in Morocco a combination of pilgrimage and picnic and provides good entertainment for young and old alike. (Actually, *Genizah* refers to both the hiding of sacred manuscripts and the hiding place itself.)

This Sephardic tradition combines mystic, religious, and social elements and is widely practiced in the communities throughout the Sharifian Empire.

In one particular year, the *Mitzvah of the Genizah* was to be held in Salé, an old pirate stronghold, once feared and flourishing, when Morocco was still the Kingdom of Fez and North Africa was known as the Barbary Coast.

It was a sunny afternoon in June. Caught in the multicolored stream of pilgrims winding down the road like a giant snake, I was half pushed and half carried by the crowd toward our destination: the cemetery.

We had left the Mellah—the North African ghetto—freshly whitewashed in white and blue colors for the occasion and decorated with the blood-red banners of the Sharifian Empire. The procession moved slowly through the narrow streets of the Jewish quarter amid delirious enthusiasm and the singing of psalms and strange, oriental chants, gay and melancholic at the same time, like the Jewish soul itself.

Soon it had passed through the heavy gates of the walled city and wound its way along a dusty road through the arid and rocky countryside.

At the center of the procession was a cart, loaded with old and torn prayer books, manuscripts and Torahs that had worn out from constant use and that were now on the way to their last resting place. The precious load had been collected patiently, from synagogue to synagogue and from house to house and was to be buried today, so that no page bearing the Holy Name would be destroyed by fire or soiled unintentionally. The wagon was surrounded by countless cars, ancient autobuses, and other vehicles. Skeletonlike horses staggered under the weight of shaky carriages into which whole families had piled.

The entrance to the cemetery was a short distance from the road. Yet these few yards led us from the dusty dryness of the desert into a different world: a green valley opened before our eyes, a gently sloping hill. The graves were not arranged in orderly rows but were dug here and there, haphazardly, which deprived the place of its austerity and, for some reason, reminded one of a picnic ground. The inscriptions were in French and Hebrew.

A variegated crowd circulated among the graves: peddlers and merchants, sporting the colorful straw hats of the Rif Arabs, sold sweets and refreshments; the place swarmed with an unbelievable mass of beggars and cripples of all kinds. They were the children of the Mellah; its filth and misery and the frequent intermarriages produced the blind, the one-eyed, the maimed.

Pitiful and repulsive at the same time, exposing their sores to the merciless light of the sun, they blessed and cursed the passersby, according to the degree of their generosity. Oldsters with parchment skin squatted in a circle and either meditated on a commentary of the Law or dreamt a dream of their own, oblivious to the commotion around them.

Jewesses who seemed to have stepped out from a Delacroix painting chatted in small groups, their necks and arms covered with bracelets and necklaces, and their features disappeared under heavy coats of paint. These oriental beauties, with opulent curves and diaphanous hands, squatted for hours, drinking their mint tea in the shade of a cyprus tree.

Elsewhere, a bereaved young mother bent in mute despair over a small, fresh grave, the joy of her life lost forever. Women in Western dress haggled for candles with obsequious merchants in Arab *djellabas*. Small groups of men in greasy, black "kaftans" had a violent discussion; the glare of the midday sun tinted their beards a reddish hue. Olive-skinned children played innocently on the graves. The whole scene, combining the delicate gravity of a Venetian print and the vulgarity of a travel folder, could be the setting for a great painter's masterpiece.

A dense crowd congregated around a small, pink stone building with a dome-shaped roof: it contains the remains of the holy rabbi, Raphael Encoua. This great scholar had been an eminent legal authority and the author of various treatises. He was also said to have performed miracles during his lifetime as well as after his death in 1935. It was rumored that even Moulay Aba al-Hafid himself, the father of the present ruler, had consulted him on many occasions. The picture of the venerable rabbi can be found in all Jewish homes in North Africa, the humble and the wealthy alike.

A score or so of pilgrims of both sexes sat in a semicircle around the tomb in the shade of a canopy. They came to pray and implore the help of the holy rabbi, the bestower of the *Berakha*.

The pungent odor of candles blended with the smoke from archaic, twisted oil lamps, which swung on chains over our heads and were decorated with Hebrew symbols and the Arabic "hands of Fatima." A cheap cake pan stood on the tomb, serving as a recipient for the donations. At a short distance other, smaller sepulchers, of brown granite, held the remains of less famous rabbis and were visited by many pilgrims. The worshipers prostrated themselves and kissed the burning hot stones fervently.

What a strange spectacle! An ecstasy, almost palpable, pervaded the air. A religious fervor possessed the crowd, similar to the mass hysteria that reigns in nearby Spain during the mysteries of the Holy Week. A young Arab, one-armed and half-blind, operated a primitive oven, topped by a stovepipe.

This eery picture had the effect of a hallucination upon the stranger; the unreal feeling of a dream or a nightmare.

Our attention was drawn toward a dense crowd, milling like ants around an open grave. We were about to witness the strangest of all auction sales, where hundreds of worshipers would "bid" on the burlap-wrapped packs of dilapidated books descending to their grave. There were dozens of such packs, weighing about a hundred pounds each. Lifting them high in their arms with blessings and incantations, the "purchasers" performed the *mitzvah* of lowering the bags into the cemented vault. The money heaped up under the zealous eye of a rabbi, acting as treasurer. The women clung to the borders of the grave and screamed hysterically.

Observing my confusion before this scene, a *R'bati* (native of Rabat) approached me. "You see, young man," he began, "this ceremony may seem childish and primitive to you or more like a meaningless superstition, if you are not familiar with its real purpose. As you well know, our Law forbids us to burn or destroy any manuscript or writings bearing the Holy Name. Our sages felt therefore that such books should be given the same kind of burial as the human body, returning to the dust from which it came. And so, the *Genizah* is practiced wherever Jews live. But while in Ashkenazic communities it is a simple and sober ceremony, performed by the rabbi and a few attendants, it has become a public event in Sephardic countries, and the whole community takes part.

There are more reasons than meet the eye for this loud celebration. You Frenchmen would call these reasons 'practical.' This is another means to collect money for our poor. Each person that donates a worn-out prayer book—and what home does not possess at least one such book—after four years of constant use—provides the means of raising money so sorely needed for our thousands of needy and helpless, for food, clothing and medicines, as well as for books. Remember what the Lord, blessed be His Holy Name, has said: 'The true obligation is not to worship Me blissfully, but to give to the poor. He who gives to the poor, gives a loan to God.' You see, Monsieur, through an act of death, we perform an act of life. But this is not all; do you know that we receive a tax for our poor on each bottle of kosher wine, on each loaf of bread cooked in our community ovens, on each piece of kosher meat? In your Western world—so well organized, protected, deodorized, and disinfected—do you take such good care of your less fortunate brethren?"

The man spoke with quiet dignity and was obviously proud of his community.

In the meantime, bag upon bag was heaped up in the vault, to a point where the old guardian of the cemetery had to climb down on a ladder and stack the packs in an orderly fashion. It seemed such a cruel reminder for a man his age . . . To my surprise, he emerged from the black hole smiling and very pleased.

These torn books, so carefully preserved during their lifetime and now carried to the grave like a beloved relative, reminded me of those other books, those hundreds of Torahs burned on bonfires on so many street corners; our devastated synagogues, where the German boots trampled the half-burned Torahs lying in the blood of their worshipers . . .

A Muslim town official, wearing the traditional white *djellaba* and red fez, presented the greetings of the Khalifa to the president of the local *Hevra Kaddisha* (burial society), who bowed deeply and repeatedly in return. My neighbor whispered: "Maybe he came to see if we're holding a Zionist meeting; it has become a forbidden word since Morocco joined the Arab League."

Arab peasant women leaned against the crumbling stone walls of the cemetery, rising on their toes in order not to lose anything of the spectacle. Whole Arab families in festive clothes, arriving as if it were a fair, greeted each other noisily, with much backslapping. A primitive orchestra produced a strange music, which combined the plaintive whining of a fiddle with the sharp tom-tom beat of a tambourine made from a sheep bladder.

At sunset the pilgrims left the cemetery, slowly, almost regretfully, swarming down the hill to pile into their rickety vehicles. Only the rabbis and a few pious stayed to pray throughout the night.

—D.G.

 ## Demons and Spirits in Jewish Tradition

From the very dawn of history the belief in demons was universal. "There are people without a God," said Huxley, "but there are no people without spirits." The idea that demons were the cause of diseases was deeply rooted among races and peoples the world over. Such beliefs were especially prevalent with reference to the eye. Its complicated and misunderstood mechanism lent itself to all sorts of speculative superstitions. Early man saw in the pupillary image of his sick friends the evil spirit that took possession. His conviction was strengthened in cases of opacities of the cornea and diseases of the media, which left the eye blind.

In classical Greek literature, demonology and religion overlap considerably. The early Greeks made no distinction between gods and demons. There were good and bad demons, depending on the work they were assigned to do. Aristotle, son of a physician, spoke of demons influencing and inspiring the possessed. The Babylonians viewed all demons as malevolent.

In the cuneiform inscriptions, demons are pictured as spiteful beings. The archdemon was known as Tiamat. He ruled over seven evil deities known as *sheidim*. Of the 660 medical texts discovered in the royal library of Ashurbanipal (668–627 B.C.E.), an unusually large number deal with diseases of the eye. Charms and incantations were prescribed to render the demon powerless.

The ancient Egyptians firmly believed that all supernatural beings controlled all affairs of life. Everything in nature, even the elements themselves, were thought to be governed by spirits. Spirits exerted a great influence on men, causing vexation and disease by stealthily entering their bodies. The Persians ascribed disease to genii and cures to the influence of good spirits. Ahriman, the archevil *daeva*, had myriads of subordinates, as did Ormazd, the chief of the benevolent demons, who endeavored to conquer the disease and death produced by the evil one. The king of all spiritual beings was known as Aeshma (Talmudic Asmodeus).

Despite the clear logic of the Greeks, the belief in spirits and their worship occupied a prominent part in their lives. In the philosophy of Plato, demons are considered inferior to the gods but superior to men. Plato was of the opinion that when a demon took possession of a person, the latter was entirely overpowered and no longer capable of thought and speech, these faculties emanating not from the person but from the demon.

The Old Testament prohibits the worship of pagan divinities. "Thou shalt have no other gods before me" is repeatedly stated. "It is the Lord Himself that sends pestilence and death." "Deber and Reshaf are (only) the angels of God." The sorcerer became a repellent subject. He was regarded as an ally and servant of the spirits of evil in league against God. The Old Testament is against occult practices, and the Book of Baruch denounces demons as the idols of paganism.

But despite the Hebrew opposition to polytheism and spirit worship, their existence is recognized in the Bible. Spirits were, however, powerless to act of their own accord. They were always subject to the will of God. Evil spirits are referred to in the Old Testament as *sheidim*. They are also known as *seirim* (goatlike), satyrs identified with the Arabian *jinn* of the desert. Other spirits mentioned in the Old Testament are *ketev meiri* and Lilith, the queen of the demons who reigns at night. In rabbinic literature she is pictured with wings, long flowing hair, and long nails and is the mother of Ahriman.

Nahash (serpent) is another biblical designation for a wicked spirit. In the story of the fall of man, the author of Genesis seems to have recorded a tradition preserved among ancient races. The serpent was always considered a mysterious and evil inciter. He is found in the mythology of Egypt, Mesopotamia, India, and Persia. "Everywhere," stated Westphal, "the serpent personifies the power of darkness." He is said to be the most ancient figure by means of which mysterious powers of evil were designated. In Talmudic literature he is often known as *Nahash hakadmoni* and is identified with the Persian Ahriman.

The most dreaded and terrible spirit was Satan. He is described as the mortal enemy of Israel—an angel of death and evil thought. In the Book of Zechariah, Satan is designated the foe of the Hebrews. In the prologue to the Book of Job, Satan plays the role of an enticer of evil and inflictor of disease. He acts as a messenger, thoroughly submissive to the will of God. In the First Book of Chronicles, Satan provokes David to transgress against the will of God and thus becomes the enemy of Israel.

The Old Testament contains only one instance that could possibly be interpreted as demonic possession—the case of Saul. However, even here the construction of the passage, "The evil spirit of the Lord troubled him," does not necessarily apply to demonic possession in the accepted meaning. Josephus reflects the popular belief of possession in the statement: "But as for Saul, some strange and demonic disorder came upon him; such suffocation as was ready to choke him."

The two spirits protecting Lot from the mob "smote the men that were at the door of the house with blindness." The blindness of Tobit, caused by a condition of the cornea, as recorded in the Apocrypha, does not seem to have been demonic in origin. The cure, however, was effected by the intervention of the benevolent spirit Raphael.

It was probably because of the belief in demonic possession that ancients regarded blindness as the lowest form of degradation. The blind were considered outcasts of society and were quarantined outside the city gates.

According to Josephus, demons were spirits of the wicked who entered men and killed them unless prevented by exorcism or by fumigating. Josephus credited King Solomon with authorship of a book on occult science and also with the supernatural power to cast out demons by incantation, "a science useful to man."

After the Babylonian exile (586 B.C.E.), the occult sciences became widely spread among the Hebrews, as is apparent from the Apocryphal and the Talmudic literature. Demons were known by scientific names, and diseases were frequently attributed to them. Philo, who endeavored to blend the Old Testament with Hellenic doctrines, asserted that there were good as well as evil demons. Angels, demons, and souls were to him identical. "Moses called those 'angels' whom the Greek philosophers chose to call 'demons.'"

Of the three sects that dominated Jewish life at the beginning of the Christian era, the Essenes exerted the most powerful influence on the followers of Christianity. They claimed the power to invoke the good spirits and exorcise the evil ones and to cure the possessed. The New Testament admonishes the Sadducees for denying the existence of angels and spirits. The Pharisees, following a middle course, confessed the existence of supernatural beings but considered them unclean and endeavored to repel them not by magic formulas or exorcism but by the study of the Torah and by the spirit of holiness. The belief in occultism never became an essential feature of Jewish theology, although the reality of demons was never questioned.

Talmudic demonology is a mixture of Babylonian and Persian beliefs. Satan is said to have six submissive demons, known as Kezef, Af, Heima, Mishbar, Mashbit, and Mechaleh. While the names are Hebraic, the idea was probably taken from Persian occultism. The Avesta mentions a similar number of *daevas* (demons) who were messengers of the archdemon Ahriman. In Talmudic literature, demons are known mostly by Aramaic names, for Aramaic was the language spoken among the Jews of Babylonia and Palestine at the beginning of the present era. They were designated as *ruchin* (spirits), *mazikim* (hurtful spirits), *malachei habalah* (angels of destruction) and *sheidin* (Hebrew *sheidim*). A demoniac was known as a *gevar sheidyan* (man possessed by a demon). There was a morning spirit, Telena, and a night spirit, Lilith. They were governed by an archdemon Asmodeus.

According to the Book of Enoch, demons originated from the union of the "fallen angels" with the "daughters of man." A Talmudic legend, which probably originated from a Persian myth, attributed their origin to the intercourse of Adam with the night demon Lilith. Still another legend attributed the birth of evil spirits to the archangel Samuel. The latter is said to have cast lascivious glances at mother Eve; the issue of this union was no other than Satan, the tempter. The spirit governing the function of the eye in the Talmud is known as Bath Chorin, but she was of a rather benign nature.

Like earthly beings, spirits were believed capable of eating, drinking, reproduction, and death and could assume either a male or female form. They could be differentiated, however, from earthly beings by the fact that they did not cast a shadow. Their dwelling place was said to be in the far north, from whence they flew to every corner of the earth. Strong northern or northwestern winds were believed either to be invisible demons themselves or to carry the demons with them. The Hebrew and Aramaic *ruah*, signifying wind and spirit, probably originated from this belief. To this day, peasants in the Baltic provinces believe that the strong gusts of wind that blow in the spring from north and the northeast are caused by the demons and witches of northern Finland and afflict people with rheumatism, colds, fever, and sore eyes. The most fatal date is said to be Ascension Day, when the wind is thought to blow the hardest. Natives on this day take care not to go out of their houses.

—B.L.G.

 ## In Yemen, *Shofar* Was Blown When Worshipers Marched Around Synagogue on Simhat Torah

Sukkoth was such a festive and popular celebration that many houses (in Yemen) were built with one room without a ceiling so as to provide a permanent *sukkah;* the roof was covered the rest of the year with mats to keep the rain out. The *sukkoth* covering consisted of *durra* or cornstalks or green cactus leaves. Inside, the floor was covered with mats and carpets, and bowls of myrtle leaves hung in the corners.

Possession of a *lulav* and an *etrog* was an imperative. Some fathers used to acquire them for all of their sons who were capable of holding them. Yemen, incidentally, grew two kinds of *etrogim:* one, edible, weighed up to fifteen pounds; the other, much smaller and inedible, was used for the Sukkoth ritual.

It was customary in some areas of Yemen for several families to buy jointly an ox or a sheep so as to have an abundance of meat for the holiday. On *Sukkoth* nights, everyone slept in the *sukkah*.

Hoshanah Rabbah differed from its observance elsewhere in the Diaspora in one major item: between each *hakkafah* (circling of the pulpit), the ram's horn was sounded.

The Yemenite boy was formally introduced to his community when his father took him to the synagogue, at the first *Simhat Torah* in his life, and had the worshipers bless the child—a joyful ceremony, which culminated with a festive *Kiddush*.

—D.–M.H.

 ## Why Bukharan Jews Used to Remain Indoors on Hoshanah Rabbah

The prescription for the Feast of Tabernacles was very much to the liking of the Bukharan Jews; the more intricate the commandment, the better they liked it. They decorated their booths with gay splendor: the walls were hung with tapestry and adorned with colorful paper garlands, and the ground was covered with thick carpets. "Elijah's chair," a symbol of welcome to the patriarchs, since according to tradition they visited the booths in spirit, stood in one corner, decorated with silks and laden with sacred books.

On *Hoshanah Rabbah** they were careful not to leave their homes, for they believed—as the Zohar intimates—that anyone venturing abroad on that night who does not see his shadow would meet with tragedy.

Simhat Torah was a day of pure rejoicing. The walls of the synagogue would be adorned with tapestry and drapery. Each Scroll of the Law was wrapped in seven coverlets. Removal of the coverlets and the bringing to light of the written parchment were considered a great honor and worthy of considerable sums to be donated to the synagogue. Removal of the last coverlet was naturally the highest honor, and the wealthy worshipers bid for it hotly, much to the merriment of the congregation. The winner would later treat his friends and relatives to a feast.

Immediately after Sukkoth, the trustees would make the rounds of the homes of the wealthy for funds to buy fuel to tide the poor over the long and bitterly cold winter.

—D.–M.H.

* Seventh day of the festival.

III
Turning Back the Clock:
A Look into History

When *Etrogim* Pelted the High Priest

The earliest account of the *etrog,* or citron, appearing in the Sukkoth ritual involves a remarkable incident concerning the unpopular Hasmonean king, Alexander Yannai.

The Talmud and Josephus both describe how, in his role as high priest, he once outraged the assembled throng in the Temple by contemptuously spilling the water libation upon the ground. The furious worshipers retaliated by hurling their *etrogim* at him.

Doubtless, Yannai's insult was inspired by his hatred for the Pharisees, a hatred that eventually provoked war in 94 B.C.E.

Does the absence of any prior record of the *etrog's* being associated with the festival of Sukkoth suggest that something else may once have represented the "fruit of a goodly tree," which Leviticus instructs the Jew to use with the *lulav?*

Some years ago, Shmuel Tolkowsky argued that the biblical phrase *pri etz hadar* should be interpreted as the fruit of the "dar tree," that is, the cedar tree, known to have been venerated in several ancient cultures.

He advanced the ingenious hypothesis that it was the known association of the cedar cone with pagan rituals that ultimately led to the substitution for it by the etrog. He believed that this was done at the behest of Simon the Maccabee, who then minted coins depicting the *etrog.*

Recent research, however, has revealed that these coins were, in fact, minted during the uprising against the Romans from 66 to 70 C.E. (several hundred years later).

Writing in the American journal *Science,* Erich Isaacs disputed Tolkowsky's contention that the *etrog* would have been unknown in Israel after the return of the exiles from Babylon.

Isaacs suggests that, irrespective of whether the citron tree was indigenous to either India or southern Arabia, the extensive trade links throughout the ancient world would have guaranteed its familiarity to the Jews before the compilation of the Book of Leviticus.

Tolkowsky paid scant attention to the unswerving insistence of the rabbis of the Talmud that the "goodly fruit" was the *etrog.* This seems unjust, for these rabbis were the inheritors of a long oral tradition. There is no better source of information about the ancient rituals.

Nevertheless, an important question remains: Why the *etrog?*

The citron tree was unique because it flowered throughout the year. This may well have convinced the ancients that it was endowed with a mystical life force. Thus, not only can we understand why it would be a "goodly fruit" for the Jews, but also why others esteemed it as a medicinal agent capable of defeating the demoniacal forces held to be responsible for diseases.

The botanist Theophrastus, a pupil of Aristotle, recommended a concoction of citron in wine as an emetic that would bring relief to victims of poisoning. On a more mundane level, he advocated it as a remedy for bad breath, something the Assyrians seem to have known five centuries earlier. The parallel between this use of "natural citron" and present-day claims for the deodorant properties of "natural chlorophyll" in toothpaste and other nostrums should not be overlooked.

With the passage of time the therapeutic claims became bolder. Not for nothing did botanists name the *etrog "Citrus medica."*

Neither victims of gout nor dyspeptic old men need have feared the future so long as citron could be purchased. The seeds were sought after as a purgative. And pregnant women hailed it as the panacea that would assuage their overwhelming desire for strange foods, succor them during their confinement, and even, as the Talmud itself testifies, ensure the birth of a male child.

Yet can we be altogether certain that our forefathers were not in some way responsible for the outrageous claims made about the medicinal properties of citron?

As the Jews settled around the Mediterranean coasts, they transformed the landscape by introducing the cultivation of the citron, which they required for Sukkoth.

—W.S.

 ## Jewish Life Two Millennia Ago: A Son Is Born and a Cedar Is Planted

The Birth of a Child. . . . In the period at which we have now arrived, we have definite knowledge that the woman in labor was placed on a birthstool that was probably the property of the midwife. The latter was called *chayo* (the one that brings life—a name that was applied also to a woman in childbed) and also *chachomah* (the wise or skillful one). She was paid for assisting in the delivery, for her skill had become a vocation transmitted usually from mother to daughter or to daughter-in-law. If no midwife were available in the locality, one of the many women who were present in the house made herself helpful. A physician was sent for in an emergency.

As soon as the child was born, even before it was bathed, the women who were standing about seized it and held it in their arms and hugged and kissed it, especially when the child was a boy. Then the midwife cleansed the babe, rubbed it with salt, and bathed it in warm water. Next, she anointed the child with warm oil and powdered it with powder made of pulverized leaves of myrtle. She then straightened the limbs of the babe and swaddled it from belly to feet. In regions infested by mosquitoes a mixture of unripened grapes was prepared and applied on the skull of the child in order to keep away gnats and mosquitoes.

In this period the Jews, like their neighboring nations, surrounded the bed of the mother with various safeguards and charms to protect her and the child from evil spirits and witchcraft. The rabbis of the Talmud were hostile to these magic folk practices. However, they had to accede to the popular demand and sanction some of them.

A new feature in this period was the cradle. Among the poorer classes the kneading trough was used as a cradle. The same word, *arisoh,* is used for both. Among the richer classes, the cradle was an adorned carriage on wheels, with bells attached to it. The ringing of the bells lulled the child to sleep and also acted as a charm to keep away evil spirits.

Planting a Tree. . . . As in biblical times, the birth of a child was not celebrated with a feast. Among the Palestinian Jews, however, it was customary to plant a tree in the garden to commemorate the birth. For a son, a cedar was planted; for a daughter, a pine. At the wedding, the bridal chamber was built from the wood of the pine and the cedar trees that the parents had planted.

The planting of a tree at the birth of a child was believed to act as a charm to ensure that he or she would grow and thrive like the tree. In the popular belief there was a mysterious relation between the life of a person and the growth of a tree. The custom of planting a tree to celebrate the birth of a child was not original with the Jews but was adopted from the Romans and other foreign nations among whom they lived.

The Jew Among the Uncircumcised. . . . When in the last centuries of the Second Temple, Antiochus Epihanes prohibited circumcision under penalty of death, the rite gained in importance among Jews. They became martyrs for circumcising their newborn males. Mothers were executed with their circumcised children. To the Jews, the blood of the martyrs enhanced the religious importance of the "emblem in the flesh" carried by the children of Abraham.

Soon the political situation changed, and when it did, the significance of circumcision underwent a temporary change. Antiochus' persecution incited the Jews to revolt against the Syrian oppression. The leaders of the rebellion, the Maccabeans or Hasmoneans, were victorious in their protracted struggle and ultimately succeeded in founding a new, independent Jewish kingdom of Palestine. The Hasmonean princes conquered many non-Jewish regions of the land and Judaized their inhabitants. In that period, circumcision became the physical means of Judaizing the new non-Jewish subjects of the Jewish theocratic state. It became an outer mark of the subjection to the rule of the Hasmoneans.

But Judaization as a means of political expansion did not last long. Rome soon conquered Judea, and the independent state of the Hasmoneans came to an end. However, the end of the Jewish state did not halt the widespread diffusion of Judaism in the pagan world. The problem of circumcision loomed large in the religious propaganda of the Jews.

In that period of early imperial Rome, the Jews were dispersed over almost the entire world, and they carried on extensive propaganda for their faith and made countless proselytes. Hundreds of thousands in higher circles of pagan society cherished a strong admiration for the Jewish religion and the Jewish way of life.

However, it was no easy task for a pagan to embrace Judaism completely. This entailed the severance of all intimate relations with friends and relatives. For men especially, circumcision was a great obstacle to the adoption of the Jewish religion. There were, therefore, proselytes of various grades. Many were satisfied with only a minimum of Jewishness. They visited the synagogue occasionally on the Sabbath or on a Jewish festival and observed this or that bit of Jewish religious life but persisted in most of their pagan practices. On the other hand, some underwent circumcision and became full-fledged Jews. Between these two extremes there were, of course, many intermediate stages of conversion to Judaism.

In those days, not all Jewish missionaries who made proselytes insisted upon circumcision in every case. The following story is told by Josephus Flavius concerning the conversion to Judaism of the royal house of Adiabene, a kingdom in northern Mesopotamia.

A certain Jew by the name of Ananias succeeded in converting to the Jewish faith many women of the highest rank in the royal court, among them the queen, Helena. She became an ardent Jewess. The king, Monobazus, showed much sympathy for the Jewish religion, but he did not embrace it. But their son, Izates, heir to the throne, completely adopted the Jewish religion, with the exception of circumcision. This he was dissuaded from doing lest he estrange himself from his subjects, most of whom regarded the Jewish religion as peculiar. But when Izates ascended the throne, he resolved to complete his conversion by being circumcised. Ananias argued with Izates that he could be a Jew and worship God even though he omitted circumcision. But when another learned Galilean Jew convinced the king that one who is uncircumcised breaks the law of Moses, the king carried out his determination to complete his conversion, and his act was emulated by many of the princes of the royal family.

In Conflict with the Outside World. . . . In the Greco-Roman world, circumcision was mistakenly regarded as an exclusively Jewish rite, and the Jews were ridiculed for being circumcised. The Greco-Roman writers had little understanding of the Jewish way of life, as glaringly shown by the fact that they derided the Jewish observance of the Sabbath. The Greco-Roman slave-holders regarded the institution of a weekly day of rest for all toilers as a manifestation of laziness on the part of the Jews.

Circumcision separated the Jews from the Greco-Roman world, and the casuistic arguments of the Christian church against circumcision only intensified in the Jews their zeal for the "indelible covenant in the flesh" of the children of Abraham. This feeling was strengthened by the persecution of Hadrian, the Roman Emperor, who, like Antiochus, three hundred years before, prohibited circumcision as one of the fundamental practices of Judaism, under penalty of death. In those years of religious persecution, circumcision was performed secretly. It was not divulged in the neighborhood. Indirectly one discovered that a circumcision ceremony would take place the following day when, on the preceding evening, he noticed the preparations for the feast.

This persecution did not last long. Antoninus Pius, Hadrian's successor, rescinded the decrees against Judaism. Circumcision was again permitted, but only for born Jews, not for proselytes. Because the Jews had suffered for circumcision, it grew in importance. A generation after the persecution, Judah the Patriarch declared that circumcision was more important than all other precepts of the Jewish religion put together, possibly reflecting the thought that the unity of a people in exile must be maintained and strengthened.

The Circumcision Ceremony. . . . Circumcision had thus become a religious ceremony of great significance. It was attended by benedictions and celebrated with joy and feasting. On the eve of the occasion, the house was full of activity— oil lamps were burning; the hand mill was clattering, grinding wheat into flour, in preparation for the important and joyous ceremony. On the next day a large company gathered to witness the rite.

The operation was no longer performed by the father, but by a special *mohel* (one who performs the circumcision operation) who used an iron knife. The stone knife of biblical times had been discarded. The version of the benedictions recited at the ceremony had already been fixed by this period. The *mohel* said: "Blessed be Thou, O Lord, our God, King of the Universe, who has sanctified us with His commandments and enjoined upon us the circumcision." The father followed with: "Blessed be Thou, O Lord, our God, King of the Universe, who sanctified us with His commandments and enjoined upon us to initiate our sons into the covenant of our father Abraham." The assembled people also responded: "As he has entered the covenant, so shall he also enter into the study of the Torah, into the *huppah* and into good deeds."

A Circumcision Feast in Jerusalem. . . . In a Midrashic tale we have a vivid description of a circumcision feast in Jerusalem shortly before the second destruction of that city. The father of the child in this tale was Avuyah, one of the wealthy nobles of the Holy City. A son was born to him, who was named Elisha. All the celebrities of Jerusalem were invited to the joyous ceremony, among them the famous sages, Rabbi Eliezer and Rabbi Joshua, the two great disciples of Rabbon Johanan ben Zakkai.

A description of the festive occasion in the house of this wealthy dignitary in Jerusalem follows:

First the circumcision is performed, followed by a sumptuous feast. There are eating and drinking in profusion. After the banquet, the guests amuse themselves in joy and merriment. In one room the people of high rank are gathering. They clap their hands and dance; they sing psalms and recite Greek acrostics. Rabbi Eliezer and Rabbi Joshua sit in another room, surrounded by pious and learned people, whose festive joy is more spiritual in character. Rabbi Eliezer and Rabbi Joshua begin to discourse on the Torah. They start with the Pentateuch and proceed to the prophets; from the prophets they proceed to the writings. The words of the Torah are spoken by them with such clarity and brilliance that to the people listening it seems that not words but a stream of light fills the room. The father, Avuyah, stands nearby and listens. He notices the tremendous effect of their words on the listeners, and Avuyah makes a solemn vow that when little Elisha grows up, he will devote his life to the study of the Torah.

Avuyah fulfilled his vow. Elisha became one of the great Jewish sages of that epoch. Later, however, he deviated from the path of Jewish Orthodoxy and was shunned by his colleagues and condemned by them as a heretic.

In general, the circumcision of a child in Jerusalem was a great festive occasion in which many people participated. Whether the father of the child was rich or poor, a large company assembled at the home whenever a circumcision ceremony was to take place. In Jerusalem there were special brotherhoods for the purpose of attending to important religious duties. There was a brotherhood to participate in circumcision ceremonies; a brotherhood to attend weddings; and a brotherhood to console mourners.

A Circumcision Feast in Galilee. . . . In another Midrashic tale we have a description of a circumcision feast that took place more than a hundred years later than the one just described. Catastrophic and far-reaching changes in Jewish life had occurred during these one hundred and fifty years. Jerusalem and the Temple had been destroyed, and sixty-five years after that disaster came the revolt of Bar Kochba. In the bloody suppression of that revolt, Judea, the southern part of Palestine, had been entirely devastated, and the center of Jewish life and Jewish learning had shifted to Galilee, the northern part of the land. The greatest city in Galilee and the center of the administration of the Jewish community was Sepphoris. Here the leaders and representatives of the Jewish community resided, and it was in the house of one of the wealthy leaders of Sepphoris that the circumcision ceremony took place.

The father invited many people from neighboring towns and villages. Some guests came from En-Teenah, a small town nearby. Among them was the famous tanna, Rabbi Simeon ben Chalaphta, an older contemporary of Rabbi Judah the Patriarch, the compiler of the Mishnah. The wealthy father treated his guests with seven-year-old wine, and at the feast he said: "I pray the Lord in Heaven that I may give you from this same wine at the wedding of my son." After the father had spoken, the throng in the house responded in unison: "As you have initiated him into the covenant, so you shall initiate him into the study of the Torah and into the huppah." We are told in the Midrashic tale that the feasting and banqueting lasted until midnight.

Naming the Child. . . . A girl was still named soon after birth, but the naming of a boy occurred at the circumcision ceremony.

After the Babylonian exile, a great change took place in the naming of children. The custom of naming a son after his grandfather, which prevailed among the ancient Egyptians and Greeks, was now adopted by the Jews. We first hear of it in the fifth century (B.C.E.) among the Jews of Elephantine and Aswan, on the southern border of Egypt. The existence of a community of Jewish soldier-colonists there, hundreds of years before the conquests of Alexander, is a newly discovered chapter in the history of the Jewish dispersion. The archives of this Jewish community were unearthed at the threshold of our century. They contained many papyri written in Aramaic, among which we find the first records of Jewish children named after grandparents.

Later we find this custom also prevalent among the Palestinian Jews. In the high priestly family we find the names of Onias and Simon succeeding one another. In the Hasmonean dynasty, Hyrcanus II bears the name of his grandfather John Hyrcanus. Still later we find the genealogy of the famous Hillel with only a few names in it, mostly those of the grandfather.

Children were also named after the brothers of their father. Two sons of Simon the Hasmonean, Judah and John, bore the names of their father's brothers, apparently after the decease of the latter. Occasionally the child was named in honor of the living. A child might be named for his father or grandfather who was still alive.

A more striking innovation was the use of foreign names, first found in the later books of the Bible. According to modern scholars, Sheshbazzar, Zerubbabel, Belteshazzar, Shenazzar, Mordecai, and Esther are Babylonian names. In Daniel-Belteshazzar and in Esther-Hadassah we have the first use of two names for one person, one Jewish and the other non-Jewish.

This tendency became more pronounced in the Greek period, when Greek or Grecianized names were favored. We find Greek names in the aristocratic circles sympathetic to Greek culture (the high priests and the Maccabean and Herodian princes and princesses). Great religious teachers of the Pharisees, the spiritual leaders of the people, bore the names Antigonus, Symmachus, and Tarphon (Tryphon). Latin names also came into vogue. Jews called their children Marcus or Justus and did not hesitate to name them Titus. Double names, one Jewish and the other Grecian, became popular, as Judah-Aristobul, Salome-Alexandra, Simon-Peter, Saul-Paul. The purists among Palestinian Jews in the centuries following the second destruction of Jerusalem considered it meritorious to bear a genuinely Hebrew name. But outside of Palestine names were mostly non-Jewish.

This was not the only innovation regarding names in the days of the Second

Temple. The common preexilic custom of compounding names with that of God was abandoned altogether or so shortened that only one letter remained of His name. Thus Jehoiada became Jaddua; Hananiah became Honi; and Mattathias became Mattai.

The biblical names, for example, Abraham, Moses, Aaron, and David, were avoided in Talmudic times. Only in the post-Talmudic era did they become popular among all Jewish groups. Biblical names, unheard of in the days of the Second Temple and in subsequent Talmudic times, became popular in Gaonic times. We find Jehiel, Joel, Jehoram, Enoch, Obadiah, and many others.

The first record of a form of prayer for naming a boy is found in Gaonic times. It was written in Aramaic. This was later changed to Hebrew among European Jews, who did not speak Aramaic; and the Hebrew version is still used today.

—H.S.

 ## How Jews Made a Living in the Early Roman Empire

The Roman Imperial Peace (Pax Romana), which endured from the time of Augustus Caesar almost to the close of the second century of the Christian era, was a golden age of economic advancement for the peoples of the ancient world. While it lasted, the entire Mediterranean basin, a considerable portion of the Middle East, and much of Europe north of the Alps were welded together into a single prosperous unit. Under conditions of stable government, effective land and sea communications, and uniform currency, there was unprecedented movement of goods, services, craftsmen, and techniques.

One of the regions that did not enjoy the full benefits of the Pax Romana was Jewish Palestine. There, after a short period of relative calm under the vassal Herod I (37–4 B.C.E.), the peace was interrupted incessantly by opposition to imperial rule, culminating in a wave of revolt and brutal suppression. Nevertheless, the populations of Judea and Galilee remained predominately Hebraic, and economic conditions were basically unaltered, even after the great uprising of 67–70, which ended in Titus' destruction of the Temple. Not until almost a century later, following the Bar Kochba revolt, did the foundations of Jewish material civilization in Palestine lie shattered—but by then the Pax Romana itself was showing signs of breaking down.

However, if Palestine continued as the core of the Jewish world for most of this period, some of the Diaspora communities (those outside Palestine) were beginning to overshadow the motherland in economic importance, and Jewish adventurers were also active far beyond the frontiers of the Roman Empire.

The Jewish population in the early Roman Empire has been estimated at between four million and more than six million. At the time of Herod, Palestine had between one and two million, followed by fairly rapid depopulation during and after the insurrections. But by the beginning of the second century more than twice as many Jews lived in other Roman provinces as in Palestine. As for the Jewish communities outside the empire, the total figure for Persia, Babylonia, and territories further afield, was probably not more than one million.

While Palestine Jewry remained predominantly rural, the Diaspora settlements of that time were concentrated in urban areas. Jerusalem, with a population of about one hundred thousand, was the largest homeland city. Considerable Jewish minorities were to be found in the great commercial centers of Asia Minor and Syria (such as Miletus, Sardis, Antioch, and Damascus), in the Aegean (especially at Delos), on the Greek mainland (Athens and Corinth), at Cyrene on the North African coast, in Sicily at Syracuse, and in Italy itself (at Rome and and the port of Puteoli). In the new city of Seleucia (on the Euphrates north of Babylon) there were fifty thousand Jews in the middle of the first century of the Christian era. By then Alexandria, with its two hundred thousand Jewish citizens out of a total of about a half million inhabitants, had become "almost as much a city of the Jews as of the Greeks."

While the Jews of Palestine remained essentially an agricultural people, farming itself showed some marked advances over the situation prevailing in biblical times. Although the soil compared unfavorably with many of the more fertile regions of the empire, the increasing pressure of population (until the trend was reversed by the Judeo-Roman War) had promoted intensive, capitalistic methods of cultivation and costly artificial irrigation projects. This had resulted in improved yields of wheat and barley, so that in good years there was sufficient to support the local population, meet demands for tributes from Rome, and provide small surpluses for commercial exports.

Much more important as export items were Palestine dates and figs, oil from the prolific olives of Giscala, and high quality wines from the vineyards of Galilee. Balsam, with its medicinal qualities, was found only in the district around Jericho and was so prized that the destruction of the balsam plantations became a powerful economic weapon during the war against the Romans.

The Sea of Galilee supported a major fishing industry, with its salted and dried fish products being sold not only throughout Palestine but in markets abroad. In the drier eastern districts pastoral farming prevailed, as in former times, but many of the shepherds and cowherds had now become commercial cattlemen, making regular visits to the large meat and wool markets of Jerusalem.

Although a class of wealthy landed proprietors had come into being in Herodian times (many members of whom enjoyed connections with the ruling house or belonged to influential priestly families), independent peasant yeomen prevailed over most of the country, and the large estates (or *latifundia*), which had become so characteristic of rural organization in most parts of the empire, were a comparatively rare phenomenon in Palestine. In part, this stemmed from the fact that ever since Maccabean times the rabbinical enactments against debt bondage and the protection of Gentile slaves (which surpassed even biblical legislation) had been rigidly enforced; and without a considerable supply of free labor, the *latifundia* were not economically profitable.

In part, too, the absence of large estates flowed from the continued observance of scriptural laws, such as those concerning land redistributions in Jubilee years. Yet the strict adherence to such moral injunctions became progressively more difficult for a farming community that had also to comply with Roman civic duties. As the ravages of revolt were superimposed on these burdens, rural prosperity tended to coexist with, and was ultimately replaced by, extreme agrarian poverty.

Handicraft industry probably occupied a more important place in the Palestine economy during the Imperial Peace than it had done in former times in spite of the fact that Jewish artisans were not able to compete with many imported wares, even when these were common items of everyday use, such as sandals, felt hats, and handkerchiefs. Nonetheless, the literature of the period mentions at least forty different types of native craftsmen, and there were many villages that had come to be associated with particular occupations.

The dignity and blessing of manual labor—continually stressed in the scriptural commentaries—meant that there was little idleness, and many members of the priestly class as well as eminent scholars supported themselves and their families by manual toil: Hillel the Elder was employed as a woodcutter; Rabbi Nehunyah was a well-digger; Rabbi Yehudah, a baker. Most crafts were passed on from father to son and were organized by guilds. Moreover, the rigid prohibitions against admitting Gentiles into holy places fostered certain branches of industry, particularly constructional work; even the irreligious Herod had been compelled to make exclusive use of some 10,000 Jewish masons for his extensions to the Temple.

The position of Palestine in the Roman world meant that many of the great international trade routes that linked the east with Rome and the provinces of the far west traversed the country. This traffic was of sufficient volume to induce the Roman authorities to establish customs houses at Jericho, Caesarea, Jaffa, and Gaza, although most of this transit business, like the port cities themselves, was in non-Jewish hands. On the other hand, in return for the many natural products that the country itself had exported, came foreign goods of wide variety and origins, ranging from Median beer and Edomite vinegar to Italian furniture and Corinthian candlesticks. These imports for the most part were handled by Jewish-owned caravans and seagoing ships manned by Jewish donkey- and camel-drivers and Jewish sailors.

Even merchants who had no contacts with the outside world frequently established commercial relations with the Diaspora through the pilgrim trade, which annually attracted many thousands of Jewish visitors to Jerusalem. In this way, the capital became the center of a flourishing tourist industry, and the financial needs of the travelers brought into being a new class of specialist moneychangers and bankers, who set up their booths on the outskirts of the Temple. (Thus, when Jesus "overthrew" their tables, Matthew 21:12, he was interfering with certain amenities that for the sake of convenience had come to be attached to the holy shrine.)

The Temple authorities themselves had come to depend on such banking services, for agents were needed to transfer the numerous endowments bequeathed by wealthy coreligionists throughout the empire and in Babylonia. Within the country, full-time bankers collected the half-shekel that every adult contributed annually for the shrine's upkeep, transmitting the proceeds to Jerusalem for a small commission.

This was a comparatively mild tax compared to the exactions of the lay authorities. Herod himself, widely recognized as one of Rome's richest vassals, had built palaces and sanctuaries not only in Palestine but all over the eastern Mediterranean, and such splendor was achieved through a fiscal reign of terror. Yet the notoriety of the king's tax-farmers was eclipsed by that of the Roman procurators who followed, although their levies on the users of roads, water, houses, and salt were probably no greater than those extracted from the natives of other countries subject to Rome. Nor was Vespasian's *fiscus Judaicus* an additional burden but merely the transfer of the Temple tax to finance the erection of a pagan shrine in Rome.

However, it was a grave religious affront, and insofar as political stability under foreign rule depended on the close coordination of priestly authority with local government, such Roman actions served progressively to impair the country's economic well-being.

While imperial rule in Palestine itself became increasingly oppressive, there remained many opportunities for personal advancement in the numerous Diaspora settlements. During the Pax Romana there was nothing to prevent an energetic

Jewish citizen from rising in the armed services from the rank of common soldier to commander or in administrative employment from petty official to a procuratorial post, even ending as a prefect. We know of at least one such case, Tiberius Julius, the historian Philo's nephew, who became prefect of Egypt in the year 69 and played a prominent part in the behind-the-scenes activities that led to the appointment of Vespasian as emperor.

Others with the necessary drive and initiative gained a footing at the top of private enterprise, particularly in Alexandria, becoming "the most active traders of that great commercial metropolis," controlling the export trades in papyrus, wheat, and dates and farming the public revenues for a contractual lump sum. Still others became important as craftsmen in the linen, silk, and metal industries, whereas the more recent arrivals in Egypt and the Asiatic provinces brought with them a detailed knowledge of the art of glassmaking. In the delta area of the Nile, along the coast of Spain, and in other parts of the empire as well, were to be found prosperous communities of Jewish commercial farmers.

Yet the few instances of opulence and great Jewish fortunes should not obscure the fact that the masses of the Diaspora often lived in dismal poverty. Even in wealthy Alexandria, Philo records the existence of dark, congested, unhealthy ghettolike quarters and a life pervaded by economic uncertainty. In Delos, the colony mainly comprised petty tradesmen eking out a marginal subsistence. In Rome itself, Juvenal made fun of the Jewish beggars whom he found swarming in the neighborhood of the sacred grove of Egeria. Indeed all over the empire Jews were prominent among the flotsam of the large cities, earning meager livelihoods from manual labor and peddling or resorting to such bizarre occupations as interpreting dreams and telling fortunes.

Of course, such economic rootlessness and poverty were by no means confined to Jews—it had become a common feature of urban life throughout an empire in which almost all jobs were monopolized by slave labor. But while the shiftless, unemployed mobs of Rome had their attentions occupied by costly bread and circus entertainments, for destitute Jews in Alexandria, Cyrene, and other eastern Mediterranean metropolitan centers, the only diversion was the fostering of a bond of solidarity with their downtrodden coreligionists in the motherland. It was a situation that led inevitably to the widespread Diaspora uprisings of the years 115–117.

These unsettling events in the provinces, together with the increasing oppression of imperial rule in Palestine itself, induced some Jews to hazard their fortunes beyond the empire's boundaries. Following the abortive revolt in Cyrene, for example, an important southward migration took place towards Senegal and the middle Niger. As a consequence, Jews became widely scattered throughout the whole interior of northern Africa and began to participate in the trans-Saharan caravan traffic. Meanwhile, the disturbances occasioned by the Jewish revolt in Alexandria not only greatly impaired the prosperity of that city, but also induced the emperor Trajan to bypass the port by building a canal from the Nile to Clysma on the Gulf of Suez.

This link between the Mediterranean and the Red Sea was now needed to facilitate a growing volume of maritime traffic with the Far East after the discovery of the monsoon's seasonal movements enabled shipping to make directly for India instead of hugging the coastline. Jewish traders had been familiar with the products of oriental commerce ever since the Asiatic conquest of Alexander, from which time linen and muslin fabrics of Indian origin had been imported regularly into Judea, and aromatic woods from Assam and China had reached the Hebrews via the Persian Gulf and Arabia. Accordingly, Jewish merchants were among the first to take part in the growing seaborne trade with the East, and by the close of the second century they were well established in Cochin on the Malabar coast, from whence they probably built up commercial ties with the districts of Lushan and Chengtu in China. Others traded with the mouth of the Indus, eventually penetrating into Afghanistan and founding a colony near Kabul.

However, the overland routes were not altogether neglected, and by the second century, too, Jewish middlemen were sharing in the caravan silk traffic from China to Europe. Most of these merchants belonged to the Babylonian communities, which then formed part of the sprawling Parthian Empire. In addition to such participation in long-distance commerce, these Jews of the Euphrates Valley were commercial cattle-breeders and carried on "trades of all descriptions." But few specific details of their economic activities have survived, although it would seem that they enjoyed a considerable degree of local autonomy and paid reasonable taxes.

Jewish economic life during the Imperial Peace, therefore, presents a checkered pattern: in the ancestral homeland it was a time of mounting anarchy accompanied by economic retrogression and emigration; beyond Palestine, though there existed opportunities of material advancement for the enterprising or lucky few, the majority appear to have been unsettled and unprosperous. Yet, in many respects, Jewish experience in this era was a prelude in miniature to what was to overtake all the empire's peoples once the Pax Romana itself had collapsed.

—M.A.

 ## What Happened to King Solomon's Treasure?

What became of the treasures of King Solomon's Temple? This question is being asked with increasing frequency in Israel, whose soil in recent years has yielded enormous archaeological treasures. The priceless finds include letters written by Bar Kochba, heroic commander of the revolts against Rome; the ruins of Hazor, once an important Middle East center; Caesaria, the metropolis built by King Herod I, whose ancient amphitheater was recently the site of a concert by Pablo Casals; and the twenty-seven-hundred-year-old palace of Uzziah.

In the course of the centuries, many legends have grown up about the disappearance of King Solomon's sacred objects. Thus, Rabbi David Ibn Abi Zimra, who lived in the sixteenth century, tells of a king who ordered a search for the Ark of the Covenant in the mountain caves beneath the site where the Temple once stood in Jerusalem, but that all the searchers were killed by poisonous emanations, whereupon the king had the caves filled with earth.

In a booklet published in Poland prior to World War II, this writer found the following nonsense offered to the public: Having invaded North Africa in the sixth century [sic], the British troops transferred the Temple treasure to London, where it is exhibited at the British Museum . . .

And only recently, an article about the treasure appeared in a number of newspapers, placing it in Rome or, more correctly, in the bed of the Tiber river, where it was said to be buried under several feet of mud and silt. When the invading Goths appeared at the gates of Rome in 410 and the panic-stricken citizens prepared to flee, the Roman Jews—so the story goes—stormed the palace where their sacred vessels were stored and threw them into the river to prevent their further desecration at the hands of the Goths. The article gave as its source an ancient Jewish chronicle in which it allegedly was recorded that before long the treasure would be brought to the surface and returned to Jerusalem. . . . Needless to say no known Jewish document or historical source describes such an event.

What historical facts are actually known?

When King Solomon's Temple was completed, about three thousand years ago, people from distant lands came to admire it, for it was unique amongst the sanctuaries of antiquity, not only for its great splendor but also because it differed in two ways from any other temple of its time: it was dedicated to the worship of one single deity, and, secondly, the stranger, scorned in Greek and Roman society as an enemy intruder, was welcomed here as a friend and a guest. King Solomon himself had made it clear in his famous dedication prayer. "Also the stranger," he appealed, "when he prays toward this House, hear his prayers . . . and do what the stranger begs for . . ."

But pious worshipers bearing gifts for the Temple were not the only visitors. Others came at the head of armies, conquering and plundering the Holy City time and again.

Solomon's Temple stood for about four hundred years when Nebuchadnezzar destroyed it in 586 B.C.E., looting it of its treasure, taking even the famed iron columns of Jachin and Boaz back to Babylon. According to the Talmud, however, the Ark of the Covenant, richly sculptured with figures of cherubim, and the two stone tablets with the Ten Commandments were hidden in a cave beneath the Temple.

The Book of Daniel mentions the stolen ritual objects in describing a drunken orgy at the court of Nebuchadnezzar's son and successor, Belshazzar: "Belshazzar, while he tasted the wine, commanded to bring the golden and silver vessels which Nebuchadnezzar, his father, had taken out of the temple which was in Jerusalem, that the king and his lords, his consorts and his concubines might drink therein" (Daniel 5:1).

The feast ended when a ghostly writing appeared on the wall announcing the fall of Babylon: *"Mene, mene tekel, upharsin . . ."*

The great Persian ruler Cyrus, who conquered Babylonia, allowed the captive Jews to return to their homeland and enabled them to rebuild their temple. He completed his generosity by returning to them their sacred objects for the new temple, which was far more modest than the magnificent house of worship of King Solomon.

But this was not the end yet, and the treasure was still to change hands many times. The Syrian king Antiochus III invaded the country in 217 B.C.E. and looted the Second Temple. The war was won by the Maccabees, but they were unable to regain possession of their treasure and had to furnish their sanctuary with new ritual objects. The temple was completely rebuilt by King Herod with such splendor that again it became one of the marvels of those times, until it fell prey to the flames with the fall of the second Jewish state, and the ritual objects of the Maccabean period fell into Roman hands.

To celebrate the hard-won victory over Judea, Emperor Titus built the famous Arch of Titus in Rome, which still stands and whose sculptured reliefs picture his triumphant return to Rome with the rich spoils: the seven-armed *menorah,* the golden table, two silver trumpets, and numerous vessels. The Jewish historian Josephus Flavius adds to it a Torah roll, and, according to the Mishnah, an incense mortar, the breastplate of the high priest, together with its ornaments, the *urim* and *thummim,* as well as the *parokhet* hanging in front of the Ark, were taken as well. It is, however, very likely that during the last three weeks of the siege, with no sacrifices taking place, the priests may have buried many of the ritual objects to prevent their desecration by the enemy.

The Romans treated the Jewish temple treasure with all respect, storing it in the Templum Pacis—the temple of peace—and the Torah roll and the Ark curtain were kept at the emperor's palace. A century later, an eyewitness, Rabbi Eliezer, the son of the famous Rabbi Yose ben Halaphta, reported seeing in Rome the breastplate and the curtain originally used for the sacrifice ritual on Yom Kippur.

But not even Rome was powerful enough to keep the treasure. Genseric, the king of the Vandals, sacked Rome in 455 c.e. and took the loot to Carthage, his headquarters, where it remained for seventy-nine years. In the meantime, the fortune of war changed, the Vandals were crushed by the Byzantines, and the Temple treasure fell this time to Byzantium—Constantinople—where it was carried through the city in a triumphal procession. A Jew who was among the crowd was overheard saying to his neighbor that he thought it was wrong to bring the treasure to the palace, for it had brought about the ruin of Rome and Carthage, and that it should be returned to King Solomon's Temple, where it belonged.

These words were reported to the Emperor Justinian, who, fearing that he, too, might fall under the curse, as did the previous possessors of the ill-fated treasure, ordered its immediate return to Jerusalem, which was then part of his empire.

The trail ends here. The treasure never reached its destination, nor was it ever heard of again. Most probably it was lost on the way from Byzantium to Jerusalem, together with the ship that carried it.

Historians believe that it lies on the bottom of the Mediterranean, whereas the Ark and the Tablets of the Law are buried in a sealed cave under the ruins of the Solomon Temple, and someday a final chapter might be added to the adventurous story of the sacred treasure, designed to serve peace but used as an offering to the gods of war.

—Y.L.B.

 Jewish Fund-raising Three Thousand Years Ago

Recently identified fragments of an ancient 850-year-old parchment letter reveal the practice of highly advanced publicity techniques by ancient fund-raisers. The letter, which contains a report of a successful fund-raising campaign waged on behalf of the famous Babylonian Talmudical academy at Pumbedita, has been deciphered from fragments now in the archives of the Jewish Theological Seminary of America. This is part of the vast literature of the Cairo Genizah, which scholars have been studying for over fifty years in the library of the seminary.

This private letter is one of the earliest evidences of an organized school fundraising campaign on record. Although, throughout their history Jewish support of charitable and educational causes has been proverbial, since this is a fundamental obligation under Jewish teachings, this letter underscores the fact that fund-raising for the support of schools was an integrated, accepted feature of community life as long ago as the early eleventh century.

The letter, which might well have been written in our own day, reflects in tone the real sense of triumph of the man who, it appears, had engineered the successful campaign for the Pumbedita academy, one Moses ben Barhum Taherti, head of a prominent family of Kairouan, the capital of the sultanate that later became Tunisia.

The Babylonian academies were a major influence in the political and legal development of Jewish life. Under the guidance of distinguished principals, the academies had become the great centers of Jewish scholarship. Among their legacies to us is the great Babylonian Talmud. The influence of the academies extended far beyond their own country.

It appears that the academy at Pumbedita (now Baghdad) had found itself in financial straits, and an emergency appeal had been issued by its principal, Hai Gaon. (*Gaon* is an honorary title meaning "Excellency.") The leaders of the Kairouan community had consulted Taherti, and in his letter he relates how he had instructed them to conduct the campaign to raise the monies for the academy.

Taherti's own account of the negotiations and "persuasions" that were involved in bringing this campaign to a successful conclusion is a lesson in expertise. As a first step Taherti had advised the community leaders to persuade a certain Ibhim ben Ata to head the united appeal. Ben Ata, a physician and a courtier of the Sultan al-Mu'izz, would appear an admirable choice; as both a professional and a politician he would be a person whose influence would carry weight in the community.

Ben Ata, one learns, was reluctant. Yet Taherti persisted in his efforts, convinced that Ben Ata's cooperation was essential to ensure the appeal's success. He writes: "I told them—this matter requires unity . . . through his joining us unity will be created and there will be general agreement." In the end, Taherti triumphed. He reports, elatedly, "I awakened his interest through open and hidden ways until he accepted." With Ben Ata at its head, the campaign was an assured success. Ben Ata himself made a handsome leading contribution—and his lead was followed and "much money was collected."

An interesting sidelight that emerges is that it was also the practice of the ancient seats of learning to reward distinguished citizens with honors—today's honorary degrees. It would seem that Taherti had awakened his (Ben Ata's) interest with some such promise. We find in later references to Ben Ata that he has been given the title of *nagid* or *negid ha-Gola,* a mark of high esteem implying a princely patron.

Owing to the fragmentary condition of the letter, it is impossible to identify with certainty the person to whom Taherti was writing. However, Professor S. D. Gotein of the Hebrew University, who identified this manuscript, attributed it to Joseph ben Awkal of Fostat, or Old Cairo, the representative in Africa of the Babylonian academy. Taherti asks ben Awkal to make sure that Hai Gaon was apprised of his (Taherti's) role in the success of the appeal.

Although Taherti's letter is one of the earliest in date on this subject, the seminary's *Genizah* literature has brought to light a number of manuscripts dealing with charitable appeals and fund-raising activities. Notable among these is an epistle in the hand of the great medieval philosopher-physician Moses Maimonides. This letter, written by him in 1170 and addressed to the North African communities, appeals for funds for the redemption of captives.

The Genizah collection, from which these documents are derived, was started by the private collection of Solomon Schechter, second president of the seminary. In 1896, Dr. Schechter, then Reader in Rabbinics at Cambridge, had been the man primarily responsible for the discovery of the priceless cache of centuries-old Hebrew manuscripts concealed in the *Genizah* (storeroom) of an ancient synagogue near Cairo.

The acquisition by the seminary in 1923 of the library of the noted British bibliophile Elkan Adler vastly enriched its collection of *Genizah* materials. Today the library of the Jewish Theological Seminary of America contains the largest collections of Cairo *Genizah* manuscripts existing in this country, approximately 40,000 items that range in size from one-inch scraps to fragments of several pages.

—News release,
Jewish Theological Seminary

 Early Medical Knowledge Among the Ancient Hebrews

The eye (*ayin*) is alluded to in the Bible many times. The pupil is known as *babat ha'ayin* (door of the eye). The eyelids (*af appayim*) are referred to in Jeremiah, in the passage "and our eyelids gush out with waters," which indicates the belief that the lacrimal apparatus is located in the lids.

Blepharitis ciliaris appears to have been a common disease among the ancient Jews of Palestine. An interesting case is that of Leah. The passage reads, "and Leah's eyes were weak; but Rachel was of beautiful form and fair to look upon."

One is led to believe that the weak eyes of Leah spoiled her appearance: they were red and swollen about the lid margins with perhaps the loss of eyelashes and the formation of concretions on the margins. Her case could not have been that of tender eyes as rendered in the King James version, for such eyes could hardly be called ugly and give rise to complaint by Jacob.

Gonorrheal ophthalmia undoubtedly existed because *gonorrhea* of the genital organs was prevalent in both sexes. As seen from the excellent account of the symptomatology and of the sanitary precautions observed, the visual organs were frequently infected by contact with the discharge.

The Hebrew words for blindness (*sanwerim* and *iwwaron*) used in the Bible are extremely vague terms; they cover all types of partial and complete blindness of a temporary and permanent nature. The prevalence of blindness is well illustrated in 2 Samuel: "The inhabitants [of Jerusalem] complained to David: Except thou take away the blind and the lame, thou shalt not come in hither; thinking David cannot come in hither."

In fact, blindness was so prevalent that special laws were necessary to protect the blind. In Deuteronomy, we read, "cursed be he that maketh the blind to go astray in the way." Whereas diagnosis was not made, there can be but little doubt that such diseases as *retrobulbar neuritis, albuminuric neuritis, optic neuritis,* and other forms of organic diseases existed.

Senile cataract has always been a prominent cause of blindness and probably occurred frequently among the ancient Hebrews. The most suggestive passage is the following, "now the eyes of Israel were dim for age so that he could not see." Both age and race are predisposing causes of cataract. The "dimness" of his sight rather than blindness is indicative of cataract. However, this case might have been the early stage of glaucoma.

Four cases of Old Testament amaurosis present the possibility of glaucoma:

1. "And it came to pass when Isaac was told that his eyes were dim so that he could not see."

2. "Now the eyes of Israel were dim for age so that he could not see."

3. "Now Eli was ninety and eight years old and his eyes were set; so that he could not see."

4. "Now he [Ahijah] could not see; for his eyes were set by reasons of his age."

In the first case, the word "dim" is confusing, for according to the biblical narrative, Isaac suffered from total loss of sight. The patriarch could distinguish his two sons, Esau and Jacob, only by the sound of their voices and by his sense of touch. In each case, the writer gives old age as the cause of blindness. The third and fourth cases are most significant. The Hebrew word *qamu* literally means "they stood still." The blind eyes of Eli and Ahijah were at a standstill. They could not fix on objects in front of them, as is characteristic in *amaurosis* following glaucoma, in which perception of light is gone; there is a peculiar stare, and the eyes either do not move or do so aimlessly.

This peculiar stare could not be mistaken for senile cataract, for in this condition there is usually some light perception, and the ocular muscles keep working in order to locate luminous objects in front of the eye or to recognize dark objects in daylight.

The etiologic factors in all the cases cited bear a striking similarity: old age is given as the main cause of blindness. It is generally agreed that the cause of glaucoma lies in those degenerative processes that are inseparable from the wear and tear of the living organism occurring in old age. In all the preceding cases, there is a history of mental and physical strain, which is recognized as a predisposing factor to ocular trouble.

All these biblical persons were living in the same environment and climate. Two pursued the life of shepherds, exposed to the hot sun during the day and to the cold and damp Palestinian air at night. The contrast between the glare of the sun by day and cold, damp night air is considered a factor in causing glaucoma. All four of the affected persons were members of the Semitic race, among whom glaucoma is especially prevalent. In the first and second cases, each showed a hereditary predisposition to glaucoma; in the first, third, and fourth cases, each suffered total loss of vision; in the second case, sight was only partly impaired, and in all the cases, the loss of vision was bilateral. If unilateral blindness, as well as *amaurosis* not contingent on old age, is barred and if senile cataract is eliminated for the previously mentioned reasons, the clinical history in the four cases cited is strongly suggestive of glaucoma.

Insanity was not unknown among the ancient Hebrews ("the Lord will smite thee with madness"). David, when visiting the Philistines, feigned insanity. An interesting feature of his guise was that he slobbered at the mouth. Saul seems to have been more furious than insane in his fits of passion against David, who, after all, from Saul's point of view, was an upstart and eventually a usurper.

Intercourse: Because intercourse does not necessarily lead to pregnancy, ancients were ignorant *of* the cause-and-effect relationship existing between intercourse and pregnancy. From the story of Onan, it is evident that the ancient Hebrews were however well aware of the fact that coitus was a prerequisite for pregnancy. Onan did not wish to impregnate his brother's widow, since his brother would be the legal parent of the child; so he, "when he went in unto his brother's wife . . . spilled it on the ground, lest he should give seed to his brother."

This is the first recorded case of *coitus interruptus* and birth control in history. Such a procedure was evidently frowned upon, for Onan was killed for this act. Since the Israelites realized that intercourse was necessary for, but did not invariably lead to, pregnancy, they felt that successful fertilization was in the hands of

God. Thus it is noted, "and Adam knew Eve his wife; and she conceived and bore Cain, and said: I have gotten a man with the help of the Lord."

Barrenness: The very derivation of the Hebrew word for barren (*akar*) gives us an insight as to how the ancient Israelites regarded the condition of childlessness. This word signified "uprooted," and the family that was left childless certainly was torn away from the root of Abraham. Strength and wealth among the ancient Hebrews were considered in terms of children, for he who had the largest number of children had the greatest security in life.

"Give me children or else I die," begged Rachel. The very fact that she gave her handmaid Bilhah to Jacob shows how keenly she suffered because of her barrenness. Hannah's rival, Peninnah, "vexed her sore, to make her fret, because the Lord had shut up her womb."

The first barren woman mentioned in the Bible was Sarah, Abraham's wife. The fault certainly did not lie with Abraham, for he had a son with Hagar. "And Sarai [Sarah] was barren: she had no child." And when Isaac was born, Sarah cried out in amazement, "Who would have said unto Abraham that Sarah should give children? For I have born him a son in his old age." Sarah had definitely undergone menopause when all this took place. The Bible says that "it had ceased to be with Sarah after the manner of women."

Since birth control was considered sacrilegious, the number of children that a woman bore depended solely on her physiological limitations. Thus whereas Leah bore seven children with Jacob, Sarah gave birth to only one.

Labor and Delivery: The Old Testament gives minute obstetrical detail in the passage concerning Tamar, who was impregnated by Judah, her father-in-law:

> *And it came to pass in the time of her travail, that behold, twins were in her womb. And it came to pass, when she travailed, that one put out a hand; and the midwife took and bound upon his hand a scarlet thread, saying, this came out first. And it came to pass, as he drew back his hand that behold, his brother came out, and she said: Wherefore hast thou made a breach for thyself? Therefore, his name was called Perez (a breach). And afterward came out his brother that had the scarlet thread upon his hand; and his name was called Zerah.*

The return of the fetus with the prolapsed hand with the delivery of its twin first should be noted. It should also be pointed out that the identification bands, employed to identify the babies, rival the technique used in our modern obstetrical nurseries, where bracelets of beads on threads are attached to the infants at birth. And the fact that the colored threads were applied before delivery indicates that a diagnosis of twins had been made in advance—by no means a simple feat even today.

The following seems to be a breech delivery, for how else could the midwife know the sex of the child before delivery was complete? "And Rachel travailed, and she had hard labor. And it came to pass, when she was in hard labor, that the midwife said unto her; Fear not; for this also is a son for thee."

Rachel gave birth to a living child, but died during this delivery.

When Rebekah was pregnant, great significance was placed on the fact that her twin fetuses "struggled together within her." The Lord said unto her:

> *Two nations are in thy womb,*
> *And two peoples shall be separated from thy bowels;*
> *And the one people shall be stronger than the other people;*
> *And the elder shall serve the younger.*

In recording the delivery, besides describing a prolapsed hand, Genesis also points out that Esau had much *lanugo*. This latter fact was taken as an omen that Esau would be hairy throughout life, no doubt, for later we find Isaac distinguishing between his two sons by touch, since Jacob was smooth-skinned, and Esau hairy. Let us quote from Genesis:

And when her [Rebekah's] days to be delivered were fulfilled, behold, there were twins in her womb. And the first came forth ruddy, all over like a hairy mantle; and they called his name Esau. And after that came forth his brother and his hand had hold on Esau's heel; and his name was called Jacob (that is, "one that takes by the heel"). And Isaac was threescore years old when she bore them.

The method of delivery practiced among the Hebrews before and after the Egyptian bondage is most interesting, but not well understood. We frequently come across passages such as the following, (1) "and she [Rachel] said: Behold my maid Bilhah, go in unto her; that she may bear upon my knees." (2) Woman reclined in a semierect position, and the child was born upon the knees of the midwife. Further than this, we can only guess at the obstetrical procedure. While it is true that the ancient Hebrews were keen observers of obstetrical detail, it is only fair to point out that they were not totally free from superstitions. They believed in the doctrine of *maternal impression*, for instance.

Menstruation: The priestly code ordains that a menstruating woman is unclean for one week from the beginning of the period, no matter how long it lasts. During the time of the taboo, her defilement is communicated to every object with which she comes in contact.

Very few infant deaths are mentioned in the Bible. No stillbirths or miscarriages are recorded. There is one case of a prostitute accidentally killing a newborn babe. Practically all recorded births survive the trials of childhood. Rather than ascribe this to superior medical care or superstock, one probably finds the answer in the fact that only important persons are noted in the Bible, and the births of the multitudes that doubtless died at a tender age are left unrecorded. This idea gains further credence when it is noted that the prophets several times revived presumed dead children, thus indicating that many others must have perished unheralded. The following lament certainly indicates that miscarriage, stillbirth, and death during infancy must have existed:

Why died I not from the womb?
Why did I not perish at birth?
Why did the knees receive me?
And wherefore the breasts that I should suck?

Midwives are mentioned in the Bible as far back as Genesis. Rachel was assisted by one. Tamar also had a midwife. The duties of the midwife after delivery were probably those mentioned in Ezekiel, "And as for thy nativity, in the day thou wast born thy navel was not cut, neither wast thou washed in water for cleansing; thou wast not salted at all, nor swaddled at all. No eye pitied thee, to do any of these unto thee . . ."

It seems as though midwives were not employed in normal cases. Rachel's delivery was definitely a hard one; and Tamar, who gave birth to twins, also had an unusual delivery. Only two midwives (*ahoyoth*), Shiprah and Puah, were employed in a community of six hundred thousand Jews in Egypt. Usually, friends or relatives aided in the delivery.

Male Births: An interesting feature of the Bible is the fact that recorded male births tremendously exceed female births. This is probably due to the fact that only the births of the great were recorded; and the women, as a rule, were not permitted to attain any greatness except that which might be reflected from their husbands. This point of view seems to be upheld by the fact that there is no dearth of wives for the excess of men mentioned in the Bible.

Among the Israelites, the first-born son was considered to possess the best hereditary makeup. This is demonstrated by the following passage:

> *Reuben, thou art my first born,*
> *My might, and the first fruits of my strength;*
> *The excellency of dignity and the excellency of power.*

—B.L.G.

 ## *Kiddush Hashem* in a Castle in York

The date of the first settlement of Jews in Britain is a matter of conjecture. There is evidence, not too well substantiated, that even in biblical times Jews came with the Phoenicians to Cornwall in the south of England, where tin had been mined for centuries, to buy the tin and to trade. Today there is a coastal town in that area named Marazion (Bitterness of Zion). Possibly even the origin of the name "Britain" can be traced to the Phoenician words *Berat Anach* (the country of tin). In the *Liber Poenitentialis* of the Archbishop of Canterbury (669 c.e.), there are enactments against contacts between Jews and Christians: for example, it was forbidden that they eat together or that Mass be celebrated where Jews were buried. A century later these prohibitions were repeated by the then Archbishop of York. On the other hand, it is felt that these enactments may have been merely copied from continental European codes. There are other isolated references dating back to the ninth century.

However, whether or not Jews settled in Britain before 1066, it is certain that Jewish immigration took place early in the reign of William the Conqueror.

England at that time was a primitive and purely agricultural country, dealings not being in currency, but in kind, by barter. The more sophisticated Norman conquerors had to introduce a form of currency to oil the machinery of commerce.

Strange as it may sound, the laws of the Church against usury were so stringent that they prevented observant Christians from not merely moneylending, but ordinary commercial undertakings. Excluded from other callings at that time, the Jews of Europe perforce had to devote themselves more and more to finance and trade.

It was in the interests of William the Conqueror to invite Jews to settle in England. He was anxious that the feudal dues should be paid to him in coin so that he could purchase the luxuries of his time and satisfy his military obligations. Jews were given a privileged status with freedom of movement of themselves: their property was excused from tolls and duties. They were permitted to buy land, with the exception of church property. To a considerable extent, their transactions consisted of loans on the security of land, and they were allowed by law to charge a high rate of interest. The king levied a tax on these transactions in return for the protection he extended to the Jews. However, there were restrictions against conversion of Christians, whereas the reverse was encouraged.

Jews became, in effect, the special wards of the king, under his protection. One of the disadvantages was that upon the death of a Jew, his wealth became the property of the king.

Of necessity, Jews kept themselves apart from the general community, if only because their appearance and customs marked them as aliens. From time immemorial, it has been axiomatic that people of every nation have tended to be hostile to alien immigrants whom they cannot understand.

However the Jews were safe so long as they enjoyed the favor of the king and he retained the control of his subjects.

So for a hundred years or so, in the main, Jews suffered neither exactions nor annoyance. They even profited in fact from the initial fervor of the First Crusade as men of all ranks, to equip themselves, sold or pledged all manner of property. Jews, practically the only people with substantial available money, were in the majority of cases the suppliers of funds.

There were occasional times when the favor of the king waned. As an instance, in 1130, the Jews of London were fined the exorbitant sum of 2,000 pounds on the pretense that one of their number had killed a sick man. At that time, Jews almost monopolized the practice of medicine in Western Europe.

Despite such occurrences, Jewish communities had sprung up throughout the country. At Oxford, Jews were both numerous and wealthy. They owned so many houses that students were compelled to become their tenants—the Guildhall was even owned by Jews. In London they settled in the area known still today as Old Jewry and lived in mansions worthy to house the nobility.

It was in the middle of the twelfth century that the period of tranquillity that the Jews of Western Europe had enjoyed gradually came to an end. The disasters encountered during the first Crusade were avenged on the hapless Jews in whatever town they were encountered. The spirit of the Crusades heightened the vague dislikes of the populace into a positive hatred.

In 1144, the first record of the Blood Libel appeared at Norwich. Others were in Gloucester (1168), Bury St. Edmunds (1181), Winchester (1192), London (1244), and Lincoln (1255). In every instance, miracles attached themselves to the burial place of the so-called victim, and the local abbey or cathedral reaped a rich harvest. It is no coincidence that the Blood Libel was made as a rule at a time when the Royal Treasury needed replenishing.

In 1189, the most formidable of all royal protectors of English Jews, Henry II, died, and the reign of Richard I began. Leading Jews as well as Christian prelates and magnates gathered at Westminster for his coronation on September 30. Several Jews attempted to enter Westminster Palace during the coronation banquet, and an altercation at the gate led to full-scale anti-Jewish riots, which resulted in the loss of at least thirty lives. Among these was Benedict of York, who had traveled south with his fellow-Jew, Josce. The danger that the coronation riots might provoke a series of nationwide assaults in other towns was real, and there is record that Richard I sent messages and letters throughout the kingdom that Jews should be left in peace.

In December of 1189, Richard I sailed for France for six months. During his absence, crusading detachments were slowly assembling with increasing religious fervor. Combined with the rising of passions during the season of Lent, this created an atmosphere of anti-Jewish intent that turned into brutal action.

At the beginning of March in York, a crowd took advantage of the confusion caused by a fire that they may themselves have started, to break into the house of the recently deceased Benedict. After murdering the inhabitants, including Benedict's widow and children, they looted the house of its treasures.

When such riots occurred, it was the pattern that Jews would take refuge in the local royal castle, where, being under the protection of the king, they remained in safety until quiet returned.

So the Jews of York took the natural step of seeking protection in York castle, except some who remained outside. The next day Josce's own strongly built house was plundered, and rioting continued throughout the night. The few Jews in the city were beaten and offered the alternative of baptism or death. But while this was happening, those who had escaped into the castle seemed safe.

Under the atmosphere of indiscriminate looting and killing in the city, confidence between the Jews and the royal representative, the royal constable, became strained. Rightly or wrongly anticipating treachery, the Jews refused to readmit him to the castle when he went out on business. Perhaps not altogether coincidentally, the sheriff of the County of Yorkshire happened to be in the vicinity with a large body of his militia. The royal constable appealed for help to the sheriff, who decided to eject the Jews by force. This led the crowd to believe that an onslaught on the Jews would have royal approval.

By the time the sheriff rescinded his order, it was too late; the mob clustered around the castle were in the grips of religious frenzy. For several days, short of food and without arms, the Jews were able to defend themselves, a tribute not only to their courage but also to the sturdy construction of the castle. However, on Friday, March 16, 1190, specially prepared siege machines were put into place, and it became obvious that the final hour was imminent and that death at the hands of the mob was certain. It was that evening, *Shabbat Hagadol*, the Sabbath before Pesach, that the fateful decision was made.

The spiritual head of York Jewry was Rabbi Yomtov of Joigny, a man of great learning, who incidentally wrote a hymn that is still recited during the *Kol Nidre* service. He spoke at length to those present and while his talk cannot be authenticated word for word, the following was written soon after the event:

> *Men of Israel, the God of our fathers, to Whom none can say what doest Thou? commands us at this time to die for His law; and behold, death is even before our eyes, and there is nothing left us to consider but how to undergo it in the most reputable and easy manner.*
>
> *If we fall into the hands of our enemies (which I think there is no possibility of escaping), our deaths will not only be cruel, but ignominious. They will not only torment us, but despitefully use us.*
>
> *My advice therefore is that we voluntarily surrender those lives to our Creator, which He seems to call for, and not wait for any other executioners than ourselves. The fact is both rational and lawful; nor do we want for examples from amongst our illustrious ancestors, to prove it so. They have frequently proceeded in the like manner, upon the same occasions.*

A few did not agree, but the great majority proceeded to follow the advice they had received. First they burned or destroyed all their property. Josce then set the first example by cutting the throats of his wife, Anna, and of his sons. The terrible responsibility of killing the women and children seems to have fallen to the fathers of each household in turn. The latter probably met their fate by the knife of Rabbi Yomtov, who appears to have finally ended the slaughter by taking Josce's life just before his own. The number of victims was in the neighborhood of five hundred, as far as can be ascertained.

Those whose courage had shrunk from the supreme ordeal spent the night defending themselves from the flames that had spread to the entire building. In the morning, they begged for mercy and offered to accept baptism if their lives were spared. The offer was accepted, but the survivors were barely outside the gates before they too were murdered by the mob.

Immediately after the massacre, the nobility made their way to York Minster, where they took from the terrified custodians the few records of their debts to the Jews deposited there for safety. From this fact, it can be assumed that the mob had been encouraged by those in authority who felt that in this manner and in the absence abroad of the king, they could rid themselves of their obligations to their Jewish creditors, even in so terrible a manner.

One can well speculate whether some part of the wealth of the nobility of northern England may have had its foundations with the spilling of Jewish blood.

—D.C.

 ## Benjamin of Tudela's Fantastic Twelfth-Century Book

This is a book of travels composed by Rabbi Benjamin, son of Jonah, from the land of Navarre, may he rest in Paradise. This Rabbi Benjamin had left his native town Tudela and traveled through many far countries, as is related in this book. In each place that he visited he wrote down things he had seen or learned from trustworthy people, things unknown in the land of Spain. He also mentioned the names of scholars and notables renowned in those places. He brought this book back with him on his return to Castile in the year 4933 of the Creation [1173 C.E.]. This Rabbi Benjamin is a wise man, well versed in Torah and Halakhah, and in each point we have verified his words and have found them to be true, justified, and correct. For he is a man of truth.

With these words of praise a medieval preface introduced the book of Benjamin of Tudela, a famous traveler of the twelfth century. Written orginally in Hebrew, it was translated into Latin and later, with the invention of printing, became an extremely popular piece of Jewish literature in many languages. The modern reader might regard it as an exotic tale. But the author actually intended to give his contemporaries a factual account of his travels and to deal with some very practical and pressing problems.

What exactly did Benjamin plan to accomplish when he started out on his fantastic journey? At first, probably nothing but a pilgrimage to the Holy Land, which, despite the Crusades, retained magic attraction for the pious Jew. A pilgrimage—an *Aliyah*—probably with the thought to stay there for the rest of his life. But the fact is that he did take the long road, stopping frequently, meeting people, visiting places, and keeping his eyes and ears open. And in each place where Jews lived, he questioned them about their numbers, their leaders and scholars, and the conditions of their life. He also wanted to know all the details about the country in which they resided: its way of government, local customs and traditions, main professions and activities, and the principal products of the land. His attentive eye spotted all landmarks, old and new monuments, and he reported on the marvels he had seen with glowing admiration. In complete contrast to the bored and critical tourist of today, Benjamin was a naïve, unspoiled traveler, full of interest and praise for the new places, making countless marvelous discoveries, all of them unique and worthy to be recorded.

Had our traveler not made any stops on the way, his voyage would have taken all of five months to Jerusalem. The delays were not caused by actual traveling, for his route followed the course of rivers or along the coast, which was the surest and thus, in the long run, the fastest way of reaching his destination.

From his native Tudela in Old Castile, he crossed the Ebro valley by way of Saragossa and Tortosa, following the coast to the north into France: Tarragona, Barcelona, Gerona, Narbonne, Beziers, Montpellier. He made a few detours inland to visit smaller Jewish communities in the south of France—Lunel and Arles —regaining the coast again in Marseilles and following the Mediterranean coast into Italy.

After stays in Genoa and Pisa, he traveled south in search of a port of embarkment for the Holy Land. Before reaching the first important port, Naples, he visited Rome, Capua, and Pozzuoli, where Jews had been settled since antiquity. The next stop was Salerno, a port farther to the south and a famous center of medieval learning. He decided to try his luck on the Adriatic coast, crossing the peninsula by way of Melfi and Ascoli and arriving in Trani, an assembly place for pilgrims to the Holy Land. But there was no room for the Jewish pilgrim, nor was there in Bari. Benjamin decided to explore the southern ports, crossing the "heel" of the Italian "boot" twice, to Taranto and then back to Brindisi and Otranto, the most eastern point in Italy, where he finally found a boat for Corfu in Greece.

It must have been one of those small coastal vessels that stopped at every small island and port. But our traveler welcomed the chance to make a tour of the Balkan Peninsula, descending to Corinth and up the coast to Salonika and Constantinople. This itinerary accounted for three months of straight traveling, not taking into account the delays in finding transportation or his frequent visits to countless Jewish communities along the road, where the visitor from faraway lands was received with open arms. It took another two months—again not counting his frequent stops—to reach the Holy Land in St. Jean d'Acre via Cyprus, Tarsus, Antioch, and Beirut.

After a prolonged stay in Jerusalem, which he thoroughly explored to the smallest details, he was on the road again, crisscrossing Palestine in all directions, in search of the ancient cities of the Jewish past.

Again he pushed on, this time to the East, possibly as far as Baghdad, which in itself was a rare achievement. But his avid adventurous mind and his vanity gave him no rest, and soon his diary began to fill with data on such unexplored faraway lands as India and China. No longer able to distinguish fact from hearsay and on-the-spot descriptions from fantasy, he included them all in his notes, quoting distances, statistics, economic and historical data, yet omitting to state clearly whether those were his own findings and observations.

The return trip was less difficult. After crossing Arabia, the Sinai peninsula and Egypt, Benjamin arrived in Sicily after a twenty-day crossing of the Mediterranean. He spent little time in Italy, choosing new territories instead, namely, France and Germany. Again, as in the Orient, his insatiable desire for new discoveries was driving him on to collect information on the legendary lands of Bohemia and Russia, but it was vague and scarce.

About 1173, our traveler returned to his native Spain, and soon his adventures were avidly read and copied throughout the whole Jewish world. His success was well deserved, for the fantastic stories of the marvels of the Orient were not only fascinating and entertaining but offered the readers a greater comprehension of the world around them, broadening their horizons far beyond the walls of their towns and the borders of states and provinces.

But the book contributed other valuable information of a more practical, tangible character. There were, to begin with, a number of "useful addresses" for Jewish pilgrims, indicating, for instance, that the community in Montpellier had "wealthy and charitable men who extended a helping hand to all who came there." A similar hospitality, Benjamin assured, would be found in Lunel, Genoa, and Constantinople. These were the places marked with three stars in this early travel guide.

The book also provided valuable information on Jewish communities: twenty Jews in Pisa; forty in Lucca; two hundred in Rome; three hundred in Capua; five hundred in Naples; six hundred in Salerno; only twenty in Amalfi, but two hundred again in Melfi and Benevento . . . The names of their notables were equally important. The forty Jews in Ascoli were headed by Rabbi Consoli; his son-in-law, Rabbi Tsemah; and Rabbi Joseph. The leaders of the three hundred Jews in Trani were the Rabbis Eliyah, Nathan, and Jacob; and the three-hundred-strong community in Taranto had Rabbi Meir, Rabbi Nathan, and Rabbi Israel at its head. This guide had to be kept up to date, for it was important to note that Rabbi Abba Mari, head of the two hundred Jews in Arles, had passed away since Benjamin's passage through that center.

The notes also proved to be a valuable students' guide, from which the young Jewish scholar could learn that "Narbonne was a city excelling in scholarship . . ." and that in Montpellier there were "houses dedicated to the study of the Talmud"; that in Lunel, "students from faraway lands were taught, lodged, fed, and even clothed at the expense of the community as long as they continued their studies." In addition to Talmudic studies, it was also useful to know that in Salerno "the Christians had a school of medicine" and that scholars in Constantinople were "well versed in the whole literature of the Greek."

The most likely travelers in the Middle Ages were merchants. In their behalf, Benjamin kept an eye open on commercial centers.

In spite of his Jewishness, our traveler had no inhibitions against visiting churches or mosques. On the contrary, his curiosity is generally awakened by anything touching the field of religion. Rome is described as "the capital of Christianity," ruled by the "Pope, who is the spiritual chief." Constantinople, he relates, is the "seat of the Patriarch of the Greeks, for the Greeks do not obey the Pope." And if our poor traveler had little success in Trani finding a ship for Palestine, he was nevertheless aware of the fact that Trani and Messina were the principal points where "(Christian)" pilgrims embark for the crossing to the Holy Land."

Even today's reader must concede that Benjamin's booklet was an extremely versatile document containing a wealth of useful and practical facts for the Jewish traveler. It was a tourist guide, an international directory of commerce, a community yearbook, and a student handbook, all in one. But do we really know what virtues it had for the contemporary readers to whom it brought the enchantment and mystery of adventure so sorely missing from their own drab and restricted lives? Perhaps the fantastic side of his report, where facts blended with imagination—the part that we rejected as unreliable—was the prime reason for the book's popularity and the most fruitful one.

For who could say that Benjamin's exotic tales of faraway Asia, which he had never seen, had not inspired Marco Polo's travels in search of the splendors of the Far East a century later?

—B.B.

Jewish Buccaneers and the Spanish Main

Jewish buccaneers once roamed the high seas in search of gold-laden Spanish galleons. One of them was Captain Subatol Deul, known as the Corsair of Guayacan, who sailed the coast of South America in the early half of the seventeenth century.

Guayacan, a small harbor, not far from present-day Coquimbo, on the Chilean coast, was discovered in 1578 by Sir Francis Drake and thereafter was a favorite refuge and meeting place for the corsairs and buccaneers who sailed the Pacific off South America.

The relations between Spain and the other European powers at that time were far from friendly, so it was not unusual for maritime nations, particularly England, to grant their subjects permission to arm and equip vessels to capture merchant ships of "other nations" (read: Spain). These were the letters of marque, and the men who received them were called privateers. The trade was so profitable, however, that many men did not bother to get official permission.

Some of the Spanish Jews, expelled by Ferdinand and Isabella, derived a special satisfaction from the capture of Spanish ships, loaded with gold and precious goods from the New World.

Sometime around 1600, two pirate ships arrived in Guayacan. The first was commanded by a certain Ruhual Dayo, of Flemish or Norman origins, and the second was mastered by Captain Subatol Deul, of whose early life nothing is known.

Later, the two ships were joined by other buccaneers, notably Henry Drake, son of Sir Francis. Together the adventurers formed an alliance, which they pompously named the Brotherhood of the Black Flag. They drew up a document that testified to the Jewishness of Subatol Deul, whose father—the document avers—was Sudel Deul, a great physician who visited many lands and spoke many tongues. According to another document, the potato was not introduced in Europe by Sir Francis Drake, but by the same Sudel Deul, who also traveled to America. This interesting statement was supported by Sir Francis Drake.

The Brotherhood of the Black Flag was gradually reinforced with the arrival of new captains. The chronicles tell that one night, as Deul sailed close to the shore, he noticed a light that blinked irregularly. Knowing the spot to be uninhabited, Deul's curiosity was aroused. The following day he returned, with some of his crew. They soon discovered a smelting furnace, fired but unattended. When the metal was examined, it was found to be gold.

After spending the night near the furnace, Deul and his men found the entrance to a tunnel, which had been camouflaged with boulders and brush. Rushing inside, they came upon several Indians who were extracting rocks with primitive hand tools, under the supervision of a Spaniard, who fled as soon as he noticed the arrival of Deul's party. Most likely, the Spaniard had been running an illegal gold mine to avoid the Royal Fifth tax to the colonial government. Deul took over the mine.

As their treasure increased to unwieldly proportions, the pirates buried it in an underground vault, where they hid some six thousand pounds of gold and an even larger amount in silver.

In 1640, the brotherhood suffered a disastrous defeat at the hands of the Spanish navy. Henry Drake lost his life, and the others barely escaped capture. Deul and Dayo, fleeing together, sought refuge among the local Indians with whom they were on excellent terms. They both married daughters of the *cacique*, or tribal chief. When the *cacique* died, Deul was elected by the elders of the tribe to fill his place. He spent most of his remaining days with the Indians. Under the guidance of Deul and Dayo, the tribe found another gold mine and prospered.

However, the call of the sea was still strong for the retired buccaneers. When some adventurers showed up at Guayacan with several captured ships, they jumped at the opportunity of rebuilding the Brotherhood of the Black Flag. They fortified the harbor with artillery and planned to extend their power to the whole Chilean coast. But their plans came to a sudden end when a fleet of Spanish men-of-war showed up and destroyed all their ships. Some members of the brotherhood were captured and hanged, but Deul and Dayo were able to return to their faithful Indian friends.

The brotherhood was now smashed. Deul would have liked to return to Europe and enjoy his fortune, but he no longer had a ship, and the Spaniards were eager to catch him. So he resigned himself to live out his days with the Indians.

In 1926, a farmer named Manuel Castro, who had heard about the buccaneers of Guayacan, tried to find the buried treasure. He didn't succeed, but he discovered instead an earthen jug, containing a large number of documents, most of them written by Deul.

The documents are written in Spanish but include a bewildering mixture of Hebrew and Roman characters. This confirms the Marrano origins of Deul, for none of the buccaneers was Spanish, yet it is known that Marranos wrote in Spanish, using Hebrew characters.

—L.M.Z.

 # When Spain Expelled the Jews in 1492

By an anonymous Italian Jew. Written in the late fifteenth or early sixteenth century.

In the year 1492 during the reign of Ferdinand, God again punished the remnant of the Jewish people, by having them expelled from Spain. Ferdinand had wrested the city of Granada from the Moslems on January 7 [actually January 2] and soon thereafter ordered all Jews to be deported from Castile, Catalonia, Aragon, Galicia, Majorca, Minorca, the Basque provinces, Valencia and Alusia, and the islands of Sardinia and Sicily. The king gave them three months' time to leave the country. On May 1 the edict was read in every city (the nineteenth day of the Omer and expired one day before Tisha b'Av) . . . I would estimate that around 50,000 families were affected. They owned homes, land, vineyards, and cattle. The majority however were artisans. There were many *yeshivot* in Spain, and some of the heads were Rabbi Isaac Aboab in Guadalajara, Rabbi Isaac Bezodo in Leon, and Rabbi Jacob Habib in Salamanca. In the latter city lived the great mathematician Abraham Zacuto, whose advice was sought on all mathematical problems that could not be solved by the Christian scholars.

During the three months left to them, the Jews tried everything in their power to reverse the decree . . . Their leaders were: the Rabbi Don Abraham Senior, the head of the Spanish communities, who always traveled with a train of thirty mules; Rabbi Meir Hamelamud, the king's secretary [a son-in-law of Abraham Senior]; and Don Isaac Abravanel, who had escaped from the Portuguese king and was appointed to the same post in the Spanish court . . . Don Isaac Abravanel was later exiled to Naples, where he was held in high esteem by the king of Naples . . . Isaac Abravanel used to call Don Abraham Senior "Soneh Or" ["Hater of Light," a pun on Senior] because he was an *epicurus* [a heretic]. He was correct, for at the age of eighty, Senior and his whole family (except his brother Samuel) were converted.

Don Abraham had arranged the match between the king and the queen . . . Because of this, he had been appointed rabbi of the Spanish Jews, but without their consent. An agreement was almost reached that the Jews would pay an enormous amount of money and be permitted to stay, but it was thwarted by an official [supposedly, Torquemada, the Grand Inquisitor] who reminded the queen of the story of the cross. The queen then gave an answer, similar to the saying of King Solomon (Proverbs 21:1) . . . adding, "Do you believe, that this was brought on you by us? It is God who controls the king's heart."

The Jews realized then that the king was out to harm them and they abandoned all hope . . . There was little time left, and . . . they sold their homes, their land, and their cattle for paltry sums. As the king did not allow the export of gold or silver, they had to convert their money to textiles, furs, and other articles.

One hundred and twenty thousand persons left for Portugal, following an agreement between the king of Portugal and a . . . certain Don Vidal bar Benevenesti del Cavallaria . . . The Jews had to pay one ducat for each person admitted and one quarter of their goods in order to stay six months . . . After the six months had elapsed, he [the king] enslaved them all and deported seven hundred children (some say fourteen hundred) to the island of St. Thomas, where they perished . . . And so it came to pass, as it is said, "Your sons and daughters will be given to another people . . ." (Deuteronomy 28:32).

Many of the exiles went to Moslem countries, to Fez and to the Berber provinces, which were under the rule of the king of Tunis. The Moslems did not admit the Jews to their cities, and many died of starvation; many were devoured by lions and bears while lying exhausted on the outskirts of the cities. A Jew of Tiemsen named Abraham, who was viceroy to the king, admitted many of the exiles into the country, spending a fortune on their behalf. The Jews of North Africa were very helpful. But many of the exiles, finding no place that would receive them, returned to Spain and embraced Christianity . . . Because they had fled to glorify God's name, only a small number were converted . . .

When the edict became known in other countries, ships arrived from Genoa to transfer the Jews. The sailors on these ships behaved atrociously towards them, robbing them and delivering most of them to the notorious pirate called the "Corsair of Genoa." Those who managed to escape to Genoa were mercilessly mistreated by the populace, who went so far as to tear children from their mother's breasts and to convert them.

Many boatloads of Jews from Sicily arrived in Naples. The king of Naples was friendly to the Jews, behaved mercifully, and gave them financial assistance. The Jews of Naples provided the sufferers with goods as much as they could and dispatched messengers throughout Italy to collect money to sustain them. The Marranos in the city lent them money without interest. Even the Dominicans showed human sympathy. But all this was not sufficient to keep them alive. Many died of starvation; others sold their children to Christians to keep them alive. Finally, a plague spread among them, and many died, and those who remained alive were too tired to bury the dead.

Some of the exiles sailed to Turkey. Many of them were thrown overboard and drowned, but those who managed to reach Turkey were warmly received by the sultan because they were artisans. He lent them money and enabled them to settle on an island where they received land and homes.

A few of the exiles settled in the various cities of Italy . . .

 ## Sabbath Among the Arabian Jews in the Fifteenth Century

The following is the arrangement of the Sabbath meal customary to Jews in all Arabian countries. They sit in a circle on a carpet, the cupbearer standing near them, near a small cloth that is spread on this carpet; all kinds of fruit that are in season are brought and laid on the cloth. The host now takes a glass of wine, pronounces the blessing of sanctification [Kiddush], and empties the cup completely. The cupbearer then takes it from the host and hands it successively to the whole company, always refilled, and each one empties it. Then the host takes two or three pieces of fruit, eats some, and drinks a second glass, while the company say, "Health and life." Whoever sits next also takes some fruit, and the cupbearer fills a second glass for him, saying, "To your pleasure," the company join in with the words "Health and life," and so it goes round.

Then a second kind of fruit is partaken of, another glass is filled, and this is continued until each one has emptied at least six or seven glasses. Sometimes they even drink when they smell flowers that are provided for the occasion; these flowers are the duda'im, which Rashi translates into Arabic by "jasmine"; it is a plant bearing only blossoms that have a delightful and invigorating fragrance. The wine is unusually strong, and this is especially the case in Jerusalem, where it is drunk unmixed. After all have drunk to their heart's content, a large dish of meat is brought; each one stretches forth his hand, takes what he wants, and eats quickly, for they are not very big eaters. Rabbi Moses brought us confectionery, fresh ginger, dates, raisins, almonds, and confectionery of coriander seeds; a glass of wine is drunk with each kind. Then followed raisin wine, which was very good, then malmsey wine from Candia, and again native wine. I drank with them and was exhilarated.

There is another custom in the country of the Arabs: on Friday all go to bathe, and on their return the women bring them wine, of which they drink copiously;

word is then brought that the supper is ready, and it is eaten in the daytime, before evening. Then they all come to the synagogue, cleanly and neatly dressed. They begin with Psalms and thanksgiving, and evening prayer is read until two hours after dusk. On their return home they repeat the *Kiddush*, eat only a piece of bread of the size of an olive, and recite the grace after meals. In this whole district the afternoon prayer is read on Friday in private, except in Jerusalem, where the Ashkenazim have done away with the custom; and the afternoon and evening prayer are said with a *minyan* as with us, and they eat at night; the evening prayer is not begun, however, until the stars are visible. In these parts the Sabbath is more strictly kept than in any other; nobody leaves his house on the Sabbath, except to go to the synagogue or to the *Bet Ha-Midrash* [house of study]. I need scarcely mention that nobody kindles a fire on the Sabbath or has a light that has been extinguished rekindled, even by a Gentile. All who are able to read the Holy Scriptures read the whole day, after having slept off the effect of their wine.

—O.Y.D.B.

 ## Witness to a Pogrom

As this eyewitness account by a British officer indicates, the barbaric attacks on Russian Jews should have shocked all civilized people. These pogroms, which were part of the government's calculated attempt to destroy its Jewish population, were the major reason for the mass exodus of Russian Jews in the late nineteenth and early twentieth centuries.

I have been shocked beyond belief. I have seldom been so angry and yet so impotent as I have been today. I would never have believed that human beings could behave worse than the most savage and cruel wild beasts; worse, because their behavior was intended to be cruel and brutal, and what they did was done with relish; I witnessed a pogrom in the streets of Odessa.

I was having dinner with our Consul General Smith when it started. There was running and shouting in the streets. Smith and I went to the front door of the consulate and saw people running excitedly in all directions and much hysterical shouting. Smith said, "I fear this is a pogrom: we had one here some years ago. We must keep off the streets as the Russians become quite irresponsible and the police become immobile. Now you will witness one of the vilest facets of the Russian character." We watched. The streets were well lit and we could see well in both directions; there was also a small square in front of the house.

Russians, many with bludgeons or knives or axes, were rushing all over the place, breaking open barricaded doors and chasing the wretched Jews into the streets where they were hunted down, beaten, and often killed. One old man was axed on the head quite close to us. I was longing to interfere and beat up some of these Russian wild beasts, but Smith restrained me—fortunately. A young woman chased by a Russian rushed frantically into the consulate and collapsed on the door mat; her pursuer pulled up short on seeing us. I abused him in English. Smith said, "For God's sake, don't provoke them; they're mad!" Another Jewish youth was chased, beaten into the gutter, viciously kicked, robbed, and left unconscious. By this time, the streets were in an uproar, but not a policeman was in sight. A large window of a store was smashed and the shop entered, looted, and its goods thrown into the street.

The climax arrived when a Russian passed the consulate dragging a Jewish girl about twelve years old by her hair along the gutter; she was screaming and the man was shouting. I have no doubt she would have been outraged and then murdered. I could not help it, I heard old Hales [headmaster of a private school] whispering, "Do something!" So I dashed out, kicked the Russian violently in the stomach with my heavy Russian boots and landed him a good blow on the jaw; he went down like a log, and I carried the child into the consulate. Smith said, "We shall get into trouble for this." Trouble, indeed, when compared with the fate of this child! I am overcome with anger and compassion this evening.

Smith has been in Odessa for ten years. He tells me that some years ago when the Russian revolution was in full swing, it was decided to have a pogrom in Odessa. Many Jews were warned of their impending danger and succeeded in bribing the revolutionary leaders not to molest them, but some four hundred Jews were nonetheless killed. The pogrom, which lasted three days, was organized by the Minister of the Interior, in order to demonstrate to the Czar that the people were not yet fit for self-government. On the first day of the pogrom all the police were withdrawn from Odessa for three days. After that time, an order went forth that the military must stop the massacres; this was effected in a few hours. Some of the rioters, on being shot in the streets, bitterly complained that they had not had the full three days promised by the authorities! Smith assured me that the above was strictly accurate and that a full report with proof had been sent at the time to our foreign office.

I am deeply moved by these terrible deeds and have resolved that whenever I can help the Jews, I shall do so to the best of my ability. There is no word in the British language to describe such vile and bestial behavior.

—R.M.

 ## Jews Have Had Their Share of False Messiahs

In the course of two thousand years of the Diaspora, many men have taken advantage of the low morale of the Jewish community, exploiting existing conditions for their own ends, often with disastrous results. Best known of these false messiahs, Shabbetai Tzevi, persuaded huge throngs of Jews that he was the true Messiah, who had come to bring them back to Israel and to redemption—and yet, when he was threatened with death or renouncing his faith, he chose to become a Moslem, producing pandemonium and national depression among large numbers of Jews. And he was not the only one.

In the thirteenth century there was a Jew named Abraham ben Samuel Abulafia, who lived in Spain, and while in his twenties reached the city of Acre in Palestine, presumably in search of the mystical-mythical river Sambatyon, which was said to cease its flow on the Sabbath. A restless soul, he wandered to Greece and later to Italy, studied the then new words of Maimonides and was also exposed to the new teachings of Kabbalah, or Jewish mysticism.

While still in his thirties, Abulafia proclaimed that he was endowed with prophetic powers and found a willing ear among the mystics who followed the Kabbalah and also among the more rational-minded Jews who were adherents of Maimonides. He wandered around Italy, Spain, Sicily, and Greece, notifying people that there was a mystical, hidden key to the teachings of Maimonides—a key that he alone held.

At the age of forty, Abulafia made his way to Rome, intending to call the Pope to task for the sufferings of his people, whereupon the Pope promptly ordered him executed. The sentence was not carried out because of the Pope's own death, and Abulafia was shipped to Sicily, where he continued to preach a strange brand of mysticism, including the prophecy that the messianic era would begin in the Jewish year 5050, which was only a few years away.

Many believed him because they wanted to and made serious preparations for an immediate return to Israel to await the Messiah. Others denounced him, complaining that he had proclaimed himself a Messiah. The leading rabbi of the day, Solomon ben Adret of Barcelona, examined Abulafia's writings and announced that the man was a charlatan, whereupon Abulafia fled to the remote Mediterranean island of Somino, located near Malta, where he persisted in his "prophetic" writings.

The movement that he hoped to launch gradually petered out, and the hopes for redemption that he had stirred in the hearts of many Jews of the time turned to ashes. By insisting that people who studied his version of Kabbalah and Maimonides' teachings of the Torah could attain prophetic powers and virtually carry on dialogues with the Almighty, Abulafia went contrary to the Jewish passion for rational explanations and interpretations of all aspects of life, and his name was added to the list of pseudo-Messiahs who rose, influenced large numbers of people for a brief time, and then receded into ignominy.

One of the most notorious and far more recent of these false messiahs was a man named Jacob Frank, who was born in the early part of the eighteenth century in Poland and who proclaimed himself quite simply the true Messiah. His mystical festivities were said to have been based on sexual orgies, which were supposed to lead to the redemption through *impurity*—and, incredibly, he attracted large numbers of followers who believed his lies, which he twisted until his anxious adherents were certain that they were the real truth.

Things got so bad that Frank was excommunicated, whereupon he appealed to the local bishop for protection. The Catholic leader agreed to extend his aid to the Frankists on condition that they refute the Talmud; Frank agreed, adding that he and his followers even accepted the Christian version of the Trinity.

In the middle of the eighteenth century, the bishop ordered a public debate between the local rabbis and the Frankists, which was climaxed with a public burning of the Talmudic tomes. Subsequently, Frank led his followers into a formal, public baptism ceremony. He spent his latter years secluded in a monastery. When he died, in 1791, his daughter carried on his work for a time.

Many of the Frankists became leaders of the Christian community, and a number were believed to have become members of the Polish nobility in the nineteenth century.

—D.C.G.

The Jew Who Was King of Poland for a Day

Radziwill, the name of the Polish princely family into which the late U. S. President Kennedy's sister-in-law married, hit the headlines when the President and Mrs. Kennedy visited their kinfolk during a European trip. Was there a Jewish connection with Radziwill, or was I merely indulging in an almost instinctive Jewish habit of linking the famous with the House of Israel?

You may shake your head, but the fact is that there is a Jewish connection that was real enough in the minds and hearts of generations of Polish Jews, and because of its kernel of truth, it is worth recalling.

The story begins in Italy. Samuel Judah Katzenellenbogen (1521–1597), chief rabbi of Padua, had a son Saul (1541–1617), who settled at Brisk, in Poland. While on a tour of Europe and the East, Nicholas Radziwill, a Polish prince, found himself in Padua, deserted by his retinue and impoverished until his needs were generously provided for by Chief Rabbi Katzenellenbogen.

When he took leave of his benefactor, Prince Radziwill promised to look up Saul in Poland and to do everything in his power to promote his interests. The prince kept his word, and under Radziwill's patronage Saul rose to be a wealthy and influential figure.

In the old Kingdom of Poland, the nobles were accustomed to elect a king when the old monarch died. The election debates were often tense and overhung with the threat of civil war. This was the case after the death of King Stefan Batory in 1586. The electoral diet met armed to the teeth, and the partisans of the candidates occupied strongly entrenched camps in the vicinity of Warsaw. The outlook became particularly threatening on the second day of the diet, and, as night was falling, it seemed likely that the passions of the nobles would not stand the tension of another adjournment.

When the tumult was at a peak, Prince Radziwill suddenly rose. "How would it be," he shouted, "if we were to elect my Jewish factor, Saul, for this night, and resume the discussion tomorrow?" The bizarre proposal caught the fancy of the assembly; with laughter and cries of "Long live King Saul!" the nobles sheathed their swords and went home.

During that night and the following day Saul devoted himself to a peaceful solution of the electoral difficulty. The more turbulent spirits having been quieted by the respite, the diet then chose Sigismund III as king. Saul was given the surname *Wahl*, which is the German word for "election," to mark the occasion. He was loaded with other honors and became a great favorite of the new king.

Saul Wahl used his wealth and position to advance the welfare of his people, and his descendants, who included both nobles and rabbis, have been found not only in many parts of Europe, but in Austria and the United States. Important in their day, the names of these merchants and dignitaries are for the most part forgotten.

The son of one of Saul Wahl's granddaughters moved to Germany, and from this branch of the family came Karl Marx, author of *Das Kapital*. The presence in this country of descendants of Wahl is brought to mind by a perusal of *Americans of Jewish Descent*, a genealogical compendium recently published by the American Jewish Archives, a historical research center affiliated with the Hebrew Union College-Jewish Institute of Religion. Tracing the descent from Saul Wahl of David Samuel, who settled in Philadelphia in the last century and whose family still exists, this volume and the journeyings of the President of the United States may remind us that there are American Jews who can claim a king of Poland among their ancestors.

—S.D.T.

 ## How the Marranos Settled in Amsterdam

During the liberation war waged by the Dutch provinces against Spain, many Marranos abandoned Portugal and Spain to seek protection in Dutch centers.

Sons of forcibly converted Jews, they hoped to escape from the nets of the Inquisition and to return openly to the religion of their fathers, which many of them still practiced in secret.

Many old chronicles describe these perilous travels to reach the safety of a land that had broken the chains linking it to Spain. Two such reports, one by Daniel Levi de Barrios and the other by Uri Phoebus ben Aaron Levi, are particularly interesting. Both relate the same event, despite certain contradictions in some places. Both deal with their flight and the day of Yom Kippur in Amsterdam.

The *Hakham* Moses Uri Ha-Levi was one of the few Jews who lived in the small seaport of Emden. His wife earned their daily bread by selling poultry, while Reb Moshe, according to tradition, spent his days in the study of the holy books; their son, Aharon, had a post at the local synagogue, leading the small Ashkenazic congregation in their prayers. Over the entrance to their modest house an inscription, "Truth and Peace are the Foundations of the World," was carved in Hebrew and Latin.

On a stormy day, two sailships approached the shores of Emden. Soon it became known that they had sailed from Castile, by way of England, and carried ten Portuguese Marrano families, with all their rich possessions.

They now had only one goal: to escape the hell of the Inquisition and to be free people again, allowed to practice the Jewish religion, which their fathers had been forced to renounce to escape death on the stake.

The storm passed; the ships were about to take to the high seas when leaks were discovered in the wooden hulls. It was impossible to stay afloat, and they rapidly turned course toward the next port on the way to Emden. The refugees went ashore and took up lodgings at the local inn.

The next day, rested and refreshed, the men walked through the streets of the little town and observed its life and its people, so strange and so different from their faraway homeland in the south.

The house with the foreign inscription attracted their curiosity. On their return to their quarters, the innkeeper explained to whom the house belonged. One can imagine the joy and surprise of the weary travelers to find Jewish people in the little port where they were stranded—friends to turn to for advice and assistance. They tried not to show their excitement until they retired for the night. Once among themselves, they discussed their situation and decided to pay a visit to Rabbi Moses Uri the next morning.

The scholar received the strangers in a friendly manner, but cautious, not understanding their language. Finally, his son Aharon was called to act as interpreter. The visitors told him of their sufferings and escape and of their great desire to return to the faith of their forefathers. Raised as Catholics under the watchful eye of the Inquisition, they needed most of all a rabbi or scholar to teach them the laws of the Torah and the prayers in the Hebrew language. They were all wealthy merchants, and the learned man who would instruct them, they said, would not suffer any need.

The rabbi was deeply moved by their faith and exclaimed: "The Lord be praised Who guided you on the right path! It is true that in our city your wish cannot be fulfilled, for most of the people are Protestants. Get ready to travel to Amsterdam, and I promise to follow you there in a short while, together with my beloved ones."

This was more than the travelers had expected, and they were overwhelmed with joy. But Moses Uri still had more advice to offer. "Once in Amsterdam, rent a house on Junker Straat, across from the tower. Put up a sign that we may recognize it. We should be there in two or three weeks." The Marranos thanked him and took leave.

It took them another few weeks to reach the capital, but they got there safely with all their goods and treasures. Once settled, they set our for their anxiously awaited goal: to become Jews again.

The first one to be circumcised was Don Jacob Tirado, the oldest and most respected member of the group. The others followed his example. The venerable Ashkenazi from Emden had kept his word and joined them with his family. And soon, with their help, the first Portuguese Marrano community was founded in Amsterdam.

The Day of Atonement had arrived. The Marranos congregated for solemn services—behind closed doors—for the deep-rooted fear of the Inquisition still lurked in their souls.

Their Christian neighbors wondered about their secret meetings and rumors began to spread. They were suspected of being Spanish "Papists," conspiring against the Protestant country in favor of the Spanish Catholics.

The mayor was alerted and sent his police to apprehend the "conspirators." Loud knocks at the door terrified the men engrossed in their prayers. Wrapped in their prayer shawls, they attempted to flee through the back door, convinced that the long arm of the Inquisition had caught up with them in the free Dutch province.

Only the head of the congregation, Jacob Tirado, had no fear. He remained and calmly told the police captain that they were peaceful worshipers, congregated in prayer on a High Holiday.

But the Dutchman was unable to grasp the meaning of the Spanish words and refused to leave until the mayor himself arrived to question the "conspirators." Fortunately, the mayor was a scholar with knowledge of Latin, and finally, Jacob Tirado was able to explain. They were not conspiring against the religion of the free province, in favor of Spain; far from that. They, themselves, were victims of the Inquisition, forcibly baptized Jews, who had fled Portugal to practice their old faith. Today was their Day of Atonement; no food and no drink were to pass their lips from sunrise to sundown. They were congregated to pray to the One God, humbly imploring His forgiveness for their sins against the Lord of the Universe and against their fellowmen.

The police, still suspicious, searched the house for any Catholic ritual objects, but found only Hebrew prayer books and prayer shawls. At that point, Jacob Tirado mentioned that he and his coreligionists were all wealthy, honorable, and capable merchants who would greatly contribute to Dutch commerce if they were allowed to stay.

The Marranos were granted citizenship and allowed to live in peace, according to their laws and customs. The handful of pseudo-Christians had returned—"unto the rock whence you [they] were hewn . . ." (*Isaiah*, 51).

The foundation was laid. Amsterdam's Sephardic community was formed. It was to develop into one of the most brilliant centers of the Jewish world.

—S.B.

 ## The Foiled Assassin: One Jew Tried and Failed to Kill Hitler in 1938

The story of this one Jew's unsuccessful effort to change the course of history came to light in a brief eulogy delivered at his gravesite on a kibbutz in Israel.

By 1938 the threat of Nazism had become widespread. Germany was rearming. The Sudetenland had been seized from Czechoslovakia. Barbaric anti-Jewish legislation had been promulgated in Germany, threatening the very existence of that country's 600,000 Jews, as well as the Jewish community of Austria that had been "annexed" by Germany.

Like Jews elsewhere, the Jews in British-mandated Palestine were deeply worried about their coreligionists. They urged those who would listen to leave Europe and join them, and of course the Youth Aliyah movement did succeed in bringing out of Germany many thousands of youngsters. But beyond that, it was a situation of waiting and watching—and hoping.

There was one Palestinian Jew, a member of the Haganah, a member of a *kibbutz*, who took a much more serious view of things. He thought Hitler was only at the beginning of his career of murder and destruction. He believed that if the Nazi tyrant could be eliminated, many Jews would be spared suffering, and humanity's prospects would be enhanced.

At a meeting of his *Haganah* group, he proposed that a squad of volunteers be sent to Germany for the sole purpose of assassinating the Nazi chief. His proposal was discussed, evaluated, and rejected. Haganah said it would be an impossible task, no matter how desirable it was. The meeting went on to the next topic on the agenda.

But this particular Haganah member was not satisfied. The threat that he saw in the growing Hitler movement would not let him rest. He brooded about it for days and weeks, and then one day, he made up his mind to act. He was a taciturn man, but he held strong convictions.

He bade his family goodbye and said he was being sent on a mission abroad, without specifying any details. He packed a few clothes and secreted two guns and ammunition in his bags. In 1938 there was no direct flight from Palestine to central Europe, so the way he traveled was by train, crossing many borders, with only one goal in mind. He first crossed the border into Lebanon and then Syria, and then the train headed west—to Turkey. The trip continued across the Bosporus, into Greece, across the Balkans, and eventually to Austria, to the country's capital, Vienna. He found a room in a modest hotel and began his period of waiting—a matter of ten days.

A parade led by Hitler was scheduled to be held in the main street of the Austrian capital, and the Haganah man's plan was very simple: to get a front-line position among the crowds sure to come out to hail their great "liberator" and to pump Hitler full of bullets. He knew he would be arrested, tried, and probably executed. He also knew he might even be shot to death on the spot by enraged Nazi followers—but he was also convinced that the deed was worth his life. He was convinced there was an impending catastrophe for mankind in general, and for the Jews in particular.

He had seen newsreels of Hitler standing up in his open car, waving at the crowds as he passed through various cities. He was a Haganah marksman, familiar with arms, and felt he could carry off his mission.

The fateful day arrived. As planned, he was among the first to arrive and found a front-line position. He was careful to stand on the side of the street where the sun would not impede his view. He felt the two pistols in his belt and knew they were ready, for he had checked them thoroughly the night before.

At last the parade began. First came the swastika-emblazoned motorcyclists. They were followed by several bands, with Nazi flags flying in the wind. The crowds all around him cheered and applauded. He remained watchful, calm, and waited. At last, there was a tremendous uproar—the Austrian Hitler-lovers were cheering; the car carrying the Führer was driving slowly down the avenue.

The *Haganah* man followed the people's gaze—and his hands froze on the guns stuck in his belt. He felt cold sweat break out all over him, for he saw that the car with Hitler was not the usual open vehicle but a bulletproof, closed car, through which a figure of Hitler could barely be discerned. All his plans, all his hopes, all his waiting—it was all in vain.

Filled with a sense of dismay, he left the crowd and went back to his room, packed, and retraced his steps to Palestine. Only a few close friends and his wife had known of his mission. He returned to his *kibbutz*, deeply grieved in spirit, totally convinced that his unsuccessful mission was an omen of a terrible Holocaust that lay in store.

From then until his death at an advanced age, he nurtured a feeling of profound anguish. He never said those two words, but they were inscribed on his face for the rest of his life: "If only . . ."

—D.C.G.

Napoleon: Champion of Jewish Rights

No other sovereign in history was as concerned with the welfare of the Jews and did as much for them as Napoleon Bonaparte. He had a remarkable knowledge of the Holy Scriptures and of Jewish history. When, in leisure moments, he would reach for the Bible, he would choose the Old Testament, which occupied the place of honor among the books he took with him on his campaign in Egypt.

It was at Gaza that Napoleon promised to return the Holy Land to the Jews and enable Jerusalem to recover its ancient brilliance under Jewish rule. Napoleon's plan to return the Promised Land to the dispersed Children of Israel was foiled by the naval battle of Aboukir (1799), where the French fleet was defeated by Nelson and the French armies decimated by pestilence.

The frustrated Egyptian undertaking may have been one of the failures he was thinking about when he said to his companions in exile: "The day will come when the greatest scientists and statesmen will regret that all my enterprises failed to have the desired success."

Several generations have indirectly been affected by his Egyptian failure. How different would matters have been if he had been victorious? Had a Jewish state emerged at that time under powerful French protection, millions of Jews would have been saved from the persecution of the past decades.

It is hard to imagine that this man could have had the leisure and the desire to think of Jewish matters. Napoleon, who vanquished kings and created new kingdoms at will, whose triumphant march through Europe and across the Alps was one uninterrupted glorious adventure, who signed the Concordat and made constitutions and the Napoleonic Code, and who settled some of the most ticklish international problems, found time to direct his genius to the plight of an ill-treated minority existing on the margin of Christian society.

When the constitution for the kingdom of Westphalia, where Napoleon's inefficient and flighty brother Jerome was to rule as king, was being prepared by the statesmen Von Müller and Dohm, the Jews were guaranteed full rights as citizens. The "Jew taxes" were abolished. It was forbidden under penalty to call a Jewish citizen names that insulted his religion.

King Jerome Bonaparte, notorious for his thoughtlessness, took the credit for the work of his brother, the Emperor. The gratitude of the Jewish community was deep, as was expressed in a prayer recited at the synagogue on King Jerome's birthday. It said: "One favor has been granted to us by God. We have a wise and honest monarch reigning over us, who does not allow discrimination between Jews and other citizens of the country. He has put an end to insult and contempt."

Recently, statements by high Jewish leaders have been made regarding the creation of a Supreme Jewish Council that would eventually become a sort of Sanhedrin. This enormous project is by no means novel, for in 1806 Napoleon conceived a plan to bring back to life this supreme authority, which had disappeared with the destruction of the Temple.

History shows that wherever the Emperor's power reached, laws were promulgated granting equal rights to the Jews. Nevertheless, a new movement of anti-Semitism broke out during his reign. The peasants of Alsace voiced their protest against their Jewish creditors. Napoleon insisted that the municipality arbitrate the controversy and presided over it personally. He later decided it would be more convenient if the Jews handled their own affairs in the future. With this in mind, he ordered elections held among the Jews of the various countries over which he ruled for delegates to a convention to be held in Paris.

Representatives came from Germany, France, and Italy. The assembly was presided over by Rabbi David Sinzheim. Twelve questions were discussed, among which the following were the most important: Do Jews recognize France as their homeland? Should marriage between Jews and non-Jews be permitted? Should Jews practice usury against Gentiles?

The answers to those questions were submitted to the Emperor. After a time Napoleon's reply came: The Jews were to be granted every right of citizenship. His decision brought new life and inspiration to the hungry hearts of a long-suffering minority in the ghettos.

Napoleon had a surprise in store for the assembly. He ordered the revival of the Sanhedrin, creating a replica of the ruling Jewish body of antiquity, with seventy-one members. The Jewish parliament would interpret the general laws and reconcile them to the Jewish law, eliminating those that were not convenient, in conflict, or doubtful. The high spirit and general happiness of the Jewish community found expression in the appeal for elections of candidates to the Sanhedrin:

> *Our fathers' fervent desire for centuries, which we never dared to hope for, will materialize before the surprised eyes of the world. The twentieth of October is the date set for the opening of the great Sanhedrin in one of the largest Christian cities and under the protection of our glorious and just Prince Napoleon.*

The reconvening of the Sanhedrin took place, and the adopted resolutions were submitted to Napoleon. The Emperor's lucky star was about to decline, however, for the war with Prussia and Russia had broken out. With it the Sanhedrin sank into oblivion. Then came the battles of Leipzig and Waterloo, and Napoleon's defeat. The Emperor was taken prisoner and carried to exile on the island of St. Helena.

—P.T.

When Palestine Was in Ashes: Mark Twain's Bleak Report

From "Innocents Abroad," published in 1867.

Of all lands there are for dismal scenery, I think Palestine must be the prince. The hills are barren; they are dull of color; they are unpicturesque in shape. The valleys are unsightly deserts fringed with a feeble vegetation that has an expression about it of being sorrowful and despondent. The Dead Sea and the Sea of Galilee sleep in the midst of a vast stretch of hill and plain wherein the eye rests upon no pleasant tint, no striking object, no soft picture dreaming in a purple haze or mottled with the shadows of the clouds. Every outline is harsh, every feature is distinct, there is no perspective—distance works no enchantment here. It is a hopeless, dreary, heartbroken land.

Small shreds and patches of it must be very beautiful in the full flush of spring, however, and all the more beautiful by contrast with the far-reaching desolation that surrounds them on every side. I would like much to see the fringes of the

Jordan in springtime, and Shechem, Esdraelon, Ajalon, and the borders of Galilee —but even then these spots would seem mere toy gardens set at wide intervals in the waste of a limitless desolation.

Palestine sits in sackcloth and ashes. Over it broods the spell of a curse that has withered its fields and fettered its energies. Where Sodom and Gomorrah reared their domes and towers, that solemn sea now floods the plain; in those bitter waters no living thing exists—over whose waveless surface the blistering air hangs motionless and dead—about whose borders nothing grows but weeds, and scattering tufts of cane, and that treacherous fruit that promises refreshment to parching lips, but turns to ashes at the touch. Nazareth is forlorn; about that ford of Jordan where the hosts of Israel entered the Promised Land with songs of rejoicing, one finds only a squalid camp of fantastic Bedouins of the desert; Jericho the accursed lies a moldering ruin today, even as Joshua's miracle left it more than three thousand years ago; Bethlehem and Bethany, in their poverty and their humiliation, have nothing about them now to remind one that they once knew the high honor of the Savior's presence; the hallowed spot where the shepherds watched their flocks by night and where the angels sang, "Peace on earth, good will to men," is untenanted by any living creature and unblessed by any feature that is pleasant to the eye. Renowned Jerusalem itself, the stateliest name in history, has lost all its ancient grandeur and is become a pauper village; the riches of Solomon are no longer there to compel the admiration of visiting Oriental queens; the wonderful temple which was the pride and the glory of Israel is gone, and the Ottoman crescent is lifted above the spot where, on that most memorable day in the annals of the world, they reared the Holy Cross. The noted Sea of Galilee, where Roman fleets once rode at anchor and the disciples of the Savior sailed in their ships, was long ago deserted by the devotees of war and commerce, and its borders are a silent wilderness; Capernaum is a shapeless ruin; Magdala is the home of beggared Arabs; Bethsaida and the Chorazin have vanished from the earth, and the "desert places" round about them, where thousands of men once listened to the Savior's voice and ate the miraculous bread, sleep in the hush of a solitude that is inhabited only by birds of prey and skulking foxes.

Palestine is desolate and unlovely. And why should it be otherwise? Can the curse of the Deity beautify a land?

Palestine is no more of this workday world. It is sacred to poetry and tradition —it is dreamland.

—M. Tw.

IV
The Bible:
The Jew's Contribution
to Civilization

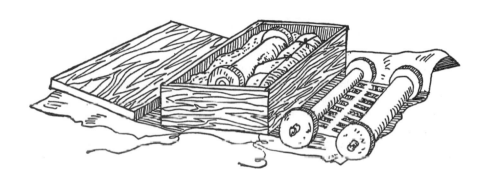

The Eternal Book

The word "Bible" derives from the Greek word *biblia*, which means "books." In the course of time the Bible came to be designated as *the* Book, the collection of the most important sacred and religious writings of both Jews and Christians. For Jews the Bible consists of that group written in Hebrew that Christians call the Old Testament. The number of books in the Jewish Bible is thirty-nine or twenty-four, depending upon the reckoning of certain groups as individual books or entire units. The usual Hebrew name for the Bible is *Tanach* although it is also known in Jewish life as *Kitebe Kodesh*, or the Holy Scriptures.

The thirty-nine or twenty-four books of the Holy Scriptures were selected from a much larger literature current at the time when the choice was made. This selection was not made at any given date; it was a process extending over about five centuries. The Torah, for instance, consisting of Genesis, Exodus, Leviticus, Numbers, and Deuteronomy, had acquired a sacred status as early as the fourth century B.C.E.; the books of the prophets were collected and organized during the period of the Second Temple; the final decision on which books of the Hagiographa (Holy Writings) were to be included in the sacred literature was not taken until after the destruction of the Second Temple, probably at the beginning of the second century; even then there were five books (Ezekiel, Proverbs, Song of Songs, Esther, and Ecclesiastes) concerning which there was considerable controversy before they were admitted into the Bible Canon.

The Bible Canon is a term used to designate the whole group of books finally selected for inclusion into the sacred scriptures. The books that were excluded fall into two categories: the Apocrypha and the Pseudepigrapha. The books that constitute the Apocrypha were hidden or stored away so as to remove them from circulation; hence, in Hebrew the Apocrypha are known as *Sefarim Genuzim* (books that are to be hidden). The Pseudepigrapha are books whose authorship is unknown but which were ascribed to earlier heroes such as Enoch or the twelve sons of Jacob or Baruch, the secretary of Jeremiah.

Comparison of the books included and the books excluded indicate three criteria that may have been adopted by the rabbis for inclusion in the Bible Canon:

1. That the books be written in Hebrew. The beginning and the end of Daniel, for instance, seem to have been hurriedly translated into Hebrew from the Aramaic in order to gain it admission into the Canon.

2. That a book to be included must have been written before the period when "prophecy ceased in Israel," that is, about the time of Malachi (fifth century B.C.E.).

3. That the content of the book must conform to the religious standard set by the rabbis.

In dealing with so sacred and authoritative a literature, it became necessary to preserve the text against possible changes, additions, or omissions, whether intentional or inadvertent. Hebrew is written down largely by consonants. The Torah scrolls in the synagogue to this day are written without vowel points. The vowel signs were invented in post-Talmudic times, that is, later than the seventh century; and they were not fixed until the tenth century. In an unpointed Hebrew text the same group of consonants may be read in more than one way, each with a different meaning. For example, HRB, vocalized *HoReB*, is the name of a mountain; vocalized *HeReB*, it means a sword. HLB, vocalized *HaLaB*, means milk; vocalized *HeLeB*, it means fat. Such a difference in reading may result in a vast difference in a law or a precept or in the interpretation of a text. There was, therefore, developed an authoritative reading to assure the preservation of the original text. The Hebrew word for tradition is *Masorah;* the authoritative teachers of the Bible text came to be known as Masorites; the official text as finally punctuated and vocalized by the Masorites is known as the Masoretic Text.

The division of the Bible into numbered chapters and verses is of still later origin than the vowel points. It was not introduced until about the thirteenth century. The original Hebrew text, as may be seen in the Torah scrolls, to this day has neither vowel points nor chapter divisions nor separations into verses.

The Bible, though generally bound between the covers of one volume, is not one book. It is a literature. It was not written by one person or in any one age. It was many centuries in the making. There are different opinions as to when and by whom the various books were written. It is the result of the work of many hands. It reflects many minds and changing historical scenes and circumstances.

A number of the books of the Bible carry identification of authorship. Thus the Torah is attributed to Moses; the books of the Later Prophets, to the names they bear; Proverbs, Song of Songs, and Ecclesiastes, to Solomon; Psalms, to David and other poets.

Rabbinical tradition attributes the Book of Joshua to the hero who bears its name; the books of Judges, Samuel, and Ruth to Samuel; Esther to the men of the Great Synagogue, who are also credited with the final editing of Ezekiel, the Minor Prophets, and Daniel. Among the rabbis of the Talmud there was difference of opinion regarding authorship of the Bible books; the majority, for instance, hold that the concluding eight verses of Deuteronomy could not possibly have been written by Moses, since they record Moses' own death. Rabbi Simon, however, clings to the opinion that Moses is the author of the whole Torah but wrote the account of his own death with tears in his eyes and at the dictation of God himself.

These assertions of the authorship of the books of the Bible are the Orthodox and traditional point of view. The modern school of historical and literary criticism, however, after having analyzed each of the books at great length, generally agrees that they are composite in authorship and assigns the final compilation of each book to anywhere from practically contemporary times in the case of the autobiographical books to one thousand years later in the case of the poetic, historical, and legal portions. It is the historic, collective experience of a people seeking to learn and to understand the ways and the will of God.

This is what makes the Bible in a high sense the book of the Jew. The heroes of the Bible are Jews, the thoughts of the Bible are Jewish, the adjustments are those of Jews, and God is represented as speaking to Jews and through them to the world.

As law the Bible is organic and fundamental; all subsequent Jewish law rests upon its legislation and its moral sanctions. As a treasure house of a philosophy of Jewish life, indeed, of a philosophy of human life, it remains unequaled.

For centuries it was the curriculum of Jewish education. The Jewish child began his schooling with the Bible and, though he continued later with postbiblical Jewish literature, he returned again and again to the Bible as the authority, the foundation upon which the rest was built.

When Jews began to create their prayer book in the days of the Second Temple, they had in the Bible a storehouse of liturgic riches. Psalms became the hymn-book of the Second Temple and, in the synagogue, was incorporated into the daily and festal ritual. Passages like the *Shema* became the battle cry and the expression of Jewish religious yearning. Daily lessons for edification and instruction were culled from the Bible, and whole sections were permanently assigned for regular reading as the central and most dramatic part of the synagogue service.

The Bible is the literary record of more than one thousand years of Jewish history. It has preserved the Jewish legends of creation, the accounts of the early history of the Jewish people, their laws, their poetry, their wisdom, their customs, and manners and their religious aspirations. Its heroes are neither demigods nor saints; they are human beings, revealed in every phase of human strength and human weakness.

To the Orthodox Jew the Bible is a book of revelation. The Pentateuch is the law of God as He dictated it to Moses on Sinai, eternal and unchangeable. Every sentence, every word of the Bible has its inner meaning and its message to teach. Therefore, to the Orthodox Jew the Bible is the supreme and unquestioned authority in religious life, and every modern interpretation must be based on its sanctions.

To the Reform Jew, the Bible is not so much a product of revelation as of inspiration. The authors of the books of the Bible shared this inspiration in varying degrees; that is why some parts of the Bible are of a higher spiritual and ethical value than others. To the liberal Jew of the Reform persuasion, the Bible is witness to the evolution of Jewish ethical and spiritual concepts from their primitive forms to their most advanced stages.

To both traditional and more modern Jews the Bible is the record of Jewish religious idealism as it emanated from the Jewish experience of over a thousand years. It is the testament of religious genius; its moral and ethical teachings are both cogent and universal and are applicable to modern social and economic problems. Thus, Orthodox, Conservative and Reform Jews are united in the judgment passed on the Bible by a rabbi of the first century B.C.E., who said, "Turn it over and over again, for everything is in it; study it and grow old in it for thou canst have no better rule than this."

—A.J.F.

 ## Bibletown: What It Was Like

Normally, we tend to think of the Bible as something sacred and apart from real life. And if the Bible were not so "holy," it would be far better known and understood. As the Bible has gained in "sanctity," it has lost in vitality. We tend to forget that the people of the Bible were real flesh-and-blood human beings, who were born and grew up and married and bore children and died, who ate and drank, slept and woke, worked and played, sang and danced, laughed and cried, who sickened and were healed, quarreled and sacrificed, failed and achieved, loved and hated.

What would a group of temporary sociologists or anthropologists have noticed if they had gone into a typical Palestinian community? Where would the city have been located? What would it have looked like? What sort of buildings would they have found there? What kind of people would have been living there? What

would they have been eating and drinking and wearing? How would they have been earning their living? What would they have been talking about? And how would they have been bringing up their children? What kind of religion would they have adhered to? And how would they have been governed? And what laws would they have obeyed—or broken?

When we speak of "Bible times," we are speaking about a period of more than 1,500 years. The people of the Bible include not only Hebrews or Israelites, but Egyptians, Assyrians, Babylonians, Persians, Amorites, Edomites, Moabites, Midianites, Phoenicians, Philistines, and Ethiopians. Peoples living in such different places differed sharply among themselves. We can hardly speak then of a "typical" community.

We limit ourselves to approximately six hundred years, from the beginning of the Early Iron Age (around 1200), when the Israelites were settling in Palestine, to the end of the Middle Iron Age (around 600), which was just before the Destruction of Jerusalem (586 B.C.E.) and the Babylonian Exile, which so profoundly changed the character of Jewish community life.

We are considering the community life of Palestine alone and not of the other Bible lands. We further delimit our scrutiny to the Palestinian communities of the Israelites, not to be confused with the "Hebrews" of earlier times or with the "Jews" of later eras. The Bible contains references to more than a thousand cities. The twenty-first chapter of the Book of Joshua lists some forty-eight cities that were given by the other tribes of the Levites. If we may assume that in this, as in other things, the Levitical portion was a tithe, ten percent, we may estimate that the Israelites of that period occupied some 480 cities. Professor Salo Baron reports that "no less than 400 localities bear the name, 'town.'" Palestine was by no means a land of wide, uninhabited spaces with four or five famous cities, as we tend to visualize it from a cursory reading of the Bible and from our knowledge of Palestine today. Not only were there hundreds of cities, but each city had several villages around it that were dependent upon it, as can be seen from Joshua 17:11 and Joshua 19:22 ("sixteen cities with their villages") and numerous other references in the Bible.

However, we have to consider the possibility that many of these references may apply to mere "settlements" or "localities" and not to "cities" in the more usual sense.

An ancient city was not determined by size. It was distinguished from a town or village in a very simple way: it had a wall. In the Book of Esther, mention is made of unwalled cities. The term "walled city" in Leviticus 25:29 implies the existence of some cities that do not have walls. This is, in fact, stated explicitly in the Song of Deborah (Judges 5:7), if we translate this verse, as some scholars have suggested, "The open cities ceased in Israel." Similar references are to be found in Deuteronomy (3:5), I Samuel (6:18), Zechariah (2:8), and elsewhere. So the Biblical distinction between "city" and "village" must indeed have reference to size, keeping in mind the reservation that the words may not always have been used with any precision.

According to the Book of Joshua, the entire population of the great city of Ai, which the Israelites destroyed, was only twelve thousand. Baron states that the combined populations of Jerusalem and Samaria, the two capital cities, never exceeded eighty thousand, or about five percent of the total population of the country. Few of the other communities, he says, had populations totaling more than a thousand. Most of them occupied areas of between six and ten acres, although cities like Megiddo and Jerusalem might be as big as twelve acres.

These little communities had definite characteristics ("socialities") of their own, which were actually recognized in "pet-names" that they bore. Thus, Jericho was "the city of palms." Damascus was the "joyous town." Sidon was "the great." Jerusalem was "the city of the great king" and "the holy city."

The average distance between towns was no more than about four miles, making it possible for the vast majority of their inhabitants to reach their places of work by walking two miles or less.

Roads that connected one city with another were narrow and unpaved. Usually, they were unplanned and simply devoted to public use by immemorial custom. If a landowner wished to raise grain in a field through which one of these paths ran, he plowed up to the very edge of the narrow path and put in his seed. There were neither fences nor ditches to separate the road from the field.

The picture of roads and paths honeycombing the countryside in the cities of Biblical Palestine indicates that much of the life of the city was carried on outside it. The communities were largely agricultural, with the inhabitants gathered together within the walls mainly for defense purposes. Their chief occupations were farming and cattle raising. The cattle were kept outside the walls, not inside, as in some cities of the Orient. Each day men, women, and children would go out of the city to their work in the fields, the vineyards, and the pasture lands. In the twenty-first chapter of the Book of Joshua we repeatedly find appended to the name of a city the phrase "and its pasture lands."

Since the main function of the city was defensive, in almost all cases, the location of a city was primarily determined by considerations of military strategy. Nelson Glueck points out, "They were always built on easily fortified and usually isolated hills, dominating perennial streams and strategic roads. The question of security was obviously paramount in the minds of the settlers . . . They chose sites for their towns . . . which might guard the fertile, irrigated plains from which they gained their sustenance . . ."

Both from the standpoint of vulnerability, requiring compensating safeguards, and from the standpoint of agricultural utility, springs and streams provided logical city sites. And the name of many a biblical city was prefixed by the Hebrew word En, meaning "spring,"—as En-gedi, En-gannim, En-dor, En-haddah, En-hazor, En-harod, En-rimmon, En-rogel, En-shemesh, and En-tappuah.

Entrance to the city was effected through gates. But the gate, which might be as much as forty feet wide, was not merely a large door of metal or wood covered with metal, with huge bars, by which it was bolted at nightfall or in time of danger. Frequently, the gate included a long passageway between the inner and outer walls, which one would have to enter by a right-angle turn to the left, between two large towers, leaving one's sides unprotected. The name of the gate might be taken from some other feature connected with it. In Jerusalem, some of the gates were: the Gate of Ephraim, the Fish Gate, the Sheep Gate, the Water Gate, the

Dung Gate, the East Gate, the Old Gate, the Horse Gate, the Fountain Gate, the Valley Gate, the Corner Gate.

These gates were important places and might be considered to represent an actual social institution in Bibletown. For the gate opened upon a marketplace, as we see from the seventh chapter of the Second Book of Kings, for instance, where the prophet Elisha prophesies that "a measure of fine meal shall be sold for a shekel, and two measures of barley for a shekel at the gate of Samaria." Here, agreements were concluded, such as Abraham's purchase of the Cave of Machpelah from the Hittites, or the bargain by which Boaz relieved the immediate next-of-kin of Ruth's deceased husband of the obligation to marry her. Here, too, were the courts of justice. Here was the general loungingplace and meetingplace, to which all the men gravitated for news, gossip, and all sorts of business. And here, also, the children played.

Passing through the gates, one would find the streets of the city narrow and crooked. The streets were not laid out in any set pattern. Probably there were several broad streets that cut through the city and led directly to the palace or the temple, but the majority formed simply the limits of a group of houses. The ruins of cities that have been uncovered sufficiently to enable us to gain a general view show a ground plan that is almost a maze. However, there is some evidence for the conclusion that occasionally attempts were made at what we today should call "city planning," as by David and Solomon in their development of Jerusalem.

Numerous passages in the Bible demonstrate that the streets were unpaved. Isaiah, for instance, refers to "the mire of the streets," as do Micah, Zechariah, and the Psalmist. From Isaiah, too, we learn that the citizens of Bibletown would throw their refuse directly into the streets, and these must indeed have been vile-smelling places, as are so many of the cities of the Orient even today. Some of these biblical cities did have at least primitive attempts at drainage systems. Such a Judean city as Debir (*Tel Beit Mirsim*) had better sanitary arrangements than are found in some Arab villages today. It has also been suggested that the prophets were not referring to actual "streets" but to broad city squares, set aside precisely for this purpose and as marketplaces. It has been pointed out that dung mixed with straw and earth and well-trodden underfoot provided ancient people with fertilizer and even fuel. This practice may, therefore, have to be understood and evaluated in an economic context rather than from the standpoint of hygiene.

The streets were usually identified either by destination, as when Isaiah speaks of "the lane to the laundrymen's field," or by occupation of the majority of its inhabitants, as when Jeremiah refers to "the bakers' street," although we must remember the possibility that he was referring to a market square of the bakers rather than to a street of dwellings. It seems clear, however, that members of different crafts did tend to cluster together in certain streets and squares.

The houses in Bibletown were sometimes built of unhewn limestone, varying in size from small pebbles to large boulders; sometimes, of sun-dried mud bricks; sometimes, of stone and brick combined; and sometimes, of wood and stone, although this combination was found only in the more elaborate homes of the wealthy. Mortar and cement were never used. But the stones were set in mud and might have wide crevices between them. Doorways were simply openings in the walls, and the door was fastened to a post set in a hollow or perforated stone, in which it was free to turn as the door swung open or closed. Sometimes the walls were plastered. And occasionally the floors were paved with small stones or by mixing lime and mud and letting it harden. More usually, however, the earth was simply smoothed off and packed hard.

Usually, these houses were merely one story high, although more luxurious houses might be two stories high. The heavy walls of some ruins would lead one to conclude that some may have been as high as three stories. The upper story or stories would then have been used for residence purposes, whereas the first floor would have been used for storage and for the domestic animals.

Generally, the outer doorway would lead into a courtyard, into which two or three (occasionally more) rooms would open up. The outer walls of the house would be blank, and the rooms would get their light and air from the courtyard. Altogether the total area of the house would be 150 to 300 square feet. Rooms were rectangular in shape and very simply furnished. At best, a few stools, a low serving table and some couches, and perhaps a chest or two for storage would constitute the sole furniture. There were no provisions for heating, but sanitary arrangements were not too primitive. However, the house was used almost solely for eating and sleeping. Otherwise, when at home, the family would spend a great deal of its time on the flat housetop, which was usually made of brush and mud spread over wooden beams.

Other structures in Bibletown might include communal and private granaries, which were usually circular structures of various sizes. Communal threshing floors were frequently associated with local sanctuaries, as we see in the twenty-fourth chapter of the Second Book of Samuel. Local shrines and high places persisted in the smaller communities, although Israelite temples were centralized in the great cities, as those of Solomon and Jeroboam.

Burial places might be located within the city or directly outside it, and these were of various types. Sometimes caves were used as sepulchers. At other times, graves might be dug in the earth, lined with cement, and then covered with massive stones and earth. Often, shafts were cut into the soft limestone for tombs. And occasionally "columbaria," or groups of "doorway" tombs or smaller niches, were cut into the hillsides.

Originally, the people who lived in Bibletown had all belonged to one *mishpahah* or clan. We see evidences of this clan organization as late as in the time of Samuel and Saul, as in verse 21 of Chapter 10 of I Samuel. Ophrah was known as the city of the Manassite clan of Abiezer, and Bethlehem was inhabited by the clan to which David belonged. However, in the Book of Judges, we can already see the beginning of the breakdown of the *mishpahah* organization, as the clan was merged into the larger tribal unit. Gradually, as the bonds of the clan became weaker, there developed greater mobility between communities, and individuals might settle in communities far from the particular domains of their own special clans. Likewise, there was the assimilation of native Canaanite groups and of mercenaries (such as Uriah the Hittite and Doeg the Edomite), who were imported into the land as soldiers and then settled down in it. Foreign merchants came to Bibletown to trade there and frequently remained there permanently. In fact, all these alien elements constituted a distinct class, known as *gerim*, which, toward the end of our period, represented quite a serious social problem, as we can see from numerous laws about them in the Bible.

A similar problem was created by the presence of other underprivileged groups. Particularly acute was the situation of widows, divorcees, and orphans. Again, biblical legislation and prophetic admonitions attempted to alleviate their unhappy lot.

Slaves were another problem group in the biblical society. The aged, far from being the problem that they constitute in ever-increasing measure in our own society, were venerated. Old people even proudly exaggerated their age in order to receive greater care. For the old folks assumed heightened social status with their years. Even government was carried on primarily by "the elders."

No doubt, in the biblical community, as in communities of all times everywhere, the property owner had special status. We can see from the story of Naboth's vineyard just how important and independent a property owner might be. Again, in Job and the other Wisdom literature we find numerous references to the special respect accorded the man of property. Although these particular citations refer to a somewhat later period than that with which we are dealing, we may assume from the picture of Naboth and of other large landowners and houseowners denounced by the prophets that conditions were not much different in this respect in the earlier period. Conversely, the poor were often held in contempt, exploited and variously oppressed, evoking the prophets' energetic defense of their cause.

The difference between the mode of life of the rich and that of the poor in Bibletown was chiefly characterized by what we today know as "conspicuous consumption," surface differences. There were differences in the qualities and quantities of the various goods consumed rather than in the kind of goods used. Rich and poor wore much the same kind of clothes, as did men and women. Even the materials of which they were made were pretty generally limited to two, wool and linen. However, there were wide differences between rich and poor in the fineness of the cloth, the care with which it was woven, and the quantity of it used in the garment. There were differences, too, in color. Unprocessed linen and wool are by no means white, and really white cloth was extremely expensive. Dyes had to be imported, and scarlet and purple became synonyms of luxury. Imported cosmetics were also affected by the wealthy, but perfumes were regularly used by men and women, rich and poor alike. Jewelry, too, was apparently common for all classes. Bracelets, anklets, earrings, perhaps nose rings, were made of gold, silver, and bronze and sometimes of iron. Beads for necklaces were made of precious and semiprecious stones, of faience, and of glass. Naturally, the wealthy had a greater profusion of these, and theirs were of better quality.

The diet of the rich was very similar to that of the poor, except quantitatively and qualitatively. Bread and wine were staples. But the bread might be made of fine flour or coarse flour, leavened or unleavened, well or crudely baked. And the wines varied from the rich, heavy "syrups" that had to be diluted with water or otherwise mixed before drinking, to the vinegar of the poor man. However, all sorts of vegetables and fruits were also on the menu. Meat was also eaten, but not in the profusion to which we are accustomed today. The slaughter of an animal was something of an occasion, even for the wealthy man.

Each community was relatively self-sufficient. And occasionally there would be enough left over to barter elsewhere. Ezekiel pictures Bibletown as shipping to Phoenicia "wheat . . . wax, honey, oil, and balsam."

The chief occupation of Bibletown was agriculture. Excavations in recent years have confirmed biblical accounts of the production of wheat, barley, oats, beans, vetch, figs, grapes, pomegranates, olives, apples, apricots, pistachio nuts, and honey. That flax was also grown is shown by an interesting calendar that has been unearthed at Gezer and according to which the names of the months are based on the agricultural year, beginning in October, as follows: "month of ingathering, month of sowing, month of the late sowing [?], month of the flax-harvest, month of the barley-harvest, month of the harvest of all [other grains?], month of pruning [vines], month of summer-fruit [figs] . . ." Unfortunately, the end of the calendar is missing.

The domestic animals raised in Bibletown were asses, several kinds of cows, sheep, goats, camels, a few horses. Pigs were, of course, anathema to these Semites. Dogs were only half-domesticated. And there appear to have been no domesticated birds. Hens did not appear in Palestine until after the Babylonian Exile.

Associated with the agricultural life were also spinning and weaving. Spinning wheels and weaving looms were apparently to be found in almost every home. However, there seems early to have developed some small amount of industrialization. Dyers, potters, and tinkers were well known, and smiths were people of considerable prestige, since the individual householder was not usually competent to take care of his needs in this regard. In fact, one of the unbearable impositions of the Philistine occupation was the prohibition against Israelite smiths. Merchants were usually foreigners and were suspected of dishonesty or at least of sharp practice. The building trades were also developed as distinct occupations, as we can see from the passage in II Kings (Chapter 12) about the skilled laborers employed by Jehoash in the repair of the Temple.

Modern archaeology has demonstrated considerable technological advancement in Bibletown. The famous Siloam inscription describes the digging of a tunnel to bring water into the city of Jerusalem. The workmen started digging precisely in the middle, no mean engineering feat. Nelson Glueck, excavating the site of the ancient Red Sea port of Ezion-Geber, uncovered some remarkable metal refineries, going back to the time of Solomon, which anticipated our own Bessemer process.

The tools and utensils used in Bibletown have likewise been unearthed by the archaeologists. These include knives of flint and of metal, saws, chisels, axes, adzes, whetstones, files, hammers, nails, baskets, arrows, spears, swords, fishhooks, needles, spinningwhorls, large keys, spoons, bowls of all sorts, baking trays, various types of ovens, mortars, millstones, olive presses, wine vats, sledges, sickles, hoes, plowshares, lamps and lampstands, combs, spatulas for cosmetics, fibulae (primitive safety pins), and even some glass containers. There was an elaborate system of weights and measures, both dry and liquid. These were far from exact, however, and as the biblical injunctions indicate, many men had one set of weights by which to purchase and another set by which to sell, all of which gives added significance to the complaint of Amos about "making the *ephah* small and the *shekel* great."

Menes adduces the twelfth chapter of II Kings, which describes the payment of the Temple workmen by King Jehoash, and also some of the laws in the Book of the Covenant, which reckon fines and indemnities in terms of money, as evidence of the development of a money economy in Bibletown by the middle of the period we are considering, in the ninth century B.C.E.

Actual standard coins were not used anywhere until almost the close of our period, and they did not penetrate into Palestine until considerably later, after the Babylonian Exile. Bibletown used barter in kind a great deal, and when the people did use money, it was in the form of weighed amounts of silver or gold or of gold and silver rings. In the latter centuries of our period, moneylenders appeared, and the social structure of Bibletown changed greatly. Social conflicts sharpened, and a criminal class developed, as is described in Psalm 10. It was this development that called forth the wrath of the great prophets, and we can understand their fulminations best if we picture them as representing a conflict between two opposing economies, which continued on in Bibletown to the very end of the period we are studying.

The operational techniques of the prophets give us some insight into the methods of communication in Bibletown. Generally, communication was by direct word of mouth. However it seems . . . that transcripts of prophetic addresses were circularized in the provinces, thus reaching countless thousands beyond the voice of the prophets. Such transcripts would, we might say, take the place of newspapers in our day. As has previously been stated, the marketplace was an important medium for the exchange of news. But for long-distance purposes, letters were exchanged. Styli were used for writing on clay and wax. Reeds were used for writing with ink on papyrus and on animal skins (leather).

When we discover that people in Bibletown communicated with one another in writing, we wonder just how many of them could actually read and write. Most of the writing was done by scribes. And judging from the volume of correspondence that has been discovered or to which we find references, scribes must have been fairly numerous in Bibletown. The evidence on this point is far from conclusive, however. The term that in much later times was applied to the illiterate, *am haaretz* or "people of the soil," implies that literacy might have been confined to city dwellers.

Radin states that there were probably no schools in Bibletown, because we find no references to them. Even in much later times, instruction was chiefly from father to son, although by the time of Ben Sirah (in the third century), a system of community compulsory education had already been established under Simeon ben Shetah. As indicated in the *Sh'ma* (Deuteronomy 6:7), it was the father's inescapable religious obligation to "drill" his sons on the divine commandments, regardless of how much else of their education might or might not be delegated to professional teachers.

Solomon Schechter describes the very active social life of people in the time of Ben Sirah. But even in the earlier period with which we are dealing, there must have been considerable social activity, such as is referred to by Isaiah, for instance.

Isaiah refers to various musical instruments that were used to enliven parties in Bibletown. We know, both from the Bible and from recent excavations, that Bibletown did have many different instruments, including reed pipes, harps, and trumpets.

Sculpture was rare in Bibletown. But there were draftsmen gifted in the carving of gems and jewelry. Some very fine ivorywork has been uncovered also, confirming biblical references, such as that to Ahab's "ivory palace."

There was also considerable cultural interchange between Bibletown and other contemporary communities in lands both near and far.

—S.Gl.

Economics in the Bible: Hard Work, Individual Freedom, Enterprise Were Encouraged

Although agriculture was the overruling force shaping the Hebrew economy during the biblical epoch, the ancient Israelites were by no means concerned exclusively with self-sufficient farming activities. The regular exportation of surplus crops, a pronounced urbanization movement (in Israel and Judah, an area covering less than 8,000 square miles, there were no fewer than four hundred settlements classifiable as towns), and, in the later period of the monarchies, the growth of large estates and the appearance of a landless peasantry all suggest that trading and industrial pursuits were not wholly insignificant. In fact, a scrutiny of the text serves to cast serious doubts on the oft-repeated assertion that the Jews were not originally a commercial people and that it was only after the dispersion that they were commercialized by force of circumstances.

Owing to its strategic location on the main trade routes, Palestine had an importance in antiquity that was quite disproportionate to its size and natural resources. The normal flow of traffic between the valleys of the Euphrates and the Nile crossed the land of Israel from northeast to southwest, and from south to north the country was traversed by the caravan road that linked Arabia with the great commercial cities of the Phoenicians. A caravan, according to William Cunningham, "not only serves to convey goods great distances, it is also a moving market or fair which is opened at successive stages" (*Western Civilization in Its Economic Aspects,* Cambridge, 1923); people living along such routes gain certain advantages from the transit cargoes—they can supply the merchants with provisions, they are able to purchase foreign luxury articles, and they have the opportunity to serve as brokers and intermediaries. Numerous allusions in the Hebrew Bible suggest that as a result of such a favorable geographical location there was a wide diffusion of "commercial spirit" among the Israelites and that, contrary to popular opinion, they were in advance of many neighboring communities in this respect.

The potential economic benefits flowing from this situation were modified, however, by the fact that for many centuries a narrow belt of foreign territory separated the Hebrew people from the Mediterranean coast. The ports to the north of Carmel were in Phoenician hands, and it was not until 144 B.C.E. that the harbor of Joppa (Jaffa) passed into the possession of Israel (in fact, this very poor roadstead is never mentioned by the preexilic chroniclers). Throughout the Hebrew Bible the sea is portrayed as a power hostile to God and man (for example, Psalm 93:3-4; Job 7:12; Isaiah 17:12 ff), and it is extremely doubtful that the Israelites ever operated trading vessels on the Mediterranean before the Persian era.

Mercantile caravans passing between Egypt and Mesopotamia and crossing the Plain of Jezreel to and from the desert southlands must have been a familiar sight to the nomadic Hebrew wanderers, even in the early days when Joseph was sold as a slave by his brothers, and there are indications in Genesis (37:25, 43:11) that these clans sometimes carried goods between Syria and Goshen or escorted cargoes passing through the district that they occupied.

For some time after the permanent settlement in Palestine much of the transit trade remained in the hands of the original inhabitants, and the term "Canaanite" became a synonym for merchant (Job 40:30; Proverbs 31:24); from them the Israelites would procure foreign goods, partly by barter, partly through plunder (one such example is the episode of Achan's mantle from Shinar, Joshua 7:18-21), while they occupied themselves with herding and cultivation. The gradual unification of the tribes promoted regional interchange (such as the livestock products of the pastures for the wheat of the grainlands), and the growth of townships encouraged commercial farming. With the establishment of the monarchy, direct Israelite participation in external commerce gained in significance.

There are numerous scattered allusions to this trade, but the leading instances are the accounts of Solomon's mercantile activities in the First Book of Kings; what is found there applied, in varying degrees, to the whole period of the monarchy. Solomon's interest in foreign commerce stemmed from a number of circumstances: close ties with the Phoenicians had made him fully aware of its likely benefits; his successful conquests had brought into the country considerable quantities of hitherto unfamiliar goods as gifts or tributes (5:3, 10:10, 25). At the same time, an increasing supply of foreign articles was needed to meet the luxury demands of the royal court, to support his elaborate program of building expansion in Jerusalem, and to equip the armed forces.

Through David's conquest of the Edomites, the Hebrews had gained direct access to the sea. Thus, in alliance with Hiram of Tyre, who supplied timber, shipbuilders, and skilled Phoenician mariners, "King Solomon made a navy of ships at Ezion-geber, which is beside Eloth, on the shore of the Red Sea, in the land of Edom" (9:26). Thereafter this fleet sailed every three years to the mysterious land of Ophir, which Prof. W. F. Albright suggests was located on the East African coast in the neighborhood of modern Somaliland. Ophir, apparently, was something of an entrepôt for the early commerce of the Indian Ocean, and the squadron would return with treasure and a miscellaneous collection of exotic items: "gold and silver, ivory and apes, and peacocks" (10:22). The land traffic, which came to be organized as a government department, included extensive imports of wood from the Lebanon ranges (5:20), linen, chariots, and horses from Egypt—some of the war steeds being resold to the Hittites (10:28–29).

Such imports implied corresponding exports: Solomon contracted to pay for the labor and materials furnished by Tyre in olive oil and wheat (5:25); in other connections we read of spices, balm, myrrh, honey, and almonds going to Egypt; other local exports may be inferred from the existence of fertile vineyards and inland fisheries. Yet an allusion in a corrupt passage of the text (10:15) seems to suggest that heavy tariffs were imposed on the transit traffic between Arabia and the Levant in order to help balance the great disparity between the value of imports and exports during Solomon's reign.

The political and civil disturbances after Solomon's death must have put an end to the Red Sea trade, since the only other reference to commerce between Ezion-geber and Ophir is the statement (22:49) that Jehoshaphat made a fruitless attempt to renew it. But this disappearance of the ocean outlet may have been offset by an upswing in the northern land traffic, for we learn that Ahab, after his victory over Ben-hadad and the Syrians, secured the right to establish Israelite trading quarters in the markets of Damascus (20:34).

The observations of the eighth-century B.C.E. prophets on the material prosperity and love of luxury in the two kingdoms (see, for example, Isaiah 2:6–7; Hosea 2:10, 10:1; Amos 6:3–6) imply a sustained demand for foreign goods. The subsequent expansion of Assyrian power and the eclipse of Samaria must have resulted in a serious shrinkage of external trade.

Since the land of the Bible was well supplied with the products of the most advanced industrial civilizations of the time, its situation at the crossroads of far-flung commerce proved something of a hindrance to the development of local manufacturing industry. Nonetheless, Cunningham's assertion that "at the time of their greatest prosperity, the people of Israel had apparently made no progress in industrial skill" (op. cit.) is much too sweeping.

Although the products of Egypt, Chaldea, and Phoenicia were all readily available, the grave risks and high costs entailed in transport in the ancient world made them relatively expensive, so that their consumption would have been confined to the wealthier segments of the urban population. In the smaller towns and villages female domestic labor took care of most family needs: spinning and weaving garments were regular tasks for the housewife (I Samuel 2:19), who also fashioned finer linen fabrics for sale to itinerant merchants (Proverbs 31:24), although the priestly code forbade the interweaving of linen and wool (Leviticus 19:19). The mention of a field outside Jerusalem named for the fullers (II Kings 18:17) suggests that some of the coarse cloths woven in the peasant cottages were taken to urban specialists to be cleaned and finished off. The art of dyeing is not mentioned in the Scriptures, but colored stuffs are referred to in numerous passages (for example, Exodus 26:36; Proverbs 31:22), so it is probable that the technique was known to the Israelites.

The art of the potter, too, was undoubtedly widespread in biblical Israel and is a favorite source of prophetical metaphor (for example, Isaiah 29:16, 45:9). There were settlements of potters in the lower city of Jerusalem, where Jeremiah found them shaping their clay, working their wheels, and attending their furnaces (Jeremiah 18:2–4). Yet recent excavations show that Hebrew potters mainly imitated foreign models in a somewhat crude fashion; except for price, the native product could not easily have competed with the wares imported by the Phoenicians from Cyprus and Crete from the ninth century on.

The extensive building operations of the monarchial period made masonry a major industry, and the measuring line, the plumb line, and the mason's level became familiar terms (Isaiah 28:17, Amos 7:7; II Kings 21:13). The detailed accounts of architectural activities in Jerusalem under Solomon (I Kings 6:1 ff), however, make it clear that in the construction of the Temple, the erection of city walls and fortifications, and the building of reservoirs, the Hebrews were heavily dependent on foreign skills and materials—especially those of the Phoenicians.

Yet the people of the Book did attain eminence in at least one industrial occupation: metalworking. During the tribal era Hebrew smiths had fashioned weapons and a variety of implements (Deuteronomy 19:5, 27:5), and the wily Philistines considered it prudent to deport all smelters, "lest the Hebrews make them(selves) swords or spears" (I Samuel 13:19). Subsequently, David's victories in the north, which brought in an abundance of iron ore (II Samuel 8:8), the development of the Phoenician tin trade, and Solomon's exploitation of the Negev's copper deposits (evidence for which was provided by the 1937 Glueck excavations) ushered in a brilliant period of metallurgy, and the Temple was embellished with adornments fashioned from molten bronze (I Kings 7:13 ff). The aptitude that the Jewish people have displayed through the centuries in the working of the precious metals also found a ready outlet in Solomon's love of costly splendor: "And all King Solomon's drinking-vessels were of gold, and all the vessels of the house of the forest of Lebanon were of pure gold" (I Kings 10:21). In addition, he ordered two hundred pounds of beaten gold, while his great throne was overlaid with gold foil (I Kings 10:16–18). With orders of such magnitude, the art of the goldsmith must have made tremendous progress, but even at a much earlier time fine priestly garments were being woven from golden threads (Exodus 39:3).

The fact that only a small number of separate crafts are mentioned in biblical literature would suggest that division of labor was not very pronounced; moreover, there was only one word, *harash* (literally, "hewer"), to designate three different kinds of workman: woodman, cabinetmaker, and stonecutter. In the cities craft specialization was more pronounced, and there was also a certain amount of occupational segregation; in Jerusalem, for instance, bread was supplied by professional bakers, who lived in a special street (Jeremiah 37:21), where separate groups of locksmiths and barbers were also to be found. Although a guild of potters is mentioned by the chronicler (I Chronicles 4:23), it was only after the Babylonian Exile—and probably as a result of industrial experience gained during the years of captivity—that the grouping of artisans in Jerusalem into such craft associations became general (Nehemiah 3:31). Since particular occupations were originally a clan affair (Genesis 4:20), it seems reasonable to assume that trades were also hereditary in certain families.

All in all, industry appears to have played a somewhat more important part in the economic life of the Israelites than most historians are prepared to acknowledge.

Scattered biblical references give some slight indication of how business practice kept pace with the development of commerce and manufacturing. There is evidence that by the eighth century B.C.E. a combination of barter and the use of money in transactions was widespread (Hosea 3:2), while even in nomadic times silver shekels had been a frequent unit of payment (for example, Genesis 23:15; Exodus 21:32). But throughout the whole period ending with the fall of Jerusalem and the Babylonian Exile no coined money was employed, and for every transaction all ingots had to be carefully weighed (Genesis 23:16). Since trading dishonesty is always a problem in an age of sporadic marketing contacts, from the time of the earliest prophetic writings on there were repeated warnings against the use of unjust weights (Proverbs 11:1; Micah 6:10 ff; Amos 8:5) and strict injunctions against falsifying the balance (Deuteronomy 25:13–16; Leviticus 19:35–36).

Since the early days of settlement in the land of Canaan the priestly shrines had served as banks to the extent of receiving money and other valuables for safe deposit (Judges 9:4), but in the Hebrew Bible there is absolutely no trace of embryo bankers to provide finance capital or credit facilities.

Yet one sign of "capitalistic" progress is furnished by the rules regulating interest. Originally interest payments on money loans were strictly forbidden (Exodus 22:25), since lending was regarded as a purely benevolent action and there was no notion of funds being borrowed for business purposes. Subsequently, as the Israelites gradually became involved in the transit commerce with Egypt, Arabia, Phoenicia, and the East, charging interest was permitted in the case of a foreigner (Deuteronomy 23:21), although this modification is mentioned with disapproval by a later psalmist (Psalm 15:5).

A further provision in the Deuteronomic code (15:1 ff) regarding the canceling of debts in the "year of release" refers to charitable loans only, not to advances for business purposes. The emphasis both in the Mosaic code and in the writings of the later prophets is on protecting the debtor against unjust treatment, and there appears to be no biblical stipulation for the recovery of a loan—although the nonrepayment of a debt is condemned (Psalm 37:21). As has been previously indicated, however, there is little doubt that toward the end of the monarchial period the large estate owners were able to lend money during bad times at exorbitant rates on the security of the borrowers' lands, which were forfeited when the repayment obligations were not discharged.

There is direct mention in the Hebrew Bible of only two or three other elementary points of business ethics, such as the duty of fair dealing (Deuteronomy 24:15), the danger of greed (Jeremiah 8:10; Micah 2:2), and the extension of hospitality to the commercial traveler (Deuteronomy 10:19).

One broad generalization that emerges from this brief survey is that in the main the ethic-religious ideals that chiefly concerned the biblical philosophers and lawgivers are not in direct conflict with the concept of economic progress. If the Book of Books displays a relative indifference toward earthly riches, it nevertheless encourages hard work, exalts individual freedom, and looks upon genuine enterprise as a virtue. Composed in a society that was disturbed more than most by spiritual matters, the Hebrew Bible reveals a lively awareness of economic affairs.

Nor are these biblical references of merely antiquarian interest: in the modern state of Israel questions of cultivation, afforestation, mineral prospecting, and industrial planning are frequently decided on the basis of exact historical information provided by a literary monument that dates back more than three thousand years. If and when the Israelites of the twentieth century surmount their economic difficulties, their success in no small measure will be due to the continuing influence of the Bible: "I will cause the cities to be inhabited, and the waste places shall be builded. And the land that was desolate shall be tilled, whereas it was a desolation in the sight of all that passed by. And they shall say: This land that was desolate is become like the garden of Eden" (Ezekiel 36:33–35).

—M.A.

 ## The Making of the Bible

What happened to the original manuscripts of the Bible?

Until the discovery of the Dead Sea Scrolls—one of which included a complete text of the Book of Isaiah—the oldest biblical fragment was the Nash Papyrus. It contains only the Ten Commandments from Deuteronomy. The Nash Papyrus dates to the second century. There is another manuscript in Damascus that is said to go back to the third century, although the claim is doubted by some. The British Museum has a large fragment from the Book of Genesis that dates from the ninth century. There is a manuscript of the Prophets in Leningrad, dated 916 of the present era. The oldest complete Bible in existence is also in Leningrad. It is dated 1009.

The three oldest fairly complete manuscripts of the Bible known to be in existence now are in Greek. Two of them were written probably at least two generations before Jerome was making his Latin translation, the Vulgate. The third was written a little later. One of these manuscripts, the property of the Vatican Library in Rome for at least five hundred years, though long jealously guarded from the public, is known as the Codex Vaticanus. It is on vellum, said to be antelope skin, with three columns to the page.

The other two manuscripts are both in the British Museum. One of them is called the Codex Alexandrinus, which came to England in 1627 and was put into the British Museum in 1757. The other has a more recent and rather exciting adventure and is known to scholars as the Codex Sinaiticus, so-called because it was discovered in 1844 in the Monastery of St. Catherine at the foot of Mount Sinai. It was found in that monastery, a great gaunt building, by a German scholar, Constantine Tischendorf, who was visiting there in 1844 in search of manuscript fragments that he thought might be around Mount Sinai. He actually found 129 leaves of the manuscript in the trash basket and was told by the monks that they were about to be burned—that two similar baskets full of rubbish had already been so destroyed. Finally the manuscript was assembled, and in 1867 it was presented to the Czar of Russia and placed in the Imperial Library. The monks received from the Czar 9,000 rubles, roughly $7,000 at that time. With the Bolshevik Revolution, the manuscript passed into the hands of the Soviet government, who sold it in 1933 to the British Museum for £100,000. It is written on vellum, four columns to the page, by three scribes, two of whom were bad spellers.

In the Middle Ages, the Church forced upon the Jews of Europe public disputations with Christian clergy over the relative merits of Judaism and Christianity. The disputations were, of course, based largely on the Bible, the Christians claiming that many passages in the Old Testament prophesied the events in the New Testament. This, the Jewish scholars denied.

In these disputations, it was frequently necessary to refer to specific verses, and it became convenient to refer to the verses in such a way that the Christian clergy should know which verse was meant. The Vulgate, the Latin Bible that was chiefly used in these disputations, had been divided into chapters and verses as early as the fourteenth century. The Jewish scholars were compelled to have a similar division. In order not to be at a disadvantage in referring to biblical passages, a Concordance of the Vulgate was written as early as 1244. Around 1437–45, a Jewish scholar, Isaac Nathan of Arles in southern France, wrote a Hebrew Concordance, in which he referred to the passages of Scripture by chapter and numbered verse. This was the first use of chapter and numbered verse in Hebrew biblical literature. From there, the system passed into the Hebrew Bible, and all Hebrew Bibles today are marked by chapter and verse.

Small parts of the Bible were rendered into Anglo-Saxon and Old English, possibly as early as the seventh century. The venerable Bede (673–735), who was considered the most learned man in Western Europe at this time, was known to have translated parts of the Bible. There is even a tradition that King Alfred (840–899) translated some of the Scriptures into Old English.

The first translation of the entire Bible into English is associated with the name of John Wycliffe, who lived from 1320 to 1384. His work was based on the Vulgate and was begun in 1379 and completed in 1382. It is a landmark in the history of the English language.

Many other English translations were done before the King James Version. There was Tyndale's Bible; there was Matthew's Bible; there was Coverdale's Bible; there was the Great Bible; there was the Geneva Bible.

Finally in 1604, King James I of England, as head of the Church of England, called a conference at Hampton Court to consider ecclesiastical matters, and there he approved the suggestion of bringing together scholars—forty-seven of them—to translate the Bible into an authorized version. The revisors and translators worked in three main groups—one at Oxford, one at Cambridge, and one at Westminster. Every part of the Bible was gone over at least fourteen times, and finally the work was finished in 1610 and published in 1611, dedicated to King James and known as the King James Version or the Authorized Version.

The King James Version remained the standard English translation of the Bible until the nineteenth century. In 1870, in response to a widespread demand for an up-to-date version of the English Bible, convocations of the Anglican Church arranged for a new translation of the Bible. This became known as the Revised Version.

In the ninth century, Saadya Gaon saw the need for an Arabic translation of the Hebrew Scriptures so that the Jews in the Arab world might be able to read the Bible. He was the first to do the Arabic translation. In the twelfth century, Joseph Kimhi and his two sons, Moses and David, compiled the Hebrew Grammar and Dictionary that were for a long time helpful and influential in the translations and understanding of the Hebrew Bible.

Not until the eighteenth century, however, was there a Jewish translation that had significant influence in the history of the Jewish people. Moses Mendelssohn was a famous Jewish scholar in Berlin who was touched by the Emancipation. He saw the need for a Bible translated into German so that Jews who understood Hebrew would be able to learn German by reading a Bible written in German but using Hebrew characters. In 1783 he translated the Pentateuch and other parts into High German. The effect of this on German Jews was incalculable, for it opened up for them the treasures of German language and inspired in them a taste for the culture from which they had hitherto been barred.

Although parts of the Hebrew Scriptures had been previously translated into English for Jewish use, the first complete Old Testament was translated by Isaac Leeser and published in Philadelphia in 1853. Leeser followed the style of the King James Version but made so many changes in text that his work is essentially an independent translation. This monumental work held its place in English and American synagogues. It was indeed, the family Bible in many homes.

It was gradually replaced by the Jewish version of 1917. The Jewish Publication Society first planned its revision in 1892, to be based on Leeser's translation, but it soon became clear that a new and independent translation based not only on Leeser's Bible, but also on the King James Version of 1611, the English Revised Version of 1885, and the work of many eminent Jewish authorities, would be necessary. In 1917 the job was finished and published by the Jewish Publication Society. A new Jewish Publication Society translation of Scriptures into English is now nearing completion, and will no doubt become the new standard English translation for Jews.

—R.C.H.

 ## The Bible and Talmud Understood and Regulated Laws of Ecology

The rabbis of the Mishnah and Talmud were acutely sensitive to the subject of ecology and the need for maintaining the amenities of city life. So they established the first codified set of zoning laws for the planting of trees.

Two apparently contradictory regulations concerning the place of trees and open spaces are to be found in the Mishnah. One is the last Mishnah of Tractate Arachin. It is based upon the biblical injunction that mandates a broad open space of no less than 1,000 cubits circumscribing the city, and, in the case of Levitical cities, 2,000 cubits.

The Mishnah postulates that one must not encroach on this area by building. The other is the Mishnah in Bab Bathra 2.7, which states that it is forbidden to plant trees within 25 cubits of the boundaries of a city. In the case of carob and sycamore trees, the distance had to be increased to 50 cubits. R. Simeon adds that this prohibition refers to fruit-bearing trees (which beautify the precincts) but not to nonfruit-bearing trees (which, apparently in his view, disfigure it), and the reason for the added distance for carob and sycamore trees is that "they have much foliage," which tends to dirty the city. The Talmud (Baba Bathra 25b) resolves the apparent contradiction between these two Mishnayot.

The apparent prohibition against planting any trees within the city boundaries is clarified by a passage in Baba Kamma 82b, which lists ten ecological prohibitions that applied only to Jerusalem, so as to preserve it as "the perfection of beauty the joy of the whole earth" (Psalm 48:3). Among them is the remarkable injunction stating, "It was forbidden to plant gardens and orchards in Jerusalem, apart from the rose garden which existed there from the time of the early prophets."

Rashi explains that the "rose" referred to was the "kippat ha-Yarden," mentioned in the Talmud, Tractate Keritot 6, as one of the ingredients of the incense used in the Temple. A subsequent discussion in the Talmud cites the reason for this strange prohibition as being on account of the stench given off (by rotting vegetation). Now, if the planting of gardens and orchards was prohibited only in the capital, it certainly suggests that it was permitted in all other cities. This stands in apparent contradiction to the statement of the Mishnah that trees had to be planted at a minimum distance of 25 cubits from the town, whereas carob, sycamore, and nonfruit-bearing trees had to be situated at least 50 cubits distant.

The solution of this apparent contradiction appears to be clear. Gardens and orchards could be planted in all cities with the exception of Jerusalem. What was prohibited was the planting of trees by private individuals lest these trees be neglected and their fallen foliage disfigure the beauty of the city.

Excluding Jerusalem, therefore, an exceedingly attractive picture emerges. Ordered gardens and orchards within the city: an open space of 1,000 cubits circumscribing the city's boundaries within which it was forbidden to plant trees or build, and beyond that open space afforestation, both natural and planted by men.

After the Jewish people was deprived of its homeland, to what extent did these Talmudic zoning laws apply, both to urban Jews living in the Diaspora and to those who remained in the land of Israel while it was under foreign domination?

Before answering the first question, one should emphasize that during the whole period of the Middle Ages, the Jews were entirely deprived of citizen rights and were regarded, at best, as resident aliens. This must be recognized since all medieval codifiers maintain that these laws apply only to cities in the land of Israel, and Joseph Karo, commenting on the bare statement to this effect in the Tur (155.27), states, "Since we have no concern with the beautification of cities outside Israel, even though they may have a Jewish majority, but only in the Land of Israel, and so wrote Rabbi Solomon bed Adret in his novellae, and so it appears from the commentary of Rashi, and it is apparent from the Talmud itself."

However, after he had completed his monumental commentary on the *Tur*, the *Bet Yosef* ("The House of Joseph"), Karo reviewed it again and made certain additions, to which he gave the cognate title *Bedek Ha-Bayit* ("The Repair of the House" or "The Examination of the House"). In his comment on that Mishnah, which is codified in the Tur, he says, "It [now] appears to me that even in the Land of Israel it does not apply [today] since the Land of Israel is in the hands of foreigners on account of our sins [and the law will remain in abeyance] until such time as we shall be vouchsafed to regain possession of it," and R. Yom Tov Lippmann Heller, the author of the commentary *Tosfot Yom Tov* on the *Mishnah*, calls the law a *"Hilcheta De-Meshicha,"* i.e., one that will become operable only in the Messianic Age.

That Messianic Age has not yet arrived, but the independent State of Israel has. The land is no longer "under foreign domination," and the law that remained dormant for so many years has not become operative. We Jews who see in Israel's renaissance the Divine intervention to ensure the revival and survival of the Jewish people refer to this as "the beginning of the flowering of our Redemption."

Thus, the Jewish National Fund has taken upon itself, as one of its major tasks, the beautification of Israel in the direction of its reafforestation. Of course, the planting of trees within the cities, the special laws with regard to Jerusalem, and the proper distance of trees from the city boundaries are outside the realm of JNF's activities. But what the JNF has achieved by beautifying Israel through afforestation outside these city boundaries is a remarkable story.

In the Tu Be-Shevat (February 12, 1979) edition of the *Jerusalem Post*, Alexander Zvielli opens his article with a statement that could easily be regarded as a commentary on the regulations of these *Mishnayot:* "The House of Israel, compressed as it is within the narrow compass of our fast-growing cities, will seek rest and comfort within the few remaining open spaces. Jerusalemites, for example, will seek the greenery and comfort of our forests, and the green belt planted to defend us from the everyday gloom of multistoried housing projects. The holidaymaker makes us remember the good work of the Jewish National Fund."

Two opposite interpretations are given for Deuteronomy 20:19, which says: "for is the tree of the field a man that it should be besieged by thee?" One states it positively, interpreting it to mean that man *is* as the tree of the field; the other makes it a rhetorical question to which the answer is in the negative, "Is then man like the tree of the field?"

Certainly, at least to some extent, the former is acceptable. The tree, like man, comes from seed: it grows, it breathes, it lives, and it dies. Sometimes it lives out its allotted span and dies only when it has attained a ripe old age; sometimes it is stricken by a fell disease and has to be treated to be restored to health; sometimes it dies prematurely, while at other times it is afflicted by a mysterious new disease that baffles the doctor-botanist, and it is left to die. And lastly, in this context, it can become malformed, stunted, and twisted by unsatisfactory living conditions, so the surgeon must come to operate on it and restore it to normalcy.

Both these phenomena have been markedly in evidence in the work of the JNF in recent years. The descent from Jerusalem to the Lowland was one of the JNF's earliest and most successful afforestation projects. The entire twenty-one kilometers of that stretch of road was one entrancing vista of trees—mostly pines and cypresses—a delight to the eye. A few years ago, however, at kilometer six a mysterious, still-unidentified malady affected these beautiful pines. All the skill of superb botanists was of no avail, and the pines died. Apart from the few cypresses that were not affected, that once luxuriously planted forest is now bare and ugly.

With regard to the second point, in some of Israel's natural forests the undergrowth and brush are so thick that they produce stunted and malformed trees, competing with them for air and mulch. The JNF has begun a long-term program that aims to free these trees from their strangling surroundings and allow them to grow to normal, uncrippled adulthood. This experiment began last year on a 300-*dunam* tract in the Yaar Ha-Yeled forest in Western Galilee. There the dominant trees are pistachio and oak. Previously the competition of the brush had restricted the height of these trees to only two to three meters whereas, had they had the desired "breathing space," they should have grown and do grow to a height of ten to fifteen meters. The operation will take from five to ten years, but, upon completion, the forest will present a gratifying picture of tall oaks and pistachios, small trees and shrubs, which also must have a right to live—but always on condition that they abide by the "Laws of Good Neighborship," by which the *Shulhan Arukh* and the other codes describe the laws of the desirable growing of trees.

And just as man justifies his existence not only by the spiritual dimension that he brings to his life, but also by the exercise of his productive capacity, so too, do the trees. Each year JNF is harvesting some eighty thousand tons of timber from the pruning of its forest. Thus, the biblical and the Talmudic laws and regulations concerning the beautification of Israel, afforestation, and considering trees as "human beings" are being fulfilled by the Jewish National Fund.

—L.I.R.

Exodus from Egypt:
The Floods _Did_ Stand "Straight Like a Wall"

The historical accuracy of the Old Testament has been verified by recent archae-
ological discoveries but many events, by virtue of their seeming physical impossi-
bility, remain the subject of speculation. One such event is the fortuitous parting
of the Red Sea during the Exodus, which permitted the newly freed Jews to es-
cape the pursuing Egyptians.

The New York *Times* for October 22, 1883, carried the following article datelined
Java, Netherland Indies ". . . The District Inspector of Telegraphs, while engaged in repairing the broken wire between Serang and Anjer . . . suddenly
descried far out to seaward a piled up wall of water, standing up like a high column and coming in upon the shore with inconceivable swiftness. When it subsided
Anjer was gone . . ."

The Book of Exodus has a similar passage in 15:8, "At the blast of your nostrils the waters piled up, the floods stood straight up like a wall."

The two passages, written some three thousand years apart, are both eyewitness accounts of the same phenomenon, i.e., a *tsunami* or seismic sea wave,
often called a tidal wave.

The writer of the *Times* article is describing a *tsunami* resulting from the eruption of the Krakatoa Volcano on August 26, 1883. The writer of the Exodus excerpt also is describing a *tsunami,* in his case resulting from the volcanic eruption
and collapse of the late Bronze Age island of Thera (Santorini) in the thirteenth
century B.C.E. Thera is the southernmost island of the archipelago of the Cyclades
in the Mediterranean. It is about four hundred and fifty miles northwest of the
area on the north coast of Egypt known today as Lake Manzala, whose marshy
southern portion was referred to in biblical times as the Sea of Reeds. The lake itself is actually a bay, open to the sea in some places and in others separated only
by a low, broken shelf of land.

Each of these *tsunamis* was caused by the eruption of a volcanic island. After
the magmatic chamber of the volcano was emptied by the pouring out of vast
quantities of material, a cavity of huge dimensions was formed under the central
parts of the island and as its roof collapsed, the sea rushed into the hollow. The
water, suddenly striking the superheated cavity, violently recoiled. The sudden
movement of such huge quantities of water, created sea waves of prodigious energy; these waves spread in all directions.

In the open ocean, wave heights of a *tsunami* are small, two or three feet at the
most. However, wave height increases greatly as the water piles up on a shallow-
ing shore line. In V-shaped bays the effect is greatly enhanced, and water heights
have been known to rise to ninety feet or more.

The initial wave begins with a recession that appears as an unusually low tide
developing in a matter of minutes and exposing the sea floor to limits far beyond
those of normal tides. An extensive tidal shallow such as the Sea of Reeds would
have its bottom exposed over a large area by such a phenomenon. The "tidal
wave" may appear within a few minutes, or it may come as much as half an hour
later. Tidal resonances, not uncommon in the confines of the Mediterranean basin,
would enhance these effects. The damage created by a *tsunami* was evidenced on

another occasion by the wave originating in the Aleutian earthquake of April 1, 1946, which produced waves up to fifty-five feet high two thousand miles distant in the Hawaiian Islands. The speed of travel of a *tsunami* in open ocean can be greater than six hundred miles per hour, but even in the shallower Mediterranean, the speed would exceed two hundred miles per hour.

In 1883, above the sea, the dust cloud of Krakatoa rose over fifty miles into the atmosphere and at night was reported to be "laced with volcanic lightning." Surely it reflected the fires of the eruption below. The top of a dust column of this height would be visible to an observer on the ground from over seven hundred miles away. On the assumption that the Thera dust cloud similarly rose to this altitude, almost two thirds of it would have been clearly visible from the area of the Sea of Reeds.

The timing of the events of the Thera eruption are difficult to determine. Volcanologists agree, however, that there was some time gap between the first eruption, which generated the preliminary ash fall, and the culminating paroxysm, which produced the *tsunami*. Some estimates put this gap at as long as twenty to thirty years. In the case of Krakatoa, the first outburst in 1883 was on May 22. The final collapse of the volcanic caldera and the resultant *tsunami* occurred on August 26. Deaths due to the resultant flooding are reported for the evening of August 26 and the early morning of August 27. As cataclysmic as the event of Krakatoa, the Thera *tsunami* is considered to have been generated by an energy source three to ten times that of Krakatoa.

The account of Exodus finds many parallels in what we now know geologically and archaeologically of the Thera eruption and in what observers have related regarding more recent catastrophes of the same type.

For example, in Thera today one can still see the thick alternating layers of red, black, and white pumice/ash resulting from previous eruptions on that island. A visitor to Thera some hundred years ago remarked on the "extreme red coloration" of the harbor waters during his stay. Consider further that the prevailing winds in that area of the Mediterranean are predominantly from the northeast and northwest. In fact, deep cores from the Mediterranean Sea bottom indicate a windblown pumice pattern from Thera that points directly toward the Egyptian Delta and the Sea of Reeds. Dust from the Krakatoa eruption in 1883 was carried over one thousand miles by sea winds, and it is not difficult to imagine the Thera dust raining down on the Egyptian Delta, only four hundred fifty to five hundred miles away.

To realize the effect of this fall of red pumice, one has only to refer to Exodus 7:20–21 and 7:24: ". . . and all the water in the Nile was turned into blood and the fish in the Nile died. The Nile stank so that there was blood throughout the land of Egypt . . . and all of the Egyptians had to dig round about the Nile for drinking water because they could not drink the water of the Nile."

The effect of a rain of black cinder and volcanic ash is also described in the *Times* article of October 22, 1883. "During the night several residents of Singapore were surprised by the appearance of a floating black dust, pungent, stifling, and so fine that even a mosquito-net was not proof against it. In Java the tokens of evil were even more awfully manifest. The sun rose in vain for Batavia on the morning after that fateful Sabbath. A thick black cloud—a cloud of darkness which might be felt—encompassed the affrighted city. The few men who returned to grapple their way about the darkened town, fell fainting in its streets."

A direct parallel in Exodus 10:21 reads, "Then the Lord said to Moses: Hold out your arm toward the sky that there may be darkness upon the land of Egypt, a darkness that can be touched." Also, Exodus 9:8–10 relates, "Then the Lord said to Moses and Aaron: Each of you take a handful of soot from the kiln and let Moses throw it toward the sky in the sight of Pharaoh. It shall become a fine dust all over Egypt and cause an inflammatory breaking out in boils on man and beast throughout the land of Egypt. So they took soot out of the kiln and appeared before Pharaoh. Moses threw it toward the sky and it caused an inflammation breaking out in boils on man and beast."

The events of the Israelites' route of march immediately before and during the passage at the Sea of Reeds also provides strong correlation with what can be surmised of the events of the Thera cataclysm.

In Exodus 12:37 we read, "The Israelites journeyed from Raamses to Succoth," a southward leg of the journey. And in 13:18: "So God led the people roundabout by way of the wilderness and they encamped at Etham." In 14:1–2, "The Lord said to Moses: Tell the Israelites to turn back and encamp before Pi-hahiroth, between Migdol and the sea before Baal Zephon; you shall encamp facing it, by the sea." Pi-hahiroth is mentioned in Egyptian inscriptions as well as in the Bible text. The site has never been located, but the name appears to mean "the mouth of the waterway," an appropriate term for many localities in the swamps of Egypt's eastern Delta. The biblical Migdol is identified with Tel el-Her, south of Pelusium on the border of Sinai.

The path of the Israelites was, therefore, south from Raamses to Succoth, then north to the Sea of Reeds along the west side of what is presently the Suez Canal, and finally south again (on the east side of the Suez) into the wilderness of Etham in the Sinai Peninsula.

Furthermore in Exodus 13:21, we read, "The Lord went before them in a pillar of cloud by day to guide them along the way, and in a pillar of fire by night, to give them light . . ." Later in 14:19–20 we read, "the angel of God, who had been going ahead of the Israelite army now moved and followed behind them; and the pillar of cloud, shifted from in front of them and took a place behind them, and it came between the army of the Egyptians and the army of Israel. Thus there was the cloud with darkness, and it cast a spell upon the night [an alternate translation is "and it lit up the night"] so that the one could not come near the other all through the night."

The Israelites' line of march carried them north from Succoth toward the Sea of Reeds. In front of them towered the Thera dust column "a pillar of cloud by day . . . and a pillar of fire by night." At the Sea of Reeds, they began their turn south toward the wilderness of Etham, and the Thera paroxysm was now at their backs, ". . . and the pillar of cloud shifted from in front of them and took a place behind them."

The Israelites probably encamped on a rise of ground south of the marshy area (there are several rises of over two hundred feet in that area) unaware of the cataclysm to which they would soon be witness. The localized temperature drop created by the shielding effect of the dust cloud (the temperature drop was ten degrees in the vicinity of Krakatoa in 1883) would have caused shifting wind patterns and, as reported in Exodus 14:21, ". . . the Lord drove back the sea with a strong east wind all that night and turned the sea into dry ground"—the first recession of the waters had occurred!

At this point in time, "the Egyptians came in pursuit after them into the sea, all of Pharaoh's horses, chariots and horsemen. At the morning watch the Lord looked down from a pillar of fire and cloud, and threw the Egyptian army into panic. He locked the wheels of their chariots so that their wheels moved with great difficulty."

The Egyptian chariots had become mired in the temporarily exposed bed of the marsh, in what their drivers had mistaken to be "dry ground." It was at this point that the seismic wave piled its waters upon the shore and upon the hapless Egyptians, ". . . and the deeps covered them . . . the water piled up, the flood stood straight like a wall."

The Israelites, observing in comparative safety from their rise of ground, watched the waters rush by them, "the waters forming a wall for them on their right and on their left." When the waters receded, the Egyptians were gone.

There have been some arguments as to the exact dating of the above events. The biblical Exodus is generally conceded to have taken place in approximately the third quarter of the thirteenth century B.C.E., i.e., 1250–1225 B.C.E. It could even have occurred over a period of years. Luce places the Thera eruption in the fifteenth century B.C.E.; Galanopoulos places the preliminary dust fall as late as 1310 B.C.E. and the *tsunami* twenty to thirty years later in 1290–1280 B.C.E. Pomerance, on the basis of studies of the economic status of the Aegean and the eastern Mediterranean, gives a date of 1180 to 1170 B.C.E.

There can be no doubt, however, that the events described in Exodus did occur. The correlations are too great to think otherwise.

—B.S.R.

 ## The Eternal Language of the Prophets

Rarely has one language traversed such vastness of time and space as has the Hebrew tongue. In the sixth century B.C.E., Hebrew had already reached one of its highest peaks in the vigorous and visionary images of Israel's prophets. The rhythms of Amos, Micah, Isaiah, Jeremiah were well suited to their particular message and reflected the soil of ancient Israel itself.

When the Jews were exiled to Babylonia, however, in 586 B.C.E., we began to hear a new note in the language: "How shall we sing the Lord's name in a foreign land?" And in truth, many of the Judean exiles soon abandoned the tongue of their fathers and mothers and began to use Aramaic, a dialect then prevalent throughout western Asia.

When Cyrus the Great, King of Persia and leader of the new world power, offered the Hebrew exiles an opportunity to return to the land of their origins, a small but faithful remnant responded and, despite tremendous obstacles, reestablished the beginnings of a new Jewish commonwealth. With these returning pioneers went the Hebrew language, although the Aramaic influence was already quite evident.

The period that followed, often referred to as the "Silver Age" of the Hebrew language, produced literary creations comparable to the magnificent achievements of the early period. It was during this time that a custom arose—usually attributed to the initiative of Ezra the Scribe—of "reading the Law" in the original Hebrew as part of the Sabbath services, although it had already become necessary to translate and interpret Scriptures in Aramaic. This custom later turned out to be quite important for the survival of Judaism and the preservation of the Hebrew language.

Although this practice enhanced Hebrew as the language of Jewish religious life, it was not successful in making it the vernacular of the Jewish people.

Aramaic, a more pliable and adaptable vehicle, first achieved a secure foothold among the lower classes of the population, but it soon also became the literary language of the Jews. The Apocryphal literature, written in Hebrew, dates from that period, although it was eventually lost in the original language and is known to us only through Greek translation. The most important and most lasting Hebrew work of this period, however, is the Mishna. Although the language of the Mishna contains some foreign elements, it does represent a natural development of biblical Hebrew.

Eventually, with the Moslem conquest of the Neo-Persian world, Arabic replaced Aramaic as the vernacular of the people. By the tenth century, Saadia Gaon, the leading Jewish scholar of his time, was writing his works in Arabic, including a translation of the Bible. However, the seeds of a new Hebrew culture were already being planted. The Karaites, who recognized only the Bible as their source of religious truth (as opposed to the Talmud), applied themselves fervently to its study. Their opponents, the followers of traditional Judaism, were thereby compelled to sharpen up their study of biblical Hebrew, and as a result, a new era opened up for Hebrew poetry and prose.

As Moorish Spain became the new center of Judaism, a whole galaxy of Hebrew writers and scholars—Yehuda Halevi, Solomon ibn Gabirol, Abraham and Moses ibn Ezra, Yitzhak Giat—left their marks on Jewish cultural life. Our *siddur* today cannot be understood adequately without their Hebrew poetry. Yet the spoken language of the Jews was Arabic. Judah ibn Tibbon (1120–1190), dean of Hebrew translators, summed up the situation this way:

Most of the geonim in the dispersion, under the rule of Ishmael, in Babylon, Palestine and Persia, were speaking Arabic, and likewise all the Jewish communities in those lands were using the same tongue. Whatever commentaries they wrote on the Bible, the Mishna and the Talmud, they wrote in Arabic, as they similarly did with their other works, as well as with their Responsa, for all the people understood that language.

Works confined to the limits of Jewish usage were, of course, written in Hebrew, whereas works of a wider scope of interest were written in the language of the educated classes, in Arabic or in Judeo-Arabic. Yehuda Halevi and Moses Maimonides may serve as typical illustrations of this linguistic partnership. Halevi, "the sweet singer of Zion's joy and sorrow," and Maimonides, "the glory of his generation," whose Hebrew Code of Laws towers mountainlike over the literature of postbiblical Judaism, wrote their philosophic works in Arabic.

The late Professor George Sarton of Harvard University, renowned historian of science, claimed that the great cultures of the Moslems and Jews in the so-called Dark Ages were responsible for the preservation of the great cultures of the Greeks and Romans. He maintained that it was the Moslems and Jews who laid the foundation of modern social structures, and he suggests that the modern investigator or student of European civilization should learn Arabic and Hebrew, instead of Greek and Latin, in order to be able to probe the sources of the Renaissance and the Reformation.

The zenith of this Arabic-Jewish culture is represented by Maimonides, and with his death began a decline that lasted almost seven hundred years—until the days of Moses Mendelssohn in Western Europe. In Germany, Mendelssohn's teachings served to reawaken a love for the Hebrew language. But it was not until the 1840s that Isaac Ber Levinsohn wrote his seminal works championing the cause of Hebrew and secular education. Almost overnight there appeared a school of talented writers who strove to present the new ideas of modern Europe in Hebrew raiment. As a result, the Hebrew language again found itself the vehicle for every branch of human knowledge.

Three writers may be singled out who placed their stamp upon that period of Hebrew literature: Abraham Mapu, novelist; Peretz Smolenskin, publicist; and Judah Leib Gordon, poet. The latter, in a moment of dejection brought on by a tendency toward assimilation that he observed among a section of Russian Jewry, lamented: "Who can foretell—perhaps the last of Zion's bards am I, and the last reader—you?"

However, the Hebrew language was never dead; it merely had to battle for its existence in every generation. Professor Tur-Sinai correctly observed:

> *A man or an animal, once dead, cannot be brought to life again. But a language, though supposed dead, can be revived . . . In the case of Hebrew, the [Jewish] people never ceased to hope and strive for a full revival of the sacred tongue of the glorious past, and out of this eternal vision, the indomitable will to revert to the language of the biblical homeland arose, together with the urge and will to return to the historic homeland itself.*

Hebrew has never ceased to live among Jews. When it was brutally silenced in Palestine by the Roman sword, it slowly grew to even greater vigor in the Diaspora. Throughout their vicissitudes during the Middle Ages, the Jews wrote their private and official correspondence in Hebrew, as well as their commercial statutes and their public and communal records. Even while they developed their vernaculars, such as Yiddish and Ladino, they never stopped using Hebrew. And of the great creative works that Jews produced in other languages, only those that had been translated into Hebrew survived as part of the national heritage.

It is noteworthy, too, that even the dialects that Jews adapted were written in Hebrew characters and retained many Hebrew words and phrases. And it was these Hebrew expressions that gave Yiddish (and other languages that Jews adopted) their unique Jewish character. Hebrew thus never remained static. Its vocabulary and its inventory of ideas continued to grow, even where it was not the spoken language of the Jews. It must be remembered, also, that Hebrew, because it was the language of prayer and study, was in daily use among many Jews who used another language as their vernacular.

In 1860 the Reverend Philip Schaff, in his book *Through Bible Lands* made this extraordinary observation:

> *A word about the Jews. They have four holy cities in Palestine: Jerusalem, Safed, Tiberias and Hebron. They still look forward to the restoration of their race and country. Their number in Jerusalem is growing rapidly and amounts fully to one-third of the whole population. They are divided into three sects— the Sephardim, of Spanish and Portuguese origin; the Ashkenazim, from Germany, Hungary, Poland and Russia, and a small number of Karaites, who adhere strictly to the letter of the written law and discard the rabbinical traditions. There are no Reform Jews or rationalists in Jerusalem. They are all Orthodox, but mostly poor and dependent on the charity of their brethren in Europe. Many come to be buried on holy ground, and outside of the Eastern wall on the slopes of the valley Kedron, which are covered with tombstones.*
>
> *The Jewish Quarter is squalid and forbidding. It ought to be burned down and built anew. The Polish Jews look dirty and shabby, and wear curls, which give them an effeminate appearance. The Hebrew language is used in Jerusalem as a conversational language, and there only. The Spanish and Portuguese Jews, whose ancestors emigrated after their expulsion from Spain*

under Isabella I (1497), still speak a corrupt German. Baron Rothschild and Sir Moses Montefiore have done much for them by building hospitals and lodging houses. They ought to buy Palestine and administer it on principles of civil and religious liberty.

It was not only a natural step for Hebrew to become the national language of Israel but also a politically necessary one. The Hebrew language represents our title-deed to the soil of Israel. It is the language in which the land was promised to our forefathers. Only by preserving and developing the language of the Bible could we have secured recognition as the legal claimant of the Holy Land.

"Verily, this book shall not leave thee forever," God instructed Joshua. The Jews preserved the Book of Books, and, in return, the Book preserved the Jewish people. The Jews in the Diaspora were able to show the world that at least this one book—in its original language—was theirs.

The Hebrew language in all generations remained a kind of "territory" for Jews outside Palestine, a spiritual homeland; and the hopes, aspirations, and visions of the Jews were chiefly expressed in that language. "One cannot understand the Jewish people without understanding Hebrew," said Edmond Fleg. For the individual Jew, a knowledge of Hebrew provided a source of identity and self-dignity.

Moreover, Hebrew has been studied and cultivated through the centuries by non-Jews as an essential component of Western civilization, many of whose ideas originate in the Old Testament. Biblical research, archaeology, the Dead Sea Scrolls—even the geography of the Holy Land—are a closed book to anyone without knowledge of Hebrew.

The basic theme of the Bible is the millennial human search for God, who is the embodiment of justice and righteousness. If need be, it is sometimes also, as we say in Hebrew, a struggle *with* God. It is a language of protest against the follies and shortcomings of people—a theme exemplified in Books of the Prophets. It is a language of challenge to people to improve themselves, to set up a society in which social justice shall be the rule rather than the exception. It is the language in which people were originally told to "love thy neighbor as thyself."

These are themes that still challenge the best minds of humanity. And in my view, one of the reasons people have been attracted to the study of Hebrew has always been that it is the original source of these ennobling themes and because they identified with the values to be found in these themes. This imposes a double responsibility on the people who inherited the language and its immortal works, an idea beautifully expressed by the poet David Shimoni:

> *O tongue of my muse, thou Hebrew of old,*
> *We are in the blood indivisible: Twin*
> *Worlds long forgotten in both of us spin*
> *Ancient stock and abandoned of kin*
> *Mysterious echoes of ages untold.*

Leibnitz once remarked that "language is a mirror of the spirit of the people." Similarly, Moritz Lazarus, the noted Jewish scholar, claimed that "in the formation of a language a nation reflects its whole conception of the world, its whole presentation of things, its moral and intellectual standard, in fact its whole sphere of ideas and thought."

The language of the Book was intertwined with the sacredness of the Book itself, and hence both were preserved. The Hebrew language is one of the few languages that has been expressing a continuous historical experience of the Jewish people for many, many centuries. The Bible has been put to every conceivable use. It has been translated with varying success (but always with remarkable devotion) into upward of a thousand languages. It cannot be regarded as merely the dead record of an ancient people. It is an account that has relevance today.

Though it is true that the Bible lives also in translation, it is only in Hebrew that the text stays truly alive and open to changing interpretation. The Christian scholar W. L. Roy writes: "The Bible can never be understood unless through the medium of the language in which it was originally written and the spirit by which it was dictated . . . Hebrew is so rich in sense that no translation can do it justice." This is one reason for the existence of so many translations of the Bible— each one is supposed to be an improvement over the others.

During all of the Middle Ages, Hebrew scholarship flourished among enlightened Latin Christians. As early as the thirteenth century disputations arose between Jewish and Christian scholars concerning exact meanings of the Hebrew text of the Old Testament and other sources. The most famous disputation took place in 1240, when a converted Jew, Nicholas Donin, called the Pope's attention to passages in the Talmud and to other Jewish words that were allegedly of an anti-Christian nature. A formal disputation took place that year in Paris. The result was what has been called "a vast bonfire of Hebrew books," a preoccupation popular throughout Europe in that period and known so well in more recent times.

But to others, the Hebrew language—and the writings in it—were to be treated with respect and diligence. The Hebrew version of the Old Testament or the Greek translations of the Bible by the Jews, Jewish-Christians, or the disciples of rabbis served as the bases of the great exegetes of the early Church. Such was the case with Origen, Jerome, and Theodore of Mopsuestia. Jerome, when criticized for his interest in Hebrew, said: "Why should I not be permitted to inform Latins of what I have learned from the Hebrews? It is most useful to cross the threshhold of the masters and to learn the art directly from the artists."

In effect, there were two major avenues for the transmission of biblical tradition to Christianity. The first was the Christian study of Jewish sources through translation; the second was the study of Hebrew sources in the original tongue by Christian scholars who had been taught the language by Jews. This reached such proportions that, during the Reformation, Hebrew learning became a sign of "enlightenment."

The motives behind the early Christian interest in Hebrew and Hebraic sources are of importance and provided the key to their impact. The initial impetus is obvious: In order to study the basis of the Gospels, it was of crucial importance to know the Scriptures in their original language. With the advent of the Jewish-Christian disputations from the thirteenth century onward, a knowledge of Hebrew enabled the Christian scholar to stand his ground with greater authority. The element of conversion was also closely linked to this; the Christian theologian felt he could better prove to the Jew "the error of his way" if he was able to bolster his claims with citations in the original tongue.

The early Christian interest in Hebrew also had its origins in the dictates of geography and in medieval Latin psychology. First of all, if a scholar intended to learn Greek, the other major language necessary for medieval scholarship, it was necessary for him to travel either to Byzantium or to southern Italy. Hebrew, however, was available from the Jew living in the same town. Even more important was the mystical appeal of Hebrew for the early Christian scholar. Hebrew was regarded as the mother tongue of all languages and the vernacular of heaven.

Hebrew thus appealed to the emotions, to the philosophy, and to the historical sense of the Latin scholar.

The traditional Jewish sources were important also because they included linguistic and grammatical material important for textual understanding. The best-known Hebrew scholar to use glossing in the vernacular throughout his works was the eleventh-century exegete Rabbi Shlomo ben Yitzhak (Rashi) (1040–1105). His work was important for the technical aids it offered, but its greatest significance in our present context is the fact that it was incorporated almost totally into the words of Nicholas de Lyra, the fourteenth-century Franciscan exegete, upon whom Luther leaned so heavily in his work.

In this manner much of the traditional Jewish interpretation of the Old Testament entered the works of Christian scholars with the appropriate Christian slant. It became commonplace for church scholars to study the Hebrew texts of Scriptures in conjunction with rabbinical commentaries. Beryl Smalley, a recent scholar, is indeed justified in noting that "the Hebrew text was no more separable from its traditional commentaries than the Vulgate was from its *Gloss.*"

Some works that were at first thought to be of purely Christian origin were later proved to be of Jewish authorship. An example of this is the classic *Fons Vitae,* a classic for medieval churchmen, which had been ascribed to "Avicebrón, a Spanish Christian writer." It was not until the nineteenth century that a scholar discovered the real author of this work to have been none other than the famous Hebrew poet Solomon Ibn Gabirol (ca. 1021–ca. 1058).

The tradition of early English churchmen who valued Hebrew is a long one indeed. The Venerable Bede, in his great work *De Temporum Ratione,* claims to have based his chronology on "the Hebrew truth" as he found it. Robert Grosseteste, the learned Bishop of Lincoln and the mentor of Roger Bacon, was a pioneer in the field of Hebrew studies. Bacon himself stated repeatedly that a knowledge of Hebrew was necessary for the proper comprehension of science, theology, and philosophy. His conviction about this was so profound that he even went to work on a Hebrew grammar.

The religious aspect was important in Bacon's attitude. Hebrew was, after all, the language in which God had revealed His presence to mankind. Bacon felt, therefore, that the origin of all knowledge was to be found in the Hebrew writings. From an academic point of view, Bacon was dissatisfied with previous translations of the Bible. He was a Franciscan monk, and his attitude toward Hebrew was so characteristic of the order that "when in a 13th or 14th Century manuscript we find any evidence of Hebrew knowledge, we may suspect a Franciscan origin."

Johann Reuchlin (1455–1522), forerunner of the Reformation, first realized the necessity of studying Hebrew when he was twenty years old. At that time he was compiling a Latin dictionary and found that he was unable to explain many Hebrew words that he was copying from older sources. But copies of the Bible in Hebrew were almost impossible to obtain.

In Florence, he met Pico della Mirandola, who impressed upon him the idea that the Kabbalah formed "the most solid foundation of the doctrine of Christianity." At the court of Frederick III he met the Emperor's Jewish physician, Jacob Loans, who agreed to help him learn the Hebrew language. In Rome, as ambassador at the court of Pope Alexander VI, he met a famous rabbi, under whose guidance he was able to perfect his knowledge of Hebrew. In *De Verbo Mirifico,* a book that he published in 1494, he characterized Hebrew as a language, "simple, holy, terse, and vigorous, in which God conferred with men face to face."

The only Christian in Europe with a sound knowledge of Hebrew, he was eager to spread its study among his friends, and for that purpose he wrote and published a Hebrew grammar, the first Hebrew grammar written by a Christian scholar. The book served its purpose admirably. "It aroused a taste for Hebrew in a large circle of scholars, who thenceforth zealously devoted themselves to it, and these studies supply a new factor towards the Lutheran Reformation."

The Reformation was to a great extent a rejection of the Catholic tradition and a return to the Bible. However, the Bible was then generally available only in the Catholic version—the Vulgate. A number of German theologians, therefore, turned to Jewish rabbis for assistance. Almost all the leaders of the Reformation were learned Hebraists: Luther, Zwingli, Melanchthon, Tyndale, Servetus, and others. Some religious sects made a knowledge of Hebrew an important tenet of their faith.

As a result of this interest in Hebrew and Hebrew scholarship, there was considerable activity from the Middle Ages on in the translation of the Bible from Hebrew into other languages. Several attempts were made to translate from Hebrew into Latin, among them a rare example of the interlinear technique. But by far the most interesting are those in Castilian. A number of people—all of them Christian—worked on these translations. One such example had an interesting history. At the end of the fifteenth century, when the Jews were expelled from Spain, they took with them to the eastern Mediterranean their native tongue. These people then required a Bible, and this was first printed for them in Ferrara in 1553.

The transition from the Dark Ages was in great measure due to the scholarship of the Moorish Arabs. The great Hellenic tradition, to all intents and purposes lost to the Western world during the Middle Ages, was preserved and cultivated by the Arabs and was particularly developed in Muslim Spain. Hippocrates, Ptolemy, and Aristotle were all studied and admired in the world of Islam. Although, as mentioned before, all the original texts were inaccessible, they were translated into Arabic. When the Christian scholars wished to avail themselves of these works, it was to the Spanish Muslims and to Saadia Gaon and Maimonides that they turned. It was here that the Jews served as a bridge between the two worlds. The Christian scholars looked to the Jews of their own country, who in turn could draw on the knowledge of their brethren across the Pyrenees in Spain.

Hundreds of these translations by the Jews of Europe during the Middle Ages have survived to our day. The thinkers and writers of Europe quickly accepted and made use of this Muslim-Hebrew version of Hellenic thought. For example, Dante's cosmogonic system is without doubt an adaptation of the Hebraic-Arabic conception of the world's origin. This intellectual exchange served as the basis for mathematical study in Europe. One can say, as well, that medicine, to the extent that modern science has its origins in the rudimentary gropings of medieval medicine, is equally in debt to this continuous transfer of a cultural and informational heritage.

The Hebrew Bible has had a strong influence on the New World. Even before the Pilgrims reached America, a bitterly persecuted people, they drew sharp parallels between themselves and the Jews. The Bible was their constant source of hope, faith, and ideas. They identified with its personages and events. From the very beginning and throughout the Revolutionary War period, they visualized themselves as fighting against the "Philistines" or the "Amalekites." If Israel had its Pharaoh, they had their King George. The Atlantic Ocean was their Red Sea; Washington and Adams were the modern Moses and Joshua, and America was the New Canaan.

As Jews recite the Haggadah on Passover night, so too the Pilgrims remembered:

Ought not, and may not the children of these fathers rightly say, our fathers were Englishmen, who came over this great ocean, and were ready to perish in this wilderness, but they cried unto the Lord, and he heard their voice and looked on their adversity. Let them therefore praise the Lord, for He is good and His mercy endureth forever; yea, let them who have been the redeemed of the Lord show how He hath delivered them from the hand of the oppressor, when they wandered in the desert wilderness out of the way, and found no city to dwell in; both hungry and thirsty, their soul was overwhelmed in them. Let them therefore confess before the Lord his loving kindness and his wonderful works before the children of men.

In his book *On the Desert* (1833), the noted clergyman Dr. Henry M. Field writes: "Perhaps it does not often occur to readers of the Old Testament that there is much likeness between the Hebrew Commonwealth and the American Republic. At bottom there is one radical principle that divides a republic from a monarchy . . . It is the natural equality of man, which is fully recognized in the laws of Moses as in the Declaration of Independence."

The Christian Hebraists quoted many proverbial phrases from Hebrew Scriptures in the original language. They delivered commencement addresses in Hebrew. And, above all, they encouraged its study and its cultural significance in colonial America. This attitude was so prevalent that it gave rise to what some scholars say is only a legend, but even as a legend it is quite revealing. H. L. Mencken, renowned student of the American language, reports: "William Gifford, the bitterly anti-American editor of the *Quarterly Review,* is authority for the story that at the close of the Revolution certain members of Congress proposed that the use of English be formally prohibited in the United States, and Hebrew substituted for it."

Along with this regard for the language of the Old Testament went a love and reverence for its political ideas. In the Bible, Colonial America found inspiration for its opposition to the principle of the divine right of kings. Jonathan Mayhew, a leading clergyman, in a sermon delivered in Boston, May 23, 1766, on the repeal of the Stamp Act, declared:

God gave Israel a king in His anger, because they had not the sense and virtue enough to like a free commonwealth, and to have Himself for their king —where the spirit of the Lord is, there is liberty—and if any miserable people on the continent or isles of Europe be driven in their extremity to seek a safe retreat from slavery in some far distant clime—oh, let them find one in America.

Thus, Moses' warning and Samuel's admonition against monarchy actuated the policy of the United States at the crossroads of Colonial life during the third quarter of the eighteenth century.

Of striking interest is the draft for the seal of the new United States. Submitted by Benjamin Franklin and Thomas Jefferson, it portrayed Pharaoh, with a crown on his head and a sword in his hand, sitting in an open chariot, passing through the divided waters of the Red Sea in pursuit of the Israelites; Moses, with beams of light radiating from his face, stands on the shore and extends his hand over the sea, causing it to overwhelm Pharaoh and his hosts. Underneath this drawing was the motto from the Book of Maccabees: "Resistance to tyrants is obedience to God."

Knowing this, we can understand why the leaders who needed an inscription for the Liberty Bell went to the Old Testament and not to Greek philosophers or Roman poets. In Leviticus 25:10, they found what they were looking for: "Proclaim liberty throughout all the land unto *all* the inhabitants thereof," a motto that has been one of the main pillars of our constitutional democracy.

Judaism and American democracy have much in common. Both teach the unity of the human race. Both have their foundation in the precept "Love thy neighbor as thyself." Both acknowledge the divine character of human personality. Both command respect for the religious convictions of others, and the practice of charity toward all. Both emphasize the conscientious observance of the laws of the state, and respect for government. Both are based upon the natural right of each human being to be different and not to be penalized for this difference. Both stand for government by the consent of the governed. Both recognize that the focal point of social process and the test of human progress are in the individual and not in the state.

—A.I.K.

 In Biblical Days
Farmers Were Protected from Becoming
Landless Serfs

The Bible means different things to different readers; it has been the source of more argument and friction, of more discussion and reinterpretation than any other text ever published. Today it still has the power of provoking a multitude of reactions, which range all the way from word-for-word literal acceptance to cynicism and absolute disbelief.

Archaeologists, anthropologists, and other types of investigators concerned with various aspects of society in the ancient world usually find themselves, at some stage of their research, trying to substantiate or refute a particular thesis by referring to specific biblical passages; and the worldwide interest in the Dead Sea Scrolls is merely another symptom of the continuing importance of biblical studies in scientific research. Anyone genuinely interested in the history of antiquity—irrespective of his or her views on religion—cannot afford to ignore the most valuable source book on the evolution of society and its institutions in the ancient Near East.

Of all these scholars, perhaps it is the economic historian who is the most fortunate: the data with which he or she is primarily concerned, by their very nature, are much less subject to controversy or ambiguity. This is especially so with the most basic of all economic activities—agriculture. Scattered about in the Hebrew Bible are continual references (some of them extraordinarily clear and detailed) to agrarian matters. These allusions not only throw a good deal of light on farming arrangements and rural conditions but also suggest that the techniques of husbandry were somewhat more complex than is generally imagined and that some of the social problems flowing from the organization that were to confront many later communities were not unknown to the Hebrews.

The ancient Israelites first emerge from the dim mists of a legendary past as a nomadic pastoral people; in fact, the association of Cain with land cultivation, whereas his brother Abel, was "a keeper of sheep" (Genesis 4:2), clearly implies disparagement of tilling the soil. Abraham is represented as a nomad par excellence, and it is only after the conquest of Canaan that the Hebrews begin to become sedentary, crop-growing farmers. Even then, in some districts not well suited to constant tillage the principal means of subsistence continued to be the rearing of sheep and goats, involving a limited nomadism because of the seasonal alternations of pasturages. This was the case in the south of Judah (see, for example, I Samuel 25) and among the tribes of the trans-Jordanic plateau (Judges 5:16), which in the days of Ahab paid a tribute of 100,000 lambs and the wool of as many rams (II Kings 3:4). Yet tillage rather than a pastoral life had become prevalent after the settlement in Canaan, and the tendency was for the peasant to sell his goats and purchase a field with the profits of the transaction (Proverbs 27:26).

A wide variety of crops came to be cultivated, the most important always being wheat. In good seasons, when the harvests exceeded local demands, considerable quantities were exported, especially to Israel's northern neighbors, the Phoenicians (Ezekiel refers to the practice in his lamentation for Tyre [27:17]). Barley was the second major crop and apparently formed the staple food of the poorer classes (see Ruth 3:17); other food crops included millet, beans, and lentils. At least one plant was cultivated for manufacturing purposes—flax, for linen and sailmaking (the hackling process is alluded to in Isaiah 19:9).

Of great importance was the culture of the vine and the olive, and figs were also cultivated extensively. To "dwell safely, every man under his vine and under his fig-tree" (I Kings 5:5) became the goal of every Hebrew husbandman. Viticulture demanded more attention and labor than the other types of agriculture, since the stony slopes, whose thin layer of topsoil was easily washed away by the winter rains, had to be carefully terraced (Isaiah 5:2). Both "grape-blood" (Deuteronomy 32:14) and olive oil became valuable export items, and Solomon paid at least part of his debts to Hiram in oil (I Kings 5:25).

By the time of Saul and David the method of tillage had advanced from hocing to plowing. The ox-drawn plow used by the Hebrews was a light, simple affair, and its modern counterpart is still to be found in many districts of Syria and the Nile Valley. It consisted of wooden beams and supports, but the wearing parts were fashioned from iron (as is clearly indicated by Isaiah's famous prophecy that "they shall beat their swords into plowshares" (2:4). The sowing season was seldom a joyful one, apparently, owing to the vagaries of the Palestinian weather and the heavy expenditure of energy on the hard, rocky soils; the author of Ecclesiastes urges the constant attention of the husbandman to the young seedlings (11:6); Isaiah advocates placing the seeds into furrowed rows instead of scattering them broadcast out of a basket (28:25), and Joel refers to new seeds shriveling under the clods in a season of severe drought (1:17).

In the interim between sowing and reaping the crops were constantly exposed to a host of natural hazards: hailstorms were not unknown during the months of March and April (Haggai 2:17); weeds were a problem (Jeremiah 12:13); crops were subject to a whole catalog of fungus diseases, among them mildew (Deuteronomy 28:22); and of course farmers were plagued by the ravages of the locust, mentioned in many contexts. The grape grower had to be especially wary of "the little foxes" (Song 2:15) and the wild pig (Psalm 80:13), but all the crops were in danger from the inroads of cattle. Clear provision is made (Exodus 22:4) for the payment of compensation if beasts have pastured in a neighbor's unharvested field.

The commencement of harvesting operations varied according to elevation, exposure, and local fertility: in the neighborhood of Jericho the cereal harvest started around the middle of April, on the coastal plains about ten days later, and in the high-lying areas as much as a month afterward, the work would continue for about forty days (Deuteronomy 16:9).

The sickle used for cutting the grain is never described in any detail by the biblical authors, but apparently two types were employed (see Deuteronomy 16:9 and Jeremiah 50:16), the more popular variant being a wooden implement toothed with flints and believed by Professor W. M. F. Petrie to have been designed to resemble the jawbone of an ox. Since the weather during these harvest weeks was usually rainless, threshing would take place in the fields themselves. When only small quantities of grain were to be handled, threshing was a simple operation with hand flails (Ruth 2:17); where large amounts were involved, a sledge of large weighted boards, with sharp stone chips attached to the underside and drawn by a team of four or five oxen, would shell out the grain from the sheaves spread out over the floor (II Samuel 24:22; Job 41:22).

When the threshing was finished, winnowing began; the grain was separated from the chaff by means of a special wooden fork (Jeremiah 15:7), with the evening wind scattering the chaff (Psalm 1:4); the straw left over after threshing served as a valuable cattle fodder (Isaiah 65:25). The grain would then be collected into large heaps, and until it could be safely stored, the farmer might have to sleep on the threshing floor to prevent theft, as Boaz did (Ruth 3:7); in addition, underground silos were known to the biblical Hebrews (Jeremiah 41:8).

The joy of harvesttime in ancient Israel was proverbial (Psalm 126:6), the festivities culminating in Shavuoth (the Feast of Pentecost), a nature festival that specifically celebrated the ingathering of the wheat (Exodus 34:22) and was gradually incorporated into the cycle of religious holidays. Sukkoth (the Feast of Tabernacles) celebrated especially the harvest from olive groves and vineyards, as well as the close of the husbandman's labors as a whole (Deuteronomy 16:13).

Although there is little specific biblical information on yields and returns, the general impression is that until the monarchial schism in the late tenth century B.C.E., the majority of yeomen farmers had little difficulty in making ends meet. Thereafter, however, the writings of the prophets indicate a steady process of social differentiation. As often happens in a predominantly self-sufficient community of smallholders when tribal cohesion and kinship loyalties become weaker in the face of more effective central government, some farmers grew richer at the expense of their fellows, and various forms of exploitation appeared. The Book of Amos, for instance, harps on the various burdens of the small farmers (public taxes, private usury, and so on) and stresses that many of them were hardly making a livelihood. The accumulated fruits of years of labor could easily be destroyed by the havoc of foreign invasion, alternating drought and floods, or locust plagues; and each such catastrophe would tend to weaken the position of the less able or less thrifty peasant and strengthen the hand of a neighbor with more skill or initiative. In fact, the situation was not basically different from what was to take place among the people of Latium in central Italy four centuries later: many farmers eventually lost their holdings altogether, and a small group of comparatively rich landowners began accumulating large estates.

Isaiah's passionate exclamation, "Ah,/Those who extend house up to house,/And join field to field,/Till there is room for none but you/To dwell in the land!" (5:8; see also Micah 2:1–2), clearly indicates that intellectual leaders were fully aware of the trend's inherent dangers. Moreover, the tale of King Ahab and Naboth (I Kings 21) shows how pseudolegal forms of expropriation were being employed by powerful landholders; the same tale demonstrates the psychological effects of such threats—Naboth persistently refused to surrender his inheritance out of fear of being reduced to the status of a landless man, which in Israel (as in ancient Babylonia and Egypt) was a far from enviable position.

Those poorer peasants who tried to stave off the inevitable by borrowing from wealthier neighbors frequently ended up by being even worse off. Since the agricultural output of most holdings would not bear the strain of prevailing high interest rates, they would be permanently ruined by such debts. The frequent warnings against suretyship found in the Book of Proverbs (for example, 6:1; 11:15; 20:16) indicate severe treatment of defaulting debtors, whereas an incident concerning a deceased husband who had incurred a moderate debt (II Kings 4) clearly reveals that the creditor had the right to exact payment from his widow in the form of labor services. This tendency must have been aggravated in the ninth century B.C.E., when the Syrian wars desolated the borders, and those smallholders who had lost their crops through the ravages of the invader (see Jeremiah 6:12) were driven to borrow at rates as high as 25 percent. Consequently, many impoverished debtors became the bonded servants of more prosperous farmers, at least for a time; and when the term of servitude was over, the only course open to them was to join the swelling ranks of landless workers and hire themselves out on the large estates.

Although there are some biblical references to annual and triennial employment contracts (for example, Isaiah 16:13; 21:16), the majority of these wage earners appear to have been hired on a day-to-day basis with little security of tenure, so that seasonal unemployment must have been considerable. Furthermore, with growing urbanization and the establishment of permanent royal courts, many of the bigger landowners were induced to live all year around in Samaria or Jerusalem, leaving the administration of their estates to professional farm managers; the upshot of such absenteeism was agricultural mismanagement and an increase in localized rural oppression.

It is not surprising, therefore, that this miserable state of a considerable segment of the peasantry should have aroused both the pity and the indignation of the eighth-century B.C.E. prophets, who rebuked the avarice of the wealthy landowners and upbraided those harsh creditors who sold their victims into virtual slavery (for example, Amos 2:6; 8:6). This prophetic campaign was not without positive results and was to culminate in a system of laws designed to protect and alleviate the rural indigent.

A whole series of statutory regulations relating to the harvested crops and noteworthy for their humanitarianism had first appeared in the Book of Deuteronomy: a tenth part of the yield of every third year was to be kept for the use of the poor (14:28); the wayfarer was entitled to pluck sufficient from the standing grain to satisfy his hunger (23:25); and any sheaf forgotten in the field was not to be retrieved but left "for the stranger, the fatherless, and the widow" (24:19).

This strongly marked humane tendency so characteristic of Deuteronomy was reinforced and carried very much further in the late priestly code. For example, the old custom of leaving the margins and corners of each field unreaped so that the hungry could benefit thereby eventually became an express grant to the poor (Leviticus 19:9). The climax in this movement was reached with the enhancement of the sabbatical year (to insure a fallow season for the land every seventh year) into a year of Jubilee, which provided that every fiftieth year all property pledged because of poverty was to be restored and that anyone who had been forced into servitude on account of debt was to be set at liberty (Leviticus 25:25-28, 39-41). There can be little doubt that these two main elements of the

Jubilee—personal emancipation and the return of mortgaged property to its hereditary owner—were intended to abolish rural poverty and to overcome the problem of a landless peasantry.

Of course, it was impossible to enforce such a utopian enactment properly; the earlier Deuteronomic legislators had displayed soberer judgment by asserting that "there will never cease to be needy ones in your land" (15:11). Nonetheless, here were the first timid gropings toward tackling a problem that has perplexed humanity down the centuries and into the era of the welfare state.

—M.A.

 ## Jewish Law Is Being Transformed from "Messianic" to "Operative"

With the modern resettlement of the land of Israel, which began approximately a century ago and culminated in the establishment, after nearly 2,000 years, of the independent Jewish State of Israel, and the mass *aliyah* that subsequently occurred, many of the laws of the Torah, which had remained dormant during the long centuries of the *Galut*, became operative once more. This is particularly evident regarding the Torah's agricultural laws, most of which apply only to the land of Israel.

The significance of these laws can be determined from the fact that of the six orders of the *Mishnah* into which the Oral Law is divided, the first, significantly called *Zeraim* ("Seeds") is, with the exception of the first tractate, Berachot, wholly devoted to these regulations. And as the land lay dormant during this period, so did the laws applying to it.

The Talmud does not differentiate between operative and nonoperative laws. For instance, it pays as much attention to the laws of the sacrifices, which also occupy a whole order, and to the laws of the Red Heifer, which is the subject of a separate tractate, as it does to the laws of the Sabbath, marriage, and other aspects of personal status and to civil law.

It was Jacob ben Asher, (1270–1340), author of the Four Turim, after which he is named the "Ba'al Ha-Turim," who for the first time distinguished between the two kinds of laws. The operative laws were called *Halachah Le-Maaseh,* "Practical Laws," and the nonoperative laws were given the Aramaic name *Hilcheta De-Meshicha,* literally, "Laws of the Messiah," i.e., laws that would only come into operation again with the coming of the Messiah and the restoration of the Jews to their land as a sovereign, independent nation living under the rule of the Torah.

Jacob ben Asher's monumental *Arba'ah Turim,* "The Four Rows," was designed to codify only the laws that applied in the circumstances of the *Galut* in which the Jews lived. Thus, whereas Maimonides, who codified both the operative and nonoperative Oral Law in his classical *Mishneh Torah,* found it necessary to divide his compendium into fourteen books, Ben Asher was able to reduce his code to only four divisions—hence its name. The four divisions are *Orach Chayyim,* the laws of daily observance, Sabbath, and festival; *Even Ha-Ezer,* laws of personal status, including marriage, divorce, legitimacy, and so on; *Yoreh Deah,* ritual law, particularly the dietary laws; and *Choshen Mishpat,* civil law. From that time onward these became the standard divisions of Jewish law.

Two centuries later Joseph Karo, after spending nearly twenty-five years writing an exhaustive commentary on the Tur, rewrote it and called his new code the *Shulhan Arukh*. However, it followed the order of the *Arba'ah Turim* chapter by chapter and clause by clause. The *Shulhan Arukh* essentially reflected the Sephardi *minhag,* so Rabbi Moses Isserles of Cracow amended and adjusted it to reflect the Ashkenazi usage wherever it differed from that of the Spanish authorities. If therefore, a law of the Torah and/or of the Talmud were not incorporated by Jacob ben Asher in his *Turim,* it is conclusive evidence that in the view of the author it did not belong to the sphere of *Halachah Le-Ma'aseh,* to practical, operative law, but rather to *Hilcheta De-Meshicha,* which would become operative only in the Messianic Age. (Incidentally, in the last chapter of his *Mishneh Torah,* Maimonides alone of all the authorities identifies the Messianic Age with the Jews achieving national independence in the Land of Israel, with the important proviso, however, that it be ruled by the Laws of the Torah.) And if Jacob Ba'al Ha-Turim omits a law in the Talmud and Joseph Karo includes it, it implies that the former believed that it had no practical application whereas the later opined that it did.

Orach Chayyim 306.11, a law codified in the *Shulhan Arukh,* states that in order to acquire land in the land of Israel from a non-Jew, it is permitted to write the deed of sale on the Sabbath. That law is explicitly stated in both the Babylonian and the Jerusalem Talmuds (Gittin 8b and T. J. Moed Katan, end of chapter 2), and the formulation of the law in the *Shulhan Arukh* is an amalgam of both these sources.

Nevertheless, the law is not included by the author of the *Turim* in chapter 306 of the Laws of Sabbath. Rabbi Jehiel Michael Epstein, author of the *Aruch Ha-Shulchan,* comments on this omission, "This omission is as though to emphasize that at the present time [i.e., when we are deprived of the land of Israel] there was no point in including it." By that very same token, the fact that Joseph Karo did include it indicates that in his time, two centuries later, circumstances had changed and that what was previously *Hilcheta De-Meshicha* had now become *Halachah Le-Ma'aseh.* What then motivated Rabbi Joseph Karo in the sixteenth century to resurrect a law that his predecessor, whose format he followed, regarded as not being operative since it belonged to all the Messianic Age, and include it in *Halachah Le-Ma'aseh,* practical law?

The answer, which has a definite topical bearing upon our position today is easily obtained. Joseph Karo (1488–1575) was among those who were expelled from Spain in 1492, the greatest calamity to befall the Jews of Europe before the Holocaust. The extent of that tragedy roused hope that it would herald the advent of the coming redemption. These hopes were heightened when, in 1516, less than a quarter of a century later, the land of Israel was conquered by Turkey. Immigrants streamed in, especially from North Africa; the communities of Jerusalem and Safed were revived. With that development came the realization of the need to redeem the soil and establish a firm practical basis of permanent settlement. This partial awakening of the land of Israel from its deep slumber—the change from the grim desperate clinging to mere vestiges of settlements to settlements of a permanent character—and the *aliyah* of the *Hasidim,* followed by that of the disciples of Elijah Gaon of Vilna, represented the turning point of "acquiring land in the Land of Israel" from non-Jews into part of *Halachah Le-Ma'aseh* in place of its former status, *Hilcheta De-Meshicha.*

When the acquisition of land became a major project, the Jewish National Fund came on the scene. Now, for the first time, land acquisition by purchase was undertaken on a national scale as part of the concerted effort by world Jewry, with the establishment of the state as its ultimate goal.

Nearly 2,000 years ago the *Midrash* pointed to an ironic paradox. Above and beyond the Jewish people's rights to the land of Israel based upon divine promise and those which accrued by conquest, there were three sites that our ancestors acquired with "hard cash": the Cave of Machpelah, the site of Shechem, and the site of the Temple. Yet, even at that time, they were barred from all three places. To a certain extent that same paradox exists today regarding these same three sites. On the other hand, however, there can be no question but that legal sale, the possession of a *kushan*, and the registry of the land in the state records constitute an inviolable claim. When Israel was established, its borders, to a great extent, were determined by the existence of Jewish settlements that, in turn, were made possible by the purchase by the Jewish National Fund of the land on which they were situated. It was this transformation of the *Hilcheta De-Meshicha* into the *Halachah Le-Ma'aseh* that made the state a reality.

—L.I.R.

 ## Second Only to the Bible: The Story of the Mishna and Its Compiler

At the end of the second century C.E., Rabbi Judah Ha-Nasi (the Patriarch) assembled and edited a compilation of Oral Law, known as *Mishna,* meaning "study." It gained immediate acceptance as the authoritative work in the field of interpreting and amplifying the contents of Scripture, including as well rabbinic enactments that particular circumstances required and that did not enjoy the ultimate authority of laws derived from interpretations of the Bible. Nowhere in the work is Rabbi Judah Ha-Nasi specified as its redactor and compiler. He is, however, universally regarded as the scholar responsible for gathering into a single text the material he believed worthy of preservation. The Mishna has retained a position of authority second only to the Bible itself.

An early account states that Rabbi Judah was born on the very day that Rabbi Akiba met a martyr's death (135 C.E.). Rabbi (as the editor Rabbi Judah Ha-Nasi is always called in the *Mishna,* in tribute to his prominence) was a descendant of Hillel. He studied under one of the distinguished teachers of his day, Rabbi Judah ben Ilai. He was a man of aristocratic bearing and spirit as well as of great affluence. He is reputed to have been on intimate terms with the Emperor Antoninus.

Rabbi Judah's compilation was the most comprehensive of its time and displaced all other similar collections. The heads of academies probably taught their students out of compilations they themselves had gathered and edited. We know, for instance, that Rabbi Akiba assembled the material available to him into a *Mishna*. The vast accumulation of material made the Rabbi's compilation necessary. The diversity of Mishnaic collections emanating from the various schools required the redaction of a text that would include the basic material and replace the variety of conflicting digests of Oral Law. From the numerous miscellaneous collections, many of them unrecorded save in the memory of devoted scholars, Rabbi Judah selected, sifted, and gathered the product of centuries of discussion and deliberation. He abbreviated, summarized, and rejected as his scholarship and editorial wisdom guided him, and he organized the laws and discussions into a systematic work.

Rabbi Judah and his associates were also moved to undertake the gigantic labor of compiling the *Mishna* by their desire to furnish a text that to some degree would function as a code by providing a norm for decisions by the sages amid the wide-ranging diversity of opinions and legal views contained in the several collections of oral law in vogue in the academies.

The *Mishna* was meant to be more than a guide for the rendering of accepted and authoritative decisions. It was meant, in the words of George Foot Moore, to be "an instrument for the study of Law, an apparatus of instruction." Hence it embodies not alone decisions but also legal principles, not alone the view of the majority that was to be followed by subsequent sages but also the minority opinion that from a strictly practical view had only academic value. Professor Louis Ginzberg (a great Talmudic authority) points out that of 523 chapters contained in the Mishna only six are free from disagreement among the authorities. The text thus provides a basis for study, for an examination of premises and conclusions, and for a comparative study of the differing views that it included. The students were to be stimulated to follow the process of reasoning used by the masters whose views are recorded in the *Mishna*.

The reasons that prompted the gigantic work that Rabbi Judah undertook in the compilation of the *Mishna* were fourfold. First, the enormous growths of oral law scattered over so many diverse collections called for a single authoritative text. Second, the desire to provide some measure of uniformity in the interpretation of the law dictated the editing of the *Mishna*. Third, there was a necessity to provide an organized text to become the basis of instruction in the academies of higher Jewish learning. Finally, there was an apprehension that a recurrence of political disturbance or oppression might endanger the survival of the Oral Law, unless it was preserved in a single authoritative collection. A gap of one generation caused by social upheaval would prove fatal to the preservation and transmission of a moral law unless it were assembled and recorded.

The *Mishna*, as it was organized by Judah Ha-Nasi, was the product not of one man or one age. Its contents are not to be regarded by any means as new and original. The *Mishna* is the culmination of the thought and teaching of the preceding generations during which the Oral Law grew and developed.

The word *Mishna* stems from a Hebrew root meaning "to learn" as a derivative of the primary meaning "to repeat," "to rehearse." Learning is achieved by a tireless process of reiteration, reexamination and recapitulation. When the term *Mishna* is used without any qualification, it refers to the work edited by Rabbi Judah Ha-Nasi. It may also mean a single paragraph or section of that work, in contrast to *Mikra*, which refers to a single verse in Scripture.

The designation *Mishna* may likewise be applied to any of the collections of earlier teachers. Thus we may speak of the *Mishna* of Rabbi Akiba or the *Mishna* of Rabbi Meir. It means the content of the teaching contained in these collections as well as the method followed. For there is an important difference between the approach of the *Mishna* and that associated with the other type of rabbinic literature known as *Midrash*. The latter attaches its elaborations and comments to a verse of Scriptures. The verse is always cited and serves as the starting point for the extended meanings that the Oral Law wove about the specific Scriptural statements.

The *Midrash* serves as a vast running commentary upon Scripture, and it attaches itself to the biblical verse whose meaning it elaborates. The *Mishna*, however, becomes, so to speak, physically independent of the text of the Bible, though in spirit and content it remains, to be sure, bound to and based upon the Torah. A verse of the Bible may be cited as proof, but a rabbinic law becomes a *Halakha* with an identity of its own, distinct from the verse. We have interpretation of the subject in the spirit of the Torah, but not necessarily associated with a specific Scriptural verse or passage. The *Mishna* is not a running commentary. It is a distinct structure of law and lore, rising upon the foundation of Torah but operating within the orbit of its own rules of interpretation, inference, and deduction. While subordinate to Scripture in authority, it is a complementary legal code, with a measure of autonomy in its own right.

The separation of the Oral Law from a necessary and direct dependence upon the actual text of Scripture permitted its development as a separate and distinct entity. The earliest teachers of the Oral Law were known as *Soferim*, "Men of the Book." The sages of the *Mishna* are called *Tannaim* (singular, *Tanna*), "repeaters," "students and teachers." The language of the *Mishna* is Hebrew though linguistic elements from Aramaic, Greek, and Latin found their way into Mishnaic Hebrew and thus testify to a significant interaction between the Jewish and other cultures. The style of the *Mishna* is compact and precise, shunning rhetorical extravagance and ornamentation. The drama of controversy is present almost throughout the *Mishna*. The clash of differing opinions and opposing interpretations enlivens even passages dealing with abstruse and technical subjects. The *Mishna* does not hesitate to venture frequently on excursions into the more attractive fields of narrative, biographical account or reminiscences, homiletical exposition, and ethical and doctrinal discussion.

The *Mishna* is divided into six main divisions called orders. In Hebrew these divisions are termed *Shisha Sedarim*, Six Orders. (The Talmud is, therefore, often called *Shass*, a word composed of the first letter of the words Shisha Sedarim.) In many synagogues of Eastern Europe there was, as there still is in some synagogues in America, a *Chevra Shass*, comprising a group of men who daily studied the text of the Talmud.

It was Rabbi Akiba who developed this arrangement in order to systematize the enormous material of the Oral Law. Each order included a number of *massechtiyot* or tractates or volumes. This Hebrew term is derived from a root meaning a weaving and corresponds to the origin of our word "text" from the stem likewise signifying weaving, as in "textile." There are in all sixty-three tractates. Each tractate is divided into chapters. Each chapter, called a *"Perek,"* is further subdivided into sections called, in the Babylonian Talmud, a *"Mishna."* A brief enumeration of the contents of each of the six orders of the Mishna suggests the wide scope of its subject matter.

I — *Zeraim* (Seeds). The eleven tractates in this division deal with laws of benedictions and prayers, laws pertaining to agriculture and fruits of the field, the Sabbatical year, tithes and offerings to the priests.

II — *Mo'ed* (Festivals). This division embraces twelve tractates devoted to the laws of Sabbath (the tractate "Shabbat" is the largest in the Mishna), the High Holy Days, Passover and the Paschal sacrifice, the Temple tax, the festival of Sukkoth, fast days, Purim, the work that may be done and that which is prohibited, the methods of observance, and so forth.

III — *Nashim* (Women). In the seven tractates of this order we have discussions centering on marriage, betrothal, divorce, levirate marriage vows, the trial of the wife suspected of unfaithfulness, and so on.

IV — *Nezikin* (Damages). This order of ten tractates deals with the phases of law that we would include under the terms civil and criminal law. We have here the laws of damages and compensation, property, trade, employer-employee relationships, real estate, inheritance, court procedures, testimony, evidence, punishment for criminal offenses, the administration of oaths, and regulations associated with the idols and pagan practices of neighboring peoples. *Nezikin* includes also the best known of the tractates of the Talmud, that of *Abot*, the "Ethics of the Fathers." This famous volume, frequently incorporated in its entirety in the prayer book, demonstrates the continuity of the Oral Law with the Law of Moses and cites ethical maxims by many of the teachers of the *Mishna*.

V — *Kodashim* (Sacred Things). The eleven tractates in this division largely treat of the laws related to the Temple and its sacrificial cult. Animal sacrifice, meal offerings, proper method of slaughtering the animals, the firstborn of man and animals, pledges and the profanation of sacred things, Temple furnishings and practices are the chief subjects dealt with in *Kodashim*.

VI — *Tohorot* (Purfications). We have in the twelve tractates of this order a treatment of vessels that are rendered ritually impure, such impurity being caused by contact with, or proximity to, a dead body. The order deals with the uncleanness of leprosy, methods of purification, the menstrual impurity of women, and with the impurity of those who are afflicted with unclean issue from their body.

Explicit Scriptural ordinances were not the only source for the vast legislation that is to be found in the *Mishna*. Practices long in vogue, oral traditions, inferences and deductions from Biblical verses, and regulations derived by a unique system of interpretation—all became part of the Oral Law, and all were regarded as invested with unquestioned authority.

The *Mishna* was not intended to be a one-purpose work. Meant to be a text for the students in the academies, it was also to serve as a guide for the teachers who were called upon to render decision in controversy and inform the people as to correct practice. Unmistakable signs are found in the *Mishna*, despite the fact that it unfailingly records both sides where there is a difference of view, as to which view is preferred and to be regarded as authoritative. Opinions that are offered anonymously, without mentioning the name of the teacher who held them, are to be accepted as the norm of practice or principle to be followed. Where an opinion is attributed to one sage, but the opposing view is introduced by the phrase "but the sages say" or "in the view of the sages," the latter interpretation is the one to be adhered to in practice.

The *Mishna* thus served an immediate purpose in establishing a basis for greater uniformity in practice. Yet there is much material in the *Mishna* that was already academic at the time Rabbi Judah issued it. The loss of political independence and the destruction of the Temple rendered inoperative that large part of the *Mishna* that deals with Temple ritual and sacrifices. It did not occur to the sages to eliminate such material from a work that addressed itself, among other aims, to a most practical goal. The ultimate basis of the Oral Law was Scripture, and its enactments and regulations are informed, it was believed, by a timelessness that their divine origin conferred upon them. The eternal cannot be upset or dissolved by the upheavals and the configuration of events and circumstances that take place on the more limited stage of human affairs. To eliminate these laws would be to refute the very theory from which the interpretations of the rabbis derived their authority.

But the reason that prompted the inclusion of such laws was not merely doctrinal. The rabbis did not regard these laws as purely academic and unrelated to life. Rooted in their world view was a firm belief in the restoration of the Temple, the sacrificial cult, and political independence. The laws of sacrifice and of criminal law were as carefully and devotedly studied as the laws of Sabbath observance, dietary disciplines, and the recitation of prayers. So compelling was the hope that all through the centuries in academies everywhere, in North Africa, Spain, Eastern Europe, students regarded the laws of sacrifices, criminal procedure, purifications, priestly ritual, as belonging properly to the category of relevant and indispensable knowledge that the faithful Jew should master.

Kindred to the *Mishna* edited by Rabbi Judah Ha-Nasi is a work known as *Tosefta*. The term means "Supplement," and it includes sections of earlier collections of Oral Law as well as material that did not find its way into the authoritative work of Rabbi Judah. Subsequent additions, originating after the death of the editor of the *Mishna*, are likewise included in the *Tosefta*.

Like the *Mishna*, the *Tosefta* is divided into tractates, though the organization of the subjects varies from that of the primary work. Isolated passages that became disassociated from the collections that had been lost and were not ingathered by the Mishna are known as *Baraitot*, meaning "external to" or "outside of." They are sometimes cited by later authorities in the discussions that developed about the *Mishna*. Thus, although Rabbi Judah Ha-Nasi's text did not embrace all the available material, it is the supreme work of the Oral Law, exerting an incalculable influence on its subsequent development.

—M.Ad.

V
Holidays, Festivals, Weddings: Now and Then

Shavuoth Services in Newport, R.I., May 28, 1773

Pentecost. Went to the Synagogue at ix h[ours] A.M. At reading the Law the Rabbi [Haijm Isaac Karigal of Hebron] was desired and read the Ten Commandments. But before reading the Law and the Prophets, the Rabbi went to the Desk or Taubauh and preached a Sermon about 47 minutes long in Spanish. It was interspersed with Hebrew. His Oratory, Elocution, and Gestures were fine and oriental. It was very animated. He exhorted them not to perplex themselves with Traditions and Criticisms, but to attend to certain capital points and principal points of Religion—he expatiated upon the Miseries and Calamities of their Nation in their present Captivity and Dispersion and comforted them under their Tribulations by the assured Prospect of the Messiahs Kingdom—he exhorted them not to be discouraged but persevere &c—he showed that Calamities and sufferings were not Evidence of their being forsaken of God—that Adversity and Judgments were the common Lot of all Nations, Kingdoms and Countries—and instanced in the Desolation made by the Eruption of Mt. Vesuvius near Naples in Italy which he said he had seen, and beheld the Deluge of liquid Matter, flowing and carrying all before it, overwhelming Villages, Houses, Temples, people &c—yet Christians did not consider this as an Evidence against their Religion; neither was the Destruction of the Temple and the City of Jerusalem by the Romans &c any argument against the Truth of the Jewish Religion. They were chastised for their Sins, but not forsaken of God, who was the common Parent of all mankind, while he had chosen Israel his peculiar Treasure. Then he enlarged with Fervor on the Divine Benevolence and seemed to be elevated with very sublime Ideas of the divine Benevolence, Mercy and Love; which he converted into an argument for their loving one another, which he earnestly pressed upon them—and closed with a serious Prayer. The Affinity of the Spanish and Latin enabled me to understand something of the Discourse—but after all I have but an imperfect Idea of it. He wore Spectacles thro' the whole Sermon, and frequently looked down on the Desk before him as if he had the Discourse written, but I don't know that he had any Writing. The Jews intend to print it. He was dressed in his Fur Cap, scarlet Robe, green silk Damask Vest, and a chintz under Vest—girt with a Sash or Turkish Girdle—besides the *Alb.* with *Tzizith.* The Jews don't admire his reading [the X Commandments], and indeed he speaks off with much greater Fluency and Ease than he reads, tho' he reads correctly. There was Dignity and Authority about him mixt [*sic*] with Modesty. After the Sermon, two Rolls of the Law were brought forward with great Solemnity, and after Elevation the *parasang* [*parashat*], including the XXth Chapter of Genesis [*sic*], was read as usual: at reading the X Commandments the whole Congregation rose up and stood. After which Mr. Rivera's little son 8 or 9 aet. read the first Chapter of Ezekiel—then prayers for all Nations, for the Jews, for the King and royal Family, for the Magistrates of Rhode Island.—The Law was then returned in solemn procession singing the usual Psalm; then Alms, Prayers and Singing concluded the Whole. The Synagogue was decorated with Flowers &c. About the Time the Rabbi began sermon which was a few minutes before x h[ours] three of the Commissioners came in, viz. Governor Wanton & Judge Oliver and afterwards Judge Auchmuty and were seated in the Seat of the Parnass or President of the Synagogue. The whole service ended a quarter after twelve.

—E.S.

 Civil War Seder

In the commencement of the war in 1861, I enlisted from Cleveland, Ohio, in the Union cause and became attached to the 23rd Regiment, one of the first sent from the Buckeye State.

Our destination was West Virginia. We encountered on the 10th of September, 1861, at Carnifax Ferry, the forces under the rebel General Floyd and were ordered to take up our position at the foot of Sewen Mountain. We remained there until we marched to the village of Fayette, to take it and establish there our winter quarters, having again routed General Floyd and his forces.

While lying there our camp duties were not of an arduous character, and being apprised of the approaching Festival of Passover, twenty of my comrades and coreligionists belonging to the Regiment, united in a request to our commanding officer for relief from duty, in order that we might keep the holy days, which he readily acceded to.

The first point was gained and, as the Paymaster had lately visited the Regiment, he had left us plenty of greenbacks. Our next business was to find some suitable person to proceed to Cincinnati, Ohio, to buy us *matzos*. Our sutler, being a coreligionist, and going home to that city, readily undertook to send them.

We were anxiously awaiting to receive our matzos, and about the middle of the morning of *Erev Pesach* a supply train arrived in camp, and to our delight seven barrels of *matzos*. On opening them we were surprised and pleased to find that our thoughtful sutler had enclosed two Hagodahs and prayer books. We were now able to keep the Seder nights, if we could only obtain the other requisites for that occasion. We had a consultation and decided to send parties to forage in the country while a party stayed to build a log hut for the services. About the middle of the afternoon, the foragers arrived, having been quite successful. We obtained two kegs of cider, a lamb, several chickens, and some eggs. Horseradish or parsley we could not obtain, but in lieu we found a weed, whose bitterness, I apprehended, exceeded anything our forefathers "enjoyed."

We were still in a great quandary. We had the lamb, but did not know what part was to represent it at the table; but Yankee ingenuity prevailed, and it was decided to cook the whole and put it on the table, then we could dine off it, and be sure we had the right part. The necessaries for the *charoses* we could not obtain, so we got a brick which, rather hard to digest, reminded us, by looking at it, for what purposes it was intended.

At dark we had all prepared, and were ready to commence the service. There being no *chazan* present, I was selected to read the services, which I commenced by asking the blessing of the Almighty on the food before us, and to preserve our lives from danger. The ceremonies were passing off very nicely, until we arrived at the part where the bitter herb was to be taken. We all had a large portion of the herb ready to eat at the moment I said the blessing; each eats his portion when, horrors! what a scene ensued in our little congregation, it is impossible for my pen to describe. The herb was very bitter and very fiery like Cayenne pepper, and excited our thirst to such a degree, that we forgot the law authorizing us to drink only four cups, and the consequence was that we drank up all the cider. Those that drank the more freely, became excited, and one thought he was Moses, another Aaron, and one had the audacity to call himself a Pharaoh. The consequence was a skirmish, with no one hurt, only Moses, Aaron, and Pharaoh had to be carried to the camp, and there left in the arms of Morpheus. This slight incident did not take away our appetite, and, after doing justice to our lamb, chickens and eggs, we resumed the second portion of the service without anything occurring worthy of note.

There, in the wild woods of West Virginia, away from home and friends, we consecrated and offered up to the ever-loving God of Israel our prayers and sacrifice. I doubt whether the spirits of our forefathers, had they been looking down on us, standing there with our arms by our sides ready for an attack, faithful to our God and our cause, would have imagined themselves among mortals, enacting this commemoration of the scene that transpired in Egypt.

Since then a number of my comrades have fallen in battle in defending the flag they volunteered to protect with their lives. I have myself received a number of wounds, all but mortal, but there is no occasion in my life that gives me more pleasure and satisfaction than when I remember the celebration of Passover of 1862.

—J.A.J.

 ## Holy Days in the Holy City

The year is 1908. The suffering and despair that were the lot of East European Jewry moved Rahel Yanait Ben-Zvi, along with other daring and inspired young men and women, to revolt against life in exile. They came home to the land of their fathers, determined to revive both country and people by their work on the soil.

The following is a moving account of her first High Holy Days in Palestine. The Avner mentioned in her story was the political alias of Itzhak Ben-Zvi, Rahel's husband and later the President of Israel.

The High Holy Days approached. The chants of *Selihot* prayers rose all around us in the nights. The poor quarters glowed with a second and sublimer soul. Jerusalem wore its holiday face.

The eve of the New Year. Everyone grew ready for the great day. At sundown we went out, looking into synagogues through the iron grates of the windows. Voices rose in prayer in the traditional chant. We went from one synagogue to the next, standing outside and listening. Somehow we did not dare to enter, perhaps because we did not have holiday clothes. I was melancholy and Avner's face was covered with sadness. Was this nostalgia for the tradition of our childhood days?

The next morning we rose early and made our way to the Old City. We went down the steps of the Street of David. The covered marketplace was bustling and noisy as always. The narrow lanes smelled of fruit and vegetables, fresh and rotten. Crowds of *fellahin* and Bedouin, with their overladen asses, jostled the Jews in their holiday finery: Ashkenazim in black silk *kapotes* or colorful velvet robes with hair *streimels* on their heads, Sephardim in their many-colored gowns. All of them had the same expression on their faces—the look of sanctity. As if walking in some higher sphere, they passed by the traders and hurried to the synagogue, to the Wall. We, too, hastened.

Stooping, we passed under the low arch and came into the courtyard of the Hurva Synagogue of Rabbi Yehuda the Pious. I tried to follow Joseph and Avner inside, but the angry looks of the gatekeeper warned me off. With a wave of his hand he directed me to the women's gallery, and I climbed the narrow wooden staircase. I was later to become better acquainted with this courtyard—in the days of Hagana. I climbed hesitantly and sat myself near the door. There were many women at prayer. I could almost have been back in my hometown synagogue. Here were the same spotlessly white silk kerchiefs on the women's heads, the mothers and the grandmothers grasping the familiar prayer book. I peered through the partition which separated the women's gallery from the men praying below. The chant was exactly like that of my old home. When the Reading of the Law was reached, I saw that Avner and Joseph were making their way out, and I hurried down the steps to join them.

Opposite the Hurva towered the minaret of a mosque. There the muezzin summoned the faithful to prayer. His call rang out as if in challenge to the sounds of Hebrew prayer. We moved on to the synagogue of the Karaites in a nearby courtyard paved with smooth stones. The ceiling was low and domed, and the two barred windows looked out to an inner court. The building was shabby and dilapidated, but in the corners of the yard geraniums grew and ivy clung to the wall. This New Year day was no festival for the Karaites, whose calendar differed from that of other Jews. I was depressed by the workday atmosphere and by the breach between us and these brothers of ours. This Karaite synagogue contained a treasure: a *Keter Torah*, one of the most ancient bound manuscripts of the Bible. Avner bent over it. Every word, every phrase excited his attention. Years later, in 1957, he was to bring it back to Israel from exile.

In low spirits we left the Karaites and went on to the Sephardic Synagogue of Rabbi Yohanan Ben-Zaccai. A few steps led down into a dimly lit hall which echoes to the sounds of prayer. I had never heard the Sephardi ritual before. The worshippers were seated on low, narrow benches covered with straw mats, and they held sprigs of fragrant herbs. A mystic emotion welled up in me. Here we stood at the very source of Hebrew melody. This was the atmosphere I was looking for with all my heart in Jerusalem. We sat there entranced by the prayers, then wandered from room to room, the dimness accentuating the sense of antiquity.

Avner turned to the hall at the bottom of the court. I followed him and stood by the door. The strains of a familiar psalm floated up to us: "From the depths I called upon thee, O Lord." I remembered it from childhood, from the time before I knew the meaning of the words. The cry seemed to be directed to us, perplexed as we were, striving for guidance in our land.

On the Day of Atonement we went once again to the Synagogue of Yohanan Ben-Zaccai. Our excitement mounted higher and higher towards noon, when we reached the *Avoda* prayer of ancient Temple times, describing the high priest's part in the Atonement service. It was a melody full of poignant longing. An unbelievable tremor flowed through the congregation when the cantor intoned: "And they who stood in the gallery . . . bent and bowed down . . . and so would he count . . ." At that moment I seemed to be in the gallery of the Temple. This wonderful chant must have come directly from the Levites who were saved from the burning sanctuary and fled to the mountain fastnesses of Galilee, there to build their famous synagogues. From them it must have gone down, generation after generation, to our brethren, the Sephardim.

It exists in all the Oriental communities—among the Kurds, the Persians, the Turks. They all sing the same chant of the *Avoda*, which I treasure in my heart with the Ashkenazi *Kol Nidre* of my youth.

On the way out of the synagogue of Yohanan Ben-Zaccai I saw women squatting outside on the pavement, near the barred, ground-level windows. The panes were broken. And this was supposed to be the women's gallery! I was sorry for my sisters.

One day after the New Year we visited Bethel of the Kabbalists. In a twist of a tortuous alley which led to Maidan Road in the Old City nestled this house of prayer in a garret, apart from the other synagogues. We climbed the narrow wooden steps, which seemed to be hanging in the air. The door opened onto Bethel—a spacious hall with open windows and gleaming white walls. Two men were praying at opposite sides of the room, each one in his own world. One was young, tall and pale, his face turned to the Wailing Wall, his fingers quivering. The other was an old man bent over a thick tome, leatherbound and dog-eared. Neither paid any attention to us. We sat in silence near the door, a prayer in our hearts. My downcast eyes strayed to the face of the young man. "The One, the One," he whispered fervently in his prayer. He seemed to be in a trance.

The Kabbalists filed in for the midnight prayers. They were mostly old men, but there was something ageless in their bearing, as if they had tasted of eternity.

—R.Y.B.-Z.

 ## Hanukkah in a Monastery

In the hard winter of 1940 I was seventeen years old. In my home town in Poland, there was no coal for us Jews of the ghetto. Day after day, I would rise early in the morning to queue up at one of the coal dealers, waiting patiently for my turn. The Germans and the Poles were given theirs first; by the time I reached the gate there was never anything left.

One day as I was returning from hours of waiting in the coal line, I took a different route home. The temperature was far below zero, and biting winds blew in my face. Passing a little monastery, I decided to enter and thaw my half-frozen limbs. A kindly monk asked me whether I wanted food. When I nodded, he motioned me to follow him. He led me through a long dark corridor and into a pig shed. He asked me to wait there and promised to return soon with some hot soup.

As I looked around, I envied the pigs, obviously well fed and not the least concerned about the German soldiers. If I had prayed at that moment, I would have asked God to change me into a pig. For them there was no queueing up. They had an abundance of food and no forced labor. They had no fear for tomorrow. They knew nothing about frustration.

The monk returned with a steaming pot of potato soup. I squatted on the floor, and my nostrils were filled with the odors of hot potatoes and onions, as well as the smells of the pigsty. When I finished my soup, the monk handed me a small piece of bread. I broke it into little pieces and used it to wipe out every last bit of the potatoes. Then I licked the spoon until it was completely dry. My hunger was

only half quelled, for I had not had a good meal in days. I thanked my newly found friend and asked him if there was any work for me on the premises. He hesitated. Finally he said that if I didn't mind sleeping with the pigs, I could stay awhile, doing odd jobs around the place—but on one condition, that I never go beyond the monastery gate.

I agreed.

I immediately started on my job, which consisted, among other things, of tending the ovens, cleaning the kitchen, and catering to the needs of the pigs.

I was happy in my new home. Every day I got to know the pigs better and found them to be more merciful than some of the people of the outside world. I did not mind their filth too much, for, after all, they were pigs.

From time to time I would be called away from my routine work and asked to substitute for one of the altar boys inside the chapel of St. Martin. I enjoyed this new status, but it made me feel ill at ease. I felt somewhat hypocritical, as a Jewish boy, carrying a big portrait of the Madonna and standing on the altar together with the faithful. At times my lips would mumble a Hebrew prayer while the brethren carried on the mass. As December approached, I became more restless then ever. Memories of home and the festival of Hanukkah at Grandmother's house flooded my heart. I could not help remembering Grandfather shining the brass *menorah* and all the grandchildren preparing the wicks. I remembered the sweet smell of Grandmother's pancakes and of the Palestinian olive oil used for frying them as well as for use in the *menorah*.

My restlessness became unbearable as the melodies of the Hanukkah holiday kept returning to my mind. The hum of them was without interruption. It was as if my phonograph of memories had gone mad and I did not know how to turn it off.

If I could only do something to chase these melodies away! I was sure that, if I could only light one candle and recite the blessing over it, the melodies and memories would disappear.

In the little monastery chapel hundreds of candles were lit every day, and here I was with not even one candle to light on the first night of Hanukkah.

From time to time, as I passed through the semidarkened nave of the chapel and noticed a candle that had been snuffed out, I wanted to take it, hide it in my pocket, but how could I? These candles were designated for St. Martin, St. Barbara, St. Joseph, and the Madonna. Certainly their donors had not brought them to be used for a Jewish festival.

One evening as I was turning off the lights and snuffing out the few burning candles, I noticed a mass of wax that had been dripping down on the floor from one of the small side altars. Aware that this would never be used again, I carefully scratched it off the floor and hid it in my pocket. I returned to my adobe, lay down, and tried to sleep. Exhausted as I was from a full day's work, sleep would not come.

Sure, you have the wax. You could even make your own candle, but where where would you light it?

It was past midnight when I fell asleep. I dreamt about Grandfather shining the old brass *menorah*. When he finished, he called on me. I was very small, and he pinched me on my cheek and said, "Tonight you light the first candle." Then I awoke and found myself still in the pigsty. At first I wanted to cry, but then I decided I was too old for that. Instead I started to search for a place where I could light my candle.

One of the smaller buildings used as dormitories for the monks had a trapdoor that led into a small attic. It was a hole used by the chimney sweep. After a lot of perilous climbing on lintels and woodwork, I made my way up through that opening. I felt my way in the darkness and found nothing but dust and gravel. In the darkness my fingers felt the outline of a chimney. I felt it from top to bottom. Where the chimney narrowed, there was on each side a little ledge, half a brick in width, and I took out my wax and began to knead it. I tore off one of the fringes of my prayer shawl and placed it in the center of the wax. When I finished rolling it, I lit the candle and placed it on the ledge.

My heart was bursting with joy as, in a barely audible voice, I chanted the *Maoz Tsur*. For a moment I thought I felt my Grandfather's pinch on my cheek. Happy memories filled my heart. The walls of the cloister disappeared. The cold, hunger, and misery of daily life vanished. Once again I was part of a link in the long chain of the tradition of Judaism. Not even a squeak at the trapdoor turned me aside from the burning taper.

Not until I felt a bony hand on my shoulder did I realize where I was.

It was the hand of Peter, a lay brother in the monastery. I had never liked Peter. I never trusted him. From the way he had eyed me, I had constantly feared he would turn me over to the Nazis.

Come on, why don't you say it?

Yes, I am a Jew. I have been hiding here, serving as an altar boy, eating your food, and enjoying your hospitality. Go ahead, why don't you call the Gestapo? I don't care anymore.

Peter's eyes moistened. Silently he stood there. After endless agonizing seconds, he said, "Let us sing together, '*Maoz Tsur*.'"

He actually knew the Hebrew words and melody. We continued together.

The two shadows on the wall merged into one.

—I.Ne.

 ## The Purim Mysteries

Almost everything about the story of Purim has been doubted. There are distinguished students of the Bible who assert that the events narrated in the story of Esther never happened, that the characters there mentioned never existed—not Esther nor Mordecai nor Haman nor Vashti—that the story is merely a story and that the holiday was not Jewish in origin.

None of the names mentioned in the Scroll of Esther has been found in any of the records of inscriptions of Persia. Of course, the available information about ancient Persia is rather meager. Most of the documents and tablets of that period were destroyed in the course of the many wars that were fought in that part of the world.

Nonetheless, many scholars argue, some mention of the event or of the people connected with it might have been found. The fact that not a trace of the Purim story exists is highly damaging evidence. The origin of the Jewish festival must, they believe, be sought elsewhere than in the story itself.

The Esther story, in addition to lacking external corroboration, also presents certain internal difficulties. Neither Mordecai nor Esther are Jewish names. The former derives from the god Marduk and the latter from the goddess Ishtar. At the same time, the story contains not a single mention of the name of God. It is apparently a secular story from beginning to end; the miraculous deliverance is achieved by purely human means; the revenge taken by the Jews and the rewards granted to Mordecai are equally human. Finally, certain differences exist between the story of Esther as told in the Bible and the same story in the Greek translation known as the Septuagint. The very name of the day is different, the Septuagint calling it *Fruria* and omitting the verses that speak of the casting of lots, whence the name Purim is derived.

Almost every Bible scholar during the past century has tried his hand at solving these seeming mysteries of the Book of Esther. They sought the solution in Jewish history and in non-Jewish history, among the stories of the ancient gods and among the literatures of Palestine's pagan neighbors.

Heinrich Graetz, the noted Jewish historian, argued that the story was mostly invention. It had been written, he held, at the time of the Maccabean revolt against Antiochus of Syria, to fortify the spirit of the Jews in that hour of crisis by showing that God does not abandon His people.

Other critics displayed even more remarkable ingenuity in finding parallels, references, and novel clues to the identification of the story's original motive, form, time, and place. A recent theory by Dr. Julius Lewy traces the story to the transformation of a pagan myth into the Jewish holiday.

The fact remains that the earliest mention of the feast of Purim dates from only the second century B.C.E. This time element is important. Judah the Maccabee won his great victory over the Syrian general Nicanor on the thirteenth of Adar in the year 161, and that day was declared a holiday. This would never have been done had the Fast of Esther, which traditionally falls on that day, already been commonly observed. At least in Palestine, Purim was evidently not yet universally acknowledged, although the Purim day itself, under the name of "the Day of Mordecai," was known.

The festival grew more important with every passing generation. Purim was generally observed in Palestine some time before the destruction of the Second Temple. Priests officiating at the Temple service were required to leave their sacrificial duties and listen to the reading of the Scroll.

About the middle of the second century of the common era, the famous Rabbi Meir is known to have followed the strict rules that had already become accepted regarding the reading of the Scroll of Esther. A regulation from that period reflects the joyful attitude prevalent at the Purim season. Nevertheless, the rabbis of that age still remembered the doubts that their predecessors had expressed about considering the Scroll as sacred as other portions of the Holy Writings.

Does all this lend countenance to the theory of the story's foreign origin and to the assumption that it has no historical foundation? Many traditionalist Jewish and Christian scholars have denied this and attempted to defend the historicity of the book.

After all the erudite deductions have been considered, the simple, unadorned story that the Bible tells still seems the most reasonable and credible. This was not the only time in the eventful history of the Jews when an enemy plotted their destruction and all but succeeded in his plans; nor was this the only time when petty, purely human motives operated both against them and in their favor. The very fact that their deliverance is not attributed to God speaks for the credibility of the story as an actual, historical event.

The story was told in Susa and spread to other parts of the empire, until it eventually reached Palestine. The dark days of Syrian persecution, during the pre-Maccabean period, afforded a favorable atmosphere for its spread. It soon became popular because it proved that, in the last moment, God intervenes to save His people and that He does so through human instruments. This actually happened in the case of the Maccabees. The subsequent loss of Jewish independence to Rome heightened the hopes for a human deliverer and thereby increased the popularity of the story of Esther. The Jew who lived in the midst of pagans, such as those of Egypt, Syria, and Asia Minor, had an even more immediate reason for finding the story interesting. There was considerable anti-Jewish feeling in these countries. It was comforting for the Jews to cite an instance—as a source of edification to themselves and a warning to their neighbors—when a pagan enemy was so thoroughly discomfited.

The fourteenth of Adar coincided with a holiday period in the pagan calendar in western Asia. Haman may deliberately have chosen a holiday of this sort for the execution of his plans. The merrymaking, half-inebriated rabble could the more easily be aroused to join in the slaughter of innocent people, especially if the latter were unprotected by the authorities and if loot were in prospect. Quite possibly, some Jews had participated in the fun and gift-giving of the pagan holiday before the Haman incident. With the example of Christmas and New Year festivities before us now, we can readily understand why the Jews of that day imitated their neighbors. They justified their actions after the incident by pointing to the request included in the Book of Esther that her and Mordecai's victory be commemorated by rejoicing, exchanging of gifts, and the giving of portions to the poor—the last probably a purely Jewish addition.

One may well imagine that the religious leaders of the Jewish people in Palestine did not like the growing popularity of the new holiday. They could not easily resign themselves to approving a book in which eating and drinking were encouraged, but the name of God was not mentioned. Nevertheless, there was no gainsaying the popular will. In time, the religious guides of the people yielded. They accepted the book into the Holy Writings, made its reading obligatory, and made gift-giving part of the celebration.

For a long time, variations in the observance continued to exist. It is possible that in some Greek-speaking countries the book was read in Greek rather than in Hebrew. For some generations, there was uncertainty about the time of reading, whether at night, in the morning, or both. The latest addition to the observance was the introduction of the Fast of Esther, on the day preceding Purim, which is not mentioned until Gaonic times, that is, after the seventh century. The "beating of Haman" was probably an early feature of the reading of the Scroll in public. It may have been taken over from the pagan festivities, when the communal fool was crowned king for a day. Hanging Haman in effigy soon turned into a popular sport and on several occasions brought trouble to a Jewish community. Miracle plays were introduced later, as were also the Purim se'udah (feast), and haman-tashen.

The frequent bitterness of life in unfriendly Diaspora lands made Purim increasingly meaningful to the Jewish people. Very early, they broadened its application and gave it universal meaning by connecting it with God's vow, as expressed in Exodus 17:14–16, to destroy Amalek, the prototype of cowardice and evil. It is, therefore, easy to understand why a rabbi many centuries ago, declared that even after the arrival of the Messiah, Purim would survive as a holiday to be observed by all mankind.

—S.G.

 ## The Dancing Jews of Brooklyn: A Simhat Torah Tableau

"The world is full of enormous lights and mysteries, and man shuts them from himself with one small hand," said Israel ben Eliezer Baal-Shem Tov ("Master of the Good Name"), who founded Hasidism in the Ukraine in the eighteenth century.

The Hasidim try to keep themselves open to all lights and mysteries, and they worship with a wholeness of body and spirit that leads them on *Simhat* Torah and many other occasions to sing and dance with a contagious abandon.

Since the years of gas chambers and concentration camps, the largest centers of Hasidism have been in Israel and in Brooklyn.

On the eve of *Simhat* Torah, I went first to the meeting place of the Modzitzer movement in the middle-class Crown Heights section of Brooklyn.

Each Hasidic group is part of a separate dynasty that goes back to a founding *rebbe* in Eastern Europe. The *rebbes* who began the various dynasties traced their antecedents to Baal-Shem Tov or one of his disciples.

The *rebbe,* who may or may not be an ordained rabbi, is considered by his followers to be an unusually noble *tzaddik* (pious man), and especially in Eastern Europe he was believed to work miracles.

The Modzitzer rebbes first established their courts in the province of Lublin, Poland, in the middle of the nineteenth century and remained in Eastern Europe until 1940.

The members of the Modzitzer community in Brooklyn are younger on the average than the other Hasidic groups, and their spirits began to rise quite early in the evening.

Applying themselves to their duty to be happy that Saturday night, they drank beer and wine, joked before the ceremony began, and even laughed freely at a mock sermon.

"This is the only time of the year," a Hasid explained hastily, "when we can have fun with the prayers."

Like all Orthodox Jews, the Hasidic men pray separately from the women, and women do not take part in Hasidic dancing.

On a joyful holiday like *Simhat* Torah, however, the children are everywhere, running and playing about the main room.

When the dancing started, boys and girls were lifted on shoulders and became part of the simple dances, which quickly generated such powerful rhythmic momentum that the floor shook.

Most of the melodies that set off the dancing are easily learned and infectiously lyrical. Many are without words, on the principle that union with God may be blocked or distorted by the interference of words.

A leader initiates the songs during the official prayers, but at other times during the night a Hasid anywhere in the room may start a song, others pick it up, and another round of song and dance has begun.

Hasidim who aren't dancing bang out the time with jubilant force on a desk or chair. I heard no other musical instruments. The harmonies that embellish the simple songs are improvised, since most of the worshipers are untrained musically but have acquired a keen ear for group singing through enthusiastic practice. At the Modzitzer and most other Hasidic celebrations, the music on this night is joyous and hopeful in contrast to the plaintive crying of much traditional synagogue music.

Music is essential to all Hasidic communities, but the Modzitzer movement has become particularly known for the vitality of its *niggunim* (songs).

Unlike many Hasidic rebbes, the heads of the Modzitzer composed their own tunes. Unable to write music, they transmitted their composition orally, and at least half have been lost.

Rabbi Saul Taub composed more than seven hundred *niggunim* before his death in 1947 and is considered to have been the most musically creative of the recent heads of the dynasty.

Modzitzer melodies have been taken over by several other Hasidic groups, but only recently have collections of them been recorded.

At one point early in the evening, a new arrival at the Modzitzer gathering told me that the Lubavitcher *Rebbe*, head of one of the largest of all Hasidic communities, would sing a new *niggun* of his own composition at about four in the morning, an event of singular importance to members of his group, because of the great pride Hasidim take in the accomplishments of their leaders. The Modzitzer people keep asking their own *rebbe* in Tel Aviv for new songs, and from time to time he sends them tape recordings.

The dancing resumed as the traditional seven circuits of the reader's desk (*hakkaphot*) were made again. At the beginning of each circuit, men of the congregation—and later, boys—were honored by being asked to carry the Torahs during the dance. The jubilation was accented by shouts and the clapping of hands with the hands rising higher and higher as the men lost themselves in the intoxicating rhythms.

Some, with white prayer shawls over their heads, seemed close to a trance. I suddenly found myself recruited into a swaying circle as a Hasid said with a grin, "All Jews are brothers," and I soon found it impossible not to yield to the swing of the melodies and the open pleasure everyone was taking in one another's company and in his own high spirits.

Hasidic melodies were rarely written down until the turn of the century. Before then it was considered "goyish" to write down the music.

There may now be two or three thousand Hasidic songs on paper but no definitive large-scale collection of them has appeared thus far.

Several Hasidim joined in the story, possibly apocryphal, of the Hasidic *rebbe* who always danced when the cantor sang a certain traditional hymn during the Friday-night services.

The cantor, however, had grown increasingly impatient at the time it took him to teach the songs by ear, and he decided to learn to read and write music.

After some months of study, he arrived one Friday night with a group of songs neatly notated. That evening the *rebbe* didn't dance.

Both the cantor and the *rebbe* were troubled, and the only explanation the rebbe could conceive was that a sin had been committed.

"All I've done," said the baffled cantor, "has been to learn to write music."

"Ah," said the rebbe, "that is the sin."

The powerful Lubavitcher movement, though no less enthusiastic about singing and dancing (on previous *Simhat* Torahs they danced in the streets of Brooklyn), is at the opposite end of the scale from the small Modzitzer unit, which is essentially a family group that has picked up several score adherents in Brooklyn.

The Lubavitcher movement, in contrast, has an active publication society; branches throughout the world, including Russia and North Africa; and an extensive network of schools with thousands of pupils in America, Israel, Europe, and North Africa.

The best organized of all Hasidic communities, the Lubavitcher movement gives economic aid to its members and even sends young students out on "Torah Missions" throughout the country to convert, not the Gentiles, but Jews who have fallen away from Orthodoxy.

The dynasty was founded in Ladi, White Russia, in the eighteenth century. The present *rebbe*, Menachem Mendel Schneerson, is on his father's side the seventh in direct line to the founder and is the son-in-law of the previous *rebbe*. He had been studying electrical engineering in Paris when the call came to head the movement, and it took him two years to decide that being a *rebbe* was indeed his vocation.

It was well past midnight on *Simhat* Torah when I arrived at the huge *sukkah* of the Lubavitcher. *Simhat* Torah comes at the end of the harvest festival of *Sukkoth,* and during that time, the Orthodox Jew takes his meals in the *sukkah.*

The singing and dancing, which would take place elsewhere, had not yet started. Hundreds of men, most of them bearded, were seated and standing, listening to the rebbe, who had been talking in Yiddish for some two hours and was expected to go on for at least another hour or two.

He was "saying Torah," talking about the religious aspects of the holiday, meanings that were deeper than the ritual, and other subjects from Jewish law and life germane to the occasion.

The *rebbe* had no written notes and was improvising in a soft, conversational voice. He was at the center of the table, his own beard streaked with gray, and wearing his authority with ease and gentleness.

At the synagogue of the Bobover Hasidim, also in Crown Heights, the singing and dancing had started a couple of hours before. Again, most of the men were bearded; and here—unlike among the Modzitzer and the Lubavitcher—many had round fur hats, some made of mink (the *shtraimel*).

The hats had been worn by many Jews in Eastern Europe and purportedly were copied from those used by Polish landowners as a symbol of status, although another theory holds they were first worn in Spain as a special designation of Jews.

At the Bobover celebration, as at other Hasidic places of worship, many men also wore handsome black holiday coats with black silken cords (*gartels*) around the waist to make the distinction between the "higher" and "lower" spheres. Although it was late, many small boys moved around the floor or sat high along the wall, watching the singing and dancing.

The custom of the Bobover *rebbe,* who came to Brooklyn after the war, was to perform the first dance of each of the seven circuits by himself.

After singing a passage of prayer, he placed his prayer shawl over his head, then, weaving, danced in a narrow rectangle that the pressing crowd cleared for him. His dance was both of measured control and an almost glowing inner intensity.

At about two in the morning I came to the Williamsburg section of Brooklyn. Many of the most Orthodox and poor Hasidim live in Williamsburg, and the synagogue that we entered—with simple murals of Jerusalem on the walls—was that of the Sattmar *rebbe*, whose dynasty had begun in Hungary and who had also come to Brooklyn after the Second World War.

Here nearly all the men were bearded and wore fur hats. Many also had long ear curls (*peyos*). The Lubavitcher, by contrast, wear trimmed beards and avoid most of what one of their members calls the older "externals" of Hasidism.

The Hasidim, even more than Orthodox Jews in general, stay within their own community and usually marry among themselves.

Of all the Hasidic communities in Brooklyn, those of Williamsburg are probably the most insular. Some can also be fiercely militant if they feel outside secular authority is threatening their way of life anywhere. A delegation from the Sattmar *rebbe* once went to Washington to ask the American government to use its influence against mixed swimming pools in Jerusalem.

Again despite the late hour, there were small boys in the synagogue with long ear curls and pale faces who were clearly long accustomed to hours of relentless daily study but seemed alert, ready for mischief, and thoroughly confident of where they belonged.

Most of the older Hasidim communicate even more clearly a wholeness of personality, an absence of anxiety. They do not have, their adherents claim, a *kera*, a split in their personalities.

The dancing had not yet started. The rebbe sang from the liturgy in a high, wailing chant that sounded Near Eastern in its piercing cry. At the end of each phrase, the Hasidim answered with words that were really sighs.

The Hasidim participate in the praying and the music as fully as their rebbes. They do not passively accept sermons, nor do they always sing hymns only on cue.

They try to give themselves spontaneously to the religious experience. All around me the men were rocking back and forth rapidly, praying with fierce devotion and creating a pressure of sound and rhythm as if to force the bursting forth of an apocalyptic vindication.

—N.H.

 ## A New Suit for Rosh Hashanah

A new suit for Rosh Hashanah depended on a number of things: if Pop's blind horse (he had a weak spot for unfortunate animals) hadn't had to go to the vet that summer, if his peddling business among the Pennsylvania Dutch farmers had been fairly good, if Mom hadn't lost any boarders over the hot months, and if she hadn't given away what little there was of the spare cash to her various charities, including her Ladies Auxiliary of something or other. For Mom, that old Jewish saying that "charity overcomes death" was a truism not to be argued. If we would say to Mom, "Look, we can't afford it," she would answer that "that's *takka* the time to give. That's really doing a *mitzvah*."

The new suit for me was Pop's chore. He was the *mavin*, being something of a "clothier" himself because he carried a "line" of men's pants—the line consisting of basic black in a single style, for that's all the Pennsylvania Dutch farmers wore for dress. But never mind. Pop would examine the seams, feel the cloth, say yes or no, the verdict being nonappealable as if handed down by Louis Brandeis himself.

As for me, all I cared about was whether an Ingersoll watch went with the suit. An Ingersoll watch, for the benefit of those who never had one and thus avoided a premature but permanent stoop or even a hernia from carrying it, was a big, fat nickel timepiece that sold for a dollar and whose determined tick never let you forget that time was indeed fleeting. You carried it in your breast pocket suspended from a chain or leather strap from the buttonhole in your lapel. It was a favorite gimmick to sell boy's suits—and the gimmick worked. In *shul* on Rosh Hashanah, the ticking of the Ingersolls was so loud you could barely hear the *hazzan*.

Suits then for boys had "knee pants," knickerbockers maybe, in New York, but knee pants in Lancaster. Long pants for kids were not yet in, parents believing that their offspring shouldn't grow up too fast, and maybe they were right.

I probably had suits of soft materials now and again, but I don't remember them, only the scratchy, tweedy kind built to last for active kids, especially at the knees, which went fast from shooting marbles, for how could you shoot marbles except down on a knee?

The suit was always at least one size too big: "You'll grow into it." I never did. It either gave out before the next suit was due, or off it went in the semiannual package to the "old home" in Shavel Uyest, Kovno Gubernia, for Pop's folks, and to Popalan in the same Lithuanian county or province to my mother's relatives. Incidentally, I have met in my wide travels lots of people who know of Shavel, now called Shauli by the Russians, but only one who ever heard of Popalan—a rabbi who said he knew my mother's people, the Pearlmans, a "fine line of rabbis and scholars." I couldn't get myself to tell him that my mother was a barmaid in a *kretchma* there, and a handsome barmaid she must have been—tall, blond, blue-eyed, high-cheekboned in the Slavic mold. She was only fifteen at the time, and married at sixteen and off to America the same year. Pop was only a year older, and a glazier by trade.

We didn't have a full-time rabbi in our *shul* in Lancaster, but our *hazzan*, Reb Moshe Mussnisky, who later changed it to "Muss" when he accepted a "call" from a Brooklyn congregation, and our *melamed-shochet-shammos* Reb Chatzkel Mishler, filled the bill nicely. I sang in the *hazzan's* choir as leading soprano until that which happens to boys happened to me and I wasn't a soprano any more and became a pretty bad combination of tenor-baritone-basso-squeek.

Reb Mussnitsky had a fine repertoire of High Holy Day airs, so good in fact, that people like Puccini, Leoncavallo, and Verdi brazenly stole his tunes, which I later heard at the Metropolitan, sung without apology to the real composer.

With the new suit came a snap-brim fedora hat, which the British call a "trilby." Only the *hazzan* and *shammos* and choir wore *yarmulkes*—the square kind, not the little round ones or the knitted dollar-size *kipot* that have become the style now—that is, except on Yom Kippur, when it became a bit too much to wear a hat from sunup until sundown, and all the men wore *yarmulkes*.

The Neilah service on Yom Kippur, which closes the solemn day and you have already been inscribed in the Book of Life, you hope, and pray that you'll be kept there, tested the memory both of the congregation and, certainly, of the choir boys, because by the time we got halfway through this service, the *shul* was dark, and no *Shabbes goy*—or, more accurately, *Yom Kippur goy*—to turn on the lights. So as the service progressed, the congregants moved closer and closer to the windows to get the last rays of light and then had to rely on memory—as did the *hazzan* and the choir boys. And I still remember a good part of the service "by heart."

The women would begin to disappear some time during the Neilah service, to go home and set the table, and come back in time to hear the *shofar* and join in the wish, loudly and clearly, *"L'Shana Habaa B'Yerushalayim"*—Next Year in Jerusalem—if not the Jerusalem of substance, for it then seemed so far, far away, then the Jerusalem of the spirit, when it would no longer be, as Sholem Aleichem put it, so hard to be a Jew.

—R.Y.

 ## Fasting on Yom Kippur Saved a Soldier's Life

The following story is attributed to Billy Rose, who heard it from General Douglas MacArthur's pilot, Colonel Anthony Story. It is a true account.

Communist North Korea attacked South Korea in 1950. Many American soldiers were part of the United Nations force that was sent to help South Korea. Among these soldiers were many Jewish boys.

The war lasted until 1953, and as in all wars, acts of heroism were recorded and told and retold. One of these stories has to do with a young Jewish soldier on Yom Kippur.

In one of the Marine Corps regiments that fought its way into the South Korean seaport city of Inchon, there was a corporal named Abrahahm Geller. Abe was the son of a rabbi and was brought up on the Lower East Side of New York.

Abe was not one of those young men who, upon entering the Army, forgot he was Jewish, forgot to pray and to observe *mitzvot* and holidays. Even though sleep was so very important to these young men who fought at the front, Abe never failed to wake a half hour before the rest of his regiment, take out his *tefillin* and *tallit* and say the morning prayers. By the time he was finished, the rest of the boys in his regiment were waking up.

During the course of the fighting, Abe's regiment crossed the Han River and cut the Seoul-Kaesong road. North Korean snipers were hidden in every rice paddy and field, and the men were constantly being bombarded with their bullets. So by dusk they were glad to dig into their foxholes and try to sleep for a few hours, although it was wet and clammy in the rice fields. They knew that their drive for the South Korean capital, Seoul, was scheduled for dawn, and so it was especially important they sleep to be alert.

It was an hour before dawn, and, except for the sentries, only two men in the company were awake: Corporal Abe Geller, bent over his prayer book, and Captain George O'Connor, who was looking over the field of battle and trying to figure out the best places to position his troops for the coming battle.

When Abe was finished praying, the captain said, "Go to the chow truck and get a cup of coffee."

"Thanks, Captain," said Abe, "but today is Yom Kippur. It is our holiest day and a fast day, and I won't eat until sundown."

"You mean to say you're going to fast the day we break into Seoul?" asked the captain.

The lad from the Lower East Side grinned. "I figure I've got enough calories packed away for at least twenty-four hours, and I won't miss it," he said.

Unfortunately, the Marines ran into a lot of trouble during the battle of that first day, trying to drive into Seoul. Along about sundown, Captain O'Connor's men were inching their way across a field with dead North Koreans all around. However, one of the enemy, though badly wounded, was only playing dead. As the officer came within firing range, he rolled over on his side and aimed his pistol.

Abe was standing a few feet from Captain O'Connor and saw the action of the North Korean soldier. He jerked his bayonet out of his belt and made a dive for the enemy soldier, but as he killed him, he was hit with three bullets intended for O'Connor.

The captain did the best he could for Abe, but at this point the situation on the field was very tense, and he had to remain in charge of the fighting. It was almost three hours before the corporal received a shot of penicillin and was carried to a hospital tent.

There he was operated on, the operation lasting over an hour, and when the surgeon finally came out, Captain O'Connor was waiting for him.

"How does it look?" asked the concerned captain.

"The kid's doing fine," said the surgeon.

"I was afraid he wouldn't make it," said O'Connor.

"So was I," said the surgeon. "The bullets went through his stomach and several loops of intestine. Wounds like that are usually fatal if penicillin isn't given almost immediately."

"I don't quite understand everything you are saying," said the captain, "but his pulling through seems something of a miracle."

"You could say that," said the surgeon, "for in a manner of speaking it is. Geller owes his life to the fact that when he was shot, there was hardly any food in his stomach."

In faraway Korea, on the front lines of battle, a life was saved because that young man fasted on Yom Kippur.

—B.St.

 ## Samaritan Passover: Ancient Rites on Mount Gerizim

Though their official status as Jews has at times been denied, though their name has been made legendary by the Christian parable of the Good Samaritan, the Samaritans regard themselves as the truest of Israelites, and their Passover service is indeed the closest approximation to the priestly sacrifice of ancient times.

Today the Samaritan community is divided between Israel and Jordan.* Known as the Shomronim, they number some four hundred and fifty souls, of whom two thirds live in Jordan in their ancient center of Shechem [Nablus] on the slopes of Mount Gerizim, their rival to Mount Zion in Jerusalem. The Jordanian Shomronim eke out a frugal existence, with the help of the Joint Distribution Committee, as shopkeepers, tailors, and tradesmen; and quite a few of the younger generation are schoolteachers. The remaining Samaritans live on the outskirts of Tel Aviv in a community established under the sponsorship of the late President Ben-Zvi, who, as a student of ethnology, made fast friends among the Samaritans.

Once a year, at Passover, the Samaritans from Israel travel en masse to Jordan to take part in the ancient rites on Mount Gerizim, known not as a *Seder* but as the *hurban*, the sacrifice. The Samaritans reenact the Exodus from Egypt in a stirring nightlong ceremony that follows the biblical description to the letter.

During the entire Passover holiday the Samaritans live in tents and booths on Mount Gerizim, which they claim is the sacred Mount Moriah, where Abraham set Isaac upon the sacrificial altar. They also identify Gerizim as the site of the blessing of the Israelites under Moses, as the site of Jacob's dream, as the gate of heaven, as the navel of the earth and abiding place of the Lord.

It is this ancient claim of Gerizim against Zion that was a basic element in the separation of the Samaritans from the remainder of the Jewish establishment. They declare that this dwelling place of the Lord was known of old, before the passage into Egypt, and was reestablished immediately after the return from Egypt and that it was an error of King David to remove the site of worship to Jerusalem.

This theological dispute actually has political origins. The Samaritans' forebears were of the northern kingdom, Israel, which did not recognize the sanctity of Mount Zion and Jerusalem, Judah's capital, but established their own religious centers and holy mountains, one of which was probably Mount Gerizim. Here the Samaritans built a temple, in the fourth century before the Common Era, which was subsequently destroyed. But they have continuously maintained their Passover on the mountain.

This year, as every year, preparations for the *hurban* began, in accordance with Scripture, two weeks before the service, when the elders went out to select the sacrificial sheep: "Your lamb shall be without blemish, a male of the first year."

A dozen or more of such animals were chosen, "according to the number of souls, every man according to his eating shall make your count for the lamb." Thus the cost of the sheep was scrupulously divided among the family clans by head count, except for the *Cohanim*, the priests, who were the guests of the other four families—Marhiv, Altif, Surani, and Tzadaka.

The sheep were brought to Shechem, washed, and placed in a special pen, and a watch was put over them. The day before the *hurban* the contingent from Israel arrived. Their movements during their stay in Jordan were strictly limited by the authorities; for instance, they were not even allowed to enter the ancient synagogue that the Samaritans of Jordan use throughout the year. Indeed they were not even allowed to stay in the town, but had to proceed up the hillside to the campsite. This was an open field near the top of Mount Gerizim.

Some of the families built small cabins or booths to supplement their tents. In high spirits, the Jordan and Israel sides of the five families reunited while tents

* Written in 1964. Now the Israeli-occupied West Bank.

were pitched and mats were spread. Family news was exchanged and the match-makers got busy.

Marriages outside the congregation are rare. When a match is made between the Israel side and the Jordan side, it is unlikely for the couple to elect to remain in Jordan, although one notable romance has gone on for several years with the engaged couple unable to agree as to which country to live in.

Well before dawn, at about 2:00 A.M., the men rose and put on their prayer robes. Some of them wore the loose white gowns used regularly in their syna-gogue, but the elders wore voluminous oriental trousers, narrow at the ankles, and jerseys or jackets, the whole in white, with white caps.

They gathered around the altar, a large flat stone, quite low, and the prayers began. The Cohen *Hagadol*, the high priest, led the chanting in the ancient He-brew. The text of many of the prayers, in praise of God, calling on God to rise and confound the enemy, were quite close in their content to familiar prayers in the Hebrew liturgy, and there was the constantly interjected choral cry, equivalent to the Shema, *"Ayn Ela Ela Ahad!"*—"There is no God but the One God." Its sound is strangely reechoed in the Mohammedan chant, *"La Allah il Allah."*

Until about eight in the morning the men prayed. Then the women arrived, bringing food. After family feasts and celebrations in the field, the groups re-turned to their tents and booths to continue their visiting. Meanwhile selected members of the congregation took upon themselves the various preparations for the *hurban*.

In each family someone prepared dough for *matzoth*. The Samaritans do not use a dry, ready-baked *matzoh;* theirs is a matzoh-cake, similar to the Arab bread, or *pitta*, baked with salt. Each family's portions of dough were brought to a cen-tral fire, consisting of a sheet of iron over stones, upon which the *matzoth* were to be freshly baked every day.

Meanwhile, in a pit by the altar, the sacrificial fire was started, and stones were heated under the eye of an expert. The pit was over two yards deep—a trench with a rounded bulge at one end. The heat was judged by the expert's practiced eye, for the perfect preparation would depend upon the exact degree of tempera-ture in the stones. First the stones became black, but afterwards they became white hot; then the fire was ready.

In the meantime, barrels of water had been heated over the fire for use in the ritual.

Shortly before sundown the entire congregation assembled on the open site, forming a procession to the tent of the Cohen *Hagadol*, to invite him and all the priestly family to the feast. The Cohen *Hagadol*, a round-bearded patriarch named Amram Isaac Cohen, took his place at the head of the procession, carrying the ceremonial Torah.

With chant and jubilation, the procession followed the Cohen *Hagadol* to the altar. The elders grouped around the stone, singing the prayers, while the younger men proceeded to their appointed tasks. Some fetched the hot water barrels and placed them on the stone. Others brought the sacrificial sheep.

All five designated ritual slaughterers, *shochtim*, then formed a row to one side of the altar. At their feet, the helpers placed the bound sheep, two or three for each man. The chanted prayers continued, and portions of Exodus were read, copied from the Samaritan scroll, which differs slightly from the Masoretic text. (The key difference for the Samaritans is in the line that occurs twenty-one times, directing that the altar shall be set up in "the place which the Lord has chosen"—hence, Gerizim, whereas the Masoretic text reads "in the place which the Lord shall choose"—hence, Jerusalem.)

As their recitation proceeded, there was little resemblance to the Haggadah as it is recited in the accepted family Seder, for the traditional "four questions" were not asked, nor were the symbolic objects displayed—the shankbone, the *charoses,* the bitter herb. Still, there were many familiar high points, such as, "With a strong hand He brought us out!"

What proceeded here was a kind of mass celebration of the beginning of the Exodus, rather than an explanation of it. The Cohen *Hagadol* mounted on a stone, so as to be seen by the whole congregation as he led the recitation from chapter 12 of Exodus:

> *And the Lord spoke unto Moses and Aaron in the land of Egypt, saying: "In the tenth day of this month they shall take unto them every man a lamb, according to the house of their fathers, a lamb for a household. Your lamb shall be without blemish . . . and the whole assembly of the congregation of the house of Israel shall kill it in the evening!"*

At these words the five *shochtim* raised their arms, then swiftly brought them down in the ritual act of slaughter. The assembled congregation cried out, "There is no God but the one God!"

This was the high point of the ritual. Behind the priests and the circle of white-robed elders stood the white-gowned men, and behind them the women and the children, and in a more distant circle stood thousands of spectators, Arabs who gather each year to behold the event.

"And they shall take of the blood and strike it on the two side posts and on the upper door post of the house," the recitation continued, and the congregation cried again and again:

"There is no God but the one God!"

The chief *shochet* meanwhile made the rounds of the sacrificial animals, examining each one to be certain it was unblemished in slaughter. Had a stranger touched a sacrifice, it would have become *tref* and hence rejected.

The accepted sheep were now handed over to a special group of older boys, assisted by a few women, and the skins were scraped clean of hair. Finally, each carcass was hung from a pole and lifted on the shoulders of two men. The *shochtim* removed the innards, which were carefully placed on the altar to be completely burned, according to Mosaic law. The sheep, again washed, were carried on the poles to the specially appointed seasoners, who salted the meat. Now the sheep were ready for the pit.

When the oven-watcher declared the moment had come, the poles with the sheep were set vertically into the pit. Another group had prepared a loam of grass, earth and water; a large wire mesh was placed over the pit, and this mesh was covered completely with loam, so as to seal the oven. No wisp of smoke was allowed to appear, for had there been smoke, the sacrificial meal would have burned.

It was now about 8:00 P.M. The worshipers returned to their family tents, where they sang, prayed, and nibbled on Passover dainties until the approach of midnight. When the pit-watchers declared the time had come, one of the Cohanim marched about the encampment, blowing the *shofar.* The celebrants emerged from their tents and again went up to the altar. Each family brought a large serving basket or a huge copper dish. The pit was opened; the baked sheep were taken out and appointed among the clans. To the Cohanim, according to Scripture, went the right forepart of each animal, the cheeks, and the stomach.

The meat was carried back in the servers to the tents. Now the celebrants gathered around, bringing their *matzoth* and their bitter herbs, and the Passover feast took place. Everything was eaten from the central server, so that no crumb or scrap might go astray, for the Samaritans strictly follow the rule, "Ye shall let nothing of it remain until morning and that which remaineth of it until morning ye shall burn with fire."

Far into the night the feasting continued, with storytelling and festivities. Many of the men stayed up all night at the altar to see that every scrap of remaining meat was burned to ashes.

Throughout the whole of the Passover the encampment continued, not only as a way of making certain that there should be no danger of contamination with leaven, or *chometz*, in the lower town, but also as a springtime holiday.

On the last day there was a procession to a still higher place on Mount Gerizim, or Mount Moriah as they believe it to be, to the altar of Abraham and Isaac. Here the final prayers were recited. The congregation then turned homeward, and the annual separation between the Samaritans of Jordan and those of Israel took place.

Contact between the two groups would be difficult during the year. As usual, radio programs on both sides will carry personal announcements, in this way sending greetings back and forth for anniversaries, weddings, births, holidays.

Since the entire priestly family lives on the Jordan side, a member of the Tzadaka family, Yefet Avraham Tzadaka, who has been appointed by the Cohen *Hagadol*, will continue to carry on services in Israel. These are held in a neat, new synagogue built at the entrance to the settlement, on the edge of the industrial area of Tel Aviv.

A good deal of literature exists on the Samaritans. The heart of the conflict over their status goes back to the building of the Second Temple, when, for political reasons, it appears, they were barred from taking part in the rebuilding of Jerusalem.

Through the centuries they, too, suffered destruction and dispersion, beginning with the Assyrian conquest, when nearly 27,000 were removed into captivity. Three hundred years ago the Samaritan community had dwindled to only forty males, and some say that not a single member of the Cohanim remained, but others say that the priestly line has never been broken. Today, even though divided between Israel and Jordan, the Samaritan population is again on the increase.

—M.L.

 Holy Days in Faraway Places

"Time for *Slihot*, Avram," "Time for *Slihot*, Yosef," the town crier called out as he walked down Jewtown Road, in Cochin, India, at 3:00 A.M. on the first of the month of Elul. He continued calling each man individually that night and for all of the forty nights through the Days of Repentance up to Yom Kippur.

Even the young boys, wishing to be in style with the grown-ups, slipped the town crier some pennies so that he would call their names, too, when it was "Time for *Slihot*."

This *Slihot* period for forty days, when penitential prayers and supplications for God's mercy are recited, is observed by many Sephardi communities. Its origin is believed to be in Moses' reference (Deuteronomy 9:16–19):

And I looked and behold, ye had sinned against the Lord your God; ye had made you a molten calf . . . And I took hold of the two tablets, and cast them out of my two hands, and broke them before the Lord, as at the first, forty days and forty nights . . . because of all your sin.

Any male child born during this forty-day period is named Rahamin (Mercy), for it is believed that during this period God is on the seat of mercy.

Kehimkar, in his book *The History of the Bene Israel in India*, tells of a custom followed by these brown Jews of the Bombay area on the last day of the month of Elul. The congregation is divided into two sections. Group A stands and reads the *Hatarah*, the prayer of forgiveness. Group B responds, "As we forgive you, so may you be forgiven from on High." The groups then change parts and recite the selections. Following this, they kiss one another's hands.

On the day before Rosh Hashanah, a sheep—or calf or cow—is sacrificed in the courtyard of the synagogue in Kabul, Afghanistan, in memory of the near sacrifice of Isaac. The meat of the slaughtered animal is distributed among the poor in the belief that "Charity delivereth from death" (Proverbs 10:2). There being no poor Jews in the community, the meat is given to poor Moslems.

Special foods are on the family's Rosh Hashanah table in this community. In addition to the usual apple coated with honey—"that we may be granted a sweet New Year"—there is a piece of the sheep's head—"that He may put us at the head and not at the tail end of things"; and some lung—"that our sins may be as light as lung." Other foods include beets, the Hebrew name for which (*selek*) denotes going away, leading to the hope "that our enemies may go away." Also on the table are carrots, whose Hebrew name (*gezer*) suggests the trust "that the harsh sentence—the *gzar din*—may be torn up." Popular also are pomegranates in the hope "that our merits may be as numerous as its seed."

In Kuala Lumpur, Malaysia, I was told no sours or pickles are used; and in Penang, Baruch Ephraim said the Sephardi community there uses sugar in place of salt in making the *motzi*, the benediction over bread. The Bene Israel use *halvah* on Rosh Hashanah. The *halvah* is made of cooked ground wheat mixed with sugar, almonds, raisins, and other nuts. With the wine of *Kiddush*, these Jews taste various dried fruits.

H. Z. Hirschberg tells of a Rosh Hashanah meal he attended in Persia in 1946. On the table was an immense platter with many vegetables, roast beef, and part of a sheep's head. *Kiddush* was recited. Then began the benedictions over each food on the platter. Aromatic herbs were also passed round, and the prescribed benediction for each repeated. Liturgical poems and excerpts from the *Zohar* were recited. Only after all this was there the ritual washing of hands and the benediction over the bread to start the holiday meal.

Blowing of the *shofar* holds its unique position everywhere during the Rosh Hashanah service. In India the form of the *shofar* is spiral in form rather than the type we in the West are accustomed to using.

Another customary Rosh Hashanah rite observed throughout these faraway places is that of *tashlikh*, deriving its name from the words of Micah 7:19—"Thou wilt cast (*tashlikh*) all their sins into the depths of the sea." There has also grown the belief that evil spirits cling to the ends of one's garments and should be shaken free to be carried away by running water.

The form of this ceremony is different in different places. Iraqi-born Jews I met in Kuala Lumpur told me that in their native country they would ride in a launch and empty their pockets into the sea. In Afghanistan, they do not go to the sea or river, but assemble at a home where there is a big well and there observe the casting out of sins. In Turkey, too, *tashlikh* is not observed in public at a riverside but at wells. In Persia, Jews gather at fishponds, with which many homes are equipped, and empty their pockets into the running water there. The goldfish dart up to swallow any crumbs falling into the water.

Reading of the Psalms on Rosh Hashanah is frequent throughout the world. As far back as the Talmudic period the Psalms came to be highly regarded as potent charms in time of need. Particularly popular is Psalm 91, known in rabbinic literature as *Shir Shel Pegaim* (Song Against Demons). Some of the verses of this song against demons read:

> *I will say of the Lord, who is my refuge and my fortress,*
> *My God, in whom I trust,*
> *That He will deliver thee from the snare of the fowler,*
> *And from the noisome pestilence.*

> *Thou shalt not be afraid of the terror by night,*
> *Nor of the arrow that flieth by day;*
> *Of the pestilence that walketh in darkness,*
> *Nor of the destruction that wasteth at noonday.*

> *There shall no evil befall thee,*
> *Neither shall any plague come nigh thy tent.*
> *For He will give His angels charge over thee,*
> *To keep thee in all thy ways.*

In Afghanistan it is customary for Jews to read the entire Book of Psalms, 150 in number, twice, thus making a total of 300 Psalms that have been read. It is believed that in this way a pardon from the Lord will be achieved, for the numerical value of the Hebrew word for pardon—*kaper*—equals three hundred.

We come now to the ninth day of Tishri, the day preceding Yom Kippur. It is a day full of rites and ceremonies. In the morning the Jews of Penang bathe at the seaside. In Cochin, people ask each other for forgiveness for any slights or hurts made during the past year. All pledges that have been made are paid. In Libya it was customary for the synagogue trustees to sit in the courtyard at tables decorated with flowers. Individuals would then pass by the tables and make their payments.

Kapparot, the offering of a fowl or other animal as substitute for oneself in atonement, is a ritual generally observed. In some places the meat of the animal thus sacrificed is given to the poor.

The Bene Israel, as do many other Jews, visit the cemetery before Rosh Hashanah and Yom Kippur to invoke the intercession of the dead on behalf of the living members of the family. The Bene Israel, however, believe that the spirits of the dead visit the homes, joining the family for this important day, and leave on the day following Yom Kippur.

Seder Malkot—the ritual of penitential flagellation—is observed in many places in the middle of the day of Yom Kippur eve. How it is enacted was described to me in Afghanistan: A man, stripped to the waist, his face to the wall, leans against a wooden pillar jutting out from the wall of the synagogue, his hands stretched out above his head. A synagogue representative ties the man's wrists to the pillar. Then, with a leather thong, the religious functionary lashes the man across the left shoulder and recites the following verse (Psalm 73:38):

But He, being full of compassion,
forgiveth iniquity, and destroyeth not;
Yea, many a time doth He turn His anger away,
And doth not stir up all His wrath.

Then the man is lashed over the right shoulder, and once more over the left shoulder. Each time the same verse is repeated. In Hebrew, this verse consists of thirteen words. Therefore, each one of the three strokes counts as if the man had been lashed thirteen times. In this way, the required thirty-nine strokes are assumed to have been applied. According to the *Mishnah,* thirty-nine strokes are the maximum number required for punishing a person by flagellation.

The food eaten by the Bene Israel on this day includes *gharies* (rice flour cakes fried in oil), *puries* (tarts made of wheat flour and sugar), liver and gizzards, fruits and wine, pistachios and almonds.

Dressed in white, people proceed to the synagogue for the evening service. *Nerot neshama* (soul candles)—six feet tall and six inches in diameter—are brought to the synagogue to burn throughout Yom Kippur in memory of the departed. Before the sun sets, *Kol Nidre* is recited as a prelude to the start of the Day of Atonement.

Synagogues are in the Sephardi style, with the *bimah* (reader's desk) in the center, and the places for the congregation around the four walls. In Isfahan's ghetto I saw a small synagogue with arches, dome, and walls of blue mosaic tiles. The reader's desk, with carved, wooden decorations, was in the usual place. Rugs were spread over the entire floor. Men left their shoes in cubicles in the entry before sitting down on the rugs with low tables, no higher than footstools, before them. The women watched the service from behind a wooden lattice work.

Elkan Nathan Adler, who once was present at a Yom Kippur service in Salonika, tells that on this day everybody was honored with an *aliyah,* being called up to the reading of the Torah. Over and over the last three verses of one portion of the day's Torah reading were repeated for each person in turn.

At the conclusion of the Day of Atonement, fathers in Libya would place their hands on their children's heads and bless them. In Afghanistan men take any bits remaining from the soul candles and offer them to wives who may be barren. It was firmly believed that chewing these bits of the *nerot neshama* would be efficacious in making a barren woman fruitful.

The day following Yom Kippur is for the Bene Israel a day of rejoicing. This is in the tradition of *Simhat Kohen*—Rejoicing for the Priest. In Temple days, the high priest entered the Holy of Holies only one time during the entire year—on Yom Kippur. To mark the high priest's safe return from the Holy of Holies, the day following the Day of Atonement was set aside for rejoicing and festivities. So the Bene Israel note the day following Yom Kippur with entertainment and visits and almsgiving to mark their remaining in life in spite of their sins.

—I.G.C.

 ## Shavuoth at the Tomb of the Prophet Nahum

From Tanura I went to Alkush [Iraq], where I arrived in 1848, two days before the Feast of Weeks.

Alkush is situated in a very unfruitful neighborhood. The town is inhabited only by Armenians and appears to be very ancient. The houses, which stand single, are like fortified towers, rising at the foot of the mountains. Several Israelites and Kurds accompanied me to Alkush in order to attend the ceremonies here, which take place at the tomb of the prophet Nahum. Quite close to one of the mountains is a large court, in the middle of which stands a spacious building, consisting only of one room, capable of containing about one thousand persons. There are two entrances into this building, which was intended for a synagogue; but, standing as it does without a community, it presents but a strange appearance. In this desolate temple on a spot, parted off by railings, is a catafalque, covered with tapestry worked in gold and ornamented with various coins, above which is a costly canopy. This is said to be the tomb of the prophet Nahum. The Jews from Mosul, Aruel, Arbil, Kirkuk, from the Kurdistan mountains and from a still farther distance of eight days' journey round, annually assemble a week before the Feast of Weeks for a ceremony, at which they spend fourteen days in religious exercises.

The pilgrims bring their manuscripts of the Law with them, and deposit them in the holy shrine of the temple. The women then enter the chamber of the prophet, and after this the service begins. First the Book of Nahum is read aloud from an old manuscript, which is laid upon the catafalque; when this is finished, they make a solemn procession seven times round the sacred shrine, singing sacred songs. After the seventh round, a hymn is sung addressed to the prophet, the chorus of which is "Rejoice in the joy of the Prophet Nahum! . . ."

On the first evening of the Feast of Weeks, the sixth of Sivan, they assemble in the synagogue, which is lighted by about one thousand lamps, and enter the chamber of the prophet, when service begins . . . As soon as it is over, they go without further ceremonies into the sacred house, where a festive and general entertainment takes place, at which coffee is plentifully served. At break of day the morning prayer is recited; and then the men bearing the Pentateuch before them, go, armed with guns, pistols, and daggers, to a mountain in the vicinity, when, in remembrance of the Law, which on this day was announced to them from Mount Sinai, they read in the Torah and go through the *Musaf* prayer. With the same warlike procession they descend the mountain. The whole community breaks up at the foot, and an Arabic fantasie, a war performance, begins. The picturesque confusion, the combatants, their war cries heard through the clouds of smoke, the clashing of weapons, and the whole mimic tumult present a fantastic spectacle, which is not without a certain dignity and makes a strange impression on the spectator. This war performance is said to be a representation of the great combat, which, according to the belief in those parts, the Jews, at the coming of the Messiah, will have to maintain against those nations who oppose their entrance into the Promised Land and the formation by them of a free and independent kingdom. The women, who remained behind in the town, come, singing and dancing to the accompaniment of a tambourine, to meet the men, and they all return together.

I was at first almost stunned by the tumult and excitement of the noisy crowd but later became quite meditative when I saw to what a degree ignorance and custom can deface a religious festival and injure even the most essential principle.

Several parts of these ceremonies are doubtless of foreign origin and give evidence of Arabic custom. I, therefore, thought it well to address some words on this subject to my brethren in the faith, who testify great respect to Jewish European travelers and consider their opinion as especially important. It was explained to me that these customs have been held in respect since ancient times and that they must be kept up until the coming of the Messiah.

The return to the synagogue took up nearly half a day as they often stopped by the way and renewed their warlike games. When at length they reached the synagogue, the Pentateuch, which they had taken with them, was replaced to the holy shrine; after which began near the catafalque the usual service for the prophet. That finished, all returned to the town, to rest themselves after the exertions of the day.

—J.I.B.

 ## A Passover Seder in a Women's Prison

The grandmother held her six-month-old granddaughter in her arms throughout the Seder and was reluctant to put her down long enough to take morsels of food. A mother held hands with her daughter and son-in-law and had difficulty letting go of one hand long enough to pick up her glass. A strikingly attractive young woman leaned to the right throughout the Seder—she was snuggling as close as possible to her fiancé. Another young woman, seated between her parents, frequently exchanged kisses and hugs with her mother.

It was a happy Seder, filled with warmth and affection. The partings at the end were sad and intense. The farewell kisses were prolonged, and there seemed to be a painful tearing of one large group from the other.

More than half the guests put on their coats and were escorted outdoors by a uniformed guard. The grandmother, the mother, the engaged young woman, the daughter, and six or seven other women who had had no family at the Seder turned in the opposite direction and were escorted by another uniformed guard down a long corridor. A heavy door with bars at the upper portion closed tight after them. The Jewish women prisoners of the Bedford Hills Correctional Facility went back to their cells to be locked in for the night.

Visiting is permitted only on weekends, so the Seder was held on the Sunday evening before Passover. Rabbi Yaacov Rone of Bet Torah Congregation in nearby Mt. Kisco conducted it from a special woman's *Haggadah*, and the guests included members of the congregation who have concerned themselves with the Jewish prisoners.

There are some ten Jewish women in a prison population of 450.

After reciting the traditional blessings and dividing the *afikoman*, the rabbi, with a twinkle, called upon "Harriet, our youngest," to ask the Four Questions. Harriet, the mother, had suddenly disappeared from between her daughter and son-in-law. Her daughter spoke to a guard and was permitted to go through the corridor to bring her back.

By the time Harriet returned, the Four Questions had been asked by others. Harriet took her seat.

"It suddenly got to me," she apologized. "I couldn't stand it—here we are celebrating the holiday of freedom and look at me." She explained to the visitor she had already served six years and had five to go.

Harriet's daughter said that her mother, like many of the other prisoners, had been convicted on a drug charge. She claimed that her mother had not actually sold the drugs but passed it on for friends: "She didn't make any money out of it. She always got involved in trying to help other people." However, state laws passed in 1973 set harsh punishments for drug dealers, even first offenders,

Harriet managed to follow the *Haggadah* carefully, even while exchanging kisses and hugs and personal information with her daughter. She noted at one point, "I like this *Haggadah;* it's very well written." It was, in fact, a fluent English interpretation, which emphasized women's roles and the Jews' long struggle against all forms of enslavement.

Harriet went on to explain that she had never been very observant, but was proud to be a Jew. "I tell everyone. They all know I'm Jewish. Some hide it." She said that she always lit memorial candles for her parents, but that last time she had lit one for her father, an attendant, possibly not understanding what it was for, blew it out.

"When I saw that, I said, 'Daddy, now you know where I am—please help me,'" said Harriet.

Harriet said that she was an honor prisoner and, therefore, had been permitted her own television set in her nine-by-seven cell, but she feared new restrictions. A recent tightening of rules at the institution meant that each prisoner could have only two adults and two children as visitors. Harriet had hoped to have her adult son as well as her daughter at the Seder, but this was not possible.

A tremulous, soft-spoken young woman with tear-filled eyes came over to chat during the course of the meal. She appeared to be about eighteen, but said she was twenty-nine and had a six-year-old child, who was now staying with her ex-mother-in-law. She had no family visitors.

"I'm a victim of circumstances," she said. When asked on what charge she had been convicted, she shook her head, apparently overcome. She repeated, "I'm just a victim of circumstances," and then told a complicated story of having taken her ex-husband into her home to help him and then being held at gunpoint by him.

"I've been here two months and I can't stand it," she said, "I . . . I'm just not used to this kind of thing. I don't belong here." She said her lawyer had been unable to do anything on her behalf. She either did not know or could not muster the courage to pronounce the length of her sentence. She only shook her head.

In contrast, the grandmother remained cheerful throughout the *Seder,* seldom glancing away from her granddaughter's face. She was uninterested in discussing anything but the infant's charms and, when complimented on the child's good behavior, she said with a charming, meaningful smile, "Well, she certainly didn't disgrace me."

Eunice and Marvin Edelman, who have been involved in helping Jewish prisoners at the women's institution and the nearby men's prison, appeared warmly attached to each individual. They said that although most of the prisoners were involved in drug crimes, one member of the group was in for homicide; another, for embezzlement.

"Most of them are fairly well educated and come from middle-class homes," said Mrs. Edelman. "I think some of the punishments are very severe, especially on the drug charges. You know, they don't get the big offenders. And then, some of them may have been guilty of something, but not what they were convicted for."

The attractive young woman with the fiancé had already served eight years. She said she had permitted her home to be used for a cocaine sale. She is serving a twenty-five-years-to-life sentence and has already been denied clemency twice. She is a thirty-seven-year-old divorcée, the mother of three children, a college graduate, and fluent in Spanish and Italian. She clung with apparent desperation to her fiancé as she bade him goodnight. He had seen her picture in a magazine, and they had corresponded before meeting and becoming engaged.

At the end of the *Seder,* when the rabbi had raised his glass of grape juice and said, "Next year in Jerusalem!" she and the other prisoners turned to their visitors with smiles of hope and the shadow of fear in their eyes.

—E.L.

 ## Jews from Eight Countries
Celebrated Seder in Communist China

The word spread quickly among the Jewish guests at the Tung Fang Hotel in Kwangchow (Canton), People's Republic of China. A *Seder* was going to be held that night in the banquet hall. Do you want to be there?

"Yes," said Ann and Stanley Lyons, of Garden City, New York, who were in China to participate in the Chinese Export Commodities Fair, an international trade show. As the sun set over Kwangchow on April 21, 1978, the Lyonses joined twenty-six other Jews representing eight countries to celebrate what was believed to be the first Seder held on mainland China since the 1949 Revolution.

"It was," recalled Lyons, who runs an importing firm on Long Island, "a *Seder* to remember."

"Here were all these Jews from all over the world who had never met each other and were now sitting down to share their common heritage and observe the commandment to celebrate the Passover," added Mrs. Lyons.

The Seder was the brainstorm of Victor DeLoya, a businessman. When DeLoya arrived in Kwangchow, he said he noticed that many of his coreligionists were "restless" and desired to celebrate Passover. He and Alvin Florea, a buyer and leader of the Hong Kong Chamber of Commerce, planned the *Seder* along with the help of the American Liaison Representative's office and officials from the Canadian Consulate, where there are several Jews employed. DeLoya arranged with the hotel's managers for the preparation of food.

Among those sitting at three large tables were Jews from the United States, Hong Kong, Canada, Switzerland, Venezuela, Mexico, Spain, and Great Britain plus one non-Jewish guest from Japan.

Improvisation was the key to the *Seder*. Hot towels were passed around to compensate for the lack of a water pitcher for the *ur'chatz* (washing of the hands) ceremony. The men wore handkerchiefs or caps on their heads to serve as *yarmulkes*. DeLoya, who was born in Morocco, conducted the service in the Sephardic style.

The one *Haggadah*, from which each guest read in turn, was supplied by DeLoya, who had received it from the chief rabbi of the Israel Defense Forces. DeLoya had visited Israel a week before arriving in China. Two boxes of *matzoh* were provided by Florea and by Ted and Sylvia Zuckerman of Los Altos, California, who had purchased the unleavened bread in Hong Kong.

Stephanie Levin, a resident of Hong Kong, had brought one bottle of Passover wine to the Seder. So instead of the traditional four cups of wine, the guests took four sips from one cup.

In addition, substitutions were made for the standard Passover fare.

"The chicken soup was Chinese style, but it wasn't as good as mine," said Mrs. Lyons, "but the *charoses*, which was made from Chinese plum jam, was delicious, and the *moror*, which used ginger root, was just as bitter as horseradish."

The meal was served Chinese style—one dish at a time—and with chopsticks.

The cooks had not differentiated between fish and shellfish and inadvertently brought out a platter of shrimp. *"Pesahdike* license," joked one guest.

Following the meal, the guests went through traditional Israeli dances and songs such as *Hevenu Shalom Aleichem.* "The waiters were quite mystified at what we were doing," Lyons said, "but I think they realized they were seeing some kind of festive occasion."

—A.E.

 ## Merrymakers at Jewish Weddings

Merrymakers at Jewish weddings occupied a prominent place in the later Middle Ages. Their character, activity, and significance changed with the social changes in the ghetto. Their influence was great and lasting, and they became an indispensable component of every Jewish wedding, irrespective of local and state regulations. The merrymaker, whether he was a jester (*letz*), *marshallik,* or buffoon (*badhan*), had one task: to amuse the guests at the wedding and to increase the merriment. The means that he employed to that end were not always too refined, and he aroused the anger of the Jewish religious leaders. His great popularity, however, ensured his survival for many generations.

It is hard to determine when the merrymaker (*letz*) first made his appearance at Jewish festivities. The first notice about Jewish jesters is found in the unpublished work of Rabbi Elijah of Carcassonne, *Asufot,* which would indicate that Jewish merrymakers were known as far back as the thirteenth century. There is no doubt, however, that their history in the ghetto is much older. The meager notice in *Asufot* gives no idea what the Jewish jester in the Middle Ages was like and with whom of the non-Jewish *vagantes* he should be compared. It is not until we reach the sixteenth and seventeenth centuries that we have fuller data on the character of the letz.

The term *letz* signified a merrymaker, comedian, satirist, and even a *jongleur,* whose function was to amuse the people at weddings (or other joyous occasions). Frequently the term also was used to denote a musician.

A Yiddish story, *Maase Bria Vezimra,* written about 1580, refers to jesters in such a manner that it is difficult to tell whether musicians or merrymakers are meant: "They prepared a magnificent wedding. The Holy One, blessed be He, pronounced the blessing and the angels were the jesters." Rabbi Jair Hayyim Bacharach in the seventeenth century referred to a musician as a *letz.*

The regulations of Hesse of 1690, which restricted extravagance at weddings and prohibited "the custom in vogue to date of riding to meet the bridegroom," as well as "crepe, gauze and liverymen," made an exception, however, for "waiters and jesters." The fact that this was a sumptuary regulation and nevertheless permitted jesters indicates that the reference must be to musicians or to performers who were both musicians and merrymakers. We hear of such musicians and merrymakers in Prague, the classical city of Jewish merrymakers, when in 1651 "the poor Prague musicians and entertainers" petitioned the king for permission to "perform music" and to entertain on Sundays and on Christian holidays.

In his *Juedische Merckwuerdigkeiten,* Schudt cites a regulation of Frankfurt of 1716 in which musicians are called jesters. The regulation reads:

No wedding shall have more than four jesters, and they should not play later than midnight. Those jesters playing beyond midnight shall not be employed any more within the year.

According to an explanation given to Schudt by prominent Frankfurt Jews, the name *letz* was applied to musicians because their playing is mere mockery of the performance of the Levites in the ancient temple.

We do not know exactly what the original functions of the marshallik were. An idea may be gained from later reminiscences from places in which the badhan (merrymaker) retained some of the functions of the marshallik. The functions of such a marshallik in the 1840s in Minsk are described by L. Levanda as follows:

The customs and ceremonies of Jewish weddings are so numerous that it is almost impossible to execute them in an orderly fashion and in consonance with tradition without a special leader and supervisor. The role of such a supervisor is usually assumed by the so-called marshallik. *He is entrusted with the administration of the wedding, for he knows in detail what is demanded in each instance by tradition, from which one dare not deviate.*

That the marshallik was originally a master of ceremonies is also clear from a report by von Kloden's that he saw in 1800 a Jewish merrymaker with a *pritsche*. The *pritsche* was a kind of scepter for the German master of ceremonies, which was in all probability taken over by the Jewish master of ceremonies.

We have information from the seventeenth century about the marshallik as merrymaker. The first source is probably the Hebrew-Yiddish-Latin-Italian dictionary of Nathan Nata Hannover, *Safah Berurah*, which was published in Prague in 1660. In *Safah Berurah*, the word marshallik is rendered *buffon, buffone,* and in Latin *scurra*, that is, merrymaker. In one of the sumptuary laws passed by the Lithuanian Council of Communities in 1673 mention is made of the marshallik in connection with limiting expenditures for weddings. It is difficult, however, to determine whether the marshallik referred to still retained his original functions or was merely a merrymaker. Another regulation of the same council, issued in 1761, indicates clearly that the badhan, who was the successor of the marshallik, also assumed some of his functions.

The *marshallik* apparently lost his peculiar character as a result of the frequent regulations limiting expenditures at weddings. The wedding was reduced from a community festivity to a small family affair. What need was there for a master of ceremonies at the wedding when ceremonies were prohibited by provincial or local decrees? The marshallik as mere merrymaker encountered the competition of the badhan, which was called forth by the circumstances of the seventeenth century.

The seventeenth century saw the flowering of a moralistic literature in Yiddish. After the Chmielnicki massacres the Jews of Poland became eager consumers of moralistic literature. The masses sought consolation for their great misfortunes and were led to believe that they had not been sufficiently pious and they had sinned excessively. In a period of national depression and search for sin the mere merrymaker was, of course, out of place. The Council of 1650, which met in Selts, ordered "that no music should be heard in a Jewish home, except on the night of the wedding." What was needed was a merrymaker who would not merely relate piquant jests or sing piquant songs, but one who would know how to comfort the depressed and afflicted audience and assuage their troubles.

Such was the badhan. He was more of a declaimer than a singer, and frequently only a declaimer. A morality preacher had to be a scholar after a sort and be familiar with the rabbinic literature, whence the badhan drew his material. Hence only people with some learning took to the calling of badhan.

To be sure the badhan was not always a mere morality preacher, playing the pious role of a chaste humorist reciting rhymes or Talmudic parables. Frequently the badhan was an entertainer according to all the rules of the art of the jester. This, however, cannot be said about all the merrymakers. Many of them regarded themselves as mere morality preachers and did not trespass the boundaries of their talent.

J. Zizmor tells the following in his memoirs about the badhan Rabbi Eliezer Sislevitch, who flourished in the middle of the nineteenth century:

> He was an eminent scholar, an ordained rabbi whose discourse was interspersed with sayings of the sages, quotations from the Midrash, and homiletic interpretations based on numerical values of the letters of given words and mnemonic devices. He deftly interpolated the names of the parents of the bride and groom in a biblical passage. Moreover, he was a God-fearing man, who always carried with him a volume of the Talmud. He refused to participate in the ceremony known as bazetsens of the bride, for that would require his presence in the midst of women. He also never announced donations of wedding gifts because he said:
>
> "How would it look if I just got through a Torah discourse—and if it is in rhyme is it not Torah?—and then followed this with shouting out the wedding gifts like an auctioneer on the mart? It would be a desecration of the honor of the Torah."

This type of badhan, however, was limited almost exclusively to Poland. He was not found in the ghettos of Germany. There the lusty and piquant merrymaker, the merrymaker-cantor or singer dominated the scene. There the merrymaker remained the "clown" (in German *Narr*).

Although the *Narr* had no specific roots in Jewish life and the term did not denote a special kind of merrymaker, the word nevertheless was very popular, especially among German Jews, as a synonym for merrymaker. We have proof from the eighteenth century that merrymakers at weddings wore special clowns' attire. One such merrymaker, Shlomo, was furnished a special clown's outfit for a wedding to which he had been specially invited. In the wedding songs the merrymaker frequently refers to himself as a *Narr*. In a wedding song of the eighteenth century the merrymaker pleads: "Give also gifts today to the clowns and to the musicians."

The Jewish merrymaker did not occupy a prominent social position. He was feared on account of the rhymes that he freely utilized to his own purposes and frequently caused embarrassment. People exploited his friendship for their personal advantage; they were amused by his apt parables, paraphrases, and merry songs and then proceeded to censure him as a sinner. The merrymaker had an inplacable enemy in the Talmudic scholar, who was offended by the former's free and sacrilegious interpretation of biblical and Talmudic passages.

The moralistic books, the most ardent advocates of a seriousness and piety that almost verged on asceticism, were strong opponents of all forms of mirth, which in their opinion was the first step towards sin. It is not surprising, therefore, that the moralists had no love for the free, irreverent, and lusty merrymakers. The *Sefer Middot* (1542) inveighed against lascivious talk at weddings. This attack undoubtedly was aimed at the merrymakers and would indicate their prevalence in the fifteenth century. The passage reads:

It is a mitzvah to amuse the bride and the groom. But they should not be amused with lascivious talk, or with levity, for modesty becomes both sorrow and mirth.

The merrymakers thus met with considerable resistance. The stubborn fight against them, however, did not bear an official communal stamp, as was the case with the theater, which was combated not only by scholars but also by means of legal regulations, which imparted to the struggle an official character. The community as a whole did not oppose the merrymakers. On the contrary, it protected and cared for them, as manifest in the many regulations dealing with the merrymakers. The community administration knew quite well how beloved and popular the merrymaker was among the people and that he was considered indispensable at festivals.

—E.Li.

 ## Bikkurim in Kibbutz Matzuba

The sea is wide and still during the hot month of Sivan. From behind the copse that faces the road there approaches a red tractor, pulling a wide platform laden with freshly cut fodder. Aboard are a host of little children wearing their holiday clothes decorated with greenery. Immediately following you see a procession of people attired in holiday costume, some walking, others traveling in vehicles.

The entire cavalcade is decked out in fresh foliage. They move slowly, the tractors and machines, the horse- and donkey-drawn wagons. The wagons are filled with workers in high spirits, dressed in their working clothes, carrying their tools and the fruits of their labors. There are broad-shouldered plowmen; workers from the orchards and vineyards wearing their wide-brimmed hats; sun-tanned vegetable gardeners and poultrymen carrying baskets of chickens and eggs; drivers and beekeepers.

Among them on foot are the dairy workers and the foddermen pulling a little bull calf. There are those who work in the banana orchards, two of them carrying a weighty bunch of ripe bananas, fastened to poles; the landscape gardeners adorned in flowers; the mushroom growers with their produce. Following on their heels, gaily singing, are the workers from the laundry, the carpentry shop, and the looms, the builders, and those who do the sewing and work in the kitchen. A band accompanies the procession and song after song spontaneously breaks forth. "Open the way for us, we bring the *bikkurim!*" . . .

The cavalcade reaches the reaped fields. On their faces you can see their pride as workers on the soil. In festive spirit they enter a square through seven gates, which are crowned with seven kinds of produce with which the land of Israel was blessed.

One after another, the workers of the various branches approach the stage and offer, with the appropriate blessing, the firstfruits contained in their straw baskets. Seven *haverim* and *haverot* stand on the decorated stage and accept the baskets, containing the produce of the fields and the garden.

Those who accept the *bikkurim* answer with festive greetings, and the leader of the ceremony totals up the income, which is dedicated to the Jewish National Fund. The children, who have also brought their firstfruits, proudly present recitations and songs. A group performs a play about the story of Ruth. The choir accompanies them with songs and special harvest dances. The time spent in the fields is enjoyed by all; the *haverim* and the children sing and dance together, there in the fields as in the days of yore. Before everyone starts back home, the sun begins to sink into the sea, the young *haverim* pass around biscuits coated with honey and glasses of milk. Thus the biblical saying is fulfilled in Matzuba: "He brought us to this place and gave us this land, a land flowing with milk and honey" (Deuteronomy 26:9).

—G.A.

 ## Pistol-Shooting Wedding in the Caucasus

In the Caucasus, in southern Russia, the marriage ceremony is always performed on Wednesday. On the preceding Thursday three or four girls, relatives of the bride, put on her clothes and invite other girls to sleep in a special room with her. Toward evening the groom sends meat and rice flour to the bride and her friends. The latter go out to sprinkle the flour on the young people, who dance while the boys and girls clap their hands. On this evening also the groom spreads a feast for his friends. On Sabbath morning the friends of the bride, among whom there must be at least five grown persons, clad in the bride's garments, go from house to house leaving invitations to the feast and receiving wherever they may stop sugar, coffee, apples, or eggs.

After the service, at which the groom is not called up to the Torah, which is read only after the ceremony, the guests accompany the pair to the house of the groom for a feast and then to the house of the bride, where the men eat first and the women afterward, the girls furnishing music with harmonicas, trumpets, and the like. On the Sabbath as well as on the following day, the bride spreads a table for her friends; on Sunday the groom, for his friends. On Monday and Tuesday the bride invites the friends of her household with her girl companions, who sing a Tatar song. She is clad in mourning to indicate her sorrow at leaving her parents' house. The visitors everywhere receive presents and refreshments. As they approach the house of the groom, his companions appear and pelt the procession with sand and small stones. The groom is similarly led about among his friends. If he is rich, he is even obliged to have silk wedding garments made for the members of his household.

On Tuesday evening the father of the groom spreads a feast for the whole community. On Wednesday the bride and groom fast. About noon the rabbi, with a male relative of the groom and some women, goes to the house of the bride in order to inspect the clothing that she has made with the money of the groom. Quarrels often arise on this occasion. If the father is wealthy, he adds a sum of money to that which has been provided by the groom.

Then the groom and bride are taken to the sea for the bath, after which they put on the wedding garments. The groom is preceded by young men, and the bride by girls, with drums and with handclapping and Tatar songs. While the hair of the weeping bride is being combed, the girls light the lamps; then the bride, kneeling, receives her mother's blessing. The brothers of the bride, if she has any —otherwise an uncle—lead her to the ceremony in the court of the synagogue, the girls following with lights, generally white candles ornamented with blossoms.

The groom is brought with songs from the sea; girls go to meet him in festive train, with dishes of confectionery and with a branch hung with silken kerchiefs and coins. Arrived at home, he is kissed on the forehead by all the women; then after having been blessed by his relatives, he is led with music to the court of the synagogue, where, under the *huppah*, the rabbi with two pupils awaits the pair. The music ceasing, the groom goes under the huppah, while the bride's parents are mourning at home for their child and those of the groom are preparing for the ceremony. The bride is led a few times around the groom, the bridesmaids and the others carrying lights. The ritual is that of the Sephardim; the rabbi sits during the ceremony, and both he and the groom hold a glass of wine during the blessings, drinking after each of them.

After the ceremony, guns and rockets are discharged; the bride, closely veiled by her attendants, is put on a horse, which a relative of the groom leads while another holds a mirror before her face; and with shouting and music the couple are led home, showered on the way with rice. Arrived at the house of the bride, the girls dance, and as soon as she crosses the sill, the doorposts are smeared with honey, while a light burns over the door; at the same time the young men again discharge pistols. The musicians are then paid, and the wedding procession is ended.

—M.Gru.

VI
Israel:
"Land of Milk and Honey"
—and Challenges Galore!

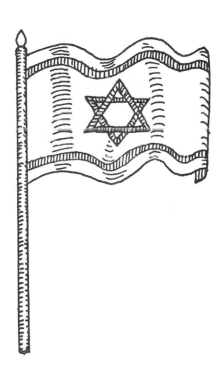

Truman Had to Wait for Jewish State's Name Before Announcing Recognition

In the General Assembly of the United Nations, meeting in the New York State building at Flushing Meadow Park, the hands of the clock were edging toward six in the evening—midnight in the Holy Land—May 14, 1948. A last-minute effort was underway, led by the United States, in contravention of President Truman's word to Chaim Weizmann, to nullify the partition of Palestine and substitute another trusteeship when the British left, a few moments hence, delaying again the end of the Jewish people's two-thousand-year exile.

The Jews at the benches assigned to them and the Arabs at their delegates' seats paid little attention to the drone of the debate which flowed on without regard to realities. The hands edged perpendicularly, and when they lined up, the Iraq delegate got up to shout, "The game is up!"

It was, but not as he wished it. To him, the Jewish dream was forever dead, crushed by the guns of the Arab armies that had already begun their assault on the Yishuv, the Jewish community in Palestine.

Abba (Aubrey) Eban rose from his seat, went to the delegates' lounge and called Chaim Weizmann's suite at the Waldorf-Astoria. Vera Weizmann came on the line and said, "Aubrey, all is well."

The Mandate had ended, the British flag was down, the Governor-General, Lieutenant General Sir Alan Cunningham, had departed from Haifa on a British destroyer and the State of Israel had been proclaimed.

A few minutes later, the word came that President Truman had given the state de facto recognition, and would have done it even earlier if he had only known its name. He called Eliahu Elath, who was to be Israel's first ambassador to Washington, to ask, but even Elath did not know and had to call Tel Aviv to find out. He took a cab to the White House to report, simply, "Israel," and Truman announced: "This Government has been informed that a Jewish State has been proclaimed in Palestine and recognition has been requested by the provisional government thereof. The United States recognizes the de facto authority of the new State of Israel."

The American delegation sat stunned. The Arab delegations were livid. The American Jewish community was jubilant, but its jubilation would not be manifest until the following day. It was a time of silent jubilation before the public demonstration let loose. Into the darkened room of the ailing Weizmann at the Waldorf crowded the people who had fought the good fight at the United Nations, the Israelis and the Americans. Weizmann lay silent. Eban tells it in his autobiography:

"Cables came from Tel Aviv telling of familiar Zionist leaders bearing new and glamorous ministerial titles. But there was no news or greeting for Weizmann. A sense of abandonment and ingratitude invaded his mood. Suddenly a bellboy appeared with flowers and fruit and—a telegram from the Zionist leaders in Tel Aviv:

" 'On the occasion of the establishment of the Jewish State, we send our greetings to you who have done more than any living man towards its creation. Your help and stand have strengthened all of us. We look forward to the day when we shall see you at the head of the State established in peace. Ben-Gurion, Kaplan, Myerson, Remez, Shertok' "—Prime Minister David Ben-Gurion, Finance

Minister Eliezer Kaplan, Labor Minister Golda Myerson (soon to be Meir), Communications Minister David Remez and Foreign Minister Moshe Shertok (soon to be Sharett).

The American Jewish community had gotten the news over their radios, and there was little sleep that night, each Jew with his own thoughts, his own attempts to absorb this greatest happening since the exile following the destruction of the Second Temple in the year 70 of the Common Era. And his radio brought bad news as well as good: Tel Aviv was under attack, the battle was on for the Jerusalem road, a state of siege had been declared by Egypt, the Arab League had voted to set up an Arab civil administration for all of Palestine and reject the British-American plea for a three-month truce.

True, the Haganah had occupied Jaffa, and Acre had fallen to the Israelis, but the picture was grim. In New York and in cities across the country, the plea went up for blood donors and Hadassah set up blood centers for the collection of plasma. In New York City, at Beth Israel Hospital, the donors were led by Fanny Hurst, the novelist, who "wanted to set an example."

The Jews rose to see the glaring headlines in their papers—*State of Israel Proclaimed! Arabs Attack from All Sides!* They also read calls to mass meetings. Many made their way to the ramshackle building of the Jewish Agency on 66th Street just off Fifth Avenue, since torn down and replaced by the school building and auditorium of Temple Emanu-El, where Chaim Shertok, fourteen, son of Moshe, who had gone on to Israel to take up his Foreign Ministry portfolio, leaned from a window and unfurled the Israeli and American flags, his mother, Zippora, standing wet-eyed beside him.

For Zippora Shertok, the tears were both of joy and sadness: Just the day before her daughter Yael, seventeen, had left for Israel to join the Haganah, and her son, Yaakov, twenty-one, was already at the front with his unit.

And as the two flags flapped in the warm breeze, Hayim Greenberg, a member of the Jewish Agency Executive and one of the most beloved of the Jewish cultural leaders in America, solemnly recited the *Shehechiyanu*—the prayer of thanksgiving to the Lord for "having brought us to this time." From below, spontaneously, came the "Hatikva," and the young people began to dance a *hora* in the street, and the five-story Agency building rocked with *"le-chayims!"*

At the then headquarters of the Zionist Organization of America, the president, Zionist sage and veteran Emanuel Neumann, expressed the wish, as he offered a *"le-chayim,"* that the American government would do all in its power to lighten the burden of the provisional government and the beleaguered people of Israel.

The reference was to the arms embargo imposed by the White House as soon as the fighting began, under the terms of the American Neutrality Law. But this was not to be lifted for some time—not until, in fact, the battle had turned in Israel's favor and the end of the fighting was in sight.

Also at the ZOA headquarters, Jacques Torczyner, now a member of the World Zionist Organization Executive and director of the Herzl Institute, made the toast to the new state and its leaders, while at the American Jewish Congress headquarters, Rabbi Stephen S. Wise, one of the prime movers and shakers for statehood among American Jews, reminded the world that the call for a Jewish commonwealth came in 1918 at the very first meeting of the Congress, which had been organized to represent the Jews at the Peace Conference.

The picture was repeated through New York and, indeed, throughout America, wherever there was a Jew.

Rabbi Abba Hillel Silver, chairman of the American Section of the Jewish Agency, and the de facto leader of the Jewish delegation at the United Nations, never at a loss for words, could only repeat over and over, "This is marvelous, this is marvelous."

And in Magistrate's Court in Manhattan, Joseph Untermeyer, nineteen, the adopted son of Louis Untermeyer, the poet—on trial, along with a friend, for possessing a large cache of arms destined for the Haganah—asked that the trial be delayed when the news of the birth of the Jewish State came. The two declared that as soon as they were freed of the charges they would go to Palestine. They were, and they did.

The American Zionist Emergency Council held a rally at Madison Square Garden. The Garden, which was then at Fiftieth Street and Eighth Avenue, was supposed to open its doors at six, but by five-thirty it was already packed with the nineteen thousand it could hold, and the fire department closed the doors while some seventy-five thousand milled outside in the rain. Most of the seventy-five thousand went home because of the heavy downpour, but six thousand stayed on in the rain, listening to the speeches and the musical program over the loudspeakers.

There was little commotion in the streets, considering the crowd; only a few broken bones, and two women were arrested for slapping a cop. The police and members of the Zionist youth movements, who helped them, managed to keep the enthusiasm under pretty good rein.

Inside, the nineteen thousand went wild as the colors were trooped—the massed American flags up the left aisle, the massed veterans' association flags up the right aisle, the Israeli flags up the center. The program began with the *Shehechiyanu*, pronounced by Dr. Neumann, but Dr. Weizmann, who was slated to be there, was asked by his doctor to stay put at the Waldorf. On the program were Henry Morgenthau, Jr., the Secretary of the Treasury under Franklin Delano Roosevelt and now the general chairman of the United Jewish Appeal; Mayor William O'Dwyer, Rabbi Silver, Senator Robert Taft, Herbert Lehman, Rabbi Wolf Gold, and Rose Halprin, then the national president of Hadassah.

But the greatest drama was being played out some six thousand miles away, on a bit of earth about the size of New Jersey but with history enough for a country a hundred times its size.

As Abba Eban has it:

"I went into Park Avenue [from Chaim Weizmann's suite, on the evening of the news that the State had been declared]. It was dark and late. Back in our hotel, Suzy and I waited until midnight when the New York *Times* with its banner headlines gave us the news: Victory in Washington and the United Nations, but danger in the Middle East. The British High Commissioner had sailed from Haifa on a cruiser with the last remaining units of the [Mandate] government. Egyptian forces had crossed the frontier and advanced into the Negev. An Iraqi column moved in strength towards the Jordan River. The Transjordanian Arab Legion was arrayed along the river bank with its main encampment at Zerka. On the upper reaches of the Jordan, a Syrian brigade was ready to attack our settlements in the hot green valley. The Arab governments sought to occupy the country, subjugate its Jewish population and strangle Israel's statehood at its birth.

"Israel was experiencing the joys of birth and the fear of death in a single taste . . .

"It was a day that would linger and shine in the national memory forever—a moment of truth that would move Israel to its ultimate generations."

—R.Y.

A Happy Man in an Israeli Village

On a hot, uncomfortable day in Israel, in an obscure village near Afula, I found a happy man in an uncertain world.

For a while it seemed that it would be a quite ordinary day, the kind usually spent by Americans in Israel who want to "do" the land. The last thing in our minds, or imaginations, was that we would meet people like Haddad, who revealed to us a kind of person—and a type of Israeli—I could not believe exists, even though I met him, spent three hours with him and carry in my mind almost every minute of the one hundred and eighty we spent with him and his family.

We were attempting to get to Nof Ginosar, which lies on Lake Kinneret in the lower Galilee. The trip itself was tiring before we reached Afula. Traveling the quickest route, my son-in-law Gav drove up along the West Bank, through the Judean Hills, into Samaria, past Nablus and Jenin before we reached Afula, an important center above which lay the rich farmland developed and curried by Israeli farmers.

It was Sunday, and the Arab-inhabited lands were dry, sparsely cultivated, even though this area was supposed to be the "breadbasket" for the Kingdom of Jordan. Many of the Arabs appeared to be Christian, for we saw, in village after village, small clusters of Arabs in Western dress returning from church services. The stone homes painted in blue and orange indicated they were Arabic, for these are favorite Arab colors. We whizzed past small children who tried to sell figs to us and all other tourists traveling by car. We felt, for more than two uncomfortable, humid hours, that we were in unfriendly territory and we were more relaxed when we came to Afula and knew that soon we would leave a hostile area.

Suddenly, the disk brakes on our French-made Peugeot jammed and we realized we were in trouble because who, in this fairly primitive region, would know what to do to fix the brakes? Where would we find a competent mechanic? When? How?

We managed to crawl to a gas station which, to our disbelief and dismay, did not even have a telephone we could use to call the Israeli equivalent of the AAA in Tiberias. The station owner, however, adventurous with cars like so many other Israelis, assured us that we could drive to Tiberias without brakes. Remembering the hairpin turns, we argued it was impossible. He shrugged. From his attitude we sensed that he had dismissed us as over-careful American tourists not worth another minute of his time.

Carefully, Gav directed the car down a small incline where we saw a pickup truck and two workers. Slowly, the Peugeot came to a faltering stop and we approached the workers. One of them joined us, bent his body slowly and carefully under our car, tapped about and probed for a time and pronounced to us all, in a piercing baritone voice, "Your brakes are shot," or its equivalent in Hebrew. This was not news to us, but we thanked him and asked if there was anything he could do to help. He couldn't—except to say that a kilometer below us there was a modest grocery store which, he knew, had a phone. From there we could make the call to Tiberias, he suggested.

Again we gambled and maneuvered downhill and came to a final stop, convinced that here we must remain until help was brought. Unhappily, the store's phone was out of order. The North African women who ran the shop—opening the door to us with a sense of suspicion—stated that the phone had been broken a few days now and they, too, were waiting for repairs. We began to feel unhinged. How long would this take? Would help ever come? We couldn't even call the desk at the guesthouse at Nof Ginosar to tell them we were stuck—where were we?

Gav started to explore the village and a few minutes later he called to us. Simultaneously, a wiry, dark-haired, black-moustached man joined him in waving and it was his voice we heard, urging us forward toward his house.

This is how we met Yousaf Haddad in Moshava Yavniel, together with six of his children and his pregnant wife, Mesuda. We remained with them for three of the most interesting hours any of us have spent anywhere and we were all fairly well traveled.

We were, of course, tired, thirsty, unhappy and uncertain when Haddad first welcomed us to his home. Perhaps this is why, in retrospect, we remember the visit with such affection and admiration for the man. But somehow I doubt it. We would have felt the same way had we come well-fed and content with everything.

Gav had obviously informed Haddad that we were having car trouble. Haddad had said that his neighbor was an auto mechanic, so why not wait for him to return from Tiberias and join the Haddads until everything was fixed? That was the basis for the invitation.

We were invited into a small, poorly furnished home. It was difficult to see how so many could live in so small a house, except that there were four daughters, all of whom could be squeezed into a single bedroom. The two boys slept on couches in what was—we later learned—the shelter from which Israelis used to watch out for Arabs on the Golan Heights. Haddad and his wife had the remaining bedroom. There was a kitchen, with a large refrigerator proudly placed almost in the center; there was also a small table with two chairs. Everyone had to eat in shifts. The single bathroom carried the odor of eight active people who constantly were entering and exiting.

During the afternoon, Haddad insisted we have coffee and, later, beer. He also urged us to remain for supper, but that was not to be. Luckily for us, the neighboring mechanic returned from his job in Tiberias a bit earlier than anticipated. He was highly skilled and that made it possible for us to leave for Ginosar comparatively quickly. What remains in the mind is the man—Yousaf Haddad—far more so than his quiet, adoring wife, his two dark-haired handsome sons and his four daughters, all startlingly attractive. Two other daughters were married and lived elsewhere—one in Tel Aviv and another in Haifa. Haddad saw very little of them.

Haddad was born in this village and has lived there all his life. He must be in his fifties. When we first saw him, he was in his working clothes, spattered with paint, his hands dirty and his hair disheveled. He was a handyman in the area and was fixing a neighbor's cracked wooden floor. I don't know when the paint got all over him. He didn't say. But he sat down for lunch and, quite imperiously, motioned to a daughter to bring him his food.

Meanwhile, he talked. "My father," he said, "came here after he saw the world. Don't think he didn't." Haddad laughed harshly and without restraint. His Hebrew was uncultured but clear and lucid. "He was born in Egypt and he worked there. Then he worked in France and in North Africa. But he came here. Why not? He was a Jew. Here he lived and here I was born. Here." He looked at me quizzically as though I were about to challenge him. "You don't see why I live here? I'll tell you. We have everything in the world that we need, or want. I talk to people who go to America. They go. But they come back. Why?" He sipped slowly from his cup. "Why?" he asked again. I played his game and said, "You tell me why."

"I will," he answered. "I will. They come back because there is nothing in America . . . anywhere . . . that we don't have. Right? And why do you and your family come here? To see how we live. We have all we need. That's why so many Americans come here." He didn't seem to realize that most Americans remain in America and that there weren't all that many American Jews in Israel, either. But this didn't stop him.

"Look at us," he urged. "We eat every day . . . eat well. I have eight children, all very good." He spoke indoors as he ate, with his wife and all but one of his daughters sitting outside in the sun. The eldest sat in the kitchen with her father and me. "And I have a good wife . . . and two sons . . . and bread." He laughed again, without softness but with deep pleasure.

He finished his food and excused himself, saying, "Soon I finish my job and the mechanic will come. You don't have anything to worry about. It will be good."

When he left, I talked a bit with the daughter sitting alongside me. Her hair was in curlers and she was shy. She was also very pretty. Remembering that North African Jews generally marry at an early age, I asked her if she was thinking of marriage. "No. I do not marry just to marry. Some day, maybe, I will find someone good for me. Not yet." She did tell me animatedly that she looked forward to the Saturday night dances in Tiberias and that she enjoyed them and she knew a great many boys. But no, there was no one special.

When Yousaf returned, he called on his wife to prepare a bath for him and to lay out his clothes. Shortly thereafter, he emerged, and was another man entirely. He had managed to wash off all the paint and dirt. He looked considerably younger than I had first taken him to be. But he retained the smile, the pleasure in living that I had recognized.

Now he was ready to spend the rest of the afternoon with his unexpected guests. He urged beer on my son-in-law and on me, but offered my wife and daughter wine. "Beer," he announced, "is for men. Wine for women." At first we were reluctant to put him out, but he persisted. It seemed important to him, so we accepted and he almost danced with excitement. Then he began talking.

The initial surprise was that when he introduced the entire family to us—his wife, Mesuda, his four daughters and his two sons—he disclosed that the youngest son was named Kennedy.

"Kennedy?" I asked.

"Yes," he replied, "Robert Kennedy Haddad," rolling the words off his tongue. "Because Kennedy was killed by an Arab. If an Arab killed him, he was a friend of ours, a friend of Israel. Mesuda was having a boy. So when he was born, we called him Kennedy."

"Is that what everyone in the village calls him?" I asked.

"Most do," he replied. "Some call him Robert, but everybody knows he is Kennedy." Yousaf giggled. "You know," he said, "when I named him Kennedy, I wrote a letter to the Kennedy family in America, but I didn't know their address. So I sent the letter to the ambassador, the American ambassador." He frowned for a moment. "I never got an answer. Not from the ambassador and not from the Kennedys. Maybe the letter never was sent to them. What do you think?"

"Maybe the ambassador can't read Hebrew and nothing happened with the letter."

"Well, I couldn't write in English. I know only Hebrew."

"Why did you write?" I asked.

A sly smile crossed Yousaf's face. "Well, I wanted the Kennedys to know what I had done. It isn't everyone who did what I did. Besides, they are rich. Who knows . . . ?" He shrugged his shoulders and spread his palms wide.

I laughed.

Kennedy is a handsome, dark-skinned boy, less shy than his sisters. When I asked him his name, he said promptly, "Kennedy and Robert. I answer to both."

Yousaf dropped the subject and was ready to offer us more beer, which we politely turned down. The mechanic was still working on the car and I thought we would soon be ready to leave, but Yousaf was not ready to relinquish us. Instead, he talked of his life on the farm, the Arabs who lived atop the Golan Heights and the possibility of another war.

I wanted to know, "Do you worry about the Arabs who live so close to you, who can look down on your village?"

"No," he answered. "It is written. What will be will be."

I wondered what he meant. He spoke in short sentences, with animation, without anxiety.

"You see, there will be a final battle. There has to be. It is written. Gog and Magog. Jew and Arab. It doesn't matter who will win. We must all die. Then the Messiah will come—and we shall all live in peace. But the big battle must come. And we have nothing to say about the final victory. It is out of our hands. So, we work, we live, we have our children . . . and we continue to do what we have to do to live."

Again, he laughed. "Don't think because I talk this way that I am religious. *Ani lo dati* [I am not religious]. You see, I do not wear a *kipa* [yarmulke]. My daughters do not wear long dresses. My wife wears short sleeves and no wig." He was telling the truth. The long-limbed, nubile daughters wore shorts and tight blouses. Mesuda did not dress like a pious woman, either.

"Still," Yousaf insisted, "the day will come when the big war shall come. The Arabs on the Heights will shoot down on us again. I do not trust them. I do not like them. Understand. But it will happen, and we will fight back, as we always do. I think we will win. But it is in God's hands."

He offered us more beer and when I said I thought we had had enough, he changed his tactic and invited us to listen to music with him. I was curious. "What kind of music do you have?" My daughter whispered, "Dad, it's usually Greek or Turkish." I nodded, yes.

Yousaf said proudly, "We have everything, you see. I have a new phonograph." Not trusting his wife to get it, he scurried into the house and emerged with a portable record player and two records. The first played Greek music, loudly and a bit scratchy. Yousaf rose, swayed, wiggled his hips and snapped his fingers.

He invited us to join in the dance. It was still very hot and we worried about the car. We were in no mood to dance, but enjoyed his performance and his pleasure in himself. He then played the second record. He knew all the lyrics and was familiar with the rhythms. He danced energetically. His pregnant wife, who had been listening silently as he talked about the Arabs, war and the Messiah, watched him with great affection. His daughters, accustomed to their father's behavior, sat and talked with my wife and daughter.

Finally the car was fixed and it was time to leave. Yousaf, who had been watching me use my camera to take pictures of himself and his children, diffidently asked me if I would perhaps send him some snapshots. I assured him I would.

"Wonderful!" he shouted to one and all. "Our pictures will be made in America and we will see them!" He asked, "How long will it be before we can get them?" I said we would remain in Israel a few weeks longer and so I couldn't send the photos for another month. He seemed a bit downcast. He couldn't project that far ahead. Then he cheered up and asked me again, "You will send them?" "Of course," I assured him.

He lined up his family to say good-bye to us all and wished us a happy journey to Ginosar. As we entered the car, he turned to his record player and placed the Greek record on the turntable. The music, strident and piercing, carried throughout the village and to our ears as we drove away. As the car climbed up the dusty hill, the musical sounds followed us. Then they died down and we continued on our trip to Ginosar, another world among our people.

—H.U.R.

 My Faith in Israel's Future

It has never seemed to me that I deserve any special credit, as an individual, for what I did about Israel when I was President of the United States.

In recognizing the new State of Israel, and in giving careful consideration to its needs and its problems after 1948, I believe I was only expressing the sentiments of the people of the United States, regardless of political party or religious belief. And I also believe I was acting as the President of the United States ought to act —that is, in the interest of the United States.

There was something deeply moving and deeply stirring to every American in the creation of the new State of Israel in the ancient land of Palestine.

Here was a country founded on the love of human freedom, just as our own country was based on the ideal of freedom.

Here was a country designed to be a haven for the oppressed and persecuted of the earth, just as our own country had been.

Here in the land of Moses and the prophets was a rebirth of a nation dedicated, as of old, to the moral law and to belief in God.

I had faith in Israel before it was established. I have faith in it now.

I believe it has a glorious future before it—not just as another sovereign nation, but as an embodiment of great ideals of our civilization.

One of the great men of Israel, and one of the great men of modern times, was the late President Chaim Weizmann. I knew him and admired him. He was a founder not only of Israel, but also of the Hebrew University.

Israel did not begin on May 14, 1948. Israel had many beginnings. One of them came on the day in 1918 when Dr. Weizmann laid the cornerstone of the Hebrew University. The university preceded the state. And that is as it should have been, for the state must be more than a political or military fact. The state must be founded on knowledge and on enlightenment. It must try to achieve the good life for its citizens—and that can be done only if its citizens are educated and enlightened.

I think I know the precious worth of a good education and university training better than most men. That is because I was never able to get a college education. I had to get such learning as I have through my own reading. And that makes one realize how important, how very valuable, university training is.

We have achieved our unity in this country, not by eliminating our differences in religion and tradition, not by hiding or suppressing our political and economic conflicts, but by holding to a concept which rises above them all, the concept of the brotherhood of man.

After the Point IV organization was set up, I asked the Executive Director of TVA, Gordon Clapp, to make a tour of the Near East, beginning with Turkey and going through Syria, Lebanon, Palestine, Arabia and Egypt. He made a survey of the Mesopotamian Valley and informed me that the Tigris and Euphrates rivers, properly harnessed and used for irrigating that wonderful plain, would support between twenty and twenty-five million people, just as it had done in the times of Babylon and Nineveh.

I asked him to investigate the desert areas between the Jordan River and the Persian Gulf, which had been great caravan routes during Roman times. There were discovered in this area old Roman concrete basins built to hold and conserve rainwater from the rainy season. But now they are filled with sand. I visualized these being cleaned and used again for pastoral projects.

I also asked Mr. Clapp to investigate the feasibility of a syphon from the Mediterranean Sea to the Dead Sea Valley. The Dead Sea is twelve hundred and sixty odd feet below the level of the Mediterranean, and I visualized a source of power there that would make an industrial area out of the whole of Israel and the immediately adjoining region to the south, which contains immense stores of metal ores.

He reported to me that this was perfectly feasible. With the aid of Point IV, Turkey has become a surplus wheat-growing country, and the establishment of an agricultural haven in the Tigris and Euphrates Valleys, with proper control and development of the Nile, and of the immense oil resources of Iran and Arabia, would make this area an agricultural and industrial dreamland.

Sometime this will be done, and there will be peace in this great area. It will be a source of satisfaction to the Greeks, Turks, Arabs and Jews, as well as to the Egyptians.

We must cherish and help those nations and cultures which support the dignity of the human individual. Only if we do this can we roll back the tide of communist aggression. A society based on respect for the individual is the only answer to race prejudice. It is the only answer to religious prejudice. It is the only answer to tyranny and oppression.

Today we must work toward the ideal of peace and progress in the Near East. That must be the goal of the United Nations and of the United States of America, for the well-being of all nations of that area and the safety and prosperity of the whole west depend upon us.

—H.S.T.

 ## Why an Arab Farmer Brought a Bar Mitzvah Present

A few months after the Six-Day War ended, an Israeli physician was driving in the West Bank, headed for home in Jerusalem. He was hurrying on the poor secondary road, anxious to return home before nightfall. He was glad that he had stopped to give a hitch to a lone Israeli soldier, who of course had his weapons with him, as he headed for a brief furlough in a Negev kibbutz.

Like so many other Israelis in those summer and early fall months of 1967, the two were exchanging reminiscences of the period that led up to the Six-Day War, when Jews throughout the world—including those in Israel—feared an all-out death blow to the young state. Instead, as history will record, the Israelis not only had emerged victorious, but also had shown the world—and themselves—that they could unite and fight valiantly for their self-defense.

Suddenly, the Israeli physician saw a figure jump out into the road, waving his hands excitedly, asking the car to stop. The soldier with the doctor cursed under his breath and advised the doctor to ignore the man in the road—to drive on. "It might be a trap," he said.

But the Israeli physician thought otherwise. Maybe it was something about the man's stance as he stood and waved his hands frantically—or perhaps it was the doctor's instinct, honed by years of medical practice. He braked his car sharply and came to a full stop. The soldier at his right kept his hands on the automatic weapon that lay across his lap.

The man in the road rushed forward. In a torrent of Arabic—which the Israeli physician understood, having picked up enough during the years he treated Arab patients in the famed Hadassah medical center—the man made it clear that he needed help, his wife was in labor, she was having a hard time, there was no doctor in the area—and as he realized that the driver of the car he had stopped was a doctor, he began to sing hosannahs to Allah.

Within a few minutes the Israeli physician was in the modest home of the Arab, less than a stone's throw from the road. The wife was indeed having a hard time and was screaming for help as she fought to deliver her child. The Israeli physician rolled up his sleeves, shushed the Arab husband from the room, and within less than an hour, the mother and child were both doing fine.

The Israeli physician would accept no payment, wished the Arab father and mother well, and, still escorted by his Israeli military companion, set off for Jerusalem, which he reached later that night, fatigued but happy that he had managed to perform an act of humanitarianism.

Several years passed; the doctor was now living in a Tel Aviv suburb and the incident was gone from his mind. On a particular Sabbath morning, he and his wife, as well as several scores of invited friends and relatives, were leaving the synagogue, at which they had just celebrated the Bar Mitzvah of their son, when they were stopped by a stranger who inquired politely, in halting Hebrew, if he could speak to "Dr. C."

Yes, the physician responded, at which the stranger bent low and kissed the doctor's hand, and began to speak, still in halting but comprehensible Hebrew:

"You do not remember me, Doctor," he said. "About seven years ago you saved the life of my wife, and you gave us a son—a fine, healthy boy. You would not take money from me, you did your work and you left, but how could I forget such a deed? I wrote down the name of your car number, and later, when I was in Jerusalem, I told the officials that I wished to know who you are, and at first they would not believe me. But then I showed them my son, and they asked me to repeat the story, and then told me your name and your address.

"Once a year I have come to this small city to ask about you, to know if you are well, and each year I have been told all is well. I have sat on the curb stone across the street from your office, during my visits, and watched you go out, and have blessed you, and have been made happy to see that you are well and happy.

"Last year, I learned that you are going to celebrate your own son's coming of age, what you call Bar Mitzvah, and I thought what can I do for this fine man, who has given me my son, that will express to him the joy and affection I feel in my heart for him? I have thought about this the whole year, and then I knew what I must do."

From inside his coat pocket he withdrew a small, gaily wrapped package, and handed it to the doctor. "This is for your son," he said, "from my son, and from my wife, and from me—with all our devotion."

The doctor was deeply touched, as were the guests surrounding him, listening to the Arab's account and expression of thankfulness. The father touched the Arab's shoulder in a gesture of friendship and handed the gift to the Bar Mitzvah boy, who quickly opened the package, revealing a glistening, gold-colored pen, bedecked with a blue stone.

"*Todah rabbah*," the Bar Mitzvah boy said to the Arab, extending his hand.

The Arab shook his hand, and then, as he had earlier, kissed the youngster's hand, too.

The story is true, not apocryphal. Other tales of warm contacts between Arabs and Israelis on many different levels abound.

Perhaps the people who sit down at peace negotiating sessions should be the Israeli physician from the Tel Aviv suburb and the Arab farmer from the West Bank.

—D.C.G.

Memoirs of a Bilu Pioneer
En Route to Palestine from Russia in 1882

Moscow, February 10, 1882

These are bad times for the Jews, yet the continuing reports of more pogroms seem to push people toward action rather than into greater distress and confusion. The terror of recent events has made it impossible for anyone among us to remain indifferent; even smug and complacent Jews have been awakened, rudely enough, from what must have seemed a sound, sweet sleep. Until these pogroms began I myself had thrust aside my Jewish origins. I lived and breathed a Russian life and every new Russian scientific discovery, every new creation of Russian literature, every victory of Russian imperial power, everything Russian filled my heart with pride. My passionate desire was to devote my strength to my fatherland, to carry out all the duties of a good and honest citizen . . . Then, suddenly, with no warning, we were shown the door and were told flatly: "The Western frontier is open to you." I am continuously haunted by the cruel, pointed question: "Who are you? Identify yourself—if you can." But what kind of a question is that? What does it mean? Who am I? Is it essential that I be somebody? Although I try to evade the answer, I still can't get away from the question. I know that I must, that I am obliged to answer—that I must decide. I answer: "Of course, I'm a Russian." But I feel that this would not be sincere. What true basis do I have for such an answer? Really, just my feelings and my dreams. But, lunatic that you are, don't you see that the Russians respond to this passionate love with the coldest and most offensive contempt? We have always been strangers everywhere in the world. We have been driven out of every country in the world. We are never accepted as members in the family of nations—only as latecomers and foreigners. Yes—whether I wish it or not, I am a Jew. But are these persecutions the only

bond I have with my people? No, we have in common a great past in which we served the world, gave it its basic ethics . . . This is so—yet what are our problems and aspirations today? Judaism does not satisfy me. What does it give me other than its memories? What does it offer me now that can be essential to my life? The only kind of life to which I can look forward makes me shudder. I see myself a fool, suffering from a passionate sense of wrong, suffering from frustrated longings, bitter insults and affronts, but worst of all, from apathy. A terrible life, and it is the lot of every sensitive Jew. My God, why must we be denied the sympathy and love of those who are closest to us?

March 2, 1882

A strong movement has started in one segment of the Jewish community for settlement in Palestine. I have thought hard about this idea and have come to the conclusion that this is the only solution for our people. My doubts have vanished. Judaism still has a great future, a glorious, historical goal and so there is still a good and fruitful field of work for honest and devoted sons of Israel. I have found a meaning in the word "Jew." This great ideal of renascence is worthy of hard work.

But to give up my education and take up the plowshare and spade in a wild country . . . I had grown up with the idea that I would get a professional education and now, not far from the goal, to go and exchange all this for the hard, physical labor of a worker of the soil! All that time a fierce struggle went on within me—it was like a fever. But now I am at peace. I know what I want.

April 25, 1882

We have organized a group of intelligent young people who intend to emigrate to the Holy Land and to devote themselves to farming there. We have no money, but we are sure that once we are there we will be helped to settle quickly. There are people everywhere who sympathize deeply with the idea of settlement [in Palestine]. Many organizations and influential people have already promised to help us. In the city of Kharkov there is a very active circle which has helped other groups to organize in many other cities. We have told Kharkov that, for the sake of unity, we would join with them, and today we had a very satisfactory answer from them.

These are the main facts about our organization: we are called Bilu, have a membership of 525 people belonging to several groups, all of which are under the leadership of the Kharkov group which is known as "The Central Bureau." This bureau will conduct all the affairs of the pioneers until the entire membership has been brought to Jaffa. The goal of the group is to set up a model settlement to serve as an example for all Jewry. Each group must be ready to set out for Odessa as soon as it receives its call from the Central Bureau.

Odessa, June 29, 1882

Our orders from the Central Bureau have come at last and we—that is, a group of six—have come [here] to Odessa. The Bureau had been transferred first from Kharkov to Odessa and then from there to Constantinople, where it is now attempting to secure enough land from the Turkish government to settle three hundred people, and it has hopes for success. We will still have to remain in Odessa for some time while arrangements are being made for our passports.

Black Sea, aboard the steamship Russia, July 19, 1882

The tumult is quieting down, the engine hisses and roars, the boat is getting ready to leave. After the last quick embraces, the passengers hurry to their places; the police leave; the third deafening whistle blows; the sailors move about briskly, pulling in the gangplanks, and gradually the ship begins to move away from the harbor. The passengers quickly gather at the stern for one last look at the home shore, from which the dense crowd of people who have come to see us off are waving hats and handkerchiefs. The boat moves sluggishly, as though it were reluctant to leave a place where it had so safe and calm a berth. But look! It is pulling itself together and, at the captain's command, "Full speed ahead!" it throws off all its doubts and rushes bravely and decisively on. The last farewells from the shore, the people, boats, houses, everything we were able to see—begin to merge and lose their contours. Gradually, little by little, the land disappears—we are out on the open sea. The S.S. *Russia* is carrying me away from Russia . . . under full steam. My heart grows heavy at the thought that I have left all my ties and aspirations behind me; have left all my dreams and desires, everything by which I have lived until now; the place where I grew up, where I learned to feel and to love . . . But you, dear homeland, pushed me away! You responded coldly, mercilessly, frigidly to all my tenderness. Oh, our lot has been cruel: eternally to sow and never to reap, abuse and mockery instead of the gratitude we might have deserved . . . But the time has come to put an end to such bitter thoughts. We have lived among strangers long enough; the time has come for us to establish our own little home.

The heat has subsided a little. Evening has come. The sun has dropped into the sea, leaving a long, golden path of light as a link between itself and us. Now a strong wind has begun to blow, and great waves are beating up against the boat, but our *Russia* moves on, without hesitation, cutting proudly through the stormy elements. I stayed on deck to fill my lungs with the refreshing, invigorating sea air. At last I remembered that it must be time to have a bite, and I found my friends, snugly ensconced in the hold inside a circle of crates and suitcases, drinking tea. We were, as I have already said, six people, G. age twenty-five, a straightforward, honest fellow from Courland who is accompanied by his pretty blonde fiancée. It seems that the first time she ever heard Russian spoken was by pilgrims on the boat, so she calls it "Die Bogomilische Sprache." C. is thirty, an exceptionally pleasing man, clever and distinguished-looking, with a high forehead and slightly mocking eyes. The other G. left a technical school, and E. is a simple but good fellow.

Constantinople, July 22, 1882

The weather was good at the beginning of our voyage, but as we continued the ship began to play tricks and consequently almost everyone suffered badly from seasickness. I had been determined to stay on my feet. I wanted to experience the feeling of facing the storm and outfacing it! But as we approached Constantinople I, too, succumbed; it still seems to me that the ground is shaking under my feet! On the night of the twentieth we dropped anchor at the entrance to the Bosporus. On the twenty-first, at six in the morning, we sailed into the Straits, and two hours or so later the ship entered the harbor. While we were still some distance away we had become aware of a flotilla of small landing craft and before we had a chance to stop, it had completely surrounded us. The boatmen, as nimble as monkeys, climbed right up the ship's sides. In a moment the deck was thick with them, and they were pestering the passengers with offers of service. But we waited, knowing that the Central Bureau would send someone we would be able to rely on. In our situation, inexperienced as we were and not knowing the language, these Turkish seamen and all kinds of agents and customs officials could have cost us a pretty penny.

Then a young man came over to ask whether we were "the students from Kharkov." After he had shown us his credentials from the Bureau, he took complete charge. He called over one of the Turkish porters, who gathered up our belongings and we were off, but an inspector went through all the other landing craft checking every passenger for sealed packages. When he came over to our landing craft, one of us produced some papers for the sake of appearances, but our escort gave him a meaningful wink and the inspector took off. When we landed, the customs officials who had come to meet us went away, likewise, after a little whispering between them and our agent. Some porters grabbed up our bags which, for obvious reasons, had not been inspected. We started out for the city through a long, narrow corridor. There we saw a half-blind official with the face of an idiot, sitting with his hand outstretched. We were amazed that this shameless *baksheesh* should exist even in Constantinople, a place where one soon ceases to wonder at what one sees. We put a coin into the outstretched hand and we stepped out into Galata Street, the main thoroughfare near the sea. The city is densely populated, and land is scarce and dear; they have solved the problem by putting up tall apartment buildings, which are very dirty. Each house floor belongs to a different owner. The streets are narrow and paved with cobblestones. Some kind of local superstition prevents the people from driving off the great number of fat, lazy, dirty dogs who lie about on the street. The passers-by walk around them. They live completely at their ease, feeding on the garbage which the apartment dwellers throw down into the street! A man has to run in front of every *konki* (horse-drawn wagon) to drive the dogs out of the way because they never move of their own accord, and they would be killed by the hundreds.

The method here of delivering milk is highly unusual, simple, direct, and an absolute guarantee of freshness. Instead of milking their animals at home and delivering the milk in pitchers, the Turks drive their goats through the city and sell fresh, steaming milk to anyone who wants it!

When we arrived at the hotel, we found our comrades from the Central Bureau still in bed, but they were delighted to see us. There are three of them now, but sometimes there are more. They jumped up, dressed, ordered tea, and talked about ordering some cake as well, but from the way they looked at each other it was plain enough that they couldn't afford even such modest luxuries. While we drank our tea they gave us a report of their financial situation, which is critical.

Briefly, they have no assets but many debts. Everything they brought with them has been pawned except the clothes on their backs. Once in a while some money does come in from various benefactors or from their parents, but in very small amounts. Yesterday they were down to their last half-franc, with no one to borrow from.

This is the story they told us: The management sends tea to all the rooms every morning, so they drink a lot of tea. But yesterday, for instance, having drunk all the tea they wanted, and finding themselves with only a half-franc at breakfast time, they were faced with a major decision. One of them said, "Look, there's no problem. It's breakfast time. Let's buy a loaf of bread."

"Fine. But what then?"

"Nothing. We'll have breakfast. After that, it's simple. We'll drink tea again tonight. If we've eaten once, it won't be too hard to go without supper. We may even have some bread left. Come on, let's eat. I'm hungry."

But the third one didn't see it in the same way. "That's all very well for you, but, personally, I'm dying for a smoke, and there's no tobacco."

"It's either bread or tobacco. We can't afford both. Take your choice."

"We'll take a vote."

Two voted for tobacco and one for bread. They bought tobacco. The Central Bureau for the Rebuilders of the Land of Israel! This is the way they live! These are the problems they discuss!

Constantinople, July 24, 1882

I have already mentioned that the Central Bureau has been petitioning the government in Constantinople for a grant of land in Syria for three hundred people (Palestine is officially a part of Syria). The petition was presented to the Minister of the Interior, but thus far they have had no reply. Since not much can be done here in Turkey without help from influential people, they turned to Osmani Pasha. He is now the Minister of War in Constantinople, but he is better known as the courageous defender of Pleven. He received them cordially and when he heard that they were students from Kharkov, he recalled that he had been there as a prisoner of war. Then, after listening attentively to their request, he promised to help them.

Oliphant had encouraged them previously with all kinds of promises, but he has recently notified them that, since the Egyptian problem has become acute, the English are no longer welcome at the Sultan's court. He is, therefore, not in a position to do anything for us now. It is all too obvious that there will be plenty of hardships ahead for us in Jaffa before we reach our goal. Under these circumstances the Central Bureau cannot possibly call out the whole group from Russia now. So far only fourteen people have come to Jaffa.

In the meantime, having heard reports that Russian and Rumanian Jews are not allowed to enter Jaffa without a *teskere* (a transit certificate through the Turkish provinces), we prepared ourselves for any eventuality by getting these documents. We have all signed an agreement by which we are obligated to live and work together with the group already in Jaffa. As Biluim in Jaffa we will manage our own internal affairs, but all our general business will be handled by the Central Bureau until the entire group has been gathered together in Jaffa. One more member of the Kharkov circle has just arrived in Constantinople and he will leave with us.

Smyrna, July 31, 1882

On the evening of the twenty-ninth we left Constantinople on the steamer *Lazarev*. By the next morning we were in the Straits of Dardanelles and saw the small town that bears the same name. Late last night we stopped in the Bay of Smyrna, outside the richest, busiest city in Asia Minor. In the morning the steamer approached the city to take on food, and for one *matlik* (about two kopeks) we were able to go ashore in a small boat. I stepped on Asiatic soil for the first time in my life. We were hungry and wanted some dinner, but not knowing the language, we searched the town for a Jew. Finally one of those creatures who belongs to no particular nationality, has no homeland, has even forgotten his own parents, whose very bones are degenerate to the marrow, spied us. You see their kind everywhere; they speak every language—after a fashion. They are men who live by their wits and are always looking for someone to make a sucker of. In short, we ran across a Jewish *makler*. He caught sight of us from a distance and then stuck to us like a leaf from a bath-house switch. All we were willing to ask him was where we could get an inexpensive dinner, and he took us to a restaurant. Having already had some experience in Constantinople with the ways of the breed, we got rid of him as soon as we could. He left us unwillingly, grumbling because we had given him only one franc.

It took all my knowledge of Greek and a fair amount of guessing to make some sense of the menu and prices, so that I could show the waiter what we wanted. He brought us some cognac first and then bouillon, roast meat and some kind of green vegetable that I had never seen before. The whole meal, which included beer, cost us only one franc each.

After dinner we set out to see the city. Smyrna lies in the lowest part of the bay. Mountains, terraced with vineyards, rise behind the city. A beautiful, wide street paved with small granite bricks runs down its length as do tracks for a train that links Smyrna with some town close by. We were stunned by the beauty of the buildings along the waterfront. They are mainly three- or four-story hotels with cafés, quite palatial, and many of them have marble facades. Their entrances are decorated with beautiful stained glass and elegant white grillwork and the upper floors with balconies. We were overwhelmed by the beautiful Oriental gardens which open out at the end of long central corridors whose inner doors lead to the interiors of the buildings. Everything—hotels, balconies, gardens—is magnificent, exotic. Running parallel to the waterfront are two or three more streets with the most luxuriously magnificent stores. Then, quite abruptly, there was no more magnificence. The streets became mean, dirty and littered with refuse. It had become a typical Turkish town!

In population, the city is heterogeneous. The Jews are mainly Sephardim, ten thousand to fifteen thousand of them, wealthy and well established. I saw their famous synagogue and a school belonging to the Alliance. There are about a hundred Ashkenazi Jews. They are heartbreakingly poor, but quite recently, under the leadership of one of their own people, they have formed an organization into which each member pays the equivalent of about one *medjidi* (or two rubles) a month. Any needy member is given aid from the treasury. They have rented a clubhouse and subscribe to newspapers. Free room and board are provided for about ten to fifteen days for any indigent Ashkenazi who comes into the community. If he wants to do business, peddling to the crews and passengers of incoming ships, he is allowed a few *medjidi* to buy notions.

Mersina, August 5, 1882

After leaving Smyrna on the evening of August 2, we reached Chios at midnight, and at dawn continued on our way for the next fifty hours to Mersina. The ocean was calm and we enjoyed the journey, but at Mersina a storm began to play about us. Even before the storm broke, the ocean had been sufficiently agitated to make it impossible to continue taking on cargo. Everyone was ordered away from the stern; the hatch was battened down; sails were unfurled, and the captain, standing on his bridge, gave orders to weigh anchor. They were raising the anchor when the ship suddenly lurched, leaped, and sprang into the air twice! I shall never forget those horrible leaps! Everything fell: suitcases, bundles, all kinds of objects began to roll across the deck; then, there was a great crash and a violent uproar. Terrified passengers fell upon their knees with cries of "God have mercy!" and the Jews recited the "Shema Yisroel." It was a solemn moment. Each one of us prepared to die, with only God knowing what we thought and felt. Then the silence was shattered by a great outburst of crying and sobbing. From the terrifying noise, we had thought that the boat had exploded and was sinking. It survived— only to start rocking madly over the water, tossing about like a playball, its masts whipping the water, the waves flooding the deck. There was water beneath us, around us, and over us and it seemed as though we had already been swallowed up by the elements. Weak and helpless, we rolled about the deck, colliding with one another in the stern. Then, amidst this great holocaust, we heard someone cry out, "Hey! Somebody call the captain!"

"What do you want him for?" someone else asked.

"I want him to get the hold filled with water. That will make the ship stop tossing and we won't be drowned!"

Only the crew remained on their feet. The captain, in hooded rain gear, closely belted and strapped, shouted his commands, drowning out the roar of the waves as though he were threatening the elements. But they simply answered him with a monotonous, "Aye, aye." For twenty hours the storm raged and then, gradually, began to subside.

G. was the first to go out on deck, but the ship was still tossing so much that his hat was torn off and he had to stand astride, hanging on tightly to a ship's cable in order to keep his balance. His bare head, his bald patch, his whole posture lent him such a serious aspect that one sailor, not understanding what G. had in mind, went up to him, took hold of his arm, and asked, "What are you trying to do?"

"To stand, to stand! I am holding up the ship!" the Courlander answered hastily; he had trouble expressing himself in Russian. The sailor looked at him contemptuously, shook his head and walked away, amazed at how astoundingly stupid those Germans were. When G. described the scene after the storm, we had a good laugh.

Alexandretta, August 6, 1882

We arrived at Alexandretta this morning, and about noon we set out for the city. We wanted to buy some meat in the city, but we were unable to find any Jews. Finally, I wrote in Greek (there are many Greeks here) on a scrap of paper, "Where is the Jewish neighborhood?" and gave the note to the first Greek we met. Modern Greek pronunciation differs so radically from the classical that I really wouldn't have been able to communicate with anyone orally. The Greek read my note and then pointed to a grilled gate. We went into the courtyard, opened a door at the opposite end, and found ourselves in a medium-sized synagogue. In one corner, at a workbench, sat a doddering old man repairing shoes.

He got up to meet us, and after the customary "Sholom Aleichem" we began to speak to him in Hebrew. But since we were unaccustomed to the Sephardic pronunciation, it was difficult for us to express ourselves well.

The old man explained to us that he was the *haham* [rabbi] of the local community. When we were finally able to make him understand what we wanted, he slid his aged feet into red slippers, locked the door, and went out with us into the street. He took us to a Greek butcher store, pointed out some meat bearing black stamps and told us that this was kosher meat. In this country—not only in cities where the Jewish community is so small that it would not be profitable to maintain a Jewish butcher store, but even in cities which have a considerable Jewish population—kosher meat is sold in non-Jewish stores. The butcher simply calls in a Jewish slaughterer, who then puts his stamp on the meat he has slaughtered, and from this stamp the Jews know that this is "their" meat. We looked at this "kosher" stamp with some little suspicion and asked, "Where is your *shohet* [ritual slaughterer]?"

"What do you need him for?"

"We'd like to get a chicken killed."

The old man nodded, pounded his chest and said proudly, "I am the *shohet.*"

"But aren't you the *haham?*"

"I, with God's help, am both—the *haham* and the *shohet.*"

And the shoemaker! we added silently.

So we went to look for a chicken! But first we bought two *okiyas* (six pounds) of fish for forty kopecks. Then we met a boy carrying a goose. We bargained with him for the goose and finally bought it for eighty-five kopecks. (Our Russian silver has been accepted wherever we have offered it.) We took our goose and carried it off to the *shohet.* My companions are not very strict about *kashruth* and they asked the *shohet* to find us a woman who would cook for us. He took us to his daughter-in-law. We gave him a half-franc and offered her another half-franc and the feathers from the goose for her labor, and she went right to work. While we waited, we talked with the old man. He gave us to understand, quite proudly, that he was not "just anybody" but that his ancestry went back in a straight line to King David himself. His father, who is still alive and served as rabbi in one of the very important Jewish communities in Syria, has in his safe-keeping all the documents and details of their genealogy—proof of their lofty origin. In all fairness to him, I must say that he knows both the Bible and Hebrew well. The total Jewish population of Alexandretta, he said, consists of five Sephardi families and one Ashkenazi.

When the goose was roasted, we took it with us, bought some brandy, wine, vegetables and grapes and returned to the ship. The few Jewish families who are traveling on the ship also provided for the Sabbath. (Today is Friday.) They have a kerosene stove, and their cooking is really extensive. We all decided to eat together, so we gave them our fish to cook and we are looking forward to a "good Sabbath."

Beirut, August 8, 1882

The women improvised a table out of benches, covered it with a cloth and kindled the Sabbath candles. Although no one is permitted to light candles, or to smoke, in the hold, no one hindered us. We made up a *minyan* [quorum] with an old man serving as cantor. The other passengers, curious about our customs, formed a circle around us. A Rumanian priest began to mock us, but the other Greek Orthodox pilgrims and the sailors put a quick stop to that. At the end of the service, we wished one another a good Sabbath, recited Kiddush over the wine, washed our hands, and sat down at the table.

I have rarely observed all the little ceremonies with so much care as we did that night. We were carried away by the fantastic setting. We ate our dinner with much good cheer that was certainly increased by the amount of wine which we drank with the meal. That night the ship reached Litania, where it stopped for two hours, and by the next morning we were already in Tripoli. Along the waterfront there are only the usual hotels, cafés, warehouses and so forth. A *konki* runs between the waterfront and the city proper, which is built up on the hills about four or five *versts* in from the sea. Nature here is enchanting. The domestic animals are unusually well kept, the vegetation luxurious, and wells and brooks are abundant. Food here is very cheap.

We left Tripoli in the evening and arrived in Beirut the next morning. We hired a boat for the four of us at a round-trip price of a half-franc per person for a trip to the city. When we arrived on shore a customs official came over and asked for our papers. To our great surprise he spoke to us in Russian. He turned out to be a Polish Tartar, a native of Novogrudok in the province of Minsk—in fact, a countryman of mine! For the past fifteen years he has been wandering about in foreign countries. He lived for a while in Cyprus, worked in Egypt, traveled through the whole Middle East and, for the past year, has been working for the Turks.

He said, "I'm living very comfortably here, thank God, if such a thing can be said of a man whom fate has doomed to eternal wandering. I am here, but my heart is where my parents and my family are." We shook hands with him feelingly and went on.

The city, inhabited mainly by Arabs, is quite large and clean. Most of the commerce is in the silk which is manufactured locally. There are literally rows and rows of stores heaped high with silk.

Since we hadn't much time we went back to the boat as soon as we had bought what we needed. But as the boatmen pushed away from shore, they asked us for their money. It is usual enough, simply an easy way to skin the Jewish passengers, a way of cheating them of their money. We had heard stories of passengers having been beaten and their money taken from them by force. We understood perfectly well where this demand was leading and simply answered that we would give them the fare when we got to the ship. At that the boatmen stopped rowing and began to threaten us.

"Oh, pay them!" C. finally shouted. "It's three o'clock already. They'll make us late for the boat."

G., our treasurer, took out two francs and handed them to the Arab, who took it and then demanded more.

"No. We agreed on a half-franc per person."

The Arab grabbed at the hand in which G. was holding his wallet, but E., who is very strong, jumped up and swung his fist hard. We heard a sharp crack, and the Arab's hand dropped limply. His friends jumped to his defense and a wild skirmish was in the making when the boat tipped and almost capsized. Since nobody wanted to drown, we all settled back and then threatened the Arab that we would go to our consul.

"Yallah! Go to your consul!" shouted the boatmen angrily and began to row back to town. There was no way to stop them from returning to shore, so we decided that we would go to the [Russian] consul with our complaint. But it turned out to be an hour's walk to the consul's office, and we had only three quarters of an hour left before sailing time. We went into the customs booth, but we found only one officer there—not the Russian we had met before. One of the boatmen, shaking with laughter, told him his version of the story while we tried to tell him in French what really had happened. But that bastard, who most certainly got his share from these little adventures, only answered, in the calmest, most good-natured way imaginable, that the fixed price for the trip was one franc per person each way, and so we owed them eight francs!

"Why so?" we asked. "We agreed it was going to be two francs for both ways."

"What can we do? It's a fixed price . . . You should be grateful that they're not asking sixteen francs for two trips. After all, you know, you have made them lose their time!"

It was, of course, impossible to hire another boat. In helpless rage we gave them another six francs and went back to the boat. As soon as we stepped up to the ship's ladder the Arabs, shrewd enough to fear revenge, shoved off quickly. G., furious, ran to the captain to complain.

The captain only laughed. "How do you expect me to help you?" he asked. "Why didn't you complain to the consul?"

"We were afraid we'd be late for the boat."

"That's a shame. The boat won't be sailing on time. You just keep on the lookout and if those rascals come back, let me know."

G. remained on the lookout without ever budging from the rail, but our Arabs didn't show up. At last he did see one of them coming back in his boat. He immediately ran to the captain to tell him, and the captain called over a strong boatswain. The moment the Arab set foot on deck, the deckhand grabbed him by the forelock, dragged him to the mast, tied him to it with a strong cable and called over a sailor to keep an eye on him. All of the passengers crowded around to watch the spectacle. The Arab struggled like a wild animal, tried to bite through the cable, ground his teeth, and spat out a string of curses on all "Muscovites."

After a while the mother of our captive arrived, accompanied by a lot of other women. She begged, implored, and swore that she was too poor to return the money, but the captain simply ignored her. Then all the women threw themselves down on the deck, crawled to his feet, kissed his garments, but the captain remained adamant and shouted, "Get them out of here, and tell the mother that if she doesn't bring back the money, I'll give her son a hundred and fifty lashes and take him away with me!"

The Arab women went away in bitter disappointment. It was growing dark when the old woman came back, sobbing and lamenting. At last, realizing that all her sighs and sobs were of no use, she handed the captain six francs, only to be told, "Two more francs."

"Why? Two francs is all that was coming to him . . ."

"No! You bring all the money and you'll get your son back."

The poor old woman shuffled back to her boat.

"Well, God be with her!" said the captain. "Untie the wretch!"

Once he was untied, the unfortunate Arab, having been kicked and cuffed on the back of the neck, darted off, leaving a torrent of curses behind him.

—C.Ch.

The Jewish Legion:
A Turning Point in Modern Jewish History

"Far away, in your home, you will one day read glorious news of a Jewish life in a free Jewish country—of factories and universities, of farms and theatres, perhaps MPs and ministers. Then you will lose yourself in thought and the paper will slip from your fingers, and there will come to your mind a picture of the Jordan Valley, of the desert by Raffa, of the Hills of Ephraim by Abu Ein. Then you shall stand up, walk to the mirror and look yourself proudly in the face, jump to attention and salute yourself—for it is you who made it."

These were the words which Vladimir Jabotinsky, a stormy petrel of the Zionist movement for nearly a quarter of a century, addressed to the first volunteers who enlisted in the Jewish Legion in 1917 because they were eager to be the first Jewish fighting force to enter Palestine since the days of Bar Kochba. In 1977 some three hundred survivors of the more than ten thousand members of the Jewish Legion came to Avi-chail, Israel, to observe the sixtieth anniversary of the formation of the Jewish Legion, at ceremonies held at Hagdudim, the Jewish Legion Museum.

Jabotinsky, who did not live to see the birth of Israel in 1948 and who was for a long time a political foe of the men and women who became the first leaders of Israel, was a militant and maximalist Zionist who fathered the Jewish Legion as a unit of the British Army during World War I, but later was treated as an enemy by the British authorities in Palestine.

When an Arab mob attacked unarmed Jewish worshipers in the Old City of Jerusalem on April 4, 1920, shouting "the government is with us," the Holy City was "stiff with troops," yet five Jews were killed and 211 were injured in three days of rioting that followed. Two companies of a Jewish self-defense unit called Haganah, made up largely of teenagers, tried to come to their rescue, but were barred by rifle-wielding Tommies at the Jaffa and Damascus gates. In the New City outside the walls, guarded by Jewish patrols, not a single Jew was harmed.

On April 7, the British military command arrested nineteen members of the defense unit, including their commander Jabotinsky. The former chief political officer of the Zionist Commission that had come to Palestine to begin implementing the Balfour Declaration had warned the military that their toleration of Arab agitation would lead to violence. A secret court-martial sentenced Jabotinsky to fifteen years' penal servitude and eighteen other Jews were given three years at hard labor. Haj Amin el Husseini, the principal agitator, later notorious as the Grand Mufi of Jerusalem whose violent anti-Semitism led him to become an ally of Hitler, was sentenced to eighteen years.

The British military who ruled in Palestine until the first civilian High Commissioner took office in 1920—it was he who amnestied Jabotinsky, and the Arab rioters—had an old score to settle with Jabotinsky, who had been irritating the British since 1915, when he and Capt. Joseph Trumpeldor had organized the Zion Mule Corps in Egypt. The Mule Corps was the predecessor of the Jewish Legion.

A widely known Russian journalist and Zionist orator and propagandist, Jabotinsky was en route to cover World War I from the Turkish side when he turned up in Alexandria, Egypt, in December 1914. There he found a motley throng of distraught and often quarrelsome Jewish refugees from Palestine, most of whom were Russian subjects. They had either been expelled from Palestine by the Turks as potential enemies or had hastily fled of their own accord when Turkey entered the war on the side of Germany in November 1914.

One of the refugees was Trumpeldor, a one-armed veteran of the Russo-Japanese War. The only Jewish commissioned officer in the Czar's army, he had lost his arm at the siege of Port Arthur and spent a year in a Japanese prisoner-of-war camp. There he became a passionate Zionist as well as a pacifist, socialist and vegetarian. In 1911, he settled at Degania, the first kibbutz, where he taught the colonists how to shoot and ride. He died in an ambush at Tel Hai on March 1, 1920, a few weeks before the Arab attack on the Old City.

Jabotinsky and Trumpeldor shared the conviction that a Jewish military force under British command would influence the future of Palestine by helping to liberate it. From the ranks of the bedraggled Alexandria refugees, few of whom had ever handled a gun, they signed up some six hundred recruits pledged "to join a Jewish Legion and to propose to England to make use of it in Palestine." In Russian, Hebrew, Yiddish, Ladino and Polish, the recruits put their names to a seven-line resolution scrawled in Hebrew on a page torn from a schoolboy's notebook.

The idea of a Jewish army to regain Palestine was not new. It had first been advanced in 1160 by David Alroy, a "false messiah," and again in 1524 by David Reubeni, another would-be Jewish redeemer. When Napoleon landed in Alexandria in 1798, he had offered land in Palestine as an inducement to Jews to join his armies. Herzl, too, had spoken of the need for a Jewish military force.

When Trumpeldor, wearing his Russian medals, Jabotinsky, and leaders of the Alexandria Jewish community went to Gen. John J. Alexander, commander of British forces in Egypt, and offered him a Jewish Legion ready to join the British Army for service in Palestine, he was astonished. He knew of no immediate or future plans for an offensive in Palestine, and he was aware that regulations barred the enlistment of foreign nationals in the British forces. The best he could offer was a suggestion that the Jewish volunteers form an auxiliary detachment for mule transport to be employed on some other sector of the Turkish front.

Repelled by the name "Mule Corps" and scorning to send a Jewish unit to any front but Palestine, Jabotinsky bowed out of the venture. Trumpeldor, however, felt that any Turkish front led to Zion, and he became second-in-command to Lt. Col. J. H. Patterson, an Irish Protestant, when a battalion of 562 Jews was officially organized as the Zion Mule Corps.

Wearing the Star of David as their emblem, and lustily singing "Tipperary" in Russian and Yiddish accents, the Zion muleteers sailed for the Gallipoli Peninsula in February 1915. Driving mules loaded with ammunition from supply dumps to the front lines was their lowly but hazardous assignment. In the disastrous 1915 campaign that failed to dislodge the Turks from the Dardanelles, they suffered heavy casualties. Evacuated and disbanded in May 1916, the survivors became the nucleus of the Jewish Legion.

To the Turks, the Zion Mule Corps was a Zionist declaration of war for which the Jews of Palestine suffered heavily. Jemal Pasha, the Turkish governor of Palestine, arrested and imprisoned hundreds of Jews and had thousands more deported or forced into exile. Retaliation against the Jews of the Yishuv became even more widespread at the end of 1915 when the Turks discovered NILI, a clandestine Jewish intelligence network working for the British behind the Turkish lines in Palestine and Egypt.

One of those jailed as an enemy of the Sultan was twenty-eight-year-old David Green, a staff member of Ha'Achdut (Unity), a Hebrew weekly magazine edited by Isaac Shimshelevitz as the organ of the Labor Zionists. In his first article Green signed himself "Ben-Gurion." As a farm laborer at Sejera, Ben-Gurion had been one of the organizers of Hashomer (The Watchman), a secret society of armed guards founded in 1907 to protect Jewish villages against marauding Bedouins. Its principal organizer was Shimshelevitz, who, as Itzhak Ben Zvi, would become the second president of Israel.

Ben-Zvi and Ben-Gurion, known as "the twins," went off to Constantinople in 1913 to study at the Ottoman University Law School and to dream of what they would do for Palestine Jewry when they became members of the Turkish parliament. They were joined by Moshe Shertok, a boy of nineteen, just out of the Herzliah High School in Tel Aviv, who would later make his mark as Moshe Sharett, Israel's first foreign minister.

All three returned to Jerusalem a few weeks before Turkey entered the war. Shertok became a captain in the Turkish Army, serving until 1918. Ben-Gurion and Ben-Zvi appeared in Alexandria while the Zion Mule Corps was being trained, but neither joined it. They left instead for the United States, where they spent two years recruiting settlers for Palestine and propagandizing for Labor Zionism among the Yiddish-speaking trade unionists. When Britain decided to enlist a Jewish Legion, they began recruiting for it.

While the secret negotiations that would lead to the Balfour Declaration were being pressed in London in 1915 and 1916, Jabotinsky became the most detested man in the London Jewish community because of his lonely fight for a Jewish Legion. Most British Jews scoffed at the idea as quixotic or denounced it as dangerous. The Russian-born Jews were hostile because it would have allied them with Czarism. The American Jews were still split over the war, with many favoring Germany not because they liked the Kaiser, but because they were anti-Russian. The British War Secretary, Lord Kitchener, wanted "no fancy regiments" and opposed an offensive in Palestine.

Jabotinsky initially tried to persuade the Russian Jews in London's East End to volunteer for the British Army. As aliens they were exempt from conscription, but the country was rumbling with complaints about Jewish slackers. Recruiting rallies in Whitechapel were broken up by mobs of anti-Zionist socialists and anarchists, and Jabotinsky himself was often stoned and pummeled. It was the remnant of the lowly Jewish muleteers, rejected by Jabotinsky, that turned the tide.

When 120 veterans of the demobilized Jewish muleteers, headed by Captain Trumpeldor, arrived in London at the end of 1916, every one of them reenlisted. All were posted to the same outfit, the 20th County of London. Jabotinsky promptly joined them, as a private, in January 1917. From his barracks he began negotiating with Prime Minister David Lloyd George and the War Office. The flow of communications between Private Jabotinsky and the War Office became a battalion joke. Whenever an orderly arrived with a brown envelope, Jabotinsky's sergeant cracked, "I suppose it's another telegram for Mr. Jug-O'-Whiskey," which is how the name sounded to some of the Cockney soldiers. Jabotinsky was a teetotaler, but the nickname stuck and followed him to Palestine.

The brown envelopes contained encouraging news. One communication advised Jabotinsky that his memorandum of January 24, 1917, to the Prime Minister, had been carefully read. Leopold Amery, who would soon be busy formulating the final text of the Balfour Declaration, sent word that the War Cabinet was interested. Another message from Amery said that Jabotinsky's plan for a Jewish force had been referred to the War Office. On a sunny April morning Jabotinsky, a private in pince-nez, and Trumpeldor, a captain with one empty sleeve, presented themselves at the War Office. Amery had made an appointment for them with Lord Derby, Secretary of War. After his first astonishment at the lowly rank of his callers, who had been vouched for by higher authorities, Derby listened politely but made no promises.

In July, Britain and the Kerensky government in Russia reached an agreement giving Russian citizens in England the choice of enlisting in the British Army or returning to Russia for military service there. On August 23, 1917, just 71 days before the issuance of the Balfour Declaration on November 2, the War Cabinet approved the formation of two regiments of Jewish volunteers in an announcement in the Official Gazette. Jabotinsky was commissioned a lieutenant and made chief recruiter. Trumpeldor had already left for Russia, where he hoped to mobilize an army of Jews who would invade Palestine by way of the Caucasus. Two years later he returned to Palestine, alone, the Bolshevik Revolution having drawn the iron curtain, before the phrase was coined, between the Jewish masses of Russia and their brethren in Palestine.

The first of the two authorized regiments was the 38th Royal Fusiliers. Its nucleus was the Zion Mule Corps veterans, with their own Colonel Patterson in command, and it was filled out by Yiddish-speaking tailors, pressers and shopkeepers recruited in London's Whitechapel. The Tommies dubbed them the "Jewsiliers." On February 5, 1918, they sailed for Egypt after having marched in full battle dress through the City of London as a band of the Coldstream Guards played "Hatikvah." Jabotinsky carried the blue-and-white flag with the Star of David and the Hebrew motto, "If I forget thee, O Jerusalem, may my right hand forget her cunning."

A second Jewish regiment, the 39th Royal Fusiliers, was organized from volunteers in the United States and Canada. Among the chief recruiters were Ben-Gurion and Ben-Zvi, who counted on the enlistees staying on in Palestine after the war. The "twins" had found themselves on the wrong continent when the Balfour Declaration was issued and the British capture of Jerusalem created wild excitement in the Jewish world. Both enlisted in the Jewish Legion in April 1918 and landed in Egypt in August. In a few weeks, Ben-Gurion was a corporal. Eager to get on with the building of the land, however, he lost his stripes when he went AWOL from a camp near Tel Aviv to call on Dr. Chaim Weizmann at the Jerusalem headquarters of the Zionist Commission. It was the first meeting of the two men, whose lifework was bound up with creating the State of Israel.

Ben-Gurion's outfit included Jacob Epstein, later the world-famous sculptor; Gershon Agronsky, a future mayor of Jerusalem and founder-editor of the Jerusalem Post; the father of former Prime Minister Yitzhak Rabin; the father of Mordechai Gur, Israeli Chief of Staff; and Louis Fisher, later an internationally known journalist. Ben-Gurion's commander was Col. Eleazar Margolin, a native of Palestine who had grown up in Australia. He was the first Jew to lead an official Jewish military force into action in Palestine since the days of Simon Bar Kochba.

Once the British invaded Palestine, they were swamped with Jewish volunteers demanding the right to help complete the conquest of the Holy Land. General Allenby, commander of the British forces in Palestine, and General Louis Bols, head of the British military government in Palestine, opposed enlisting Palestinian Jews and only reluctantly permitted the formation of the 40th Royal Fusiliers. It was organized by Eliahu Golomb, later chief of the underground Jewish militia that became Haganah, and was commanded by F. D. Samuel, an English Jew.

When the fighting ended in Palestine in October 1918, the three regiments, known collectively as "The Judeans," numbered over five thousand men. In their ranks were many future officers of Haganah and builders of the Jewish state. Official dispatches cited their gallantry during the conquest of southern Palestine and the Jordan Valley, but not a word of their heroism was permitted to be published in the Palestinian or Egyptian newspapers. By the beginning of 1919 the Judeans constituted about one-sixth of the British army of occupation in Palestine.

Threats of Arab violence made the existence of the Jewish regiments crucial to the defense of the Jewish community. Jabotinsky saw the Jewish Legion as the core of the permanent Jewish militia of a future Jewish government. The British wanted the Legion demobilized as quickly as possible, and did everything they could to speed its liquidation. For more than a year the Jewish troops languished in idleness at an Egyptian camp. By the end of 1919 the force had dwindled to four hundred men. Discharges were being accepted as soon as offered because of the violent Jew-baiting by British officers. They treated the Jewish soldiers like foreigners and potential troublemakers whose chief they mocked as "Mr. Jug-O'-Whiskey." Two companies of Americans and Canadians, who made up more than half of the Jewish Legion, mutinied in protest against open discrimination. Jabotinsky defended them at a court-martial.

Jabotinsky's cockiness and militancy reached a climax with a sensational letter he addressed to General Allenby, the conqueror of Jerusalem. "Anti-Semitism," he charged, "is permeating the whole administration and military atmosphere" in Palestine. The efforts of the Jewish Legion, he wrote, were "breaking into pieces under the intolerable burden of disappointment, despair and broken pledges."

Jabotinsky became a marked man with his warning to Allenby that "the common opinion is that you are the enemy of Zionism in general and of the Jewish Legion in particular." Adding that he still wanted to believe "that this is not true," and conceding that perhaps things were happening without Allenby's knowledge, Jabotinsky ended the incredible letter by requesting a personal interview "as the last attempt to stop a process which threatens to impair forever Anglo-Jewish friendship throughout the world."

On August 9, 1919, British General Headquarters in Cairo ordered Lieutenant Jabotinsky forcibly demobilized. Things had changed since Private Jabotinsky was invited to confer with the Secretary of War, although London had sent him a decoration for his war services.

Once the Judeans were demobilized early in 1920, the Zionist Commission grudgingly agreed to Jabotinsky's proposal for a permanent Jewish defense organization. The Labor Zionists held out for a secret militia patterned on the Hashomer, but Jabotinsky's insistence that the unit be public won a bare majority. Once again he became the chief recruiter. Among the early members of the small underground force Jabotinsky established around a core group called Haganah, created by Zionist teenagers and youths in February 1920, were Ben-Gurion, Ben-Zvi, Zalman Shazar, Levi Eshkol, Nehemiah Rabinowitz (father of Yitzhak Rabin) and Gershon Agronsky.

Guns for Haganah were obtained from an Armenian smuggler and cached in Jabotinsky's apartment and in the residence of his aide, Jeremiah Halperin. Demobilized officers from the Jewish Legion drilled the recruits in night hikes and grenade-throwing. Training was entirely in the open. Ronald Storrs, Jerusalem's military governor, was kept fully informed.

A few days before the Moslem festival of Nebi Moussa, members of Haganah staged maneuvers on the slopes of Mount Scopus, where the Occupied Enemy Territories Administration had its headquarters. It was this tiny Haganah force, the heir of the Jewish Legion, that tried to defend the Jews of the Old City during the pogrom of April 4–6, 1920.

—B.P.

 ## "You Felt As a Partner in the Act of Creation"

As soon as I had disembarked and passed through the Turkish customs, I hurried to Petah Tikvah. Friends pressed me to stay a few days in Jaffa, but I could not restrain an overmastering urge to see a Jewish village, and toward evening of the same day I arrived at the oldest and largest of Jewish colonies.

That night, my first night on homeland soil, is engraved forever on my heart with its exultation of achievement. I lay awake—who could sleep through his first night in the homeland? The spirit of my childhood and my dreams had triumphed and I was joyous! I was in Eretz Yisrael, in a Jewish village, and its name was Petah Tikvah—Portal of Hope!

For a year I sweated in Judean colonies, but I had more malaria and hunger than work. All three—work, hunger and malaria—were new and full of interest. Was it not for this that I had come to the homeland? The fever would visit me every fortnight with mathematical precision, linger for five or six days, and then disappear. Hunger, too, was a frequent visitor. It would stay with me for weeks, sometimes for months. During the day I could dismiss it somehow, or at least stop thinking of it. But in the nights—the long racked vigils—the pangs would grow fiercer, wringing the heart, darkening the mind, sucking the very marrow from my bones, demanding and torturing and departing only with the dawn. Shattered and broken, I would drop off to sleep at last.

But the enthusiasm and joy did not fade. Who worried about malaria in those days? The few who did not suffer from it were a little shamefaced before the rest of us who did!

That was in 1907, at the time of a new *aliyah;* every ship brought more young people. Most of the new laborers settled in Petah Tikvah, and although the farmers there had recently issued a ban on Jewish labor, our numbers grew from week to week.

After a day of work, or maybe of fever, we would gather in the workers' kitchen, or in the sandy tracks between the vineyard and groves, and sing and dance in a circle, sing and dance arm in arm and shoulder to shoulder.

The interminable hoeing and spading did not satisfy me fully. It was too mechanical and monotonous. The ceaseless thumping and thudding smacked of a factory. I yearned for the wide fields, for waving stalks of corn, for the fragrance of grass, the plowman's song—and I made up my mind to go north to the Galil.

From Judea I came to Sejera. Here, at last, I found the Land of Israel. Nature, people, work—here everything was wholly different, more of Israel; here one inhaled the aroma of homeland at every step.

Sejera almost monopolized the diverse lovelinesses of created scenery with which the land is clad. Mountains surround it and enclose it on every side.

The settlement is built on the slope of a hill—two rows of houses one above the other, encircled by thickets of eucalyptus and pepper trees, and looking from afar like rungs of a ladder mounting to the peak. The farm itself stands there.

The people of the village were as diversified as its environment. Among the fifty-odd farmers and laborers were tall, broad-shouldered Kurdish Jews, as unlettered as their non-Jewish neighbors in Kurdistan; thin, bony Yemenites, highly learned in the Hebrew language and in traditional Judaism; young Russians, disciples of enlightenment and revolution; native-born Ashkenazi [German Jews] and Sephardi [Spanish Jews], who had left the yeshivot of Safed and Tiberias to take up the spade and the plow; Russian farmers from the shores of the Caspian Sea, who had embraced Judaism and come to labor in the homeland of their new faith; young Sephardim, educated in the schools of the Alliance Israelite. This motley community had Hebrew, Arabic, Aramaic (spoken by the Kurdish Jews), Yiddish, Russian, French, and Spanish. But this miniature "ingathering of exiles" was cemented and made one by a firm and powerful bond—the land and its cultivation. In Sejera—and in those days it was unique of its kind—there was nothing but Jewish labor, the labor of the farmers themselves and their children; even the farm, which belonged to the Jewish Colonization Association (ICA), employed only Jewish workers.

The officials and laborers lived on the hilltop; the villagers, the farmers, lived below, on the slope; but the relations between the two sections were very cordial. Almost all the farmers were young men who had formerly worked as laborers on the farm, and when they acquired land of their own, went on working it themselves. We, the workers, would meet them often, in the field and at home. There was no sign here of the rift that divided farmers from laborers in Judea. On Sabbaths and festivals we would celebrate together, and on workdays we would meet in the fields, plow side by side and help one another.

Here I found the environment that I had sought so long. No shopkeepers or speculators, no non-Jewish hirelings, no idlers living on the labor of the others. The men plowed and harrowed their fields and planted the seed; the women weeded the gardens and milked the cows; the children herded geese and rode on horseback to meet their fathers in the field. These were villagers, smelling wholesomely of midden and ripening wheat, and burned by the sun.

The work, too, was more satisfying. There was none of the deadening monotony that attends the rigors of the hoe in Judea. You follow and guide the plow, turn the sod and open furrow after furrow; and soon the very soil you plowed and planted would clothe itself in green. Before your very eyes it would bring forth its crop. No sooner were the rains over than the grain would ripen and out you would go to reap the harvest and carry the yield to the threshing-floor. You felt as a partner in the act of creation.

—D.B-G.

 Operation Magic Carpet:
Bringing Yemenite Jews to Israel

The car drew up alongside our faithful Skymaster on the hot desert airfield at Aden. We could see our patient passengers waiting in the shade of the outstretched wings. There were about one hundred fifty in the group, about half of them children. Many were dressed in colorful Arabian costumes—flowing robes and stunning headdresses.

I was struck with their stunted, wizened appearance. Many were emaciated from the ordeal of their long trek from Yemen and, although they had already received considerable care at Hashed Camp, it was clear that they would need a good deal of care when they arrived in Israel. Now I could understand how we could carry so many of them and still not be overloaded.

Most of them were barefoot, but some wore tennis shoes provided by the camp at Hashed. They had very dark hair, rather wiry, and many, including the men, wore it in curls and sidelocks with ringlets down about their ears. Most of the men were bearded and many looked as though they might have stepped right out of the pages of the Old Testament. They sat under the wing, some of them smoking water pipes which stood about three feet high. . . . If they were excited about the trip it certainly was not apparent from their actions. The women and children also sat around in small groups, the children quietly disciplined to remain with their parents and keep out of the way of the ground crews. Their interest in the aircraft appeared casual and they did not wander around, touching and fingering the strange marvel of flight, as might have been expected. It seemed as though they accepted this great metal bird poised on the desert as a part of the Bible and prophecy in which they were so well versed.

They presented a strange picture, squatting in groups on the sand. Some wore the exquisite silver filigree jewelry for which the Yemenites are renowned—bracelets, earrings and necklaces. Many were beautiful, deeply tanned, with fine features and aristocratic faces. They were deeply religious, and . . . many were carrying with them their Bible scrolls, some probably hundreds of years old. They had little else.

One swarthy fellow, barefoot in a red-and-white headdress and brown-and-white striped robe, approached me while I was inspecting the craft . . . I could see his black curls hanging inside his headdress. He had dark features, bushy eyebrows, piercing black eyes that flashed in the bright sunlight and a hawk nose. He held out for me the most beautiful silver filigree bracelet I had ever seen, probably the only thing he owned besides his clothes. I could not understand what he said, but I'm sure he wanted to sell the bracelet. Unfortunately I did not take advantage of the opportunity.

Before long they climbed the wooden ramp to the main door of the Skymaster and were seated on the plywood benches. An attendant who spoke Yemenite Arabic and also knew some English remained with them in the cabin.

One by one the engines were started, and thus began our first flight back to Lydda Airport. Much was demanded of the straining engines as we took off in the hot desert air, and almost all of the runway was used up before we were airborne. The load of passengers was noticeable in the performance of our plane, and our rate of climb was low . . . We finally leveled off at nine thousand feet and, after cruise power was set and all was functioning in good order, I took leave of the cockpit for a look at our passengers. Upon opening the door, I saw a scene of crowded tranquillity. Most of the passengers had been lulled to sleep by the droning engines. Some were staring through the windows in a relaxed manner, perhaps looking for the Promised Land, which they would not see until another seven hours had passed. What a short link of time in the chain spanning thousands of tortured years ere their return! An eternal link forged from the ultimate in a modern technology and fitted to an ancient prophecy which even now was drawing up the anchor of a forgotten age. I thought of the marvel of flight and wondered what they thought of it. I saw one woman thoughtfully touching the circular frame of a window, her delicate fingers vibrating in tune with the quivering pulse of the plane. A mechanical phenomenon, explained in the intricate formulae of vibration mechanics, but, to her, was it perhaps evidence of a living pulse coursing through the great eagle that was winging her homeward?

The flight was quite beautiful, flying up in the middle of the Red Sea toward the Gulf of Aqaba. The sky was a clear turquoise blue and, below, an occasional ship could be seen plying its way along the sea lanes where, three millennia before, the ships of King Solomon had sailed. As we droned along in the sky, I thought of the patient people in the cabin behind us . . . and how many centuries they and their ancestors had waited for this moment. No more blocks to their return to Israel now . . . This time no Red Sea would have to part. . . . We were high above, and somewhere down there, west of Suez, there was a crossroads in the sea where only time separated two epochs of history.

Presently we were flying up the Gulf of Aqaba past the rugged terrain of the Sinai Peninsula. Off our left wing in the distance I could see Mt. Sinai, where Moses received the Ten Commandments, which even now were riding with us on ancient Yemenite parchments, and where the Lord had called unto Moses saying, "Ye have seen what I did unto the Egyptians and how I bore you on eagles' wings and brought you unto Myself." Suddenly I understood the attitudes of the other pilots I had met on the airlift and their quiet devotion to their work in this inspired airlift. I became at this moment an integral part of "Operation Magic Carpet."

Late afternoon and fatigue can do queer things to a pilot, even two in the cockpit at the same time. We were descending over the Negev Desert toward Lydda when what appeared to be Lydda Airport came into sight. We called Lydda Tower and were cleared to land, although we were advised they did not have us in sight. This meant nothing to us until, as we swung into final approach and were over the end of the runway, we realized too late and with embarrassing suddenness that we were landing at the wrong airport. It turned out to be Aqir Field, an Israeli military airfield.

During the landing rollout on the runway I could see a number of varied types of aircraft on either side of the field. These were of the primary basic and advanced trainer category such as Piper Cubs, BT-13 basic trainers, and AT-6 advanced trainer types. Nowhere, however, could I see evidence of planes of up-to-date combat capability, and I was amazed to think that the Israeli air force had been able to carry on a successful war in the air with such modest equipment.* The courage and skill of the Israeli pilots must have been great indeed to have enabled them to do so well with so little. As we came to a halt, a military jeep loaded with Israeli Air Force brass raced over to our plane, and it required some rather talented explanation to account for our predicament. The officers were very understanding, however, and in fact took a rather humorous view of the situation, although perhaps a little too much so to suit our ruffled pride . . . We were permitted to depart for Lydda, where we landed about ten minutes later . . .

Our Yemenite passengers deplaned in orderly fashion, their shining, radiant faces portraying their joy in being at last in the Promised Land. As if in a dream they quietly proceeded to the JDC center at the airport . . . For these good people the prophecy of Isaiah had been fulfilled: "But they that wait for the Lord shall renew their strength; They shall mount up with wings as eagles; They shall run, and not be weary; They shall walk, and not faint" (Isaiah 40:31).

—E.T.M.

 Tel Aviv: 99 Percent of Its Citizens Are Jewish

Kikar Malchei Yisrael, Tel Aviv's City Hall plaza, is now Tel Aviv's favorite site of mass rallies and celebrations. Be it the dove-ish Peace Now or the hawkish-religious Gush Emunim political assemblies, Purim or celebrations of Simchat Torah or Independence Day, the folks congregate by the tens of thousands to demonstrate solidarity or dance in tune with the occasion. The "happenings" of Abie Nathan, the maverick peace pilot, always drew an audience when aided by a bevy of big-name entertainers. As for the stately building itself, it stands unshaken by the blare of speeches and music or the squeaks of plastic hammers the revelers bounce off each other's heads. Only its glassed front twinkles with the reflections of projectors and fireworks, as if musing silently about the city's past.

* This article was written in 1948.

It all started on April 11, 1909, when sixty families set out to build their sixty homes on 110 *dunams* (about 27 acres) of sand dunes north of Jaffa. In seventy years this has grown to 350,000 people occupying tens of thousands of housing units on 50,000 dunams, with 350,000 vehicles daily choking its 550 kilometers of roads. Tel Aviv, having absorbed its mother city Jaffa in 1949, is now known as Tel Aviv-Jaffa and is the hub of a metropolitan area populated by more than a million people—one out of three Israelis. It has the distinction of being the only large city in the world whose population is 99 percent Jewish.

On a bright Saturday morning a "Hassid" (pious Jew) wearing a *shtreimel* (fur hat), with a prayer shawl across the shoulders of his black *kaftan* (long coat) might be seen window-shopping the elegant Dizengoff Street stores on the way home from synagogue. His less observant neighbors are packing the sandy beaches or picnicking in the spacious Yarkon and Clore parks. The culture-minded flock to the Tel Aviv or Haaretz museums, where entrance is free in deference to the Orthodox, who oppose the sale of tickets on the Sabbath.

Symbolic of the social gap created over the years, the Shalom Shabazi slum, whose name honors a Yemenite to Hebrew poet, nestles in the shadow of the Shalom Mayer Tower, an edifice glorifying the name of a business tycoon from Romania. While a youth center wall collapses in the poor quarter, the affluent continue to enjoy the swanky facilities of the Tel Aviv Country Club. An inevitable breeding ground for crime and degeneration, such slums, unless rebuilt, could threaten to upset the moral fabric of society. This and other problems, like illegal squatting and construction, are a constant worry for the city administration.

Elsewhere, it is a daytime nightmare to try and drive through the business center. With parked cars lining both sides of the narrow streets, the only way to make deliveries is by double-parking, with the accompanying horn-blasting bottlenecks. In vain are drivers urged to use public transportation; many buses are old and overcrowded, with too few passengers paying heed to by-laws prohibiting smoking and littering. An ambitious bus station, intended to be a showplace of the Middle East, and meant to replace the present ramshackle facility, which defies description, was close to completion when work was halted for lack of funds.

Started thirteen years ago, it may remain in its ghostlike state until it is made obsolete by a subway now suggested as a solution to the traffic snafu. Meanwhile, Acre and Afulah have pleasant, modern and adequate bus depots and Tel Aviv does not. However, the ambitious Ayalon Project, with such daring steps as the diversion of one of the two riverbeds within the city, a system of cloverleafs, bridges and tunnels, and the recently completed Hayarkon road serving the beachside hotels, go a long way toward speeding up transportation.

Although it willingly relinquished to Jerusalem its brief status as the national capital after the establishment of the State, Tel Aviv-Jaffa remains the vortex of the country's every sphere of activity. Famous for its Israel Philharmonic Orchestra and Habimah Theatre, the large Tel Aviv and Bar-Ilan universities within its metropolitan area head a host of other secular and religious learning institutes. Not only is it the theater and film center; it is also a focal point for popular as well as classical and modern dance and for opera. Even overseas circuses open as a matter of course in Tel Aviv. It is well equipped for international sporting events with a fifty-thousand-seat Ramat-Gan stadium, an Olympic-size swimming pool, and the Ramat Hasharon Tennis Center, to name a few. There is even an iceless skating rink invented by an Israeli.

T.A. is Israel's major banking and financial center, the site of much of the country's commerce and industry, and a mecca for tourism with its extensive hotel, dining and entertainment facilities. Visitors are equally attracted to the oriental Carmel market and the Exhibition Gardens, often displaying the latest technological marvels; the Beit Hatefutzot Museum of the Diaspora is a "must" for the serious. Most Israeli books and newspapers are published within the city limits.

During the seven decades of their history the people of Tel Aviv-Jaffa have learned to "overcome." There was exile by the Turkish masters in 1917, repeated bloody Arab riots, and even some Italian air raids in World War II. Who can forget preparations for dealing with possible victims of the 1967 war or the grim atmosphere of the first days of the Yom Kippur War?

In more recent incidents like the Savoy Hotel attack, the seaside bus carnage and the Carmel Market bombing, each produced its heroes and the true moral fiber of individuals came to the fore. It was the same people who more than thirty years ago bore the brunt of the victorious struggle for independence against tremendous odds; here they rejoiced when the State was born and here they saw death and destruction dealt out mercilessly and haphazardly on their own coastal road, over thirty years later.

A visitor recalls arriving at night during a blackout when Tel Aviv was at war in 1948. When morning broke the gloom of the night, he took a walk along Rothschild Boulevard. To his amazement, he saw several men on stepladders busy trimming the trees lining the street. What other proof is required of the spirit of citizens who came in peace and are here to stay?

The average Tel Avivian is an equally strong critic and patriot of his city. To live elsewhere is unthinkable, for he enjoys being the biggest and best and feels somewhat sorry for the "provincial" Jerusalemites (who have exactly the same feelings toward them). Tel Aviv may be hot and crowded, but it is alive, up-to-date, ambitious and dynamic.

Speaking of peace, the greatest challenge is still to come. The name Tel Aviv—Hill of Spring—was taken from a novel by Theodore Herzl depicting his utopia of a Jewish State. Having achieved part of the dream, how will Herzl's heirs muster the stamina to carry on the struggle of the prophets of Israel for a just society, with equal opportunities for all? If the past is any proof, they certainly will.

—S.Y.

 ## Egypt and Israel Were Once Military Allies

Now that a treaty has formally been signed, and prospects for a peaceful new era in the Middle East certainly seem to indicate that a time of peace, progress and prosperity is on the horizon, it is interesting to see what have been the relations between Israel and Egypt in years gone by.

The Israelites' first contact with the Egyptians was biblical, of course, when famine swept the whole region, driving people south, toward Egypt, which was endowed with fertile lands, granaries and apparently ample staples for large numbers of non-Egyptians.

The result of the ancient Israelites' sojourn in Egypt during the famine period was like a double-edged sword: they obviously were grateful for the help extended them during their time of need, and they seemed to like the ambience of the historic country. At first they tarried, then they stayed a little longer before returning home, and then they stayed on—and finally, when a new Pharaoh arose who had not known of the help that Joseph had extended to the Egyptians when he was virtually prime minister, the Israelites were rounded up and enslaved.

The slavery of the Jews in Egypt continued until Moses arose and, moved by Divine guidance, led the Israelites out of bondage, back to the ancient land that had been deeded to the Jews by God when He made a covenant with the founding father of the Jewish people, Abraham.

Although at one time, some two millennia before the Common Era, Egyptian hegemony extended as far north as Beth Shean and Megiddo, and included Jaffa and Gaza, a text of the times written by an Egyptian includes mention of "Israel," indicating that Israel was a nation definitely located in what used to be called Palestine. Some eleven hundred years before the Common Era, historians note that Egyptians ended their exploitation of the famed Timna copper mines, found in the southern Negev. Prior to that time, Egypt had extended its rule and influence across the waters separating Africa and Asia, and in turn had been influenced internally by Semitic and other cultural forces from the Asian continent.

After David had solidified his reign, Egyptian forces seized the city of Gezer, but peaceful relations continued thereafter right through the reign of Solomon, David's son and heir. Around 950 B.C.E., a Libyan-dominated group had seized control of Egypt and, working in tandem with the Israelite pretender to the throne, Jeroboam, invaded Judah, looting and ravaging. This incursion was followed by an attack on Israel in the north, inflicting the same cruel treatment on the inhabitants. The invaders, satisfied that they had demonstrated their capacity for conquest and rapacity, returned home, leaving the area much weakened.

The ruling powers of Egypt changed over a period of time. The Libyans were supplanted by Nubians, and several centuries later, when Assyria invaded Israel, Hosea the Prophet appealed to Egypt for help. The aid sought was given, but it was of no avail—Samaria fell to the enemy. In the ensuing years, King Hezekiah of Judah again sought help from the Egyptians; during this period, Israel and Egypt apparently were allies.

Centuries later, there was a period in Egyptian history when Egypt used Jewish mercenaries to help repel attacking forces. A whole colony of these soldiers-for-hire later set up a southern fortress city in Elephantine to help defend the country. The Egyptians provided some support for Jerusalem when the Babylonians attacked in the sixth century, but again it was not effective. In the year 586 B.C.E., the first of the Holy Temples was destroyed; the Jews were taken into captivity and carried off to Babylonia.

In the year 332 B.C.E., following the conquests of Alexander the Great, large waves of Jewish migrants reached Egypt, and again the Jews stayed on, working as merchants, farmers, mercenaries and government officials, and apparently doing well. By the first century of the Common Era, it was believed that the Jewish population of Egypt numbered one-eighth of the total population. For the next several hundred years, the fate of the Jews in Egypt depended largely on the ruling families, most of whom treated the Jews well, although there were instances of attempted massacres and anti-Jewish agitation fomented by the government.

By the third century of this era, synagogues were established in Alexandria and others followed soon after. The advent of the Greeks in Egypt brought on a rapid Hellenization, and the Jews, who up to that point spoke only Aramaic, soon switched over to Greek.

Interestingly, the Roman destruction of the last vestiges of Jewish independence in Israel, culminating in the fall of the second Holy Temple in 70 C.E., was followed by the near deterioration of the Jewish communities of Egypt, especially in Alexandria.

From the time of the Arab conquest of Egypt in the seventh century until the end of the tenth century, little is known by historians about the fate of the Jews in Egypt. The advent of Islam seems not to have subjected the Jews to undue pressures; for a while, the Egyptian Jews and the culturally advanced Babylonian Jews maintained close ties. It was in Egypt also that Maimonides worked, and composed his immortal works of Jewish scholarship.

In more recent times, it is true that the Egyptians, and the Arabs as a whole, preferred during World War II to see a Nazi victory over the Allies. Their eagerness to throw off the yoke of European imperialism appears to have been greater than their opposition—if indeed they were opposed—to Hitlerism.

With the new Israel-Egyptian treaty now a fait accompli, one can only hope that modern Israel and modern Egypt will succeed in cementing a formal bond of amity into a true, mutually beneficial peace that will recall the ancient days when, if only for brief periods, the two nations were indeed friends.

—D.C.G.

 ## Bees in the Land of Milk and Honey

Beekeeping, the art of caring for and manipulating colonies of honey bees so that they produce and store a quantity of honey above their requirements, is one of the oldest forms of animal husbandry. It was practiced widely at the time of the Second Temple. Today beekeeping, or apiculture, has become a major industry in modern Israel.

Bees like "settling" in Israel because of the country's clement climate and its profusion of nectar-bearing flowers. And Israelis, the livelihood of thousands of whom depends on the little insect, fully appreciate the honey bee.

There are in Israel today more than fifty thousand bee colonies, which amounts to an average 12.5 hives per thousand habitants. The bees in this land of milk and honey provide the raw material for up to two thousand tons of honey annually— of which 80 percent is consumed locally and 20 percent is exported.

Thanks to ultramodern methods, Israelis have managed to double the production of honey in the past ten years. Equipment such as mobile extracting plants on wheels, just being introduced, is capable of collecting 1,000 to 1,500 kilograms in an eight-hour day. While the average yield per hive is 30 to 40 kilos (65 to 90 pounds), some farmers in the Upper Galilee region are reported doubling this— harvesting 60 or more kilos per year.

A veteran Israeli bee fancier and researcher, Y. H. Blum, has devised a revolutionary method to augment the world's threatened food supplies, which could affect both the production of honey and world flora. His suggestion, not treated very seriously by some local academics, but well received by delegates at the twenty-sixth World Apiculture Congress in Australia, involves transporting swarms of bees from place to place.

According to Blum, the proposed transport will utilize the bees' "pollination power" much more efficiently and will increase tenfold the production of honey in the world. Equally important, he says, the system will vastly stimulate the growth

of vegetation across the globe, thus providing more nectar, the raw material for the production of honey.

A method used in Israel with considerable success is the system of artificial insemination of the queen bee. Because the queen bee flies to the height of ten to twenty meters, where she mates with several males, there is no control over her mating habits, the results of which are vital to her hive. Thus artificial insemination under the control of the beekeeper, practiced in many beekeeping colonies in the country, may help to assure the healthy continuation of that particular hive.

Further research in Israel which may lead to control of the all-important mating process is going on now at Hebrew University's Faculty of Agriculture Bee Center. Young scientist Michael Notkin has pinned down valuable information about pheromones, a substance emitted by male bees or drones when mating, which attracts other males to the scene of action. New knowledge about the drawing power of pheromones could assist beekeepers in more controlled breeding.

Other research currently going on at the Bee Center in Rehovot under the direction of Professor Yaacov Lensky is investigation into the question of which factors determine whether a bee larva becomes a queen or a worker. The professor, who, together with his fellow researchers at Hebrew University, has been studying this problem for eight years, believes that one of the main factors deciding the bees' caste is the nutrition the bee receives while still in the larva stage.

Honey production is only one of the talents, albeit the most visible, of the "wee bee." Her extraordinary efficiency in crop pollination is valued in the Israeli economy at millions of dollars each year. As a crop pollination agent of the first order, the bee helps to increase the yields in Israel's diversified agriculture, particularly in avocado and deciduous fruit tree plantations. Bee by-products include royal jelly, flower pollen and beeswax, both for local and export use. Israeli know-how of apiculture is also exported; Israeli experts travel to developing countries to set up bee colonies and to teach the people living and working there how to manipulate them.

Export of queens is still another branch of beekeeping. Israel's temperate climate permits the breeding of queens much earlier in the year, and they are subsequently exported to beekeepers in Europe and in Asia. Under strict control by professional authorities, the owners of large apiaries breed their queens from locally grown, selected Italian strains.

—L.E.

The Menu of Israel

One of the nicest and most distinct Israeli traditions is food. But what is "Israeli" cooking? Jews coming from the Middle East and the Far East, from Europe, down under in Australia and in South Africa, across the oceans from North and South America—all had adapted the local cooking habits to their dietary laws and passed them on to their children and their children's children. The cooking style of their native countries came as part of their baggage when they made their way to Israel.

Coming to Israel, some cooks have maintained the culinary traditions of the Ashkenazim, those who originally lived in Germany and France but later on in other predominantly Christian countries—Poland, Hungary, Lithuania, Romania, the U.S.S.R. and the United States. Others have retained the traditions of the Sephardim, originally those from Spain and Portugal, then those of the Middle Eastern Moslem countries as well as North Africa, and finally Italy, Greece and Bulgaria. Today, one is as likely to find borsht, gefilte fish and kugel (pudding) on the menus of Israeli restaurants as to find bourekas, eggplant and stuffed vegetables.

The strong character of the Middle East dominates Israeli cooking—*falafel* (fried chick-pea balls), *humus* (chick-pea dip), *t'china* (sesame seed paste) and *pita* (Arab pocket bread).

The ready-to-eat and packaged food industries of Israel are young, yet *humus* and *t'china* in plastic containers are widely available, as are packets in supermarkets and grocery stores. *Pita* sits alongside wide varieties of white and dark breads and rolls. Likewise, *humus* is among the few packaged mixes available; one adds only water and spices before using the mix.

What other foods are considered Israeli foods? Eggplant salad (in fact, eggplant in a hundred different ways!), vegetable salad (with lemon juice and oil dressing), *kabab*, *shishlik*, *schnitzel* (boneless breaded and fried chicken or turkey), roast chicken, fruit soup, pickles and olives, strong Turkish coffee.

Whether one is Ashkenazic or Sephardic, undoubtedly these would rate high on a list of "Israeli" foods. Interestingly enough, though, many people consider the Ashkenazic-European cooking as "Jewish," while the Sephardic-Oriental-Middle Eastern is referred to as "Israeli."

Let's take a look at what some other typical Israeli and Jewish foods are. To a North African, it's *couscous* (farina or semolina), *shahshouka* (Spanish omelet with vegetables and hot sauce) and *ful* (broad beans).

To the Iraqi and Kurdistani, *kibbee* (cracked wheat cake stuffed with meat and fried or baked) and *bulgur* salad (cracked wheat with tomatoes) would rate high, along with rice, lentils, beans, eggplants and squash.

My Yemenite neighbors would tell you that *hilbe* (fenugreek dressing) and *skhug* (the hot paste made of garlic, cumin, hot peppers, coriander and cardamom) are Israeli, as well as tea with mint and cardamom in coffee.

Other Middle Eastern groups would tell you *bourekas* (stuffed turnover-type pastries with cheese, potatoes, spinach or meat inside), *hamindas* (browned hard-boiled eggs) and stuffed vegetables (with rice or meat) are Israeli.

Russians will list herring salads, *kasha* (buckwheat groats) or *borsht* (beet or cabbage and meat soup).

Romanians mention *mamaliga* (corn meal pudding).

One cannot forget *tzimmes* (stewed carrots or carrots and meat with prunes), knishes, gefilte fish, *kreplakh* and *cholent* (the Friday-night-to-Saturday-lunch bean-meat stew)—all from Eastern Europe—or goulash and stewed vegetables from Hungary.

Besides these, most people consider the fruits and vegetables and other foods so widely available locally as "Israeli"—avocados, eggplant, green peppers, squash, fruit salads, dishes using oranges, fish, omelets, cheeses and yogurts, artichokes, cheese cakes, and fruit juices.

If you want to try Israeli food, remember that we have absorbed immigrants from nearly a hundred lands—and for each newcomer Israeli food is what he eats in Israel.

—S.Z.

 ## The Rabbi Who Loves Soccer—Even on the Sabbath

Rabbi Behar, his arms flaying the air, sweat streaming down his face, his blue eyes throwing sparks, was cheering his boys, who were exerting themselves on the soccer field. It seemed miraculous that his black homburg hat stayed put on the curly white head of this portly gentleman in his sixties. It isn't often one comes across a rabbi who enjoys a soccer game, but when one considers that soccer games take place on Saturday afternoons, that traveling on the Sabbath is forbidden and that —there being no public transportation on that day (in Israel)—the rabbi hires a bus and travels with the Jaffa Maccabi team, which he was instrumental in organizing, then Rabbi Behar stands out as a most unorthodox rabbi, and a rather brave man, to thus defy the rabbinical establishment. Indeed, he has become something of a celebrity because of his liberal views. There have been newspaper stories about him and he has been interviewed on television.

I'm no soccer fan myself, but I had come to Ramat Gan's open-air stadium with an open mind—despite a somewhat skeptical feeling about mixing soccer with religion, as if by kicking a ball very hard, one could get through to God.

Getting to the stadium wasn't exactly easy. Thousands of young men streamed toward the stadium on foot, on bicycles, on motorbikes, or via *sherut*—Israel's collective taxi, which does a booming business on the Sabbath. There were surprisingly few cars in the parking lot. Scores of policemen were keeping some kind of order in the thick, jostling crowd.

By the time I managed to squeeze through the proper gate, the game had al-

ready started, and the rabbi was much too absorbed to pay any attention to me. As he said later, he forgets everything when he watches a game. Although he no longer plays, he was a pretty good goalkeeper in his younger days.

So I took some time to study the crowd of working-class Israelis having fun. Boys, young men, fathers with their children—most of them rather poorly dressed —plus peddlers selling popcorn and ice cream. What would they do on long, dreary Saturday afternoons if it weren't for the soccer games? The policemen sprawled on the grass, mopping their brows, relaxing at last. Neither the Jaffa Maccabi team nor their adversaries were very good, and the spectators shouted encouragements, interspersed with boos and catcalls.

The rabbi lustily cheered his boys, regardless. At the half-time break, they surrounded him, making it evident that they loved him as much as he loved them. There was something warm, lovable and gay about this man, something very different from the cold, rigid demeanor that seems characteristic of many rabbis in Israel. To those scrawny, pimple-faced, ball-playing lads, he wasn't standing way above them to pass judgment—he was a human being—one who could holler and stamp his feet, one they could talk to, who would understand them.

After the game, I went to visit Rabbi Behar on his home territory—at the Sinai Synagogue in Jaffa. Located on Jerusalem Avenue, the town's busiest and noisiest thoroughfare, the modest one-room synagogue had little to commend it. In fact, the dusty display of cult objects in the front window made me think, at first, that it was a bric-a-brac shop. But the sign unmistakably announced: *Beit Knesset Sinai.*

I hardly recognized Rabbi Behar in the calm and composed gentleman, dressed in a pearl-gray suit, who sat at the desk, speaking into the telephone. Then he turned to me. "Yes? How can I serve you?"

The phrase startled me—it's not frequently used by Israelis. I said I would like to find out a little more about him and his synagogue, and perhaps write a story.

"I'm busy right now—but if you'd like to stay a while and look around, you're very welcome," he said. "Sit anywhere you like, we don't stand on formality."

It was odd. Women aren't supposed to sit in the main part of an Orthodox synagogue where men pray, but here it was accepted. Yet this didn't seem to be a Reform temple—it had the air of a quite ordinary, rather poor Sephardic house of worship. The traditional synagogue guardian was old and bedraggled, with a bad eye. Some people sat around on folding chairs, chatting in Ladino—a Spanish dialect spoken even today by the Jews expelled from Spain. They didn't look too prosperous. They just enjoyed being in the synagogue, together, before evening services began. In the back of the room, the Holy Ark where Torah scrolls are kept was hidden by a worn red velvet curtain, and the back wall was covered with marble plaques inscribed with names, some followed by *Zihrono Lebraha*— "blessed be his memory."

People kept dropping in to see the rabbi. Some wanted to make arrangements for children's circumcisions or confirmations, or for memorial services. Others wanted to invite the rabbi and his wife to a party celebrating the engagement of a son or daughter. Most old people who came had worried looks on their faces and pieces of paper in their hands. Rabbi Behar wrote a letter to a sick-fund for one man, promised another to investigate the snag with his welfare check, filled in forms for an old lady who wanted to enter an old-age home, jotted down addresses and telephone numbers and promised to handle many similar matters.

When the people left, they looked relieved. Obviously, Rabbi Behar felt it was part of his duty to give comfort and help, to solve those everyday problems that befuddle people who are old and poor, or who don't know their way around. He was efficient and quick, but also courteous and friendly. Clearly, what attracted people to him were the humanity and warmth he radiated.

Perhaps, I mused, soccer was a way of establishing similar contact with that segment of youth—mostly poor and from the Oriental communities—that drops out of school before learning much about any job or profession.

When I went to interview the rabbi the following week, he led me up a rickety flight of stairs to the women's gallery of the synagogue. "Many women prefer to sit up here, but I don't insist on it," he said. "Neither do I insist that men cover their heads. When boys come in belligerently, heads uncovered, I merely show the sign that states this is a house of prayer. I know most of them have skullcaps in their pockets. In time, they put them on. The main thing is not to push them away. We must try to understand these youths, to help them . . ."

Pointblank, I queried, "You go along with these kids for the soccer games. Isn't it forbidden to travel on the Sabbath?"

"It is explicitly forbidden," Rabbi Behar answered quietly, closing his eyes. "But what is more important? To be strictly observant? Or to try to do something about these youths that roam the streets, play cards, linger in cafés and often take drugs? There is such emptiness in their lives! The first thing is to get these youngsters interested, to integrate them in a healthy, constructive framework. I encourage them to join sports clubs, to swim and play soccer. Every Saturday our team plays some local team. We travel to Natanya, Haifa, Ashdod, Beersheba. The youngsters see something of the country and get to know one another. You see, young people nowadays can't and won't be coerced. They draw away from religion because it seems to forbid most of the things they enjoy. They hardly realize that humans still need to commune and pray. First, we must try to establish contact with these kids. Then they may come to the synagogue. I tried to persuade the Rabbinate to condone these Sabbath games, but they wouldn't hear of it."

Rabbi Behar explained that the interdiction of traveling on the Sabbath came about in days when most Jews were farmers. Since animals, too, were entitled to their weekly rest, travel was forbidden. Now, machines do the work. Also, life was very different when people lived in small communities; now, they're cooped up in crowded city flats, with no place to go to on their days of rest. The rabbi suggested that a law that once had meaning but was not adapted to modern life might be changed. He concluded, somewhat rhetorically, "What is more important: To get closer to youth, to try to have a pure heart, or to rigidly enforce observance of religious law?"

"It seems your relationship with the rabbinical establishment is rather strained," I asserted.

Rabbi Behar laughed good-humoredly. "I manage to get along."

Most synagogues in Israel receive funds from the Ministry of Religion, the Rabbinate and the municipalities, to help them defray part of their costs—and rabbis get salaries. Rabbi Behar and his synagogue have no such financial assistance, but the rabbi has staunch support from his predominantly Bulgarian congregation. He commented, "Without my brave Bulgarians, this synagogue wouldn't have existed. Do you know why it is called Sinai? No, not because of Moses and the revelation of Mt. Sinai. It's named for the boys who fell in the Sinai Campaign—their parents were the first to donate money which made it possible to establish this synagogue. The names of those boys are inscribed on some of the marble plaques. Other plaques are inscribed with the names of great rabbis."

When I asked Rabbi Behar whether he was born in Bulgaria, he said he actually was born in a typical Sephardic community of Turkey. Both his mother and his father were killed during fierce bombardments along the Dardanelles during

World War I. Only five then, he was sent with other war orphans to a Jewish orphanage in Plovdiv, Bulgaria—which boasted a strong, ancient and dedicated Sephardic community.

"I grew up there," the rabbi recalled. "In the orphanage, I learned Hebrew, Talmud and Torah. At twelve, I was already the school's cantor. Then I was sent to Sofia, the capital, to rabbinical school. I also learned the professions of circumciser and ritual butcher, and was self-supporting by eighteen, long before being confirmed as a rabbi. Actually, I still work as a circumciser.

"It was 1948 when I came to Israel with my family. Most Bulgarian Jews reached Israel at about the same time: 1947–48. I know most of them, and many of those in Jaffa come from Plovdiv. I tell you, they are the finest of Jews! You can always depend on them!" The rabbi's face glowed as he spoke of his special people. "Say I have an old sick woman who needs special food or medicine, twenty *liras* to tide her over until her welfare payment arrives. Almost any Bulgarian in Jaffa will immediately open his pocket and give what is needed. We also have good clubs, and a model old-age home. All who come here are welcome, naturally, but most of its support comes from Jaffa's Bulgarian community."

When Rabbi Behar first came to Israel, he worked as most people did in those days, at anything that came his way. He picked and packed oranges, had a job in a fish cannery, and then started his own business and did rather well but, as he put it: "There was no spiritual joy in it." He missed not having a synagogue, working with and for people. Money wasn't all that important.

Once he established the Sinai Synagogue, he began making a living by performing confirmations and circumcisions and reciting special prayers for the dead. These he recites both in Hebrew and Ladino, as is the custom with many Sephardic communities. "God gives," he commented, saying he and his wife lacked nothing. "We don't need much. Both our children are grown. Our daughter works for El Al and our son is studying the hotel trade in Canada. Neither of us smoke. Our needs our few." Since the Rabbinate refused to recognize him as a rabbi, because of his unorthodox views, he does not have the right to perform marriage ceremonies. The members of his community thus need another rabbi for the ceremony, but they always ask Rabbi Behar to attend.

I was surprised to learn that he performed confirmations for girls, as well as boys—in the old days, this had been unheard of in Sephardic communities.

"In Israel, the tendency to treat boys and girls alike has spread to most communities," Rabbi Behar explained, "and Bulgarian Jews are inclined to have liberal views."

Rabbi Behar opined that it was particularly in regard to women and their status that religious law could do with some changes. "The woman must be respected," he said. "Loved and respected."

Unless certain religious laws—such as personal status issues—are interpreted less rigidly, he fears that public pressure for civil marriage and divorce will grow to the point where an accommodating law would have to be enacted. He is among the few rabbis who sees the need for the evolution of laws which, once codified, didn't change in hundreds of years.

Since his views are in many ways closer to Reform Judaism than to Orthodoxy, I asked him if he had links with the "Progressive" movement now represented in Israel. He replied that he had been approached, but saw no need to identify with any particular ideological movement. He and his congregation wanted to manage their own affairs, he said, without being drawn into controversies.

Bulgarian Jews constitute a cohesive community and combine a strong feeling of Jewish identity with a strong sense of social commitment. Honest and hardworking, few are very rich, but almost none are really poor; few are in the upper echelons of power, but almost none are found at the bottom of the social ladder. Decent, sensible, independent-minded, they form a solid middle class.

I trailed along while Rabbi Behar set out on a round of duties in his battered car. One morning, he said prayers for the dead in the Holon cemetery outside Tel Aviv. One family was of rather modest means; the other, judging by clothes and manners, belonged to the upper middle class. Rabbi Behar knew them all. The prayers were read in Hebrew and the old Castilian dialect, which even most of the young people still knew. Four generations were gathered around the tombstones— from an old gnarled grandmother in her black crocheted shawl to boys and girls in army uniform. Somehow, I had a feeling of continuity of generations and of communal ties.

In the early afternoon, the rabbi was to officiate at a circumcision. En route, he gave me some of the family's background. "Like most of us, this family first lived in a transit camp. They didn't have a penny. They worked hard and—praise God —now they live in nice flats, and when a grandson is born, they can afford to rent a hall and offer their friends a sumptuous meal. We've all done rather well in Israel."

When we arrived, the people immediately surrounded Rabbi Behar, greeting him affectionately. Assisted by the nurse who always works with him, he donned a white satin gown and a head cover, then slipped on a surgeon's white coat. The instruments were ready, sterilized. He scrubbed his hands thoroughly, then stood on the dais looking both dignified and jolly. The infant cried, adults intoned prayers and everybody seemed happy.

—J.K.

 ## Israel and the Single Girl

In the early years of Israel, there was a widespread impression that the country had a surplus of males. Actually, in many of the communal settlements, this was true. Men in one kibbutz even went so far as to advertise and publicize their need for mates. Today, however, the situation has changed. Although recent statistics still indicate a slightly larger number of males in the twenty to thirty age group, after thirty, women have the edge—numerically speaking, that is.

These statistics have not deterred the ever-increasing number of unattached females (divorced, widowed or never married) who continue to come to Israel, seeking the mate they did not find in their home country. Their search is not doomed to failure. Many do meet and successfully marry, either native Israelis or other newcomers like themselves. As one Canadian girl said, "I had to come all the way from Montreal to meet my husband, a native Torontonian."

Not all find husbands and some even leave the country, discouraged by the reality that it is no easier to find a husband in Israel than anywhere else. For those who remain, however, there are compensations which far outweigh the fact that they do not achieve their initial goal. "I like living here," said one English secretary, "because you feel that you're part of something bigger than yourself, that your mere presence is important. The country is dynamic—there is always something happening."

She recalls the welcome home party the Mayor of Tel Aviv gave the local Maccabee basketball team, honoring them for their victory over the Russians. "Imagine, 150,000 people crowding into the city square to cheer and sing."

Her roommate, who works for a travel agency, seconded her remarks. She prefers cafés, such as Cafe Exodus in the north of Tel Aviv, "which attracts a university crowd. After you have been in the country for a while, you find your favorites, discover that certain cafés cater to certain groups."

Israel's cultural patterns are steeped in the Jewish tradition, which is oriented to family living. Throughout Jewish history, the rabbis and the sages have regarded marriage as a primary religious duty. Even those who do not regard themselves as observant adhere to this ideal. Similarly, the precept "Be fruitful and multiply" is ingrained in the national consciousness. As a result, young people in Israel are pressured toward early marriage.

Those of Afro-Asian origin—or Sephardim, as they are colloquially called—strive to marry girls off young before they can be tainted by the modern world which is threatening to destroy their value system. Ashkenazim do the same, fearing that their daughters' chances for marrying decrease with every passing year. "Even as a newcomer," says a new immigrant from the States, "you're pressured on every side to get married. It is as if the country were one huge 'Yiddishe Mama'!"

"Once you adjust to this family-oriented atmosphere," says a graphic artist, now in her early thirties, "you can ignore it and enjoy Israel for what it is, a country where you have a contribution to make, where there is a definite sense that you, as a Westerner, are bringing skills and experience that the country needs." She had visited Israel twice before settling permanently.

"Each visit I felt a closer tie. I discovered that I liked being in a Jewish state, being among my own people. You can say that in Israel I discovered my Jewishness, found a purpose and meaning to life that I hadn't experienced in New York."

She has not sensed any discrimination on the part of the government authorities. "All privileges and rights are given on an equal basis, including customs allowances, rental subsidies and mortgage money. True, you get less as a single than couples do, but there is no discrimination because you are female. In the States, when I went to rent an apartment, I often had difficulties. Not everyone wanted to rent to me. Paradoxically enough," she adds, "in the States, where there is stringent legislation forbidding discrimination on grounds of sex, color, etc., many landlords do manage to get around these restrictions. In Israel, where there doesn't seem to be such overt legislation, in practice there isn't any discrimination. Not that I didn't run into some amusing encounters on this score. The painter, for example, did not want to give me a price estimate. 'I'll discuss this with your husband,' he said, casually dismissing my attempts at negotiating. He seemed genuinely surprised to hear that I had no spouse, that I lived alone and liked it."

After five years in Israel, this graphic artist—and others like her—is sensing a change in attitudes. "More and more, single girls are being accepted, perhaps because there are more of us." She notes the existence of a singles society, "more perhaps than most people know about. There are home parties, run by and for the unattached, and an increasing number of lecture programs and Bible study groups where we meet people." She also has made friends on trips sponsored by the Society for the Preservation of Nature, "rough camping and hiking tours which are fun as well as instructive."

"Don't come to Israel just to meet a husband," advises a librarian who had the exciting privilege of setting up one of the country's best university-affiliated law libraries. "Find your satisfaction in doing your job well and in fulfilling yourself as a Zionist. You may also find a husband"—as she did—"but that should not be your main motivation. Come with an open mind plus a willingness to bear a possible year or so of loneliness until you find your circle and your place. But when you do, then Israel can be a very wonderful place."

—R.S.

A "University to Evoke the Respect of Cultured Mankind"

(From an address in March 1925 marking the opening of the Hebrew University in Jerusalem)

The opening of our Hebrew University on Mount Scopus, at Jerusalem, is an event which should not only fill us with just pride, but should also inspire us to serious reflection.

A university is a place where the universality of the human spirit manifests itself. Science and investigation recognize as their aim the truth only. It is natural, therefore, that institutions which serve the interests of science should be a factor making for the union of nations and men. Unfortunately, the universities of Europe today are for the most part the nurseries of chauvinism and a blind intolerance of all things foreign to the particular nation or race, of all things bearing the stamp of a different individuality. Under this regime the Jews are the principal sufferers, not only because they are thwarted in their desire for free participation and in their striving for education, but also because most Jews find themselves particularly cramped in this spirit of narrow nationalism. On this occasion of the birth of our university, I should like to express the hope that our university will always be free from this evil, that teachers and students will always preserve the consciousness that they serve their people best when they maintain its union with humanity and with the highest human values.

Jewish nationalism is today a necessity because only through a consolidation of our national life can we eliminate those conflicts from which the Jews suffer today. May the time soon come when this nationalism will have become so thoroughly a matter of course that it will no longer be necessary for us to give it special emphasis. Our affiliation with our past and with the present-day achievements of our people inspires us with assurance and pride vis-à-vis the entire world. But our educational institutions in particular must regard it as one of their noblest tasks to keep our people free from nationalistic obscurantism and aggressive intolerance . . .

A special task devolves upon the university in the spiritual direction and education of the laboring sections of our people in the land. In Eretz Yisrael it is not our aim to create another people of city dwellers leading the same life as in the European cities and possessing the European bourgeois standards and conceptions. We aim at creating a people of workers, at creating the Jewish village in the first place, and we desire that the treasures of culture should be accessible to our laboring class, especially since, as we know, Jews, in all circumstances, place education above all things. In this connection it devolves upon the university to create something unique in order to serve the specific needs of the forms of life developed by our people in Eretz Yisrael.

All of us desire to cooperate in order that the university may accomplish its mission. May the realization of the significance of this cause penetrate among the large masses of Jewry. Then our university will develop speedily into a great spiritual center which will evoke the respect of cultured mankind the world over.

—A.Ei.

 ## Time Stands Still in Safad

Time stands still in Safad, this weathered city of antiquity, with its crooked oriental alleyways and labyrinths of winding, cobbled streets. It is an ancient bastion of Jewish scholarship and mysticism, whose houses are perched precariously one atop another, stitching a tapestry of style and symmetry.

There lingers the unmistakable aura of venerated age, of a remote, hallowed past, fraught with the wisdom of the sages, creating an undeniable suspension of secular concerns and reflections. It is a scene of sanctified timelessness, with no beginning, as though the place might already have been consecrated, yet crumbling, when the prophets first appeared.

"In Safad," it was said, "is the purest air of the Holy Land and there is not a place where they understand better the profundities and the secrets of the Holy Torah."

Whether purity of the air was responsible for the mystics nurturing an affinity for the Divine, or the claim is largely legendary—no matter. For certain, this quaint, crowded town, with its magnificent view of the surrounding mountains and shimmering Galilee, was among the four sacred cities of the Holy Land.

It was here in Safad in the year 66 C.E. that Josephus Flavius, then known as Ben Mattatia, led the Jewish rebels in their war against the Romans and fortified the town. In this period, Galilee had the largest population in Palestine. It was here that the priestly families settled after the destruction of the Temple.

Safad's origins are irrevocably rooted in the past, but the influence of its historical heritage is not the prime reason for people's attraction to the city.

Ask Beni Becher, who owns the local theater, Kolnoa Tzil, on Rehov Yerushalayim, the main street. Every child knows Beni. The kids run after him. "Beni, Beni, Beni, you got *mastic* [chewing gum]?" Beni, born in Chomsk, Russia, first saw Safad in 1943, while on vacation. He succumbed to the enchantment of the area immediately. "My first visit to Safad, I fell in love with it and since then I am here," he explains exuberantly.

Beni is infatuated with the beauty, the splendor of the scenery, but above all—the people. "Most of my friends are artists, very talented persons," he emphasizes. Within the artists' colony, occupying the old Arab quarter, creativity is at its optimum. The area abounds in splendid virtuosity—more than forty resident artists, employing various media: oils, lithographs, water colors, ceramics.

Rehov Yerushalayim runs the length of the city, circling the top of Safad. Citadel Hill, at the center, has been converted into a public park. From its terraced garden is an overwhelming panorama of the Galilee down to Lake Tiberias. Ancient pine trees and twisting paths accompany the climb up to Givat HaMetzuda, built over the ruins of the Crusaders' fortress, which rests on the foundation Josephus laid, almost two thousand years ago.

On the summit is a simple war memorial, commemorating a miracle, the famous "Davidka," the mortar which tricked the Arabs into believing the Jews had a secret weapon during the War of Independence. Against insurmountable odds, 130 Palmach commandos infiltrated Arab lines and drove the enemy out.

Synagogues stem from the Middle Ages, although many have been rebuilt in part, because of repeated earthquake damage. Down a narrow lane is the sanctuary of Joseph Caro, where he compiled the *Shulchan Aruch*, the codification of Jewish law, from 1555 to 1563. Of simple design, the *bima* is enclosed by a wooden railing on floor level. Congregants sit cross-legged on cloth-covered couches against walls of delicate blue. Women are segregated behind a lace curtain.

Two of the synagogues are named for Rabbi Isaac Luria, the famed mystic who fathered the Cabbalist movement. Ari-Ashkenazi has an unusual and highly decorative interior. The Aron Kodesh, the Holy Ark, is resplendent with intricately carved fruit: apples, pears, fat clusters of grapes. Painted columns are crowned by elaborate carvings. A majestic chandelier hangs from the domed, vaulted ceiling in this "Hall of Sacred Apples." Extensive reconstruction was necessary after the 1837 earthquake in which four thousand people were killed. Ha'ari Hasephardi, which withstood the devastation of the earthquake, has beautifully carved doors, served as a Haganah barricade, and is adjacent to the old cemetery, the resting-place of its saintly medieval scholars.

At nearby Mount Meron, Israel's highest peak, are ruins of a synagogue from the third century, quarried out of a cliff. Two huge blocks of stone support a central slab, whose fall, it is believed, will herald the advent of the Messiah.

Every year at Meron a pilgrimage takes place to the tomb of Rabbi Shimon, a second-century scholar. Thousands congregate from every region, an observance unbroken for four hundred years. Just before nightfall the celebration starts with prayers in the shrine and dancing in the courtyard of the tomb. Throughout the night, bonfires are kindled. Following a Cabbalist tradition, little boys get their first haircut under a tremendous tree and the clippings are ceremoniously cast into the flames.

From earliest times, Safad has figured prominently in the chronicles of the land. Genizah documents confirm the existence of a Jewish community at the beginning of the eleventh century.

At the start of the sixteenth century, when Ottoman rule was initiated, Safad became the spiritual center of the country and of Judaism. Following their expulsion from Spain, multitudes of Jews found asylum there. They arrived with business acumen and religious devotion.

L'cha Dodi, the song of greeting to the Sabbath Queen, a refrain that still forms part of Sabbath eve services, was composed here by Rabbi Shlomo Halevi Alkabetz. The first printing press in Asia Minor was established in Safad by a father and son from Prague who printed the Book of Esther in 1577. In the early 1700s, Polish Jews, fleeing the persecution of the Cossacks, sought refuge here.

Miraculously, despite catastrophic assaults by man and nature, Safad has survived.

—G.C.

Baseball Comes to Israel

What a strange congregation of people: tennis-shoed and baseball-gloved young Jews from cities and towns across the United States and Canada; a slightly older crew, hailing from Venezuela and Mexico, now residents of Tel Aviv and Ashkelon; battle-hardened American Marines and young, clean-shaven recruits; journalists from the New York *Times* and the Washington *Post;* and the American Ambassador to Israel, Mr. Samuel Lewis. What could possibly bring all of these people together at a small kibbutz halfway between Jerusalem and Tel Aviv?

The New York-accented voice projecting over the loudspeaker system provides the answer: "Welcome to the game. And now batting . . ."

The game—an undisputed title understood by all—is softball, that stepchild of baseball originally intended as a substitute for the parent sport. It was brought to Israel by Western Hemisphere *olim* (immigrants) who came supplied with bats, balls and gloves.

On Saturday, March 17, 1979, the Israel Softball League opened its first official season of play at Kibbutz Gezer. The Jerusalem *Post* and *Maariv* announced the event beforehand, and both carried postgame coverage on Sunday.

After several years of informal exhibition play, the idea of a serious, organized baseball league was put forward by a young lawyer whose *aliya* to Israel had only barely begun. Edwin Friedman, formerly a Jewish student-movement activist, was used to discussions about "the potential contributions of American *olim* to Israeli society"; usually the theorizing revolved around American pluralism in religion and politics. But baseball?

One might ask: Is this what Israel needs? Isn't this particular American import unlikely to strike roots in a soil hitherto unfertile and unreceptive?

The advocates of the new league might reply, "No more so than basketball"—an American game that is now played around the world and has gained great popularity in Israel, especially with the success of the Tel Aviv Maccabi team, which took second place in the European League.

Those who question the validity of importing baseball to the Middle East run the risk of discovering, to their own eternal dismay, that even soccer—Israel's own beloved *kadur regel*—is not found in the Bible. In fact, there is a perhaps apocryphal epilogue to a true incident that occurred when interested parties asked Rabbi Avraham Yitzhak Kook, may his memory be blessed, then Chief Rabbi of Palestine, for a ruling to permit the playing of soccer on Shabbat, a ruling which

he subsequently granted. He asked the petitioners to describe the game, so that he might understand the nature of the beast on whose "kashrut" he was being asked to pronounce. After hearing the description, Rabbi Kook inquired why, if it was so difficult to put the ball into the net at the other end of the field, one didn't simply put it into one's own net.

During the spring, summer and fall of 1978, several teams around the country, all now part of the new league, visited each other and played "for the heck of it." The South Americans, the American Embassy squad, the New York State medical students (on a four-year program at Tel Aviv University) and the journalists were all part of the action, as were several kibbutz teams, including Gezer's.

Shortly after Friedman's *aliya* in the winter of '78, he began to visit Gezer, driving in just before Shabbat, and managing to string an *eruv* around the baseball field of the kibbutz before dark. (An *eruv* permits one to play on Shabbat within the sectioned-off area.) Rabbi Wolf Kelman, a recent visitor to Gezer, didn't think the *eruv* was necessary, but Friedman persisted, in spite of tractors and pedestrians repeatedly trampling the strings so meticulously placed.

At this point, Friedman and John Broder, a Mideast correspondent for the Chicago *Tribune*, decided to take the initiative in forming a league: "We placed an ad in the Jerusalem *Post* announcing a meeting in Broder's apartment, and about fifty people showed up." Among these was Phil Grad, umpire deluxe from the American Midwest, now living in Tel Aviv. Grad umpired the opening games at Gezer, earning everyone's respect for his no-nonsense style, although many batters ruefully concluded, "He calls 'em low."

Friedman and Broder then contacted other groups and, with a list of about ten teams, they went to the Ministry of the Interior to apply for incorporation. "We are now incorporated and recognized," Friedman pointed out, "by both the Ministry of the Interior and by the Israel Sports Authority, as the Israel Baseball League." The Ministry was never one for fine distinctions: softball, baseball, what's the difference?

"We are now the forty-third sport in Israel, up there with badminton, rugby and tennis," Commissioner Friedman proudly reported, not without a hint of irony at the reduction of the game to such lowly company.

Transportation loomed as a major obstacle because the teams are spread out all over the country. The only day off in Israel, and therefore the only day when games can be organized, is Shabbat, when there is no public transportation. So far, however, the teams have successfully made the rounds on their own momentum, up to Degania, out to Tel Aviv. On any given Shabbat, furthermore, the medical students may have a critical test coming up, the kibbutzniks are sure to be exhausted from a rigorous work schedule, and the journalists are liable to be called to fly off to Teheran or Beirut at a moment's notice.

As the league has shaped up, the franchises are equally divided between city and kibbutz. There are five teams based in kibbutzim: Ein Dor, Galon, Adamit-Shomrat, the Emek team (based around Degania) and Gezer. And in Tel Aviv there are another five franchises: the South Americans, the American Embassy team, the Tel Aviv medical students, a group from Kfar Shmaryahu, and the journalists.

As the playing season approached, the teams sought to spruce up their respective images. Gezer obtained hats and T-shirts. The journalists took on the name "Typoz." The South Americans, aided by the Maccabi organization, and the Embassy team (outfitted by its PX) really suited up.

The journalists, currently in last place, might have been the source of good publicity for the league. Last summer, AP carried a story, picked up by several papers, about baseball at Gezer. The assumption about publicity, however, failed to take into account the deleterious effects of being in last place. Nice guys may finish last, but they rarely write about it.

The journalists' team includes reporters for the New York *Times*, the Washington *Post*, UPI, AP, the Chicago *Tribune*, the Jerusalem *Post* and CBS, and the English-language press officer with the office of the Prime Minister—there to play ball and to keep an eye on his teammates. Once an exhibition game was almost interrupted by a dispute between the press officer and a *Tribune* reporter over an article the Chicago paper had printed that the Prime Minister's office considered unfair.

Much deliberation went into plans for an opening day ceremony that would be sufficiently festive without too much pomp. Some thought that, following the American tradition, Israel's President Yitzhak Navon should be invited to throw out the first ball of the season. This idea was discarded, however, because of the political complications it might engender, due to the game's taking place on the Sabbath.

An idea with equal appeal, but one which struck the organizers as equally wishful, was the suggestion that American Ambassador Samuel Lewis be invited to toss out the first ball. Much to everybody's surprise, Lewis wrote back that he would be happy to attend "this historic event," but he diplomatically gave himself an escape clause lest "pressing matters" prevent his coming. The whole league was elated.

But then President Jimmy Carter came to Israel, seeking a peace treaty, just a slim week before opening day. Ambassador Lewis became busier than ever, and the league braced itself for an embassy substitute. But the President came and went, and on opening day Ambassador Lewis not only showed up on time and threw out the first ball, but stayed around for three hours and displayed a delightful sense of humor. After tossing out the first ball, a bit high and over the head of the waiting catcher, to hearty applause, the Ambassador chuckled, "Now you know why I'm an ambassador and not playing baseball today."

The presence of Ambassador Lewis added immensely to the festivity of the league opener, and perhaps his being there contributed to the first-day victory of the Embassy staff team.

In the first game, the South Americans got off to an early lead, but stealing was permitted, and this resulted in some sloppy play. Lack of control by the South American pitcher and errors by his teammates late in the game finally tipped the balance in favor of the Embassy staffers.

In the second game, the journalists started off getting four runs early on; but the Gezer team, led by first baseman Ken Bob, the kibbutz treasurer, and Elliot King, a tall ex-Philadelphian playing short centerfield, came back to win the game.

Elsewhere around the country there was other action as well on opening day. Now, with the season underway, many questions remain unanswered: Will the currently disputed steal rule be adopted? Will the teams stay with it, or will rapid turnover and declining enthusiasm as the novelty wears off undermine the durability of the new enterprise? In a larger sense, this latter question relates to the ongoing dilemma of American—and South American—*aliya*.

But the uncertainty at the top of everyone's mind at the present is: Who will win the coveted first league championship? At the current writing, the medical students are in first place.

So in Israel, too, at least for now, it will happen every springtime.

—D.T.

Israel's "Mother of the Sons" Was Singled Out at White House Peace Ceremony

Who? Who was that?

In one of the most dramatic moments ever seen on television, against a backdrop of the White House, where the historic Israel-Egypt peace treaty was being signed, Prime Minister Begin of Israel paid his respects to Presidents Carter and Sadat, to numerous other officials and dignitaries—and to "Mrs. Guber." And everyone asked—who?

For the many people who have never heard of this remarkable seventy-seven-year-old woman, who was invited to join the Begin entourage that was to participate in the peace treaty ceremonies, her story is a reminder—poignant and at the same time heroic—of what Israel is all about.

Rivka Guber grew up in Russia in an agricultural colony dedicated to Zionist ideals. Together with fellow idealists, she went on *aliyah*. It was not an idyllic situation for Jews that then permeated the old-new nation's atmosphere; quite a few of the pioneers felt they couldn't make a go of it and left, some for the United States, others for South America. Still others even returned to Russia.

But not Rivka Guber. She settled in a small colony near Rehovot, known as Kfar Bilu. Life was very difficult. Attacks by Arabs drove fear into the hearts of many Jews; she joined in the defense of her home, working alongside the men. Time passed, conditions improved, but news from Europe was ominous, and by 1939 the Nazis launched World War II.

When the British finally acceded to the demands of the Yishuv and allowed a Jewish Battalion to be formed to fight the common foe, Rivka Guber volunteered to serve. Her friends chided her: she was a mother of small children—how could she leave them to fight a war many hundreds if not thousands of miles away? Her response, when she was invited to speak to a women's convention in the winter of 1942, was straightforward:

"I am not a heroine, and not a Joan of Arc—but when I am called on to help my brethren who are defending me, how can I not respond?" She said to friends and neighbors when she left for her military service: "I believe that those of us who are as 'insane' as I am are the only ones who are being realistic, and that the so-called 'normal' ones are denying what is before their very eyes—a monstrous threat to the continued existence of the Jewish people."

After demobilization, she returned to the family farm, only to find that her seventeen-year-old son, who had for a time run the farm while she was in uniform, had enlisted and fought with the Jewish Battalion on the Italian front. He returned home to Palestine on the same day that the British authorities rounded up the Yishuv's leaders and imprisoned them in Latrun. The son, Ephraim, immediately joined Haganah, and helped so-called illegal refugees trying to smuggle themselves into Palestine. He was caught and imprisoned in Cyprus, alongside thousands of other Jews seeking a haven in the Promised Land.

In March 1948, two months before the establishment of Israel, when Arab assaults against isolated Jewish settlements had been intensified, following the United Nations partition decision, Ephraim Guber commanded a Haganah force that defended the small village of Tirat Shalom. When the defenders ran out of all ammunition, he ordered a retreat. All of the Jews got away safely except Ephraim, who was covering the retreat. He died on the spot. His sixteen-year-old brother, Zvi, immediately following the traditional *shiva* week of mourning, joined the Palmach striking force. Three months later, with Israel barely a month old, he fell in action in a battle against the Egyptians in the Negev.

When Rivka Guber, in her halting English, was interviewed by reporters in Washington, she said that at least she is consoled that her sons died for a just and noble cause, the establishment of Israel, and not like the young Jewish men and women who lost their lives in the Holocaust. She spoke without bitterness or rancor, gratified to have lived to see a day when peace and friendship are on the horizon. Her only regret, she said, was that her friend Golda Meir had not lived to this "wonderful day."

Rivka Guber rebuilt her shattered life by helping others. She moved to the Lachish area—in Israel's early years a remote, sparsely populated region desperately in need of people who would transform the area into a thriving agricultural sector. She worked with heart and soul, as a teacher, as a librarian, introducing the world of books to the children of immigrant families, many of them from backward countries. Mrs. Guber helped them to know the pleasures of reading, to learn and to grow into idealistic future citizens of Israel. Ben-Gurion called her the "Great Mother in Israel." In Lachish, about which she wrote a book, the people know her lovingly and admiringly as Rivka.

There is a village in Israel named for the two Guber sons—Kfar Achim, the Village of the Brothers. Rivka Guber has written about Israel and about her fallen sons. Once, to a friend, she wrote:

"I have taught my sons to be good Jews, to take little and give much, to choose the hard paths happily, if it must be so; and, above all, to battle for that which is right until the last breath, for man is duty-bound to fight for what he holds dear in life."

A full cycle has been closed now, for the Mother of the Sons has witnessed the signing of a peace treaty that took more than thirty long years of bloodshed to attain. It is fitting that she was invited to attend the Washington ceremonies, and to know that she at least, if not Golda Meir, did indeed have the privilege to witness what, it is hoped, will be the first official, covenanted day of peace.

—D.C.G.

 Israel's Wild Wheat

"After skirting Rosh Pina, take the right fork," advises a best-selling guidebook to Israel. Fortunately for bread eaters—about a third of humanity—on June 18, 1906, a young agronomist named Aaron Aaronsohn decided not to skirt that sleepy village on the lower slopes of Mount Canaan, near Safad, and thus made one of the most significant discoveries of modern botany: he found a single stalk of wild grain growing out of the crevice of a rock. From a distance, it looked like ordinary wild barley, the weed that grows in almost all empty lots in Israel's cities. On second glance, however, he recognized it for what it was: a wild wheat, the first specimen of its kind ever to be found growing in nature.

It took Aaron Aaronsohn two years of scouting throughout northern Israel, Syria and Jordan to collect samples of wild emmer wheat—known to scientists as *Triticum dicoccoides*—and determine its distribution in these areas. By that time

Aaronsohn was sure that his newly discovered wheat was the direct progenitor, the "mother," of all cultivated wheats, a conjecture that was later proven to be correct by detailed genetic studies.

Israel is more likely to be associated, in the modern mind, with oranges, olives, melons and avocados. But in Biblical days, people thought of the country in terms of wheat.

Moses, addressing the Children of Israel before they entered the Promised Land, took care to explain: "For the Lord your God is bringing you into a good land of brooks, pools, gushing springs, valleys and hills; it is a land of wheat." There would be plenty of water and wheat; other crops and natural resources came farther down the list. Because wheat was a main—if not the major—crop in ancient Israel, hindsight indicates that it was not unlikely that "mother wheat" should be discovered there. In the nineteenth century, however, archaeologists assumed that the domestication of wheat occurred somewhat farther to the north and east, at the very center of the Fertile Crescent, or perhaps in Europe or even in the Gobi Desert of Central Asia.

Aaronsohn's discovery sent waves of excitement through the academic world. Historians, knowing that the domestication of wheat had been a crucial factor in man's transition from hunting to cultivating—i.e., that it had radically altered the course of civilization—were fascinated. Biologists, too, were ecstatic about the discovery. Because of the specialized characteristics of agricultural wheat (including its inability to disperse its seeds), the plant no longer propagated itself in the wild. Unconsciously man had guided its evolution, choosing for continual cultivation only those plants convenient for his purposes, thereby creating a species that depended entirely on human agriculture for survival. After years of searching in vain, biologists had given up hope of ever finding the "mother wheat"; it had been lumped along with the thousands of other species into the category of the extinct. Now, suddenly, there was an opportunity to study the biological development and evolution of wheat.

But Aaronsohn (who had established Israel's first experimental agricultural station at Atlit, south of Haifa) looked at his discovery with the eyes of an agronomist, envisioning the transfer of desirable genetic characteristics found in wild emmer to cultivated wheat, thereby improving its nutritional quality and yield. Noting that the species grew—with equal sturdiness—high on cool Mt. Hermon at an altitude of six thousand feet and in the scorching heat of the Dead Sea five hundred feet below sea level, he realized that it was highly drought- and disease-resistant and able to survive even in poor soil.

Some ears were black, others white; some had long hairs, known by biologists as beards, while others were clean-shaven. Some were short, others tall. The diver-

sity of characteristics boded well for the possibility of discovering valuable properties that could be introduced into cultivated species.

In 1909 Aaronsohn was invited by the United States Department of Agriculture to visit the United States and lecture on the properties and importance of wild emmer. He distributed samples of grain to scientists there so they could study the wheat themselves and use it in their own breeding programs. The severe conditions under which the plant grew in Palestine were similar to those found in many parts of the United States and Aaronsohn hoped that wild emmer would soon be adapted by American agriculture experts. However, though genetic and general biological studies on wild emmer continued, Aaronsohn's vision of using the plant for wheat improvement was soon forgotten. One explanation for this comes from Prof. Moshe Feldman, of the Weizmann Institute's Department of Plant Genetics, and his colleague Dr. Lydia Avivi, who have picked up the thread that was dropped fifty years ago.

"In those days, the knowledge and techniques of breeding were very primitive. Scientists in Europe and in the United States, as well as Aaronsohn himself, using emmer wheat, had failed to produce viable offspring. The hybrids suffered from partial sterility and did not produce good grain. Additionally, they were busy gathering thousands of samples of different cultivated wheats, which also contained hidden and valuable characteristics. These plants, whose genetic structure was identical to the bread wheat then in use, were easier to employ in breeding programs. Why should work be done on problematical plants when striking improvements could be obtained with more suitable starting materials? But perhaps the most serious blow was Aaronsohn's death at forty-three in 1919 in a mysterious plane crash over the English Channel. A powerful personality, whose perseverance and expertise had brought wild emmer to the attention of the scientific world, was eclipsed, and with it his vision of a new wheat."

The Weizmann researchers are not only carrying forward Aaronsohn's scientific work, but also his prophetic vision. "I think that the discovery of wild emmer occurred prematurely, in a sense," says Prof. Feldman. "Its practical implications can only be fully realized now."

Seventy years have done much to change the world's wheat-breeding situation. Scientists have now incorporated nearly all of the economically valuable features found in various cultivated wheats, and today the chances of finding new traits are dwindling fast because primitive farmers everywhere are switching to modern seeds, which means that the rich genetic pools of their traditional crops are being lost to humanity forever.

The decrease of genetic resources combined with the increase of human population make it essential for grain and other seed producers to boost both the yield and the nutritional value of their crops, but so far science has failed, despite using radiation and other mutation techniques, to produce these. One of the last remaining natural stores of such traits is Aaron Aaronsohn's *Triticum dicoccoides*. Like Aaronsohn before them, Prof. Feldman and Dr. Avivi have made dozens of wheat-gathering trips throughout Israel. Their particular interest: determining the nutritional quality of wild emmer and its wild relatives.

—E.L.T.

VII
People:
Whatever They Were,
They Were Originals

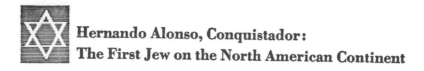 Hernando Alonso, Conquistador:
The First Jew on the North American Continent

A history of the Jews in Mexico from 1521 to the present has never been written in any language. Few have written on any aspect of the life of the Mexican Jews during the colonial period. What little has been written has concentrated upon the life and family of the conquistador and governor Don Luis Carvajal y de la Cueva (1539–90), and one other Jew, Tomás Trevino de Sobremonte, who was burned alive in the Grand Auto-da-Fé of April 11, 1649.

The focusing of attention on the Carvajals has obscured the fact that Jews had preceded them into Mexico by sixty years and that Jews have inhabited Mexico uninterruptedly since 1521. Little note has been made of the fact that Jews had been victims of the Inquisition prior to 1590.

Hernando Alonso, the first Jew to come to Mexico, arrived in 1521. His religious faith was disclosed publicly in 1528. He accompanied Cortes, was a ship's carpenter and was instrumental in the construction of the thirteen bridges that Cortes needed to attack Cuauhtemoc, the last Aztec emperor, in his palace in the middle of Lake Tenochtitlán.

After the defeat of the Aztecs in 1521, Alonso, as one of the conquistadores, was rewarded with the grant of an *encomienda*. Alonso has a double distinction. He was the first Jew to live on the North American continent proper, and he was the first Jew to be burned at the stake there—in 1528, seven years after he was rewarded for his work with Cortes. He was not alone in 1528. One other Jew, Gonzalo de Morales, his brother, shared the stake.

There are two principal accounts of his story. One was written in Spanish by Baleslao Lewin as a chapter in his book, *Mártires y conquistadores judíos en la America Hispana*. The other is an article by G. R. B. Conway, in the Publications of the American Jewish Historical Society, volume XXXI (1928), entitled "Hernando Alonso, a Jewish Conquistador with Cortez in Mexico."

Lewin is a Jew who lives in Argentina and who has made studies of the colonial era in Latin America. Mr. Conway, now deceased, was a Christian Canadian who lived and prospered for many years in Mexico. As an avocation, he became a devoted student of the Mexican Inquisition and did a considerable amount of research.

Both writers are in accord on the facts of Alonso's life prior to his arrival in Mexico and upon the evidence on which he was convicted for heresy and sentenced to be burned alive at the stake. The major differences lie in the emphasis they place upon the facts. One stresses economics and the other religion.

The charge against Alonso was composed of three counts: 1) His child was baptized twice, once by a Franciscan friar and then later "according to the ritual of the law of Moses." (Apparently the child was never circumcised. There is no indication of the fate of the child or its mother, who may be presumed to have been a *nuevo Cristiano*.) 2) He refused to permit his wife to go to church on Sunday to hear Mass. (Alonso was heard to say to his wife, "Señora, in your present Condition [i.e., during her menstrual period] thou wouldst profane the Church," to which his wife replied, "These are old ceremonies of the Jews which are not observed now that we have adopted the evangelical grace.") 3) Many years prior to 1528, someone had peeped through a window and had seen Alonso and a friend take a two-year-old infant, pour water over its head and gather the water which dripped down into a cup and drink it. Hernando Alonso confessed to this when threatened with torture on the rack and explained that "it was done in mockery of the sacrament of baptism."

Conway, an engineer, an entrepreneur and a person of means, was interested in Alonso's position in the commercial and political community. He wrote that Alonso's name appears with frequency in the municipal archives of Mexico City between March 1524 and March 1528, with regard to the bidding for the contract to supply meat for the city. Conway was obviously impressed by the fact that the first Jew became the wholesale supplier of beef and pork for the city. He reports the keen business rivalry between the Jew and others in the community. Conway narrates that, when there was a question of Alonso's bid being the lowest, adjustments were made by the city fathers or new bids were called for, with the result that Alonso usually secured the contract. It is obvious that he was friendly with the members of the City Council and the acting governor of Nueva España, Alonso de Estrada.

Conway makes no comment on the interpretation of the Mosaic or Jewish laws that may have been involved. He completely ignores the obvious religious contradictions touched upon by Lewin and apparently had little knowledge of Jewish customs and ritual.

Lewin, the Jewish author, gives scant words to Alonso's business and political activities. He was interested in the validity of the religious charges.

With respect to the last of the three charges, Lewin adds that the witness heard Alonso and his friend singing a psalm that referred to Israel's Lord God of Egypt, "o una cosa de esta manera." In fact, Lewin slightly gilds the lily by saying that it was likely that the song heard was Psalm 114, which is part of the Hallel (Hymns of Glory) recited by Jews in the synagogue on holy days. Lewin contends that the evidence was a mixture of fact and myth. He says that the second baptism and the dripping of water was to erase the effects of the Christian baptismal rites.

Lewin rightly asserts that Alonso was possessed of little knowledge of Jewish law, since he equated a Christian place of worship with a Jewish house of prayer. There is no proscription on Christian women going to church during the period of their "uncleanliness." The complete absence of anything Jewish, such as prayer and other ritual, in Alonso's life makes paradoxical his concern for the religious sanctity of his faith. This and similar comments and observations are absent in Conway's account.

Conway and Lewin wrote more than four hundred years after the events occurred. Each saw the identical reports of the summary of the evidence before the Inquisitor. The image that each created and the emphasis placed on the facts, however, differ according to their background, ethnic interests and religion. Coincidentally, each ignored the historical background of the 1520s in Mexico.

Conway presents the inference that the motivation for the charges against Alonso stemmed from unsuccessful business rivals. Since they could not underbid him or replace him in the favor of the City Council, they resorted to the use of the Inquisition to dispose of him. Nowhere in Lewin's chapter can there be found anything that might hint at causes for the Inquisitor to have suspected Hernando Alonso of heresy against the Catholic faith.

Both Conway and Lewin have ignored, in their respective writings, a plausible motivation for initiation of the prosecution of the Jew, which supplies a third important aspect to the affair. By 1525, the struggle for power had begun between secular society, including representatives of the Spanish Crown, and the Church. Later, it was to become a struggle between the Dominican Order against the array of society, the secular clergy and the Jesuits, Franciscans, etc.

Cortes conquered Mexico for the Spanish King and the Church. He sought more than territory, riches and the subjugation of the autochthonous population. He insisted upon the destruction of their idols and their conversion to Christianity, even if he had to kill hundreds of thousands in the attempt. If credence is to be given to contemporary accounts, Cortes was most zealous for the Church. His troops were battle-scarred warriors who sought the sanctity of religious rites when in danger and in the first moments of victory, when the reality of danger still lingered. In normal times, they caroused, drank, gambled and debauched, as all mercenaries have done since time immemorial. These were not men seeking the salvation of Indian souls.

Those who decided to remain in Mexico were rewarded in a fashion similar to that of Hernando Alonso. Many became landowners and constituted the first society in the New World. They did not regard those who followed them as equals. They never forgot that they were the conquering heroes. They did not change their innate character because they had become people of substance. Their wives were Indians, and their servants and slaves were Indians. The entry of each into his own home was regal and constituted a reminder of the great military feat in which he had participated. The subservience of their spouses and households continued to inflate their egos. The early years in Mexico have been termed "Gangster Interlude."

They could not and did not forget that they were Spaniards and white. The adulation of the defeated was not sufficient; they had to impress the newcomers from Spain. Victory had not given them learning or manners, and they were still uncouth. They were still profane in their language and crude in their expression. They could not discard their habits. The utterance of the Lord's name as part of curses and imprecations was a common practice. They gave no heed to the admonition that this constituted violation of the Ten Commandments and Church dogma.

The Church Fathers, and in particular the Dominicans, sought to establish their hegemony. The Dominicans succeeded in having one of their own, Fr. San Vicente de Maria, sent to Mexico in 1528 to act in all matters against the Faith as well as to establish the first monasteries.

In the Middle Ages, the Church sought secular as well as spiritual power. Cortes's company took orders from no one except Cortes himself. Many of his men were hailed before the Church on charges of blasphemy and other sinful acts. While Cortes was in Mexico, punishment of his men was mild, but he returned to Spain in May 1528 to air certain of his own grievances before the King.

One can find a meaningful coincidence between the approximate time of Cortes's departure and the burning of Alonso. Alonso was the most vulnerable of Cortes's company. Because of his faith, no one could come to his defense. It is likely that the Church took advantage of Cortes's involvement in his own affairs or his departure to strike a blow at the practical inviolability of the conquistadores that had existed until then. While others could escape with a small penance or insignificant fines, he who was a Jew might not have enjoyed even the protection of his former comrades-in-arms. To be a Jew was to be the worst form of heretic prior to the advent of Protestantism. More specifically, to be a Jew in Mexico in 1528 was to have been present in violation of the Royal Decree, forbidding Jews or Moors or even their descendants from being in Nueva España.

—S.B.L.

When Dickens Apologized for the Character Fagin

Oliver Twist is one of Charles Dickens' most popular works, but the reaction of Jews to this work has always been one of keen disapproval.

Jewish objection to *Oliver Twist* is directed against Fagin—the fence, the corrupter of youth, the arch-villain of the story. He is the only Jewish character in the story, and his very name, like that of Shylock in *The Merchant of Venice,* has become a term of insult and anti-Jewish abuse.

It would be unfair to the memory of Dickens the writer to leave uncorrected the reputation of anti-Semite that he has among Jews. *Oliver Twist* was one of his earliest works—appearing first in monthly installments in 1837. In 1863 Dickens' attention was drawn to Jewish resentment of the portrayal of Fagin. This was in a letter from a Mrs. Eliza Davis, who, fortunately, kept all Dickens' letters to her, and copies of her letters to him. Although this correspondence was known to students of Dickens' work, it was not published in full until 1918.

Under the title of *Charles Dickens and His Jewish Characters,* it was printed by the Chiswick Press, London, in 1918. Opposite the title-page is printed: "The conquest of Palestine and the fall of Jerusalem has directed the attention of the civilized world to the problem of the Jewish people."

Mrs. Eliza Davis was the wife of James P. Davis, to whom Dickens had sold his London house in Tavistock Square in 1860. In her first letter, dated June 22, 1863, Mrs. Davis asks Dickens for a donation to the memorial for Judith, Lady Montefiore, "a lady who conjointly with her husband exerted herself at great personal sacrifice to relieve her oppressed people in distant lands." Mrs. Davis, as though she had been but awaiting this chance to declare what had long been in her mind, added: "But there are other oppressions much heavier, other things far sharper, than the fetters and goads of Damascus, Lebanon or Russia. In this country, where the liberty of the subject is fully recognized, where the law knows no distinction of Creed, the pen of the novelist, the gibe of the pamphleteer is still whetted against the 'Sons of Israel.' It has been said that Charles Dickens the large-hearted . . . has encouraged a vile prejudice against the despised Hebrew. . . . Fagin, I fear, admits only of one interpretation; but while Charles Dickens lives, the author can justify himself or atone for a great wrong on a whole though scattered nation."

Having relieved her mind thus, Mrs. Davis reverts to the Lady Montefiore memorial, asking permission to place Charles Dickens' name on the list of donors. The memorial was to take the form of a convalescent home for the Jewish poor, "whose dietary laws exclude them from participation in the existing institutions for the recovery of health."

The amount of the donation was unimportant, declared Mrs. Davis; she ended with a note that Sir Moses Montefiore was the first, with a munificent gift, to open the subscription for the relief of the Syrian Christian sufferers from the cruelty of the Druses.

Dickens' reply, from Gad's Hill, Rochester, Kent, is dated July 10, 1863. He declares emphatically: "I must take leave to say that if there be any general feeling on the part of the Jewish people, that I have done them what you describe as 'a great wrong,' they are a far less sensible, a far less just, and a far less good tempered people than I have always supposed them to be . . . But surely no sensible man or woman of your persuasion can fail to observe—firstly—that all the rest of the wicked *dramatis personae* are Christians; and, secondly, that he is called 'The Jew,' not because of his religion, but because of his race. If I were to write a story in which I pursued a Frenchman or a Spaniard as 'the Roman Catholic,' I should do a very indecent and unjustifiable thing; but I make mention of Fagin as the Jew because he is one of the Jewish people, and because it conveys that kind of idea of him, which I should give my readers of a Chinaman by calling him a Chinese."

The letter ends by stating that the donation enclosed for the Lady Montefiore Memorial, though nominal, "may serve to shew [*sic*] you that I have no feeling towards the Jewish people but a friendly one. I always speak well of them whether in public or in private, and bear testimony (as I ought to do) to their perfect good faith in such transactions as I have ever had with them. And in my *Child's History of England* I have lost no opportunity of setting forth their cruel persecutions in old times."

Mrs. Davis replied to the above letter on July 14, venturing some remarks on the Jewish character. After thanking Dickens for his letter and donation, she writes: "It is a fact that the Jewish race and religion are inseparable. If a Jew embrace any other faith, he is no longer known as of the race, either to his own people or the Gentiles to whom he has joined himself."

Referring to Dickens' statement that the other criminals in *Oliver Twist* were Christians, she declares that "they are at least contrasted with the character of good Christians. This poor wretched Fagin stands alone, 'The Jew.' How grateful we are to Sir Walter Scott . . . for delineations of some of our race, yet Isaac of York was not all virtue!

"I hope we shall not forfeit your opinion of our good sense and good temper; perhaps we are over sensitive, but are we not ever flayed? Are we not constantly irritated by the small gnats who may fret us, yet are in themselves too insignificant to be annihilated? It is only when a great mind appears against us that we so plaintively appeal."

Warming to her subject, Mrs. Davis enlarges on the general ignorance concerning Jews and states: "We dwell in this country very little known, our domestic customs entirely unknown. I have myself been greatly astonished at the ignorance of my countrymen concerning what they appear to think an entirely foreign people. Look at the blood accusations from time to time rising up against us, even such a popular paper as *Chambers* disseminating that calumny. I hazard the opinion that it would well repay an author of reputation to examine more closely into the manners and character of British Jews and to represent them as they really are . . ."

And once more thanking Dickens for his donation—"Your name . . . will be a high gratification to the whole body of British Jews"—she promised not to trouble him with further correspondence. She did not keep this promise.

In May 1864, the first monthly installment of *Our Mutual Friend* appeared. When the seventh number was published, Mrs. Davis wrote to Dickens. In this chapter the Jew Riah, the good Jew, in contrast to Fagin, the bad Jew, was presented to the public. Mrs. Davis' suggestion had, surprisingly enough, been taken seriously by Charles Dickens. Instead of resenting her criticism of his work, he—the great, the successful, the established writer—had taken her remarks to heart. He had sought to atone for the wrong he now felt he had done to the Jewish people in his portrayal of Fagin as "the Jew."

But once again Dickens revealed himself as ignorant of Jews and Jewish life. Like all his characters not actually based on his own life experience and observation, Dickens' Jewish characters are unreal and not true to life. Having made

Fagin a villain of the deepest black dye, to restore the balance he made Riah a soul of purest white, so good that no reader can believe in either his goodness or his actuality.

On the appearance of Riah in the seventh installment, Mrs. Davis writes to Dickens (November 13, 1864), "breaking though a promise . . . to thank you very earnestly for what I am so presumptuous as to think a great compliment paid to myself and my people." But this did not prevent her from correcting certain errors that Dickens had made, such as making Riah refer to God as "Jehovah"—"no Jew ever utters this appellation of the Creator, even in his prayers"; she explains in detail, with use of Hebrew letters, the substitution of the word Adonai for the Ineffable Name.

Mrs. Davis further corrects Dickens as to the dress of English Jews and the use of uncharacteristic phrases: ". . . I am acquainted with an aged Hebrew living not far from the house in St. Mary Axe whose physique and courteous deportment it [the story] very well describes. The costume, however, differs; ordinarily these people dress as their neighbors do, and before the present fashion of beards prevailed did not wear theirs unless, indeed, they are Polish Jews. I conclude from his language that Riah is an English Jew, but the action of kissing the hem of a garment is strictly Polish. A Turkish Jew might use it, but we have few of them in England. I have never myself seen it practiced but by a Polish Jewess, these also will kiss the hand of a benefactor.

"The phrase 'generous Christian Master' is not characteristic. The kindness to the two girls, the indifference whether they be of his own faith or another is very truthful. I believe we do perform the enjoinder to 'shew kindness unto the stranger because ye know the heart of the stranger for ye were strangers in the land of Egypt'—and to a certain extent we are strangers here."

Three days later, on November 16, 1864, Dickens hurried off a short reply: "I have received your letter with great pleasure, and hope to be (as I have always been in my heart) the best friends with the Jewish people." The errors pointed out to him had been noticed by him too late for correction. "The peculiarities of dress and manners are fixed together for the sake of picturesqueness."

Riah was the antithesis of Fagin. And if, indeed, he graces the pages of *Our Mutual Friend*, as he surely does, and Dickens was the creator that fashioned him, the words and sentiments Riah utters belong as surely to Mrs. Eliza Davis. Riah, in a fine speech, declares "It is not, in Christian countries, with the Jews as with other peoples. Men say, 'This is a bad Greek, but there are good Greeks. This is a bad Turk, but there are good Turks.' Not so with Jews. Men find the bad amongst us easily enough—among what peoples are the bad not easily found?—but they take the worst of us as samples of the best; they say, 'All Jews are alike.' If, doing what I was content to do . . . I had been a Christian, I could have done it compromising no one but my individual self. But doing it as a Jew, I could not do but compromise the Jews of all conditions and all countries. It is hard upon us, but [as] it is the truth I would that all our people remembered it!"

Most gratified was Mrs. Davis for the change she had helped to bring about in the presentation of Jewish characters by the leading English writer of her day, the most popular and widely read novelist of the century. In February 1867, she sent him a handsomely bound volume of Scriptures in Hebrew, with English translation, enclosing an inscription to be inserted on the title page. It read: "6th Feb. 1867. Presented to Charles Dickens, Esq., in grateful and admiring recognition of his having exercised the noblest quality man can possess; that of atoning for an injury as soon as conscious of having inflicted it, by a Jewess."

In the letter accompanying the Scriptures, Mrs. Davis, referring to the inscription, writes: "It does but faintly express how highly I appreciate and how profoundly sensible I am of the nobility of character evinced by him who depicted 'Riah' in contrast to Fagin. Most gratefully do my people accept the spirit of the work."

To this, Charles Dickens answered, March 1, 1867, from Bradford, Yorkshire, where he was giving a series of readings: ". . . The terms in which you send me that mark of your remembrance are more gratifying to me than I can possibly express to you; for they assure me that there is nothing but goodwill left between me and a people for whom I have a real regard, and to whom I would not wilfully have given offense or done an injustice for any worldly consideration."

Mrs. Davis was not personally acquainted with Charles Dickens. But we must be grateful to her for treasuring and keeping the letters and copies of the correspondence as witness to later generations of the atonement and vindication of a great writer.

It is well for Jews to know of this atonement of Charles Dickens before we stigmatize him as a Jew-hater.

—B.Z.A.

 ## Harpo Marx and the Doorman

One spring afternoon in New York, Harpo (Marx) was deploying down Fifth Avenue encased in a bright yellow overcoat and topped by a blue hat with a little feather in it. Around his middle he wore a sash such as Brazilian maxixe dancers favor. His throat was bared, and the ends of a Byronic collar lay low on his chest. The details may sound a bit eccentric, but the ensemble was one of great elegance —particularly since it was Harpo's fancy when out for a stroll to arrange his plastic features so that he resembled exactly the late Kaiser Wilhelm.

In front of a very famous jewelry store, Harpo came to a resplendent halt. An argument was in progress between a taxicab driver and the doorman of this awesome emporium. The doorman was tall, blond and uniformed. The taxi driver was none of these things. He was chiefly Jewish. And Harpo stood listening owl-eyed to the strange barrage of insults to which the doorman was treating the driver.

"Get away from in front here, you dirty Jew," said the doorman. "Go on before I break your dirty Jew head. There'll be a law soon keeping you and all Jews off this street. Go on, get back to the ghetto where you belong."

Harpo vanished from the scene. Fifteen minutes later our Preposterous Knight reappeared, walking on Fifth Avenue. His pockets were filled with five-and-ten-cent-store emeralds, rubies and diamonds. He paused before the doorman and fixed upon him his finest Kaiser glare. The doorman bowed, opened the door obsequiously for Harpo and beamed ingratiatingly on this arrogant customer. Harpo glared back at him, barked once, and entered the store, leaving the flunky soul of the Nazi stirred to its depths.

Twenty minutes later Harpo emerged, and as he stepped into the street he tripped. The horrified door-opener saw this elegant customer fall flat on his face. And he saw something even more horrifying. Out of the pockets of this high-born shopper rolled a score of emeralds, rubies and diamonds. They bounced across the pavement in all directions. The paste jewels were worth all of three dollars. But the doorman didn't know this.

With a cry of anguish the doorman threw himself to the sidewalk and darted wildly after the bouncing jewels. He scurried about on hands and knees for ten minutes. He retrieved rubies from the gutter, snatched emeralds from under the feet of startled pedestrians, and plucked diamonds from the pavement cracks. He arose after the ten minutes, out of breath but beaming, and approached the elegant customer with the rigid face.

"Please," he panted blissfully, "look quick. See if they are all there."

Harpo examined the jewels coldly as the doorman handed him the glittering handful.

"Yes," Harpo barked, "they are all here."

"Thank God!" said the doorman and mopped his brow and stood by vibrating joyfully.

Harpo strode to the curb. A cab was waiting. At its wheel sat the same Jewish driver at whom the doorman had been screaming insults a half hour before. The doorman limped eagerly beside Harpo and opened the door of the vehicle with a happy bow.

Harpo paused before the opened door. He examined the jewels still in his hand and selected the largest diamond from among them. He handed it to the doorman.

"Here," said Harpo. "For your trouble."

The doorman gaped.

"And give this one to your best girl," said Harpo, selecting another huge diamond, "and to your dear mama this ruby."

To the cabby Harpo suddenly cried in a voice all business: "Drive me to the synagogue. I am late for my afternoon prayers."

The doorman was discharged later that afternoon for screaming at the assistant manager.

—B.H.

 ## The Jew Who Saved the Chinese Revolution

Dr. Moses Schwarzberg, who passed away in Tel Aviv at the age of eighty-three in March 1964, was one of the most colorful figures in recent Jewish history, and an inveterate cloak-and-dagger adventurer to boot. Shortly before his death, Dr. Schwarzberg was offered a fabulous sum in return for his testimony in Peking's border dispute with Moscow. The Soviet Embassy in Tel Aviv also contacted the

aged Jewish physician, offering him twice as much as the Chinese did for keeping mum about a promise made by Moscow in 1924 to hand over several Siberian border districts to China.

Dr. Schwarzberg turned down both proposals, leaving the unpublished manuscript of his adventures in China with friends and instructing them to publish it after his death. Now it can be told.

In the early 1920s, a young refugee from revolutionary Russia, Moses Schwarzberg, found himself wandering across the frozen land of Manchuria. As a student of medicine at the University of Moscow, he had been active for many years in the left-wing social revolutionary movement, which was outlawed by the Communists after an attempt on Lenin's life in 1918. When social revolutionary activists were being rounded up for execution by Communist secret police squads, Schwarzberg fled east to the town of Samara on the Volga River, where revolutionary leaders proclaimed the short-lived "Russian Democratic Republic" and demanded free elections all over the country.

The rebellion was crushed by the Red Army under the renegade Czarist officer Mikhail Tukhachevski (who was later executed by Stalin on trumped-up charges), and Schwarzberg fled east to Siberia, then ruled by various anti-communist Russian generals, freebooters and bandit leaders. Refugees were robbed and murdered, women raped, villages razed and crops destroyed in the fighting, which raged for three years.

Schwarzberg hoped to get to some Far Eastern port and board a ship for the United States, where relatives were expecting him in San Francisco. China itself was rent by a bitter and protracted civil war fought between the National Republic of Dr. Sun Yat-sen and the powerful warlords who ruled North China and Manchuria.

"I was walking along the railroad tracks to Hailar station when I came upon the prostrate body of an elderly Chinese, half covered by the drifting snow," Dr. Schwarzberg recollected. "I felt his pulse and saw that he was still alive. There was a small farm near the tracks, inhabited by Russian Cossacks, who used to work on the railroad before the war. I dragged the frozen Chinese to the farm, asked the woman to boil us some tea, and massaged his limbs with snow. He came to after a while, drank the tea and looked at me for a long time without saying anything. I had learned the North Chinese dialect during my travels in Manchuria, and I asked him who he was. To my great surprise, he replied in fluent Russian. He said he was sent by the Soviet People's Commissar [Minister] of Foreign Affairs, Chicherin, with an important message to President Sun Yat-sen.

" 'If you are from Moscow,' he said, 'you must know me, or at least the place where I used to work—Li's Chinese Laundry on Pereyaslavski Street. I served with the Chinese Regiment in Kiev, until Comrade Chicherin sent me with the message to Dr. Sun Yat-sen. I feel I am dying. I certainly can't go on. And the message must be delivered. Comrade Chicherin gave me five hundred gold rubles to bribe my way across the borders. Here, take the money and the message, and swear on your honor that you will deliver it.' " He tore the lining of his cotton-padded jacket to extract a thick brown envelope with red wax seals, and a heavy money bag, Schwarzberg remembers. "He pushed both into my hands and closed his eyes. A few minutes later, he was dead. My first impulse was to grab the money, destroy the message and make a beeline for Tsingtao, where passage could be bought on ships sailing for the United States. For some reason, perhaps because I was superstitious and feared the old man's curse, I did not destroy the envelope. It took me six weeks to get to Tsingtao. There I learned that the next ship for the United States was not due for another two weeks. I thought I might as well jump to Shanghai and deliver the message to Dr. Sun Yat-sen. After all, a man had died to bring it across the border. I booked passage aboard a small coastal steamer and arrived in Shanghai. The North Chinese warlords were threatening the coastal regions, and the Government of the Chinese National Republic was getting ready to move south to Canton.

"It took me some time to meet Dr. Sun Yat-sen. His bodyguards were on the lookout for enemy agents, and had a nasty habit of shooting first and asking questions later. But one day, while I was waiting for the President to come out of his residence and enter the car, flanked by tough-looking guards who eyed me suspiciously, a huge man with a shaved head and two pistols in his belt crossed the street and approached me. I could see he wasn't a Chinese, but could not have known that he was Jewish—'Two-Gun' Morris Cohen, Sun Yat-sen's chief bodyguard and, later, a famous general with the Chinese Nationalist Army.

" 'Who the hell are you, and what the hell do you want?' he barked in English. I said I had an urgent message for Dr. Sun Yat-sen. Cohen questioned me in English, but when he learned I was a Jewish refugee from Russia, he switched to Yiddish. *'Dein nummen is Moishe? Mein nummen is oikhet Moishe. Kum arein tsum President.'* *

"He introduced me to Sun Yat-sen and waited until I handed over the envelope and repeated the story of my encounter with the anonymous Chinese messenger near Hailar. Dr. Sun Yat-sen tore open the heavy seals and extracted three typewritten sheets of poor-quality paper, embossed with the Soviet state insignia, and bearing Commissar Chicherin's signature. The message was written in Russian, and neither the President nor 'Two-Gun' Cohen knew the language. I was asked to translate from Russian to English, which the Chinese President spoke well.

"Chicherin's first message spoke of the historic friendship between Russia and China, of the revolutionary bonds uniting the Chinese National Republic with the Russian Socialist Republic, the common interests in the struggle against White Russian and North Chinese warlords in Siberia, Mongolia and Manchuria, and the hatred of imperialism and colonialist exploitation. In the name of the Soviet Russian Government, Chicherin suggested a military alliance with China, and proposed joint action against the warlords and guerrilla bands, offering military aid to the Chinese Republican Army.

"The Chinese President then asked me to wait outside, in a big room crowded with officers, administration officials and Kuomintang Nationalist Party big shots, who were curious to learn what were two 'foreign devils' (that's how the Chinese call all foreigners) doing with their Chief of State.

" 'Two-Gun' Cohen came out and motioned me to follow him. We went up to his room, he gave me a shot of gin and poked a stubby finger at my midriff. 'Listen, kid, how would you like to stay on as Dr. Sun Yat-sen's confidential secretary? He likes you and wants you as his personal interpreter. This Russian offer is more serious than you think, and someone with a perfect knowledge of the Russian language is needed to conduct all the negotiations and correspondence. What do you say?'

"The alcohol made me drowsy and I must have nodded, for Cohen clapped me on my shoulder, shook my hand and poured another drink. The next day, we

* 'Your name is Moishe? My name is also Moishe. Come inside to the President.'

boarded a special train for Canton. I spent most of my time in Dr. Sun Yat-sen's private coach, drafting the text of his reply to Chicherin: The Republic of China welcomed the Soviet offer of military aid and political alliance. Because of the fighting which raged across North China and Manchuria, the message was sent by ordinary mail to Cohen's relatives in London, with a request to pass it on to the Soviet Legation in Latvia. It arrived in Moscow towards the end of 1922, and Soviet military aid arrived by sea, from Vladivostock to Canton, as of October 1923.

"Two months later, the Soviet-organized and -trained Army of the Republic of China smashed the northern warlords and entered Peking. Another meeting with Ambassador Karakhan took place aboard President Sun Yat-sen's private train at the Peking Railway Station. I was again present as the President's personal interpreter. Karakhan brought with him the draft of the Soviet-Chinese Border Rectification Treaty, as suggested by Moscow. Its main point was that a plebiscite, jointly supervised by Russia and China, would be held in all disputed border areas. If the majority of the inhabitants wished to be united with China, the boundary of the district would be changed accordingly. Dr. Sun Yat-sen appeared to be satisfied with the treaty suggestion. He did not realize the Reds were planning to double-cross him before the ink was dry on their signatures.

"But he died of cancer on March 12, 1925, before he had time to sign the preliminary agreement with Moscow. The Soviet 'advisers' moved in to exploit the chaos and fill the vacuum created by Dr. Sun Yat-sen's death. They took over the Whampoa War Academy near Canton, and diverted all modern equipment to pro-Communist units of the Chinese Army. From my friends in the Kuomintang Nationalist Party, I learned that 'Two-Gun' Cohen and I were on Soviet 'liquidation lists.' Moscow regarded us as potential enemies who knew too much about behind-the-scenes deals arranged by the Russians in China.

"I was inclined to disregard the warnings and stay on in Canton, where I fell in love with the daughter of a prominent Jewish banker in the nearby British colony of Hong Kong. But 'Two-Gun' Cohen was more experienced in these matters. He took off for Canada, after persuading me to flee China until the Reds cooled off.

"I went to Berlin, finished my medical studies there, practiced for some time in Vienna, and returned to Hong Kong in 1929. I got married and tried to practice medicine in peaceful surroundings, but 'Two-Gun' Cohen sent one of his men with an urgent message to meet him in Shanghai. Cohen had returned to China two years before I did, in time to join Chiang Kai-shek's famous coup against the Reds.

"The Russians and their local Communist stooges were so sure of success that they did not bother to hide their plans of creating a Soviet Republic in China. General Chiang Kai-shek and the right (Nationalist) wing of the Kuomintang party decided to crack down before it was too late. The Chinese Civil War broke out, and lasted—with minor interruptions—for more than twenty years, till the Communist victory in 1949.

"I divided my time between Hong Kong, where our daughter Rita was born in 1933, and where I had a fashionable medical practice, and Peking, where I continued to serve as Generalissimo Chiang Kai-shek's personal adviser.

"When the Japs attacked Hong Kong in December 1941, the Generalissimo had us flown to his temporary capital of Chungking. After the Second World War, when I heard of Israel's struggle for independence, I organized the Shanghai Regiment of some twelve hundred Jewish volunteers resident in China. Despite the Civil War then raging between the Communists and the Nationalists, I used my connections to obtain exit permits for the volunteers, and secure airline passage via India, Persia, Turkey and Italy, to bypass Arab-controlled airfields. When Nationalist resistance collapsed, I joined Generalissimo Chiang Kai-shek in Formosa. My beloved wife died during the evacuation, but I managed to send my daughter to Israel with the last group of volunteers who left Shanghai before the Reds marched in, and followed her in 1951.

—L.H.

 ## A Yiddish-Speaking FBI Agent

Enter the name of Harvey Burstein into the roster of ingenious and creative Jews.

At first glance, the scholarly, bespectacled Mr. Burstein gives the impression of holding a chair devoted to the Greek translation of the Bible, or Jewish Hellenism. He doesn't. But he knows these subjects too.

Mr. Burstein also can rhapsodize freely—and in fluent Yiddish—on what was once, in the pre-Hitler era, "the wonder of the *shtetl*": the Jewish city-within-a-city in old Europe.

He will talk to you of Yiddish journalism that flourished in this country, in the not-too-distant yesteryear. Reverently he intones passages from the works of Sholom Aleichem, Peretz, Sholom Asch, David Pinski.

Today, Mr. Burstein is general counsel for a contract firm, living a sedate life with his wife in Mamaroneck, New York. He devotes time to consulting work on loss prevention programs. He measures five feet eight inches, tips the scales at 165 pounds, and just became forty-one years old.

Who would guess that the gentleman was a special agent of the Federal Bureau of Investigation during the war years—that he had the distinction of being the first Yiddish- and Hebrew-speaking FBI agent!

To be sure, the FBI has employed many Jews, but Mr. Burstein was the only one with the ability to handle Yiddish and Hebrew in their written form as well as orally. The files of the FBI attest to his contributions to the nation's welfare because of his knowledge of Yiddish.

It was 1941. Harvey Burstein was assigned to all aspects of espionage and foreign intelligence. The war was raging in Europe, and tensions were mounting between Japan and the United States.

On Fifth Avenue, a man, walking slowly, glanced down. A metal container glistened at the corner of a building. The alarmed citizen quickly picked it up. He was convinced that this was a coded message being passed between enemies of the United States. He rushed to the New York offices of the FBI. Washington was notified.

A courier hastened to Washington with the "coded message." "Get Burstein on the double," rang out the order. Agents were crowded around the desk when agent Burstein entered, took one look at the container and said, "Gentlemen, this is the *Sh'ma*, the basic credo of the Jewish faith—nothing to worry about." The container was a *mezuzah*.

Down the long corridors of the FBI went the word that if "anything comes across any desk in a foreign language, call Burstein." From then on it was Burstein, the Yiddish agent.

To what illegal uses can Yiddish be put? Well, agent Burstein was handed an alleged extortion letter written in Yiddish and proceeded to translate—but was stumped by one word. He delved deep into books in the Hebraic Section of the Library of Congress, but was still baffled.

Back at the office, the answer suddenly dawned. "The word," he recalls, "was neither Yiddish nor Hebrew, but it was an English word written out phonetically in Yiddish characters."

Agent Burstein found himself in Chicago on an investigation on the eve of Passover. He entered an apartment house occupied mainly by Jewish residents. He knocked on a door. The door opened about an inch. In a Jewish accent, a woman replied through the crack that she had no information for him.

Agent Burstein resorted to Yiddish. "I told her how sorry I was for interfering with her preparations for Pesach, how difficult for her to answer questions in the midst of cleaning and cooking, in the midst of grinding her gefilte fish."

The door literally flew open. Agent Burstein was invited in. She had no information to give, but agent Burstein got a piece of gefilte fish for Passover lunch, and a delicious glass of tea. And, anytime he was in the neighborhood he was "to be sure to call for a good Jewish meal." Yiddish opens many doors.

One time the Chicago police raided a large bookie establishment. They seized records, racing forms, and other items connected with the ring's operations. One particular book confronted the local constabulary with a vexing problem. The entries were in a strange language.

Agent Burstein was summoned. The entries were in Yiddish. The bookmaker was keeping a record in Yiddish of all bets, with the names of the horses, the odds—everything—spelled out phonetically in Yiddish.

One horse was "Shtarke Yingel" (Strong Boy). The odds on Shtarke Yingel were 3–1, a near favorite—only the odds were listed in Yiddish as *gimel* over *aleph*. (Hebrew numerals are based on the order of the letters in the Hebrew alphabet, which is used in Yiddish. Thus, *gimel* is three and *aleph* is one.)

Confronted with this bit of evidence, the bookmaker changed his plea from "not guilty" to "guilty" and placed himself at the mercy of the court—or in this case, *"di rachmonis von di bet din."*

Former agent Burstein is quick to stress that Jews are "very definitely in the minority where crimes of violence are involved."

He has felt no qualms about using Yiddish "against my people," because he believes that a person who becomes part of a criminal activity so discredits the Jewish community that there is no reason to have a conscience about the arrest of a Jewish gambler.

Agent Burstein did not stay in Chicago long. Members of Congress were confronted with problems calling for knowledge of Yiddish. J. Edgar Hoover, the FBI chief, ordered him back for the assignment.

In 1954, Mr. Burstein resigned from the service—after receiving the highest commendations from the heads of the FBI.

—I.S.

 # The Rabbinical Sherlock Holmes

Among the most unique occupations in today's bewildering world must be numbered that of Israeli Rabbi Shimon Katz, who finds himself cast in the true-life role of a clergyman-detective. He was assigned by the Chief Rabbinate to the

Ministry of Justice and given the official task of tracking down deserting husbands who have fled Israel.

He is so successful at his job that he has earned the title of "The Rabbinical Sherlock Holmes." He plies his trade all over the world and, during the past year, caught up with fugitives who had sought to disappear in such widely scattered places as Paris, Rome, London, Sofia, Berlin and New York City.

On one occasion he crashed the summit conference between Nikita Khrushchev and President John F. Kennedy, causing considerable embarrassment to the KGB, the dreaded Russian secret service. Another time, he made a perilous journey into the isolated mountains of Turkey, trekking halfway up the slopes of Mount Ararat—where Noah's Ark is supposed to have come to rest.

Rabbi Katz owes his assignment to the fact that divorce laws in modern Israel are still oriented toward the five-thousand-year-old canon which appears in Deuteronomy, Chapter 24, verse 1:

"When a man taketh a wife and marries her, then it cometh to pass, if she finds no favor in his eyes because he hath found some unseemly thing in her, that he writeth her a bill of divorcement and giveth it in her hand and sendeth her out of his house."

In short, when a man decided he was through with his spouse, he put it in writing and pushed her out of his tent. It was as uncomplicated as all that in the ancient male-oriented society.

Subsequent rabbinical interpretation has modified this considerably, of course, so that marriages cannot now be whimsically dissolved by the husband. Nevertheless, it remains true to this very day that no Orthodox Jewess can remarry unless and until she can flash her former husband's signature at the foot of a bill of divorcement.

Naturally, when a husband takes French leave in the middle of the night, the deserted wife—called an *Agunah*—is literally sentenced to a lifetime of loneliness, often complicated by the struggle to support the children of the still-undissolved union. To prevent the *Agunah* from leading a life in limbo, neither married nor single, is Rabbi Katz's principal motivation.

With the dislocations of recent wars, the hasty marriages and the equally precipitous flights from them, the number of abandoned brides in the State of Israel increased to an alarming extent. It was to correct this situation that Rabbi Katz was tapped by his superiors in the Rabbinate. Without ceremony, they drafted him from his peaceful pastorate in Petach-Tikvah, where his father is chief rabbi.

Pursuit of one such fugitive husband brought Katz into contact with the late Soviet premier Nikita Khrushchev.

The meeting itself took place in 1961, but its roots go back to 1958, when one Max Planski took as his wife a certain Sarah Fasciak, who, like himself, had migrated to Israel from Poland. Before long, an attack of restlessness seized Max and, heedless of his marriage vows, he disappeared without going through the formality of signing the bill of divorcement. Signs pointed to his having returned to Poland.

Once inside that vast land, the rabbi found himself hampered by the traditional reluctance of the Russian citizen to chat freely with foreign visitors and even more so by the well-known official disdain for active practitioners of the Jewish faith. Ultimately he found himself obliged to leave Russia empty-handed.

When he read, early in 1961, of the impending summit meeting between President Kennedy and Premier Khrushchev, to take place in Vienna, he thought immediately of Max Planski and began to lay plans to take up the matter with the one man in all the Soviet Union who could help him complete his mission successfully.

But how to reach him? Katz's letters requesting an interview went unanswered. His telephone calls to the Soviet Embassy brought only polite evasions. In desperation, Rabbi Katz took his problem to Abraham Fingerhut, Chief Rabbi of Paris and himself a member of the French delegation to the summit conference in Vienna. Between them, the two clerical gentlemen hatched a plan.

When the Russians threw a party for the French envoys at the Soviet consulate in Vienna, Rabbi Katz came through the front door as an official member of the delegation. And, when Nikita Khrushchev turned from lifting a brimming beaker of vodka from the tray of a passing waiter, he found himself unexpectedly face-to-face with a tall, bearded man who also held a glass in his right hand.

When Rabbi Katz finished explaining his problem to the Soviet premier, Khrushchev turned to a uniformed, bemedaled aide and exploded a furious barrage of Billingsgate, the sum total of which added up to one burning question: "How in blazes did this guy get through your security and corner me here?"

While the aide hemmed and hawed, Rabbi Katz fought hard to keep from showing the little thrill of pride that he felt. The pride soon evaporated, however, when an aggravated Khrushchev turned on him with a gruff: "Why should I do this? It is none of my business."

Patiently, the rabbi explained that civilized nations did not dismiss lightly the careless fracturing of the marriage vows. The premier shrugged but, looking around the room, found that the entire delegation of visitors seemed to be examining him as though they, too, knew what was being asked of him and were wondering how he would measure up to this test of common decency.

Finally, he growled, "I will see." That was his final word and Rabbi Katz had to content himself with it.

The long-distance telephone wires to Moscow must have burned that night, however, for the following evening, a sheepish-looking Max Planski turned up at the rabbi's hotel. His escort consisted of a group of angry KGB operatives whose duty it was to see that their charge signed the paper.

Meekly he placed his scrawl on the last line of the legal paper and departed. From the way he was jostled along, it was apparent that his secret service superiors were far from pleased with the way he had embarrassed them in the eyes of the big boss.

"I couldn't help feeling sorry for him," Rabbi Katz says, his gentle voice belying the implacability of his pursuit. "I feel sorry for so many of them. After all, it is not always the man's fault. Sometimes a woman is hard to live with . . . refuses to adjust, to make allowances."

He sighed. "There are so many other problems as well. It is such a new country and the people have come from all over the world. There are differences of language, of custom. Sometimes the barriers are too high to cross.

"But what can we do? We cannot let them walk out on their obligations. We do not insist that they come back. But the woman has a right to live, too. The least a man can do is to grant her her freedom . . . a chance to find happiness in a new life."

Despite his genuine sympathy for his quarry, Rabbi Katz has organized a tight net of detection. He travels throughout the world on a diplomatic passport, can make himself understood in at least ten languages and, when necessary, has available to him the services of Interpol, the international police organization, of which he is a member.

In addition, he has his own organization, which consists of the entire Israeli diplomatic corps, its ambassadors and consuls in every city where they maintain legations. In addition, he can count on the help of the rabbinate in whatever country he visits, as well as an informal network of salesmen, journalists, the clergy of many different faiths and travelers of every kind.

It was an itinerant salesman of ladies' lingerie who casually mentioned to a rabbi in St. Louis that a customer of his on a farm outside Des Moines was being courted by a man who once had lived in the Holy Land. The rabbi, from the salesman's description, recognized the man as a runaway husband. A meeting of the rabbi and the peripatetic farmer was arranged between rows of ripening corn, where the frightened man put his signature on the divorce papers.

In Paris, an exotic dancer who was the rage of the nightclub circuit told a newspaper friend that a certain café owner wanted to marry her. The reporter, who covered the Israeli consulate on his foreign news assignment, knew that the prospective groom already had a wife in Israel. In fact, the man once had been confronted by Rabbi Katz and had refused both to sign the divorce papers and to offer financial aid.

Israeli officials in Paris quietly notified Rabbi Katz, who flew in immediately. The rabbi visited friends at the Sureté and arranged for the full cooperation of the French police. The dancer went through with the plans for her marriage, but as soon as the judge at the civil ceremony had concluded, a man stepped forward and showed his badge. The nightclub owner, he explained, had committed bigamy and as such was a most undesirable visitor. Of course, this marriage was void. The groom was hustled off to the police station. Anxious to ingratiate himself with his captors, he readily agreed to sign the papers for Rabbi Katz.

On another occasion, the vital piece of information came from a Catholic priest in Italy. In this case, a British soldier stationed in Palestine had married an Israeli girl during the period of the Mandate. Their union was blessed with six children. When Israel became independent, the British constabulary force was returned to England.

The soldier's wife, with the six children, accompanied him back. Unfortunately, the marriage, which had worked so well in the Near East, was thrown out of joint by the change of location. The couple could not agree and, finally, by mutual agreement, the wife left, taking the children back to the land of their birth.

That was in 1954. Five years later she met a widower who wanted to marry her. Unfortunately, she could present no signed bill of divorcement—and therefore was unable to marry. When Rabbi Katz tried to locate her British husband, he could learn only that he was no longer in England.

A friend remembered that he had said something about going to Italy, possibly somewhere in the neighborhood of Milan. It was all very vague, but there were no other clues to pursue.

Rabbi Katz alerted his far-flung network of agents. He also wrote letters to all the priests in the Milan area, giving a full description of the missing man. Two years later, at Christmastime in 1961, he received a telephone call from a priest.

The missing man, he was told, was a member of the annual pilgrimage made from the diocese of Milan to the Holy Land. As a result of the call, when the train carrying the group back from the Holy Land puffed into the Milanese railroad station, Rabbi Katz was waiting with the inevitable divorce papers in his hand.

"He made no fuss," the rabbi said. "He didn't want his new found friends to know anything about his past. Naturally, I wouldn't betray him, either. My great obligation was to the woman he had ignored. When he did his duty by her, I was through with him."

Actually, the rabbi makes it clear, there is one thing that pleases him even more than getting the signature on the divorce papers. This is to relaunch a marriage that seems to have foundered irrevocably.

Such a case occurred with Heinrich Gross, who had been a fine violinist until Adolf Hitler dispatched him to a concentration camp. When released at the end of the war, Gross found his way to Israel, chose a mate and, for a long time, seemed very happy. Then the marriage began to show signs of strain and, one day, Heinrich Gross was among the missing.

Fourteen months later, Rabbi Katz received word from a source in Argentina that the missing husband had turned up in Buenos Aires and was playing in a small concert group there, as well as giving private violin lessons. When confronted, Heinrich Gross absolutely refused to sign the papers that would mean the dissolution of his marriage. He didn't want a divorce, he explained tearfully. He would have been perfectly happy living with his wife and children, but he couldn't stand his in-laws—they kept butting into his family life. In short, it wasn't his wife he was running away from: it was her mother and father.

Rabbi Katz checked the records of Gross's home kibbutz and found justification for the violinist's claim. "We are no different from the rest of the world," he explained. "Sometimes the parents, without meaning to, do make trouble for their married children. But, in Israel, we have the means to do something about it."

What was done was this: The offending in-laws were called before the kibbutz's rabbinical committee. They were sternly ordered to desist from meddling. They were warned that if they continued to make trouble, they would be sent to another kibbutz at the opposite end of the country.

"So far," the rabbi reports, "it seems to be working out. Gross is back home and things are going well."

Unlike Heinrich Gross, Israel Lisaboda wanted no more of his marriage. After twelve years of wedded bliss, this father of two children applied for a job with the Israeli steamship company, ZIM. In New York, he promptly deserted ship.

Pursuing him, Rabbi Katz arranged for the Jewish newspapers in the United States to publish the fugitive's picture. Among the many replies was one from a merchant in Milwaukee, saying he had seen Lisaboda. A query from Rabbi Katz was sent to the local rabbi, who confirmed the identification.

Rabbi Katz took the first jet out, but by the time he arrived in Milwaukee, Lisaboda had left. Rabbi Katz turned his attention to Chicago. There hadn't been time for the man to go much farther. Quickly, there came a response from Rabbi Abraham Abramowitz with news of the quarry and Katz caught up with his man.

Cornered, Lisaboda blandly agreed to cooperate. He hadn't meant to make any trouble. Sure, he'd sign the divorce papers; first thing in the morning. Alas, came the morning and Lisaboda had flown the coop again without so much as a farewell *"shalom."*

But he didn't realize the mettle of the man he was up against. "I felt I had a pretty good insight into the way he was thinking," Rabbi Katz explained. "He had escaped once on a ship; he would try it again."

"I hurried back to New York and got in touch with all the steamship companies. Sure enough, one of the lines serving South America advised me that a seaman answering to Lisaboda's description had applied for a berth." The rabbi paused, then added grimly, "This time he signed the papers before he was allowed to go anywhere."

Perhaps the most unusual case was that of the man who called himself Efrem Nawarli and who had come to Israel from Turkey. Soon after his arrival in 1946, he succumbed to the considerable charms of a beautiful Yemenite woman and married her.

A dozen years later he flew the nuptial coop. Efforts to find him proved unavailing.

In 1960, however, the International Red Cross identified a picture of Efrem Nawarli as that of a man who had been released after two years in a Jordanian prison as an Israeli spy. Thus was Nawarli's two-year disappearance accounted for. But, the Red Cross report continued, the man had claimed to be a Turkish national and it was to that country he had been repatriated.

Rabbi Katz got in touch with all his Turkish rabbinical sources, but no information was forthcoming. He widened his net by enlisting the aid of traveling salesmen and businessmen, both Jew and non-Jew.

A Christian businessman advised Rabbi Katz that, while en route to Bethlehem on a pilgrimage, he had encountered a man answering Nawarli's description. He had seen him in a small town in Turkey.

Rabbi Katz sped to the place, but soon found that Nawarli was not a resident of that Turkish town. A minor police official, however, recognized the man in the picture and said that he was living in a tiny hamlet high up on Mount Ararat.

The condition of the roads made travel by automobile impossible, but Katz was not to be daunted. He hired an oxcart and a native guide and set out on his wearying trip up Mount Ararat.

The fugitive at the end of the trail was Efrem Nawarli, all right. But he had shucked his Jewish identity completely and was living in this remote village as Kamir, a member of the Moslem priesthood.

To Rabbi Katz's plea for a signature on the divorce papers, Nawarli was quietly, but aggressively, defiant. First of all, he insisted, he never had been a Jew, he had merely acted as one in order to get the Yemenite girl.

Secondly, he was now tired of her and had no further interest in her—but he'd be damned if he'd make it possible for another to get her.

Third—and this was offered in a menacing tone—Rabbi Katz had placed himself in a position of great personal danger by coming there alone. It would not be the first time, Nawarli hinted, that strangers unfamiliar with that wild Turkish mountain terrain had accidentally fallen off a cliff during the night.

The smartest thing Rabbi Katz could do, Nawarli suggested, was to turn around and go home, forgetting that he ever had located this missing husband.

Rabbi Katz considered the bleak situation. While Katz sipped the rich, aromatic Turkish coffee, he was struck by a sudden thought and smiled confidently at Nawarli.

The Kamir met his new attitude with a probing stare. "Something amuses you, Rabbi?" he asked.

"I was thinking of how happy you seem to be here."

"It is my boyhood home, Rabbi," he said warily. "It is always good to return to the land of one's birth and settle down."

"I'm sure it is."

"I was never comfortable in Israel," Nawarli explained. "Although I must admit I do miss the children sometimes."

"I can understand that." Rabbi Katz kept his tone casual. "You are happily married now, no doubt."

"Oh, very. Turkish wives are so devoted—" Nawarli stopped suddenly in mid-sentence, literally biting the words off.

"I'm so glad. And I'm sure you've told your wives about your marriage in Israel and the lovely children. They have forgiven you, haven't they?"

This time Nawarli had no answer—just an ever-reddening flush that crimsoned his sun-darkened face.

"You haven't told them?" Rabbi Katz pretended surprise. "Well, that's understandable. They get pretty fiery about things like that, don't they?"

Nawarli remained mute, but his glance kept shuttling to the doorway in obvious fear that the ladies in question might walk in.

"And your superiors in the Moslem hierarchy," Rabbi Katz went on easily. "I'm sure you've told them all about your little escapade with a wife of another faith. And of the children you left behind to become Jews. And of how you yourself lived for a long time as a good Orthodox Jew . . . going to synagogue regularly, saying your prayers in Hebrew."

The "rabbinical Sherlock Holmes" chuckled, recalling the incident. "There was no trouble after that," he said. "He couldn't wait to put his signature on the bill of divorcement. He personally escorted me all the way down the mountain, watched over me like a mother guarding an only child. He kept saying he wanted to be sure no harm came to me. But I rather think he also wanted to be sure I didn't stop to tell my story to anyone on the way."

His face lighted up at another thought. "It was good to be able to give those papers to the *Agunah*," he said. "She was free after that—and she soon was able to make a good marriage and a good home for the children."

It was obvious from the way he talked that moments such as this made up for all the unpleasantness of the job of man-chasing.

"People always tell me that our Israeli divorce laws are too stringently archaic and should be liberalized. We, on the other hand, feel that marriage is such a sacred contract that it is not to be dissolved easily. But we do not want to see innocent victims made to suffer by our fidelity to the laws of our ancestors.

"That is why I try so hard to find these men who have run away. First and most important, to try to restore a broken marriage. But if that cannot be, then I want the innocent victim to be free to gather up the shattered pieces of her life and try to build a new and better one."

 ## The Incredible Saly Mayer

Saly Mayer was a retired manufacturer of lace who lived in Saint Gallen, Switzerland. About sixty years old when the Second World War began, he was of modest means and had given all his time since 1937 to the protection of German refugees.

He had become well known to the Swiss government as a stubborn negotiator, and to the Joint Distribution Committee (called "the Joint") as a friend deserving of all possible support. He was a deeply religious Orthodox Jew and was president of the Jewish community of Switzerland. He was tall, robust and tireless.

When Morris Troper and Joseph Schwartz emerged from Hungary into Switzerland in June of 1940, they met with Saly Mayer and arranged for closer relations between the Joint and Saint Gallen.

By the autumn of 1942 Switzerland had become a second Lisbon, with refugees from France and Czechoslovakia, and even a trickle from the Polish ghettos who had escaped on the Italian trucks bought in Galicia. Saly Mayer had resigned as president of his community and was giving all his time to the Joint.

The refugees who had been lucky enough to reach Switzerland were now receiving money directly from New York, so most of Saly Mayer's life was devoted to helping the forlorn remnant in Occupied Europe. He was on good terms with the International Red Cross, whose agents could travel freely. He had friends in the Swiss and Swedish embassies, who helped him to keep in touch with the remaining Jews of Europe and to learn where money or medicine might still be useful.

As a neutral, dealing in the most valuable of European neutral currencies, he could get money to any destination so long as the Joint had permission from the United States Treasury to buy Swiss francs. Sometimes he could even put his dangerous cash into a Swedish diplomatic pouch. And, best of all, Swiss medical-supply houses were allowed to send their representatives into Occupied Europe— another rich source for news and another route for smuggling. Thus Saint Gallen became a main clearing house for information coming in and for Swiss francs and medicine going out.

The Joint told the United States Treasury exactly what it was doing, and within reasonable limits was allowed to do whatever it could. The "reasonable limits," of course, were reached when private charitable aid could be suspected of helping the German economy.

Washington was generous, and London niggardly, in appraising these limits, for the British had more faith than the Americans in the economic blockade. In 1943, for example, the Treasury Department made a ruling that private organizations such as the Joint might transfer funds to their agents in neutral countries for use in rescue operations, and that the agents might enter into communications with people in enemy or in occupied territory. The money might be Swiss francs bought for dollars, or it might be raised among the peoples under the German heel against the promise of repayment after the war.

The British government protested, but Washington replied that the saving of even a few lives outweighed the tiny financial aid which might accrue to the Germans, adding that no payment of ransom, direct or indirect, would ever be permitted.

Thus the Joint's favorite system of raising money under the nose of the Gestapo, on its own postwar credit, was given official sanction. Thus also Saly Mayer was unleashed to do the most good possible. During eight months he managed to distribute 4,434,000 Swiss francs in France, Belgium, Holland, Bulgaria, Romania and Slovakia—a small sum, to be sure, but the number of Jews in Europe was rapidly diminishing. Some of the ghostlike people who survived the camps may well have been kept alive by this money.

In May of 1944 Saly Mayer got 800,000 Swiss francs into Hungary, and another 200,000 into Bratislava, where the Jewish population was starving and where all other contacts had been cut for over a year. By the end of 1944, he also had moved 237,000,000 Chinese dollars into Shanghai.

Saly Mayer would telephone Lisbon that his spies told him some Jews were still alive and hiding in Krakow, but desperate for medical supplies. Joseph Schwartz would send the money; Saly Mayer would buy the medicine in Switzerland and smuggle it into Poland through one of his secret routes. Or he would learn that Austrian Jews had escaped to Budapest. If the Joint would send money he would promise delivery. Or Lisbon would telephone to him: Could anything be done in Yugoslavia? Within a few days his multinational spies would have the answer.

The Swiss were not entirely happy about these telephone conversations. Saly

Mayer had devised a code—the usual substituted names, plus a confusion of Hebrew and Yiddish words. One day the censors asked him about this continuous telephoning, not only to Lisbon but to his agents (Jewish and non-Jewish) all over Europe. What did it mean?

He asked the censors why they did not study Hebrew.

"Don't worry," was the answer, "we are."

Yet the telephone and the money-smuggling were never seriously interrupted. The government put up a brave show of impartial neutrality, but, as the news from the death camps became increasingly hideous, few people could keep to the pretense that the Germans were no better and no worse than their neighbors.

The Joint could never induce Saly Mayer to accept an expense account, although his expenses must have been cripplingly high for a man whose private fortune was on the scale of a hundred thousand dollars. Mr. Schwartz begged him at least to allow the Joint to pay for the telephone calls.

"I talked it over with my wife," he answered, "and we decided that we could not live with ourselves if we let the Joint reimburse us for anything we do."

His view on this was absolute: If people gave money for charity, it must be spent on charity. If he was privileged to help spend it, he must pay for the privilege. After the war, when his work became even more burdensome, he permitted the Joint to send him an American assistant—but he added, "Please don't send anybody who is brilliant."

On the wall over his desk at Saint Gallen was a large sign, "O. P. M.," which meant "Other People's Money"—in English, presumably, because the "Other People" spoke English. No one has ever been more meticulous with O. P. M. After the war, when accountants from the Joint visited Saint Gallen, hoping to get a general notion of how the money had been spent, they found an exact record of every transaction, aboveground and underground, with every penny accounted for. Full reports had also been given to the American legation at Bern on all the money spent, and on the sometimes devious methods of spending it. Since Saly Mayer was often disposing of a million dollars a month, such accuracy is noteworthy.

This dedication of his, and this insistence upon detail, sometimes made trouble. The Joint, in its dealings with Occupied Europe, was a conspiracy, from the German point of view, since it sought to frustrate a major policy of the Reich. Conspirators have to make use of rough human material: adventurers who may not have a Swiss businessman's respect for money or an Orthodox Jew's devotion. Yet, if Saly Mayer lost confidence in a man's integrity, or in his blind adherence to the cause of the Joint, nothing could induce him to deal with that man again. Not even Joseph Schwartz could break down this stubbornness and, being a wise man, Mr. Schwartz did not try more than once.

—H.A.

 Maimonides' Day

Samuel Ibn Tibbon came from a family of scholars and scientists. His family had its origin in Granada, but he lived in Marseilles. Ibn Tibbon is known for his translations of Maimonides' works. In 1199, or shortly before, Samuel decided to translate his famous Guide of the Perplexed *from Arabic to Hebrew. In order to*

get Maimonides' help and approval in this project, Ibn Tibbon wrote to him for an invitation.

Maimonides' reply follows:

"I cannot but say how greatly your visit would delight me, although I am worried about your taking such a dangerous sea trip.

"Yet I must advise you not to expose yourself to the perils of the journey for, beyond seeing me, and my doing all I could to honor you, you would not receive any advantage from your visit. Do not expect to talk with me on any scientific subject for even one hour, either by day or by night, for the following is my daily occupation:

"I dwell in Fustat and the Sultan resides in Cairo; these two places are four thousand paces distant from each other. My duties to the ruler are very heavy.

"I must visit him every day, early in the morning; and when he or any of his children, or any of the women of his harem, is sick, I dare not quit Cairo but must stay the greater part of the day in the palace.

"Therefore as a rule I go to Cairo very early in the day and, even if nothing unusual happens, I do not return to Fustat until the afternoon. Then I am almost dying with hunger. I find the antechambers filled with people, both Jews and Gentiles, important and unimportant people—a mixed multitude who await the time of my return.

"I dismount from my animal, wash my hands, go forth to my patients, and beg them to bear with me while I eat some slight refreshment, the only meal I take in twenty-four hours. Then I go forth to attend my patients. Patients go in and out until nightfall, until eight o'clock or even later. I converse with and prescribe for them while lying down on my back from sheer fatigue; and when night falls I am so exhausted I can scarcely speak.

"Therefore no Israelite can speak with me except on the Sabbath. On that day the whole congregation comes to me after the morning service, when I instruct them as to their doing during the whole week; we study together until noon, when they depart. Some of them return and read with me after the afternoon service until evening prayers. In this manner I spend that day. I have related to you only a part of what you would see, if by God's aid you were to visit me.

"Now that you have begun your book you ought to finish it—I beg that you will come joyfully to visit me, but not with the hope of deriving any advantage for your studies, for I have very little time.

"May your happiness, my dear son and pupil, increase and grow great, and may salvation be granted to our afflicted people. Written by Moses, the son of Maimon, the Sephardi of blessed memory."

Humanity Was His Heir

"There is no possibility for doubt that the possession of great wealth lays a duty upon the possessor. It is my inmost conviction that I must consider myself as only the temporary administrator of the wealth I have amassed . . . It is my duty to contribute in my own way to the relief of the suffering of those who are hard-pressed by fate. I contend most decidedly against the old system of alms-giving, which only makes so many beggars. I consider it the greatest problem in philanthropy to make human beings who are capable of work out of individuals who otherwise must become paupers, and in this way to create useful members of society."

So wrote Baron Maurice de Hirsch in 1891, in an article on the "Obligations of Wealth," published in the influential *North American Review*. The legendary philanthropist was born in Munich, in 1831, son and grandson of bankers to Bavarian royalty. He moved to Brussels as a youth and there he married Clara Bischoffshein, daughter of a senator and banker, in 1855. A daring young financier, Baron de Hirsch undertook railroad building in Austria, Russia and the Balkans. Where others had failed to build the first railroad to Constantinople, de Hirsch succeeded. His financial wizardry won him in short order an international reputation. His personal fortune came to be rated as one of the largest in his day. He enjoyed to the full the brilliant elegance and luxury of an aristocrat. His racing stables were considered the greatest of the period, but all of the substantial winnings of his pedigreed horses were turned over to the support of hospitals. All of this was in an age when income taxes were not the motivation for giving.

During his Constantinople railroad venture he discovered the degradation and poverty of his Jewish brethren in the Middle East. In Constantinople Baron de Hirsch met Immanuel Veneziani, whom he named as his liaison with the philanthropic endeavors of the Alliance Israelite Universelle. When Veneziani acquainted the Baron with the fine work of the Alliance schools, de Hirsch undertook from 1880 onward to cover the annual deficits sustained by the Alliance.

But Baron de Hirsch was not satisfied with mere almsgiving. He was determined to channel his munificent benefactions into constructive, productive channels. This profound notion was given fullest impetus in 1887 when he lost his only son. "I have lost my son," said the bereaved Baron, "but not my heir. Humanity is my heir."

At this stage in his unique career of princely giving Baron de Hirsch, together with his wife, created a pioneer foundation with a capital of $2.5 million to establish modern schools for the Jewish children of Galicia and Bukovina. The modern quality of the Baron de Hirsch Foundation is attested to by its charter, which stated its purpose as "the establishment of nursery and primary schools and of children's recreation-grounds and their maintenance—the establishment of commercial, technical and agricultural schools—the apprenticing of Jewish youths to handicraftsmen and agriculturists—the granting of loans, free of interest, to artisans and agriculturists." The Baron also stipulated that the doors of such schools should be opened to non-Jewish students as well.

The fullest fruition of Baron de Hirsch's varied philanthropy came in 1891 as a result of the renewed Russian persecutions of Jewry. It was now his single-minded determination to plan the exodus of Russian Jews. Having been acquainted with the success of Jewish farmers in south Russia, the Baron believed that thousands more of fleeing Russian Jews could be directed into agriculture in the virgin territories of lands across the Atlantic. His sights were initially set upon the Argentine.

For this undertaking Baron de Hirsch hoped that he could secure the cooperation of the Czar's government in organizing resettlement commissions in Russia whose task it would be to organize and supervise the emigration of Jews. Moreover, in discussing the Baron's proposals with Russian authorities, his emissaries proposed that the Jews be trained for agriculture before they emigrated. Wanting to leave nothing to happenstance, de Hirsch arranged that the large tracts of Argentine lands be prepared in advance for the new settlers.

In London, the Baron established the Jewish Colonization Association, endowing it initially with a capital of $10 million. The new association was incorporated under British law. Its charter set forth as its purpose: "To assist and promote the emigration of Jews from any parts of Europe or Asia, and principally from countries in which they may for the time being be subjected to any special taxes or political or other disabilities, to any other parts of the world, and to form and establish colonies in various parts of North and South America and other countries for agricultural, commercial and other purposes."

Broad of vision, Baron de Hirsch saw to it that the Jewish Colonization Association be allowed wide scope in its enterprises. In its charter the Association was empowered not only to establish and maintain agricultural settlements, but also to organize educational institutions of all types, loan banks, industries and factories. The Association's leadership had only to be guided by the purpose "to fit Jews for emigration and to assist their settlement in various parts of the world, except in Europe."

It was likely this latter portion of the charter's clause—"in various parts of the world"—that motivated another grand visionary, Dr. Theodor Herzl, to seek out Baron de Hirsch to propose to him that Palestine, too, be considered as an area for Jewish resettlement. In June 1895, Herzl interviewed the Baron at his palatial Paris residence. Burning with messianic zeal, Herzl attempted to persuade Baron de Hirsch of the rightness of his Jewish State idea. The Baron listened respectfully, but remained unpersuaded.

In his diary Dr. Herzl wrote, "Actually we are of two natures, the likes of which emerge at the beginnings of a new era. He is the captain of money. I am the captain of spirit. If only we could move together we could alter the course of our time."

As it evolved, each of these men did help to alter the course of Jewish history, the philanthropist in the direction of the western hemisphere, the visionary in the direction of the Promised Land. In our time the spirits of these two unique Jews have merged in that Land, for in recent years the major efforts and resources of the Jewish Colonization Association have been redirected to Israel. Some twenty-one Negev farm settlements derive their financial support from the Association. Moreover, a variety of Israel's agricultural schools and institutions are subsidized by this organization. To mark appropriately the merger of Hirsch's and Herzl's ideals, the board of directors of the Jewish Colonization Association met, for the first time in the organization's seventy-year history, in Israel.

Baron de Hirsch had a particular philosophy behind his philanthropy. The magnanimous Baron appreciated the philanthropies of Andrew Carnegie in endowing libraries, parks, museums and churches. Such philanthropy, de Hirsch recognized, had its place in a land where all of "the absolute necessaries of life are so well supplied" that the rich and generous individual can devote his wealth to a country's esthetic needs.

But Baron de Hirsch's philanthropic motivation was different: "In relieving human suffering I never ask whether the cry of necessity comes from a being who belongs to my faith or not; but what is more natural than that I should find my highest purpose in bringing to the followers of Judaism, who have been oppressed for a thousand years, who are starving in misery, the possibility of a physical and moral regeneration?—than that I should try to free them, to build them up into capable citizens, and thus furnish humanity with much new and valuable material? Every page in the history of the Jews teaches us that in thinking this I am following no Utopian theory, and I am confident that such a result can be attained." Toward this noble end, Baron Maurice de Hirsch gave gifts, bequests and endowments amounting to $150 million.

On April 21, 1896, this great prince died at his Hungarian estate. In his diary Theodor Herzl wrote, "his death is a loss to the Jewish cause. Among the rich Jews he was the only one prepared to do something great for the poor ones."

—A.A.C.

 ## Why Luther Turned Anti-Semite

There are various theories as to why Martin Luther, in his later years, turned anti-Semite, not only using the vilest language against the Jews but actually advocating their expulsion and their being placed outside the law. One is that he was hoping the Jews would "see the light" and accept his presentation of Christianity, but when his hopes did not materialize he turned against them. Another theory has it that he simply wanted to placate and appease authority, which he certainly did in every conceivable way. Luther preached obedience and submission to authority, replacing the medieval Universal Church by the *Landeskirche* (state church) under the tutelage of the sovereign of the land and his court. "If authority tells you that two and five is eight, you have to accept it even against better knowledge," he wrote.

Whatever the explanation, there can be no doubt that latter-day German anti-Semitism found a good deal of "inspiration" in Luther's writings concerning the Jews. Heinrich Graetz, the historian, referring to Luther's pronouncements on the Jews, observed: "He poisoned the Protestant world for a long time to come with his Jew-baiting testament. Protestants became even more bitter against the Jews than Catholics had been . . . It was reserved to him to place Jews on a level with gypsies . . ."

This was not always Luther's opinion. In his condemnation of Papism he even posed as a defender of the Jews. Thus he wrote:

> The papists have so demeaned themselves that a good Christian would rather be a Jew than one of them; and a Jew rather be a sow than a Christian.
>
> What good will it do when we constrain them [the Jews], malign them and hate them as dogs? When we deny them work and force them to usury— how can that help? We ought to use towards them, not the Pope's, but Christ's law of love. If some are stiff-necked, what does it matter? Not all of us are good Christians.

Later, however, his hatred of the Jews exceeded all bounds. In his two pamphlets, *About the Jews and Their Lies* and *Shem-Hamphoras* (1542–3) he gave vent to it in such passages as the following:

Burn down their synagogues, take away their books including their Bible. They should be condemned to forced labor. Food and shelter should be denied to them. It would be best to banish them altogether. If they dare pronounce the name of God, denounce them to the authorities or pelt them with sow dung!

Moses already said, Don't suffer an idolater; were he alive he would be the first to burn their temples down. May they follow him and return to Canaan.

I would rather be a pig than a . . . Jewish Messiah, for a pig is not afraid of the devil and his hellfire.

Every one of the anti-Jewish Nuremberg Laws of Hitler's Third Reich were anticipated by the admonitions contained in the following list of measures Luther offered "for good counsel":

What shall we Christians do with the depraved infamous people, the Jews? I offer this for your good counsel:

1. that their synagogues or schools should be burned by fire;

2. that their houses and dwelling places, too, be broken up and destroyed, for the evil they commit in their schools they perpetrate at their homes also;

3. that we take away their prayer-books and their Talmud which teaches them all their idolatry, their lies, sacrilegious wickedness and blasphemy;

4. that their rabbis are forbidden, on pain of death, to teach forthwith;

5. that Jews are refused the right of way and the use of our streets;

6. that they must not be usurers, and that all their riches—money, gold, silver or jewelry—be taken from them;

7. that tools are given to all young and healthy Jews and Jewesses, such as hatchet, pickaxe, spade, spindle and distaff, and that they have to earn their living, and in the sweat of their long noses shall they eat their bread . . .

If however, you are afraid lest they could harm us even when working for, and serving us . . . then let us settle accounts with them by taking back what they have taken from us through usury, and have them expelled from the country for good!

—O.W.

 The End of the House of Herzl

A few minutes before dawn on August 14, 1949, the remains of Dr. Theodor Herzl, and of his father and mother, were exhumed from the family vault in the Doebling cemetery in Vienna. They were to be transferred to Israel in accordance with Dr. Herzl's testament and the specific instructions of the Israel government.

Gathered around the grave, some thirty to forty people at most, we were overcome by a strange, almost mysterious, feeling.

We were witnessing the fulfillment of the last wish of the leader. Even Moses had been barred from entering the Promised Land, not only during his life, but also after his death. In this respect Providence had favored Herzl more than the first great liberator.

Standing before the open grave of the Herzls, I was struck by the depth of this family's tragedy.

There was not a single direct descendant of the Zionist leader. I looked around me to find even a distant cousin through marriage, but could discover none. The extinction of the house of Herzl was complete.

That evening I met Dr. Isidor Schalit, Herzl's first secretary. Then eighty-one, Dr. Schalit was one of the last surviving delegates to the First Zionist Congress. We drank coffee at the very same café which Herzl used to frequent in his youth.

Dr. Schalit told me about Herzl's funeral on July 4, 1904. It was a very hot day, yet thousands of people, Jews and non-Jews alike, paid their last tribute to the Zionist leader.

Herzl had requested a "proletarian" funeral and forbade his friends and followers to eulogize him or to strew flowers upon his coffin. Hundreds crowded around the grave, mostly relations and intimate friends.

His mother stood erect and dignified without shedding a tear. Herzl's wife, on the other hand, sobbed continuously. His children stood there too, bewildered; the eldest, Pauline, was fourteen and her younger sister, Trude, was eleven.

The son, Hans, who only a few weeks before had celebrated his Bar Mitzvah, intoned the Kaddish. David Wolffsohn, Herzl's dearest friend and successor to the presidency of the Zionist Organization, took the oath of loyalty, and asked Hans to repeat the words: "If I forget thee, O Jerusalem, let my right hand forget her cunning . . ." Hans's oath would echo in his ears until his last day on earth, Dr. Schalit told me.

I had not seen Dr. Schalit more alert and vigorous than during the telling of this story. When I asked Dr. Schalit why the remains of the children had not been transferred with those of their father, his face grew tense, as if he meant to scold me for trying to uncover a hidden secret.

The fact is that the Zionist leadership seems to have done its best over the last fifty years to envelop the tragedy of the Herzl family in a veil of mystery.

Any mention of the human aspect of the Herzl story was considered taboo. Herzl was known to the world at large as the great Zionist leader, and as a noted journalist and playwright, but nobody seemed to know much about Herzl the husband and the father. Even his most intimate friends shunned discussion of his private life.

There may have been some justification for maintaining this silence out of consideration for members of Herzl's family, but today not a single member of that family is alive, so there is no question of hurting the feelings of any of them.

Theodor Herzl and his wife, Julie Naschauer, never got along very well together. They were temperamentally unsuited to one another from the very beginning.

She was lighthearted, if not frivolous. She wished to enjoy life and was skeptical about Herzl's great mission—for any sensible person could see that it was an unattainable dream. She was all for the "now" of life, definitely refusing to associate herself with anything that depended on the future, however bright its promise. She fell in love with Herzl precisely because of this enticing "now." This handsome young man with the dreamy eyes was adored by many a young girl in Vienna. He was a rising star of the Austrian theater and newspaper world. Life could be wonderfully exciting with a man like this.

Herzl, on the other hand, was an idealist by nature. Even when he was struggling for success on the Viennese literary scene, he felt an inner restlessness which would ultimately result in his vision of the Jewish State. He was increasingly inclined to sacrifice the ephemeral benefits of success for a soul-satisfying cause.

Herzl married Julie in 1889. The first years of their marriage ran smoothly enough, if not entirely harmoniously. The three children born to them in quick succession helped to bridge the gap between the couple. Herzl was a very sentimental father, and some of his finest essays centered on the children's room. But when Zionism entered his life, his relationship with his wife deteriorated, and there was almost an open rift between them.

It was often said that Julie was bitterly antagonistic to Zionism and hated everything that it stood for. Actually, she was opposed to Zionism in the same way that she regretted any idea that was "not feasible." Moreover, after Herzl published *The Jewish State* in 1896, he plunged into political activities, leaving very little time for Julie. He was often away on lengthy visits to various European capitals.

"These Zionists," she used to complain, "robbed me of my husband." She was also jealous of the women he met at the various conferences and during his calls at the courts of the mighty. She did not care to attend the Zionist Congresses, and absented herself from Zionist society.

Julie also could not get along with her mother-in-law. The feeling of dislike was mutual. Here again was a vast difference in temperament. Herzl's mother was majestic, strong-willed and domineering. Julie was over-tender, pampered to a point of weakness, and later tended to be hysterical. They clashed on many occasions, and Herzl was often torn between two loyalties. However, he nearly always sided with his mother, whom he adored. He would undertake nothing of importance before consulting her. On returning from his meetings with the great personages of the day he always rushed first to his parents. Julie found that somebody else "owned" her husband.

Then there was the question of finances, although it is doubtful how much Julie knew about their monetary situation before Herzl's death. He received a salary from the *Neue Freie Presse*. Yet this could hardly have sufficed even for the bare minimum of his expenses in connection with the Zionist movement.

The fact is that, in pursuing his Zionist work, Herzl spent his wife's dowry (the Naschauers were quite wealthy); indeed, this later proved most detrimental to the welfare of his children. He maintained the Zionist organ, *Die Welt,* the managing editor of which was Julie's brother, Paul. When Paul died at an early age in 1900, the Naschauers referred to him as "the first victim of Zionism."

Herzl's father, Jacob, supported him steadfastly until his death in 1902. Herzl never forgot that it was his father who had lovingly copied the final draft of *The Jewish State,* and that the old man had always been a fervent believer in his ideas. On this account, too, Julie often clashed with him. She was tired of his stories about the devotion of his parents.

Julie's fate was sealed with the death of Herzl. She was helpless and lonely, and even lost the inner strength to fight for her rights. The last vestige of self-confidence disappeared. The wave of grief which swept over Jewry meant little to her; her personal loss was irretrievable, and no condolences could comfort her.

Herzl's last testament was a blow. It was indeed a strange document where she was concerned. Julie was ignored almost entirely, as if she had meant nothing to Herzl. He apparently didn't think her fit to bring up their children, for he removed them from her care by appointing guardians. Pauline was to stay with Herzl's close friend, Johann Kremenetsky, the industrialist; Hans was to be sent to England to live under the guardianship of another personal friend, the English Zionist Joseph Cowen; and Trude was to become a kind of adopted child of the Wolffsohns at Cologne.

In her bitterness Julie stormed against the Zionists for having deprived her of her husband, for having left her poor, for having taken away her children. She survived Herzl by only two years, dying at the age of thirty-eight. During those two years, she saw very little of her mother-in-law, who could find no comfort after the "fall of her prince," although outwardly she still maintained her majestic bearing. She died in 1911.

The tragedy of the house of Herzl does not end here. Herzl's three children now began their odyssey of suffering. Hans, the "crown prince" of Zionism, was brought to England toward the end of 1905. He was fourteen years old and found it a very strange country; although he was to spend most of his years there, his personality simply could not adjust to the English way of life. He proved to be a capable student, diligent and painstaking, and particularly gifted in languages, but socially he was terribly ill at ease.

Until after his graduation from Cambridge he never really lacked funds—Wolffsohn saw to that by launching the "Herzl's Children Fund"—but money could not solve Hans's emotional problems. He was extremely sensitive and suffered from a feeling of inferiority in the shadow of his famous father. He knew that he would be unable to live up to anything resembling his father's reputation and soon developed a morbid belief that all kindnesses which people showed him were not due to him in his own right, but really belonged to his father.

In his own shy fashion he was proud, and he would not accept favors indiscriminately. All who knew Hans well would testify to his kindness and delicacy, but because of his "oddness," awkwardness and asceticism, he was in time not considered a welcome guest even in the London offices of the Zionist Organization.

Following the First World War, Hans longed for a tender hand to lead him. An almost penniless but refined vagrant who could find no place for himself in this world, he lived in a dark attic in a poor district of London, working as a janitor for a free lodging. He often went hungry for days.

Hans's softness and insecurity led him to seek his salvation first through psychiatry and later in religious experimentation. He managed to scrape together money for visits to Professors Jung and Freud. When Jung and Freud proved unable to help him he plunged into religious studies, but was soon completely adrift in the world of mysticism.

He had never really been taught Judaism in his childhood, for Theodor Herzl was himself not deeply rooted in the Jewish religion. Hans developed the notion that Zionism and Jewishness were separate and distinct ideas, arguing that "one can be a Zionist nationalist and a Catholic at one and the same time."

Within a brief period he was a Methodist, a Catholic and an Anglican. After the first of his conversions, he lost even the little sympathy that some Jews had had for him in former years. He was now lonelier than ever. While he no longer saw any clear purpose to his own life, of his own volition he assumed responsibility for the welfare of his eldest sister.

Pauline was unstable, flippant, not very particular about morals, and seemingly intent on drawing from life whatever earthly pleasure could be had. While still under the guardianship of the Kremenetskys, she became quite unruly. She recognized no authority but her own, for after all she was Herzl's daughter! At the same time, she hated the Zionists and refused to have anything to do with them. Her marriage to a Viennese engineer, Joseph Hift, was a complete failure.

She was divorced some two years before the First World War, and lived a disreputable life until the end. Hans's exhortations and attempts to improve her conduct came to nothing. She died in Bordeaux, in September 1930.

Hans held himself to blame as an indirect cause of his sister's death, believing that his efforts on her behalf had been insufficient. He had no more "duties" to discharge, and soon afterward he shot himself in his hotel room. He was not yet forty years old; Pauline was one year older. Both are buried at Bordeaux in the south of France, almost forgotten, their graves untended.

Trude, Herzl's younger daughter, survived until 1943, but her life, too, was tragic. She was not as aggressive as Pauline. Superficially she resembled her father in a few respects—she was profound and sentimental. In fact, she often suffered from melancholia; for a time she was in a mental institution. Trude married a Jewish cotton manufacturer from Czechoslovakia named Neumann, and had a single child by him, Stephen Theodor.

Stephen was thirteen when he was brought to England in 1931. Some years later he entered Cambridge and was graduated from the faculty of law, but did not quite know whether he should make a career of the legal profession. He resembled his illustrious grandfather to a very noticeable degree, but did not get to know about Theodor Herzl's importance in history until he was already in his teens. He had Anglicized his name to Norman. Zionism was almost a closed book to him until he visited Palestine while serving in the British Army during the Second World War.

Stephen Norman was a capable young man and, for the most part, he led a quiet life of his own. Only occasionally did Professor Selig Brodetzky, who was his mentor, discuss Zionist problems with him. Stephen planned to settle in the land of Israel. In 1946 he came to the United States on official business for the British Army. In November of that year, in Washington, he committed suicide by jumping off a bridge. The reports of his death contained no indications of a motive. However, his aunt in London—his father's sister—put forward a quite reasonable explanation when I discussed the tragedy with her.

A day or two before his death Stephen had received a letter from his mothers' maid in Vienna, describing the last days of his parents. They had been seized by the Nazis in 1943 and interned in the Theresienstadt concentration camp. They did not survive long. Stephen's father died of pneumonia and Trude passed away barely three months later. The maid had been sending them food parcels twice weekly, until she was told by the Nazis that there was no longer any purpose to this practice.

Until he received this letter, Stephen believed he would one day find his parents alive. In 1945 he had obtained special leave from the British Army to visit Frankfurt in order to trace his family. These efforts were in vain, but he did not give up hope. The finality of the maid's report may well have driven him to suicide.

Stephen Theodor Norman was the last direct descendant of the house of Herzl.

—J.N.

 # My Favorite Hero: Commodore Uriah P. Levy

My favorite American hero is a sailor named Uriah P. Levy. I was first attracted to him through his family. Levy's great-great grandfather, Dr. Samuel Nunez, was a refugee from the Portuguese Inquisition who landed in Savannah in 1773 just in time to save Oglethorpe's new colony from being swept away by a devastating epidemic.

I wish we knew more of this courageous physician, this American pilgrim, who, for the sake of religious conviction, sacrificed comfort and luxury in Europe for the poverty and hardship of the Georgia frontier.

Levy's grandfather, Jonas Phillips, refused to go to court and take an oath on Saturday because it was his Sabbath. The judge who presided obviously had no respect for other men's beliefs, for he fined the observant Jew fifty dollars.

One can well understand why, with such an ancestry as this, young Uriah P. Levy would be plucky and self-reliant. At the age of ten he went to sea as a cabin boy, and when he was twenty was captain and one-third owner of the *George Washington*.

While he was in Europe his mutinous crew ran away with the ship and cargo and left him stranded. He returned to America, secured the requisite warrants, and followed the rebels to the very ends of the earth, dragging them back to Massachusetts Bay, where he had the grim satisfaction of seeing their ringleader pay with his life for the crimes he had committed. This twenty-year-old sea captain was anything but a milksop.

That same year, as the War of 1812 began, Levy joined the United States Navy and participated in the bold raids which the brig *Argus* made on enemy shipping off the coast of England. He was captured and imprisoned by the British, but on his release he joined the Navy permanently and started the painful climb to rank and distinction. He met with prejudice because he had the courage of his convictions, because he rose from the ranks and because he never denied his Jewish religion.

Quick, decisive action was the mark of the man. Once, in Rio de Janeiro, the young officer rallied to the help of a fellow American who was being impressed into the Brazilian Navy. Levy suffered a saber wound for his intervention but saved the man. The next day, the Emperor of Brazil, Dom Pedro, came to see the young American Jew, and offered him command of one of the largest battleships in the Brazilian Navy, a sixty-gun frigate.

Levy thanked the emperor, but in words that will ever echo in the breast of every American he said that he loved the American Navy so well that he would rather serve as a cabin boy in the service of his country than a captain in any other fleet in the world. This man would not allow the pettiness and meanness he had experienced at the hands of individual officers to obscure his vision of the ideal America.

Because he believed that flogging American sailors as a disciplinary measure was both scandalous and cruel, because he believed that no American citizen should be humiliated by being whipped like a beast, he worked for decades to do away with this degrading form of punishment in the United States Navy. In his will, he enjoined his executors to carve these words on the stone marking his last resting-place: "Father of the law for the abolition of the barbarous practice of corporal punishment in the Navy of the United States."

Twice this audacious officer had to face boards of inquiry: six times he was court-martialed by his fellow officers and even ordered out of the Navy. To defend himself from attack and humiliation he had to challenge his assailants and to defend himself by force of arms.

Levy also fought for the right of a Jew to a career in the armed services of his country. In so doing he not only fought a battle for himself but for every American. Addressing a court of inquiry in 1857, he spoke these words: "My parents were Israelites, and I was nurtured in the faith of my ancestors. In deciding to adhere to it, I have exercised a right guaranteed to me by the constitutions of my native state and of the United States, a right given to all men by their maker, a right more precious to each of us than life itself. But while claiming and exercising this freedom of conscience, I have never failed to acknowledge and respect the like freedom in others . . ."

In continuing his heroic defense, Captain Levy said that he was an officer struggling to regain the privilege, wrongfully wrested from him, of serving his country while he lives and of dying in her defense. He added that there was only one serious impediment to his success in this struggle, and that was to be found in the fact of his religion.

If you enter on this course, he warned the court, think not that it can be limited to the Jew. What is my case today, if you yield to this injustice, tomorrow may be that of the Roman Catholic or the Unitarian, the Presbyterian or the Methodist, the Episcopalian or the Baptist. There is but one safeguard: that is to be found in an honest, wholehearted, inflexible support of the wise, the just, the impartial guarantee of the Constitution.

These are the words of a heroic officer, and evidently the court of inquiry deemed them just and right, for on January 29, 1858, he was restored to the active list as a captain in the United States Navy. Two years after that he became Commodore of the Mediterranean Squadron, thus enjoying the highest rank then possible for any officer in the American Navy.

—J.R.M.

 ## Albert Einstein, Jew

Of the three Jews who have played a crucial role in shaping the central ideas of our modern life and culture—Einstein, Marx, and Freud—only Einstein, both publicly and privately, was extensively and intricately involved in coming to terms with his Jewish identity.

The young Albert was neither very knowledgeable of, nor very involved in, Jewish liturgy, ritual, and customs; his parents, Herman and Pauline Einstein, as assimilated Bavarian Jews, had sent their son to a Catholic elementary school in Munich. Although he was for a time "intensely religious, both spiritually and ritually . . . and he took it amiss that his parents were lax in their Jewish observance" (according to biographer Banesh Hoffmann), this period was short-lived. Einstein apparently was never a Bar Mitzvah and his first wife, Mileva, was Greek

Orthodox; near the end of his life, he requested that, contrary to *halachah* (Jewish law), he be cremated after death. (He died at Princeton in 1955.)

In the *gymnasium* (German high school) Einstein chafed against the compulsory nature of Jewish religious instruction and went on to eschew what he saw as Judaism's overemphasis on the legalistic and compulsory. Between 1920 and 1924, his rebellion against an imposed religious or communal discipline was expressed by his refusal to pay the "mandatory" Jewish communal tax in Berlin, although he did make a voluntary "contribution" for welfare needs and during these years he became a committed Zionist.

In this period Einstein had begun to confront his deepest feelings about being a Jew, as well as his emerging sense of his obligations to his heritage. One trigger was a visit in 1919 from a Zionist group; shortly afterward he became committed to the cause. By 1920, when his theories on relativity were proven, he was subjected to vicious anti-Semitic attacks; his theories first were called part of a "Jewish conspiracy," then of a "Jewish Communist plot." Shortly after winning the Nobel Prize (in 1921), he accepted a request from Chaim Weizmann to go to America on a fund-raising tour on behalf of Jews in Palestine and the Hebrew University. In 1923, he visited Palestine and delivered the inaugural address at Hebrew University.

A strong spokesman for human rights, Einstein fought publicly throughout the thirties for the cause of Jews in Germany, fleeing that country himself in 1933. At the 1939 World's Fair in New York, which heralded the technology of the future, he opened the Jewish Pavilion.

Like I. B. Singer, Einstein was greatly influenced by that great excommunicated Jewish pantheist, Baruch Spinoza. In a 1929 letter, he wrote: "I believe in Spinoza's God, who reveals himself in the orderly harmony of what exists, not in a God who concerns himself with the fates and actions of human beings."

Einstein did have certain strong religious impulses. He believed in "cosmic religion," something he never elaborated on in detail or with much clarity, but which seems quite similar to what was once called "natural religion"—a belief in the moving and inspiring harmony and order of the universe. In his *Einstein, His Life and Times,* Philipp Frank quotes him as observing that:

> *The cosmic religious experience is the strongest and noblest, deriving from behind scientific research. No one who does not appreciate the terrific exertions, the devotion, without which pioneer creation in scientific thought cannot come into being, can judge the strength of [this] feeling.*

Although Einstein was not particularly observant, he was unquestionably proud of his Jewishness. In his two major collections of nonscientific writings, there are major sections on Jewish themes, and he gives succinct voice to the roots of his Jewish pride:

The pursuit of knowledge for its own sake, an almost fanatical love of justice and the desire for personal independence—these are the features of the Jewish tradition which make me thank my stars that I belong to it.

Einstein exulted in the prophetic ideal of *tzedek tzedek tierdofe* ("Justice, justice shall you pursue"—Deuteronomy 16:20), which he expressed this way:

The bond that has united the Jews for thousands of years and unites them today is, above all, the democratic ideal of social justice . . . [as expounded by] Moses, Spinoza and Karl Marx.

As an internationalist and one who sometimes alluded to the "Judeo-Christian tradition," Einstein rejected the idea of the "chosen people." Like Hermann Cohen, the leading German-Jewish pre-World War I thinker, he valued Judaism primarily for its ethical teachings—not for classical texts, *halachah,* or customs and holidays. The Torah and Talmud he viewed as "merely the important evidence of the manner in which the Jewish concept of life held sway in earlier times."

Einstein's negative view of the concept of a personal, transcendental, commanding God was strikingly similar to that of Freud in *The Future of an Illusion* (1920). According to Einstein, "the Jewish God is simply a negation of superstition, the imaginary result of its elimination. It is also an attempt to base the moral law on fear, a regrettable and discreditable attempt." All people might share the joy in the beauty and grandeur of the world expressed by the psalmist, he added, but "to tack this feeling to the idea of God seems mere childish absurdity."

Yet, like Voltaire, who reportedly once addressed the Almighty with the words, *"Entre nous, monsieur, vous n'existez pas"* ("Between us, sir, you do not exist"), Einstein had a whimsical and often affectionate relationship with the God in whom he did not believe. Thus, he is perhaps best known for his aphorism that "God does not play dice with the universe." Addressing a 1940 Princeton University meeting on the relation of science, philosophy, and religion to democracy, he uttered the conviction that "God is sophisticated, but he is not malicious," adding later, "science without religion is lame; religion without science is blind."

A pacifist most of his life, Einstein saw this ideal as largely rooted in the Jewish commitment to the supremacy of the intellect and language over the forces of power and coercion. Addressing a 1929 meeting of Berlin Jews, he remarked that "Jewry has proved that the intellect is the best weapon in history. Oppressed by violence, Jewry has mocked her enemies by rejecting war and at the same time has taught people." If Einstein did not see the Jews as the "chosen people," he sometimes spoke and wrote of them as though they were, or should become, what might be called "the exemplary people," calling on them "true to the ethical teachings of our forebears, [to] become soldiers in the fight for peace, united with the noblest elements in all cultural and religious circles."

But the most important and most influential manifestation of Einstein's Jewishness was his Zionism. Indeed, his 1921 "conversion" to the movement, and specifically his accompaniment of Chaim Weizmann on a fund-raising trip to America, was as important to European Zionism as Louis Brandeis's 1917 endorsement of the idea of a "Jewish homeland" was to American Zionism. In both cases, the involvement of a prestigious intellectual provided what had been a minority and seemingly marginal movement with new "clout."

What motivated Einstein's relatively late (he was forty-two in 1921) involvement in Zionist affairs was, as was mentioned earlier, the anti-Semitism he encountered upon returning to Germany from Switzerland in 1914:

> *When I came to Germany fifteen years ago, I discovered I was a Jew, and I owe this discovery more to Gentiles than Jews . . . I saw Jews basely caricatured and the sight made my heart bleed. I saw how schools, comic papers, and innumerable other forces of the Gentile majority undermined the confidence even of the best of my fellow Jews, and this could not be allowed to continue.*

Then came the August 1920 meeting of "German physicists," who inveighed against "Jewish physics"—i.e., Einstein's theory of relativity.

Influenced by the Russian-Jewish philosopher and polemicist, Ahad Ha'am ("one of the people," the pen name of Asher Ginzberg), Einstein saw a Jewish homeland in Palestine more as a spiritual and cultural center that would regenerate Judaism, than as a "normalized" state or simply a refuge for oppressed Jews. For him, Zionism represented nothing less than "the reawakening corporate spirit of the whole Jewish people," as he wrote in 1933. In an appeal to Hungarian Jews on behalf of Keren Hayesod a year later, he summed up his vision of Palestine as a regenerative force in Jewish life:

> *Palestine will be a center of culture for all Jews, a refuge for the grievously oppressed, a field of action for the best among us, a unifying ideal, and a means of attaining inward health for the Jews of the whole world.*

Like Martin Buber, his fellow refugees (the late philosophers Erich Kahler and Hannah Arendt) and the idealistic Zionists of the Bar Kochba university student group he had befriended while teaching in Prague around 1910, Einstein was particularly sensitive to the "Arab problem." In a letter written in early November 1929—only a few weeks after Arab pogroms killed 133 religious Jews in Safed and Hebron, and at a time when rage, panic, and confusion reigned in Zionist circles—he nevertheless insisted that, "Without an agreement and cooperation with the Arabs we shall not succeed. There can be no talk of forcing the Arabs from their land."

As he had incurred the hostility of German nationalists for his original involvement with the Zionists, so Einstein was sharply criticized by many religious and revisionist Zionists (followers of Vladimir Jabotinsky and, after 1940, Menachem Begin) for focusing too much on solving "the problem of living side by side with our brother the Arab in an open, generous and worthy manner," as he put it in a 1931 newspaper article.

In general, then, Einstein's Zionism was highly idealistic. As late as 1938, in a speech before the (American) National Labor Committee for Palestine, he asserted that:

> *The essential nature of Judaism resists the idea of a Jewish state with borders, an army and a measure of temporal power no matter how modest. I am afraid of the inner damages Judaism will sustain—especially from the development of a narrow nationalism.*

However, with ever darker clouds gathering over Germany and all of Europe, he added that, "If external necessity should after all compel us to assume this burden, let us bear it with tact and patience."

By no means was Einstein's Zionist commitment only rhetorical and polemical. Repeatedly he helped raise funds for the United Jewish Appeal. Several times in the late 1940s and early 1950s, he spoke over national radio on behalf of the UJA, the Jewish National Fund, Keren Hayesod and, especially, his beloved Hebrew University, one of whose governors he became at Chaim Weizmann's suggestion. These involvements soon prompted requests from other organizations aiding Jews abroad for Einstein's help in raising funds. Many years earlier he had supported ORT and the Joint Distribution Committee. In fact, Einstein's second wife, Elsa, served as first Honorary President of Women's American ORT.

For these reasons it was hardly surprising that, following Weizmann's death in 1952, David Ben-Gurion invited Einstein to become Israel's second president. In declining (Einstein had too many scientific commitments to honor at Princeton's Institute for Advanced Studies and elsewhere, and did not see himself as a national leader), he observed that "my relationship to the Jewish people has become my strongest bond, ever since I became fully aware of our precarious situation among the nations of the world." This awareness was the basis of his thirty-five years of intensive practical and polemical activity on behalf of a safe and just Jewish homeland in the Middle East.

In sum, far more than Marx, and significantly more than Freud, Einstein "exuded" his Jewishness. With his sometimes absentminded or distracted intellectuality, his intense eyes, shock of white hair and large forehead, Einstein in fact created the stereotype of the ultimate "Jewish scientific genius." In addition to his love of pranks and sailing, Einstein had at least as great a love for classical music, books, letters, and good conversation; some might say he possessed the post-Emancipation European-Jewish "craving for culture." His widely known traits of modesty and generosity were in a way typical of the Jewish tradition of *rachamim benei rachamim* ("compassionate children of compassionate parents"). Of course, his persona as a scientist and pacifist-socialist-internationalist also was of great importance in shaping Einstein the private and the public man. Seen in perspective, though, Einstein's Jewishness seemed to have played a predominant role in influencing his self-perception, his ideals, and his myriad nonscientific activities.

—D.M.S.

 ## The Hasid from New Hampshire

He came into my office and the word incongruity flashed into my mind. Lean of face, of average height, with a decided New England twang to his speech, he was dressed in the traditional attire of the Hasid: his dark, somber hat and dark, somber suit both accentuated the stark difference between his speech and his full, heavy beard.

He talked of a manuscript—not something he had written, but the work of another; a book of mystical power that would open up Jewish hearts and minds to the truth and beauty of Judaism, and would reveal its innermost powers.

The accent fascinated me, recalling New Hampshire hills. The man's look was steady and sure. One wondered: how did this man, resident in the isolation of New England, far from Jewish population centers, remote from the turbulent activities of the Jewish community, become so obviously devout and sincere a Hasid?

He was modest and self-effacing and obviously did not enjoy speaking about himself, but gradually the story emerged.

"I was born in New Hampshire," he said, "in a small town where my father had settled more than fifty years ago. We were the only Jewish family in town. My father built a successful printing company that prospered and grew over the years.

"I knew I was Jewish, but it meant nothing to me. I had no Jewish friends, seldom saw a relative, never observed a holiday, skipped Bar Mitzvah—I simply grew up in a town where I had friends and neighbors and eventually went to college and entered the family business.

"In the course of time, I got married to a local girl whom I had known all my life. God blessed us with children, and soon we had a family of four, and of course they kept us busy. My life, I thought, was full—my family, the business, the town. What could be missing?

"But I suppose something was missing, only I didn't know it. From time to time I would come to New York or Boston, on business, and eventually it dawned on me that there were more Jews in those cities than in the community where I was born. Once, in Boston, for the first time in my life, I entered a Reform temple, and realized that I enjoyed an experience I had never known existed before.

"Another time, in New York, I read in some detail in a daily paper about the Holocaust, about six million Jews who had been massacred just because they were Jews, and I realized that I knew nothing about my background, my past. The empty, void feeling began to trouble me.

"I tried to talk to my father about this, but he shrugged me off. He said, more or less, that 'all those things' were Old Country things, this was America, we had to blend into the mainstream, all people are basically the same, and so on. I took his advice and tried to ignore the annoying little questions that kept gnawing at me, but somehow they persisted.

"On my next trip to New York, I walked into a bookstore on Fifth Avenue, and found what I was looking for—a whole section of books dealing with Judaism and Jews. I bought about twenty books, took them home and began to read. My wife was surprised at the titles, but didn't say anything. For the next few weeks, I read a history of the Jewish people, a book about Jewish religious practices, a book on the ethical codes of Judaism, a book by Elie Wiesel about his experience in the Holocaust. I had also obtained a book on how to study Hebrew, and slowly I taught myself the alphabet, first the reading and then the writing. I still remember what a chill I felt the first time I wrote my name in Hebrew—it was my English name, because I still didn't know that such a thing as a Hebrew name existed, but spelled out in the ancient letters of the Hebrew tongue, it looked magical to me.

"For the next few months, I was restless, disturbed, not my normal self with my family, and I couldn't concentrate on the business either. I felt my soul was crying out to me, and saying, 'Release me, recognize me, you are a Jew!'

"Finally, I went back to New York, this time not on business, but to find an answer to my troubled inner self. I really didn't know where to turn, with whom to speak, but I phoned a rabbi—I got his name from the Manhattan phone book, at random—and he agreed to see me. I sat and talked in his study for two hours, trying to explain that I was a married man, with a wife and four children, with a successful business, but that here I was nearly forty years old, deeply disturbed because of this feeling that I had betrayed myself and my people by living all these years as a virtual Gentile. I wondered if he could help me.

"Well, we talked a few more times, and one day he introduced me to a representative of the Lubavich organization. I sensed immediately that this man's serenity was what I had been looking for—his serenity and his sense of rootedness. Next to him, I felt like a lost, floating soul; soon, I decided to enter the special yeshiva for people like me that the organization maintains, and I began my studies."

For more than a year, much to the consternation of his father, his wife and children, his friends and neighbors, he studied at the yeshiva, along with other adults who had returned to Judaism late in life. He lived in the dormitory, associated with fellow students and then, one day, made his decision.

It was a painful thing to do, but he informed his wife that he had decided to live the life of a full-fledged Jew, in the Hasidic tradition, and urged her to study, undergo conversion and convert the children, so that they could reestablish themselves as a family, but now as a *mitzvah*-observing Jewish family. His wife refused; his father at first thought that he had been brainwashed; his children felt rejected.

Today, he carries on some business for his father's plant in New England, and the father has begun to understand that his son's new way of life is one that has brought him great satisfaction.

The erstwhile New Englander mused, and sighed. "I miss my wife terribly," he said. "I miss my children more than I can say—but how can I now live with a Gentile woman and Gentile children? I pray daily that they will understand and join the community of the Jewish people. Then my life will be complete."

It was late, the sun was beginning to set. He excused himself, went off to a corner of the room, and began to recite the *mincha* and *maariv* services.

—D.C.G.

 Israel's Musical Ambassador to the World

Itzhak Perlman has the kind of face that makes one want to have him as a friend, to know him personally: sweet, kind, impish, fun. Picture him at a concert of the Israel Philharmonic Orchestra at Carnegie Hall, where he is to be the soloist in a concerto. In he walks, on his aluminum crutches, followed by Zubin Mehta, carrying Perlman's Stradivarius. Perlman seats himself, Mehta hands him his violin, and Perlman hands Mehta his baton, which he has been carrying. Both bow solemnly. Suddenly, both faces light up in broad smiles. The audience roars. Everything's off to a good start. Each person anticipates having a good time.

Perlman was four years and three months old when he contracted polio, "and the thing was that I wanted to play the violin before I was four; I wanted to play when I was three and a half," he said.

This, of course, was in Tel Aviv, where he was born thirty-four years ago and of which he remains a proud citizen, although he doesn't get there as often as he wishes.

He talks freely of that dreadful time, and from what he says emerges a picture of parents who knew exactly what to do about a handicapped son to make him feel wanted, loved, and a useful human being.

"What my parents did was so simple and so obvious," he said. " A lot of parents really have the tendency to send their kids to institutionalized situations.

"And I feel it is a problem not only with children but with a lot of situations today that the handicapped person tends to be isolated from society. As a result, some of them tend to lose belief in their abilities, whatever they may be."

In his case his family moved to within a few blocks of a school "so I could walk to school every day. So, in my case, I had sort of a double dose of unusual kid life: I practiced every day for a couple of hours, and went to school, and had friends, and so on. So, for me it was not a very unusual childhood. I did have friends, and I hated to practice, as very healthy children should, I think. I think that if someone likes to practice, well, it's a little unusual."

Only a couple of hours a day? There are stories of kids practicing six, eight, nine hours a day, he was told. "Well, that was definitely not the case with me," Perlman said. Practice, he said, is an "individual thing." Some of his colleagues practice up to six hours a day, others for only an hour. "When I was a child, I never practiced more than three hours a day. But then, come to think of it, to concentrate, for a child of eight or nine, for three hours a day is really quite enormous."

He carried a full load of homework from his public school and had no such thing as specialized tutors, "or anything like this during that time."

In a situation such as a handicapped child, "really, it depends on your parents. If the parents know what they are doing, and if they have good instincts, and if they don't feel they don't want to face someone who's disabled in the house, then you don't have anybody who's disabled in the house. It's really a question of attitude."

There has been progress in attitudes toward the disabled, but Perlman has been making a "sort of survey" of what is being done for the handicapped people of this country, "and what's not being done." And "just to give you one statistic, there are approximately thirty million handicapped people in America alone," and only "eighty thousand are in the work force, no more than that. So I feel that that's not enough progress for me."

He agreed that his parents were "remarkable people." They were not musicians, although they liked music "very much." They knew his talent, but they treated him as a normal child, and encouraged him to play with other children. "Practicing was not the most terrific thing I liked; I liked to play hide-and-seek much better."

So, it was a "natural environment for me, because I was not what you call a *wunderkind*—a wonder child—when I was seven, eight and nine. Definitely not." He was not playing for the public, concertizing as a wonder child. He considers that "lucky, because I felt that being a—if you want to call it a genius or something—at the age of eight is sort of abnormal, a terrible burden on the child" as well as a burden on the parents, because "society is not built for abnormal children."

He admits he was gifted, but his progress was "slow and even" and he feels that that is the only way to "really develop properly."

His family came from Poland, arriving in Israel (then Palestine) in 1930, thus escaping the Holocaust. He is an only child.

Although he steadfastly refused to admit that he was a child prodigy, he was reminded of his appearance at the age of thirteen on the Ed Sullivan television show in a program made up of Israeli artists whom Sullivan had recruited on a visit to the Jewish State.

He doesn't know why he was chosen for the show except, perhaps, that Sullivan needed someone in the "fiddle department." So he came, but "actually, at that time, I really didn't start playing seriously." However, he went out on a three-month tour of the country, in an act called "The Ed Sullivan Caravan of Stars." The experience led him to want to stay in New York and study at Juilliard, and that's what he did.

He was asked how it was that Israel was producing such a bumper crop of violinists—himself, Pinchas "Pinky" Zuckerman, Miriam Fried, Shmuel Ashkanazi.

Perlman replied that the question really is "Why are there so many Jewish violinists?" His answer was "I don't know." He said he thought it had to do with "a traditional sort of way that people study in Israel. You know, when you think of a musical instrument for someone in Israel, you immediately think of a violin or piano. I don't think you will think of a trumpet, or a French horn or an oboe. And you can see that trend. It is reflected in the orchestras in Israel, which are rich with string players. When it comes to wind players and brass players, they still have to scrounge around here and there, import people from the States—but it's getting to be better."

At Juilliard, Perlman studied with Ivan Galamian and Dorothy DeLay, who was at that time Galamian's assistant. He commented that both had "a system that worked." He spoke about winning the coveted Leventritt Competition, and noted that an artist never played as well afterward as he did during a competition. At least, he did not, although he said he maintained a "fairly good level" in the year afterward. The "adrenalin really makes you perform better than you really are under normal conditions," he said. Also, he is always stimulated by audiences: "I just perform better" before them.

That was in 1964, when he was nineteen, a date he remembers because the fiddle he was using was stolen at Carnegie Hall. It was a Guarneri belonging to Juilliard, and the thief got fifteen dollars for it at a hock shop whose owner, reading about the theft, notified the music school and returned the violin to it. Now Perlman plays a Strad of his own, made during the king of fiddlemakers' golden period, in 1714. It has no particular history, having been owned by no one particularly glamorous, he said.

When asked to tell how he met his wife, Toby, Perlman replied that he had gone to a music camp in the Adirondacks for about seven or eight years in the summer, and "that's where I met Toby for the first time. Our first meeting was really quite interesting. You wouldn't believe it, but I played at one of the student concerts and she came backstage and she said, 'Hi there, I'm Toby. Will you marry me?'"

That, he said, is "absolutely true."

Toby was an aspiring violinist, "and a very good one, but the minute we got married she gave it up. She said 'that's enough.'"

There are three young Perlmans—Noah, who is ten; Nava, who is eight; and Leora, nearly five. Noah, who loves music, apparently loves tennis more. Nava, who is studying the piano, "shows lots of promise."

"Are all three of them getting a Jewish education?" Perlman was asked. "Well, they're getting tradition," he replied. "Traditional Judaism—what's in our house." There are "so many different kinds of Jews, and I think that a Jew is what you feel you are. I mean, I feel Jewish. I'm an Israeli, and of course that's another discussion as to what's an Israeli and what's Jewish. Are they both the same? The house is definitely Jewish, and so you can't help but carry it to the children. I think that's the most important thing.

"And they are getting some tutoring in Hebrew and in Jewish history and so on. A little bit, so that they know who they are. But they definitely know who they are."

He himself studied Bible, and Hebrew, of course, "is our native tongue," but he wasn't introduced to other aspects of Jewish scholarship, such as the Talmud. The Perlman family belongs to Rodeph Shalom, a Reform temple, and he goes to synagogue on High Holidays, including when he is out of town or out of the country. Perlman has cut down the number of concerts on the road because he wants to spend more time with his family; he teaches music at Brooklyn College, where he has the rank of professor.

He talked about how it felt to come back to Israel after being away. "The feeling is really indescribable. You feel this is really my country. I'm an Israeli, will always be." The feeling, he repeated, is "quite indescribable. Even just landing and going into the terminal in Tel Aviv. And the smells, you know the smells when you go outside; you can't describe what it smells like. But it smells like your country. I remember this when I was a kid. That's what I smelled. And it hits me every time I come back."

He talked about playing in Germany, and speaking to Isaac Stern, who has said he would never play there, before going. Stern did not tell him not to go. Perlman found the German audience "marvelous." He said that he felt the people were aware of the horror of the Nazi regime, and he found it significant that so many Israelis were conducting German orchestras. He spoke about being on stage with Pinky Zuckerman in Berlin: "When you think that there were two Israelis alone on the stage, playing for this audience, there is something about that that is quite incredible." But, he added, "Whenever you look at a person who is over a certain age, you always wonder, 'Where were you?' "

The bottom line is, however, that "I am an Israeli, and I am a Jew, and I'm representing what I am in a place that not long ago wanted to get rid of me."

—R.Y.

 ## The Man Behind "Hatikvah"

December 1956 marked the hundredth anniversary of the birth of a poet who is immortalized by a song that has become the national anthem of Israel. The name of Naphtali Herz Imber is known to but a few, but his song, "Hatikvah," has become among the most famous of the world hymns.

Imber was an interesting personality—"a character." He was an alcoholic, but he had many unusually fine qualities. He was born in Zloczov, Galicia, in 1856, lived for a time in England, then came to the United States. He died in a New York hospital in 1909, and his remains were taken to Jerusalem. The author of

"Hatikvah"—meaning "Hope"—thus had his dream fulfilled. At his funeral, thousands of people chanted the "Hatikvah." The song already had become the rallying hymn for millions of Jews who prayed and hoped for Israel's redemption.

The Imber story reads like a romance.

In "The Neo-Hebrew Poet," the seventh chapter of his *Children of the Ghetto*, Israel Zangwill introduced one of his heroes, Melchitsedek Pinchas, in the following telling paragraph:

The poet was a slim, dark little man, with long, matted black hair. His face was hatchet-shaped and not unlike an Aztec's. The eyes were informed by an eager brilliance. He had a heap of little paper-covered books in one hand and an extinct cigar in the other.

The prototype of Zangwill's Melchitsedek Pinchas was the man who was destined to gain immortality with a song that struggled for nearly thirty years for recognition as a national anthem. Melchitsedek Pinchas was none other than Naphtali Herz Imber, author of "Hatikvah"—the Zionist song of hope that originally appeared under the title "Tikvathenu" ("Our Hope").

"Hatikvah" did not become the national anthem of the Zionist movement, in our day the national anthem of the State of Israel, until the Zionist Congress of 1907. There were other challenging songs that competed with "Hatikvah" for historic honors.

"Dort Vu Die Tzeder" ("Shom MeKom Arozim") for a time had more adherents than Imber's song. But the sentimental words and the catchy tune of "Hatikvah" gradually caught the imagination of the masses of the Jewish people. As time passed nothing could stop its becoming Jewry's anthem and chief song of hope.

Imber's name was not kept a secret in Zangwill's *Children of the Ghetto*. Chapter XV, "The Holy Land League," describes the formation of a Zionist society in London before the days of Herzl. Guedalyah the greengrocer was named president. Melchitsedek Pinchas failed not only in his aspiration of becoming treasurer, but also in being named Collector. "All felt the incongruity of hanging money bags at the saddle-bow of Pegasus. Whereupon Pinchas re-lit his cigar and muttering that they were all fool-men betook himself unceremoniously without."

In the course of the discussion, during the organizational meeting, the student and cigar commission agent, Joseph Strelitski, delivered an impassioned address in which he said:

Poets will sing for us . . . journalists will write for us . . . There are no obstacles—but ourselves. It is not the heathen that keeps us out of our land—it is the Jews, the rich and prosperous Jews—Jeshurun grown fat and sleepy, dreaming the false dream of assimilation with the people of the pleasant place in which their lives have been cast. Give us back our country; this alone will solve the Jewish question.

The stirring address of the young student in the great Zangwillian story proceeds to say:

And if gold will not buy back our land we must try steel. As the National Poet of Israel, Naphtali Herz Imber, has so nobly sung (here he broke into the Hebrew "Wacht Am Rhein," of which an English version would run thus) . . .

Zangwill at this point included in *Children of the Ghetto* Imber's "The Watch on the Jordan," in its entirety. It is a translation that helped to make that great song famous. The pioneers in Palestine preferred this song—Mishmar HaYarden —to "Hatikvah" and many Palestinians still retain this preference. "Mishmar

HaYarden" is superior to "Hatikvah" as a literary creation. This is the first stanza in Zangwill's translation:

> Like the crash of the thunder
> Which spilleth asunder
> The flames of the cloud,
> On our ears ever falling,
> A voice is heard calling
> From Zion aloud:
> "Let your spirits' desires
> For the land of your sires
> Eternally burn.
> From the foe to deliver
> Our own holy river,
> To Jordan return."
> Where the soft-flowing stream
> Murmurs low as in a dream,
> There set we our watch.
> Our watchword "The sword
> Of our land and our Lord"—
> By Jordan there set we our watch.

The first stanza and the refrain of Imber's "Hatikvah," translated by Nina Salaman from the Hebrew, are considered among the best. They read:

> While ever yet unchanged within his breast,
> The inmost heart of Israel yearns,
> And seeking still the borders of the East,
> His loving gaze to Zion turns—
> So long our hope will never die,
> Yea, this our hope, through ages felt,
> Back to our father's land to fly,
> Home to the height where David dwelt.

In the Jewish State—in the settlements preceding the proclamation of the State of Israel—the refrain has been changed, the authorship being unknown. The text in free translation, used in Zion, means:

> We have not abandoned our hope
> The hope of two thousand years,
> To be a free people in our land—
> The land of Zion and Jerusalem.

While the music of "Hatikvah" has on occasions been traced to the *Bohemian Symphony* of Smetana, the Czech composer (1824–1884), it has been definitely established by the eminent Jewish musician, Zwi Mayerowitch (1882–1945), late lecturer on Jewish liturgical music at Jews' College, London, England, that "Hatikvah's" music was composed by Henry Busato or Russotto, a Sefardic Jew, who based his composition on the tune used by Sefardic Jews in their synagogues for many years for Psalm 117 in the Hallel service.

Mayerowitch maintained that this tune was published in 1857—twenty years before Smetana composed his *Bohemian Symphony*—in *The Ancient Melodies of the Liturgy of the Spanish and Portuguese Jews: Harmonized by Emanuel Aguilar, Prefaced by the Rev. D. A. DeSola.*

Imber was a most unusual personality who possessed a great gift for humor and satire; his instant repartee made him famous wherever he lived. Many of his eccentricities are recorded in Rebecca Kohut's *As I Know Them.* Mrs. Kohut relates that the original of "Hatikvah" was presented by the eminent Hebrew poet to her son, Dr. George Alexander Kohut. This original text of "Hatikvah" was presented by Dr. Kohut to the Library of Yale University. Another copy of Imber's "Hatikvah," in the author's handwriting, has been presented to the Hebrew University in Jerusalem by a non-Jewish singer, a Mrs. Murphy, who is said to have known Hebrew. We are told that Mrs. Murphy gave a concert at a New York hospital where Imber was a patient, that she included "Hatikvah" in her repertoire and asked Imber to write the words down for her.

Imber, a member of an ardent Hassidic family, first won acclaim in his native community in 1870, for a Hebrew poem that dealt with an Austrian patriotic theme; the government of Austria rewarded him with a cash prize.

His wanderings began after the death of his father. He went to Vienna and from there proceeded to Constantinople, where he met the eminent Christian lover of Israel, Laurence Oliphant (1829–1888), who advocated the restoration of Zion to the Jewish people nearly twenty years before Dr. Theodor Herzl wrote *The Jewish State* and organized the Zionist movement and the World Zionist Congress.

Imber and Oliphant—both mystics—became great friends and together left for Palestine, Imber serving as Oliphant's secretary. Oliphant bought large tracts of land near Haifa. He especially endeared himself with the Zichron Yaakov colonists, whom he encouraged in their hours of stress.

Imber lived in Palestine for six years (1882–1888). During these years he also lived among the Bedouin and came to know them well. He wrote essays and poems for Hebrew periodicals and in 1886 produced his collection of Hebrew poems under the title *Barkai* (Morning Star). This book, dedicated to Oliphant, included "Hatikvah."

Leaving for England after Oliphant's death, Imber came to London and there befriended Israel Zangwill, who contributed to the eccentric poet's immortality by transforming him into the Melchitsedek Pinchas of *The Children of the Ghetto.* He came to the United States in 1892 and died in dire poverty in New York City on October 8, 1909. During his residence in this country he visited numerous cities, notably Chicago, San Francisco and Los Angeles.

His brothers, still in Zloczov, published another collection of his poems in 1902 under the title *Barkai HeHadash* (The New Morning Star). Unfortunately, most of the copies of this volume were destroyed by fire. A third volume of his poems was published in New York City in 1905, after the Kishineff pogrom.

Imber dedicated this volume to the Emperor of Japan; that country was at war with Russia at the time. Five years earlier, in 1900, Imber had written a booklet prophesying the Russo-Japanese War and predicting Japan's triumph. Apparently the anti-Semitism of Czarist Russia made him an ardent supporter of Japan.

After leaving Palestine, Imber stayed for a while in Egypt and evinced a deep interest in mysticism. He became an authority on esoteric subjects, his pamphlets on mysticism drawing wide attention. Among them were *The History of the Golden Calf* and *Keynote to Mystic Science.* He was the translator of Targum Sheni under the title *Treasures of Ancient Jerusalem* (1898) and was the author of *The Education of the Talmud,* which was supplemented by *The Alphabet of Rabbi Akiba.* Reference to the latter work appears in the reports of the U. S. Commissioner of Education for 1895–6.

Imber possessed great mastery of the Hebrew language. His rhetorical phrases in "Hatikvah" helped to give the song the great merit of being chanted throughout the world, wherever there are Jews. It became the symbol of what the title denotes: hope.

Among those who reminisced in their writings about Imber were Louis Lipsky and Philip Cowen. In his *Memories of an American Jew,* Cowen recalls: "I shall never forget a Zionist meeting at Cooper Institute where Imber was thrown out because he was in his cups and had become obstreperous. I had come late to the meeting and he buttonholed me outside. As the meeting was about to close and they sang 'Hatikvah,' he opened the door and leered through the crack and said to those about him: 'They may kick me out, but they must sing my song.'"

Cowen also wrote:

It was difficult to separate Imber from his bottle, much to the chagrin of his friends. He was always half-seas over. Whenever we wished to find him it was only a question of which favorite tavern he was in. He was welcome at a number as trade followed him. Mayer Sulzberger befriended him, and he soon became absolutely dependent upon the judge's bounty. In an effort to redeem him, Judge Sulzberger insisted on his going to live in one of the colonies in South Jersey. Money was sent to one of the colonies with instructions to pay his board weekly and to give him liberal sums from time to time for his liquor and tobacco. While on a periodic visit to one of the colonies I met him upbraiding his almoner for keeping his money from him; robbing him, as he said. He caused much trouble at the colonies by advising the people that the committee was keeping from them the money that Baron de Hirsch sent for their individual use. I heard him say it.

We also are told by Cowen, "In 'Bohemia,' Imber loved to tell of his life in Haifa, and speak of the Oliphants, fancifully, as his 'foster parents.' He spoke of Lady Oliphant as 'mother.'"

Eccentric, but a great idealist; "in his cups," but a devoted lover of Zion; living the life of a semi-vagabond, but nevertheless a great linguist and scholar—Imber's name will live among the very great in Zion and Israel. His song gave hope to millions and continues to inspire the people of Israel with the genius that emanates from the reborn State of Israel. Only the words of his song were known until now; from this point on his name, too, must be listed affectionately wherever there are Jews.

—P.S.

 # First General in Army of Israel Since Judah Maccabee

Last summer I made an extraordinary pilgrimage to the battlefields, cities, and settlements in Israel where Colonel David "Mickey" Marcus made history in 1948. The purpose of the trip was to round out research for a full-length biography of the West Pointer and World War II hero, the only man buried in the venerable cemetery at the military academy who was killed fighting under a flag other than the Stars and Stripes.

Mickey Marcus was at various times the intercollegiate welterweight champion, New York Commissioner of Correction under Fiorello La Guardia, Commander of the Rangers' Training School in Hawaii, volunteer paratrooper in Normandy and a Pentagon legal adviser to two Presidents. His ten military decorations included the Distinguished Service Medal and Commander of the British Empire.

The crowning achievement of his life, though, came in the Holy Land, where, although lacking previous identification with Zionism, he blazed a trail of leadership and inspiration from the moment of his arrival on February 2, 1948. Haganah was short of manpower, arms, field equipment, training—in brief, everything but courage; its loosely grouped platoons could hardly be called an army. Arab battalions buttressed with tanks, British Spitfires and heavy artillery were massing for invasion. Haganah itself was split by differences over military doctrine: the World War II veterans of England's Jewish Brigade, steeped in traditional staff methods, were ranked against the guerrilla-trained, devil-may-care youngsters of the Palmach.

At the urging of David Ben-Gurion, Marcus undertook to forge the scattered *Haganah* formations into a single powerful "striking fist." He toured the bases and future battlegrounds; twice intercepted by British patrols, he slipped through their hands by bold ruses.

Returning, he plotted with Yaacov Dori and Yigael Yadin about restructuring the Israeli troops into self-contained brigades, and developed the blueprints for a modern supply system. Then he complied a comprehensive military manual that became the cornerstone of a new Officers' Training Program and a vital bridge between the Palmach and the Jewish Brigade.

He lectured to fledgling field commanders and ate beans with the troops at remote Palmach bases. By April the impact of his gutsy personality and vigorous, confident leadership had penetrated to every corner of the *Haganah*. Then, the illness of his wife forced his abrupt return to Brooklyn.

Back in the States, Mickey was solemnly decorated in Washington—for outstanding services in World War II—by the very British Government whose patrols he had been dodging in Israel.

In May, as invasion approached, Moshe Sharett interceded with Mrs. Marcus to let her husband go overseas once more—for the thirteenth time. A few days later, Mickey was back in the Galilee, supervising antitank preparations.

Then, as Egyptian tanks crunched across the Negev, he was dispatched southward to introduce a daring plan of his own invention: Cavalry-type harassing actions by jeep squadrons mounted with machine guns. The maneuver worked.

On the central front, the Old City sector of Jerusalem had fallen; the one hundred thousand Jews in the New City were all but cut off. At this crucial moment, Mickey Marcus was appointed to Supreme Command of the entire area—the capital and its corridor to the west—thus becoming the first general in the armies of Israel since Judah Maccabee. Between the memorable battles against the Arab Legion at Latrun, he constructed the Israeli "Burma Road," the incredible cliff-hurdling highway that decisively shattered the enemy stranglehold on Jerusalem. Then, a few hours before the first truce, death came to the gallant West Pointer who was described by David Ben-Gurion as "the best man we had."

In preparing my book, I spent nearly a year talking to Mickey's family, friends, ex-classmates at West Point, and such World War II colleagues as Generals Maxwell D. Taylor and Lucius Clay. The time had come to reconstruct at first hand Mickey's climactic months in Israel.

Square-hewn, blunt-spoken Chaim Laskov, the former Jewish Brigade officer who had been Mickey's protégé in 1948 and had later risen to be Israeli Chief of Staff, was the guide for my first field trip. Laskov had been close to Mickey on both of his trips to Israel: the February-April jaunt, devoted mainly to surveying the problem and restructuring Haganah, and the return in May for active duty against the invaders. We were joined outside Laskov's house in Tel Aviv by Gaby Anakov, a wiry, moustached man who had been Mickey's jeep driver in the Jerusalem campaign.

Laskov told me how, in a few short weeks of March 1948, Mickey had written out in longhand the four-hundred-page Military Manual that became the basis for officers' training in Israel. The Israeli commander was not surprised to learn that Mickey, in 1942, had organized the first large-scale movement of American forces to the Pacific, and later was the Pentagon's Chief of Planning for postwar military governments.

As Laskov dwelt on the warmth and modesty of his erstwhile teacher, Anakov chimed in with a remark I was to hear echoed in a dozen places: "Mickey Marcus was a man you could know ten minutes—and would remember a lifetime."

At Hulda, a cypress-shaded kibbutz that was the main base for Israeli offensive operations on the central front in 1948, Laskov pointed out the staff HQ—a kindergarten room still boasting the blackboard on which "Brigadier Stone" once drew his battle diagrams.

We drove up through scrubby foothill country to the high ground from which the famous assaults were launched against Latrun, the Arab Legion complex of strongpoints throttling the main highway to Jerusalem. During "Operation Ben-Nun—2," Laskov had led an armored battalion in Mickey's divisional command.

Laskov put aside his pipe and, taking out his field glasses, showed me the layout of still-fortified Arab Latrun in Transjordan across the valley. As he pieced together the savage night battle of May 30, 1948, Anakov again spoke up. "Our command post here was right in the middle of Legion shellfire. But that wasn't enough for Mickey. He had to go down the slope to bring water to our boys. We had one helluva time getting back in one piece."

For my next expedition, to the Negev, my guide was Colonel Israel Carmi, the beefy commando whose Palmach night raiders had roamed the desert with Mickey and a score of jeeps immediately after the tank-led Egyptian invasion, taking the steam out of the enemy advance.

As Carmi showed me traces of the trenches from which Palmach youngsters, following Mickey's example, fought off diving Spitfires with their rifles, he summed up tersely, "The impact of Mickey's presence was tremendous. We didn't need Napoleon in the Negev; we needed Mickey Marcus." I also retraced the route to the Galilee taken by Mickey and Yigael Allon, then chief of the Palmach: across the Jezreel plain; down to the Sea of Galilee and Tiberias, where sniper fire had dented Allon's armored car; up the coiling mountain road to the former Palmach HQ on cloud-high Mt. Canaan. At Rosh Pina, I examined the spot where the two Haganah commanders had bluffed their way past a British roadblock with a cargo of illegal arms.

In a book-crammed, high-walled study near the government offices in Jerusalem, Yigael Yadin talked of Mickey's grasp of Israel's military problems: "He provided a balanced view that was invaluable." Shlomo Shamir, the Haganah commander who first "recruited" Mickey in the United States, offered a fascinating glimpse of the complex motives that led this hitherto non-Zionist Jew to the embattled Jewish State: a compound of West Point, Talmudic ethics and the United Nations. The army archives yielded not only original drafts of Mickey's training manuals, but the texts of numerous military directives and top-secret operational messages from the period when he took command of all three brigades in the Jerusalem area on May 28.

Amos Horev, the Palmach scout who first convinced Mickey that a back road could be carved across the mountains to Jerusalem, willingly volunteered to retrace his original jeep route. At long last, I would be able to explore the "Burma Road." We piled into a jeep near the deserted Arab village of Beit Jiz, east of Hulda. A weed-covered, bumpy mountain trail—the first stretch of the "Burma Road"—took us to Beit Sussin. Here, at a fig patch near an ancient watering place, the donkey trail stopped.

Pointing the nose of the jeep up the steep, jagged incline to the north, he stepped on the gas. Up we shot, crashing through scrub trees, hurdling gullies and climbing slabs of slippery limestone—until we jolted to a halt on the edge of the plateau. A rear wheel had snagged on a boulder.

We heaved the jeep loose. Horev got out and guided us foot by foot, while the driver wrestled with the wheel and I hung on to anything in sight. The descents were worse, with the jeep threatening to overturn and send us plunging to the bottom of four-hundred-foot cliffs.

By the time we stumbled out of the 110-degree heat into a cafe on the Hartuv highway, I knew all that was necessary about the terrain of the "Burma Road." In broad daylight, the trip was a nightmare. What it must have been under the original conditions of blackness punctuated by Arab Legion artillery fire is beyond conjecture.

The road that saved Jerusalem was completed by Mickey's forces on the night of June 7, 1948. Three days later, the Supreme Commander of the Central Front met his death near the Arab village of Abu Ghosh, on the grounds of a lovely monastery—Notre Dame de la Nouvelle Alliance. The clergy had been evacuated because of Arab shellfire and the monastery was serving as a rear HQ for the Palmach.

I drove up the winding path to the garden of sycamores and tamarisks where the monastery stands, perched on a hilltop of biblical serenity. We were greeted by an angular, black-cassocked Benedictine monk of Gallic mien. Softly, and with marked respect, he pointed out the straggling stone fence, where, in an almost incredible confluence of ironic circumstances, like Stonewall Jackson of American Civil War fame, Mickey Marcus was accidentally shot down by one of his own sentries.

The Catholic convent, Père Joseph told us, pointing out faint but magnificent old floor mosaics, was built over the site of a pre-Christian synagogue. The location went back even farther in Jewish history. Here had stood the "house of Abinadab in the hill," where, according to the Book of Samuel, the Holy Ark of the Covenant was kept for twenty years after its recapture from the Philistines. Then it was brought back to Jerusalem by King David.

David "Mickey" Marcus had fallen within a hundred feet of the spot where, two thousand years before, the immortal warrior-king for whom he was named had danced and sung in praise of the Lord.

—T.B.

 ## Reb Nachman Remained Silent for Forty Years

When a man died in Jerusalem recently, the whole country mourned—and wondered. He was a Hassidic Jew, a member of the Bratzlever Hassidim, who could be seen in the Holy City on his way to the synagogue, or to the Western Wall. His long, white beard matched perfectly the equally long *payot* lifting slightly in the breeze; a round, black hat rested firmly on his head.

Those who knew him or knew of him, wondered about him: why, for forty years, had he become known as Reb Nachman *Shotek*, Reb Nachman the Silent One? What had caused him to enter a world of never uttering a sound, never speaking to his family, never giving vent to his joys or sorrows?

Soon after Reb Nachman's passing, a long, inquisitive article appeared in the Tel Aviv afternoon daily, *Yediot Ahronot,* but it failed to shed much light on the enigma of this strange man and his life of abstinence from human speech. Whatever his secret, Reb Nachman took it with him to his eternal resting-place.

This much is known: forty years ago he vowed never to utter any word of a mundane, secular character. All kinds of strange stories grew up around him, as people tried to penetrate his self-inflicted veil of silence. Many Jerusalemites, observing his diligence in prayer and study, were convinced that he was one of the proverbial *Lamed Vovniks*—the thirty-six righteous people whose utter goodness sustains this sinful world.

He took a vow of virtual total silence when he was twenty-five years old, already a husband and father. He never spoke to his family nor to his large number of acquaintances, but he could be heard whispering words of Torah—to his Creator. At other times one could hear him reciting, in a whisper, verses from Psalms.

If one visited the Wall at night, or ascended to King David's tomb on Mt. Zion, there would one see Reb Nachman, whispering Psalms, whispering prayers. After the Six-Day War, when the West Bank, including Bethlehem, was again in Israeli hands, he could also be found at Rachel's Tomb, his arms embracing the Matriarch's resting-place, whispering prayers.

For the nearly two decades, from 1948 to 1967, when the Old City was in Jordanian hands, Reb Nachman could be seen climbing to the highest point on Mt. Zion and standing silently, staring at the ancient section where the Holy Temple had stood. He stared, and his lips moved in silent prayer. Sometimes, it is said, he sang about the Old City—but no one heard him.

Reb Nachman subsisted on bread and water. He slept not more than a few hours every night, disdaining a pillow and blanket, preferring the cold, hard floor of his modest apartment in the Katamon quarter of Jerusalem. Sometimes he caught a few winks while remaining on his feet.

Why? Why did Reb Nachman, whose family name was Hellman, remain silent for forty long years? Had he been a sinner who now chose to punish himself with absolute silence? Nobody knows, not even his wife, his father-in-law, or his two sons, Meir and Reuben, who are also Hassidim, studying at a local yeshiva.

"*Der tata,*" the sons explain, "Father never told us why. When we were born, he was already silent. We knew he was not mute; we were told he had taken a vow of silence. He was a truly holy man, a penitent with every bone and fiber in his body."

The biographical details of Reb Nachman do not help. He was born in Praga, near Warsaw, and was brought to Palestine after World War I while he was still a small child. The family settled in Tel Aviv. As a youngster, Nachman showed an innate talent for music, and played the guitar and violin. He was a good student and a good soccer player. He transferred to a school in Jerusalem to continue his Jewish studies and also took up painting, at which it is said he excelled, but not a single one of his works remains.

After vowing to remain silent, Nachman gave away all his wordly possessions to various family members, and others simply came and appropriated some of his things. He didn't mind, his sons recall.

Once, when he was on Mt. Zion, he was asked by some people why he remained silent. Nachman took a slip of paper and wrote on it a quotation from the Bratzlever Rebbe, in which he stressed the importance of being quiet. He also wrote down a rabbinical dictum that said one hour of self-imposed silence is better than a day of fasting.

Speculation about the real reasons for his silence continued for years. One story persisted that his silence was caused by the fact that he had had an unhappy love affair—there was a girl who married another, and even after he himself got married, he remained deeply troubled about his first, unrequited love. Others said the Holocaust, and the death of six million Jews, caused a profound spiritual crisis in Reb Nachman's life, which led him to a life of total silence.

Nachman's mother, who was known as a woman of great righteousness, called him into her room as she lay dying on her sickbed. They bade each other goodbye behind the closed door. What she said to him, no one knows, but when the door opened, and Nachman was leaving, she called after him, "And you—be quiet!" After she died, and after the week's period of *shiva*, Reb Nachman announced that he was undertaking a vow of silence.

From that moment on, he spent his life studying Torah, Talmud and the works of the Bratzlever Hassidim. His day began at midnight, when he would rise, immerse himself in the Katamon *mikveh*, and go off to the Hassidic *shtibel*, where he would recite all of Psalms, and await the regular morning service worshipers. He would join the worshipers for the *shahrit* service, and then proceed home to his few hours of self-imposed isolation.

Once in a very great while, his fellow worshipers would persuade him to break his silence and lead them in prayer. Only then, as the *hazzan*, would his lovely voice be heard, in prayer, but never in secular speech. The worshipers all remembered his service with great enjoyment.

After a few hours at home, he usually went to the Wall, often twice a day, as well as to David's tomb, to recite prayers. For the remaining few hours of the day, Nachman studied the Talmudic tomes found in the synagogue, and often he also pored over the works of the mystics, notably the Zohar. From time to time he journeyed to the grave of Rabbi Shimon Bar Yochai in Miron and Rabbi Meir Baal Haness in Tiberias.

Occasionally, Reb Nachman would appear at David's tomb with his violin, and would play beautiful, haunting melodies, to the delight and astonishment of the visitors and tourists. Some people said they had seen him reading books in Russian, English, Hebrew and Yiddish—both old volumes and modern literature.

When he died after having been ill for nearly a year, his funeral took place in the middle of the night, soon after midnight. Hundreds of Jerusalemites came out of their homes to accompany him to his last resting-place.

Whatever his reason was for a life of silence, Reb Nachman never explained. He took his secret with him, to the silence of the grave.

—D.C.G.

He Gave New Life to Two Hundred
Victims of the Holocaust

World War II ended in 1945, and to many people under the age of 50, Jews in-cluded, it was something that occurred a long, long time ago. But to those over 50 or so, and especially, of course, to the tiny remnant of Jews who can be counted among the survivors of the Holocaust, the Nazi era is as vivid today as though the events took place only last week.

Reports of what transpired in those horror-filled days have appeared in books and films, on stage and in novels, in countless newspaper and magazine articles. Courses on the Holocaust are being given in colleges. Visitors to Israel who pay their respects to the Six Million when they visit the Yad Vashem memorial in Jerusalem come away from an experience that they can never excise from their memories.

And yet, not all of the stories have been reported, even at this late date. Some even have a happy ending, just like in storybooks.

In the frantic months of the spring of 1945, just before, during and after the Nazis finally surrendered to the Allied forces in April, an act of dedication and lovingkindness—true *chesed*—was carried out by a small, publicity-shy group of Orthodox Jews in the Williamsburg section of Brooklyn, which helped to rescue several hundred Jewish young women from postwar despair and helped them on the road to a new and decent life.

These young Jewish women, who had been interned in the so-called model Theresienstadt concentration camp, are now more than thirty-five years older. In most cases they are married and have families of their own, and perhaps the events of 1945 are receding into the background for them; but the fact is that they owe their lives to the selflessness of a small handful of Jews in Brooklyn who were determined to act, at a time when action was badly called for.

The notorious Heinrich Himmler, somewhere late in 1944 or very early in 1945, realizing that the Nazi reign of terror and bloodshed was soon coming to an end, made representations to the Swedish Red Cross. In effect, he said that if he were to release several hundred Jewish young women from Theresienstadt, would the postwar authorities please remember that he had a plus sign on his personal ledger of lifelong evil.

The Swedish Red Cross, at the time working closely with the Joint Distribution Committee and the wartime Vaad Hatzalah (Rescue Committee), lost no time in assuring Himmler they would remember his act of kindness. Within a few months, somewhere around February or March, while the war was still on, several hun-dred Jewish young women were allowed to cross the sea to neutral and safe Sweden. It was like leaving hell and reaching heaven. The girls were physically, mentally and emotionally exhausted and drained, and the Swedish and Jewish authorities did everything they could to nurse them back to health.

Word of the transfer of the survivors reached Brooklyn, and one unassuming man, Rabbi Abraham Kaplan, who at the time directed a Beth Jacob teachers' seminary, was stirred. An idea occurred to him and he set about putting it into motion. He visited a number of New York State legislators and proposed that a special bill be introduced, allowing these girls to enter the United States immediately, without waiting for any quota numbers, on the grounds that they would enter his teachers' seminary and be trained to become educators. At the time there was a severe shortage of qualified teachers.

Things moved very quickly; the bill was introduced, passed and voted into law. People were approached and asked for funds; within a matter of a few short months—by June of 1945—the nearly two hundred Jewish young women were in the Beth Jacob teachers' seminary. All of the former inmates of Nazi concentration camps lived in makeshift dormitories, studying English, American history, Judaic subjects, pedagogy—and being encouraged and supported by the good rabbi and his wife, who were themselves the parents of some eight or nine small children.

The girls themselves represented virtually a kaleidoscope of European Jewry: there were Nordic-type blondes and Semitic girls; some knew Hebrew and Yiddish perfectly, while others had no Jewish background and could converse only in Hungarian or German or Czech. Some were determined Zionists who had agreed to come to the United States only because it was difficult to even think of reaching Palestine at the time. There were among them girls who never smiled, while there were others who were typical teenagers—effervescent, laughing and full of life. The great majority of them had tattoo numbers on their arms; all of them were still in a mild or heavy state of shock, after the years of Nazi incarceration.

The hope of the small group who had brought them here was that time would heal their wounds, that they would see that the Jewish community cared deeply about them, and that sooner or later they would go out into the world and make new lives for themselves. Almost without exception, the young women were quite alone in the world, although later a number found distant relatives in America.

Some of the girls had been totally atheistic and others had been rigidly Orthodox. A bond of shared experience linked them all together and, in the first few months of their stay in America, they seemed to form a cohesive unit, challenging one and all to penetrate their ring of bitter memories.

Some of the girls were true students and took to their studies with alacrity; others were content merely to learn a smattering of English. Some were anxious to earn money; others were content to remain in the small, sheltered world of Rabbi Kaplan's teachers' seminary and delayed the time when they would have to leave and face the cold world outside.

For more than a year the girls studied, while receiving the loving care of their teachers and of volunteers who came to help them in any way they could. Gradually, a few at a time and sometimes singly, they left and moved to other parts of the country. A great many settled in Israel.

Rabbi Kaplan and his small group of supporters never sought publicity or credit. They wanted nothing more than to sustain and strengthen the survivors, to help them set out on a new road. By all reports, they succeeded beyond their wildest hopes. Very few of the girls ever went into teaching, however. Most of them got married and had children.

Working with the young women in those difficult postwar months was an experience that no one ever forgot. It was a positive, humanitarian act and proved once again that one single person, possessed of courage and determination, can work miracles.

—D.C.G.

The Rabbi Who Outlawed Polygamy Among Jews

Rabbenu Gershom (960–1028), better known as the "Light of the Exile," was one of the builders of Judaism in the Western world. He especially devoted himself to the establishment of a correct text of the Bible and the Talmud. The great Biblical and Talmudic commentator, Rashi, recognized him as his precursor, saying, "Rabbenu Gershom has enlightened the eyes of the Exile; we all live by his instruction and all Jews of these countries call themselves the disciples of his disciples."

Although his literary contributions to Judaism were great, Rabbenu Gershom's fame rests preeminently on the Takkanot, or enactments, which he promulgated. They greatly changed the family life of the Jewish people for all time and immortalized his name. His most famous and significant ordinances are those aimed at heightening the status and prestige of the Jewish woman.

The first decree of Rabbenu Gershom that was of monumental importance in raising the status of woman was his enactment prohibiting polygamy on pain of excommunication. Neither Biblical nor Talmudic legislation formally proscribed polygamy. Although Biblical and Talmudic Judaism tolerated plurality of wives, the ancient Jewish conscience always had regarded monogamy as the ideal state of marriage.

In the Creation story, the first man is given only one wife, and a later verse speaks of man cleaving "to his wife" and not "wives." The Prophets and scribes looked upon polygamy with disfavor. Whenever a Prophet speaks about marriage, he is thinking of a monogamous union, lifelong and faithful. Polygamy, the scholars claim, nearly disappeared during the Second Commonwealth. They buttress their argument by showing that out of the twenty-eight hundred rabbis mentioned in the Talmud, perhaps one was bigamous.

However, one cannot judge the manners of a people by the standards observed by the intellectual class. Polygamy was practiced in Talmudic times by a section of the common people. One finds many discussions in the Talmud devoted to the question of polygamy. One rabbi claimed that a man may take as many wives as he can support, while another recommended that no man may marry more than four. However, it redounds to the glory of the sages that they endeavored to discourage the practice, by demanding not only that the husband should ensure to each wife adequate maintenance and love, but that each wife could claim a separate domicile. Such restrictions made polygamy not only unattractive but impossible for most, except for the few affluent ones. Maimonides, in his Code of Jewish Law, states that it is lawful for a man to contract many simultaneous marriages. Nevertheless, he personally disapproved of the custom, and in a letter to the Provençal rabbis, he castigates them for permitting the practice in their communities. Thus, despite Talmudic and rabbinic opposition to plural marriage, Jewish law reached the Middle Ages with polygamy still permitted, though not widely practiced.

There is no doubt that women have always opposed polygamy and hoped for its interdiction. No one has convincingly explained why the official abolition came in the tenth century, by Rabbenu Gershom. Some scholars claim that it was introduced into Judaism under Christian influence. Israel Abrahams, in his enlightening book, *Jewish Life in the Middle Ages,* proves that this contention is erroneous.

When Rabbenu Gershom established the principle of monogamy in Jewish life, the Church was still permitting, under certain circumstances, simultaneous marriages. The practice of polygamy continued, especially among royalty, until the time of Martin Luther.

The decree may have been precipitated by the fact that the position of women in this period had undergone great changes. It began to be customary in Germany for women to be active in the economic sphere, while their husbands devoted themselves to the study of Torah. Women began to be the breadwinners in the family, engaging in all kinds of commercial occupations and operations. The most significant consequence of this important role played by women in the economic world was to raise their status in the eyes of the Jewish community. Women began to be conscious of their increased importance and started to agitate for more rights. Perhaps it was the demands of the women, in conjunction with the traditional Jewish scorn for the plurality of wives, that finally enabled Rabbenu Gershom to forbid polygamy. Although he promulgated the writ without any synodal authority, it was immediately accepted by the communities under his jurisdiction, and eventually by all Western Jews.

The influence of Rabbenu Gershom's enactment was felt even beyond Western Europe. Accordingly, a custom developed in Spain and the Orient to insert a clause into the marriage contract in which the husband solemnly covenanted not to marry another woman during the lifetime of his wife. Despite this precaution, polygamy among Oriental Jews living under the influence of Islamic culture, which tolerates polygamy, continues until today.

Rabbenu Gershom realized that no real and lasting benefit would accrue to the status of women through marriage reform unless it was accompanied by changes in the law of divorce. Although Judaism consistently endeavored to raise the status of women, the laws of divorce were nevertheless unfavorable to the wife. The husband, according to Biblical legislation, could divorce his wife at will. This prerogative was not set aside by the Talmud, though its severity was tempered by numerous restrictions. An effective check on the exercise of the arbitrary right of the husband to divorce his wife against her will was the law compelling him to repay her dowry and the sum agreed to in the marriage contract. In many cases these economic factors acted as a bar against divorce. On the other hand, the Talmud recognized the following as valid reasons entitling the wife to demand a bill of divorcement from her husband: refusal of conjugal rights, cruel treatment and unnecessary restrictions upon her personal liberty.

The rabbis also used moral persuasion to dissuade a man from divorce, stating that "Even God's altar sheds tears for the one who divorces the wife of his youth." However the rabbis might disapprove of divorce and seek to impose restraints upon it, though, the law in Deuteronomy recognized the husband's right to dismiss his wife if she did not please him. Therefore no court was empowered to restrain a husband who, unmoved by sentimental or monetary considerations, was intent on divorcing his wife against her wish. It was Rabbenu Gershom who finally decreed that "Even as a man does not put away his wife except of his own free will, so shall the woman not be put away except by her own consent."

This enactment, together with the official prohibition of polygamy, produced a veritable revolution in the status of the Jewish woman. No longer was the wife placed at the mercy of the husband through fear that she might incur his displeasure and thus suffer the introduction of a rival into the home, or banishment through divorce. With these measures and those of older times, which permitted a wife to apply to a Jewish court for a writ of divorcement under certain circumstances, the status of the husband and wife was practically equalized in regard to marriage and divorce. The precedent set by Rabbenu Gershom was followed by other rabbis, who continued to introduce changes advantageous to women.

—L.Bro.

Holocaust Survivor
Behind the Wheel of a New York Taxicab

You step into a New York City taxicab, you look at the driver's name—Wolfgang Silverberg—and you begin to talk. Then, you listen, and your throat begins to feel choked.

You have read about the Holocaust, you have seen the gruesome photos, you remember the swastika-clad brownshirts pounding down the streets of one captured European capital after another—and all of it serves merely as a backdrop, until one lone cabdriver opens up to you and tells you of himself, of his life before, during and after, and his fears for the future in America.

A short, toughened-looking, blue-eyed man in his fifties, grateful for a chance to talk about something that is apparently never far from his thoughts, Silverberg explained that he was named Srul Velvel by Polish Jewish parents who were living in Leipzig, Germany, and so he was dubbed Wolfgang. After all, Germany was one of the great cultural and industrial nations of the world, and a young man with a name like Wolfgang would have a better chance to advance than one known as "Srul Velvel."

"I was a good student, learned English, which I loved, and played the drums, and I was crazy about the new American jazz music that had come to be known in Germany," he explains. "We lived in a pleasant suburb and life was good, except for the time when my mother died, when I was seven, and father went back to Poland later, and came back with a new wife. But that was all right, too. I had my own interests, and I thought of becoming a lawyer.

"In 1937—I was nineteen—the Nazis threw me and all the Jewish students out of school. *Kaput!* Just like that. Why? Because we were Jews. I got a job as a drummer in a band, and although the Nazis had decreed jazz was decadent, we played it, and other American music, and we also played traditional German dance music at German functions.

"But everything changed after November 1938, after *Kristallnacht,* when they destroyed thousands of Jewish-owned stores and synagogues and other places. We Jews knew now that Nazi madness was serious—maybe we had been hoping it

would go away, but now we knew different. My parents had never changed their Polish papers and were now deported back to Poland—only the Poles didn't want them. For six weeks, they and hundreds of other Jewish families remained in the no-man's-land between Germany and Poland until the Poles gave in to American and British diplomatic pressure and allowed them to return.

"I was born in Germany and had a citizen's passport, with the letter 'J'—for *Jude,* Jew—stamped into it. My bandleader, who was a German-American, now decided he wanted to get all of us out of Germany; he didn't like what was happening, so he booked a date at a club in Holland, and there we were, about sixteen of us. I was the only Jew. The boss put all our passports together, mine with the 'J' in the middle of the pile, hoping that the guards—who at this time were all Gestapo men—would just shrug us through.

"The guards had other ideas. They found my passport, passed everyone else through to Holland, and sent me to the Gestapo headquarters for questioning. They kept accusing me of *rassen shande*—racial shame—claiming I had besmirched the reputation of German womanhood by taking out German girls, and not telling them I was Jewish. I kept telling them I never went out with German girls, but they ignored me. I was beaten, found guilty, and sentenced to hard labor in a maximum prison for the most hardened criminals—murderers, rapists, gunmen, all of whom refused to believe me when I said that I was in jail only and solely because I was a Jew. But eventually they did believe me, and many of them watched over me, to make sure I would survive.

"The war broke out while I was in jail. In 1941, a group of us were shipped to another jail, only this one was called the Auschwitz concentration camp. It was a hellish place—no words can describe it. I survived because I knew languages, and again because some of my criminal-cronies kept an eye out for me. I remember talking to the great Christian, Pastor Niemöller, who was also a prisoner; what a fine human being he was! Life went on, one day at a time, each more horrible than the one before. The camp had political and criminal prisoners as well as Jews, and the former had a little influence in getting better conditions, at least to some extent.

"And one day, it was now 1943, a Gestapo officer examining the prisoners stopped in front of me and stared hard and long. Suddenly I knew who he was. Our old neighbor—we had grown up together, played together, visited each other's houses. He asked about my father, and I told him he had been deported to Poland, and I had not heard of him since. A few days later he sneaked me out of the camp, handed me some cigarettes (it was better than money at the time), and told me to save myself, and go off and work as an auto mechanic.

"I joined up with a few other people, but eventually we were back in a concentration camp, this time Buchenwald. What can I tell you? Somehow, I survived, until the early months of 1945, when the Americans came and set us free. I became a guide for the American brass. I can never forget the look of horror on Eisenhower's face, or the tears that were streaming down the cheeks of Patton. For four weeks they fed me Ovaltine. I couldn't eat anything else. My weight was eighty pounds. I remember seeing Leon Blum, the former Premier of France, who was also in Buchenwald, and the sister of La Guardia. They got a little better treatment.

"Anyway, I went to Leipzig to search for my family, and I knew beforehand what to expect. Nothing. Everyone was gone. For a while I worked for the American military government, and then in 1947, the sense of horror at what had transpired finally choked me. I decided to start a new life for myself, and left for the United States. And nobody knows what to expect the next day or what's around the corner, but on the boat coming over, I met a young lady, a survivor of Bergen-Belsen, and we got married.

"Her story is as unbelievable as any you'll ever read in a work of fiction. She and her brother were descended from a long line of wealthy German Jews, who had been assimilated. When Hitler came to power, he was sent to England, and she remained behind. For a while he was treated as an alien, and then war broke out and he joined the British Army and she eventually was sent to a concentration camp. The brother was with a group of British officers who liberated a hospital, and through a coincidence he found her there, as a patient. Through his help, she became a passenger on the same boat as I. Now we are married and the parents of two children.

"Here I found an aunt and uncle I had never known about. For a while I worked in a restaurant, and when that folded I started driving a taxi. It's a living. Maybe you saw my picture in the papers a few years ago? I had gone to see *Fiddler on the Roof,* and there outside the theater were a bunch of Nazi punks, saying not enough Jews had been killed in the concentration camps. I charged in with both fists, there was nothing else I could do. I was arrested, taken to court, handcuffed like a common criminal. Of course, the case was thrown out.

"I've been to Israel a few times. How can I describe it? It's wonderful. Maybe I should have gone there after the war, but then I wouldn't have met my wife. America, it's a free country, you've got to take the good with the bad. Anti-Semitism? There's plenty around. Not so long ago I picked up a Texan at the airport, and by the time we got to the Fifty-ninth Street Bridge, he had gotten me so enraged by his cracks about Jews this, and Jews that, I just took him and his bag and baggage, and left him right there in the middle of the bridge, and told him to get himself another driver.

"So, what does it all mean?" He swung around and faced me. The tattooed concentration camp number was clearly visible on his arm, resting on the back of his seat. "You got to be tough and kind, and watchful and lucky."

He wouldn't take my tip. When we shook hands, his grip was firm and steady.

—D.C.G.

 ## The Colonial Jewish Peddler

In 1655 three New Amsterdam Jews—Abraham de Lucena, Salvador Dandrada and Jacob Cohen—requested permission of the Dutch authorities to trade and travel on that high road of commerce, the South River, as the Delaware River was once known, but their request was stubbornly refused by Peter Stuyvesant. Although they were permitted to send two representatives to dispose of the stock which they had already shipped, they were not allowed to barter or trade their goods as they had hoped. This incident, a cause célèbre in American Jewish history, is probably the first instance of peddling by Jews in the mercantile economy of seventeenth-century America. The Dutch restrictions against the Jews engaged in retail trade explain the absence of similar peddling expeditions. Later, when the ban was lifted, it became possible for Lucena to travel along the banks of the Hudson River, trading with the white settlers and the Indians. The pursuit of peddling was Lucena's apprenticeship in a business which he began shortly after his arrival in Dutch New Amsterdam. After the English had conquered the Dutch in

1664 and subsequently lifted other restrictions, Lucena became a full-fledged tradesman.

The economic conditions of the colonial peddler differed greatly from the conditions that confronted the tens of thousands of Jews who became peddlers during the nineteenth century. There were no brilliant successes among the colonial peddlers, none who rose from rags to riches, no Gimbel or Guggenheim, no Straus or Seligman, but only those who stepped up a rung or two on the ladder of success. The Jewish peddler in the colonies was more than a pack carrier. Often he was a sutler, an Indian trader, a drayman, a mule driver and an itinerant of many occupations. When he sold his wares traveling on foot, or with a horse and cart, he differed little from his nineteenth-century counterpart and, if good fortune persisted, he climbed farther up the ladder to become a shopkeeper and perhaps a merchant. Colonial sutlery was a branch of peddling. Sutlers like Manuel Josephson specialized in supplying English troops at the isolated forts with the seemingly insignificant items so vital to daily life.

The Jewish peddler at the end of the seventeenth century and in the first half of the eighteenth century is an elusive figure, but there were enough peddlers generally to be of concern to the colonies. In Massachusetts the wandering peddler required more than a license to sell his goods: he had to furnish a bond of assurance that he would not become a dependent. The Jew, in addition to these restrictions, was classed as an unwelcome stranger. Rhode Island, despite having a religious climate a bit warmer to its Jewish merchants, did not lure Jewish peddlers to its coast. In Connecticut in 1659, a Jew was fined for peddling to children in the absence of their parents. By 1670 Jacob Lucena of New York had extended his trade to Hartford, but the subsequent history of Jewish activity in colonial Connecticut makes no mention of Jews specifically engaged in this trade. Before the Jew inherited the mantle of the Yankee peddler, or before he was to become a major force of peddling, a war for independence was to be fought and a revolution—perhaps no less great—was to take place in the manufacture, sale and distribution of retail goods. New York and Pennsylvania became the active centers for Jewish peddlers, once they were properly licensed.

Although the Jewish peddler was by no means as common in this period as the Yankee, he was already being drawn into the same comic and anecdotal literature which had begun to envelop the Yankee. An account of a "Jew Pedlar" in a New York journal of 1753 was, with the substitution of a word, the Yankee himself.

In the course of this decade the Jewish peddler emerged as a specific figure in the colonial economy. The opening of the West in the 1750s demanded mobile merchants with ready goods to go to the Pennsylvania outposts, and the French and Indian War invited adventure and trade at the forts and stations in and around Albany, New York. The French and Indian War was to the New York peddler what the Pennsylvania outposts were to the Philadelphia peddler. Sutlery and the Indian trade were easily stimulated. The sutler became involved in the marginal economy that was dependent on troops and the fortunes of war; on the other hand, the Indian trader, lured by the barter of furs and pelts for trinkets and hatchets, envisioned lucrative opportunities.

Colonial sutlery attracted a number of Jews who, if they did not distinguish themselves by wealth, attained considerable prestige in the eighteenth-century Jewish community long after they surrendered the frontier post for city shopkeeping. Among these was Manuel Josephson, linguist, scholar and synagogue president. Josephson was a sutler during the French and Indian War and witnessed the results of the Indian massacres at Fort Edward in 1757. Jonas Phillips, in the years to come, was no less distinguished than Josephson. His first years in America were spent along the Hudson River, supplying the military with groceries and dry goods that he carted from New York in exchange for furs when money was not available. Later in life, when he settled in Philadelphia, his auction house became one of the very first peddlers' supply outlets in the country. The comparative successes of Josephson and Phillips, about whom an extensive literature exists, dwarf the failures of those about whom few records have survived or whose destiny it was not to be remembered. The few contemporary notices that allude to peddling deal with the trade's occupational hazards, such as financial failure, disappearance or murder on the highway. Levy Jacobs was among those whose fate remains unknown. He disappeared in the winter of 1759 and his partner, Mordiky Levy, advertised for him in vain in the New York press.

Others in the area of Dutchess and Ulster counties encountered financial difficulties. They could not or would not pay for the merchandise which they had obtained on credit. Philip Samuel, who was expelled from Boston in 1756, possibly for peddling without a license, was being hunted in New York in 1760. He, along with the partners Israel Joseph and Henry Mordicai, was publicly accused of absconding with merchandise of considerable value. Before they could be apprehended the trio fled to Holland.

The system of licensing of peddlers and hawkers in the colonies was carried over from England. Most of the colonies had their own system of licensing and established scales of rates or special fees for those who traveled on foot or by horse, or with a horse and cart. Since there was no reciprocal recognition of peddlers' licenses among the colonies, it is likely that the Connecticut Yankee who invaded New York State frequently did so without a license, as the New Yorker may have done when he went peddling in Pennsylvania.

Few records of colonial licenses have survived to indicate the total number of peddlers, and the Jews among them, for New York State. Jewish peddlers do not appear in Pennsylvania's records of licensed peddlers until 1765, when Moses Abraham and Abraham Moses applied for a license to travel by horse. In the six years that followed, all other licenses that were issued went to Irish or Scotch-Irish peddlers.

Of the eighteen licenses granted in 1771, only one was applied for by a Jew. But in the peak year of 1772, when forty-nine licenses were recorded, five Jews were recipients. In 1773, twenty-seven licenses were issued, four of them to Jews: renewals to Joseph Solomon Cohen and Abraham Levy, and licenses to two newcomers. The following year eighteen licenses were issued, of which four went to Jews, three being renewals from the previous year. In 1775, the last year for which there is a record, only one Jewish peddler appears among the eight licenses —Lyon Nathan.

Nathan, a former resident of Reading, Pennsylvania, moved to Philadelphia in 1770. He was one of a small group of Jews who had emigrated from Germany after 1750 and settled in eastern Pennsylvania. Unlike his fellow immigrants, whose business careers show the evolution from peddling to shopkeeping, the sequence of Nathan's career was the opposite. He began as a shopkeeper, then became a peddler and an Indian trader.

The contribution of the six Jewish registered Indian traders to the development of the western trade was minor alongside the vast enterprises of David Franks, the Gratz brothers or Joseph Simon. It was from the Lancaster old-timer Joseph Simon, or from Moses Heyman, who operated country stores in New Hanover and Reading, that the peddlers, shopkeepers and Indian traders obtained or sold their goods. A chain of country shops were conducted in Goshenhoppen, New Goshenhoppen, Tulpehocken, Womelsdorf, Hanover, New Hanover, Reading,

York and Lancaster. Their business was not always done for hard cash or paper money.

About this time the Jewish merchants of Philadelphia were stunned by the news that Jacob Isaacs and Emanuel Lyons had become involved in an incident similar to that which confronted the New Yorkers in 1760. Unable to adjust themselves to the ways of colonial society, these two peddlers, who had already proved themselves unsuccessful at a number of other occupations, absconded with a wagonload of goods in 1772. Isaacs, who had come from Ireland, and Lyons, a bearded, German-speaking Hebrew teacher, were last seen driving their loaded cart in the direction of Lancaster.

The absence of the Jewish peddler in New England was due chiefly to his being viewed as an undesirable stranger. In the South, with the exception of Georgia and South Carolina, Jews were made unwelcome by religious tests or by the restriction of their economic opportunities. In addition, the geography of the South, with its swamps and plantations and its small, sparsely populated towns separated by great distances, was not encouraging to a peddler seeking fresh communities in which to vend his goods. Perhaps for these reasons, the literature of southern Jewish history is remarkably silent on the subject of Jewish peddlers.

If the British Committee of Council for Plantation Affairs had acted on the petition of the chiefs of the Sephardic community of London, the "floating mass" of Jews, "consisting of hucksters, hawkers, journeymen and others, either verging on pauperism or steeped hopelessly in the abyss" would have been the first body of Jewish settlers in South Carolina. The plan to transport London's underprivileged Jews to South Carolina was thwarted by inaction, and only because of this did the colony escape receiving a community of Jewish peddlers. Instead, the first Jewish settlers who came to Charleston, while not affluent, did not depend on peddling as a means of earning a livelihood. Still, the venturesome nature of colonial Jews makes it impossible to believe that an occasional peddling foray was not made. It is likely, for example, that the Pennsylvania peddler and Indian trader, Jacob I. Cohen, who joined Captain Lushington's militia company, peddled his way to Charleston in time to join the American army.

As the American War of Independence became a certainty, the Jewish peddler was found again in the role of sutler. Among the new sutlers was Haym Salomon. In the late spring of 1776 Leonard Gansevoort informed General Philip J. Schuyler that Salomon was a man whose loyalty to the American cause was irreproachable, and he could be depended upon as one fit to sutle to the soldiers at Lake George. When Salomon returned to New York City he was imprisoned by the occupying British for his sympathies with the colonies. Released in order to serve in a Hessian commissary, Salomon worked as an American agent and, when discovered, was forced to flee for his life. It is likely that he crossed paths with another sutler, Alexander Zunz, the Hessian Jew who followed the army of General William Howe. Zunz stayed in Philadelphia during the British occupation of the city and later moved with the British to New York. Other Hessian sutlers operated in the South. After the war, Samuel Levy and Levy Solomons, who had come in with the British, settled permanently in Charleston, South Carolina.

The American revolution brought to a close the minor role of the Jewish peddler just as it rescinded the legislation that limited his activity. Fifty years were to pass before the Jewish peddler seized the reins from the Yankee and began to penetrate into every nook and cranny of American territory with his packs, bags, trunks and bulging wagons of goods. Meanwhile, the old legislation was replaced by new laws, in a sense no less restrictive, but based on the economic needs and changes of a vastly expanding nation. The Jewish peddler entered into the literature of America, the travel books of the Germans and the frequently contemptuous observations of the British. He became the direct retailer to the nation and at one time constituted one-third of the peddlers in the United States. Lauded as a forerunner of the department store, he was actually the precursor of the five-and-ten-cent store. The doors of Southern and New England farmhouses were opened to him; he became a common sight in the Ohio Valley, and no stranger on a Mississippi River boat; he crossed the Plains, penetrated the passes of the Rockies, fought with the Indians, and buckled sacks of gold dust to his belt. He was an integral part of American life.

—M.W.

VIII
Holocaust:
Amidst Darkness
Some Rays of Light

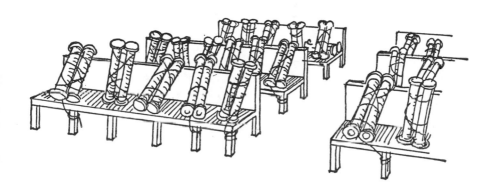

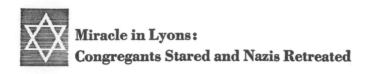

Miracle in Lyons:
Congregants Stared and Nazis Retreated

Not so very long ago, in the year 1940, soon after France had been overrun by the Nazis, a miracle took place.

Thanks are due to noted educator and author Dr. Azriel Eisenberg for uncovering this almost unknown account.

In the fall of 1940, several months after France had become yet another of the European countries seized by the Nazis, a small congregation of Jews was preparing to usher in the Sabbath; despite the black cloud that dominated virtually all of Europe at the time, they were getting ready for Sabbath eve services in their synagogue in Lyons. The city's population, Jewish and non-Jewish alike, was numbed by the events of the war, by France's defeat, and by the overriding sense of despair that had begun to permeate all of Europe.

France was divided, north and south, between occupied France and the so-called "free" Vichy government run by Marshal Pétain. Several thousand French Jews had fled before the Nazis' arrival and had found refuge in the Vichy region, although for many it was to prove only a temporary haven.

Lyons was fortunate because France's chief rabbi, Jacob Kaplan, had also left Paris and settled in Lyons, and one of the first things he did was organize a new congregation. Life for all of the Jews in that city, in those fateful days of the Nazis' ascendancy, was very bitter, and it was with genuine gratitude that the Jewish refugees gathered once a week in their modest Lyons house of worship for a few hours of Sabbath prayer and study and at least some surcease from the terrifying scourge of Nazism that loomed ever closer.

The city of Lyons, like other parts of Vichy France as well as Nazi-occupied France, had no small number of pro-Nazi groups. These were fascistic Frenchmen who shared the Nazis' attitude towards the Jews and were ready to support the Nazi plans to put an end to the Jewish people. Side by side with these groups there were in Lyons and in both parts of France ever-growing cells of sympathizers of the Free French movement, then led by General de Gaulle, who had reached safety in London.

Jews were quite prominent in the anti-Nazi maquis movement that had sprung up to combat the Nazis' takeover of France. There were also Jews who deplored the anti-Nazi actions of their fellow Jews, fearful as they were of possible consequences to the whole Jewish community.

On this particular Friday evening in the city of Lyons the small congregation of refugees from northern France had gathered to bid the "Sabbath Queen" welcome. As the service drew to an end, the congregants chanted the traditional *L'Chah Dodi,* which talks of "[soon will come] tidings of redemption day."

As is customary in many synagogues, at the conclusion of this part of the service the entire congregation turns around, facing the back of the sanctuary. The Lyons worshipers were no exception. They had just about-faced when the last phrases of the ancient hymn were suddenly stilled. Facing them was a group of pro-Nazi sympathizers, all masked, their hand grenades at the ready and clearly visible—a potential massacre in the offing.

And yet the would-be murderers stood transfixed, for they had not expected the Jews to about-face and stare at them clearly and directly. Apparently they had planned to sneak in behind the congregation, hurl their deadly weapons, and lurch back into the shadows from which they had come.

But the French Jews just stood there, staring, incredulous, transfixed, and the Nazi-lovers had a sudden change of heart. Grenades still in their fists, they backed out of the synagogue, except for one man who threw his weapon, which exploded on impact against a wall of the synagogue, causing no injuries.

It was all over in a moment. Drained, still terrified by what had just transpired, the congregants once again turned around, this time facing the Holy Ark, and took their seats. Some people were sobbing, others had broken out into a cold sweat, and still others just sat as though frozen in time.

Rabbi Kaplan moved to his position at the lectern, a slight tremor audible in his voice. "Fellow Jews," he declared, "we are witnesses to a miracle. We are safe because at the moment of gravest danger we turned to face the door, to welcome the Sabbath, the Bride of Israel. The men of evil intent are gone now, but the Bride remains. Let us greet her."

Finding its voice, the congregation sang the closing verse: "Come, O bride, let us welcome the coming of Sabbath."

We shall never know, of course, what thoughts crossed the minds of the would-be murderers as that small congregation of French Jews stared at them en masse, frightening them out of their planned act of murder. In Lyons today older Jews still talk of the miracle of *L'Chah Dodi*.

—D.C.G.

 ## The Physicians of Warsaw

In 1940–41 certain physicians in Warsaw had an unprecedented opportunity to observe the pathological effects of starvation. This is what happened.

On October 16, 1940, the German occupation forces in Warsaw established an official ghetto. All Aryans were evacuated from the area. Eight-foot-high brick walls topped with broken glass closed the exits. Only one gate was left open for closely watched contact with the outside: the *Transferplatz*, where once a week food was delivered—bread made from wormy flour mixed with plaster, sawdust, and rotten potatoes. Otherwise there was complete isolation for approximately 500,000 men, women, and children. (Before the war there were 330,000 Jews in Warsaw, but their number increased after the German invasion.)

As soon as the Warsaw Ghetto was established, the Jews began to organize their existence. A Society for the Promotion of Health was formed to give medical aid. Soup kitchens serving bread-and-water and potato-and-water gruel were set up. House committees collected supplies for children. Schools were started, textbooks being copied by hand by the boys and girls. Illegal newspapers appeared in Hebrew, Yiddish, and Polish—all this in the midst of a tremendous struggle simply to exist. Living quarters were unbearably crowded; there was scarcely a square yard of empty space in the whole walled-in section. And there was no soap, no fuel, no gas or electricity, and often no water.

At the end of a year all reserves of food were gone—the last bag of rice from the shelf, the last bit of sugar, the last piece of dried fruit, the last little tin of fish.

All the horses had been eaten. A day's ration by then consisted of eight hundred calories. The mortality rate, of course, rose very high—about five hundred every twenty-four hours. When a man, a woman, or child died, his clothes were removed —after all, there was no way to buy cloth; every rag must be saved—and the naked body was then placed in the street. This was to escape the Germans' exorbitant burial tax. Later the bodies would be collected on carts and dragged by starving fellow citizens to anonymous mass graves.

On July 21, 1942, came the first order for deportations from the ghetto. By four o'clock each day so many Jews must be ready—for death. First went the sick and the aged, to be poisoned, gassed, burned; then the intellectuals, who were systematically hunted down and killed. Next went the unemployed, followed by those who did not work for the war effort. Even in the ghetto the Germans had set up war plants; for a time some ten thousand young workers were exempt from the general order, segregated in a so-called "small ghetto" of their own. But for the most part, their parents and children were taken from them, snatched out of their arms and dragged away to be killed. After six months of deportations the ghetto population had gone down from five hundred thousand to seventy thousand. The mayor of the community, Adam Czerniakow, had committed suicide in despair.

But during this period the Jews had secretly mobilized. Guns, revolvers, and hand grenades had been smuggled into the district. Underground arsenals had been built, elaborate plans for street combat worked out, and a system of medical stations set up for expected casualties.

The first armed resistance began on January 19, 1943. SS and Latvian troops had entered the ghetto in the morning for an attack on the remaining seventy thousand Jews. They found barricades manned by fighters, fighters who fired on them and killed them—killed Germans! A call was sent out for tanks, and a thousand or more Jews were killed; then the troops withdrew, apparently stunned by the unexpected resistance. For a while even the daily deportations ceased; but during this period, which lasted several months, a force of approximately nine thousand German soldiers was collected and equipped with artillery, armored trucks, tanks, flamethrowers, and airplanes. Finally, on April 19, 1943, the final assault began: the proud German Army against the wretched ghetto Jews. During the first days three thousand Jews were killed. On April 21 snatches of a radio broadcast were heard in New York, although it was quickly cut off: "The last thirty-five thousand Jews in the ghetto of Warsaw have been condemned. The people are being murdered. Women and children are defending themselves with their naked arms. Save us!"

The battle lasted forty-two days. Nazi arsenals were seized and blown up. Five hundred Jews slipped out of the district to break open the Pawiak jail, and all prisoners (including German deserters) went over to the ghetto fighters. Suicide squads of Jews crawled under German trucks with high explosives. Single individuals attacked tanks with hand grenades. Finally, the Germans decided the whole district must be destroyed with incendiary bombs.

It is almost impossible to imagine those last nightmarish days, with entire families rushing from flaming houses into the face of machine guns, with streams of a city's inhabitants cornered in narrow streets and run down by tanks. Hospitals were invaded and the patients were killed in their beds. Thousands were burned alive. There was nowhere to step but on corpses—and this, day after day, with no escape, and no expectation of help from any side, or kindness, mercy, pity, or hope. Every building was a fortress until it lay in ashes. At last, on the forty-second day, only one was left standing, with the Jews' blue-and-white flag still waving above it. The battle went from floor to floor, until at the end, on the roof, the last ghetto fighter wrapped himself in his flag and threw himself down onto the burning ruins.

In the face of the systematic degradation and destruction of the Jews, their physical resistance is surprising. Still more remarkable is their moral courage. Perhaps the most dramatic evidence of this is the story of a group of ghetto physicians who launched a cooperative research project to study the effects of starvation on the human body—their own bodies included.

Dr. Milejkowsky, health commissioner of the district, organized a committee that established special wards for adults and children and rebuilt the laboratories (completely destroyed by the 1939 Nazi invasion) as well as possible. Many essential instruments were, of course, lacking; these had to be bought outside the ghetto and smuggled in at the risk of death. Practical work began in February 1942, and monthly sessions were held to discuss the observations of the physicians. Two age groups—one from six to twelve and the other from twenty to forty —were decided upon in order to exclude from the investigation the biochemical disbalances of infancy, adolescence, and advancing age. Everyone knew that this work could be interrupted suddenly by individual death—the doctor's own or his patients'—or by mass catastrophe. Everyone knew that the work was likely, in any event, to conclude only in death. But the doctors worked feverishly, without a day's interruption, and in the months at their disposal they accumulated a quantity of observations about experiments that would have taken many years to collect under normal conditions. At last, as the approaching crisis grew desperate, it became clear that the manuscript containing the results of these experiments must be removed from the ghetto while there was yet time. It was delivered to Dr. Witold Orlowski, professor of internal medicine at the University of Warsaw.

Except for a single individual, none of the twenty-two collaborating physicians survived. The only one still alive after the battle of the ghetto, Dr. Emil Apfelbaum, died in January 1946 as a result of his experiences.

I saw a copy of the document for the first time two or three years ago and was deeply moved by it—a treatise that must surely be unique in scientific history. The manuscript was carefully written in longhand in Yiddish on official German Army stationery. A friend translated parts of it for me at the time. There were six studies: "The Pathology of Starvation," "The Clinic of Hunger in Children," "Clinical Studies of the Circulatory System in Extreme Hunger," "Blood and Hunger," and "Eye Disturbances in Hunger." The papers have been translated into French under the title *Maladie de Famine* and published in Warsaw by the American Jewish Joint Distribution Committee. The book was sent to me a while ago.*

There is no mention of Hitler in the 262 pages of this work. The word "Nazi" does not appear. There is no discussion of politics and no note of self-pity. The only reference to anything not strictly scientific is at the head of Dr. Apfelbaum's contribution: "I dedicate this work to the memory of my daughter, Irene, who died the death of a martyr." There is also a short editorial footnote on page eighty-four to the effect that the dermatologist of the project, Dr. Raszkies, was sent to Treblinka (an extermination center), where he died in the "cyclon chamber" in 1942. His paper apparently was lost.

The complete scientific detachment of the authors of these studies from their own fate, and from the infernal background and surroundings of their studies, is almost incredible. The content of their findings is amazingly copious in view of

* An English-language edition, edited by Myron Winick and translated from the Polish by Martha Osmos, was published by John Wiley in 1979.

the great lack of research facilities. There are a few pictures of patients in the final stages of starvation that give a clear impression of the miserable poverty of the hospitals. (The accusing, hopeless, insane stare of the pitiful children will haunt all readers of the book.)

From the actual papers:

DR. A. BRAUDE-HELLER: *The mental changes and attitudes of the children are among the earliest symptoms of hunger: their apathy, which increases with the progress of starvation. The child loses his alertness, does not play, his movements grow slow. At the same time one observes changes of character: The children become disagreeable and quarrelsome; they seem extremely sad; their intellectual development seems to stop; sometimes they appear almost insane. In the most advanced stage of the disease the children lie on their sides, bent, their legs folded. Such a sickroom full of children covered up to their necks, even in summer (because of their constant chilliness), is quite characteristic. They don't move, act very quiet, but they do not sleep; they suffer from insomnia. In advanced cases they can neither walk nor sit.*

DR. J. STEIN: *The hunger in the ghetto surpassed everything we have seen or heard on the subject. The official diet of 800 calories daily contained virtually no fat, very small amounts of vegetable protein, and almost no vitamins. It was little but carbohydrate. The average weight of the adult patients who had lived on this diet was between 30 and 40 kilograms (from 70 to 90 pounds), 20 percent to 50 percent less than normal. The lowest weight observed was that of a 30-year-old woman, 152 centimeters tall (about 5 feet) weighing 24 kilograms (about 64 pounds).*

DR. APFELBAUM: *The organism that is destroyed by prolonged hunger is like a candle that burns out: Life disappears gradually, without a visible shock to the naked eye. The hunger sufferer grows lazy. He is a miser who avariciously guards what is left to him—that is, his last physical reserves. His motions are calculated, his slowness—sometimes even the complete lack of motion for several days—are very characteristic; his tendency to remain in a lying position, the somnolence, the silence, the sluggishness of the reflexes, the mental drowsiness: This is the customary picture of cachexia due to hunger.*

Our study has aimed at an understanding of the mechanism that regulates this economizing of energy. The results should throw some light on the pathology of hunger. The material that was at our disposal cannot be compared with any thus far known because of its magnitude and duration and the advanced degree of starvation.

The orderly, scientific experiment of the ghetto physicians, which proceeded through the first period—starvation—was interrupted by the second period—extermination. Their laboratories were smashed; their hospitals were burned; and, most important, the object of their study, man, was destroyed wholesale.

Nonetheless, the work went on as best it could. Up to the end there was a little group of physicians, gathered in a basement by the ghetto cemetery, discussing, writing, editing, correlating their facts and their conclusions until they themselves died of the symptoms they so accurately described, were led away to slaughter, or perished in the fighting. They have given scientists a book that will be a rewarding source of information. Even more, they have left the world an abiding testament to human self-respect and dignity.

—M.Gu.

The Tattooed People

Bea is working on *Remnants* [a publication] without her photographer. She is interviewing and documenting survivors of the Holocaust. She finds them everywhere. They drive taxis, dangerously turning around from the front seat to tell her their stories. They lunch on the old train, built during the Turkish rule, offer her cucumbers, yogurt, fresh Israeli bread, and their stories. Their arms are blue-tattooed, this special breed, baring their marked arms; these middle-aged, aged, bald people; these men with thick, graying hair on their heads, Brillo-like hair springy on their chests; these women who push crazily on buses, changing seats, disturbing the conductor. These survivors are still elbowing their way to air on the cattle cars; they are still filling their starving stomachs.

She sees the women in the Turkish baths. They are eating cheese-filled pastry. They are lying voluptuously naked on the carpets or sunning on the roof. They are bare-armed, bare-legged, bare-thighed, bare-breasted, but they are tattooed. They are dressed in numbers.

Her German florist and his wife are tattooed. The Polish bakery lady is not only tattooed but her face is half burned off. Neighbors across the street from her rented Jerusalem apartment rest tattooed arms on the railings of their balconies and watch their children playing soccer in the street.

She sees them at all the memorial places, looking into mirrors, at Yad Vashem, the Memorial to the Holocaust, at Holocaust museums, watching the Holocaust in films. Their children come, their grandchildren, their cousins in the Diaspora.

"It can never be seen enough," they explain.

Not everyone tattooed is marked as Superior Product, Grade-A Beef. Not everyone is Blue Ribbon, but they are remnants, streamers from other lands, banners of another time, these streaming ribbons of people crossing the Mediterranean. No one led them out. No one divided the sea for them. In fact, the world was unified in preventing their departure.

One red-haired fifty-year-old, the treasurer of his village, and his widowed sister tell Beatrix their tale. In their twenties, some twenty-five years ago, they sailed to Palestine on a coal boat. The British turned them back. They were fleeing the Nazis, who had already killed their parents and their younger sister. But the British turned them back. For five months they tried to land, five months not to be returned to Poland. Black with coal dust, coughing, their eyes streaming, they finally landed.

The sister holds up a photograph of her family. She is in uniform. They are the Socialist Youth Group. There she is, under her heavy chins, her thinning hair, twenty-five years ago, soft, round face, light eyes. Her brother, wearing a worker's cap, is next to her. The youngest sister poses in Youth Group uniform, with her hair braided on top of her head, her hands folded in her lap.

"She was *lacachet*," taken, says the sister, and wipes her eyes. She presses her thumb on her sister's face and leaves her print on it.

The fishman at the Super Sol* is numbered.

She sees other numbers. An Air Force security agent and his young daughter sit next to her on the train from Haifa to Jerusalem. They are going to the Mac-

---

* A supermarket in Jerusalem.

cabees games. Air Force security kisses and pets the young daughter who has his own face.

"If you want to keep your daughter," he advises Beatrix, "give her everything she wants and don't bind her wrists, and you will keep her forever."

But he is afraid he will not keep his fourteen-year-old forever. She has blood clots in her legs. After the soccer games they will go to the Western Wall to pray for the success of her leg operation. The child sleeps on his shoulder. He encircles her head with his tattooed arm.

They are circus people. The Tattooed People. The Experimented-On People. Still, they live.

—E.M.B.

 ## When Spain Rescued Jews from Hitler

The winter of 1944 witnessed one of history's strangest journeys. In February of that year a small band of Jews, miraculously released from the Nazi death factory at Bergen-Belsen, fled southward toward freedom, to asylum in Spain, the country that had once expelled their ancestors. Now this very same Spain was accepting them with open arms, giving them the most precious thing that Jews could find in a Europe gone mad—their lives.

What lay behind this grant of asylum? Why did a country that the world regarded as religiously intolerant intervene to save the lives of these Jews and many more? Why did she incur the enmity of her Nazi ally to save the lives of Jews? To understand the apparent paradoxical behavior of Spain, it is necessary to understand her historical relations with the Sephardim, the Jews of Spanish origin.

Over 450 years ago Spanish warriors destroyed the last pockets of Moorish occupation on the Iberian Peninsula and united the various kingdoms of Spain under a single rule. The Jews were the first and obvious target of the consolidators. In 1492 the Edict of Expulsion of all Jews was ordered by Ferdinand and Isabella, monarchs of Spain.

An ancient and honored community was uprooted and scattered across the face of Europe and North Africa. In every place that these Jews finally came to rest they formed little Spanish colonies and continued to speak fifteenth-century Castilian, as they still do today.

For over four centuries they could not forget their Spanish heritage. Spanish family names were proudly guarded and passed on. Spanish, together with Hebrew, was used in the house of prayer, spoken in the homes, and used in daily commerce. Throughout this long period Spain continued to maintain some tenuous contact with, and recognition of, these groups. In the training of Spanish diplomats great emphasis had always been placed upon a knowledge of the Sephardim, their history, and their culture. Although Spain had expelled its Jews, Spanish consulates all over the world kept records of the names of descendants of the exiles. These Sephardim had registered themselves as seeking Spanish protection and the Spanish Government continued to protect them even though they were no longer Spanish citizens. Every large Spanish-Jewish colony also maintained an honorary vice-consul to Spain. All this appears to indicate a reluctance on the part of both Spain and the Sephardim to cut the final ties, despite a legal disassociation of over four centuries.

In 1924 Primo de Rivera, the Spanish head of state, made it possible for Jews of Spanish background to obtain Spanish citizenship regardless of their domicile. To acquire this citizenship the first requirement was a formal declaration of intent. Of those Jews who availed themselves of this right, most went no further than to merely file the declaration. As a result, at the outbreak of World War II they theoretically had no legal status with the Spanish Government. When the Nazi authorities began deporting Jews from the occupied countries in the Balkans, the Sephardim appealed for assistance to Spain. The Spanish authorities decided to extend its protection to those who had applied for citizenship regardless of whether or not it had been granted. Spanish protection was also extended to those Jews whose names had previously appeared on embassy lists, together with the honorary vice-consuls.

Thus Spain eventually granted the rights of protection to Sephardim whose families had not seen Spanish soil in almost five hundred years. In addition, on more than one occasion the Spanish Government openly flouted the bestial policies of its ally, Germany, demanding fair play and the release of all Sephardim under Spanish protection. Since Spain had but a tiny Jewish community at that time, these acts were not the result of reaction to a pressure group.

In every European country where Sephardic communities existed, the Spanish Government stretched every interpretation of international law to grant aid where any minute legal excuse existed. In 1940, by granting protection to Parisian Sephardim who qualified, Spain spared them from wearing the yellow badge. Sephardim alone were exempt from Nazi confiscation of Jewish properties. Their property was protected and in some cases it was even administered by representatives of the Spanish Government. Such incidents were repeated in Rumania, Bulgaria, Hungary, Greece, and other countries.

The climax of these policies of the Spanish Government was the release of a group of Salonica Jews after they had been interned at Bergen-Belsen in 1944. Permission was granted for them to leave for Spain after a diplomatic agent of the Spanish Government negotiated their release as protégés of Spain. Before their release by the Nazis, these Sephardim had all their property confiscated. When Spain protested, their property was restored after the refugees reached Spain. The Government's representative in Athens took charge of the valuables, forwarding them to Barcelona.

On July 19, 1945, a few scant months after the close of the war in Europe, the first neutral ship to traverse the eastern Mediterranean plowed the now peaceful sea, bound for Haifa. The ship flew the Spanish flag and its passengers were homeless Jewish refugees seeking Palestine and a new life.

The overwhelming majority of European Jews was destroyed once it was apprehended by the Nazis. This was true of both Ashkenazim and Sephardim. The Germans operated with such efficiency, cunning, and speed that those who were in a position to assist could not even begin to help. As a result, the greater part of the Sephardic community was decimated. But Spain's efforts to save the lives and property of those it could aid stands as a shining light in Jewish history.

—H.A.E.

How the Warsaw Ghetto Revolt Began

Excerpts from testimony given at the Jerusalem trial of Adolf Eichmann

Lubetkin: The eighteenth of April 1943, was the day before *Pesah*. Two days earlier the Gestapo man, Brund, walked into the Community Council [the *Judenrat*] office and said he believed that the Council did not take enough care of the Jewish children.

There was not enough food and not enough vegetables, and he suggested that the kindergartens be opened so that the Jewish children could play and laugh because he was certain that the Jews who remained in Warsaw were productive and there was no danger of deportation. From our experience we knew that if there were any rumors and there was such a promise, it was a bad sign.

There had been rumors in the ghetto during the last few days before *Pesah* that the Germans were making ready to liquidate the ghetto in Warsaw. Others had heard from one German or another the same words of encouragement that we should stay. But on the eighteenth our Jewish policeman, who was a member of the underground, informed us that the Polish policemen had told Jewish policemen that something would happen that night, although they did not know exactly when.

The Jewish Fighting Organization which existed in the ghetto, and had fighting units, declared a state of alert. That night, at about twelve, this policeman came and told us that the ghetto had been surrounded.

Attorney General: At this time the Jewish Council no longer had any control. You were in control. Is that correct?

Lubetkin: That was even earlier, between January and April, or even earlier. The *Judenrat* itself obeyed the orders which we issued and published in Warsaw. This was a time when Jews obeyed.

We split up. I went to a post at 33 Nalewki Street. The commander of the group was Zechariah Auster. The other comrades, Anilevich and others, went to their posts. Mordechai Anilevich came to 29 Mila Street. That night we told the Jews: Whoever has arms will fight. We had arms, not only the Fighting Organization but Jews who did not belong to the organization. We said: Whoever has no arms will go down into the bunkers. And at the first opportunity, in the chaos of the fighting, let them make their way to the Aryan section of the city. Let them take to the woods. Some of them would be saved.

To the fighting groups we did not have to issue orders. The young men and young women had been waiting for months for the moment when they would be able to shoot Germans. Morning came. I was in an attic at 33 Nalewki Street, and I saw the thousands of Germans armed with machine guns surrounding the ghetto. All of a sudden they entered the ghetto, thousands of them, armed as if they were going to the front against Russia. Our unit numbered twenty men, women, and youngsters.

Each of us had a revolver and a grenade and a whole squad had two guns— and some homemade bombs, prepared in a very primitive fashion. We had to light them with matches. It was strange to see those twenty Jewish men and women, standing up against a great armed enemy, happy because they knew their end had come. We knew that they would defeat us, but we also knew they would pay a high price for our lives.

Many of you will not believe it, but when the Germans advanced upon our posts and we threw those hand grenades and bombs and saw German blood pouring over the streets of Warsaw after we had seen so much Jewish blood shed, we rejoiced. What would happen tomorrow did not worry us.

Those German heroes retreated, afraid and terrorized by homemade bombs and hand grenades. An hour later we saw an officer ordering his soldiers to collect their dead and wounded. We took their arms later. Thus, on the first day we, a handful with our poor arms, drove the Germans away from the ghetto. Of course they came back. They had enough arms and ammunition, bread and water, which we did not have. They came back again on the same day, reinforced by tanks, and we, with our petrol bombs, set fire to a tank during this fight. When we met in the evening and reported, we saw that the number of our dead was negligible: no more than two. We knew that on that day hundreds of Germans had fallen, dead and wounded.

A year later, when I was on the Aryan side of the city, I met a German who told me that on that day he lost an eye at 33 Nalewki fighting the Jews. It was a big battle, he told me, because they had many dead. I could not appreciate how we fought at that time, but if one can do so years later, there was some consolation in that fight when I say that my people set out on their last journey.

The fighting continued like that for a number of days. The Germans could not defeat us, and from time to time they withdrew. But not all the days were like the first days. We had more casualties and we killed fewer Germans. Then the Germans changed their tactics, and they forced us to change ours. From fighting from our posts on the streets we began to fight in small groups. We separated into many small groups that during the night would simply lie in ambush for the Germans.

The Germans did not come in large numbers but only in small groups. And just as we came to seek them out, they came after us—we had our feet wrapped in rags to muffle our footsteps, they in rubber-soled shoes. But we knew the terrain well. We knew the houses. We knew where to hide, the attics and the cellars. The Germans did not know.

Thus for days the fighting continued. Life in the ghetto during that week is difficult to describe. I had lived in the ghetto for years. Jews were waiting, embracing, kissing during the first days. Although it was clear to every one of us that we should not survive, there was this feeling that Jews had lived to avenge their brethren. But there is no revenge. We fought for our lives, we fought back. That made it easier to die.

The second day of the uprising was *Pesah*. In one of the bunkers I met Rabbi Meisel. We, the underground, had connections with him also on ordinary days. The underground was not always helped and encouraged by Jews. We were not always well received. Some of them thought we harmed the Jewish community. There was the sense of responsibility that the German terror had succeeded in instilling. When I came into the bunker the rabbi stopped the Seder and said, "You are welcome. I die a happier man now. I wish we had done this earlier."

From the very first day we were looking for contacts with the Aryan side. We had a number of friends on the Aryan side whom I knew. Yitzhak Zuckerman [*Lubetkin's husband*] was our representative there, maintaining contact with the Polish underground with a view to securing arms. After some time he did succeed in getting hold of arms.

But the question was how to smuggle the arms into the ghetto. At that time we had telephone communication besides contact through the men of the *hevra kaddisha* [the burial society]. Our cemetery was not within the ghetto walls, and since the men of the *hevra kaddisha* were overworked, they always had to leave the ghetto and come back, and so we received arms. We received news from Zuckerman that he had got hold of a number of guns which would be smuggled in within a few days.

We also sent letters outside the ghetto through these men in the burial unit, and we sent a letter from Mordechai Anilevich. And then this contact was also stopped.

We began looking for ways and means to send out a number of comrades—we had very few on the Aryan side—to try and get arms and food and to find a hiding place for us if any of us should remain alive. We were told that there was a bunker near the wall separating the ghetto from the Aryan side of the city, and from the bunker a sewer leading to the Aryan side. I was ordered to inspect this bunker.

The ghetto was surrounded at all times by German sentries and artillery, and every movement in the ghetto would draw a volley of shots. The approach to the house was difficult, but we did reach the house. We found a bunker full of food, and there was a way out to the Aryan side.

Besides the Jewish Fighting Organization, which included all the Jewish youth from [the] right to [the] left, there was a Revisionist group in Muranow Street, and they had prepared this exit a few days before, after difficult and brave fighting, and decided to cross over to the Aryan side. We met one of them later, and he told us the story. They were all captured and killed.

Through this same exit, and without knowing the story of the Revisionist youths, we sent two comrades to establish contact with our comrades on the Aryan side—Simha Rathieser, now in Jerusalem, and another comrade who is dead. When they came to the Aryan side, a Polish sentry saw them and, believing they were Poles, said, "Do you know what happened here an hour ago?" and told them about the fighting that had just transpired.

The place was full of Germans and no one was allowed in or out. Yet their courage—and maybe their good fortune—helped them to evade the German guards and contact Yitzhak. They were an important reinforcement to this small group, many of whom were killed on the Aryan side during the first days of our fighting. They helped to evacuate the fighters and assisted in all underground activities that continued until liberation.

The Germans could not defeat us in open battle, so they adopted other tactics. Certainly, to fight fires was quite impossible. They did not have to fight us, because the fire fought us.

Attorney General: And then there were these scenes of people jumping out of the upper stories, out of the fires. Is that correct?

Lubetkin: Yes. There are these pictures of men and women. Previously we had called on the Jews to hide in the bunkers, but when all of a sudden an entire building was set on fire, when the smoke reached the bunker people would jump from the fourth and fifth and sixth story, generally with their children in their arms.

Attorney General: People would be driven out of buildings with flamethrowers?

Lubetkin: Yes. People often jumped from one fire into another and German machine guns, which were posted all around the wall, shot every Jew, wherever he was, on the spot.

Attorney General: What happened to the people who broke out of the bunkers?

Lubetkin: They looked for hiding places in other bunkers. Many of them entered sewage canals, found shelter in some of the ruins. Some were captured by the Germans. They were taken by the Germans to the death camp at Treblinka.

Attorney General: When you started this uprising, did you know how it would end? Had you any hope of defeating the German Army?

Lubetkin: No, we did not have a fighting chance. It was in April 1943. There were only the beginnings of the Russian victory on the front and it was quite clear to us that we did not have any chance of winning in the accepted sense of the word. But, believe me, it is not just a phrase. In spite of their strength, we did know that eventually and finally we should triumph. We, the weak, because that was our strength, our belief. We believed in justice, in man, in a different regime than that which they professed.

—Z.L.

 ## The German Who Personally Saved the Lives of Over One Thousand Jews

In 1947 three women—all newly arrived Jewish displaced persons from Germany —approached the Rescue Department of the World Jewish Congress in New York with a request.

"Please," they asked, "can you send food packages to this man?"

The official took one look at the name and address on the card and then exclaimed in amazement: "A German! After all the Nazis did to you?"

"Oscar Schindler saved our lives," replied the women. "He saved over eleven hundred Jews. Now we must help him."

This unusual episode opened the file on the story of a remarkable Gentile industrialist who helped balk Hitler's insane plan to wipe out European Jewry.

Although many other Christians throughout the continent risked death to save Jews from the Nazi terror, there was one startling difference in Oscar Schindler's case. As a loyal German producing war materials, he operated directly under the eyes of the Gestapo and the SS.

Yet every day, from 1940 to 1945, he personally fed, clothed, and protected an ever-increasing flock of Jewish men and women marked for death. At any moment he might have been executed for treason. Miraculously, his scheme worked; every one of his eleven hundred charges survived.

Until the 1938 Munich Pact, Oscar Schindler appeared destined for a prosperous but uneventful career as the son of well-to-do German Catholic parents who owned a farm-equipment factory in Zwittau, a city in the Moravian section of Czechoslovakia. When the Nazis marched into the Sudetenland, Oscar was twenty-eight—tall and powerfully built, with reddish-blond hair and blue eyes.

At this point Schindler made the first in a series of momentous decisions. He joined German Army Intelligence as a civilian employee at Breslau. Here he formed lasting friendships with a number of career officers. Many of them, he discovered, secretly detested Hitler—and their attitude rubbed off on him.

With the outbreak of war, Schindler made a second fateful decision. He could keep his job, he was informed, only if he joined the Army. Instead, he chose to enter war production; he and his wife went to Nazi-occupied Poland in 1940 to obtain a factory. The Germans were then busy seizing Jewish-owned property and forcing owners into "bankruptcy."

Schindler acquired a small "bankrupt" plant at Cracow, which, with twenty-five Polish and seven Jewish workers, was turning out kitchen equipment. Unwittingly he had now found the "cover" for his future rescue operations.

Polish Jews were being abducted from their homes and herded into ghettos and brutal labor gangs. Only by working at a German-owned firm could these people hope to escape forced transfer.

Schindler's rescue efforts began on a small scale when he took over the factory and hired the former owners and other competent Jews who desperately sought work. At first he had no conscious plans for rescue. He retained warm memories of Jewish friends during his school days and he deplored the persecution around him.

Gradually his distress turned to sorrow. Every day his Jewish employees came to plead for a father, a brother, a neighbor. "Bring him around," Schindler would answer. By the end of 1941 he was employing 190 Jews.

In 1942 Hitler's diabolical "solution" to the Jewish "problem"—a blueprint for the systematic murder of six million men, women, and children—was put into operation. Able-bodied Jews were forced into slave labor, and the young, weak, and sick were thrown into concentration camps.

A peremptory notice went out to industrialists: All employers of Jewish slave labor would be responsible for housing them in barbed-wire compounds, to be guarded by SS troops. Unless barracks were built within five days, even able-bodied Jews would be consigned to the death camps.

Schindler was angered and revolted by the senseless cruelty. As a loyal German he would gladly work around the clock for the war effort. But as a human being he considered himself morally bound to use every means possible to defy Hitler's program of slaughter.

Courageously he ordered and paid for the immediate construction of oversized barracks. Here he settled his own flock of 190 Jews and 450 Jewish slave workers of other German factory owners. The number of his Jewish employees was to grow from over 600 in 1942 to approximately 800 in 1943, 900 in 1944, and 1,100 in 1945.

Not all these were bona fide workers. Some were the wives or parents of employees; others were people smuggled into the plant, with Schindler's assistance, to hide out until the Jewish underground could smuggle them out of the country. When SS officers made inspection tours, these nonproducers had to be concealed or disguised as employees.

Once every month Schindler had to submit carefully doctored lists of workers to draw the meager food rations allotted to slaves. For the privilege of "renting" each slave, he had to pay their SS masters five Polish zlotys per day, then worth about a dollar.

The cost of preserving this small army mounted every week. The SS factory and barracks guards were regulars on Schindler's payroll, and he paid huge bribes to influential Nazi officials. He was also lavish with presents, liquor, parties, women, and well-timed favors—all proffered in a calculated effort to build goodwill.

Schindler's quick thinking saved many lives. One day an SS officer became irritated by the slow progress of an elderly man who was trying to push a heavy wheelbarrow.

"Malingerer!" shouted the officer. "Execute that Jew!"

As the doomed man was led out to a back courtyard, Schindler smilingly told the SS bully, "I've just received some fine French cognac. Let me get some for you." He walked away nonchalantly.

Once out of sight, he ran to a storeroom, seized a bottle of cognac with one hand, a bottle of vodka with the other, and raced to the backyard. There an SS guard was just raising his gun. Schindler waved the vodka in the guard's face.

"We're alone out here," he whispered breathlessly. "Nobody can see us. Forget about the execution. I'll hide the man and accept all responsibility. You take the vodka."

The guard lowered his gun, took the bottle, and disappeared. Still holding the cognac, Schindler untied the trembling worker, told him where to find a hiding place, and returned briskly to his SS "friend."

On another occasion Schindler came back from a business trip to learn that in only three hours two of his Jewish workers were to be executed at the nearby Plaszow concentration camp. The day before they had inadvertently broken an old press. The accident had been witnessed by a Gestapo informer, who had rushed to the Plaszow commandant with a story of "sabotage." In Schindler's absence the men were sentenced to hang, and all thirty thousand inmates of the camp were ordered to attend the execution.

Schindler sped to Plaszow and burst into the commandant's office. "These are two of my best men," he shouted. "If you hang them, I shall report to the War Office that you are impeding the war effort."

The commandant was unmoved. Silently Schindler took a thick wallet from his pocket and dropped it casually on the officer's desk. The commandant eyed the wallet. After a long pause he said, "All right. Take your Jews and keep your mouth shut about this."

Feeding and caring for the Jews was the responsibility of Mrs. Schindler, who organized a kitchen and even a hospital staffed by slave laborers—six Jewish doctors and two dentists. A woman of tremendous courage, she frequently upbraided the guards for their cruelty and steadfastly refused to be intimidated by the Gestapo.

Three times during the war the Gestapo found pretexts to arrest Schindler. Each time Mrs. Schindler indignantly appealed to high army officials in Berlin—friends from their Breslau days—and forced the Gestapo to retreat.

Despite these arrests, the industrialist's personal courage never faltered. One morning Erna, Schindler's German-Jewish secretary, was invited to have coffee at the breakfast table. A moment later in walked an SS officer. Schindler began to pour him a generous glass of schnapps—which the Nazi coldly declined. "My honor as a German will not permit me to drink in the presence of a Jew," he sneered.

Angrily Schindler leaped from his chair, grabbed the armed officer, and, with enormous force, flung him across the room and through the swinging doors. Then he returned to his table, explaining to Erna: "How dare he talk of 'German honor'? The man's a pervert, a drunk, and a sadist. What does he know about honor?"

By 1944 Schindler realized that Germany had lost the war. If he could hold out for just a little longer, his Jewish charges would be safe. But the German Army was abandoning Poland. All factories were to be evacuated and moved westward. Slave laborers were ordered to the death camps, where the grisly incinerators and gas chambers were working on twenty-four-hour shifts.

It was at this moment that Schindler performed his greatest feat. He obtained permission to switch his production from kitchenware to strategic armaments for the Luftwaffe, and to relocate his factory in the Sudetenland. Then he demanded that all his nine hundred skilled workers accompany him. Time was too precious, he insisted, to assemble and train new workers.

After weeks of waiting, his request was approved—and he received an unexpected bonus: He could transfer not only his nine hundred Jewish workers but also an additional two hundred from the Plaszow camp in order to fulfill his quota.

Late in October 1944 Schindler went to Brunnlitz, Czechoslovakia, to set up his plant. The eleven hundred Jews had not arrived. According to Nazi regulations, they had to be reprocessed first at central camps—the eight hundred men at Gross-Rosen, the three hundred women at Auschwitz. The men arrived on time, but not the women.

After three anxious weeks Schindler learned that, due to an administrative mix-up, the women had been thrown into the execution section of the Auschwitz concentration camps.

Schindler rushed to Auschwitz. These women were essential skilled workers, he protested. Their death would cripple vital war production! The authorities were indifferent. "Never mind," they assured him. "We'll supply three hundred others."

Schindler raced to Berlin and appealed to his army friends. Amazingly, in the only known instance of its kind, an order went out directing that his three hundred women workers be transported at once to their original destination! The order was issued by the Reich Security Office of the SS at the Army's insistence.

The last six months of the war were harrowing. Guarding the Brunnlitz factory were some of the most vicious SS men Schindler had ever encountered. Despite his many gifts to them, he felt that at any moment they might massacre the Jews for the sheer pleasure of killing. To prevent such a catastrophe, Schindler quietly distributed guns and ammunition among his men. Fortunately the weapons were never used. In late April 1945 the SS guards retreated before the advancing Russians.

Now Schindler saw that he, too, would have to escape the oncoming Russians. As he prepared to leave, the Jewish leaders drew up documents in Russian, German, English, and Polish describing what he had done and expressing their gratitude. They insisted that their employer take copies with him; other copies were sent to major Jewish relief organizations.

At five minutes past midnight on May 9, 1945, certain that his eleven hundred Jewish friends were safe at last, Oscar Schindler bade them farewell and headed for the American lines.

His story has a heartwarming postscript. In June 1957 Schindler, at present a resident of Frankfurt, Germany, visited New York, where more than two hundred of his former Jewish workers, now living in the United States, overwhelmed him with gifts and undisguised affection.

But the most touching tribute, perhaps, was an announcement by several former SS slaves, now American citizens. As the builders of a housing development, they had found a way to honor their benefactor. Today, in the Elmwood Homes section of South Plainfield, New Jersey, there is a street called Schindler Drive that will perpetuate the name of a noble human being.

—K.R.G.

 # I Was Buried Alive and Dreamt of Potatoes

This chapter from the writer's record of experiences in nine different camps in Europe recalls with starkness the fate of millions of our people. The author today

lives in Johannesburg. This chapter has been translated from the Hungarian, her native tongue.

In June 1944 several thousands of us came from the Riga concentration camp to Dünaburg, where we found thousands of unfortunate Jewish prisoners from the Baltic States.

The camp consisted of the bombed-out premises of a former factory and our special task was to separate the iron and the bricks from the tangled rubble. This wasn't particularly difficult. The SS soldiers were not beating us too unmercifully and the weather was pleasant and warm. We would have worked almost contentedly had we not been suffering the torments of hunger.

I seem hardly to be standing on my feet; I am faint and dizzy with hunger. Hungry . . . I keep on closing my eyes and all sorts of colored circles seem to be dancing before me. Pink, yellow, green, black circles.

Somehow when it is the black circle's turn to appear I seem to feel the hunger more acutely. I have a sudden feeling as if at any moment I'll be thrust down by the wind. The color of the circles keep on changing, but the black ones remain dominant . . . But one cannot shut one's eyes too often, as the heap of shambles in front of us must be cleared by midnight and the SS sentries' searching glances are ever upon us.

At this morning's rally several hundred women were selected from among us and they left the camp with spades on their shoulders, accompanied by about 20 SS men. What sort of work could they have gone to? Well, I shall know later, when they return . . .

Suddenly it flashes across my mind that for a number of days I hadn't seen any of the prisoners who had been taken away in this manner in the morning return to camp. Well, I thought, perhaps they had come back late at night. Who knows. Maybe . . .

At this morning's rally thirty of us were lined up separately. I was among them. The others had already commenced work, but we thirty were given empty buckets or large jam containers. On a high-pitched command of the SS sentries we started off and left the camp.

The buckets were light; swinging them by our sides, we walked on briskly. Although the sky above was cloudy, it was warm and we were glad to at least be out in the fresh air after all the dust that we continuously swallowed.

We had scarcely covered a few miles when we reached a clearing in a forest. Here there was a truck and upon it a barrel of slaked lime.

We were ordered to form a chain leading from the barrel to an area covered by branches—the distance was approximately twenty yards.

The order was then given to pour the slaked lime onto this patch. Adjoining this ground there were squares cut out of earth covered with grass. We filled our buckets with the slaked lime and covered the area. It was not strenuous work and it was soon completed. Then we were ordered to place the squares of earth next to each other so that they covered the branches and the lime. At times our feet sank into the soft earth, but we were heedless of what lay underneath.

This work, too, we finished quickly. The truck with the empty barrel left and we were lined up. The empty buckets hung from our hands and in our hearts there fluttered the hope that we would not arrive too late at camp and miss the distribution of food. Before leaving we were given the command that at the next morning's rally we were to stand aside separately from the others. We reached the camp just when the bread was being distributed.

Of the several hundred fellow women prisoners who were lined up with us, not one asked us where we had been or what we had done. True, nothing was really important except the hope of receiving some bread and the thought that the soup might be thick, with a lot of potato peelings. We said nothing. After all, what was there to tell—that we were pouring lime somewhere on something?

This morning we, the thirty of yesterday, lined up separately as we had been warned to do. But now several hundred were added to our number. Each alternate one was given a spade.

When we were lined up in rows of five instead of the usual two or three, more than twenty SS sentries joined us—and we started off.

Why so many sentries? But this thought kept our minds occupied only for a few moments, because the news that was whispered in the latrines was far more exciting. The rumor spread that there would be peeled potatoes that night.

About four miles from our starting point we stopped at a clearing that had burnt grass; surrounding it was a forest of young trees. The rustling of a gentle wind, the fluttering of butterflies, and the humming of insects suddenly reminded me of our Saturday excursions from my home town, Ungvár, to the forest of Radvanc.

I remembered so well how my mother used to put her cool, beautiful white hand on my forehead every few minutes to see that I wasn't getting too hot. This time, indeed, I did feel hot, but nobody was solicitous about me.

The sentries marked out a large area and those of us who carried spades began to cut out the squares of earth covered with grass, which we placed on one side in a large pile. The second group broke off small branches and twigs and these, too, had to be piled up in one place. This accomplished, we were ordered to dig out the marked area.

What a big air-raid shelter this will be, we told each other as we dug the soft earth. It was not difficult work. Time was flying and the sandy earth was also flying from the pit to the surface . . . Tonight there will be peeled potatoes!

But soon the pit becomes deeper! It's more and more difficult to throw the earth up . . .

Evening was closing in upon us when the SS men agreed that the ditch was deep enough. Then a truck arrived and we put the spades and the earth upon it. We sighed with satisfaction that the work was done. Weary and exhausted, we waited for the command to line up.

A command came through: thirty prisoners to stand in one row facing the forest; then another thirty and another thirty, and again and again—with an SS sentry at the end of each row. We gazed at each other, terrified. We had never lined up like this before.

I stand at the edge of the wood and look into the twinkling rays of the sun as they penetrate through the trees. I listen to the noisy little twitterings of the birds and am gladdened by the beauty and innocence in nature, forgetting for a few moments that I am a prisoner and that an SS sentry stands next to me with a rifle in his hand, with his finger on the trigger.

Suddenly shrieking screams and the crackling reports of rifle fire fill the air. Spine-tingling and heart-chilling shrieks! And the screams continue. "Don't shoot. Don't shoot."

But the sound of the shooting follows in rapid succession. Then silence. The prisoners and the guns are equally silent. "Go on. Turn around!" shouts the SS soldier next to us, and the next thirty unfortunates turn and start towards the pit.

My feet are trembling, my back stiffening into a cramp. Oh, there will be peeled potatoes tonight and I have to die. There will be winter and spring, there will be summer and autumn, and I must die.

I am terrified. I would like to scream in my horror, but dread weighs heavily on my chest, like a big, gray animal, and my scream grows faint and ever fainter, to a scarcely audible whine.

The rows become fewer and fewer and soon it will be my turn. I want to run, to shout, but I stand stiff and motionless. The rifles are already being reloaded and one bullet will be mine . . .

Now the last row of prisoners in line with me turns round and drags itself towards the pit. Some are running to the right, some to the left, but they can only make a few steps and then they are bullet-ridden.

I stand in front of the pit with trembling feet. For a fleeting moment I see with dimmed eyes my companions in the pit, some of whom are still moving convulsively. I hear the loud report of guns, then silence and darkness.

Nothing seems to hurt me. Is this death? Is this what we fear throughout life? But if I am dead, why do I hear wailings? Or is this only heard by the soul?

So there is a soul after all! And there is another world as well! If there is another world then I shall see my parents again . . . And, having regained my peace, everything relaxes within me.

Oh God! Oh God! Something moves beneath me. I try to lift my arm but fail. I open my eyes but see nothing. Am I blind? Am I alive or dead?

I lie prostrate in the dark. There is something heavy on my feet. I cannot move them. At moments I feel a waft of fresh air . . . I am breathing. I am alive.

Alive. Alive! I rejoice within myself. But where? In a pit? Together with hundreds of unfortunate women—dead or alive?

I shake something off from my head. I try to sit up and I find myself sitting. Around my head there are fresh branches. It is dark and there are stars above me. The wood, silhouetted in the darkness, can be seen dimly and not a living soul around me—not even an SS soldier.

Consciousness comes back to me and my mind begins to clear. I must get out of this grave that I helped to dig for myself.

Shivering and weeping I cry out with a faltering voice. Are any of you alive? Come out of this pit. And on the other side of the pit a dark figure is sitting.

"It's me," says Charlotte, but from the pit no one moves. We two, the only survivors—survived, through a miracle.

Charlotte and I stand at the edge of the pit rearranging the branches and the twigs, but we are at a loss to know who are the more fortunate ones, we who survived or those others in the pit.

Above our heads the stars slowly disappear and at the crack of gray dawn rosy clouds emerge from the east. We are standing at the edge of the pit. We stare into each other's faces, speechless.

Perhaps we ought to pray? Perhaps we should recite the prayer for the dead over our unfortunate sisters? But Charlotte knows only the morning prayer and my mind is a blank. Desperately I force myself to remember, but with no success.

While Charlotte murmurs the morning prayer, I stand there with folded hands, without a prayer, without a thought, and without tears.

We drag ourselves away to the edge of the wood and drop to the ground while it becomes lighter and lighter. Only then do we see each other's bloody faces, bloody arms. Our rags are covered with blood.

We seem to be full of blood everywhere, but without any wounds. With the help of the dewy blades of grass we try to clean off the blood from each other. We become no cleaner with this effort, but instead we are covered with mud.

Time passes. We sit behind the shrubs on the ground, shivering and broken.

The birds begin their new songs. The butterflies begin their gay dances and we do not know what to do or where to go, and morning is nearly here.

I think it was a pity to survive—by now it would all have been over.

Suddenly I find myself shouting to Charlotte. I poured lime on a similar pit yesterday. If that was done yesterday, it will be done again today.

"Look, Charlotte. Look at the squares of grass that we cut with so much care for our own graves. Charlotte, as soon as the prisoners arrive with a barrel of lime we shall lose ourselves in the crowd. We shall work and return to the camp."

"What for?" says Charlotte. "Only to dig a new pit tomorrow and be shot into that one? No, I won't go. I shall remain here, sitting on the ground in the wood, come what may."

In my heart I know she is right, but I try to convince her that we will find ways and means of getting back to the camp.

"Charlotte," I say, "I have a feeling that something different will happen to us. You will see . . ."

"Yes, but what if the SS soldiers take a count and realize that there are two more?" Now I too say come what may.

After a little while a truck arrives and soon after the prisoners with their buckets. Hidden among the shrubs, we listen with throbbing hearts. The chain is formed and the lime is being poured on the branches over our unfortunate companions who lie beneath.

Suzy, the wife of a physician from the town of Dés, is near and says, "Step out." We sign to her to be silent. She is quiet, believing that we went into hiding to avoid work, which most of us sometimes tried to do. When she completed her work, we returned with her to the group, as we would have done normally.

As I place the grass squares on the pit, I listen to the low voices of the others. Last night there were no potatoes, but there might be some tonight. These are their hopes. And through my mind runs the thought: What will happen when we have to line up? Oh, if only there will be no count today!

We have finished our work. Nice, neat squares of turf cover the unmarked grave of our sisters. Goodbye, forever . . . Marge, Ella, Rose, Claire, and the hundreds . . . Sweet young girls and mothers . . .

"Rally," sounds the hoarse voice of the SS sentry. I am startled from my thoughts. "Go on!" the hoarse order is repeated. And we start.

We are all on the way. Charlotte and I among the group, and there has been no count. Oh, it wells up from the depth of my heart and I don't think of anything anymore—except "Will there be potatoes tonight?"

—R.G.W.

 ## The Synagogue with 1,564 Sifrei Torah

The unique Jewish collection of the Czechoslovakian State Museum in the proud and ancient city of Prague is at once an exhibition of treasured beauty and a memorial of the Nazis' murderous "final solution."

The museum in Prague contains relics of the destroyed communities. Many Nazis fancied themselves as apostles of culture. Their looting of art treasures wherever their marauding armies marched was on an unprecedented scale. In the

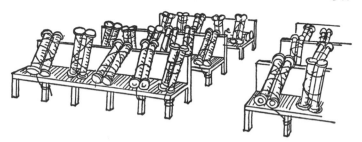

city of Prague, the capital of the "protectorate" of Czechoslovakia, they gathered together the gold and silver ornaments, vestments, pictures, books, and manuscripts from the desolated synagogues of Bohemia, Moravia, and Slovakia. It is said that they contemplated a permanent exhibition of the works of "an exterminated ethnographical group." The task of arranging and cataloging was assigned to talented Jews, who received a reprieve for the appointed labor before being shipped off for extermination. Among the treasures here gathered was a huge number of Sifrei Torah.

When the "thousand-year Reich" came to an end, the great store of Jewish treasure remained in Prague. The decimated Jewish community was helpless. The Prague Museum was eventually taken in charge by the Czechoslovakian State and has since been honorably maintained as a witness to what the Czechs call "the glorious history of Czechoslovakian Jewry," as an enduring appeal to the conscience of humanity.

The Prague Museum consists of a variety of ceremonial objects, and indeed many secular records and mementos as well. But in Jewish eyes the treasure of incomparably greatest importance was the Sifrei Torah. Other objects—precious metals and jewels, intricate and exquisite needlework or craftmanship—may have greater commercial value, but the Sifrei Torah are in a special category. In a sense, all the rest serve only as their frame and adornment.

Sefer Torah (Sifrei is the plural form) is usually translated as "Scroll (or Book) of the Law." It contains the books of Genesis, Exodus, Leviticus, Numbers, and Deuteronomy written on parchment. "Law" is an inadequate translation of "Torah"; Jews generally prefer to use the Hebrew term. It means the ancient classical teaching, which is basic in Jewish tradition and from which the massive body of millennial Jewish learning, direction, morals, and inspiration draws its first roots. It is prized for its intrinsic worth and authority, but also as a sign and a standard of the interpreted, applied, developed, universal faith that is the Judaism of past, present, and future.

For these thousands of years the Sefer Torah has been copied by thousands of pious hands. The skins of certain animals are prescribed, and they are to be prepared according to definite rules. Only the best black ink may be used. The form of the letters is laid down, as is the arrangement of the columns and the spacing of the various sections and divisions—even the proportion of the margins. Poetic portions must be set out in a definite pattern. Only the Hebrew consonants may appear: no vowels, accents, or punctuation are permitted.

Only qualified scribes are to be engaged in the sacred work of copying the scrolls; and through the ages every effort has been made to confine this labor to men of not only the highest skill but also of impeccable character. However many times a scribe may have written a passage, he is forbidden to write from memory. He must have a perfect text before him and copy letter by letter. If a scroll is damaged slightly—and the kind and degree of damage is defined—it may be repaired. If, however, it is too badly spoiled, it cannot be used. In accordance with definite rules, the sections of parchment are shaped, stitched together, and then fastened at either end of the long strip to rollers. These may be either of plain wood or adorned.

The elaborate directions for writing the scroll and for its maintenance have insured, throughout these two millennia and more, an amazing accuracy of transcription. At the same time, they testify to and support the people's esteem for this embodiment of the Jewish heritage. Much else that appears in the Prague Museum is explained by the veneration of the Sefer Torah, which accounts for the very existence of the coverings and "crowns" and other accessories on which so much imagination and clever workmanship have been lavished to afford "dresses" worthy of their subject.

In every synagogue in the world, as through all of history, the Sifrei Torah are kept in an Ark, a cupboard, usually ornamental, traditionally in the east wall of the building, whence they are ceremonially taken out for the reading on Sabbaths and many other occasions. They are indeed the synagogue's only essential ceremonial object. In the countless tragic episodes of Jewish history the rescue of a Sefer Torah occupies a special place. In pogroms and banishments no picture is more poignant than that of the saving, in danger and in flight, of the sacred scroll.

In the Prague Museum, where most of the prized objects are beautifully displayed, the Sifrei Torah themselves proved to be somewhat of an embarrassment. To display even one scroll in its length would take a huge hall. And scrolls are perishable. To keep them in storage, rolled up and unused indefinitely, would be tantamount to passive vandalism. And a proper disposition of the scrolls would require labor for which the Czechoslovakian state authorities would not claim either the competence or the taste.

The original handling and transporting of the scrolls by the Nazis caused damage; more damage has been done by the long period of storage since the time of collection. Under the circumstances, this was inevitable. But for nearly twenty years after the war no alternative to the continued storage and deterioration of the scrolls was found. The only authorities that would possess the means and the will to cope with the challenge which the scrolls presented would be found "on the other side of the iron curtain." And although attempts from the West were made, they were unsuccessful, because, aside from the Czech authorities' general reluctance to do business with capitalist agents, they were conscious of a sacred trust and were unwilling to consider an offer from a source that they thought might exploit the enterprise for profit.

Eric Estorick, the well-known London art dealer, has for some years enjoyed enviable success in showing, in London, paintings and sculpture from communist countries. He was able to gain the confidence of Artia, the official agents of the Czechoslovakian Government for cultural properties, and eventually negotiated with them for the Sifrei Torah. Mr. Estorick secured the patronage of a London philanthropist who supplied the wherewithal for purchase, packing, and carriage, arranged for an expert, Chimon Abramsky, to go from London to Prague to investigate the proffered treasure, and engaged experienced packers to transport the scrolls. With Mr. Estorick's approval the patron offered the scrolls to Westminster Synagogue, and the offer was solemnly accepted. A Memorial Scrolls Committee was set up.

On February 7, 1964, 1,564 scrolls—certainly by far the largest shipment of Sifrei Torah known in history—began to arrive at their destination in Westminster. In the synagogue, in three rooms, shelves were erected and numbered, one space for each of 1,564 scrolls. Each was given a number and placed in the space with the corresponding number. This task of merely affording the appropriate accommodation took some months.

In the summer of 1964 the second stage, the work of examining and classifying the scrolls, began. With the cooperation of the Haham, the very Rev. Dr. Gaon, and others, several skilled scribes are engaged in this task of inspecting each scroll from beginning to end and making entries of their findings regarding the condition of parchment, writing, and of any noteworthy distinguishing features. Everything about each scroll is of interest, and the record is made as complete as possible.

But the primary object of the present study is to separate the scrolls into those in good condition, those beyond repair, and those that can be made right with greater or lesser effort. It is proposed that when this study is completed and the results assembled, a certain number of the scrolls will be distributed. Hundreds of requests for them have come to the synagogue from every quarter of the globe. It is the desire of the donor that some be kept at Westminster Synagogue as a permanent memorial; some of special historic interest may be given to the museums. But the great majority of those that are, or can be made, good will be allotted to synagogues in Britain and abroad, wherever, in the judgment of the committee, the need is greatest—to find their places in the sacred Arks, to live and breathe again.

Meanwhile the scrolls lie in their appointed places in their Westminster "waiting rooms," where thousands of visitors have viewed them, most people leaving the scene overwhelmed with emotion. A Christian Czech was awestricken and shaken as he gazed upon what seemed to him "hundreds of corpses in transparent shrouds," as he counted over the synagogues from which the scrolls had come and which he had known, and as he brought to mind his "small Jewish schoolmates, later friends, who must have looked with religious fervor on the scrolls." And yet this same visitor, becoming more calm, saw "a mountain of dead books, spiritual bodies, so to speak, and yet a mountain glowing with the life of revelation, law, promise."

A Jew from Jerusalem, standing before the scrolls, seemed to hear "the wailing of the Jews being led to the slaughter. The cry of the hundreds of communities, ravaged and slain, echoed in my ears." Such sentiments were expressed again and again by scores of visitors, English and foreign, Jewish and non-Jewish.

—H.R.

 ## The Strangest Encounter of My Life

We—that is, a group of men, all of whom had suffered at the hands of Hitler— were sitting in a circle, discussing some of our strangest adventures during the Second World War. Some had been in Hitler's concentration camps; others had been in jail, awaiting execution, only to be saved by some miracle; still others had been fighting with the Resistance movement and had many times faced the icy, pitiless mask of death. There was a fourth category to which I belonged: refugees, victims of double persecution—first of the Third Reich and then of the French Vichy government, its satellite.

When my turn came to tell about my strangest adventure, I had no trouble recalling it. It has remained before my eyes like a clear snapshot, and I remembered it in every detail just as if it had happened a few hours before.

During the summer of 1944, near the village of St. Julien in France, the SS troops who had murdered the whole population of the village, including schoolchildren, in the horrible bloodbath of Oradour-sur-Glane, were combing the countryside for surviving victims.

After days of pursuit by Himmler's unchained warriors, I was hiding in haystacks and barns, bushes and hedges, bursting with helpless rage, just waiting for their final withdrawal. I had fallen asleep in my haystack when a prodding bayonet awakened me and a rough voice yelled, *"Aufstehen!"* (Get up!) Bending over me was the hateful, grinning face of an SS man. Then, suddenly, the expression of the hovering man in the dreaded black uniform changed. His eyes, wide and questioning, showed such a bewildered amazement that the ferocious mask seemed to disintegrate and give way to an expression of shy sympathy.

"Yes," was all I could utter, since I, too, had recognized him. "This is truly a strange meeting, Walter."

Destiny had played a masterful prank on both of us. The SS man who had found me hiding in the hay was Walter Berndt, one of the best friends of my younger years. Together we had belonged to the youthful group of inspired pioneers of democracy and progress in the lazily stagnating Weimar Republic that was Germany after the First World War. He was constantly with me, staunchly supporting me whenever I spoke at public meetings or at conferences. Once I was suddenly attacked in a "hall battle," where chairs were used to prove theories and defend ideals. Walter was in the thick of it, right behind me, fighting off my attacker. I knew I could depend on him.

When I emigrated in 1933 because of Hitler, we lost all contact. Now I saw him again, a familiar face on a now total stranger.

I got up. He dropped the arm that held the bayonet when I faced him. Watching my eyes glued to his SS insignia, he laughed nervously.

"I guess this must bother you a little?" he muttered.

"I am shocked," I replied. "How could it happen to you, of all people? After all . . ."

"Never mind, Kurt," he interrupted me with a tired defensive gesture. "It would be too long to explain. Many things have changed since you left Germany. After all, I am a German."

"That I know. But I remember what you used to be. How does it happen that you wear this uniform of disgrace?"

Walter was silent. Then, talking more to himself than to me, he said, "No one could judge it who was not present . . . At first I felt awfully strange and lonely. But there was nothing else for me to do. I did not want to leave Germany. I joined the party to protect myself. They pressed me to join the SS. To tell the truth, I was horrified at first, but then I gave in. I still did not like it, but it did not matter anymore. Finally I even enjoyed belonging to the privileged."

"And otherwise?"

"Otherwise," he replied hoarsely, "there was nothing. I did not become a Nazi; at least not in your meaning of the word."

"Did you really believe that you could silence your conscience so easily?" I asked.

"They all did it! Besides a conscience will not help you in the struggle for survival! You have kept your conscience because you had no other choice left!"

"Still," I ventured, "you used to believe in certain ideals . . ."

"Those are not valid anymore. They were a cardhouse of illusions . . . Then the Fuehrer, I mean Hitler . . . What I want to say is that even if there are a few dark spots, there is much light, too . . ."

"Does it mean that on the whole you have endorsed him and become one of his followers?"

"He made Germany great, didn't he?"

"He will make it smaller than ever before!"

"Maybe . . . but this is not our fault . . . We only did our duty."

"How about the crimes committed in his name?"

"I do not know anything! But suppose we did know about them, how could we prevent them?"

"What is being done to the Jews?"

"I am deeply sorry about it. I am sure it was, and is, a tragic mistake . . ."

"You think you can manage to keep your conscience pure to the very end?"

"At least no less pure than the others."

"What happened to your love of freedom?"

"It is not dead, but this is my private business. I had to choose between freedom and security. I chose security, for myself and for my nation."

This was indeed a strange discussion—unreal, ghostly, and ridiculous all at the same time, this verbal duel in a hayloft in France. On one side the armed man in uniform, trying to salve his conscience with realistic ambiguities; on the other the homeless refugee, resigned but still trying to bind the present to what he had left in 1933, who knowingly overlooked the abyss that had opened between him and his lost friend.

Suddenly voices approached, German voices of Walter's comrades.

"Now you must deliver me to the other murderers," I heard myself saying. "This is your duty, you know." I turned pale and waited.

He looked at me for a moment. His eyes sought mine searchingly. There was a deep frown across his brow as he faced this dilemma. Then he repeated slowly, "Yes, I suppose it would be my duty."

A terrible heavy silence fell. The voices were coming closer.

Walter pulled himself together and, turning to leave, stretched out his hand to me. I did not take it. He hesitated for a moment and then, with a short military salute, he turned and went outside. I could hear his voice telling his comrades who had joined him, "There's no one here. I have searched all over. Let's go." The footsteps grew faint. A deathly silence fell over the hayloft. Later I heard that Walter was killed near the end of the war.

My heart still aches when I remember our discussion. I deeply regret that I did not shake his hand. He had been my friend, and even after he had sunk to the low level of the SS, he remembered our friendship and, at the risk of his life, had saved my own.

—K.K.-B.

 ## A Visit to Ness Amim:
A Christian Colony in Galilee

The road from Naharia to the Christian colony of Ness Amim, which is inhabited by a group of Dutch, Swiss, and Germans, is one of the finest in Upper Galilee. The road cuts through fields covered with varieties of vegetables and fruits. Long stretches of fertile fields lie roundabout as far as the eye can see. On both sides of

the road are trees of various kinds. The silhouettes of farmhouses outlined against the distant horizon lend a grace and a harmony to the landscape.

The car stops on the open road before a sign in Hebrew reading "Ness Amim," where it turns in. A few moments' further driving and we are inside the Christian colony of Ness Amim, which is immediately next to the Kibbutz Lochamei Hagetaot, the "Kibbutz of the Ghetto Fighters." We have arrived during the rest period after lunch and people are sitting around in the library, which is located in the dining room. Mme. Machledt, one of the members of the *merkaz* (secretariat), receives us very pleasantly, inviting me to lunch, assuring me that it contains no pork. I now begin to study the dining room, which apparently is the center of all activity. The walls are hung with various slogans in Dutch, and objects among them include a Chanukah candelabrum, a large tablet with the Hebrew letter *beth* and other Hebrew inscriptions.

The reading section was occupied by several persons absorbed in newspapers and periodicals. Among these was an elderly aristocratic-looking woman who was introduced to me as Dr. De Junge. She had been the physician of the Tiberias Hospital, had returned to Holland, but had come back to settle permanently in Israel and had chosen to live in this colony.

Among the various periodicals were several Hebrew-language publications. When I was introduced to the readers, they responded in a resounding *"shalom."* After I scribbled a few words in my notebook, Mme. Machledt said, "Our main goal is to atone for the sins committed by the Church against the Jews, not only with respect to the killing of six million Jews by the Nazis but to heal the wounds in helping to build up the Jewish State.

"It has not been easy," she went on. "It took time to win the confidence of our neighbors, especially of our immediate neighbors, the Kibbutz of the Ghetto Fighters, with whom we share our borders. It was because they were immediately nearby that we decided this was the proper place to express our sympathy in the great Jewish tragedy. Even when, after great effort, we succeeded in gaining their confidence, there was still sharp opposition to the idea of Germans settling here after Dutch and Swiss had already settled. The Swiss were the first to come." Through the window she showed me a bus that stood transfixed like a monument, saying, "That's where the first Swiss couple stayed who settled here before the first house was erected.

"We did not overcome this opposition until 1968, when Professor Heinz Kramer of the Hebrew University in Jerusalem settled here for a period of four months. He broke the ice for the Germans. Our neighbors at the Kibbutz of the Ghetto Fighters allowed Germans to participate in the work after Otto Busey arrived."

Busey was a German who saved hundreds of Jews at the time of the Nazi slaughters in Bialystok, where he had a factory and maintained close links with the partisans. His name is commemorated in the "Avenue of Righteous Gentiles Who Rescued Jews" in the Yad Vashem memorial. Former partisans now living in Israel had looked him up, brought him to Israel with his family, and built a house for him—the finest in the colony.

"Since then our relations with our neighbors have been friendlier. We borrow machinery from each other. Now that we have undertaken a new project to grow avocados, for which we need water, they gave us a water pipe. When the Lochamei Hagetaot holds its memorial service for the six million who perished at the hands of the Nazis, we provide the flowers and wreaths that adorn the platform."

Mme. Machledt led me to the center of the colony and pointed to the monument, which is directly opposite the Kibbutz Lochamei Hagetaot, with the inscription in Hebrew *Maavak Unetzachon* (Struggle and Victory). "Our 'rabbi' (she pronounced the word *rebbe*, as in Hebrew), Shlomo Bezek, a Dutch Jew who has lived for years in Ayeleth Hashachar died a year ago, but before that he greatly assisted in the development of our colony and in our relations with the surrounding Jewish settlements. He was very active on our behalf. We observe two days of rest a week, Saturday and Sunday. On Friday night we have an *Oneg Shabbat* in which we eat together at one table and carry out a cultural program."

I received more information about this remarkable colony from the wife of Dr. John Pilon, one of its leaders. Dr. Pilon was abroad and Mme. Machledt took me to his handsome dwelling, located in the very center of the colony. Mme. Pilon received me pleasantly and showed me her husband's library, where, among other volumes, I noticed the works of Abraham Joshua Heschel, the poems of Itzhak Katzenelson, and those of other Hebrew writers, as well as works in Dutch and German about Jews and Judaism.

Our conversation began in English, but when her eleven-year-old son returned from school in the adjoining colony and greeted us in Hebrew, we switched to Hebrew, which she speaks fluently. In reply to my question as to where she acquired such excellent Hebrew, she answered, "Yes, many of us know Hebrew; after all we are residents of Israel now. There is a kindergarten in the colony and the children get the rest of their education in the schools of the neighboring colony, as far as high school."

She first mentioned the long-established bond of the Dutch people with the Bible and their old friendship and reverence for the Jewish people, reminding us that there were Jews in Holland as far back as the fourteenth century, and that at the time of the Inquisition in Spain and Portugal Jews fled from those countries to the Netherlands, where they settled and enjoyed full freedom. This was repeated under Hitler's bloodstained rule when thousands of German Jews escaped to Holland. Later, when the Nazis occupied Holland, the Dutch showed solidarity with the Jews and helped conceal many, saving them from the crematoria.

"Of course," she remarked, "there is a guilt feeling on the part of many Christians in relation to the Jewish people, especially in the younger generation. They cannot understand why civilized nations behaved so passively when the mass murders of the Jews were so brutally perpetrated by the Nazis. And so we Christians from various countries, as an expression of solidarity with the Jewish people, decided to come here ourselves and help build up their ancestral land, which they have now restored." She then quoted a passage from the prophet Isaiah that foretold that there will come a day when the seed of Jesse will stand as "a banner for the nations" (*ness amim*) and all the world will turn to it. "That is why," she said, "we chose the name Ness Amim."

What do the occupants of this remarkable colony do? They follow the model of the *moshav shitufi* (cooperative settlement) in their structure. Their produce is flowers for international export. I was shown the flower plantation, was taken around to study the various varieties of roses, and saw the experimentation carried on to improve and expand production. I was shown how the temperature is controlled in the greenhouses and how the produce is later dispatched in special aircraft whose air is carefully controlled to keep the flowers in a state of freshness.

There is a special procedure for cutting and packing the flowers for the importers in various European countries where they are sold that takes a very short time —less than twenty-four hours. However, even in so short a space of time such delicate growths can wither if they are not looked after properly. "No matter how fresh and clear the flowers look now," I was told by the man who was doing the packing as he pointed to glorious-looking bunches of roses in containers of water that were in half bloom, "they will look just as fresh and appealing when they're sold in the florist shops after they arrive by the special climate-controlled airplanes."

The cultivation of flowers for export is a new industry in Israel, having only taken root in recent years, but it is already a project involving millions of dollars.

The history of this remarkable colony of Christians in Israel provides an interesting chapter in itself. It began in the years between 1956 and 1960, when the reverberations of the Nazi mass murder of Jews were still fresh and the young Jewish State was establishing itself. The synod of the Dutch Reformed Church announced at that time that some understanding or rapprochement must be sought between Jews and Christians, and that there must be a change made in their mutual relations.

In 1960 a conference was held in the Netherlands in which delegates attended from that country, Switzerland, Germany, and the United States. This conference considered the formation of an international Christian settlement in Israel as one of the means of seeking this reconciliation.

The primary purpose was to atone for the sin of Christianity in the mass murder of six million Jews and for the persecutions, in the course of centuries, for which the Christian Church bears responsibility both directly and indirectly. This had created an abyss between the two religions that could only be repaired by spiritual and moral concord. It was stressed that the measures used previously by Christians reaching this accord between the two camps, which included efforts to convert Jews to Christianity, had only served to exacerbate the situation and provoke suspicion and distrust among Jews. Fifteen Dutch congregations in Holland participated in this conference.

In order to fulfil this goal, a project was formed in which a new company would buy a territory of twelve hundred *dunams* (three hundred acres) of land in an appropriate area offered by an Arab sheikh with whom negotiations had already been going on. It was to be an agricultural and industrial settlement organized on a solid economic foundation. It would be geared toward export and was to be under the supervision of people experienced in agriculture and manufacturing. Christians were to participate in the project both as specialists and laborers.

A memorandum was submitted to the Israeli Government on the purposes of the project, in which the moral aims were stressed to persuade the Jews of Israel that its purpose was a sincere approach to Jews out of respect to the Jewish people, that a broader experience by Christians of the problems, values, and achievements of Jews in Israel would help familiarize the Christian world with the new Jewish commonwealth and its justified struggle for existence.

The memorandum was handed to former Prime Minister Levi Eshkol. It took considerable time, however, before permission was granted. In certain circles there was some suspicion that this was another guise for missionary activity. The project was under discussion for two years. Only after its sponsors had convinced the government that their program was totally opposed to any missionary work, and after a special delegation had come to Israel and had carried on the negotiations, was it approved.

The work then began in earnest. In 1964 twenty-five young people from Holland and Switzerland began to work the land, using their own farm machinery. Prefabricated housing was brought in for them and four thousand meters of greenhouses were erected for raising flowers for foreign export, along with other products.

There are now twenty-five families in Ness Amim, including a number of unmarried people. All of them have their own private dwellings. New houses are being erected for those arriving. The work is carried on either by volunteers who come for a limited period or by the permanent members, all of whom receive the same payment. The parent organization of Ness Amim, to which the land belongs, is located in Zurich (and is also registered in Israel), and the executive committee is in Holland. Each of the four countries involved—Holland, Switzerland, West Germany, and the United States—have 25 percent of the shares. The settlement is controlled by the international association that provides the funds.

—J.B.

 A German Officer Saved Us from the Nazis

My daughter, Alma, and I survived World War II because of the devotion and humanity of a gallant German officer. I have kept silent until now because I did not wish to involve one of my wartime benefactors, the German General von Beutel. An outspoken anti-Nazi who was later imprisoned by the Soviets for many years, von Beutel is now dead. The officer who saved me has visited Israel on the invitation of the Israeli Government.

I was born in Palestine, in the village of Zichron Jacob, the only daughter of a well-to-do farmer. Despite my parents' objections, I went to live in Jerusalem, where I graduated from the Teachers College. While working for a youth organization, I met and married a geologist, but before we could settle down my husband accepted a position with a Polish oil company and we moved to Warsaw. There my daughter, Alma, was born shortly before World War II began. Before I left Palestine I had learned perfect German by spending several summers with a family of German-Jewish refugees at Nahariya, north of Haifa. When I came to Poland I spoke not only Hebrew and German but also Arabic, English, and French.

As the Luftwaffe was pulverizing Warsaw in 1939, I fled on foot with my husband and infant. Drunken Polish soldiers shot down my husband. But somehow I managed to cross wartorn Poland, swimming rivers, crawling over minefields and under barbed-wire barricades. I begged for bread, stole food, evaded German,

Polish, and Russian patrols, and finally reached Lemberg (Lvov), in the Polish Ukraine, where my husband had relatives.

After one look at my British-Palestinian passport, the Soviet security police arrested me as an "English spy." A friendly Ukrainian woman hid Alma in her house until I escaped from prison, changed my identity, and found a job as a nurse in a Soviet military hospital, with my precious passport still in my possession. I was waiting for a chance to contact the British embassy in Moscow and to get back to Zichron Jacob. But in June 1941 the Wehrmacht smashed through Soviet lines and occupied Lemberg.

Ukrainian mobs were running amok in the streets, raping women, looting apartments, and killing Jews on sight. I and my baby hid under hospital beds, but the Ukrainian nurses in the hospital knew I was Jewish. They called in a group of Ukrainian militia, who were accompanied by a German security officer.

In the hospital's personnel files my card had the words "nationality Jewish" in red ink. Somehow I had to destroy that card or be torn apart by the Ukrainian soldiers, who were already discussing the division of my clothes. I approached the German officer and, addressing him in German, introduced myself as an Arab Christian from Palestine. The officer was visibly impressed but asked, "What is an Arab woman doing in Lemberg?"

I told him I was the daughter of a sheikh, that I had married a Jew in Palestine and followed him to Poland. Since he was now dead, I was waiting for German victory and repatriation to my homeland. One of the Ukrainian nurses interrupted me, shouting that a Jewish woman should not be permitted to address a German officer. The Nazi officer was embarrassed but finally asked if I could substantiate my claims to Arab nationality.

"Of course," I replied, "but first will you honor me by drinking some Turkish coffee with me? I'm brewing it in the oriental Arab style." The officer agreed and I rushed to the hospital kitchen to grind some coffee beans and boil them over a slow fire. While the water simmered, I stole into the office where the hospital records were stored. With ice-cold fingers I searched for my personal dossier. When I found it, I tore the card into shreds and flushed them down the toilet.

Among the papers strewn on the floor by the departing Soviet officials I found a clean personnel identification form. I also came across a bottle of standard red ink and the pen used by the Russian commissar in charge of the hospital. Working feverishly and hoping not to make mistakes or printing errors in the unfamiliar Russian language, I filled out the form, adding the words "Nazionalnost Arabskaya" (Nationality Arabic). Then I carried the pot of Turkish coffee, two cups, and the forged file card on the same tray to the impatient Nazi security officer.

He sipped the coffee, studied the card, and patted me on the shoulder, saying, "You have nothing to fear from us, *Gnaedige Frau*. We Germans are very gallant toward Arab ladies. Please call at my office tomorrow morning and bring your passport. We shall be glad to issue you a regular German identity card, food ration coupons, and other necessary documents. Lemberg is not a very healthy city now. There are too many Jews around, and it is necessary that all your papers be in order. *Auf Wiedersehen.*"

While I was a nurse at the Soviet military hospital during the Russian occupation, I had helped some nuns and priests from a monastery across the street. Now I was able to hide little Alma with the nuns while I went to see a Jewish chemical engineer, a friend of my late husband. His wife had been missing for five days and he was sure she had been raped and killed by the Ukrainians. He himself had orders to report for work at the Janowski camp, where thousands of Jews were dying every week of hunger, disease, beatings, shootings, and exhaustion.

He agreed to help me. He mixed some chemical solutions, applied them to my British-Palestinian passport, and the original ink evaporated without a trace. He then wrote my new identity: Christian El Nassari; nationality Arabic; religion Roman Catholic; born in Faradis village, near Zichron Jacob, Haifa District, Palestine. El Nassari was a sheikh in the Arab village of Faradis near my home. His sons worked for my father and I now adopted him as my father.

The forged page was dry when the expert lifted it to an electric bulb. He nearly fainted. "I spoiled your passport," he exclaimed. "The chemicals were too strong. They ate right through the paper. Now everyone can see it's a forgery if the page is held against the light." I had a fit of hysterics but returned home when I recovered, knowing I had nothing to lose and hoping to distract the Gestapo officials so that they would not subject my passport to close scrutiny.

At Gestapo headquarters in Lemberg the Nazi officer had a surprise for me. A Moslem soldier from Azerbaijan, who had deserted the Soviet Army to join the SS Moslem auxiliary formations, was brought in to check my Arabic fluency. Luckily he knew little Arabic himself and spoke it in a Persian Azerbaijanian dialect. Soon I was able to talk him into kissing my hand and joining me in singing an impromptu version of a Moslem religious song. This satisfied the Gestapo investigators. They checked my passport without holding its pages up to the light and then issued me the necessary documents.

But too many Ukrainians and Poles in Lemberg knew my real identity. I had to find some safe haven to escape the dragnets of the SS and Ukrainian militia. That week a German rear-area services headquarters in charge of supplies, garrison duties, troops in transit, and convalescent soldiers moved into Lemberg. The unit was commanded by General von Beutel, an old-school German officer. In charge of the unit's administration section was Hauptmann Peter Benchen from Hamburg.

When the headquarters took over a row of apartment buildings and ordered all civilians to move out in twenty-four hours, my apartment was also affected. I then went to see Hauptmann Benchen. He heard me out in silence and then gave me a six-room apartment that formerly belonged to a Polish university professor and offered me a job as his chief secretary and housekeeper. I accepted with thanks and moved in with Alma and a Ukrainian woman, Irena, who was so helpful when things were worst.

Within the week I realized that while I had fooled the Gestapo, I had not deceived Captain Benchen. He knew from the start that I was Jewish. I could not understand why a German officer was risking his life by harboring Jews in his office. But he never so much as hinted that he doubted my Arab identity. Encouraged by his friendly attitude, I assembled some twenty fugitive Jews— scientists, poets, composers, architects, and professors—and hid them in the spare bedroom in my apartment.

One day Captain Benchen called me into his office. "Frau El Nassari," he said in his quiet voice, "your visitors are making too much noise. I don't care about it myself, but I think it would be better for you and all concerned if you insisted on standards of behavior befitting an Arab princess." When I protested I was no Arab princess, Benchen smiled and said, "But yes, I think you are. I looked up your name in some Arab genealogy books and found that El Nassari is the name of an ancient line of princes and emirs. In any case, the prefix 'El' in Arabic is like 'Von' in German, so it's all right, too. Think of the protection princely status would give you. No one would dare enter the apartment of an Arab princess without permission."

Then I understood how he was trying to help me. One of the Jewish architects hidden in my spare room drew a large sign in German. Topped off by a small coronet, it proclaimed the residence of Princess Christina El Nassari, chief secretary of Etappe administrative section. It looked impressive enough to keep all police patrols and sudden-search Gestapo squads away from my door.

With Captain Benchen's assistance, I kept the twenty Jewish fugitives hidden in my room for nearly three years. Among them were married couples, lovers, and bachelors. And there was love, romance, jealousy, tragedy, hate, and envy among the score of adults in one small, cramped bedroom, isolated from the rest of the apartment by a heavy cupboard through which Irena and I had cut a hidden door.

There were illnesses and even epidemics which I tried to cure with stolen medical supplies. A prominent Jewish professor died in the hidden bedroom. A surgeon who slept beside him dismembered the body with the help of the professor's wife; limb by limb and bone by bone the body was smuggled out of the house in Irena's shopping basket and scattered over the parks of Lemberg. The widow could not even weep because her crying would have alarmed the guards pacing the street below.

Feeding twenty people in wartime Lemberg was a problem, too. Without Benchen's help they would have starved to death. He himself suggested issuing special requisition orders to the Wehrmacht food-supply stores under his control. "We have to drink tea and coffee during office hours," he told me, "so please type out orders for tea, coffee, milk, cream, and sugar, and don't forget bread, butter, jam, biscuits, and chocolate either."

One day in 1943 Benchen called me into his office, looked over the requisition orders, and remarked casually, "An overzealous supply officer of the stores suspects you are stealing food. He wrote me a letter saying that three people—you, General von Beutel, and myself—could not have consumed forty-two pounds of sugar requisitioned last month, so you must be stealing it to sell on the black market. He wanted to complain to the criminal police, but I shouted at him that an Arab princess would never stoop to such things. I ordered him to drop the matter, but please be more careful in the future, my girl."

It was General von Beutel who saved me from another Gestapo investigation. The general must have known who I was and what I was doing. He never mentioned it, however, but he always cursed Hitler and the Nazis in my and Benchen's presence. One day the general stormed into the office waving a letter. He said his daughter had been expelled from school for refusing to join the Nazi BDM [Bund Deutscher Mädel] youth organization. "The Nazis are barbarians, worse than the Huns, Mongols, or Tartars," the general said to me and Benchen. "But, believe me, my dear Mrs. El Nassari, there are quite a few honest Germans left to uphold the traditions of German civilization and culture after Hitler and his gang are gone."

If reported to the Gestapo, such talk meant an immediate death sentence, but it showed that von Beutel had implicit trust in Benchen and me. Benchen was an old and trusted friend of the general, but an Arab woman known for her open pro-Nazi sympathies was hardly the ideal audience for the general's anti-Nazi views unless he knew who I really was.

When Gestapo headquarters decided to screen all civilians employed at German military installations, they once again came up against the problem of checking the Arab identity of Princess El Nassari. Professor Said Bey, a pro-Nazi Persian Moslem who taught oriental languages to German security officers, was invited to investigate Lemberg's mysterious Arab princess. General von Beutel and Captain Benchen were present in my apartment when the professor arrived, escorted by two senior security officers. The nineteen hidden Jews, crouching on the floor behind the massive cupboard, listened fearfully to the conversation which could doom them.

I lowered my eyes, as a modest Arab woman should in the presence of a distinguished man, and curtsied deeply. *"Salaam Aleikum, ya Khwajja Said, keef hallak?"* (Peace be with you, my master Said, how are you?), I asked him in Arabic. "I am happy to meet a real Arab princess," he replied in the same language, with a slight Baghdad accent. "My eyes are hungry for the sight of an Arab woman." Quickly I switched to German, saying that von Beutel and Benchen should not be left out of the conversation. "Yes," Said Bey agreed, "it is not polite to speak a strange language in the presence of people who do not understand. Let us converse in German."

Then I served Turkish coffee Arab-style, sticky honey and nut cakes I had baked myself, sweetmeats, sherbet, peanuts, and more coffee, unsweetened and very bitter. After the refreshments I gave the guests clean white towels and bowls of orange-scented warm water to clean their hands in the traditional Arab manner. The professor was satisfied. He held a lively conversation with the German officers, and while I was singing the Arabic love ballad *"Ana bahebaak, Ya Muhammad"* (I love you, my Mohammed), he fell on his knees and kissed my hand.

In the summer of 1944, when the Russians broke through on the Ukrainian front and rolled towards Lemberg, Benchen again invited me to his office. His wife had joined him in Lemberg some months before to escape the British and American bombing attacks in Hamburg. She, too, was very friendly and helped me gather food for my hidden fugitives, but she never admitted to being aware of their presence.

"The Russians are coming," Benchen told me. "I know you would like to stay here and wait for liberation. But think of the dangers. Officially you are a pro-Nazi Arab princess who worked for a German headquarters. Before you have time to explain anything, you'll be raped or killed. You must get away and wait for the war's end in a quieter place. I hope to see you after the war if both of us are still alive."

Captain Benchen then gave me a letter recommending my services and sent me and Alma on a German army truck to Cracow. The nineteen Jewish fugitives were hidden in the cellar of the German headquarters, behind a pile of coal. Amid the coal was enough foodstuffs to last until the Russians arrived.

In Cracow I went to work for the German labor service, which sent me to Rabka, a resort in the Tatra Mountains. I met the Russians there in January 1945. Drunken Cossack cavalry troopers were raping women in the streets. When I saw two burly Russian troops riding toward my house, I went to meet them, carrying two bottles of vodka. By the time they had drained the vodka, they were so drunk they went to sleep on my porch.

I then went back to Cracow, where I met my second husband, Dr. Arad, an expert in international economics. After we were married we moved to Prague, where my husband helped reorganize the shattered Czechoslovak economy. From Prague we came home to Israel. My husband is now attached to the Israeli embassy in London. I divide my time between London and my daughter's home in Jerusalem.

Alma is now twenty-four. This year she received her M.D. from the Hebrew University of Jerusalem. Her husband is a doctor, too. When they were married five years ago, I insisted that they spend their honeymoon in Germany so that they could find General von Beutel and Captain Benchen. They found Benchen in Hamburg and honeymooned in his house.

When the Israeli Government learned how Benchen had saved us and other Jews at the risk of his own life, he was invited to visit Israel. He came to see us in Jerusalem a year ago. Older and gray-haired, he was still the same Peter Benchen.

—R.A. (as told to L.H.)

 ## The Blue Rug

This is the strange story of the blue rug that was among the seven huge oriental carpets spread out on the moist sand of Megiddo Hill in northern Israel, where Pope Paul VI met Israeli President Schneour Zalman Shazar and Prime Minister Levi Eshkol in 1964.

Six of the rugs had the traditional crimson background associated with the "red carpet" treatment for VIPs. The seventh, which had an intricate gold and silver design on a pale blue background, was out of harmony with the others and out of place as well. It had to be pushed in sideways, between the fourth and fifth red carpets.

Hillel Dar, one of the officials in charge of the Megiddo reception arrangements, revealed that the pale blue carpet was brought to him by Mrs. Sarah Cohen of Haifa, who begged him to spread it out on the ground for the pontiff to step upon. At first Dar refused. When Mrs. Cohen persisted, he decided she was a crackpot and had his hand on the phone to call the police when she told him a story that persuaded him to place the blue rug among the six red ones.

When Mrs. Cohen, her husband, and two children fled from Austria in 1938 after the Nazis occupied the country, only Fascist Italy, still resisting Nazi policies of brutal anti-Semitism, was willing to grant them temporary-residence permits. In a small village of northern Italy the Cohens waited for the certificates that would enable them to immigrate to Palestine. Mr. Cohen, a professional photographer, eked out a living of sorts by taking pictures of peasant weddings and religious ceremonies. Trapped by the outbreak of World War II, the Cohens no longer had any hope of getting their certificates to Palestine.

In 1941 the Nazis asked their Italian allies to deport to the Third Reich all refugees from Austria, Germany, Czechoslovakia, and Yugoslavia. For the Cohens, as for other Jews, this meant death in the concentration camps. The local police chief let the Cohens overstay their temporary-residence permit by five months, but ultimately, under German pressure, he was ordered to hand the refugees over to the Nazis at the border.

Mrs. Cohen took her children to Father Anselmo, the village priest, saying that she and her husband had decided on suicide rather than going back to Nazi-controlled Austria. She begged the priest to care for the children and to send them on to their people in Palestine after the war. The priest heard her out and then went to see the police chief. He told the startled official he would excommunicate him if he handed the Cohens over to the Germans.

The police chief said he didn't like to do it, but what choice did he have? "Lend me your official car," Father Anselmo said. The Swiss border was only forty miles away. Father Anselmo put Mr. Cohen and one of the children in the car trunk, in the bottom of which he drilled ventilation holes. Mrs. Cohen and the other child were instructed to lie face down on the car floor, behind the front seat. The priest then covered them with a threadbare blue carpet from his church, placed some vestments and candlesticks on the back seat, and drove to the Swiss frontier.

Parking the car near the barrier separating Italy from Switzerland, the priest told the frontier post commander that he and his men should line up for confession. While the officer and a few sergeants tried to improvise a confessional booth, Father Anselmo engaged the sentry at the barrier in conversation and gradually led him away from the car. He had at the same time managed to open the trunk and the right-hand door that faced the border. Tapping three times on the hood while the sentry's back was turned, the priest signaled the Cohens, who with their children had time to dart across into neutral Switzerland and freedom.

"We owe our lives to Father Anselmo," Mrs. Cohen explained to Dar. "We wrote him recently and heard that a younger priest had taken over from Father Anselmo, who was getting old and infirm. We remembered the worn blue carpet with which he had covered us in the escape car and decided to buy a new one for his church.

"It took us months to find the right kind of carpet, like the one that had shielded us twenty-three years ago. We had it embroidered with a quotation from the Bible—"Blessed Be The Righteous Ones"—in Latin and Hebrew. The letters formed part of the intricate design.

"When we heard that the Pope was coming to Israel, we decided to spread the carpet beneath his feet and then send it to Father Anselmo as an expression of our gratitude."

Acting on his own authority, Dar decided to include Mrs. Cohen's blue carpet among the six official red rugs. His Holiness walked over it twice, once on the way to the battery of microphones and again on the way back to his car. That same day the blue carpet was rolled up in a triple cardboard container, sealed by Haifa customs-control officials and sent by registered parcel post to Father Anselmo's church in the village of Laterina, Italy.

—L.H.

 ## How Rumkowski Died: A Holocaust Memoir

On August 30, 1944, I left the Lodz Ghetto together with my whole family, including my father, my mother, my older brother, and my younger sister. They had somehow succeeded in surviving the most horrible times in the ghetto. By this time there were only a handful of Jews left in the ghetto. We were sure that we were the last to leave. This conviction was confirmed when we saw, waiting on the same platform, Rumkowski, Rosenblatt, and all the other *Judenrat* elite. We were gathered at the railroad station outside the city—the one used for freight, not the station in the center of town, which was for passengers. Nevertheless, the mere presence of these "invincibles" gave us courage, a little hope that maybe the situation wasn't as bad as we suspected in our hearts.

Much has been written about Chaim Rumkowski, most notably Adolf Rudnicki's study *Kupiec Lodzki* (*The Lodz Merchant*), published in Warsaw in 1963. Rosenblatt has received less attention. He was a Germanized Polish Jew who, along with all the other Jews without German citizenship, was evicted from the Reich in 1938. In the Lodz Ghetto he became chief of police, not just of the ordinary police, whose function was merely to maintain law and order, but of the most horrible group of police, the *Sonderabteilung*, which cooperated with the Germans in the evacuation of the Jews from the ghetto to the camps. One story will suffice to indicate the extent of the hatred that existed in the ghetto toward Rosenblatt.

Some criminals from the Jewish underworld—which was very well established in Lodz even before the war—joined the ghetto's Jewish police force. They were needed for their strength, ruthlessness, and lack of moral scruples. Not all criminals chose to collaborate, however. One such was Moishe Hussid. A tough, heavy-set, gorillalike man, Moishe had once been a *yeshivah bocher*, hence his sobriquet "Hussid." After leaving the yeshivah for some undisclosed reason, he went on to become one of the most celebrated figures in the Jewish underworld of thieves and criminals. One day early in 1943 the German Kripo (criminal police) visited the Lodz Ghetto, as they did every week, confiscating any gold, silver, diamonds, or money that their network of informers led them to, and incidentally beating and even killing the unfortunate "hoarders" along the way. This particular day they collected a whole suitcase of valuables, locked it in their car, and left it for a short time. When they returned the suitcase was gone! The Kripo gave Rumkowski and Rosenblatt exactly twenty-four hours to find the suitcase and the thief. If the piece of luggage was not found, one hundred Jews would be publicly hanged. Special wall posters were quickly plastered all over the ghetto, imploring the burglar to come forward and save the lives of one hundred Jews. Unbelievably he came forward. It was Moishe Hussid.

Moishe Hussid was brought before Rosenblatt and, as the story (which spread like wildfire through the ghetto) is told, said to him, "I am a Jew with a Jewish heart. Jewish lives are worth more to me than gold and silver. You, you send thousands of Jews every month to Chelmno to die in gas chambers, and you do this to save your own skin. To me the lives of one hundred Jews are more important than my own life." Naturally he was arrested and deported.

And now, on August 30, 1944, this all-powerful Rosenblatt stood on the platform with the rest of us, waiting to enter the cattle cars just like the many thousands he had sent before him. Our journey to Auschwitz, which normally should have taken six or seven hours, took about fifteen hours. Our train was stopped many, many times in order to let "more important" traffic pass. We left in the evening and arrived in the late morning of the next day. As soon as we arrived at our destination, the doors were opened and everyone was immediately divided into two groups consisting of men and women. Then came the selection: to the right and to the left.

It is almost impossible for anyone who was not there to appreciate the depth and persistence of our ignorance. In retrospect it is clear where we were being taken, what *"Arbeit Macht Frei"* stood for, what it meant to go to the left or to the right. The reader will probably be incredulous when I insist that I, a sophisticated resistance leader, did not understand where I was and what was happening around me. We all knew in a vague way that there were death camps, but we had no idea where we stood in the process at any given moment. I was clutching my father so tightly that I did not even see which way the SS man was directing me with his baton. I wanted very badly to stay with my father, but at the last second —I don't know why—I went to the left, where my brother had gone, and not with my father to the right. I never saw my parents again.

Those of us on the left were ordered to march five abreast, flanked by a double column of German guards with dogs. Suddenly we saw a most amazing sight. There, to our left, was a special platform, a reviewing stand, like a small amphitheater, with three or four steps leading up to the dais. In the center sat Rumkowski, surrounded by Rosenblatt and their entourage, looking for all the world like heads of state reviewing their troops, while we, their "troops," marched past, a most bedraggled military parade. Thus did the Germans cynically keep up the charade of *Judenrat* power until the bitter end.

We were marched to a place in Auschwitz called "Canada." Canada, even more than the United States, had been the symbol in Eastern Europe for a land flowing with milk and honey and, indeed, those prisoners who lived in "Canada" led a very good life. They were the primary helpers of the Germans. They served in the disinfection process, in the gas chambers, removing the bodies, and so forth. Every half year or so they were themselves killed and replaced by others. The Germans wanted no witnesses. But while they lived there, they lived "well," if one can use such a term under the circumstances. At least they never went hungry. A few of them, possibly because they had proved their worth to the Germans, managed to establish very strong positions for themselves within "Canada" and survived the periodic turnovers. Such a one was Moishe Hussid.

No sooner did we arrive in "Canada" than our hero from the Lodz Ghetto appeared. For the first time we realized that the Germans had not killed him after the "suitcase" affair. Prisoners weren't allowed to speak, but a ripple went through the crowd, whispering his identity to those who didn't recognize him. The first words he growled were, "Where is Rosenblatt?" To my surprise Rosenblatt was standing a few rows behind me, to my left. *Sic transit gloria mundi.* The massive, bearlike Moishe Hussid gently took hold of Rosenblatt by the wrist and, like a cat relishing its captured mouse, delicately led him to the front row. In a voice dripping with mock politeness Moishe Hussid cooed in Yiddish so that all could hear:

"Aaah, Rosenblatt, finally you are here. I have been waiting for you a long, long time. I was determined not to die until I saw you again. Now I have a proposal for you."

Here he stooped down and picked up a shaving razor from the ground. Handing it to Rosenblatt, he continued:

"You are such an important Jew. You are such a hero. You had so much courage when it came to killing thousands and thousands of Jews. Now, please, have the courage to kill yourself."

Rosenblatt took the razor and stared at it, frozen, in a state of shock.

"I am doing you a big favor, Rosenblatt, by giving you this chance to kill yourself. Because if you don't do it, I will do it for you; but I warn you, it will be a horrible, horrible death."

Rosenblatt could not make a move.

Then Moishe Hussid started in on him. He began by making him jump up and down, froglike, with knees bent and arms outstretched, I don't know how many times. This was followed by some relatively mild torture, clearly the hors d'oeuvres. Meanwhile the rest of us were herded inside a huge barracks for disinfection. Our heads, armpits, and pubic hair were all crudely shaven and into our painfully raw skin was rubbed benzol, a harsh, irritating fluid. All our clothing was taken away. We were left standing naked, except for our belts, which we were allowed to keep. I happened to have a special belt, the kind without holes that closes automatically. At that moment Moishe Hussid came into the barracks, dragging the by now bloody and beaten Rosenblatt. Moishe Hussid had the look of a half-crazed animal. He was in a virtual ecstasy of violence. He looked wildly around for a belt. His eyes lit on me—he took my belt! (For a long time thereafter I had no belt—in Auschwitz no easy thing to obtain.) He made a noose out of my belt, placed it around Rosenblatt's neck, and swung him around and around until his eyes bulged and he was blue in the face. He stopped at the brink of death, threw cold water on him to revive him, saying, "No, no, you cannot die yet," and proceeded to put his barely conscious victim into a steaming hot shower. Rosenblatt's screams were horrible. When he was taken out, he looked like a scalded chicken, his skin red and broken. He was unconscious but somehow still alive. Moishe Hussid began to jump and dance on him, breaking his bones with his heavy wooden shoes. Finally a German in civilian clothes entered, tapped Moishe in a comradely way on the shoulder, and calmly said, "Moishe, *genug.* Enough. Finish with him."

There were two places in Auschwitz where the Germans disposed of Jewish bodies. One was the crematorium, the other a huge open pit in which a fire blazed twenty-four hours a day. Into this pit were thrown "surplus" Jews for whom there was no room in the gas chambers when the daily transport was too large. (Toward the end, eight such huge pits were dug.) They also threw children, old people, and invalids—from whom they feared no resistance—into the pit. This also saved on expensive gas. The pit was about thirty or forty meters from the barracks where we were disinfected. When, that night, they took us to see the pit in order to break our spirit, its fiery flames against the sky made me absolutely sure I was in hell. Not in a place that metaphorically resembled hell, but really in hell itself. And it was into this pit that Moishe Hussid threw the unconscious Rosenblatt.

Earlier, during the torture of Rosenblatt in the hot shower, there was an interruption, and Moishe Hussid was seen carrying an old man with a shock of white hair, also unconscious, on his back. It was Rumkowski! Moishe Hussid took him out the same door that led to the pit. When he came back, he said to us with great satisfaction, "Now I have finished with the two of them." Describing with a mixture of glee and contempt the last minutes of the former "dictator," Moishe Hussid added that Rumkowski had been so terrified that he was *"bekakt un hot geshtinken."* In other words, fear had made him lose control of his bowels. *"Der Alter,* the Elder—he stunk something awful."

After the war I sent my testimony to the Institute of Jewish History in Warsaw and to Yad Vashem in Jerusalem. However, I never could find out what happened to Moishe Hussid. Twenty years passed and I immigrated to Israel. Nine more years passed. One night I happened to be on neighborhood patrol duty. My partner was my downstairs neighbor, also a Jew from the Lodz Ghetto, who had relatives in Munich. To pass the time I started telling the story of Rumkowski. As soon as I mentioned the name Moishe Hussid, he interrupted me excitedly. "What? Moishe Hussid? I know him! I talked with him two years ago in Munich!"

"He is in Munich? I am ready to fly there immediately!"

"You are too late. He died eight months ago."

Discreet inquiries to his widow in Munich revealed that not even she knew anything about Rumkowski and Rosenblatt. So Moishe Hussid died without telling a single soul about how he killed Rumkowski and Rosenblatt in Auschwitz.

—M.C.

 ## A Polish Jew Thanks the Polish Pope

It was a day in July. From the hills of Jerusalem I was driven to Ben-Gurion Airport, bound for Rome. It was a trip I had made before, but never in such a curious emotional state.

My mind focused not on Rome, the modern European capital I knew, but on the imperial city of Titus. The plane I boarded became a time capsule taking me back to witness the Hebrew captives being led in chains by the triumphant Roman legions, the precious vessels of the Temple profaned in the hands of the conqueror.

Was this a pilgrimage to weep over bitter history? To redeem my ancient brethren? Vivid as the images were, I realized that I was concerned not with the ancient martyrs but with the haunting ghosts of my own generation.

Jerusalem to Rome, from my Eternal City to "theirs." No, not "mine" and "theirs." *Both* cities played a role in the lives and history of Jews and Judaism, and in that sense *both* are part of me. Jerusalem gave Jews life and spirit and glory; Rome taught Jews to survive, despite slavery and persecution, so that we might return to freedom.

But I am a survivor in a literal as well as a spiritual sense. I am a survivor of the Holocaust, saved as an infant by a devout Polish Catholic woman who changed my name, claimed I was her child, and had me baptized. For the first few years of my life I did not know I was a Jew, that my real parents were in concentration camps, and that most of my family had been killed by the Nazis.

Now I was to participate in a private audience with the pope, granted to a small delegation of Americans, Jews, and Polish Catholics. I was to meet the personification of the Christian world, His Holiness, Pope John Paul II, like me of Polish birth. I thought of the role played by the Catholic Church in the persecution of my people. I thought of the silence and indifference of most of the Catholic world to Hitler's "final solution." I thought of the manifold indifference to the anguished cries for help from the Jews sealed behind the walls of the Warsaw Ghetto, of the complicity of segments of the Polish population in the "accomplishments" of Treblinka and Auschwitz.

Why, then, this sense of anticipation, this inner desire to meet a Polish pope? Was it because I had survived the Holocaust while a million and a half other Jewish children perished?

My survival was a miracle, but the instrument of that miracle was Bronislawa Kurpi, the Polish Catholic woman who risked her life to save a human being. To me this pope I was to visit represented not the history of the Catholic Church but the embodiment of my own survival. I was going to meet another Pole, a Catholic priest who had also risked personal safety by opposing the evils of Nazism in his native parish. I looked forward to expressing my gratitude for that part of Christianity that had motivated Bronislawa Kurpi to act as she did.

But my emotions were mixed and tempered by the knowledge that after the liberation my adoptive mother refused to return me to my parents and to Judaism and forced them to litigate the question of custody. I was pained by the thought that possibly hundreds of Jewish children, perhaps thousands, who had been saved by Christians would never know that they were Jews. I wondered if they were part of the throngs of devout Catholics who had lined the streets of Poland to catch a glimpse of the pope I was going to meet.

The audience had a formal purpose—to honor Janusz Korczak, a brilliant Polish-Jewish educator and physician, a pioneer in the field of child welfare. Although he might have survived, he had chosen to perish in the Treblinka gas chambers rather than abandon the orphans in his charge. To honor his memory and his ideals, the Anti-Defamation League, on whose staff I have served for fourteen years, and representatives of the Polish-American community had cooperatively established the Janusz Korczak Prize, an award to be made annually to the author of a children's book exemplifying Dr. Korczak's principles.

We arrived in Rome. The next day the Malta Guards saluted us as we entered the gates of the Vatican. We were led through magnificent rooms, full of religious art and artifacts, to an antechamber that looked out on St. Peter's Square. From there we were escorted into the pope's library, where, standing at the door, he greeted us warmly and individually. He then proceeded to an elevated chair in the center of the library, our delegation flanking him on either side.

The purpose of our visit was explained. Gifts were presented. I stepped forward.

"Your Holiness," I said, "I was born in Baranowicze, Poland; I am a survivor of the Holocaust. I am alive today because of the compassion and humanity of a Polish Catholic woman who risked her life to save me from the Nazis. I want to again express my thanks to her through you. I ask that you bless her soul."

The pontiff leaned forward on his chair.

I continued: "I have just come from Jerusalem, the reestablished capital of the State of Israel and world Jewry. I bring you as a gift a soon-to-be issued Israeli Pilgrims Medal expressing the concept of *Yerushalayim, Ir Hakodesh,* Jerusalem, the Holy City, and *Yisrael, Eretz Hakodesh,* Israel, the Holy Land." The medallion has a sixteenth-century map in which Jerusalem appears at the center of three continents. There is also a verse from Isaiah: "They all gather and come to you."

He stood with his arms outstretched. "Thank you, it is a beautiful medallion," he said. "Thank you for your very moving words. Thank you for what you have said, for you are bearing testimony to human kindness." Speaking slowly and deliberately, he told us he was pleased that Polish-American Catholics and American Jews had joined forces in a project to pay tribute to Janusz Korczak.

"It is important in our age," he said, "to find symbols of human kindness, human dignity, and human rights—and you have chosen well." He blessed us for our efforts.

He chatted informally as a photographer recorded the meeting. "We are delighted with your courage and your forthright statements on human rights," a member of our delegation told him. "Don't thank me yet," he said, "I have only begun."

As we prepared to leave, we expressed our appreciation for his visit to the Warsaw Ghetto and to Auschwitz, and for his statements there. He shook hands with me, squeezing my hand in his. "Thank you for your precious words," he said softly.

It had lasted forty minutes—forty moving, touching minutes with a spiritual leader who exuded sincerity, trust, and understanding. From Jerusalem to Rome.

A memorable encounter between a Polish-born survivor of the Holocaust and the first Polish-born pope, Janusz Pawal II.

—A.H.F.

 ## Vengeance or Justice? An Israeli Sailor Kills His Parents' Nazi Murderer

There is a Rumanian Jewish immigrant in Israel, a man now in his forties, who stood trial for deserting his ship while it was on a voyage to Marseilles, and who was exonerated because of rather unusual extenuating circumstances. He is well, working, and would probably like to forget a chapter in his life that spanned the period when he was a boy of ten and ended when he was in his thirties. It is a footnote to the history of the Jewish people of the past half century and deserves to be remembered.

The story begins in a small town in Rumania, where the Israeli was then a small Jewish child living with his parents. There had been a tiny, thriving Jewish community in that town for as long as anyone could remember. When reports of the rise of nazism in Germany began to filter into the town, they seemed to emanate from a distant planet. Little notice was taken of the reports by the local Jewish population.

Even after the war broke out in 1939 and Poland was invaded by the Germans, the Jews in that particular town felt secure in their remoteness. But by 1942 things changed. Jews living in the Balkans now began to feel threatened. Reports that the Nazis planned to exterminate all Jews in Europe had begun to circulate.

One day a local policeman who had known that particular family all his life arrived at the family home, accompanied by a patrol of uniformed Nazi followers. They demanded money, began to ransack the premises, an argument ensued—and the boy of ten watched with disbelief as both his mother and father were shot and killed in a matter of moments. What happened after that is not clear, except that the child was taken in hand by relatives and a few years later, just prior to the establishment of Israel, he managed to reach a haven in Palestine.

For a while he lived in a youth village. Later he joined a family from his hometown that helped raise him. He became an ardent, patriotic citizen of Israel, and except at night he never thought of that terrible day when his parents were murdered in front of his eyes.

But the nights were something else. He had continuing nightmares and often awoke in a cold sweat; the name and face of the policeman, wearing a swastika armband, who had destroyed his family continued to haunt him.

When he was of age he entered military service and was assigned to the fledgling Israeli Navy. Once, on a goodwill visit to France, he and his fellow crew members were given shore leave at the port of Marseilles. As sailors are wont to do, the young Israelis paid a visit to several local bars. Conversations were struck up among the Israelis and the French patrons, and talk turned to the French Foreign Legion, at the time still an active force recruiting volunteers for service in North Africa and Indochina. One of the Frenchmen mentioned that the week before there had been a large group of Rumanian ex-Nazis in the bar, enjoying themselves just before taking up their new posts as Legionnaires in Algeria.

The young Israeli sailor felt a chill run down his spine. He had a sudden thought that the policeman whose name and face he could never forget was among them. Without planning to do so, he found himself drifting away from his fellow crew members. As though driven by an impulse over which he had no control, he stepped into a men's clothing store, purchased a suit, shirt, and hat, deposited his Israeli uniform in a trash basket, and within a matter of hours—when he was certain that his ship had sailed without him—he presented himself at the nearest office of the French Foreign Legion and offered his services. He described himself as a former Rumanian and asked that he be assigned to any unit where he could be with fellow Rumanians.

Within a matter of weeks the young man was wearing a French Foreign Legionnaire's uniform and had been assigned to a unit replete with ex-Rumanian Nazis in a camp not far from Algiers. Gradually he made friends with his ex-countrymen. One lazy afternoon he casually dropped the name of the policeman he now realized he was chasing with murder in his heart.

One of the ex-Rumanians knew him and volunteered the information that he was now a sergeant and had been stationed in that very camp until about three months ago, when he was transferred to the Indo-Chinese front, where the French were still deeply embroiled in what was to be a prelude to America's tragic Vietnamese adventure.

The young Israeli posing as a Rumanian waited a few days and then asked for a transfer to Indochina, announcing that he wanted to see some action. His wish was granted and in a matter of a few weeks he was stationed in a Legion camp deep in the Indo-Chinese fighting zone. He began to make inquiries, to look at lists of sergeants, and then, only a few weeks after his arrival, he spotted the man's name. He was located in a camp a few miles away.

Somehow the Israeli deserter made his way to the camp, and somehow he found his quarry alone, sitting in his tent, writing a letter. The young Israeli recognized him immediately, but of course the Rumanian had no inkling as to who his visitor was. According to the trial records, the Israeli announced to the Legionnaire sergeant that he was the little boy who had witnessed the murder of his parents in a small town in Rumania many years ago. While the Rumanian tried to understand what had been said to him, the Israeli plunged a knife into him, killing him on the spot.

Although he was half expecting to be apprehended, nothing happened. It had all taken place quietly and quickly. No one saw him enter the tent, there was no outcry, no struggle. The Israeli left the camp, made his way back to his own headquarters, succeeded in doing what few ever succeeded in doing—deserting the Legion and getting away with it. Posing as a seaman who had lost his papers in a barroom brawl, he managed to return to Israel and immediately gave himself up to the Israeli naval authorities.

A secret trial was held and the young man's story was checked and rechecked. His voluntary return to Israel and his perfect record up to that point counted in his favor. The court ordered him dismissed from the service, quietly, and his having gone AWOL was ignored. The records of the case were sealed.

The Israeli's name is known to a small number of people, and because Israel is a small country, word of his act of vengeance gradually filtered down to a wider circle. Whether or not his years of nightmares have finally left him is not known.

—D.C.G.

A Rabbi Saved Priests Who Earlier Had Saved Jews

A letter written in Latin and postmarked Vatican City was delivered a few months ago to the desk of Colonel David Kahana, chief chaplain of the Israeli Air Force. It was signed by a cardinal of the Roman Catholic Church, who is the head of a permanent commission that investigates beatification claims and makes final recommendations concerning eventual elevation to sainthood. The communication sought information about the late Count Andrew Sheptytsky, metropolitan of the Ukrainian Catholic Church.

To millions of Ukrainians the count is a true Christian saint, but Moscow is trying to prevent his beatification at all costs. Because the Ukrainians venerate the count as their greatest nationalist leader, the Soviet leaders want to prove that he was not a saint but a pro-Nazi collaborator and war criminal. Books, films, and other propaganda have been employed by Moscow to vilify the late metropolitan as an agent of the Gestapo.

The only surviving witness who personally knew the late count and who can disprove the Soviet charges is Rabbi Kahana. I met the tough-looking rabbi-colonel, known as the "fighting rabbi" throughout the Israeli armed forces, in the concrete-and-steel building that houses the general headquarters of the Israeli Air Force.

When I brought up the name of the count, Chaplain Kahana was visibly moved. For a moment the clock of history seemed to turn back to July 1942, in the Ukrainian city of Lvov (Lemberg), where Nazi officers amused themselves by using Jewish children for target practice. Placing his right hand on the Holy Book, Colonel Kahana said, "I am willing to swear on the Bible that Count Sheptytsky was one of the greatest humanitarians in the history of mankind, certainly the best friend we Jews ever had. I say this not just because he saved my wife, my child, and myself but because he was instrumental in rescuing hundreds of other Jews from certain death.

"When I met him, he was over eighty, paralyzed, and near death, but not broken in spirit. He was well past the need to seek 'respectability insurance' or political gain. And he was aware that when the Nazis found Jews hiding in a church or monastery, they shot all the priests and monks and either razed the buildings or converted them into barracks. If the metropolitan was willing to risk his priests and churches, he was moved by true Christianity, by love of our Jewish people, and by a sense of national responsibility. He realized that the enemies of the Ukrainian people would blame the actions of pogrom mobs and ragtag militia on the entire Ukrainian nation. He therefore decreed that it was the sacred duty of every nationally conscious Ukrainian priest to save as many Jews as possible. Sheptytsky was a Zionist sympathizer and a firm believer in the messianic mission of the Jewish people. In 1942, when Jews were being butchered in the gas chambers of Auschwitz and Treblinka and slaughtered in the lime-filled pits on the outskirts of a thousand European towns and cities, Sheptytsky predicted the creation of an independent Jewish state in the Holy Land."

Pausing only to brush away tears of emotion from his steel-gray eyes, Chaplain Kahana recalled that before World War II Lvov was part of the Polish Republic. "I was the Jewish military chaplain attached to Lvov garrison troops," he said, "and the rabbi of the Syxtus Street Synagogue and Jewish theology teacher in the city's high schools. One of my best friends was Dr. Gabriel Kostelnik, a Ukrainian priest who filled comparable posts on behalf of the Ukrainian Catholic Church.

"After the German invasion of Poland, the Nazis tried to wipe out the two hundred thousand Jews of Lvov and the surrounding hamlets with the aid of pogrom mobs, drunken peasants, and locally recruited militia. But when the Nazis saw that there was more looting than actual killing, and that criminal elements were fighting each other over the spoils rather than murdering Jews, the Nazis brought in the notorious Einsatz-Kommando Lemberg and got down to business with Teutonic thoroughness. Slave-labor roundups, street massacres, and mass executions followed with agonizing frequency.

"Helpless against the tidal wave of murder and destruction, we sought to save our Torah scrolls, synagogue records, and various sacred books. The only safe place was in the crypts of Catholic churches and monasteries. Together with Rabbi Hamaydess, a famous leader of Polish Jewry, I went to see Dr. Kostelnik and asked for an introduction to Metropolitan Sheptytsky. We had already been herded into a ghetto, forced to wear yellow badges, and forbidden to enter the city proper on pain of death. Rabbi Hamaydess could not pose as a Christian, but I shaved off my beard, tore off my yellow badges, and stole out at night to see the metropolitan in his palace on Mount St. George.

"In the old-fashioned, high-ceilinged room that was the metropolitan's office I saw him pushed in in his wheelchair. Grasping my hand in his two hands, he said gently, 'I see trouble brings you to me, my son. Please sit down and tell me about it.'

"When I described the suffering of my people, he broke down and cried. 'I know all about it,' he told me quietly, 'and I have sent several letters to all priests with orders to have them read to their congregations in all churches. I have warned my people that any person helping the Nazis to persecute or kill Jews will be doomed to eternal damnation. But I am sorry to say that there is little more I can do than protest. I have also sent notes to all German officials of the Occupation Administration and to Himmler himself, protesting against the use of Ukrainian troops in anti-Jewish actions. These young Ukrainians volunteered to fight communists, but instead of deploying them at the front the Nazis are forcing them to participate in the massacres of helpless Jews. The answer I received was an insulting warning to mind my own business, and that but for my age I would have been shot for interceding on behalf of the Jews. My son, I can only pray for you and your people and hope that prayer helps. Tell me how I can help, besides praying, and I'll do everything in my power . . .'

"I asked the metropolitan to save the Torah scrolls from the synagogues, and the children whose parents had been killed by the Nazis and who were due to die themselves in the next German roundup. The metropolitan called in his brother, Clement, who was in charge of all Ukrainian monasteries, and the Ihumena Josepha, the head of all convents. Both declared themselves ready to help. But since the Nazis were raiding Christian orphanages and ordering all boys to parade naked to see whether any of them were circumcised, I was asked to select mostly Jewish girls for the first rescue operation.

"The first rescue operation took place on the night of August 14, 1942, when two hundred Jewish children, including the sons of Rabbis Hamaydess and Levin and my own daughter, were smuggled out of the ghetto to monasteries and convents, where they were concealed in crypts and given forged certificates of baptism and Ukrainian-sounding names. Then they were dispersed among convent schools and Catholic orphanages in and around Lvov. All of them survived the Nazi occupation and the war because the priests, nuns, and monks risked torture and death as they played a deadly game of outwitting Nazi spies, collaborators, and stool pigeons. The greatest satisfaction of my life was to gather these Jewish children after the war and smuggle them out of Soviet Russia to Israel via an underground Zionist railroad, and then to watch them grow up in a land of their own, serve in the armed forces, get married, raise families, and forget their tragic past.

"After hiding my daughter safely, the Ihumena Josepha asked me to bring my wife to the convent. The mother superior took my wife to the priest in charge of administration registers, who provided her with forged documents identifying her as a native-born Ukrainian Catholic. He also furnished her with a false birth certificate, threw a nun's homespun brown robe around her shoulders, and escorted her to the German Population Registry Office. There my wife received a Ukrainian identity card, stamped by the German Occupation Administration, food ration tickets, a domicile permit, and other essential documents.

"Thanks to the mother superior and the priest, whose name I never learned, my wife was able to pose as a Ukrainian nun and to move freely about the city. She was my prinicipal contact between the ghetto and the monasteries. When the ghetto was liquidated, she maintained a liaison between fugitive Jews and the Ukrainian Church leadership. She slept in the Ihumena Josepha's own cell at the convent, went to church to avoid suspicion, and thus avoided exposure and capture for two years.

"When the Nazis liquidated the Lvov ghetto, I was among the Jewish men grabbed by the Nazis and thrown into the Janowski concentration camp. Each day thousands were killed by the Nazi guards while others were crippled and emaciated by hunger, beatings, and disease. During those terrible weeks in Janowski I lost all faith in humanity, and I might have lost my faith in God, too, but for the shining example of Metropolitan Sheptytsky, his brother, Clement, the Ihumena Josepha, and hundreds of nameless Ukrainian monks, priests, and nuns.

"Desperately looking for a chance to escape before the Nazis killed me in one of their cruel and senseless games, my opportunity came during a sudden rainstorm that flooded the drainage ditches and turned the camp into a morass. While the guards huddled in their watchtowers, studded with searchlights and machine guns, and the police dogs took cover beneath the watchtower trestles, I crawled on my belly through mud and puddles to the northernmost corner of the fence. Earlier I had noticed that some ricocheting bullets fired by the guards into a group of Jewish prisoners had torn down a few strands of the barbed wire and had not yet been repaired.

"It took me an eternity to get through the gap in the first fence of wire and to disentangle myself from the twisted concertina wire of the second security fence. Rolling in the mud to hide from a searchlight's probing beam, and burrowing through excrement and pools of coagulating blood to kill the scent of a human body whenever a dog barked, I managed to reach the dilapidated wooden buildings of a Lvov suburb. From there I ran uphill towards the metropolitan's palace on Mount St. George.

"When a sleepy monk finally opened a small barred window in response to my frantic knocking at the night gate, he took one look at me—ragged, dirty, emaciated, bleeding from wounds and scratches, and evil-smelling—crossed himself, and shut the gate in my face. I knocked again but there was no answer. Just as I heard the jackbooted steps of a Nazi patrol approaching, the gate was suddenly opened and another monk dragged me inside. 'Brother Mykola almost fainted when he saw you,' the monk explained. 'He thought you were a ghostly apparition.'

"I must have been a repulsive sight as I followed the monk to the metropolitan's private apartment. But the prelate of the Ukrainian Catholic Church embraced me and kissed me and ordered his secretary to take me to a hot bath, burn my rags, and dress me in a monk's robes. The metropolitan was still waiting for me, despite the late hour, when I came out of the bath. He wept again and asked me to tell him of my life in the Nazi camp. For two hours I talked, until at dawn the metropolitan asked me to join him in prayer. I helped him out of his wheelchair and supported him as he knelt before the crucifix. He prayed in his way and I in mine.

"I remained hidden in Count Sheptytsky's private library. Food was brought to me there. Only at night did I go out for a walk in the walled palace garden. In the spring of 1943 the metropolitan was taken down in the garden every day at dusk. He sent away the monk who was his guide and I pushed the chair for an hour through the flower-rimmed garden paths as we talked about politics, philosophy, psychology, and theology. Needless to say, the metropolitan never tried to convert me. Once he gave me an old book to read. It was a Ukrainian priest's account of a visit to the Holy Land, which ended with a description of Jewish suffering throughout the ages and a prediction that the Jews were doomed to weep forever because they had rejected Jesus.

"When the metropolitan inquired if I had finished the book, and I replied in the affirmative, he suddenly seized my hand, kissed it, and, in a voice choked with tears, apologized. Everybody kissed the metropolitan's hand, and he himself had to kiss only the pope's hand, so I could not understand why he was apologizing so tearfully to a fugitive rabbi. The metropolitan explained that at a time when the Nazis were butchering Jews, it was a tactless mistake on his part to let me read a book whose author denied the Jewish people all hope unless they accepted Christianity. He insisted that I accept his apology.

"When I tell you that Andrew Sheptytsky was a saint, I do not exaggerate. I am a professional officer, with twenty years of military service—five in the Polish army and fifteen in the Israeli armed services. I am an Orthodox rabbi and a doctor of philosophy and theology. I know human nature and I know that the qualities which make a saint are so rare as to be almost nonexistent. But Count Sheptytsky possessed them all.

"Besides the count's brother, Clement, the Ihumena Josepha, and the hundreds of Ukrainian clergy who risked their lives to save Jews, there was Father Marko, a village priest who rescued more than forty Jewish children from Nazi firing squads. Later I had an opportunity to help him escape to the United States.

"After World War II, following Count Sheptytsky's death and the suppression of an anti-Soviet uprising by Ukrainian guerillas, the Soviet authorities imprisoned, exiled, or executed most of the Ukrainian priests. I was then a colonel in the Polish Army and also associated with an underground Zionist organization which operated an escape route from Russia across Poland and Czechoslovakia to the American occupation zones in Germany and Austria.

"To avoid certain death the Ukrainian priests who had helped me masquerade as a Ukrainian now had to pose as pious Jews with beards and sidelocks. After crossing the River San into Poland, they made their way to Warsaw, where they contacted me. Now I was able to repay their kindness. When elderly, pious-looking 'Jews' were seen entering my apartment, the [local security] officers assumed that leaders of surviving Jewish congregations had come to ask me for assistance or to discuss religious problems.

"I gave the priests false identification cards and smuggled them out of Poland with transports of Israel-bound Jews. When the transports passed through western Germany, the priests were guided to Ukrainian displaced persons camps, where they received new documents and visas for the United States and Canada. I compiled a list of over 240 such priests and monks who had rescued Jews from the Nazis. But the list is not complete.

"The Kremlin is ruled by the same kind of gangster regime which brought shame and ruin to Nazi Germany. That is why it is my duty to tell the truth about Count Sheptytsky, the only saint I recognize."*

Outside, supersonic Israeli jet fighters streaked across the sky. Rabbi Kahana pointed upwards and said, "You see this fighter formation? Four pilots in this squadron are among the children saved by Metropolitan Sheptytsky and his aides."

—L.H.

 ## Between Rosh Hashanah and Yom Kippur the Danes Saved Their Jews

While most of the nations under the Nazi yoke either stood by passively or, indeed, actively collaborated in the dispatch of six million Jews to the death camps during the ten Days of Penitence, between Rosh Hashanah and Yom Kippur, in the year 1943, the people of German-occupied Denmark managed to evacuate the country's entire Jewish population to a safe haven in neutral Sweden.

Bent Melchior, today the chief rabbi of Denmark, remembers the sequence of events during that period as though they had occurred yesterday. The Nazis had planned a roundup of the country's eight thousand Jews on October 1, 1943—it was the second day of Rosh Hashanah that year—when everyone would be conveniently assembled in the synagogue or at home, easy prey for the Sonderkommando (special commando) units of the Gestapo, handpicked by Eichmann himself for the mission.

German troop ships were anchored in Copenhagen, ready to transport the intended victims to the depot on the German coast where freight cars had been assembled for the final stage of the journey to the crematoria of Auschwitz and Bergen-Belsen.

But when the storm troopers, in a series of carefully executed simultaneous raids, descended upon the synagogues and the Jewish homes, they found that their quarry had vanished. The Danish underground had uncovered the plan in time, and all of the Jews of the country had been hidden away in the homes of fellow Danes—in basements and attics, in churches and hospitals.

In the course of the next ten days the refugees were smuggled out of Denmark and conveyed by an improvised fleet of rowboats and fishing vessels to sanctuary in Sweden, less than an hour away across the narrow waters of the Oresund.

As a teen, Bent Melchior was among those who escaped and found refuge in Sweden for the remainder of the war. A few years later, as a young man, he was

* Count Sheptytsky was not beatified.

one of a group of Danish Jews who made their way "illegally" to Palestine to join the Haganah in the 1948 War of Independence.

A "Thanks to Scandinavia" committee keeps alive the memory of the historic rescue in the United States. The group, founded by Richard Netter, a prominent New York lawyer, and Victor Borge, the pianist (and a Danish-born Jew), has raised more than one million dollars to provide scholarships for Scandinavian students studying in the United States.

Rabbi Melchior notes that the "living, most enduring tribute to the rescue is our community in Denmark—there are now ten thousand of us, the greatest number of Jews there has ever been here, and they are young, involved, more religiously committed."

—G.L.

 ## Is Swedish Savior of Forty Thousand Jews Languishing in Siberia?

Is Raoul Wallenberg alive? Has he been secretly imprisoned by the Russians for more than thirty years? And if so, why? Is this man's life—if he still lives—to be sacrificed because Soviet officials are too embarrassed, after so many years, to admit that he was arrested without cause in the first place, and would rather let him languish in a Soviet jail than admit they had unjustly imprisoned not a criminal but a truly remarkable hero who personally saved the lives of thousands of Hungarian Jews at the time of the Nazi takeover of Hungary?

The story reads like something out of a *Catch-22* mold, and yet no one has been able to shake the Russians loose from their constantly repeated denial that Swedish diplomat Raoul Wallenberg is still alive. The Moscow statements over the years have never varied: Wallenberg is dead; case closed.

But is he? And who is this martyred man whose life—if he still lives—has been so cruelly destroyed, after he himself rose to the highest peaks of human potential by courageously jeopardizing his own life and enabling large numbers of innocent men, women, and children to survive and to live out their allotted years?

One Hungarian Jew who was saved by Wallenberg claims that the total number of Jews who were rescued by the Swedish diplomat is not less than forty thousand. Over the years the Swedish Government, which had remained neutral in World War II, has been severely criticized for having abandoned its own national to this fate. More recently, after a growing number of revelations and reports have surfaced—including those of Nazi hunter Simon Wiesenthal and a former Soviet Jewish prisoner in a Siberian labor camp who is now a resident of Israel—claiming that Wallenberg is alive, a strange new twist to this already convoluted story emerged.

A bare outline of Wallenberg's life and deeds has been documented and substantiated:

In May 1944, a full year before the Nazis surrendered, Wallenberg was a young Swedish diplomat stationed in Budapest. The situation of the Jews had steadily worsened as the war wore on, but now insane energy seemed to seize the Nazis as they drove ever harder to round up the Jews of Hungary and ship them off to death camps—impending defeat staring them in the face or not. Appalled by the prospect of mass murder of the Jews—and racing against time, since he was convinced the Nazi tyranny would terminate soon—Wallenberg concocted a Swedish "protective passport," thereby saving forty thousand Jews.

The next month he placed eight thousand Jewish children in a Swedish "camp" located in Hungary, thus assuring their safety. Immediately thereafter, getting some help from the Vatican, he created an "international ghetto," enabling some twenty-two thousand Jews to survive.

As the Russians approached Hungary from the east, the Germans became more panic stricken and ferocious. In December 1944 German units surrounded the two zones of safety established by Wallenberg, now housing some forty thousand Jews, and threatened to destroy all the inhabitants. Wallenberg threw diplomatic niceties out the window: Unafraid for his own life, he confronted the Germans, warning them that if they initiated any attack whatsoever against the Jews, he would see to it that every one of those involved would stand trial as war criminals. The Germans retreated, abandoning their plan of destruction of the Jews, and Wallenberg breathed a sigh of relief when the Soviet troops finally reached the Hungarian capital in January 1945.

His relief was short-lived: when Wallenberg, who now felt himself responsible for the lives and safety of his forty thousand Jewish charges, tried to buy urgently needed food supplies from the Russians, he was arrested. The pretext they used was that he was carrying large amounts of valuables; his explanation that he had been entrusted with these by the Jews for safekeeping fell on deaf ears. The Russians seized the valuables, arrested the Swedish official (regarded by the Jews as their personal saint), and shipped him to the Soviet Union.

The war ended in the spring of 1945. From then until 1957 the Swedish Government sent diplomatic missives to Moscow: Release Wallenberg, they said. The Soviets' customary reply was simply "We don't have him."

Then, lo and behold, in 1957 Moscow issued a death certificate claiming that Wallenberg had died in prison ten years earlier! The document was considered a fabrication; former Russian prisoners who managed to contact the West reported that Wallenberg was alive and in jail. In 1974, not quite three decades after the war ended, the acclaimed Russian author Solzhenitsyn wrote of having seen Wallenberg in prison, of talking with him, and learning from his own lips the man's incredible story. Two years ago Simon Wiesenthal wrote that Wallenberg was now incarcerated in a Siberian hospital for the mentally ill. Although a Christian, in a real sense Wallenberg, too, is a full-fledged victim of the Holocaust.

To this day the Swedish Government has still not succeeded in prying loose the truth from the Russians and getting Wallenberg released. People like Wallenberg come along very rarely in human history, and they should be defended and watched over with zeal.

—D.C.G.

IX
The Precepts of the
Jewish Way of Life

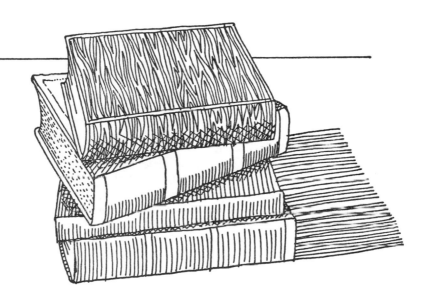

Resurrection: A Jewish View

The belief in resurrection vis-à-vis Judaism and the nature of such belief have been constantly changing. Among the early Hebrews there was no belief in resurrection. Shortly after Daniel, who lived in the fifth or sixth century before the present era, there appears to have been a definite belief that there would be resurrection for the righteous.

Along with the development of the thought of a Messiah who would lead the Jews back to Palestine and there re-create the Jewish nation in an ideal kingdom under ideal conditions, there arose the belief in resurrection.

The Jews envisioned a reconstituted world where all the discord of life would vanish, all disappointment disappear, and where the good and the faithful, who had suffered so much, would rise from their graves and come back to a life of peace and happiness.

Their faith was deep and their hope fervent. They did not seek to explain how this phenomenon of resurrection would occur, nor did they endeavor to picture the details of the new world. It was sufficient for them that it had been promised.

At or about the time of the commencement of the present era, there were three Jewish sects: the Sadducees, the Pharisees, and the Essenes. The Sadducees rejected the belief in a Messiah, while the Pharisees and the Essenes maintained such a belief. Accompanying the belief in a Messiah was the belief in resurrection.

The Pharisees and the Essenes deeply believed in a physical resurrection, and the common people, who were the forgotten men of that time, embraced this belief. Many who had been bereaved held the belief that with the coming of the Messiah there would also occur the resurrection of their beloved dead, and that reunion between the deceased and the living would then take place.

The concept of resurrection varied over the years. There were those who believed that resurrection would consist of bringing a body back to life. They believed that although upon death the body and the soul were separated, resurrection would bring them together again, that such a reunion would occur with the coming of the Messiah, and that this condition would exist during the entire Messianic period. There were also those who believed that resurrection would come only to the spirit, that the spirit would be resurrected and clothed in a body of glory and light.

There also existed at one time a controversy as to whether resurrection was the privilege of the Jews alone, or whether it applied to all humanity, regardless of their beliefs. There was also a difference of opinion as to whether resurrection would come only to those who were righteous or to the righteous and unrighteous alike.

Those Jews who devoutly believe in resurrection rely upon the belief that God is a God of justice. They say that since God selected the Jews as His instrumentality for bringing to the world the concept of His unity and His laws for the guidance of humanity, He will reward them for the pain, agony, torture, and untimely deaths suffered by them over the ages.

They believe that it is consistent with their thoughts of God that those who have been devout and have suffered persecution and even martyrdom because of their insistence in keeping the faith and enunciating it to the world should be rewarded, or at least made whole. From this reasoning they induce the concept that there will be a physical resurrection, a resurrection of the body with the reincorporation of the soul, and that thereafter there will be a long period of life on earth during which they will be rewarded, or made whole, for their devotion and suffering.

During the Middle Ages this belief was especially prevalent. One country after another took a hand at persecution. There was probably not a single country in which the Jews dwelt during this period that did not torture and kill Jews because of their religion. It was largely their passionate belief in resurrection that sustained the Jews during their afflictions, tribulations, and martyrdom. Nothing could make them deny their faith, their belief in the one God who would in His own time bring them back into this world.

The thought that there will be a physical resurrection and that this physical resurrection will take place in Palestine when the Messiah comes has persisted to the present day, and there are many Jews today who have faith in this belief.

There have been Jews who, upon reaching old age, have journeyed from all parts of the world to Palestine. Their purpose has been to spend their remaining days in that country and to be buried there, in the Holy Land, in order that when the Messiah arrives they will rise from the dead and live again in Palestine.

The modern trend in Judaism is definitely away from the belief in resurrection, particularly physical resurrection. The thought of resurrection has been merged in the Reform synagogue, and to a large extent in the Conservative synagogue, with the belief in the immortality of the soul. Immortality of the soul rather than resurrection can now be considered an integral tenet of Judaism.

It has been said that faith in God seems to point not to the fulfillment of the promise of resurrection but rather to the realization of those higher expectations of personal immortality which are sown in every human soul and are part of its very nature.

—C.-B.G.S.

 # The Least Difficult Way of Being Truly Human

When our children or our grandchildren put us to the acid test and ask, "Why be a Jew?" we shall be in a position to answer. I do not believe it is a coincidence that the major areas of crisis in the modern world are precisely the fields in which Jewish tradition has something specific to say to the world that is distinctive either in content or in emphasis. These elements are either missing or muted in the dominant world-view both of the East and the West, which are too busy wrestling with major ills.

It is true of the disaster area that encompasses the intimate relationships of men and women, the whole field of personal morality, the attitudes toward sex, love, and marriage. It is true of the problems of ecology and the preservation of our natural resources, the dwindling gifts of land, air, and water. It is true of the problems of religious tolerance and freedom of thought in a pluralistic society struggling to survive. It is true of the troubled issues of race relations, aggravated by poverty, drugs, and crime. It is true of the arena of international affairs, the rise of nationalism, and the goal of world peace.

Above all, it is true of the tension between the ideals of social justice and personal freedom, both enunciated by the Prophet of Israel. On all these critical issues the Jewish tradition has something significant to contribute. Its roots are in the millennial experience of the Jewish people, but its fruits are for all the world.

If we make ourselves truly at home in the Jewish heritage, educating ourselves and then our children, we shall be able to contribute to the world on a level worthy of the people who gave the Bible to humankind. It will then be borne in upon our children and grandchildren that loyalty to Judaism is nothing narrow, outmoded, and parochial but, on the contrary, is a perennial source of blessing to humanity.

We possess a precious legacy rich in content and beauty, in which idealistic aspiration is blended with realistic understanding. This distillation of thirty-five centuries of human experience can help rescue us and our fellow human beings from the cynicism and despair, the cruelty and violence, the corruption and hypocrisy that are the sins besetting our age.

We shall then go even beyond the great injunction of George Santayana, who said, "A man must stand with his feet firmly planted in his own country, but his eyes must survey the world." Our hearts and minds will embrace the world.

The Duke of Marlborough was raised to the peerage by Queen Anne because of his extraordinary services to the British Crown. One day, when he was at court, a nobleman decided to twit him upon his lowly origin. He turned to the duke and said, "Your Grace, whose descendant are you?" "Sir," Marlborough replied, "I'm not a descendant, I'm an ancestor."

The time has come for us to rise above nostalgia and be less concerned with pride in the past than with the quality of the future. We must resolve to be not merely the descendants of yesterday but the ancestors of tomorrow. We shall then discover, as did a great French Jew, Bernard Lazare, a long time ago, that being a Jew is the least difficult way of being truly human.

—R.G.

 A Jewish View on Homosexuality

Homosexual conduct between males is mentioned much more frequently and is more heavily condemned in the traditional Jewish sources than such conduct between females. The emphasis is on the sexual act between males rather than mental homosexual tendencies, as in Leviticus 18:22: "Thou shalt not lie with mankind, as with womankind; it is an abomination." And in Leviticus 20:13 we read: "And if a man lie with mankind, as with womankind, both of them have committed abomination; they shall surely be put to death; their blood shall be upon them." Some scholars have suggested (though it is not certain that they are right) that the "price of a dog" in Deuteronomy 23:19 ("Thou shalt not bring the hire of a harlot, or the price of a dog, into the house of the Lord thy God for any vow; for even both of these are an abomination unto the Lord thy God") refers to the hire of a man by a man for sexual purposes. While the men of Sodom (Genesis 19:5) wished to abuse the two men who stayed with Lot, the main sin of Sodom, according to the Jewish tradition (Ezekiel 16:49), was its injustice and cruelty, so that a term like "sodomy" for homosexual acts between males is not found in the Jewish sources. The term *kadesh* in Deuteronomy 23:18 is rendered in some English versions as a "sodomite," but the New English Bible renders the verse more accurately as: "No Israelite woman shall become a temple-prostitute, and no Israelite man shall prostitute himself in this way."

A debate dating from the second half of the second century is recorded in the Mishnah (*Kiddushin* 4:14). R. Judah here forbids two unmarried males to sleep together, while the Sages permit it. The reason given (*Kiddushin* 82a) for the ruling of the Sages is that Jews are not suspected of engaging in homosexual practices. The *Shulhan Arukh* (*Even ha-Ezer* 24), however, though recording the opinion of the Sages as the law, continues: "But in these times, when there are many loose persons about, one should avoid being alone with another male." The Polish commentators to the *Shulhan Arukh* (*Helkat Mehokek* and *Bet Shemuel*) argue that the author of the *Shulhan Arukh* was speaking of his own milieu, but "in our lands" it is only a special act of piety to refuse to be alone with another male. Nonetheless, they say, two males should not sleep together in the same bed.

According to the rabbis, gentiles, too, are commanded by the Torah to abstain from homosexual practices. This belongs to the special Torah laws for gentiles, the "seven laws of the sons of Noah." It is said that even those gentiles who indulge in these practices at least have the decency not to draw up a formal marriage contract between two males (*Hullin* 92a-b). In rabbinic legend Nebuchadnezzar used to submit the kings he had conquered to sexual abuse (*Shabbat* 149b).

Female homosexuality is referred to in the comment of the *Sifra* on the verse: "After the doings of the land of Egypt, wherein ye dwelt, shall ye not do; and after the doings of the land of Canaan, whither I bring you, shall ye not do; neither shall ye walk in their statutes" (Leviticus 18:3). The *Sifra* observes that this does not mean that one must not copy the architectural styles, for instance, of Egypt and Canaan but refers only to their sexual practices. "What did they do? They allowed a man to marry a man and a woman a woman." The Babylonian teacher R. Huna said (*Shabbat* 65a-b) that if a woman performs a sex act with another woman they are no longer considered to be virgins and could not, therefore, marry a high priest, who must only marry a virgin (Leviticus 21:13). From the discussion it emerges that the concern is not with whether they marry a high priest (in any event the high priesthood had ceased long before the third century, when R. Huna lived), but with the immorality of the practice. This is Rashi's explanation of the passage in question, but, in fact, the term used is "for the priesthood" and not for "the high priesthood," so that the Tosafists understood R. Huna to mean that women who indulge in these practices are treated as harlots who are forbidden to the priests (Leviticus 21:7). However, elsewhere in the Talmud (*Yevamot* 76a) it is said that R. Huna's ruling is not followed. The women would not be treated as harlots but as indulging in obscene practices.

Maimonides (*Yad, Issurei Biah* 21:8) rules, on the basis of the above, that lesbian practices are forbidden, but a married woman who is guilty of them does not thereby become automatically forbidden to her husband. Maimonides continues that a husband should object to his wife's indulging in such practices and should furthermore prevent his wife from associating with women who are known to be addicted to such practices.

It is clear, then, from the above sources that homosexual practices are severely frowned upon, but that female homosexuality is treated less severely than male homosexuality. Why this should be is not stated in the sources, but it would appear to be due to the fact that in the nature of the case the possibility of physical contact is less in the former instance. The sources, moreover, do not seem to recognize either male homosexuals or lesbians as distinct groups, or in any event there is reference only to practices and not to some men or women having homosexual natures.

—L.J.

 ### Rearing a Family
Is the First of Judaism's 613 *Mitzvot*

Marriage is that relationship between man and woman under whose shadow alone there can be true reverence for the mystery, dignity, and sacredness of life. Scripture represents marriage not merely as a Mosaic ordinance but as part of the scheme of Creation intended for all humanity.

They do less than justice to this divine institution who view it in no other light than as a civil contract. In a contract the mutual rights and obligations are the result of agreement, and their selection and formulation may flow from the momentary whim of the parties. In the marriage relation, however, such rights and obligations are high above the fluctuating will of both husband and wife; they are determined and imposed by religion, as well as by the civil law. The contract view fails to bring out this higher sphere of duty and conscience, which is of the very essence of marriage.

The purpose of marriage is twofold: posterity and companionship.

The duty of rearing a family figures in the rabbinic codes as the first of the 613 mitzvot of the Torah (Genesis 1:28: "Be fruitful and multiply"). To this commandment is due the sacredness and centrality of the child in Judaism. Little children are "the Messiahs of mankind," the perennial regenerative force in humanity.

Companionship is the other primary end of the marriage institution. Woman is to be the helpmate of man. A wife is a man's other self, all that man's nature demands for its completion physically, socially, and spiritually. In marriage alone can man's need for physical and social companionship be directed to holy ends. It is this idea that is expressed by the term *kiddushin* applied to Jewish marriage—a term that, aside from its original sacerdotal meaning, signifies the hallowing of two human beings to life's holiest purposes. In married life man finds his truest and most lasting happiness; and only through married life does human personality reach its highest fulfillment.

It is astonishing to note the amount of hostile misrepresentation that exists in regard to woman's position in Jewish life. Yet the teaching of Scripture is quite clear: "God created man in His own image; male and female created He them" (Genesis 1:27)—both man and woman are in their spiritual nature akin to God, and both are invested with the same authority to subdue the earth and have domination over it. Nothing can well be nobler praise of woman than Proverbs 31; and, as regards the reverence due to her from her children, the mother was placed on a par with the father in the Decalogue, Exodus 20:12; and before the father in Leviticus 19:3.

A conclusive proof of woman's dominating place in Jewish life is the undeniable fact that the hallowing of the Jewish home was her work; and that the laws of chastity were observed in that home, both by men and women, with a scrupulousness that has hardly ever been equaled. The Jewish sages duly recognized her wonderful spiritual influence, and nothing could surpass the delicacy with which respect for her is inculcated.

—J.H.H.

 ## What Is a Jew?

What is a Jew? This question is not at all so odd as it seems. Let us see what kind of peculiar creature the Jew is, which all the rulers and all the nations have collectively and individually abused and molested, oppressed and persecuted, trampled and butchered, burned and hanged—who, in spite of all this, is still alive. What is a Jew, who has never allowed himself to be led astray by all the earthly possessions that his oppressors and persecutors constantly offered him in order that he should change his faith and forsake his own Jewish religion?

The Jew is that sacred being who has brought down from heaven the everlasting fire and has illumined with it the entire world. He is the religious source, spring and fountain out of which all the rest of the peoples have drawn their beliefs and their religions.

The Jew is the pioneer of liberty. Even in those olden days, when the people were divided into but two distinct classes of slaves and masters, even so long ago had the law of Moses prohibited the practice of keeping a person in bondage for more than six years.

The Jew is the pioneer of civilization. Ignorance was condemned in olden Palestine even more than it is today in civilized Europe. Moreover, in those wild and barbarous days, when neither the life nor the death of anyone counted for anything at all, Rabbi Akiba did not refrain from expressing himself openly against capital punishment.

The Jew is the emblem of civil and religious toleration. "Love the stranger and sojourner," Moses commanded, "because you have been strangers in the land of Egypt." And this was said in those remote and savage times when the principal ambition of the races and nations consisted in crushing and enslaving one another. As concerns religious tolerance, the Jewish faith is not only far from the missionary spirit of converting people of other denominations. On the contrary, the Talmud commands the rabbis to inform and explain to everyone who willingly comes to accept the Jewish religion all the difficulties involved in its acceptance, and to point out to the would-be proselyte that the righteous of all nations have a share in immortality. Of such a lofty and ideal religious tolerance not even the moralists of our present day can boast.

The Jew is the emblem of eternity. He whom neither slaughter nor torture over thousands of years could destroy, he whom neither fire nor sword nor inquisition was able to wipe off the face of the earth, he who was the first to produce the oracles of God, he who has been for so long the guardian of prophecy, and who transmitted it to the rest of the world—such a nation cannot be destroyed. The Jew is everlasting, as is eternity itself.

—L.T.

Israel, Greece, and Rome

For a philosophic mind there are not more than three histories of man's past that are of real interest: Greek history, the history of Israel, and Roman history.

Greece has an exceptional past. Our science, our arts, our literature, our philosophy, our political code, and our maritime law are of Greek origin. The framework of human culture created by Greece is susceptible of indefinite enlargement. Greece had only one thing wanting in the circle of her moral and intellectual activity, but this was an important void: She despised the humble and did not feel the need for a just God. Her philosophers, while dreaming of the immortality of the soul, were tolerant toward the iniquities of this world. Her religions were merely elegant municipal playthings.

Israel's sages burned with anger over the abuses of the world. The prophets were fanatics in the cause of social justice and loudly proclaimed that if the world was not just, or capable of becoming so, it had better be destroyed—a view that, if utterly wrong, led to deeds of heroism and brought about a grand awakening of the forces of humanity.

One other great humanizing force had to be created—a force powerful enough to beat down the obstacles that local patriotism offered to the idealistic propaganda of Greece and Judea. Rome fulfilled this extraordinary function. Force is not a pleasant thing to contemplate, and the recollections of Rome will never have the powerful attraction of the affairs of Greece and Israel; but Roman history is nonetheless part and parcel of these histories, which are the pivot of all the rest, and which we may call providential.

—E.R.

 Even from Their Graves
Fathers Sought to Impart Jewish Ethics

In these days of complex inheritance and tax laws, the preparation of a last will and testament centers around financial and material considerations, with the final document almost exclusively reflecting the expertise of accountants and lawyers. But in simpler times, when material wealth was more likely to be passed in accordance with a traditional order of inheritance, many Jews sought to pass on a personal heritage as well through the medium of the "ethical will." For they longed to convey to their offspring the ideals toward which they had striven in their lifetime.

Such men were following in a tradition modeled after the deathbed statements of Jacob, Joseph, Moses, and Joshua, and based on Genesis 18:19 where God says of Abraham, "For I have known him, to the end that he may command his children and his household after him that they may keep the way of the Lord to do righteousness and justice . . ." This text was held to require every father to leave moral exhortations for his children's guidance.

The tradition of the deathbed statement—the verbal ethical will—prevailed until the Middle Ages, when surviving records of Jewish literature reveal what

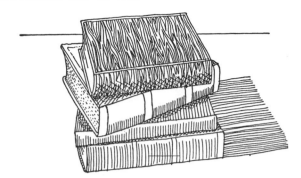

may have been the beginning of the written ethical will, in addition to the oral one. Written with the urgency of waning breath and strength, these wills were pointed ethical and personal essays, practical and usually free of ideology or underlying theological discourse. They generally dealt with matters of family life and behavior, disclosing to us the culture and mores of the authors and their times. They were revealing human documents whose content spans the ages.

In a classic ethical will of the eleventh century, Judah Ibn Tibbon, a scholar of some note, struggles with an independent and sometimes willful son, incorporating reprovals for laziness and lack of interest in books with practical instructions on moral behavior:

> *Thou knowest, my son, how I swaddled thee and brought thee up, how I led thee in the paths of wisdom and virtue. I fed and clothed thee; I spent myself in educating and protecting thee, I sacrificed my sleep to make thee wise beyond thy fellows, and to raise thee to the highest degree of science and morals. These twelve years I have denied myself the usual pleasures and relaxations of men for thy sake, and I still toil for thine inheritance.*

At a time when libraries were rare, Judah was well known for his book collection, and his description is probably not exaggerated:

> *I have assisted thee by providing an extensive library for thy use and have thus relieved thee of the necessity of borrowing books. Most students must wander about to seek books, often without finding them. But thou, thanks be to God, lendest and borrowest not. Of my books, indeed, thou ownest two or three copies. I have besides procured for thee books on all sciences. Seeing that thy Creator had graced thee with a wise and understanding heart, I journeyed to the ends of the earth and fetched for thee a teacher in secular sciences. I neither heeded the expense nor the danger of the ways. Untold evil might have befallen me and thee on those travels, had not the Lord been with us!*
>
> *But thou, my son, didst deceive my hopes! Thou didst not choose to employ thine abilities, hiding thyself from all the books, not caring to know them or even their titles. Hadst thou needed one of them, thou wouldst not have known whether it was with thee or not without asking me; thou didst not even consult the catalogue of the library.*
>
> *All this thou hadst done. Thus far thou hast relied on me to rouse thee from the sleep of indolence, thinking that I would live with thee forever! Thou didst not bear in mind that death must divide us, and that there are daily vicissitudes in life. But who will be as tender to thee as I have been, who will take my place—to teach thee out of love and goodwill? Thou seest*

how the greatest scholars, coming from the corners of the earth, seek to profit by my society and instruction, how eager they are to see me and my books . . . May thy God endow thee with a new heart and spirit, and instill into thee a desire to retrieve the past and to follow the true path henceforward!

In typical passages of practical guidance, Judah advises his son

Contend not with men, and meddle not with strife not thine own. Enter into no dispute with the obstinate, not even on matters of Torah. On thy side, too, refrain from subterfuges in argument to maintain thy case even when thou art convinced that thou art in the right. Submit to the majority and do not reject their decision. But, my son, honor thy comrades, and seek opportunities to profit them by thy wisdom, in counsel and deed. Choose upright men for friends, with them take counsel, but the fool despise.

The contrast between the two following passages reveals the extremes of Judah's values:

Show respect to thyself, thy household, and thy children, by providing decent clothing, as far as thy means allow; for it is unbecoming for anyone, when not at work, to go shabbily dressed. Spare from thy belly and put it on thy back.

All the honor I ask of thee is to attain a higher degree in the pursuit of wisdom, to excel in right conduct and exemplary character, to behave in friendly spirit to all and to gain a good name, that greatest of crowns, to deserve applause for thy dealing and association with thy fellows, to cleave to the fear of God and the performance of His commandments—thus wilt thou honor me in life and in death!

These examples from Judah Ibn Tibbon's will differ somewhat from those of Eleazar of Mayence, a simple Jew with no pretensions to learning. His fourteenth-century will mirrors the social and religious attitudes of his time:

These are the things that my sons and daughters shall do at my request. They shall go to the house of prayer morning and evening, and shall pay special regard to the tephillah *and the* shema. *As soon as the service is over, they shall occupy themselves a little with the Torah, the Psalms, or with works of charity. Their business must be conducted honestly in their dealings both with Jew and Gentile.*

They must be gentle in their manners and prompt to accede to every honorable request. They must not talk more than is necessary; by this they will be saved from slander, falsehood, and frivolity. They shall give an exact tithe of all their possessions; they shall never turn away a poor man empty-handed but must give him what they can, be it much or little.

My daughters must obey scrupulously the rules applying to women; modesty, sanctity, and reverence should mark their married lives. Marital intercourse must be modest and holy, with a spirit of restraint and delicacy, in reverence and silence. They must respect their husbands, and must be invariably amiable to them. Husbands, on their part, must honor their wives more than themselves, and treat them with tender consideration.

As to games of chance, I entreat my children never to engage in such pastimes. In their relation to women, my sons must behave continently, avoiding mixed bathing and mixed dancing and all frivolous conversation, while my daughters ought not to speak much with strangers, nor jest or dance with them. They ought to be always at home, and not be gadding about. They should not stand at the door watching whatever passes. I ask, I command that the daughters of my house be never without work to do, for idleness leads first to boredom, then to sin. But let them spin, or cook, or sew.

I earnestly beg my children to be tolerant and humble to all, as I was throughout my life. Should cause for dissension present itself, be slow to accept the quarrel; seek peace and pursue it with all the vigor at your command. Even if you suffer loss thereby, forbear and forgive, for God has many ways of feeding and sustaining His creatures. To the slanderer do not retaliate with counterattack; and though it be proper to rebut false accusations, yet is it most desirable to set an example of reticence. You yourselves must avoid uttering any slander, for so will you win affection. In trade be true, never grasping at what belongs to another. For by avoiding these wrongs —scandal, falsehood, moneygrubbing—men will surely find tranquility and affection. And against all evils silence is the best safeguard.

As to whether such exhortations had their desired effect, history offers few clues. We do know that Judah Ibn Tibbon's son Samuel, the one of such laziness and disinterest in books, became the distinguished scholar who translated Maimonides' *Guide of the Perplexed.* We also know that in certain families the custom of succeeding generations of sons amending and adding to their fathers' ethical wills served to create a unified body of continuous ethical thought that influenced certain trends within Judaism and so presumably affected the lives of thousands. To go beyond these documents is speculation.

—H.H.A.

 ## The Jewish Roots of Western Culture

A popular pastime today is to search for one's roots. I wish that more of us Americans realized that our Christian roots—and the sources of Western civilization—reach back into the roots of the Jewish people.

Just think of the many ways in which we have been affected by the many contributions Jews have made to our Western civilization.

The Jews gave to us our ethics in the Ten Commandments, which have stood the test of time for three thousand years.

They gave us the greatest book of all—the Bible—which is still a best seller.

The Jews taught us to be monotheistic and worship one God, and their God became our God.

The law of Moses has been a basis for legal systems of the Western world.

The greatest teacher of all the ages was a Jew—Jesus of Nazareth. He taught the fatherhood of God, the brotherhood of man, and that we should do unto others as we would have others do unto us. It is the saddest blot on our Western history that we, as Christian nations, have failed so miserably in living up to the teachings of this great Jew.

The Hebrew prophets proclaimed the ideals for a righteous, just social order that we have not yet begun to reach. They demanded the right of free speech and insisted that individuals be responsible for their own actions.

Our own America was built from a blueprint provided by the ancient Jews. Thomas Jefferson was asked how he knew how to create, out of thirteen colonies, a democratic republic when there never was one before. Jefferson answered,

"Why, we went to the first Jewish Commonwealth as described by Moses in the wilderness . . . and we copied the format."

Moses said, "Choose ye wise men from among you to represent you," and that's what we have done with the Supreme Court, the Senate, and the Congress.

The Jews set a precedent for the equality that Western women are still striving for. I am nearly ninety and I vividly recall my years of extensive travel through many countries. I have seen firsthand how other, older religions have perpetuated the masculine conspiracy against womanhood.

When I lived in China, I saw how for centuries women had been crippled by foot-binding. (Confucius said, "Woman is a human being, but is of a lower order than man.")

In Arab countries I saw how formerly if a married woman showed her face to a man other than her husband, the husband could (under Moslem religion) kill her. I saw enacted a Moslem philosopher's teaching that "woman is the toy with which man plays when and as he wishes. In him is light and understanding . . . in her is darkness and ignorance."

I learned from an Indian scholar that for as long as three hundred years women were burned on the funeral pyre along with their deceased husbands.

Yet here in the West women have had a more abundant life and liberty. Why? Again the answer goes back to our Jewish roots, back to Moses in the wilderness.

The daughters of Zelophehad came to Moses and said, "Our father has died and left no sons, and the elders say that we cannot inherit because we are girls." And Moses said, "I will issue a decree that henceforth girls will have equal rights of inheritance with boys." Because Moses gave extra dignity to women and girls, the prophets also dignified women.

Jews number among our greatest scientists, writers, scholars, and physicians. They have developed serums to do away with the curse of polio and the blindness of trachoma.

As American Christians, we need to remind ourselves of the spiritual and cultural kinship we have with the people of the Holy Land. And we need to understand some historical facts.

For a thousand years Jerusalem was the capital of ancient Israel. In 1918 the British Mandate established forty-five thousand square miles of this ancient land for a modern Jewish homeland. In 1922 Britain took away four fifths of this area and set up the Arab kingdom of the Jordan River.

In the 1948 War of Independence Jordan seized the West Bank by an act of aggression. The West Bank never has been Arab land. Israel has won four wars against neighbors determined to destroy her. And, unlike any other victor in world history, only Israel is being pressured to give back the secure boundaries she gained for herself.

During the years I, as a Christian, lived in the Holy Land, I witnessed Israel's treatment of defeated Arab enemies. No nation in history has been so humane. In none of her wars has Israel gloated, looted, or raped. I saw how Israelis provided bread and milk for besieged Arabs, provided health care for Arab children to fight against polio and trachoma, assisted Arabs with agricultural services, and paid Arab farmers the same prices that Jewish farmers received for crops.

When Christians remember that their roots and historic memories are tied to the Holy Land, we will understand why it is crucial for us to help Israel continue to be a strong, independent democracy in the Middle East. Israel's safety and security is the key to peace in the Middle East—that part of the world where Christianity was born.

—I.M.L.

Chief Rabbi Kook Allowed Yom Kippur Desecration for Sake of Land

Yom Kippur, the Day of Atonement, is beyond question the most solemn day of the Jewish calendar. It is the day of communion between man and his maker, the day of fasting, repentance, and return to God. So great is its universal appeal that there is hardly a Jew, however far he may have removed himself from Jewish loyalties and observance, upon whom this day does not have a profound impact.

As such, it is surely the most personal and individual of festivals. It is the only festival that takes precedence over the Sabbath and for that reason is called "a Sabbath of Sabbaths" (Lev. 23:32).

In ancient times, however, once every fifty years the shofar was sounded on Yom Kippur. What was that occasion? After seven cycles of seven years, the end of each cycle being a year of *Shemittah*, the fiftieth year was proclaimed "a year of release" by the sounding of the shofar. The "release" consisted not only of the slaves, who thus regained their liberty, but also of the soil of the land of Israel, which thus reverted to its original owners from whom it has been alienated by sale or other means. It was the Jubilee year when "ye shall return every man unto his possession."

In view of this law, the Jewish National Fund does not make outright sale of the land that it acquires. The land is leased for forty-nine years and in the fiftieth it reverts to its "original owners," the Keren Kayemet, on behalf of the Jewish people.

Thus, every half century Yom Kippur became in every sense the "day of the land." In his commentary on the Bible, Dr. J. H. Hertz rightly and beautifully calls the Jubilee year "a rare and striking example of the introduction of morals into economics." True though this is, it was in addition a "striking example" of a continuation of the golden thread that runs through the whole of Jewish thought; the emphasis on the sanctity of the principle of national ownership, under God, of the soil of Israel, and the bond between the land and the people.

It surely does not need an excess of imagination to attempt to recapture the emotions of the people on that Yom Kippur that occurred once every fifty years. It was not only the day of the return of the individual Jew to God but the reunion of the Jew with the soil. And so significant is this link with the land that on one unique occasion permission was even given to violate the sanctity of Yom Kippur for the sake of Israel's holy land. This is the story of Emek Hefer.

The acquisition of the area that was once called Wadi Hawaret and is now the Emek Hefer is a fascinating story because of the area's size and laborious complexity of the negotiations. Emek Hefer comprises the central part of the Sharon Plain between Hedera and Natanya, and originally consisted of eight thousand dunams (about two thousand acres). Not only were the legal aspects the most complicated imaginable, but serious obstacles were placed in the way by the hostile British administration.

Everything was against that acquisition, although the almost legendary Joshua Hankin took the leading part in the negotiations. For a detailed account of those wearying negotiations, which were finally crowned with success, concerning what has become the most flourishing agricultural area in Israel, one can read *Sixty Years of Land Acquisition in Israel,"* edited by A. Ashbel. Among those who played a prominent part in these negotiations were Aaron Donin and his brother,

Hiram. In a lecture delivered by Hiram some time ago, he added a detail of which I had been completely unaware: In the course of these long, drawn-out negotiations, one of its critical phases took place on Yom Kippur; the Jewish representative received permission from the late Chief Rabbi Abraham Isaac Kook who gave him permission to violate Yom Kippur in the sacred cause of acquiring land for Jewish settlement.

It seemed too incredible, so I decided to investigate whether this remarkable statement could be confirmed. I communicated verbally and in writing with him, and asked whether there was any written evidence to this effect. In his reply he stated, *inter alia*, "I have no evidence in writing or in print of this permission, but I have communicated with my brother, Aaron, who worked with Joshua Hankin in the office of Hachsharat HaYishuv at that time, and he repeated that in one of the final phases of the public sale of the land, which was effected by the Execution Office connected with the District Court of Shechem (in 1929), he was requested by Hankin to journey to Shechem in order to be present at the last moment for receiving offers at the public sale of the land. He does not remember whether the late Abraham Chone, who represented the Keren Kayemet, accompanied him, but he does remember that when he passed in his car through Petach Tikvah the irate inhabitants pelted him with stones for traveling on Yom Kippur, and I myself remember that the late Abraham Chone told me on more than one occasion that before he undertook that journey to Shechem on Yom Kippur he asked the late Rabbi Kook for advice and the rabbi told him that he was obliged to do so in the interests of the redemption of the land."

These categorical statements cried out for verification, so I turned again to Ashbel's detailed account. Ashbel gives a number of dates for the critical stages of these negotiations and at least three of them are significant and relevant to this topic.

The first is that in order to facilitate the public sale of the land, decided upon by the court on September 23, 1928, orders were sent to all the illegal squatters to vacate the land by the date fixed for the sale. When that day came, and many of the squatters had not complied, the president of the Executive Office issued an order of expulsion. It is in every way reasonable to assume that the expulsion order was issued the day after the order and expiration date, namely, on September 24; and in 1928 September 24 was—Yom Kippur!

I then examined the second date. The account concludes with the details of the last desperate attempt by the opponents of the sale of the land to the Jews to obtain an order canceling the expulsion order. This was, of course, opposed by the Jewish representatives. The court decided to postpone its final decision until Friday, October 3, 1930. Yom Kippur that year fell on Thursday, October 2. Therefore, there appears to be no doubt about the "desecration" of Yom Kippur in the course of these protracted negotiations. The only point on which there is no actual evidence, apart from the recollection of the late Abraham Chone, is whether, indeed, the saintly late Rabbi Kook actually gave permission.

But I am prepared to believe that Rabbi Kook, passionate Zionist and profound mystic, realizing that side by side with its status as the great day of reconciliation Yom Kippur is also the great day of return of the land to its rightful possessors, did grant permission.

—L.I.R.

Sexual Decency

Nowhere in ancient literature is the institution of sacrifices as the essential and supreme form of worship condemned or even questioned, as was the case with the prophets of Israel. One searches in vain for a clear call to distinguish the true worship of God from ritual and sacrifice, and to identify it with ethical conduct.

The God of Judaism was not interested in worshipers trampling His court, in incense and offerings, "in thousands of rams and ten thousand of rivers of oil." His sole requirement was that men should "seek justice, relieve the oppressed, defend the orphan, plead for the widow" (Isa. 1:17).

Occasionally one catches a fugitive note in the ritual texts of Babylon and Assyria suggesting a conception of sin as moral offense, as in the Shurpu series of incantations, but little more than that. No line is drawn between taboo sins and moral sins, and there is certainly no attempt, as with Judaism, radically to subordinate one to the other. By making this distinction, Judaism gave new dimensions to man's spiritual world.

Nowhere is there a revulsion against the sex motif, which is so central to the mythologies of ancient religions, or against the institution of sacred prostitution, which was connected with their worship, or against the unbridled orgiastic rites of their nature festivals.

Judaism alone called these practices and their sex symbolism obscene. "There shall be no cult prostitute of the daughters of Israel, neither shall there be a cult prostitute of the sons of Israel. You shall not bring the hire of a harlot, or the wages of a dog [Sodomite] into the house of the Lord your God . . . for both of these are an abomination to the Lord your God (Deut. 23:19).

Professor Albright, the noted Christian Bible scholar, states that "it was fortunate for the future of monotheism that the Canaanites, with their orgiastic nature worship, their cult of fertility in the form of serpent symbols and sensuous nudity, and their gross mythology were replaced by Israel, with its nomadic simplicity and purity of life, its lofty monotheism, and its severe code of ethics."

Along with the banishment of all sexual rites and sacred prostitution, Judaism at the same time refused to sanction vowed chastity as a form of worship—a religious institution which was common in antiquity.

Laxity in sexual matters, which characterized so many of the peoples of antiquity and which was sanctioned by the example of their gods, was execrated by Judaism in an unparalleled way. Purity of family life, to a degree practically unknown in the ancient world—even among its advanced circles—became the norm for the Jewish way of life, and it has remained a characteristic of Jewish behavior throughout the ages.

To perceive the difference one needs but recall the recommendation of Plato in his *Republic* (Bk. V) and his *Laws* (Bk. V) on the basis of the ancient saying, "Friends have all things in common," that women should be held in common, and children as well—a practice that would destroy family life altogether. The utility of the proposal, in Plato's mind, was beyond question; only the possibility of effectuating it remained in doubt.

Lycurgus, the reputed founder of the constitution of Sparta, decreed for his countrymen the honorable practice of giving "the use of their wives to those whom they should think fit, so that they might have children by them" for the purposes of breeding strong men and soldiers, or simply as an accommodation, since the matter was not worth fighting over.

That women are by nature common property was a theory widely held in the ancient world, and Plato therefore did not advance any shocking new proposal when he advocated the community of women for his warrior-saints. This view was also subscribed to by many Stoics. Zeno, the founder of the Stoic school at Athens, advocated it, as did the Stoic Chrysippus. So did Diogenes the Cynic, according to the testimony of Diogenes Laërtius.

Epictetus, who opposed this view of his fellow Stoics, reports that the idea was very popular among the women of Rome: "At Rome the women have in their hands Plato's *Republic*, because he insists on community of women."

From the writings of Clement of Alexandria it appears that such ideas were entertained even by some of the heretical Christian sects, like the Carpocratians, whose founders derived them from their Hellenistic environment and traced them back to Plato. The orthodox church denounced and repudiated these sects.

The writings of Seneca, Juvenal, Martial, Tacitus, Suetonius, and Dio Cassius all reveal the moral degeneration of Roman society, in which promiscuity, sodomy, and lesbianism were widely practiced. So also do the writings of Paul (Rom. 1:24–27). They help us to realize the violent contrast between the standards of this society and the Jewish standards of sexual decency, the sanctity of marriage and of family life.

Modesty was urged upon men and women by Judaism. The principle laid down was: "Sanctify yourself even in things permitted to you." New concepts were introduced: *zni'ut*—modesty, moral delicacy; *boshet*—reticence, sensitiveness to all that is gross. "There is nothing more beloved of God than *zni'ut*"; and "He who does not possess the quality of *bushah*, it is certain that his ancestors were not present at Mount Sinai."

This code of *boshet* (Eccles. 41:16) did not result from any prudery on the part of the people of Israel. It was an expression of reverence for life itself and for the dignity of man. It was the esthetics of morality that Judaism introduced to the ancient world, the "beauty of holiness." Three thousand years of Jewish literature are distinguished by a remarkable freedom from vulgarity and lubricity. "It is man's duty to keep away from unseemliness, from what resembles unseemliness and from the semblance of a semblance."

Such a concept makes it inconceivable that the obscenities of Attic comedy, for example, which so delighted Athenian audiences, would have been tolerated in any city in Israel. Socrates was a sage of unimpeachable moral character, "the best, wisest, and most upright of his age." But what sage in Israel would have boasted, even playfully, of being a lifelong victim of Eros, a "lover" of Alcibiades, and would have spoken of homosexual perversion as complacently as Socrates did? And what was the moral tone of a people who would show no aversion to this?

John J. I. Dollinger, in *The Gentile and the Jew*, said: "With the Greeks this phenomenon [*paiderastia*] exhibited all the symptoms of a great national disease, a kind of moral pestilence . . . In very truth, the whole of society was infected with it, and people inhaled the pestilence with the air they breathed."

It was from the Greeks, according to Herodotus, that the Persians learned this perversion. And as for the Romans, "by the time the last days of the free republic were reached, the vice had attained a fearful degree among the Romans."

To the sages of Israel sexual perversion was under the curse of God. It was so rare among the people, and regarded with such abhorrence, that "a Jew was not to be suspected either of pederasty or bestiality."

Even unclean speech was condemned. Gehenna is made deep, declared the rabbis, for the man who speaks lewdly, and for him who listens to it and is silent. Throughout they urged men to use the *lashon nekiah*—the clean, chaste speech, the *lishna ma'alya*—the euphemism, to avoid the coarse vulgar term.

Many of the biblical and later rabbinic injunctions that have been characterized as "particularistic" and "exclusive" were in fact motivated by this overriding concern to keep the life of the individual Jew and the Jewish family clean and uncorrupted.

Man never quite disentangled himself from the dim memories of his subhuman life. Ancient man was aware of a common lineage with the animal, though he was aware also that he was something more than an animal. But no clear boundaries were recognized between man and beast and between man and his gods. In his mythological world there roamed beings who were half man and half beast, and his ancient legends told of cosmic struggles between beasts and gods in human form. His closeness to the life of animals even reached the point of carnal commerce with them. Biblical law punished such perversions with death (Exod. 22:18 and Lev. 20:15–16).

The prohibition against partaking of the blood of animals (Deut. 12:16, Lev. 3:17) was in all probability also motivated by the desire to cleanse the nature of man and to remove him from affinity with the beast, for the blood was regarded as the seat of the soul or the life of man and beast. "And you shall not eat the life with the flesh" (Deut. 12:23).

—A.H.S.

 ## "The Pill" and Jewish Law

The discovery (or rediscovery) in recent years of hormone preparations highly effective as contraceptive agents, and now widely used by millions of women, has presented an altogether new challenge to the halachic attitude on birth control. Hitherto the general consensus of the innumerable rabbinic responsa on the subject published during the past two hundred years or so has been to permit contraceptive precautions only for the most urgent medical reasons, and then only on submission of every individual case to competent rabbinic judgment.

In our times, however, birth control is far less a medical than a social practice —and problem. But so long as only physical or chemical preventives used vaginally were available, the exponents of Jewish law felt constrained almost completely to disregard any indication other than some threat, whether more or less remote, to the mother's life feared to result from a pregnancy. This extremely limited scope of rabbinic verdicts on contraception has inevitably led to an immense widening of the gap between Jewish law and practice. Indeed, it has resulted in virtually ignoring one of the most acute sociomoral questions of our age, at least to the extent of failing to relate Jewish teachings to the relevant facts and pressures as they exist. But given the restrictive religious attitude as it has evolved in recent centuries on the basis of some rather scant and arguable earlier sources (none are to be found in the principal codes of Jewish law), there was little else to do or write about.

The availability now of "the pill" may well open the way to an entirely new appraisal of birth control in the light of Jewish law. To any student of the halachah, oral contraceptives are very familiar through their frequent mention, as "the potion of roots" or "the cup of sterility," in the ancient and medieval classics of Jewish law. While the composition and existence of any such potion designed to produce temporary sterility (or, in different dosages, to promote fertility, just as our modern hormones do) remained unknown, the law on its use was often stated in clear and simple enough terms. The Talmud formulates it thus: "A man is not permitted to drink a cup of roots to render him sterile, but a woman may drink such a potion so that she will not bear children" (*Tosephta, Yevamot*, 8:2). The *Shulhan Arukh* codifies the law in almost identical terms, adding only that the administration of such an oral sterilizing agent to males, while an offense, is not culpable in contrast to sterilization by other (i.e., surgical) means (*Even Ha-Ezer*, 5:12). The obvious reason for this leniency is that this method involves no direct impairment of the reproductive organs (*Be'er Ha-Golah*, a.1.). This liberal ruling on the female use of the potion is qualified by but one commentator, who limits the sanction to women who fear the pain of further births (Solomon Luria, *Yam shel Shelomo, Yevamot*, 6:44), a rather immaterial qualification.

Naturally, a sweeping sanction such as this cannot suffice, by itself, to determine the Jewish religious attitude to so complex a matter as birth control, even if restricted to oral contraceptives. To define such an attitude, one must also take into account numerous broader considerations on procreation and marital duties in general, as reflected in various haggadic as well as halachic statements. For the identification of the talmudic potion with the modern pill, while probably quite sound in a narrow legal sense, is hardly tenable from a practical point of view. In the past the sanction was no doubt mainly of theoretical value, or at best to be applied in very rare cases, whereas now it would radically change the entire pattern of family life and demographic trends. The spirit as well as the letter of the law must be most carefully investigated before such a far-reaching innovation can be authentically evaluated in the light of Jewish teachings.

The first tokens of such an investigation are so far very meagre indeed. The only responsa on the subject that had appeared until recently dealt not with whether, and under what conditions, it was intrinsically permissible to use oral contraceptives but with their side effects in tending to cause irregular bleeding; in view of this, women were cautioned against their use to prevent any complications in observing the purity laws (R. Moses Feinstein, responsa *Igrot Mosheh*, vol. IV, *Even Ha-Ezer*, no. 17).

But with the constant improvement of these pills, and adjustments in their dosage, this problem can now be eliminated in most cases. The only other previous reference in recent responsa to "the potion of sterility" is a suggestion that this may be legally identical with spermicidae jellies (*Igrot Mosheh, Even Ha-Ezer*, nos. 62, 63). But this identification or analogy hardly seems tenable, for there is a great difference between the indirect action of an oral contraceptive suspending ovulation and the direct action of a spermicide vitiating the potency of the semen and impeding its progress to unite with the ovum. Nor is this isolated opinion shared by other authorities who, while they prefer such jellies to any physical impediment (such as a diaphragm), do not place them in the same lenient category as oral contraceptives. (See, e.g., R. Menchem Mannes, responsa *Chavatzelet Ha-Sharon*, note following *Even Ha-Ezer* part; and R. Mordecai L. Winkler, responsa *Levushei Mordekhai, Even Ha-Ezer*, no. 27; cf. also Rabbi Joseph J. Z. Horovitz, in *Festschrift für Jacob Rosenheim* [Frankfurt: J. Kauffmann, 1931], p. 110f. [Hebrew part]).

The halachic attitude to oral contraceptives as such is now the subject of an article entitled "Contraception by Pills" by Rabbi Samuel Hubner in *Ha-Darom*

(Tishri 5725). But unfortunately the article is disappointing on the question it purports to discuss. The bulk of it is simply a review of the much-debated arguments on conventional birth-control methods, based on the various interpretations of the famous talmudic passage dealing with the right of women endangered by a pregnancy to use a tampon as a precaution against conception (*Yevamot* 12b).

Recognizing the legal difference between tampons (which some authorities condemn, even in cases of danger, if inserted before intercourse) and pills, he prefers the latter for two reasons: (1) The tampon interferes with the natural act, whereas the pill does not; and (2) by inserting the tampon, one directly acts to destroy the seed, while the pill works indirectly. The author adds that this explains the legal distinction between direct sterilization and the use of "the cup of sterility" as expressed in the *Shulhan Arukh* (see earlier discussion), but he does not state that this "cup" is, in fact, the equivalent of today's pill and therefore to be adjudged as such in the halachah. He merely concludes that he is inclined to permit its use by a woman who is warned by doctors not to become pregnant if this may prove dangerous to her, but he warns that the existing pills, because they caused staining, should not be taken, "as their advantage would be outweighed by their disadvantage" over other methods.

The whole subject, with its wide ramifications, is clearly in need of a very wide-ranging reexamination. A far more enlightening treatment of the subject is contained in an article on "Hormone Medications for Women and Religio-Halakhic Problems" contributed to the eighth volume of *No'am* (Jerusalem, 5725) by Dr. Jacob Levy, who has written extensively on the Jewish attitude to birth control since the early 1930s.

Thus the article discusses the latest data on the administration of female sex hormones to correct irregularities in the menstrual cycle as an aid to women whose menstruation and purification period would otherwise interfere with their wedding (delaying the consummation of the marriage) or render their marriage sterile by restricting conjugal relations to their infertile period.

Above all, such hormones could be used as a preferable substitute for other contraceptive devices, which, Dr. Levy claims, are often medically as well as halachically objectionable. He, too, identifies the law on these pills with that on "the cup of sterility" mentioned in the Talmud and the codes, but he warns against their indiscriminate use and sale, recommending them only for pressing health reasons and advocating their availability at drugstores only on doctors' prescriptions.

Dr. Levy emphasizes particularly the demographic considerations in favor of large Jewish families, citing figures to show the "terrifying decline" of the natural increase among Jews.

—I.J.

 # What Does Judaism Say About Astrology?

Judging by the popularity of horoscopes and fortune-telling, along with books on the subject, many people still believe in astrology, though it is often looked upon as no more than a parlor game. It is notorious that Hitler consulted professional astrologers to guide him in the conduct of war. They cannot have been very good at it. There is no doubt that in a pre-scientific age Jews did believe in astrology.

The talmudic rabbis, for instance, believed in it, though some of them held that the stars had no influence over Jews, who were under direct divine influence. Traces of the belief are still to be found in words used by Jews, notably the expression *mazal tov*, literally "a good star" or "planet." An unfortunate fellow is still called a *shlimazal*, "one who has no *mazal*," one on whom fortune does not smile. Even when the belief in astrology was strong, however, it was taught that the Jew should leave the future to God and not, therefore, consult astrologers. The *Shulhan Arukh*, the standard code of Jewish law, states categorically: "One should not consult astrologers, nor should one cast lots (to determine the future)" (*Yoreh Deah* 179:1).

There are two reasons why a belief in astrology lost its respectability in modern times. First, the use of scientific methods made astrology increasingly improbable, since empirical investigation does not demonstrate that a man's life is influenced by the star under which he was born. Secondly, the whole elaborate astrological scheme is based on the notion that the earth is at the center of the universe, with the spheres, containing the stars and planets, revolving around it. One of the achievements of modern astronomy was the demonstration that the universe is not geocentric. Before the rise of modern science, astrology did seem to be convincing, and a belief in it was entertained by highly sophisticated persons as well as by the credulous.

It is one of the examples, therefore, of the extraordinary independence of mind of the great Maimonides that virtually he alone in the Middle Ages rejected the belief in astrology. In a letter on astrology written by Maimonides in reply to a query from the rabbis of southern France, he distinguishes between astronomy, which is a true science, and astrology, which is sheer superstition. He states further that according to the Torah man's fate is determined by God directly and not by the stars, and that, moreover, man has free will and can choose good and reject evil—otherwise the commands of the Torah are meaningless. As for the references to astrology in the Talmud, these cannot be taken literally when they contradict reason. Man was created with his eyes in front and not behind, in other words, he must act according to reason, rejecting astrology even if it is mentioned in rabbinic sources.

Until modern times very few Jewish thinkers agreed with Maimonides. Nowadays, for the reasons mentioned above, the whole astrological scheme has been rejected by the vast majority of thinking Jews.

—L.J.

X
Off the Beaten Track:
Wandering Jews,
Now and Then

The Most Southerly Jewish Congregation on Earth

Where is the most southerly Jewish congregation in the world?

It's a congregation few travelers ever visit and is one of the smallest in the world with a synagogue: just twenty families, only fifty souls.

In few communities in the world is the ratio of Jews to total population so small: one to every 2,200. (The only place I know with a slimmer ratio is Elko, Nevada: one Jew among 7,620 other people.)

The most southern Jewish congregation in the world is Dunedin (pronounced Duh-KNEE-din), New Zealand, a Scottish-looking city (because it was settled by Scots) at the lower tip of the South Island. Latitude 46, with almost nothing between it and the South Pole but water and ice.

The little Dunedin congregation has a proud history, which any of the fifty local Jews will relate at the drop of a yarmulke. In the mid-nineteenth century, New Zealand had a gold rush. People flocked to the South Island from Australia and even from Europe. Among them were some Jews.

By 1880 there were two hundred Jews in Dunedin, making it the largest Jewish community in all of New Zealand. Because everyone was prospering and because they were certain the community would continue to grow, they built a synagogue large enough to accommodate five hundred congregants, on a valuable piece of land in the center of the city.

However, early in the twentieth century, the gold ran out and the fortune hunters began leaving. Year by year the size of the congregation dwindled. The young people, as soon as they had some education, went off to places like Wellington, Auckland and Australia; some went to far-off Israel. One reason they left was because they did not want to marry out of their religion and the chance of finding suitable Jewish partners in Dunedin was obviously limited.

There was a temporary upsurge in the Jewish population immediately after World War II, when several dozen families came from the DP camps of Austria and Czechoslovakia.

When the worldwide campaign to "Save Soviet Jewry" began, Dunedin's twenty families—"the last outpost of Judaism," as they call themselves—offered to support any Russian Jews that HIAS would send them. They made only one request: "Please send us young people. Couples with children."

What Dunedin got was a Russian dentist, who confessed he was a confirmed bachelor, and a woman doctor. Both are happily still practicing in Dunedin.

By 1966 the congregation was down to its present size, so a decision was taken to sell the five-hundred-seat synagogue and build a modern structure seating one hundred, because at that time New Zealand's only medical college was in Dunedin and there were always many Jewish students who attended services.

So they built the new synagogue with the medical students in mind and almost immediately a medical college was built in Auckland, New Zealand's largest city, where most New Zealand Jews live. Now there are only two or three Jewish medical students a year at Dunedin University and the synagogue is twice as large as it need be.

The average age of the Dunedin Jew is about sixty-five. They have no rabbi. The head of their community, who conducts the weekly service, is Ernest Hirsh, a gentle intellectual, who was a businessman in Germany before he left there in 1938. Why did he choose to go to New Zealand?

"Do you remember what was happening in nineteen-thirty-eight?" he asked. "Now, look at a map. New Zealand is as far from Germany as it is possible to go and still be on this earth."

The community was larger then and the average age was much younger. Hirsh's eyes sparkle as he reminisces. "Then there were twenty children in the Hebrew class." He bites his lower lip. "Now . . . of course, now there are none."

The most important event of the year for the Dunedin Jews is the community Seder, held in a rented hall. Attendance is greater than at either the Yom Kippur or Rosh Hashanah services.

In all of New Zealand there are just 3,736 Jews affiliated with congregations— in Auckland, Wellington, Christ Church, Dunedin and two smaller towns. That's a ratio of little more than one practicing Jew per thousand people. (New Zealand has as many people as Israel.)

In addition, there are about two thousand Jews who pay no congregational dues but sometimes attend High Holiday services. Then there are thought to be another five thousand who are not counted as Jews at all, because they are partners in mixed marriages.

Except for several hundred families belonging to liberal Jewish congregations in Auckland and Wellington (who describe themselves as "something like members of Conservative congregations in your country") the other practicing New Zealand Jews are all Orthodox. Their rabbis will not convert anyone to Judaism if there is even a suspicion that it is for the purpose of marrying a Jew. (As the Orthodox rabbi in Wellington explained it to me: "Love exists today, but not tomorrow.")

Also, no Jew who has married a non-Jew is permitted to retain his membership in a congregation.

Perhaps because of the small size of the Jewish community; perhaps because New Zealand is a land without serious problems of any kind; perhaps because New Zealanders are people with few built-in tensions; perhaps because the relationship between New Zealand Pakehas (whites) and their large minority of Maoris (the dark-skinned indigenous people) is a model the rest of the world could well study—perhaps for all of those reasons I was unable to find any sign whatsoever of anti-Semitism in this amazing little down-under constitutional monarchy so close to the South Pole.

—R.S.J.

The Jews of Jannina:
An Ancient Community in Greece

In Jannina, Greece, today are a small remnant of native Greek-speaking Jews who are largely unknown in other parts of the world. Their first settlement in Jannina goes back to prehistoric times; however, historians identify them as Romaniot Jews, since they are descendants of the Greek Jews of the Byzantine Empire established in the fourth century C.E. Their basic prayers are Sephardic; in language and culture they are Hellenized or Romaniot Jews.

The Byzantine Greeks proudly called themselves *Romaioi*, a name which goes back to the founding of the Byzantine Empire, then known as the Eastern Roman Empire. When Constantine the Great (288–337 C.E.) became ruler of the East Roman Empire, the Hellenes were still subjects of Rome. In time, the word *Romaioi* lost its original meaning, but many Greeks still speak of themselves as *Romaioi*, a name which has survived since the days of the East Roman Empire.

Many histories have been written about the Spanish-speaking exiles whom the Sultan Bayazid II invited to settle in his Ottoman Empire in 1492. The late eminent historian Joseph Nehama wrote seven volumes on the history of the Sephardim of Salonika alone. Occasionally, a magazine article has appeared describing the customs of some holidays as observed by one of the Greek-speaking Jewish communities which has survived the ravages of persecutions, invasions, wars and the recent Holocaust. Up to this writing, however, no complete history has ever been written on any of these Greek-speaking communities, from their first settlement on Greek soil.

The Romaniot or Greek-speaking Jews are different historically, culturally, linguistically and even liturgically to a degree (certainly in their liturgical songs and melodies) from the Spanish Sephardim who found a welcoming haven in the Ottoman Empire in the late fifteenth century. To begin with, the Romaniot Jews were on Greek soil more than a thousand years before the arrival of the Sephardim. Their history is not merely longer than that of the Salonika Sephardim. As Diaspora Jews they had to adjust first to a pagan Greece, then to Byzantine Christianity, to Venetian, Serbian, Bulgarian, Norman and Italian invasions (all preceding the extended Turkish occupation of the Balkan peninsula). Each of those groups battled ceaselessly to seize a part of Greece for themselves. The native Greek-speaking Jews were subjected to an endless change of regimes, which often threatened their very survival as Jews.

Only two Romaniot communities are in existence in Greece today: Chalcis and Jannina, capital of the province of Epirus. Arta, located in the same province, used to be the Romaniot community most closely related to Jannina, not only because of its proximity, but because of similarities in their language, customs, mores and liturgical practices. We know this from two books which have been preserved, *Pirke Avoth* (Sayings of the Fathers) and *Shir Hashirim* (Song of Songs), published in Salonika during the nineteenth century with this note on the title pages: "Keminhag Jannina veArta" (According to the Customs of Jannina and Arta). The Jewish community of Arta was completely wiped out by Hitler's soldiers in World War II.

Elis, a port city in the northern part of the Peloponnese (its fair harbor served as a port of embarkation for thousands of Greek Jews who immigrated to New York in the first decade of this century—my father among them) also had a

Romaniot community with a long history on Greek soil. Another important community existed in Patras, capital of the province of Achaea. The Hebrew inscriptions found in the local church of St. Anastasia reveal that there were Jews living in Patras in ancient times. Benjamin of Tudela, who traveled to Greece in the second half of the twelfth century, reported that fifty Jews were living in Patras, but in the seventeenth century, during the Turko-Venetian war, they fled the town and did not return until 1715, when Turkish rule was reestablished. During the Greek War of Independence (1821–29), the Jewish community of Patras ceased to exist and was not restored until 1905. In 1940, just before the Germans occupied Greece, there were 337 Jews living in Patras. In 1947, 152 survivors returned to their native city, but today there are only two Jewish families living in Patras.

Chalcis (also known as Egripo and Negrepont), a seacoast capital on the island of Euboea, on the Aegean Sea, also had a Romaniot community long before the Sephardim settled in the Ottoman Empire. Benjamin of Tudela found two hundred Jews living there, "with merchants from every quarter"; the merchants of Chalcis were silk manufacturers and dyers. We also have the testimony of Jews living in exile, from a Hebrew inscription on a gravestone marked 5086 (1326 C.E.), which is set in the city walls at the entrance gate. Only a few Sephardim were attracted to Chalcis, and thus the community retained its Romaniot traditions. In 1940, there were 350 Jews living in Chalcis, 170 of whom survived the Holocaust. Today only 102 Jews have chosen to rehabilitate their lives in this ancient city.

Jannina has always been the most representative Romaniot community in Greece. To begin with, it has always had the largest Jewish community, which was uniformly Romaniot in its traditions. Older Jannina natives boast that during the triumphant years of the Ottoman Empire in the sixteenth and seventeenth centuries, Jannina had a Jewish population of seven thousand Jews. In the early years of the first decade of this century, the Jewish population of Jannina was reduced to four thousand; by the end of the decade there were three thousand. After the second Balkan War in 1913, two thousand Jews remained in Jannina; the others migrated to America, Athens and Palestine. In 1940, just before the Nazi occupation of that city, there were 1,950 Jews living in Jannina. It was still the largest Romaniot community in Greece.

Even more significant, perhaps, is that the Jannina émigrés continued to observe their Romaniot traditions wherever they resettled. Those who resettled in Athens founded their own Jannina synagogue on Melidoni Street, directly across the street from the Sephardic synagogue. Those Jannina émigrés who settled in New York had their own synagogue built under the leadership of Yehuda Colchamira, at 280 Broome Street on the Lower East Side. This synagogue is actively functioning to this very day. More recently, a new synagogue known as the Mapleton Synagogue was built in Bensonhurst, Brooklyn, for those Jannina Jews who moved to Brooklyn. Those who left for Palestine founded their own Romaniot synagogue in Jerusalem, known as the Beth Avraham and Ohel Sara Synagogue.

The Jannina Jewish community has always been regarded as the most important Romaniot center in the Levant. Even as late as 1910, the commerce of Jannina was left completely in the hands of the Jannina Jews. The late Greek Professor Nikos A. Beis calculated that the financially and culturally important Romaniot community of Jannina was a considerably larger Jewish center than anywhere else in the Levant. It was the foremost community of indigenous Greek-speaking Jews. "This Jewish center of Jannina," wrote Beis in 1921, "is on Greek soil with a past of an unbroken millennium."

I visited the Jannina Jewish community four times before World War II. This is the city where both of my parents and all of my grandparents were born; I learned much about this community from my parents at home, during my growing years. I have visited Jannina eight times since World War II and have been most impressed by the community's remarkable rehabilitation. Most remarkable, however, is that all through the centuries, despite invasions and wars, despite changes of regimes and religions which, in some periods, brought forcible efforts to convert Jews to other faiths, the Jannina Jews have remained steadfast to their faith as Orthodox Jews worshiping in their Romaniot tradition.

—R.D.

How Should Jews Behave on the Moon?

How should Jews behave on the moon?

This is not a hypothetical question—at least not in the Israeli armed forces. The military rabbinate has devoted two top-level sessions to a scientific-religious discussion of the problem.

Both sessions were organized to formulate draft laws and regulations for Jewish astronauts engaged in interplanetary space travel. Held at the Haifa Officers Club on Mount Carmel, the sessions were attended by Army chaplains, religious affairs officers, and top Israeli scientists and professors.

"The fact that the Israel Army Rabbinate organized a discussion of religious problems arising out of man's penetration of space should not be interpreted to imply that the Israeli Army is preparing to launch a manned moon rocket, or some kind of Venus Sputnik," Colonel Shlomo Goren, the bearded, tough Chief Army Chaplain explained with a smile, "but the way we see this business, Jewish military personnel of other armies and air forces may soon be hurled into space with manned interplanetary vehicles. If they are observant, they may ask their own Jewish chaplains how to behave on the moon, for instance. Their chaplains will ask us, and we want to have all the answers ready. It is also possible, of course, that as man conquers space, Israel will contribute to interplanetary research and penetration. But for the time being, we have more pressing problems right in our own backyard, and we formulate rules of behavior for Jews in the U.S., Canada, Britain and other countries who may soon have to observe the Sabbath on the moon . . ."

In addition to Rabbi Goren, who presided over the sessions, the discussions

were shaped by Lieutenant-Colonel M. Piron, Colonel Goren's deputy and Chief Religious Affairs Officer, Lieutenant-Colonel Y. Meir, head of the Religious Holidays Section, and Professor Nathan Rosen, head of the nuclear physics department of the Haifa Institute of Technology (Technion).

A former associate and assistant of the late Professor Einstein, Professor Rosen agreed to advise the military rabbinate on all problems connected with nuclear energy, space penetration and universal relativity.

The first four questions considered by the more than fifty assembled Army chaplains were the following: If Jews find themselves on the moon, how will they be able to tell eves of holidays, and how will they be able to celebrate and observe Jewish holidays and festivals, since there are no twenty-four-hour days, seven-day weeks and twenty-eight-day Jewish months on the moon?

All Jews on earth must "Sanctify the Moon" (*Kiddush Levana*) when a new moon shows itself at the beginning of each Jewish month. The questions arise: If Jews are on the moon itself, how can they greet a new moon, and do they have to do it at all?

The ends of Jewish prayer shawls must be blue to signify the blue color of the skies. However, the sky on the moon is not blue, but ink-black. Does that mean that the tassel ends of *taleisim* will have to be changed from blue to black?

Finally, and most important, all Jewish laws and regulations, rituals and commandments were made for human beings living on earth. Therefore, it is a moot question whether Jews on the moon or on other planets are outside the jurisdiction of the Torah and its laws. If they meet other beings on one of the planets —creatures which cannot be classified as either animal or human by earth standards—how should Jews behave toward such beings?

"We are proud to be the first official body in the world, and—it seems to me— in the history of the world, to devote an official session to a serious discussion of religious problems raised by man's penetration of space," declared Colonel Goren in opening the debate on the four problems named above.

"Science and knowledge advance by great leaps and bounds," he said. "A few hundred years ago, every century brought some new important invention or scientific development, idea or theory. In the last century, every decade brought something new and important in the realms of knowledge and science. In our own century, every year brings something new. And now it seems that hardly a month passes without some new invention or development. Therefore, it would not be an exaggeration to assume that man's penetration of space is near and that we are on the threshold of a new era in the history of the world. Does that mean that religion as such is outmoded, or that our ancient rules, laws, customs, rituals, rites and regulations are no longer suited to the present-day modern realities? The answer is no, no and again no. No matter how deep and far-reaching the progress of science, there is a certain limit beyond which not even the most advanced scientists and professors dare to proceed, and where they must admit that they know just as little as our fathers and forefathers. The scope of our activity may change to embrace the moon, the planets and perhaps even the stars, at least some of them, but God, religion, faith and the dividing line between good and bad, right and wrong remain the same now as they were at the time of Moses, David and Solomon . . ."

Rambam (Maimonides), ancient Sanhedrin sages, and great rabbis were cited and quoted during the debate which followed. The first session adopted a unanimous resolution which is of momentous importance to all future spacemen:

"Since space has been penetrated by human beings who use the earth as their base of operations and initial starting point, and since the moon, planets, et cetera will be conquered by individuals coming from, or originating from earth, these people will observe religious holidays, laws and customs just as if they were on earth. Earth laws will apply to any place where earthmen may arrive no matter how far away from our globe, since as far as our earth human beings are concerned, the earth is their center of universe . . ."

This resolution takes care of the remaining questions. Holidays and festivals will be observed on the moon, on planets or in interplanetary rockets hurtling through space, just as they are observed on earth, and at the same time. Since it is assumed that space travelers and moon explorers will be in constant radio communication with earth, they will receive messages telling them of holiday eves and festival deadlines.

One day on the moon is fourteen earth days, so that Jews on the moon will have to observe the Sabbath twice a (moon) day, said another resolution. Should radio communications with earth be broken or interrupted for any reason, the space travelers will use their own watches to keep sunset prayers, first moon celebrations, et cetera, even though the sun shines all the time, the military rabbinate decided.

Concerning the attitude to be adopted toward other beings, Colonel Goren formulated a draft law which says that man is the ruling being of the world, since man was created by God to rule the world. The best proof of this, Rabbi Goren says, is that man penetrated space and will be the one to conquer moons and planets, if that happens. Therefore, any being encountered by man on other planets must be automatically considered to be inferior to earthmen, and not human by earth standards. But since the Jewish religion teaches us to be kind toward all living beings, including animals, Jewish earthmen will behave toward beings on other planets according to the Jewish law. This draft law was adopted by the military rabbinate, and is now being studied by Israel's Supreme Rabbinate.

The tassel ends of *taleisim* will be just as blue on the moon as they are on earth, for our religion was made on earth for earthmen who have to observe it, no matter where they go.

With Professor Rosen and a staff of army scientists explaining all technical problems, the session that followed was devoted to countless questions and answers.

"To avoid confusion, space travel and moon time will be kept by radio in accordance with Greenwich Mean Time (GMT)," one young army chaplain said, "but Jews on earth regulate their holidays and prayers not by GMT, but by sunrise and sunset. How will our radio communicate with Jewish spacemen?"

A draft resolution was adopted deciding that all Jews in space or on the moon will have to observe holidays and prayer times just as they are observed in the Holy City of Jerusalem. Therefore, they must tune in to the Israeli radio station for Jerusalem Standard Time, or, if that is impossible, add two hours to Greenwich Mean Time signals broadcast to them.

Concerning the observance of Jewish holidays on the moon, the meeting ruled that Jews outside the earth's orbit will strive to observe all holidays and prayer times. After reception of a radio signal saying that the sabbath is about to begin, for instance, they may not work, write or desecrate the sabbath unless it is absolutely necessary for the physical existence of themselves or their companions. In that case, desecration of the sabbath, Yom Kippur or other holidays would be permitted conditionally under the "Pikuach Nefesh" (saving of souls) rule.

The military rabbinate believes that Jews on the moon will be even more religious than they were on earth. Even if they did not observe all aspects of the

Jewish religion on earth, the military rabbinate believes, they will do so on the moon, because of their emotional ties with earth.

—L.H.

 ## Czechoslovakia's Jewish Treasures

For more than a thousand years Jews have lived within the borders of what is now the Czechoslovak Socialist Republic. Their eventful history (not quite 5 percent survived Hitler's occupation) is recorded not only in documents such as the Raffelstetten customs regulations of 933 and 936 C.E., but also in communal structures such as ritual baths, synagogues and cemeteries, and in works of art.

The collections of the State Jewish Museum in Prague have become the richest of their kind in the world. Together with the "Old-New Synagogue," and the most famous Jewish cemetery in the world—the cemetery of the Prague ghetto—the museum forms a kind of reservation of unique Jewish records and memorials. A number of items of Jewish interest, however, are found outside this area and even outside Prague.

A complete underground cemetery, above which a main traffic artery runs, tram cars clang and buses rumble, existed for more than three centuries on the steep slope of the Bratislava Castle hill, near the banks of the Danube. Jews, often driven from one part of Europe to another, found their peaceful rest here after a stormy life; here were the tombs of such well-known talmudic scholars as Chatam Sofer, rabbi of Pressburg.

In 1942, this three-hundred-year-old cemetery had to give way to the requirements of modern traffic, when the construction of a tunnel beneath Bratislava Castle and the strengthening of the Danube embankment were begun. However, the Jewish burial society succeeded in preserving the tomb of Chatam Sofer and the surrounding tombs of the rabbis and elders of the community.

Before the entrance to the tunnel, alongside the road, the visitor sees three iron gratings. Under them, there is a staircase descending about 16 feet below the surface of the road and ending in an iron door. Behind the door is an underground cemetery. In an area of about 120 square yards is a mausoleum containing untouched graves and tombs. On the graves and on the cornice around the mausoleum, candles burn.

Prague's town hall has the unique distinction of being adorned with the statue of a rabbi. At the entrance to the town hall, hewn into stone by the master hands of Ladislav Saloun, towers the figure of Rabbi Loew, maker of the Golem.

In 1920, Prague joined with the surrounding suburbs to form Greater Prague. A new coat of arms was created, which incorporated the existing Prague emblem —three towers and city walls with a hand holding a sword—and the emblems of the formerly independent towns and villages. Among them was the red banner of the old Jewish town, with its Magen David.

The flag of the Prague Jewish community is preserved in the Old-New Synagogue, and is a unique historic relic. The Prague ghetto obtained the privilege of flying its own flag from the Emperor Charles IV, in 1354. The privilege was confirmed in 1648 as an expression of recognition for the help the Jews gave in the defense of Prague against the Swedish siege.

The former town hall of the ghetto, seat of the "Lord Mayor," has a unique tower clock with two dials; one has Arabic numerals, while the second has Hebrew letters and hands that move counterclockwise. The Hebrew inscription "Kadosh, Kadosh, Kadosh" above the head of a statue of Jesus on the cross is certainly bizarre, but there is such a crucifix on the old Charles Bridge in Prague. The accompanying explanation, written in Latin, Czech and German, says that the gilding of the Hebrew letters was paid for by a fine imposed on a Jew who spat in front of the crucifix.

After 1945, a part of the main street of the small town of Lazne Kynzvart, near Marianske Lazne (Marienbad), was paved with tombstones from the Jewish cemetery, with the Hebrew inscriptions upward. This act of vandalism was committed by the Nazis, who devastated the time-honored Jewish cemetery and used the historically valuable tombstones as paving blocks. After their liberation from Nazi domination, Czech citizens dug out the tombstones and stored them. They are to be used for a memorial which will serve to remind future generations of the horrors of Nazi rule.

Other Jewish monuments in Czechoslovakia also serve as war memorials. In 1867 construction was begun on a new synagogue in Prague, on the former site of the oldest synagogue of the ghetto, the so-called "Old Schule," probably founded in the eleventh century. This was the first modern building to be built in the former ghetto and it incorporated novel architectural elements. The central ground-plan, basically a square, was new both with respect to synagogue architecture and with respect to the style of Prague ecclesiastical buildings in the nineteenth century. An equally interesting phenomenon was the use of cast iron to help support the vaulted ceilings.

The synagogue, built in Moorish style, was embellished with heart-shaped motifs, rosettes, shells, latticework and other designs copied from the Alhambra in Granada. The interior is richly gilded and complemented with red and green, giving the impression of rubies and emeralds.

The rich Spanish decoration gave rise to the legend that, in the old synagogue that had previously occupied the site, exiles from Spain had said their prayers. Thus the building acquired the name "the Spanish synagogue."

In this synagogue are stored about twenty-two hundred curtains for the Ark, decorative Torah mantles, and cushions on which the scrolls were unrolled for public reading. This immensely valuable treasure was collected relatively quickly, during the six years of the Nazi occupation. Curtains for the Ark and Torah mantles were often the only objects which remained of the synagogues razed or burned by the Nazis in the 168 destroyed and completely deserted Jewish communities in Bohemia and Moravia.

In this way, a unique collection of rare old textiles which had served Jewish liturgical purposes was assembled. This is a huge historically and artistically valuable exhibit which covers three centuries. The director of a famous London museum stated that it had no equal in the world; the dates embroidered on the curtains offer the possibility of precise dating, and facilitate comparison of the techniques used in creating these works during various periods.

The visitor sits comfortably in a seat and the exhibits pass before his eyes. The *parachot* are hung as curtains on a system of brackets. The decorative mantles are affixed to cardboard sheets and form an unusually large album whose leaves turn. A system of floodlights and reflectors enables the smallest details of the embroidered patterns and techniques of work to be seen.

During the Nazi reign of terror almost all the medieval synagogues in Germany, Poland and Italy were destroyed. In occupied Czechoslovakia many were preserved, and those possessing historic or artistic value are now supported by state funds.

The Pinkas Synagogue in Prague houses a memorial to the victims of Nazism. It stands on the edge of the old historic cemetery of the former Prague ghetto. A marble plaque in the synagogue vestibule states that it was built in 1535 by Aron Meshulam and his wife, the daughter of Rabbi Menachem. Some experts, however, argued that the synagogue, which had been rebuilt, was actually much older.

They were proven right when a general survey of the building, begun in 1950, showed that under the walls of the synagogue, which had been rebuilt in the seventeenth century, was a sixteenth-century synagogue, which again covered a synagogue-type structure from a still earlier date. Researchers uncovered, between fragments of baroque and rococo work, cornices of the Gothic period. When the walled-up Ark of the Law was examined, early Renaissance marble pillars and Gothic arches were found. The paving from the seventeenth century covered the remains of a substructure and flooring that date back to the thirteenth century.

Detailed study of the discoveries made it possible to reconstruct the appearance of the building during the various stages of its existence. Its eighteenth-century form, of which most elements were preserved, became the basis of the restoration. Nine years of exacting research, conservation and reconstruction followed. The Pinkas Synagogue now appears in the form of a medieval Jewish house of prayer.

This attempt at reconstruction is the first of its kind in the world. It has resulted in a medieval synagogue with all of its typical features, which are otherwise known only from old engravings. According to the latest expert opinion, the Pinkas Synagogue is probably the oldest Jewish building in Prague—even older than the Old-New Synagogue.

In this historic building, a unique memorial has been set up to the Czech Jews deported and murdered by the Nazis. On the walls of the restored synagogue two artists have inscribed the names, birth dates, and deportation dates of 77,297 Czech-Jewish victims of the racial bestialities of the Nazis. Among them were 15,000 children. All of them lost their lives in the Nazi concentration camps. It took five years to inscribe the names and dates upon the walls of this symbolic cemetery of unburied dead.

—R.I.

 ## Adventurer Extraordinary:
In Search of the Lost Ten Tribes

More than seventy-five years ago, in Budapest, died one of the most famous adventurers and explorers of the nineteenth century, a man now belatedly recognized in Israel as a forgotten Jewish genius. He was Armin Vambery, who was born to an impoverished, ultra-Orthodox family in the Hungarian town of Szentgyorgy in 1832. Crippled at the age of three, Vambery, whose original name had been Aaron Weinberg, is reputed to have been converted to Islam as a youth and in later life became a Protestant, but throughout his life he was known as a Jew.

His diaries, manuscripts and travel notes, which are supposed to shed light on the so-called disappearance of the Ten Lost Tribes of Israel some three thousand years ago, are now the property of the Budapest National Library and Archives.

A year after he had been enrolled in his hometown *heder,* Vambery knew Hebrew well, but ran away from school, announcing that he wished to study mathematics, languages and geography. His father beat and starved him, but the boy was adamant, threatening to enroll in a Catholic orphanage school. This so alarmed the father that he permitted the youth to attend a secular village school. Young Aaron changed his name to Armin, cut off his sidelocks, and completed the six-year course in three.

Ostracized by his own family, who suspected that he had become a convert to Christianity, the crippled, ragged ten-year-old made his way to Budapest, where he applied to the local *gymnasium* for a scholarship, despite the rule that the minimum age for admission to the school was twelve. When the boy addressed the school officials in fluent Latin (acquired from books he had borrowed from a monastery library) and demonstrated that he was also proficient in Hungarian, Slovene, German and Hebrew, and knew some ancient Greek, he was accepted. To stay alive, Vambery scrounged meals from kindly Jews and slept on the floor of a Hasidic synagogue, whose beadle had known his grandfather. He began to acquire a mastery of English and French.

When he was fourteen, he applied for a job as tutor to the nineteen-year-old son of Count Stefan Janoshazy, a young nobleman denied admission to the university because of mental weakness. Sixteen tutors had already tried and failed to teach the count's son, and when Vambery appeared on the scene, the nineteen-year-old amused himself by beating and insulting his Jewish tutor. Vambery reached an agreement with his charge: he would let himself be tortured only after the nobleman showed some progress in his studies. Two years later, the count's son was finally admitted to the university.

Vambery now threw away his crutches and bought a walking stick, explaining that the injuries he had suffered at the hands of his pupil had inured him to the pain in his crippled right leg. Thereafter he depended on the sturdy cane and his own fortitude to hobble through his long life, which led him over mountains, across roaring rivers and into the wild canyons of central Asia.

He was seventeen when he completed the course at the Budapest Gymnasium. The new languages in which he had become proficient were Russian, Turkish, Italian, Swedish, Arabic and Persian. A wealthy Turkish potentate he met on a cruise invited him to teach English and French at a Moslem religious college, and before long Vambery was both teaching and studying at the school, which trained *cadis*, Moslem religious judges, for service throughout the Moslem world. Although only pious Moslems were granted the title *cadi*, the designation was conferred on Armin without any formal conversion to Islam.

While in Turkey, Vambery wrote a dissertation in which he tried to trace the ancestry of the Hungarian Magyars to a common ancestry with the tribes of central Asia. The Hungarian Academy of Sciences granted him a stipend to pursue his studies and underwrote an expedition to central Asia for that purpose, which he would lead. Vambery was then twenty-nine.

He set out by boat and on horseback for the foothills of the Caucasus, en route to Mosul, Teheran, Samarkand and Bokhara. While he and his team were struggling across rugged mountain passes, war erupted between Turkey and Persia. Moslems of various sects attacked one another, and Europeans were assaulted by all sides in the conflict. Only caravans of pilgrims returning from the holy city of Mecca were allowed to pass in safety.

Attaching himself to one of the pilgrim caravans, Vambery wound a green turban around his head, indicating that he had been to Mecca, and passed himself off as Haj Mahmoud Rashid Effendi, a dervish of the fainting-and-foaming sect. Abandoning his walking stick and deliberately leaning on his crippled leg so that the pain became unbearable and he fainted, Vambery was able to convince the Moslem populace that he indeed was a dervish.

Thus disguised, he made his way to the forbidden cities of central Asia. The feudal rulers of Bokhara, Samarkand, Khiva, Merv, Mesht and other central Asian principalities had devised cruel tortures for all foreigners. Carrying only a few well-hidden gold coins and the stub of a pencil, he spent six years roaming through central Asia, subsisting mostly on rice and water, since the dervishes he presumably belonged to did not touch meat or fish. He cleansed himself with sand only, fearful that water would expose him as a European if the grime were removed from his skin.

He never did find any evidence linking the Turkestan tribes with the Magyars of Hungary, but he claimed to have solved the mystery of the Ten Lost Tribes of Israel. He made shrewd, careful and hidden notes of everything he saw, writing in Hungarian but using the Arabic alphabet. His memory was virtually photographic; he retained vast amounts of the information he collected.

At the time of his visit, there were some eighty thousand Jews in Bokhara. He longed to enter a synagogue, but was afraid to enrage the Moslems. After strolling through the ancient Jewish quarter for nearly a month, listening to conversations in Turkish dialects, biblical Hebrew and Arabic, Vambery called on the area's chief *cadi*. He offered to convert the Bokhara Jews to Islam, which amused the Moslem judge, who said that neither fire nor the sword could swerve the Jews. The *cadi* said that neither Genghis Khan nor Tamberlane had succeeded in destroying the Jews, adding that so long as they resisted conversion they were deprived of all civil rights, but even that did not seem to move them. The *cadi* then said that the "Jews were here long before us—when our tribes came here from the mountains of Pamir, we found the Jews trading in the desert oases of Khiva, Merv and Bokhara."

On the pretext of finding a new approach to converting the stubborn Jews, Vambery obtained permission to study ancient manuscripts in Bokhara's oldest synagogue, which the Moslems had turned into a mosque in the eighteenth century. Without disclosing his identity, he talked with rabbis and elders of the Jewish community, and learned from them that the two hundred thousand Jews in central Asia believed they were descended from two of the lost Israel tribes—Zebulun and Naftali.

This in turn led Vambery to conclude from the writings of Saadya Gaon that the Jews of far-off Yemen were the offspring of the tribe of Asher, while the tribes of Gad and Dan had moved eastward to India and Japan. The descendants of the tribes of Benjamin, Issachar, Simeon and Manasseh had settled in Mesopotamia, Persia and Armenia, Vambery theorized. He claimed that the Jews who returned to Jerusalem from Babylonian captivity were mostly from the tribe of Judah, with several thousand also from the Levi and Ephraim groupings.

On his way home to Europe, Vambery spent some time in Teheran, where he produced a 4,300-page account of his travels, as well as nearly one hundred maps and two hundred linguistic charts. One of the maps showed the tiny oasis of Natimah, where the frontiers of Russia, Iran and Afghanistan meet today. He learned that the tiny community was the home of some three hundred Jews who had become famous as superior gunsmiths and armorers. Their weapons were in great demand, Vambery learned, because they turned out their swords and daggers with what are now known as industrial diamonds, which were plentiful in the riverbed of a stream that coursed through the oasis. Vambery tried to induce the European powers to utilize the "secret Jewish skills" in weaponry, but no one paid any attention.

The Hungarian Academy of Sciences ridiculed his reports and stripped him of the title of professor. The Moslem college voided his designation as a *cadi*. His writings on the Jews of central Asia were ignored. Vambery fled to England, where his reports were given greater credence in political, scientific and journalistic circles. Britain was then engaged in a struggle with Czarist Russia for control of central Asia, and in a short time Vambery was named chief advisor on central Asia to the British Foreign Office. He subsequently drafted a plan for the British conquest and occupation of the central Asian emirates and sultanates, and trained British secret agents on how to spearhead an invasion.

By now Vambery had a perfect command of twelve European and twenty-two Oriental languages. He produced seventeen books on Oriental languages, and twenty-nine volumes on central Asian politics, economics, folklore and anthropology. Perhaps his most unique piece of writing is an unpublished 919-page manuscript on the Lost Ten Tribes of Israel, a work in his own handwriting; it rests to this day in a vault in the Budapest National Library. Vambery's travel notes and diaries turned out to have modern political value when Soviet intelligence agents studied them before infiltrating Afghan and Persian border tribes at the close of World War II in an attempt to seize the industrial diamond field in Natimah.

He has long since been forgotten, but whatever the value of his theories, Aaron Weinberg, better known as Armin Vambery, who died in 1913, deserves at the least a belated entry in the roster of Jewish adventurers and explorers.

—L.H.

 # The Last Chinese Jew Is Hiding Out in Taiwan

The last Chinese Jew?

It sounds like the title of a suspense thriller, but it is not: there is a Chinese Jew, i.e., an authentic descendant of the once thriving Jewish community of China, who believes he is the last of his people and that, with his death, the saga of Chinese Jewry will come to an end.

The man's name is Shih Hung-Mo, and he is Oriental in appearance; although he acknowledges openly that he is Jewish, as were his parents and siblings, he lives today on the island of Taiwan and for reasons of expediency lives as a "Marrano," keeping his Jewish life securely isolated behind closed doors.

He speaks Hebrew, and soon after the establishment of Israel he wrote a letter to a prominent rabbi asking for help in reaching the Jewish state, but received a rebuff. The rabbi claimed that there were no more Chinese Jews and that the letter writer, ipso facto, must be a fraud. Years later, full of remorse, the rabbi wrote to him and offered his deepest apologies.

Shih Hung-Mo, a bachelor in his fifties, lives a quiet life, pursuing his academic career. When he fled the mainland, his parents were still alive, but he is certain that they have since died. He recalls his father showing him gravestones in a cemetery with Hebrew inscriptions.

The last Chinese Jew was discovered by Rabbi Marvin Tokayer, who heard rumors about him while stationed in Tokyo as spiritual leader of the local Jewish community. The rabbi flew to Taiwan to investigate and found that there were many people who had the same name. Turning to the son of Chiang Kai-shek, "who owed me a favor," Rabbi Tokayer asked for help.

Since the names of all the residents on the island are stored in a modern computer, it was not very difficult to generate a roster of all the people with the same name—and then merely to sift through them, looking for one who had listed Hebrew as his second language.

Rabbi Tokayer found that taking leave of the last Chinese Jew was a painful experience, but understood the man's reluctance to leave his life as a "Marrano" on Taiwan and to proceed to an unknown life many miles away.

"When I bade him *shalom*," the rabbi said, "it was the most painful farewell I had ever uttered."

—D.C.G.

 # The Jewish Slaves of Malta

Malta, the former British Crown Colony that joined the world family of independent states on September 21, 1964, is a name not unknown to Jewish history, for it appeared on many a page telling of Jewish suffering and of man's shameful cruelty to man.

The small Jewish colony, which dated approximately from the thirteenth century, was expelled from the island in the early 1500s, but a strange and tragic fate kept bringing Jews back—very much against their will. During the course of two and a half centuries, an almost incredible relationship developed between the Jews and the powerful Maltese Knights, ending only with Malta's surrender to Napoleon Bonaparte in 1798.

In 1530, Emperor Charles V presented Malta to the Knights of St. John, also known as the Knights Hospitalers, a religious-military order dating from the Crusades. Using the island as their stronghold, the noble warriors, who wore monks' robes bearing the eight-pointed Maltese Cross, engaged in piracy, crisscrossing the seas and attacking any merchant vessel that had the misfortune to fall into their power. The ship was plundered; the crew and passengers were sold as slaves. Hardest hit were the Jews, since most of the Levantine merchants were Jews. They became victims of the Knights of Malta in large numbers.

For more than 250 years the Knights of St. John engaged in their lawless traffic free and undisturbed; the Maltese Cross flying from their ships' masts was as dreaded as the Jolly Roger of the common pirate. To the Jews—their favorite prey—the Maltese Cross was a symbol of cruelty, of inhumanity, of the most shameful abuse, in complete contrast to the original dedication of the Hospitalers to the care of the sick and wounded pilgrims in the Holy Land. A Jewish prophecy from the early seventeenth century predicted liberation for the Jewish people following the fall of four godless kingdoms, with Malta being first among them.

The Maltese pirates entered Jewish history for the first time in Rabbi Joseph Hacohen's famous chronicle, *"Emek Habakhah,"* (The Valley of Weeping). "In 5312 [1552 c.e.]," he relates, "the ships of the Maltese Knights had come across a ship carrying seventy Jewish passengers from Salonika. The ship was captured and taken to Malta, where the unfortunate Jewish prisoners were forced to appeal all over the world to raise the ransom demanded by the infamous Knights. Only after the blood money was paid were they allowed to continue on their voyage."

All the ingenuity and the resources of the Jewish people were mobilized to relieve the misery and sufferings caused by this traffic in human lives. In Venice, the commercial metropolis of the Mediterranean, the *Chevrat Pidyon Shevuim* society was founded to raise funds for the release of Jews held for ransom. The society was famous in all the Diaspora and in emergencies did not hesitate to turn to the wealthy communities of London and Amsterdam. Its appeal never went unheeded. The Portuguese Jewish community in Hamburg had a similar institution, called the *Camara dos Cautivos de Venezia* (Chamber of the Captives of Venice), to which the local German Jews also contributed.

The field of activities and tasks facing these societies was enormous, for in addition to the victims languishing in Malta, there were other Jews in equally desperate situations. For instance, in 1686, when the Christian armies reconquered Ofen (the old name for Budapest) from the Turks, its Jewish population was sold into slavery by the victorious imperial troops. Then there were the Jewish galley slaves in the Adriatic and the Tyrrhenian; prisoners held for ransom in Marseilles and in Xanthos; Jewish slaves in Persian and Tartar hands. The "Parnassim dos Cautivos" did all they could to rescue their unfortunate brethren.

In view of the great distances and the urgency of each case, an important Gentile merchant in Malta was nominated as "Consul" by the Venetian Rescue Society and was empowered to act in its behalf. Thus, when a captured Jew set foot on the island, he received from the consul a little money for his immediate needs, as well as one piece of gold weekly and an additional allocation for the holidays, especially Pesach. When a certain number of captives were brought in, the consul dispatched a messenger to Venice with a detailed report announcing the numbers, the names and the amount of ransom demanded by the noble Knights of St. John.

Negotiations then began, leading to ransom payment and release. In 1675, for instance, the society offered to pay 300 piasters for a Rabbi Yizchak Moreno of Belgrade and his family, rather than the 575 piasters demanded by the pirates. The *Parnassim* wrote to their Maltese representative: "The Maltese are in error in believing they can ask more for an old man, unfit to work, a sick woman and three children, one of them blind . . ." The Knights retorted by threatening to baptize one of the children.

The payment of the ransom, officially called "sale," was accompanied by a legal document drawn by a notary and required the formal consent of the Grand Master of the Knights. At times, the Knights decided to "make delivery" in Venice, by sending the hapless victims as galley slaves to their destination. In 1706, the community in Livorno (Leghorn) appealed to Venice for help in raising 1,000 ducats for three galley slaves "whose sufferings were more cruel than death."

Malta had a Jewish cemetery and a synagogue. The captives were sometimes forced to work on the sabbath and on Jewish holidays. This was, however, reported to Venice and a protest was lodged in each instance. Thus, on March 3, 1673, the Jewish community in Rome complained to the heads of the Order about similar transgressions of the Maltese Knights. The appeal was successful and was followed by an ordinance from the Inquisitor of Malta prohibiting forced labor for Jewish prisoners on their religious holidays.

In 1798, when Malta surrendered to the French, the rule of the Knights and their shameful traffic in human lives ended. The last Jewish prisoners languishing on the island were released on May 15, 1800. Jews had learned to overcome countless sufferings and vexations visited upon them throughout the centuries of dispersion. As time went by, the terrible wrongs caused by the Maltese Knights would have faded into oblivion, were it not for a reminder of those cruel times still found in the pages of the prayerbook. Following the reading of the Torah on

Mondays and Thursdays, a prayer is said for the release from bondage of those brethren in need or in captivity, on the seas or on firm ground.

The chapter on Malta is one more terrible record from Jewish history, which already abounds in tragedy—but the tireless efforts of Jewry in the rescue of its unfortunate brethren also offer one of the noblest examples of Jewish solidarity.

—Y.L.B.

 ## Life and Death of the Jews of St. Eustatius

Here lye the Remains of the Worthy youth Haim de Leon who departed this Life on Sunday being the Eve of the Grand Day of Atonement in the year 5547 of the Creation which Answers to the 7(th) day of October Anno 1787 he was for his Virtues his fear of God Obedience to his Parents fair dealings with all mankind beloved by every one who had the Pleasure of his acquaintance he was snatched from this troublesome world to Enjoy Eternal bliss at the Age of Nineteen.

These are the words carved on a slab of marble that marks the last resting-place of Chaim de Leon. "Statia," as Chaim probably called this place, is a tiny dot on the map, just nine miles square, 125 miles southeast of the Virgin Islands and about five hundred miles northeast of the South American mainland. Statia, which in the latter part of the eighteenth century played a significant role in a forgotten episode in the early history of the United States, also has a place in the history of the Jews of the Western Hemisphere.

Chaim de Leon's home was a place of picturesque and striking tropical beauty. On the west coast of this tiny island was a deep-water anchorage that harbored sailing ships of many nations. For almost two miles, a double row of warehouses with thick stone walls lined the waterfront. These walls bulged with merchandise of all kinds, brought from Europe for transshipment to the ports of the American continents. In the warehouses were large stocks of bronze and cast-iron cannon, muskets, cutlasses and gunpowder, all guarded day and night.

In 1776 Statia had a population of 150 white settlers and twelve hundred Negroes, but it was destined to grow in a few short years until its nine square miles were packed with thirty thousand people. By then it was bigger than Boston and its commerce outranked any North American port, but bloodshed and disaster intervened. Its prosperity vanished, its commerce ceased and its population declined to barely more than one thousand, including its important Jewish community. The island's residents gradually drifted away to find other homes on islands in the West Indies or in the new United States.

On the morning of November 16, 1776, Chaim de Leon, then a lad of eight, stood with the other citizens of Statia watching a drama unfold. The whole population of the town of Oranjestad had gathered on the ramparts of Fort Oranje, several hundred feet above the harbor and the warehouses below, to get a better look at the man-of-war coming about into the wind, preparatory to anchoring in the roadstead. Across the stern of the brigantine could be read her name and home port; she was the *Andrew Doria* out of Philadelphia. From the ship, anchored a few yards offshore, a shouted command came across the water as an ensign was hoisted at her mainmast. Caught by the brisk breeze, the banner was extended to its full breadth to reveal alternate horizontal red and white stripes and a design of thirteen stars in a circle on a blue background.

Standing on a stone observation platform at the highest point of Fort Oranje was Johannes de Graaf, the acting governor of St. Eustatius and the representative of the States General of The Netherlands. He was troubled and bewildered, for though the flag was strange, he rightly conjectured that it was the emblem of the thirteen colonies struggling for independence from Great Britain. Courtesy demanded that a salute be fired from the guns of the fort, but to fire such a salute to the rebels would be to commit an overt act of unfriendliness to Great Britain. International courtesy called for a thirteen-gun salute, but de Graaf, seeking a compromise, ordered the gunners to fire eleven guns as a gesture of recognition that also satisfied his own indecision. Johannes de Graaf didn't know it, but he had earned a niche in history, for he had ordered the first salute by a foreign power to the flag of the United States.

Other witnesses to this event were the crew members of a small sailing vessel that immediately weighed anchor and headed for the nearest British island of St. Kitts. There the British governor was informed that the Dutch had recognized the American rebels. He, in turn, relayed the news to London, where the British Admiralty learned of this unfriendly act toward the Crown. This was the forerunner of death, destruction and disaster for St. Eustatius. It was also the first act in a tragedy that caused the dissolution of the island's Jewish community.

Five years elapsed before Admiral Sir George Rodney led a powerful British fleet into the harbor of Oranjestad on February 3, 1781. The British systematically tore down the walls of the strongly built warehouses, confiscated their rich stores of goods and condemned the island of St. Eustatius to oblivion in world affairs.

As a result, twelve to twenty-five Jewish families, descendants of refugees from the Spanish Inquisition, found themselves in the role of fugitives. For them no further livelihood was possible. With overwhelming sadness, they abandoned the synagogue they had so proudly built and took leave of their dead, buried in a cemetery on the edge of the town. Tenderly and reverently, they removed the Torahs from the Ark and extinguished the Ner Tamid. Then, old and young, sick and well, hopeful and despondent, they left St. Eustatius forever.

Where had this Jewish community come from? What had brought them to this tiny Caribbean island? The answers take us back to 1492, the year Spain expelled the Jews and the year Columbus discovered America. Estimates of those compelled to leave Spain range from 250,000 to 800,000, but modern historians believe the figure was closer to 150,000. Portugal followed Spain with an expulsion order in 1497, and the next year the Kingdom of Navarre also ordered the Jews ousted from its domain.

Most of the refugees went to North Africa and Turkey. Some remained on the Iberian peninsula as Marranos or crypto-Jews, practicing Judaism secretly while outwardly professing Christianity. Some of the exiles made their way to London and others to Amsterdam. It is on the latter that our attention focuses.

In 1622, with the strong support of the Dutch Government, the Dutch West India Company was founded to trade with the Caribbean islands. In this large and powerful enterprise, Dutch Jews owned or controlled 25 percent of the stock. The reason was simple: these Jews had friends and relatives in the Spanish and Portuguese possessions of the Caribbean.

Whether the objective was trade or a military expedition, such an arrangement was bound to yield benefits to the Dutch West India Company. As a convenient and important example, the Company captured the Brazilian port of Recife or Pernambuco from the Portuguese in 1631. Recife was large and prosperous, and by 1640, Jews outnumbered all other Europeans by a margin of two to one. In 1648 there were more than five thousand Jews in this community, but in September 1654 Recife was recaptured by the Portuguese and the Inquisition was again destined to carry out its work of persecution and death.

The date 1654 is significant not only because it marks the death of the Recife community, but because it is the birth date of numerous other Jewish communities in the New World, not the least of which is New Amsterdam, a Dutch settlement the Indians called Manhattan.

There were other settlements too: in 1650 there were twelve Jewish families in Curaçao, the Dutch island off the coast of Venezuela. This community prospered and today its Jews are the bankers, merchants and shipowners of that island. Its original congregation, Mikveh Israel, is still serving its members, and a Reform Congregation, Temple Emmanuel, has celebrated its one hundredth anniversary.

The year of Recife's fall, 1654, not only dispersed Jews throughout the Caribbean, but led to a move into this area by other Sephardic Jews from London and Amsterdam as well as the flight of Marrano Jews from Spain and Portugal, who were anxious to resume their true identity. They not only settled in Curaçao, but they went to Surinam (formerly known as Dutch Guiana) and to Barbados, Jamaica and Martinique.

In the French colony of Martinique, one Benjamin Da Costa, of Marrano origin, introduced the culture of sugar cane and cocoa. He prospered and so did the island, until he incurred the jealous wrath of the local Jesuit fathers and finis was written to his enterprise in 1683. Two years later Louis XIV promulgated his infamous *Code Noir*, or Black Laws, which expelled all Jews from the French colonies. These Jews sought new homes in the Caribbean and it is believed that this accounted for the settlement at St. Eustatius.

In 1738 the Jews of Statia erected a home for the Congregation *Honen Dallim*, which means "Gracious to the Lowly." We know very little of their affairs until 1772, when a hurricane razed the synagogue and necessitated an appeal to other congregations for help. The minutes of Congregation Shearith Israel in New York tell us that a freewill offering at Passover yielded thirty-eight pounds, ten shillings and six pence—then about eighty dollars—which was sent to aid the stricken congregation.

Many such appeals reached Shearith Israel, also known as the Spanish-Portuguese Congregation of New York. One of the appeals from St. Eustatius was for a rabbi, and in 1774 Rabbi Ezekiel was sent to the little Dutch island as its spiritual leader. In those days, New York Jews who were unsuccessful were given another chance by being sent to various Caribbean islands, while those islands sent not only their unfortunates, but also their young and promising people, to New York. A sort of two-way Jewish family-and-children's bureau sprang into primitive operation with these practices.

Actually, there is not too much known about Jewish life on St. Eustatius. There is a legend that members of the family of Baruch Spinoza who left Holland and disappeared in the West Indies may have settled in Statia. Unfortunately, no detailed cataloging of burial monuments has been carried out on this island, as was done by E. M. Shilstone in Bridgetown, Barbados. Some early observations on Statia are part of a volume entitled *The Travels of a Lady of Quality in the West Indies* (author unknown). This eighteenth-century tourist visited the island prior to its sacking by Admiral Rodney. She described life and trade there and mentioned seeing two human derelicts of the Hebrew faith, victims of the Spanish Inquisition.

The Congregation *Honen Dallim* of St. Eustatius is mentioned occasionally in the history of Shearith Israel of New York. Although the lower town of St. Eustatius and all its commercial buildings were torn down by Admiral Rodney in 1781, he cannot be charged with anti-Semitism. The synagogue destruction was the result of a hurricane; there is no evidence of fire or willful destruction in the ruins as they can be seen today.

The Jews, as did their Dutch Christian fellow nationals, lost their property and businesses as well as their contacts with the Dutch West India Company. With characteristic energy and disaster-fostered courage, they decided to move to another island where fortune would be kinder. In 1796, they settled their families in St. Thomas, then under friendly Danish rule. Here a congregation already existed and, with the aid of the Statia Jews, a synagogue was erected. St. Thomas's community of twenty-two families, supplemented by arrivals from England and Statia, ultimately grew to sixty-four. In 1804 the St. Thomas synagogue burned with many valuable records, but by 1812 a new house of worship was built and a still-larger one was erected on the same site in 1823. Fire again destroyed the sanctuary in 1831, but two years later a new building was erected. It can be seen today in Charlotte Amalie, the principal city of the now American island of St. Thomas.

The history of the Jews in the Caribbean encompasses a great deal more than this brief glimpse. In general there is a similarity in the rise and decline of each of its many communities. St. Eustatius is barely known to the traveler today; even the ubiquitous American tourist does not include it in his itinerary. The grave of young Chaim de Leon is still there; the inscription on the stone is just as I have presented it above. Although the grave is seldom visited, it has a message for those who contemplate the unbroken continuity of Jewish history. The first name of the nineteen-year-old youth buried there is Chaim—a reminder of life, not of death.

—S.S.S.

 ## Mexico's Indian Jews

Calle Caruzo is a narrow, unpaved street in an impoverished area on the outskirts of Mexico City inhabited by working-class Mexicans. Number 254 is a small brick building adorned with the Star of David. It is the spiritual center of one of the oldest Jewish communities on the North American continent. Almost two thousand bronze-skinned Jews of Spanish-Indian descent are members of this congregation.

The synagogue is a one-floor edifice comparable in size to the living room of an average home in the United States. *Shema Yisrael Adonoi Eloheinu Adonoi Ehod,* the Jewish affirmation of faith, has been painted in Hebrew on the eastern wall.

Behind a table that serves as a pulpit, there is a holy ark which houses a Sefer Torah dating from the fifteenth century. Other physical appurtenances of the Temple are about forty low wooden benches and a cardboard carton that serves as a receptacle for the traditional skullcaps.

Sabbath attendance is largely confined to a group of about thirty, mostly women and children. The main reason for this small turnout is that the majority of members of the congregation live outside Mexico City and can afford to attend services only during the High Holy Days.

Poverty is no stranger to these Indian Hebrews, who are members of Mexico's laboring class. A new pair of shoes is a luxury to a family whose income does not exceed six dollars a week. Prayer books are in Spanish and Hebrew, but the service is conducted entirely in Spanish. It is not difficult to understand how the Hebrew language was forgotten by a community which had to maintain itself for over three hundred years in secret.

Baltasar Laureano Ramirez is a fifty-year-old civil lawyer who acts as rabbi during his free time. He is an amiable gentleman whose services are rendered to his followers free of charge. Besides his native tongue, Ramirez has a working knowledge of English and Hebrew.

With most of the congregation living in different villages throughout Mexico, Ramirez makes annual trips throughout the country, at which times he performs circumcisions and marriages and answers other spiritual needs of his congregants. This is all done at his own expense. Not too long ago, a friendly American tourist contributed a Sefer Torah, which will be used in a synagogue to be opened in a village in southern Mexico.

Ramirez is a sincere and dedicated Zionist. When the Israeli Ambassador visited Mexico, a special conference was arranged with Ramirez. At every sabbath service, a prayer is offered in honor of Israel. There are some members of the congregation who hope to immigrate there in the future.

What are the origins of the Indian Jews of Mexico? This is probably one of the most fascinating pages in the history of the Jewish Diaspora. Since there are still many questions which have yet to be answered, the community expects a historian to visit Mexico and make a comprehensive study.

The following information is available and can be authenticated by records in the National Archives of Mexico. The expulsion of the Jews from Spain took place in 1492 and in 1497 there was a compulsory conversion of the Jews in Portugal. In the hope of escaping the terrors of the Inquisition and returning to their ancestral faith, many of the new Christians immigrated to Mexico.

There is evidence that as early as 1521, a Jew named Hernando Alonso who accompanied Cortes was given a land grant as a reward for his participation in the conquest of Mexico. Since so many Marranos, or new Christians, were immigrating to the Spanish colonies, a papal bull of 1537 forbade the immigration of new Christians.

In 1571, an Inquisitional Tribunal was established in Mexico City for the purpose of *"liberar el país, contaminado por judíos y hereticos, especialmente de la nación portuguesa"* (freeing the country contaminated by Jews and heretics, especially of Portuguese origin).

It has been estimated that no less than a thousand Marranos were condemned to death by the Inquisitional Tribunal in Mexico for secretly practicing the Jewish faith.

One of the most famous cases handled by the Inquisition was that of Luis Carvajal, a Marrano who settled in Mexico in 1567. Carvajal was appointed governor of Leon, a tremendous area of land extending from Tampico, Mexico, to what is presently known as San Antonio, Texas. A special privilege was granted by the King of Spain whereby Carvajal was allowed to bring one hundred of his relatives and friends from Spain.

In 1596, Governor Carvajal and most of his relatives were denounced to the office of the Inquisitional Tribunal for the crime of "living by the law of Moses." Subsequently, they—including Carvajal—were condemned to death and many were burned at the stake. One of the officers of Mexico's Indian synagogue bears the name of Carvajal and is one of the descendants of this illustrious sixteenth-century governor.

By the time the Inquisition was suppressed in 1820, Jewish life in Mexico was almost completely eradicated. In spite of all the dangers involved, many Marranos, ostensibly practicing Catholics, continued to observe Jewish rituals. They were the ancestors of the present-day Indian Jewish community.

There is evidence that a newspaper, *El Sabado Secreto* (The Secret Sabbath) was published in 1889 for the benefit of those Marranos who were still aware of their Jewish background.

It was not until 1910 that the Indian Jewish community of Mexico felt secure enough to announce its existence to the world. It is almost incredible that this group survived and was aware of its identity with the House of Israel after more than three hundred years of maintaining themselves in secret and in the shadow of the Inquisition.

While religious freedom has become an actuality for these Mexican Jews, there are formidable problems facing the small community. With no funds available to hire a teacher or establish a school, the Indian Jewish children are being deprived of a Jewish education. Knowledge of Hebrew was almost completely lost after centuries of living in fear of the Inquisition. Ramirez justly feels that a Jewish education for the youth is the only way to prevent the assimilation of his group with the Mexican Catholic population.

Another basic problem involves the fact that the tiny community does not have sufficient funds to own a cemetery. Consequently, the members of the community must be buried within Christian burial grounds. The Indian Jews have been very disheartened by this situation and hope that some aid will come from sympathetic brethren in the United States.

At the present time, Ramirez is trying to select a young man in the congregation who can become his successor. It is his hope that the person chosen will be able to receive rabbinical training in the United States. The service of a full-time spiritual leader is an indispensable need for the Indian Jews.

In spite of all these problems, Ramirez and his followers feel optimistic as far as the future is concerned. During the past few years, many American Jewish tourists have found their way to the little synagogue on Calle Caruzo and have been impressed by the devotional sincerity of their Indian brethren. Ramirez is hopeful that eventually the much-needed financial aid will come from the American Jewish community.

Ramirez has stated that there are as many as fifty thousand Mexican Catholics who are aware of the fact that they have Jewish ancestry. He has spoken to some of their leaders, who have expressed an interest in returning to the faith of their forefathers. Since most of these people are concentrated in the vicinity of Monterey (part of the territory governed by Carvajal in the sixteenth century), he hopes that someday a synagogue will be established there.

The Indian Israelites are living proof of the survival of the Jewish faith and the failure of the Spanish Inquisition to eliminate the Law of Moses.

—N.F.

The Port of the Smiling Jews

The port I call my favorite exists to this very day, but only on the map. Every port is a combination of landscapes, atmospheres and people. I doubt if the landscape has altered much, but I know that the atmosphere has changed completely —because the people who lived, worked and loved in my favorite port are all dead.

Against the backdrop of the sun-scorched Jaffa skyline, near the ridge of dreaded rocks where beautiful Andromeda was chained and Jonah the prophet embarked on his voyage of destiny, there the keel of the voyage that led me to my favorite port was laid.

The call of the sea proved stronger than all other calls, and at the outbreak of the World War, I found myself sailing on a Jewish-manned vessel, attached to the British Admiralty, supplying the Australian troops in Libya.

After a few shuttle runs, I transferred to a Norwegian tanker bound for a rendezvous with Allied aircraft carriers thirsty for high octane.

Off the isle of Crete, on the twelve-to-four watch, we caught a "tin fish." It was my watch below, and when I got on deck I found a nightmarish turmoil of smoke, flames and the screams of trapped men. Without too much deliberation I dived over the side and made a point of putting as much distance as possible between me and the inferno that once was a comfortable Norwegian tanker.

After more hours than I care to remember now, I was picked up by a fishing boat where, to my surprise, I was greeted by three members of our crew who had transferred earlier from one of the rafts. Fortunately for us, the flames had attracted the attention of the fishermen, who came with their boat to pick up survivors. They were very friendly, but since none of us understood their language, nor they ours, no conversation could develop.

Daylight was breaking on the horizon and the closer we came to shore the more excited I became. When the small harbor came into sight a shiver passed through my body. If it hadn't been for the high, distant mountains, I'd willingly have wagered a round of drinks that we were heading toward the familiar shore of my home port of Jaffa, or at least a fairly accurate replica of her. I was amazed to see the square white houses hugging the side of the small hill, and the same ridge of forbidding crags. Even the wind was permeated with the fragrance of distant citrus orchards. And . . . some sixth sense told me that the fishermen were not

Greeks. I find it difficult to explain, but something in their faraway expression urged me to ask them who they might be. However, the fear that the question would seem silly and the lack of a common language prevented me from inquiring about their identity.

A group of men, women and children were awaiting us on the small boat quay when we landed. An old man separated himself from the standing people and greeted us warmly in English.

"Who are you all?" I inquired curiously. "Are you Greeks?"

He smiled good-heartedly, and while my shipmates were led to one of the houses, asked me, "And who are you, son?"

When I told him where I came from he was stunned. He stopped walking, clenched my hand and murmured a prayer in cracked ancient Hebrew. Luckily for me, I was able to continue the passage, which excited him to such an extent that he began shouting to the people. Before long I found myself surrounded, hugged and kissed by every man, woman and child within hearing distance.

"But who are you?" I insisted.

"Cretan Jews," answered the old man. "Our forefathers came here a very long time ago."

The next day the three Norwegians went to town to report to the shipping authorities. I stayed to take my survivor leave there and it wasn't long before I joined one of the old man's boats. He was, according to the tradition of his family, a descendant of the tribe of Levi—the tribe that I belong to, as well, according to the tradition of our family.

After many days and nights of hauling in fish and drinking good Cretan *raki* and wine with my new brethren, I learned that those people were a remote tribe of seagoing Jews. According to tradition, their forefathers came there with King Solomon's Tarshish ships to act as marines and guardsmen of the Hebrew-Phoenician colonies founded on the island.

"After the second Temple was destroyed by the Romans," the fisherman said to me once in a legend-telling tone, "a wave of refugees from your own town of Jaffa came here. Because this was a stubborn maritime rebel base of Judean fighters, the Romans did all they could to destroy this place and exile its inhabitants."

The sea was the center of the life of these people from birth until death, and no seafarer could have been prouder of his way of life. In a confirmation ceremony that I was invited to, I marveled and appreciated the way in which a thirteen-year-old boy had to prove his manhood. He was put in a boat and had to row her out to sea, return, anchor and make her fast in a perfect seamanlike way. After he passed this task successfully, he was called not only by the traditional Jewish expression, *Bar Mitzva,* but also (in Greek) *Kalos Kaiagatos*—a good and able seaman.

I noticed that as soon as the children could read they were taught by heart all the Bible passages referring to seamanship, like "those who go down to the sea in ships," etc. I'll never forget the wonderful "Nauta" feast—the maritime "day of Jonah," when all grown-ups and children danced, sang and sailed in their boats until late at night; nor can I ever take out of my mind the two well-varnished oars that were put in a dead man's grave so that when "time comes" he could row his way to the land of Israel!

I have sailed the seas ever since. I have been to practically every continent and had wonderful times in London and Durban, in Sydney and New York, but none of these ports was my favorite as was that tiny little port of the Cretan seafaring Jews. Every homecoming was to me a special thrill.

One day I received an urgent message from the Norwegian consul to come see him at once "with kitbag and all." "The Germans invaded Greece," he said. "We are clearing away all stranded seamen. You'd better leave soon. I got a ship for you."

"I am not stranded at all," I answered him, "but I guess I'll have to leave." I went back to the place that had become my home and gathered all the men to tell them of the developments.

"Let's take the boats and leave the island at once."

"We can't do that," snapped the old man. "Where shall we go? The gates of our land are locked by the British, as you say. If we sail they'll exile us to rot on some African island as they did other Jewish refugees. We are seafaring people. We can't be prisoners! We either live honorably or die. Besides, why should Hitler bother with a few poor fishermen . . . ?"

So I sailed away alone, with the intention of coming back after the war to bring them to Jaffa where they belonged.

Some time later, on my way to the Gold Coast, I heard over the radio that the island of Crete had been invaded by the Germans and that thousands of Australian, British, New Zealand, as well as Palestinian Jewish soldiers serving with the British forces in separate units had been taken prisoners.

Needless to say, my heart and mind were always with these people. As soon as the island was liberated I managed to get to Alexandria and join a small British coaster bound for Eraklio, Crete.

None of the crew nor the old man understood why I signed to join their dirty old coal-burner.

When we dropped anchor in Eraklio I went up to the old man. "Sir," I said, "I want three days off."

"Are you daft?" said he. "You want to waste three good days in this olive-oil stinking hole? What for?"

"Well, it just happens that I have some relatives here," I said, "whom I'd like very much to see."

"Relatives," mimicked the chief, sitting on the old man's settee and sipping his whiskey and soda.

"Yes," I said. "Relatives. And you'll be surprised—they've followed the sea as a way of life for many, many generations."

"Go 'way, Jack. Don't give us this malarkey," laughed the chief scornfully. "The only Jews that I have ever seen near the sea were clever ship chandlers."

Eventually I got my three days and hurried to the place. It was ruined. The white stone houses were bombed, shattered. No boat, no sail, not a soul. No, there was someone—an old fisherman. I went over and looked at him. He was trying to catch some oysters among the rocks.

"Where are they?" I asked. He shook his head. "The *Ovreos* [Hebrews]?" I tried my long-forgotten Greek.

"Oh," he replied sadly, passing his forearm across his throat as if with a butcher's knife, "they are all gone. The Germans killed them. Paratroops by the thousands. Goering's division. The rest were sent to the gas chambers in Poland with the rest of the Jews who lived in the towns."

"Well," smiled the old man to me when I came down the fo'c'sle stairs. He was doing some sort of inspection with the mate. "Met your Jewish seagoing relatives, did ye?" He gave me a wicked wink. "I bet she was good, the Jewish relative of yours."

The chief roared with laughter.

For a moment I looked at them.

That was the world I lived in.

Then I went inside the cabin and slammed the door. I approached the porthole and looked away toward the sea.

—Y.R.

 ## The Good Samaritans: Somehow They Have Survived

Fifty years ago they were a dying community. Decimated by wars, massacres, disease and poverty, the Samaritans of the West Bank town of Nablus, Jewry's oldest dissident religious sect, numbered about 130 persons. Many of them foresaw their eventual disappearance. Ancient manuscripts from the days of Samaria's glory and faded photographs of their Passover sacrifice of the paschal lamb would, it seemed, be all that remained.

Yet this small sect, which clung so tenaciously to its holy sites for thousands of years against overwhelmingly hostile odds, has managed to survive. Since 1949 they have been citizens of Israel. Today more than five hundred Samaritans, one-fourth of them born since the Six-Day War, live in equal numbers in Nablus and Holon. (Holon Samaritans, who are Israeli citizens, serve in the Israeli army.) Poised between dreams of regaining their former status as the dominant people of an independent nation in Samaria and recognition of their present precarious situation, they lead an ambivalent life. On the one hand are the political realities of the situation in the West Bank that are likely to affect their future; on the other, the strict rules governing their lives, to which they cling as the only guarantee of survival.

"We are really too small a nation to be of interest to anybody," says Zebulon Altif, an English teacher in Nablus. Very much the circumspect Levantine, he hesitates, weighing the possible consequences of each word. "We are, nonetheless, a nation with a language of its own, an alphabet and literature of its own, and a centuries-old history and tradition."

The concept of nationhood is central to the entire community's thinking. The Samaritans prefer to put questions of official nationality aside and declare themselves Samaritans—neither Arab nor Jewish. However, the British, who once controlled the region, and the Jordanians, who took their place, and now the Israelis, couldn't make up their minds whether the Samaritans really are a separate people. Most Arabs have traditionally considered them Jews, the remnant of an ancient people. The Israeli governor of Nablus treats them as a special sector of the population and gives special attention to their problems, but they have neither a separate ethnic status nor official religious representation.

The Samaritans' identity problem goes back to the schism between the Jews and themselves in the fifth century B.C.E., one hundred years after the Jewish return from exile in Babylon. According to Biblical and Talmudic sources, they are the descendants of foreign peoples brought into ancient Israel after the Assyrian conquest in 701 B.C.E., who adopted the religion and customs of the people among whom they lived. Samaritans and modern Biblical scholars, however, insist that only a small elite group of Israelites was expelled by the Babylonians and that the Samaritans are, in fact, descendants of the Israelite peasantry who remained behind and preserved the old ways. Whatever the truth, and to distinguish themselves from the Jews in Judea, the Samaritans took a separate name, *Shomronim*, from the Hebrew *shomer* (to conserve). They rejected the new religious texts, including Joshua, Kings, Judges and Samuel, recognizing only the first five books of the Pentateuch as authoritative. They also ignored the square, Assyrian script introduced by the priest Ezra in the fifth century B.C.E., continuing to use the original Hebrew Canaanite script. Unyieldingly, they preserved ancient Israelite laws and practices. (Among those still maintained is the custom of praying on the ground while kneeling.)

Around the time of Jesus, when they probably numbered some seven hundred and fifty thousand, the Samaritans are believed to have reached their peak. After the Bar Kochba revolt in the second century C.E., the Samaritans expanded into Jewish areas, creating friction and leading to criticism by Jewish sages of their laxness in religious observance—which in turn caused them to be increasingly regarded as non-Jews. By 634 C.E., on the eve of the Moslem conquest and after centuries of incessant warfare with the Byzantines, there were three hundred thousand Samaritans, dispersed in cities from Damascus to Cairo, with large concentrations in Gaza and Nablus. Thereafter their community continued to dwindle.

Modern Samaritans maintain a rigorous observance of the sabbath, and many of their practices—including circumcision, Bar Mitzvahs and kashruth—are almost identical to those of Jews. Central to the Samaritans' code are annual pilgrimages to Mt. Gerizim, their holy site and capital of their nation, during Passover, Shavuoth and Sukkoth. Those who do not participate are automatically excluded from the sect. This, along with foreign oppression by various conquerors over the centuries, contributed more than anything else to the population's decline. Authorization for these pilgrimages was granted reluctantly under Jordanian rule to the Samaritan community in Holon, south of Tel Aviv. With prospects for a peace agreement between Jordan and Israel on the distant horizon, the Samaritans are extremely worried that, unless they are recognized as a distinct people, with special religious status and access to Mt. Gerizim guaranteed to them, they will be forgotten. "We have no political ambitions," says Altif. "The only really essential matter for us is that our continued link with Mt. Gerizim should be preserved. Without that link, we shall cease to exist."

Huddled in a neighborhood of small, two- and three-story houses under the bright Mediterranean sun at the western edge of Nablus, next to the steep cliffs that ring the city, is the Samaritan quarter. With its narrow alleyways and the synagogue surrounded by homes, it evokes the impression of a North African *mellah*. Below it lies the crowded cluster of the city's buildings and behind it is Mt. Gerizim. For the Samaritans, the mountain is the true site of Abraham's attempted sacrifice of Isaac; it is the place where God chose his gate to heaven and called for his temple to be built. These Samaritan convictions long ago exacerbated the split with Jewry and with Jerusalem.

Samaritans in Nablus are virtually indistinguishable from Arabs and are treated by them with a mixture of neighborly friendliness and unease, augmented by the common knowledge that a sizable number of the city's Moslem families were only recently converted to Islam and are themselves of Samaritan origin. How many?

"Many," Altif tells me, smiling evasively.

Among the Samaritans, despite their lack of political ambitions, there is an unspoken resentment of their dispossession—by Assyrians, Persians, Greeks, Romans, Byzantines and most recently Arabs—from a city and a region that were once completely theirs. The formerly crowded old quarter, abandoned after a 1927 earthquake, and the old Samaritan synagogue, now converted into a mosque, still hold nostalgic memories. With space a precious commodity, and fearing that the Samaritan community might expand, no Arab will sell land to a Samaritan. On Mt. Gerizim, many Samaritans have built second homes on 150 *dunams* of land near the peak, which King Hussein decreed is communally held religious property that cannot be touched. They hope to set up a new district once water and electricity can be supplied. Within the quarter, plans have been drawn up for a housing project to provide homes for more than twenty couples who have put off marriage until apartments are available.

"We really lead two separate lives," notes Altif. "One as part of the greater society we live in and the other with our own people." A Samaritan child begins to experience this reality at the age of four, when he starts studying the Samaritan language and reading the Pentateuch. All Samaritan children attend state schools and religious classes in the afternoon. As they grow up, like Jews, they rapidly assume the characteristics of the people they live amidst and, like Jews, continue to remain apart. No one language is really theirs; they switch swiftly from Arabic into Hebrew, dropping into Samaritan and Samaritan Aramaic (the only languages that may be used for these subjects) when discussing liturgical and religious questions. Their "double life" and the element of detachment and danger accompanying it have heightened the Samaritans' powers of observation and have made them extremely perceptive and mentally flexible.

As with the Jews, they have learned over the centuries to keep a low profile and to carry themselves with the restrained, withdrawn demeanor common to other Middle Eastern minority peoples—such as the Armenians—who for centuries have had to cope with the vagaries of unpredictable authorities. For example, Sukkoth bowers are discreetly set up inside their homes rather than outdoors, and *mezuzot* are hung behind the doors instead of facing the street.

When Altif brought out an eight-hundred-year-old Torah to show to us, we asked if we could photograph it. "Only inside the house," he replied. In the courtyard, perhaps? "Well, in the doorway, no farther."

Some 25 percent of the Nablus Samaritans are members of the "priestly class," who are entitled to become priests. Actually there are only seven priests, whose salaries are provided by the Israeli Ministry of Religious Affairs. Heading the group is ailing ninety-one-year-old High Priest Amram Ben Itzhak, who acts as a judge, fixes dates for religious holidays and leads holiday services. Few of the "priestly class" have independent professions; most are government clerks and office workers who, like other West Bank residents, continue to draw both their Jordanian and Israeli salaries—which has lifted the standards of living of some of them in Nablus dramatically during the past decade. (Nablus Samaritans draw at least double the average Israeli income; Holon Samaritans earn about the same salaries as do most Israelis.)

In personal relationships, the ways of the modern world have penetrated the community. The traditional patriarchal family pattern is beginning to weaken. One evidence of change: marriages are no longer arranged by the parents of the bride and groom.

"We believe that the role of parents is to advise," says Altif. "Parents can no longer expect to impose their will on their children. Our children are proud of their faith and assimilation is not a problem. We are changing. We may change more in every aspect except for one thing—our religion."

Samaritans have traditionally banned all marriages with outsiders, except for Jews. Seven Samaritan men are now married to Jewesses who, according to present practice, have declared their willingness to adopt Samaritan religious customs, have lived in their bridegrooms' homes for at least six months to become familiar with the community's ways and have been approved by the High Priest.

Although the Samaritans are avowedly disinterested in politics, a strong undercurrent of pro-Israel sentiment runs through the community. Since 1967 Hebrew has become the Samaritans' lingua franca; they use it freely among themselves on Nablus streets. They admire the Israelis and to a great extent identify with them. This sentiment reaches even to the children scrambling in the narrow alleyways of the quarter, who have painted on a courtyard wall a flag with the Star of David. Underneath, defiantly, is daubed one word in Arabic letters—"Israel!"

The Samaritans in the Holon community exhibit the same ambivalence of identity as those in Nablus, in more muted form. Spread over a flat stretch of land in the humid heat of the coastal lowlands, the single-storied, red-tile neighborhood dates to 1954, when Yitzhak Ben Zvi, then President of Israel, personally arranged to provide the Samaritans with a place where they could all live together.

The coastal community was founded shortly after the turn of the century, when a Samaritan merchant from Nablus set up his home in nearby Jaffa. Several other families came in the 1920s and 1930s; after the Six-Day War four more families arrived from Nablus. While natural increase has raised their number to 250, Samaritan families here, as in Nablus, are small, with an average of three children. Despite the decades-long disproportion between male and female offspring (five to three) they have retained the Oriental preference for sons.

With nearly half the community's members under the age of twenty, Holon Samaritans have, to all appearances, blended into the larger Israeli society. This is especially true of the youth—who are Hebrew-speaking and in dress and manners identical to Israelis of their age—except for their religion. However, there are distinct gaps between them and their elders.

"The older generation had very little ambition," remarks red-haired, freckled twenty-three-year-old Naim Tsedaka. "They were very much content to let things lie as they were." Still, Naim, an accountant at the Bank of Israel, acknowledges that he prefers to remain at home until plans for new housing on community land materialize, since "We need to remain within the community in order to preserve our special way of life."

Young people such as Naim, who have grown up in Israel, have gone to Israeli schools and now work within Israeli society, find they have very little in common with the community in Samaria, even though they frequently visit relations in Nablus. About two years ago another young Holon Samaritan, Miriam Tsedaka, a social science student at Tel Aviv University, caused something of a scandal with an article in the community's biweekly newspaper, *Aleph Beth*, in which she declared that common interests were few between the two groups of young people, and criticized the conservative ways of her parents' generation.

The establishment of *Aleph Beth* with Israeli government assistance in 1969 was a significant turning point for the community. Its editors, the brothers Binyamim and Yefet Tsedaka, who are unofficial spokesmen for the Samaritans, run the paper as a combination newsletter, historical research chronicle and forum for discussion of community problems. Appearing in Hebrew, English, Arabic and the ancient Samaritan script, and publishing items of topical as well as religious interest, plus reprints of articles about the Samaritans from Israel and abroad, it has become a vehicle for a small-scale cultural renaissance.

Bushy-haired, bespectacled Binyamim Tsedaka is married to a converted Jewess; they have three children. His Romanian-born wife, Miriam, has successfully integrated into the community. This included learning how to prepare his favorite Samaritan dishes, which are based on seasonally available foods—mainly fruits and vegetables—always fresh.

"Intermarriage constitutes a radical change in the life of any person," he explains. "My wife had to accept the special religious framework within which we live. But once that was accomplished, there were virtually no other obstacles."

The other Miriam Tsedaka, the student, also talks about this special religious framework. "I have Israeli friends who come to visit and I go to see them in their homes. We find that we have very few differences, but that doesn't mean they don't exist. They have a great deal more freedom than I do. I don't eat out because of the kashruth laws. I don't call up in the afternoon to let my parents know that I'll be spending the night at a girl friend's home. But when you are bound up in a special religious framework, your life will automatically have certain limitations, and in the end you find it is better to have a faith within which to live."

While the palpable tension in the Nablus community is absent in Holon, none of the young people can envision changes in their way of life and, along with their elders, remain very much apart from their neighbors. Sometimes there is friction, even minor incidents. The Neot Yehudit controversy is a case in point.

Relations with the residents of Neot Yehudit, a high-rise housing project near Holon for young couples from Tel Aviv, have been far from tranquil over the past few years and were exacerbated several years ago because some Samaritan youths constructed a basketball court on the small public garden that divides the two neighborhoods. A noisy Samaritan Bar Mitzvah party led to an open confrontation when Neot Yehudit families, whose apartments overlook the Samaritan synagogue, complained about the noise from Saturday evening prayers, which peaked in volume at two in the morning, disturbing their sleep. Emotions calmed after a visit by the Holon mayor and meetings between residents of both communities. However, the Samaritans, with the tenaciousness that has helped them survive for thousands of years, adamantly declared they have no intention of praying at either a more convenient hour or of lowering the volume of their prayers.

"Others can choose or change their way of life," says young Miriam Tsedaka, "not us. We have a special responsibility to preserve it."

—J.Kr.

 Incident in North Africa

Early in World War II my company, part of a combat engineer regiment, was stationed in Tlemscen, a small city of some importance in Morocco, North Africa. We were billeted in a public, centrally located building within the city limits.

The usual kitchen facilities and security guard details were set up and the company settled down to what was to become a stay of about forty-five days. Tlemscen was as far removed from active battle conditions as the times could permit and, in fact, we were the first American troops that the great majority of Tlemscen inhabitants had ever seen.

One early morning I set off toward the center of town. As I left the building, two young lads—they couldn't have been more than ten or eleven years of age—jumped up from their seated position on a curbstone and began walking alongside me, staring up at my face. Their gaze bored into my eyes as if trying to relay a message. I walked briskly on and soon left them behind.

Later that day, during the late afternoon, I again ventured forth and, sure enough, the two youngsters were sitting in the very same spot they had occupied earlier. As I came abreast of them they fell into step beside me and kept pace with me. Their black, penetrating eyes drilled into my very mind, and yet no word had been spoken, no sound made. These two ill-clad lads wanted something of me, I was sure, and I reached into my pocket, bringing out two packages of gum. (The Americans always had plenty of candy, gum and cigarettes, and I am convinced that, if any one thing was responsible for hurrying the war on, it was the enormous amounts of candies, gums and cigarettes doled out to the natives.)

The boys took possession of the gum, still making no sound. There was only that steady, intent gaze.

The next morning I was out again, not at any appointed time, and there they were, my walking companions of the previous day. Again they fell into step beside me, their penetrating gaze focused on my own eyes. Suddenly—and this was the first uttered word in our walks together—one of the boys said, "Yud," or so it sounded to me. I just kept on walking and soon left the youths behind, each with a package of gum in his hand and a disconsolate look on his face.

That afternoon curiosity began to get the best of me; these two boys had a purpose in their attachment to me, their speechless walks, their intent, concentrated gaze. All this had a meaning and I was determined to penetrate it—if no other way, then by sign language. This time I walked up to them and handed each a candy bar to cement friendly relations. Their smiles assured me that the gesture was appreciated.

We walked along in silence and then, again, the bolder of the two looked up into my eyes and, this time with a finger pointed straight at me, said, "Yud." Good God—suddenly it dawned on me what they had been trying to convey. I had never been greeted as "Yud" in my entire life—only by the term "Jew." How could I make known to them that I was, indeed, a Jew, a "Yud"?—as apparently they were too. They spoke no English and I didn't understand their language.

Then I knew how. I reached beneath my shirt and drew out from next to my chest the *mezuzah* I wore on a chain.

At once pandemonium broke loose; both lads jumped into the air, exuberant, and when they came down on firm soil they were different individuals. They were smiling, they cried, they laughed, they were in hysterics. When they quieted down enough to do so, they each grabbed me by a hand and led me through the streets to a building on the far side of town, a building on which was affixed, of all things, a Star of David.

It was, indeed, a synagogue; these two lads were Jewish, and they were, in obvious glee, taking me to their rabbi.

The building, like most synagogues, housed a classroom, and a class in Hebrew was in progress. As my two newfound friends burst into the room with me in tow, one of the students glanced up at me and at once pounded the top of his desk—a signal, I learned later, indicating to the rabbi that a personage of importance had entered the room. Well, no need to elaborate on it, but the class terminated at that moment; all of the boys in the room surrounded me, swarmed and jumped on me, tried to kiss me, wanted to touch me, everywhere at once. Finally I was rescued by the rabbi, whose shout of authority asserted the strict discipline they were accustomed to.

That moment warmed me more than any since I had entered the service. The boys could hardly contain themselves, so the rabbi dismissed the class, after which he sat with me. Being a very learned man, he was able to converse in many languages, English among them. We spoke of many things. The rabbi asked me where my parents were born, and when I told him my mother was from Kiev and my father from Odessa, he said he spoke Yiddish, too, and asked if I would like to continue conversing in Yiddish. Well, I can't say why I felt the urge and the need, but I replied in the affirmative. Although I had never learned the language properly, I spoke and understood Yiddish because of a strong Jewish home background.

The rabbi agreed with me that although it was unexplainable, it was an emotionally wonderful happening, a spiritual phenomenon, that these two youngsters attached themselves to me, out of more than one hundred men stationed there in Tlemscen, a group such as they had never seen in all of their young lives—how they sensed and knew and persisted until they confirmed their instinctive feelings that I was, as they were, a "Yud"—for it so happened that in the entire detachment of soldiers stationed there in Tlemscen I was the only one of Jewish origin.

—S.L.

 ## The Japanese Planned a Jewish State—in Manchuria

The two events that dominate the past half century of Jewish history are of course, the Holocaust, in which one-third of the Jewish people were murdered and, on the obverse side of the coin, the establishment of Israel, the realization of a national dream and hope of nearly two thousand years.

Thousands of books have been written about the events that preceded and occurred during the Holocaust, yet somehow we still do not know the full, incredible, heartbreaking story. Now, a Long Island rabbi has produced yet another work, from which we can learn for the first time an aspect of those dark days that had remained hidden until now.

Rabbi Marvin Tokayer, a fortyish, straightforward kind of man whose formidable biceps make one think that, had he lived in Israel, he would have become a kibbutz founder or a Haganah commander, spent ten years in Tokyo, serving as spiritual leader of the local Jewish community. His original plan was to stay only two years, but somehow they kept stretching out, until one day he realized he had been living and working in the Japanese capital for a full decade.

He expanded his synagogue, which serves Ashkenazic and Sephardic Jews. Some of them are permanent residents who have been living in Japan for two or more generations; others are stationed in Japan on a temporary basis, working or teaching or studying. These Jews have come together for worship, study, celebration of *simchas*, socializing and to maintain their Jewish links. (Rabbi Tokayer pooh-poohs any serious talk of Japanese who wish to convert to Judaism, although here and there some rare persons, out of conviction or sometimes through marriage with a Jew, do join the Jewish community and are fully welcomed into its ranks.)

Rabbi Tokayer (with Mary Swartz) has published a book with the improbable title *The Fugu Plan*, the result of many years of painstaking research into the situation of the Jewish refugees who found haven in Japan and in Japanese-occupied Shanghai during the period of World War II, when Japan, of course, was a full partner of Hitler Germany. It is an absolutely compelling narrative that opens up a hitherto untold chapter of World War II, and sheds light on the Jews, the Japanese, the Americans, and human nature itself.

The Fugu Plan reveals that prior to the war, in the tumultuous, tense Thirties,

when Nazism was on the rise—and when Japan was being more and more isolated from the Western world because of its growing militarism, especially its invasion and conquest of Manchuria—the Japanese "discovered" Jews.

There were never many Jews living in Japan—a handful in Tokyo and a small
number in Kobe. Many had strong ties in Far Eastern commerce; some were Russian Jews who had fled the Soviet revolution and struck new roots in that virtually
unknown country. The Jews, by and large, were financially well off, kept a low
profile vis-à-vis the Japanese population, and were generally regarded by the Japanese people and authorities as oddities, with whom peaceful relations were maintained, in the spirit of traditional Japanese politeness and emphasis on privacy.

Nevertheless, the Japanese, in the Thirties, came to the conclusion that Jews
were superbly clever, had immeasurable worldwide financial clout, and were just
the right people to invite into the empty spaces of conquered Manchuria—to
which the indigenous Japanese refused to migrate—and turn that area into a vast,
productive, industrial stronghold. The fact that Jews were being ejected from central Europe by the Nazis seemed to play right into the hands of the Japanese. The
plan was to offer the exiled Jews an opportunity to settle Manchuria—in effect, to
set up their own Jewish state and populate the barren landscape.

However, since they were allied with the Nazis, and because they knew that the
plan was fraught with risks on the diplomatic, economic and political fronts, the
Japanese proceeded very carefully with their plan. (The term "Fugu" was used
because the Japanese word for a blowfish, *fugu*, implied that while the caught and
prepared fish was very succulent to the taste, it was also very risky to go fishing
for, since it could, if not handled skillfully, destroy the would-be devourer.)

The book traces the moving stories of a number of Jewish and Japanese personalities, from the time of the outbreak of the war in 1939 up to the freeing of
Shanghai after the Japanese surrender in 1945. Virtually every page is deeply
moving, as the reader comes to understand that among the Japanese there were
very humane people (one young counsel, stationed in Kovno, Lithuania, personally
handed out six thousand visas to destitute, desperate Jews who had fictitious visas
to Dutch-affiliated Curaçao, saving them from certain death), while among the
Jews there were, in addition to a whole army of heroic, self-sacrificing, dedicated
people, also some whose sole aim was to save their own necks, without regard for
others.

There are many chilling moments in the book. At one time, the Gestapo's
"Butcher of Warsaw" arrived in Shanghai, which then held a concentration of
nearly twenty thousand Jews, and proposed to his Japanese allies that all the Jews
be rounded up on ramshackle ships rotting in the harbor, stripped naked, and sent
out to sea, where they would then be torpedoed. The diabolical plan was rejected
by the Japanese, despite their close ties to the Nazis.

A Chassidic *rebbe*, loved and admired by the Jewish refugees in Kobe, was
summoned one day for an interrogation by Japanese naval officers who apparently
were greatly influenced by Hitlerian racial theories. Medals glistening, their uni-
forms sharply creased, the officers confronted the *rebbe* and posed one question:
"Why do the Germans hate the Jews so much?" Unflustered, stroking his beard
for a moment, the *rebbe* replied: "Because we, like you, are Asians." He explained the Germans' idolatrous regard for blond, Nordic, blue-eyed people. The
Japanese listened, pondered and ended the interview, abandoning any thoughts
they might have had of launching an anti-Jewish campaign.

One of the Japanese described in the book, Setsuzo Kotsuji, always a staunch
defender of the Jews, proceeded to Israel, embraced Judaism, and when he died

was buried in Jerusalem. His funeral was attended by Mir Yeshiva students whom he had aided during the years of peril.

—D.C.G.

 ## When a Jewish Kingdom Ruled Southern Russia

In the Middle Ages, fanaticism, ignorance and anarchy reigned in Western Europe while wild nomadic people roamed through Eastern Europe and the vast reaches of Russia. By contrast, the kingdom of the Khazars enjoyed all the privileges of civilized nations, a well-constituted and tolerant government, a flourishing trade and a well-disciplined army. The Khazars could boast of their just and broad-minded administration, and all who were persecuted because of their religion found refuge in their kingdom. The most remarkable feature of the kingdom of Khazaria was that Judaism was the dominant state religion for several hundred years.

The Khazars' history is interwoven with that of the Jews of Russia, since their settlement on the shores of the Black and Caspian seas in the first centuries of the common era. By the second half of the eighth century, the Khazar empire's zone of direct influence extended all over the immense plains of southern Russia, stretching from the northern shores of the Black and Caspian seas to the Urals and the Volga beyond Kazan.

Historians disagree on the details of the conversion of the Khazars to Judaism. According to some scholars, the conversion took place in the year 620; according to others, in 740. An outstanding Jewish scholar and statesman, Hasdai Ibn-Shaprut, who was foreign minister for the Sultan of Cordoba, wrote to King Joseph of the Khazars in the year 960, seeking information about the geography of Khazaria, its internal constitution, the customs and occupations of the inhabitants and, especially, the history of Joseph's ancestry.

In his reply, Joseph gave the following account of the conversion of his ancestors to Judaism:

> *Some centuries ago, King Bulan reigned over the Khazars. To him God appeared in a dream and promised him might and glory. Encouraged by this dream, Bulan went by the road of Darlan to the county of Ardebil, where he gained great victories (over the Arabs). The Byzantine emperor and the caliph of the Ishmaelites sent envoys to him with gifts and sages to convert him to their respective religions. Bulan invited also wise men of Israel and proceeded to examine them all. As each of the champions believed his religion to be the best, Bulan separately questioned the Mohammedans and the Christians as to which of the other two they considered the better. When both gave preference to that of the Jews, Bulan perceived that it must be the true religion. He therefore adopted it.*

Some scholars suggest that Jewish traders from the Caucasus or Greece influenced King Bulan to embrace Judaism. Others place the origin of the Judaism of the Khazars in Babylon or in Byzantium. Still others maintain that King Bulan was influenced by Jewish mercenaries from Khwarezm (a region in Persia). The mercenaries allegedly were invited by King Bulan to the land of the Khazars early in the eighth century and brought their religion with them; Bulan supposedly embraced it in the form in which they presented it to him.

From the correspondence between King Joseph and Hasdai Ibn-Shaprut, it is possible to reconstruct a continuous genealogy of the Khazar kings: Bulan was succeeded by Obadiah, who regenerated the kingdom and strengthened the Jewish religion. He invited Jewish scholars to settle in his dominions and founded synagogues and schools. Obadiah was succeeded by his son, Hezekiah; the latter, by his son Manasseh; Manasseh by Hanukkah, a brother of Obadiah; Hanukkah by his son Isaac; Isaac by his son Moses (also known as Manasseh II); the latter by his son Nisi, and Nisi by his son, Aaron II. King Joseph was a son of Aaron II.

Five years after the correspondence between the king of the Khazars and Ibn-Shaprut, the Russian prince Swyatoslaw attacked Khazaria and destroyed a number of its key cities. Four years later the Russians conquered all the Khazarian territory east of the Sea of Azov. Only the Crimean territory of the Khazars remained in their possession when they were attacked in 1016 by a joint expedition of Russians and Byzantines.

A. N. Pollack, an outstanding Jewish historian, concluded, on the basis of Jewish and Arab sources, that the Jewish state of Khazaria was not annihilated in one stroke, but survived in a contracted form for two and a half centuries. Not until the hordes of the Mongol Genghis Khan wrought havoc through western Asia and Eastern Europe in 1224 did Jewish Khazaria cease to exist as a state. Thus, it really lasted in one form or another for five hundred years. Even after its political destruction, some remnants of the Judaized tribes found refuge in the mountainous retreats of Caucasia and others migrated to Hungary. In both places the tradition of Khazarian origin is still extant.

In 1953 Hungary issued a series of postage stamps honoring its ethnic groups. One blue-green stamp clearly identifies a costumed young lady as belonging to the Khazars. According to authoritative Hungarian sources, the Khazars of the Sopron district of Hungary, although no longer adhering to the Jewish faith, still relate the tradition of their origin in the Jewish kingdom of Khazaria.

—S.D.

 ## In Rome Jews Still Live in Ancient Ghetto

On Sunday, June 5, 1977, a "happening" took place in Rome's Via Portico d'Ottavia, the main street of the oldest Diaspora community in the world. The ghetto of Rome celebrated its first official *festa,* timidly launched under the subdued title of "Rendezvous at Portico d'Ottavia."

Throughout the day, at least half of Rome's twenty thousand Jews, and thousands of curious non-Jews, milled up and down in the area right behind Rome's main synagogue.

About a thousand Jews still live in the ghetto and proudly recall that they are the only "real Romans" alive (*i veri romani di Roma*), their ancestors in all likelihood having first come to settle in 161 B.C.E. as diplomatic emissaries from ancient Jerusalem. That was, of course, before the main tide of Jerusalem Jews were brought over as prisoners by Emperor Titus in 70 C.E.

Unlike the ghettos and *shtetls* of Eastern Europe, this ghetto of Rome still exists for the city's Jews, both physically and spiritually. Regularly on Sundays, the old, winding streets burst open with bustling family clusters—sons, daughters, aunts, uncles, cousins, children of all ages dressed in their frilliest best. They come to pay homage to bittersweet memories of childhood and, beyond, to feel united in an overpowering yet undefined sense of self, based on an awareness of common roots.

Until 1870 the ghetto's population was kept under lock and key from sundown to sunrise, forced to work at trades despised by or forbidden to the Christians, such as moneylending or rag peddling and mending. Today's well-to-do owners of the elegant Jewish shops spread all over Rome have a hard time remembering that they owe their genesis to the hard and humble work of their ancestors who once lived "right here." No wonder the figure of "the wandering Jew" is a foreign archetype to Roman Jewry.

What made the day so special was not just the enormous turnout, not just the fact that, for once, there had been a legitimate excuse for a happy formal reunion and not just the sad anniversary of some tragic date in Jewish history—but that everyone had come, and come with pride. The 1967 Jewish refugees from Libya (about twelve hundred in Rome today) were well represented; so were the many "non-community" Jewish intellectuals, drawn by curiosity and who knows what other subliminal stimuli; the wealthy *makhers;* and, above all, what is known in Rome as "the Base" (a polite word for blue-collar workers), renowned for their absenteeism from what they would normally consider a "highbrow waste of community tax money."

Taxation, it must be admitted, is a sensitive issue for Roman Jewry. The community is still organized on the basis of a 1929 agreement between Mussolini and the Jews, which was originally designed to ensure Jewish survival, but which today has a certain authoritarian flavor to it. In return for self-government, all Jews must pay Jewish community taxes, besides what they owe the city and national revenue services.

The amount levied by the community's tax offices seems to be calculated according to effective conspicuous consumption. "If we had to base taxation on statements of declared income, we'd be broke by now," Chief Rabbi Elio Toaff once said wryly. Of course, the truly poor are exempted, but the able and *not* willing are punished by the community's legal power.

The only way for a Roman Jew to get out of paying Jewish taxes is for him to write a formal letter stating that he wishes his name to be cancelled from the Jewish community registry. He thereby gives up his rights to all religious services, including the right to burial in the Jewish cemetery. Such cases are very rare.

A portion of the tax money is used to support the three Jewish day schools, huddled together right across the Tiber River from the Great Synagogue and the ghetto. About fifteen hundred students—40 percent of the Jewish children of Rome—attend these schools from nursery through the elementary and middle grades; some continue on to the Jewish science high school nearby.

A focal point for community spirit came into being a few years ago after the Yom Kippur War when Arab terrorist letter bombs were in fashion. This is the School Guards, composed entirely of fathers, mostly from "the Base," voluntarily organized for the protection of their offspring throughout the school day. Security reasons aside, it is a reassuring sight to find these men cheerfully greeting our children every morning and opening the car doors for us as we arrive at school from the four corners of Rome.

My husband, Franco, comes home from his monthly School Guards stint with stories brimming over with humor and variegated insights into Jewish life in

Rome. During those eight hours of association among Jewish men united in an act of shared responsibility and love, a lot of pent-up steam is released. Here is living proof that the *shtetl* characters of Jewish literature are still in our midst.

About four hundred youngsters, ages fourteen to twenty, attend the youth clubs —on an on-and-off basis. At Kadima, the largest club, a turnout of 150 at a Purim party is considered a success, while lectures draw an average of no more than 20 students, including Israelis in Rome and young Jews from Libya.

Last year Kadima suffered a split-off from its "leftists," a small but active group now associated with the Radical Party. *Aliya* from Italy is very low and mostly confined to the Hashomer Hatzair and B'nai Akiva groups. About thirty prospective *olim* were sent from Rome to Israel last year, but 80 percent of them are expected to find their way back to Italy eventually.

Perhaps the biggest dilemma that young Roman Jews must face today is choosing a stance concerning the Left's hostile attitude toward Israel. Jewish youth, with its natural and traditional ideological sympathies for the Left, now finds itself in a no-man's-land of conflicting loyalties to Israel and to the Marxist groups, which consider Israel "an imperialist tool." The majority, however, feel an unswerving loyalty to Israel. Unfortunately, most students are not able to combat anti-Israel propaganda with facts.

Government pamphlets are available at the Israel Embassy and are occasionally requested by youngsters with problems, but the real battle in Italy is fought against the relentless barrage of the mass media. The schools, for example, have been invaded recently by an onrush of books in which Middle East history is presented in highly distorted terms. A partial remedy for this situation will, it is hoped, be provided by an Italy-Israel Cultural Agreement, which foresees a special joint commission whose job will be the elimination of slanderous texts from the schools.

The cultural gap between American and Italian Jewry is wide. American Jewish tourists can help overcome the sense of isolation and irrelevance felt by the younger generation here by visiting Jewish institutions and monuments and showing our youth that we are one people. Rome has much to offer the Jewish tourist.

A strong impetus for unity, on the other hand, is provided by a universal love for Israel, on the deepest levels. Roman Jews give very generously to Israel— proportionately more than American Jews do, although official figures are not published. Individual families have been known to donate thousands of dollars a year, and the less wealthy give as well. After the Yom Kippur War, in 1973, the teachers of the Jewish schools voluntarily gave up the "thirteenth month" salary they were entitled to by Italian law in December of that year, contributing it all to Israel. The parent-teacher association, which collects money annually to buy Hanukka presents for all our children at school, decided to buy gifts for Israeli children instead. However, perhaps the outstanding example of the spirit that moves Roman Jews is the story of what took place immediately following the news of the outbreak of the Yom Kippur War.

October 16, 1944, is the date of a tragedy still fresh in the memories of the Jews of Rome. On that day, 2,091 Jews, mostly from the ghetto, were dragged out of their beds at dawn by the Gestapo and deported to concentration camps. This act was not only barbaric, but also pure treachery, especially on the part of SS Colonel Herbert Keppler, who won sanctuary in West Germany after his recent escape from an Italian military hospital.

On September 26, 1944, Keppler had given the Jews an alternative: come up with fifty kilos of gold as blood money for your lives, or the Nazis will exterminate the community. After much panic and even a plea to the Vatican (which offered fifteen kilos), the community managed to round up the sum by themselves, only to be betrayed ten days later.

When the Israelis were attacked on Yom Kippur, an idea spread like wildfire through the Rome Jewish community.

"Israel is in danger," people said. "We once managed to squeeze out fifty kilos of gold, hoping to save our own skins, and we gave them to the Nazis. Now let's show ourselves and our loved ones in Israel that we're capable of doubling that amount for Israel's survival."

In the next few days, the line outside the main synagogue was a sight to see. People from all walks of life, the rich side by side with the souvenir peddlers, waited patiently, some with tears in their eyes, to hand in some treasured family heirloom of gold or simply a wedding band, or else to sign a check "worth its weight in gold." The poorer the family, the greater the pile of trinkets that appeared, because in Italy, gold has always meant consolation and security whenever the Italian *lira* has shown signs of faltering. Within a few hours, the goal was reached—and surpassed.

—L.P.-B.

 ## The Proud Jews of Finland

In a single New York City housing development, there are more Jews than in all of Scandinavia . . . fourteen thousand in Sweden, eight thousand in Denmark, fourteen hundred in Finland, one thousand in Norway, none in Iceland.

There are few organized Jewish communities geographically more isolated than the Finnish. The scarcity in numbers and the great distances from any Jewish center of significance have created problems of a special nature. Despite their paucity in numbers, or perhaps because of it, Finnish Jews manifest a forceful Jewish pride that is very moving. On my visits with them, many have stressed, "We are not religious Jews but 'national *Jude*,' proud of belonging to the Jewish people."

Such expressions of sentiment stem from the little-known historical fact that the older generation of Finnish Jews, now practically extinct, was more steeped in Jewish traditions and practices than the majority of those in neighboring Scandinavian communities. More recently, these attachments have been expressed by the younger generation in what they would call a more "nationalistic" spirit. Twenty-nine young men fought in Israel's 1948 War of Independence—the highest proportion from any country. More than a hundred Finnish Jews have settled in Israel, many as farmers.

From about the eighth century C.E., Finland was a Swedish province. Swedish Jewry recently celebrated a bicentennial. Two hundred years ago, that remarkable pioneer, Aaron Isaac, secured permission to settle in Stockholm and hold religious services there. Until then, Jews had been permitted residence only on the explicit condition that they would convert to Christianity. Something of the strength and individuality of this unusual man is reflected in his *Memoirs*, written in a distinct type of Yiddish. If you seek the eternally human element in the mainstream of Jewish life and history, you will find it in the torrent of memory overflowing in the pages of Aaron Isaac's *Memoirs*. The pioneering Aaron Isaac was also active in Finland from 1787 to 1790, functioning as a buyer of foodstuffs for the

Swedish army, then fighting in Finland against the Russians. The Swedish defeat resulted in a Russian takeover of Finland in 1809.

The first Jewish settlers came to the country in 1830—against their will. So-called Cantonists or "Nicolaievskis," they were young Jewish boys, between the ages of twelve and twenty-five, who had been drafted into the Russian army for a period of twenty-five years. They were assigned to garrison duty in remote outposts of the Czarist empire, like Siberia and Finland. The harsh conscription law had been designed in the reign of Czar Nicholas I as a means of alienating these young recruits from their own people and their religion.

Each Jewish community within the Pale of Settlement was assigned its quota of the young draftees. There were special Jewish officers, known in Yiddish as *chappers,* who had the task of impressing the conscripts. As there was a reluctance to draft older youth, who might already be married and supporting families, often boys as young as eight or nine would be chosen in their stead—with witnesses on hand to swear that the eight- or nine-year-olds had actually reached the statutory age of twelve.

These were the boys who would become, twenty-five years later, the first Jewish settlers in Finland. Assigned to garrison duty in Helsinki, the capital, or to Viipuri on the Russian border, many chose to stay in Finland when their quarter-century of service had ended. However, life was not any easier for them even after their return to civilian status. Until Finland gained its independence from Russia in 1917, the Jews were subjected to severe restrictions, which limited their place of residence, curtailed their freedom of movement and narrowed the occupations open to them to such enterprises as peddling secondhand clothes.

As late as 1908, the restrictions still remained in force. The famous Danish-Jewish literary historian, Georg Brandes, who went on a lecture tour in Finland that year, stated ironically in an interview with the Finnish press, "I have committed three serious sins here. As a Jew, I was permitted to stay in your country for only three days, however I have stayed here for four consecutive days; as a Jew, I was permitted to trade only in rags, however, here I lectured on world literature; and as a Jew, it is forbidden for me to marry here, but in spite of all this no one prohibited me from courting in your country . . ."

In 1917, after 108 years of occupation, the Finns declared themselves independent. In this period of revolution and civil war in Russia, Jews streamed into Finland. During the rise of Hitler, a small number arrived from Germany.

Something strange and unprecedented happened to Finnish Jews during World War II, when Finland allied itself with the Germans and attacked Russia, hoping to regain territory lost in the Winter War of 1939–40. Strange to relate, Jewish soldiers served in the Finnish army, fighting together with the Germans, without any form of discrimination against them. I know several Finnish Jewish soldiers who, in fact, reported to German officers, without being discriminated against. As in the better-known case of the Danes, a firm and determined "no" to the Germans by Field Marshal Mannerheim saved Finland's Jewish population.

Within Finland today, the Jews are fully integrated citizens. Max Jacobson has headed Finland's delegation to the United Nations and was president of the U. N. Security Council in 1969, as well as a serious candidate for the post of Secretary General at that time. His mother has been head of Finland's Women's International Zionist Organization for many years.

For such a small Jewish population, the Jews of Helsinki are rather well organized. A synagogue, a community center and a day school with a system of Jewish education from kindergarten through high school ensures each child's opportunity to learn about his or her religious and cultural heritage. However, anxiety exists over the continual decrease of the Jewish community. Many young people leave for new homes in Israel; some go to Sweden and the United States. The immigration to Israel is very much encouraged by the entire community, but is at the same time a source of worry. No immigration occurs from other countries. Finland's politics balance precariously between east and west. Unlike the other Scandinavian countries, it is not in a position to invite refugees from the Soviet bloc, because of the delicate balance in its relations with Moscow. Mixed marriages take a toll.

While a student at the Jewish Theological Seminary of America, I was privileged to occupy the pulpit of the synagogue in Helsinki for the High Holy Days. (Not knowing Finnish, I preached in Swedish and Yiddish, so that both young and old could understand me in at least one language.) Discussing the probability of securing a future for Finnish Jewry, a local leader pointed out to me, "Much has to be done and in many respects the help of world Jewry will be decisive."

—F.E.W.

 ## Are the American Indians a "Lost" Tribe of Israel?

In II Kings, chapter 17, the Bible records: "In the ninth year of Hoshea, the king of Assyria took Samaria, and carried Israel unto Assyria . . . unto this day."

To this day people speculate about the fate and whereabouts of the "carried away" Samaritans. Thus Jewish legend has it that the lost tribes of Israel continue to live in the regions of the legendary river Sambation, which is said to flow six days and rest on the seventh.

Cadillac, the founder of Detroit, was an adherent of the theory that the American Indians were the descendants of the ancient Jews. In a document dated 1718, and entitled "Description of Michilliamackinac; Indian Tribes of that Region," Cadillac describes the Indian practice of nose-piercing as follows: ". . . the word Outaous means in our language 'the nation of the Nez Percez' [pierced noses], to which they attach a small stone well ornamented, which hangs down in the middle of the mouth between the lips. This is a custom among them, and they would not consider themselves properly adorned without this ornament. Some of the elders maintain, however, that it is a preventive against 'medicine'—that is to say, the spells that their enemies and their evil-intentioned persons might cast upon them, to poison them or cause their death."

This practice, Cadillac maintained, was proof "that it is an idea of the ancient Jews; for we read in history that one Eleazar delivered people possessed of the devil, in the presence of his son, and of several princes and noblemen of his court. He proceeded as follows: he pierced the nose of the possessed one, and passed through it a ring hollow inside, wherein he placed an herb; and as soon as the devil smelled it, he threw the body of the possessed one upon the ground, and fled, without daring to return to it. The same Eleazar also did this frequently in the name of Solomon; so that these savage nations may well have retained this custom of piercing their noses, and have forgotten the purpose for which it was introduced."

As further proof that the American Indians were the descendants of the lost tribes of Israel, Cadillac presents the following evidence: "There is a place near Missilmakinak, called Essolon . . . I inquired of some savages the reason it [the name] had been given to the place; they replied that their ancestors had given it that name . . . Thereupon we may recall that Reuben had four sons: Henoch, Hesron, Phallus, and Cormi. How could the savages give the river the name of Essolon, if they had never heard of it? It is not likely that this was done by accident, but rather because it was the custom of the Jews to bear the names of their estates, or to give their own names to property of which they were in possession."

Cadillac cites another Indian habit as additional evidence of the Indians' Jewish descent: ". . . it seldom happens that a Sioux is taken alive; because, as soon as they see that they can no longer resist, they kill themselves, considering that they are not worthy to live, when once bound, vanquished, and made slaves. It is rather surprising that people so brave and warlike as these should nevertheless be able to shed tears at will, and so abundantly that it can hardly be imagined. I think that it could not be believed without being seen: for they are sometimes observed to laugh, sing, and amuse themselves when, at the same time, one would say that their eyes are like gutters filled by a heavy shower; and as soon as they have wept, they again become as joyful as before, whether their joy be real or false. The chief occasion of their tears is when their enemies have killed some of their people; thereupon, they address themselves to their allies. . . . Bending their heads they utter horrible yells, and shed a deluge of tears, after which they cease to weep and yell, and their eyes are as dry as if they had not wept. They afterward represent the state of their affairs, so that one may say that they are the same Jews who dwelt on Mount Gerizim, who were called Mourners, because they had the gift of tears." Gerizim, a mountain in Ephraim, has since ancient times been the sacred place of the Samaritans.

Cadillac was neither the originator nor the final expounder of the theory that the Indians are the descendants of the lost tribes of Israel. In all likelihood the Spanish priests who migrated to America after it had been discovered by Columbus were the first to suggest it. It was soon espoused by the historian Las Casas, a contemporary of Columbus, known as the apostle of the Indians, and by F. Lumnius in his *De extremo Dei Judicio et indorum vocatione*, libri iii (1569).

Even Manasseh Ben Israel, the Dutch rabbi who persuaded Oliver Cromwell to readmit the Jews to England, advocated it in his book *Origen de los Americanos* (1650). He based his support of the theory on the assertions of a certain Montesinos, who claimed to have discovered a Jewish settlement in Peru.

Other protagonists of this theory were such outstanding New England divines as Cotton Mather and Roger Williams, the founder of Rhode Island. In 1697 Samuel Sewall championed it.

Mordecai Manuel Noah, the first American Zionist and the founder of the proposed Jewish state of Ararat on Grand Island near Niagara Falls, proclaimed this theory in his discourse on *The Evidences of the American Indians Being the Descendants of the Lost Tribes of Israel* (1837). Again in 1908 "convincing proof" of this belief was offered in a treatise entitled *The Mound Builders and the Lost Tribes.* Excerpts from this paper are quite illuminating:

"According to the new hypothesis, the tribes reached the western hemisphere by way of an isthmus believed to have existed where the narrow waters of Behring Strait now divide the continents. Giving color of truth to this theory is the fact that ethnologists who have sojourned among the natives inhabiting the great region south and east of Behring Strait assert that many Greek and Hebrew words are distinguishable in the language employed by the natives of that region today."

A 1957 book asserted that the Mandan Indians were the direct descendants of the tribe of Naphtali. Proof follows: "The one outstanding word running through the warp and woof of tribal lore was the word 'Nuptadi.' The name phonetically has changed little from its original 'Naphtali' in 2,000 years—it has been handed down to us practically on a silver platter."

The author concludes, ". . . We believe that after twenty-seven centuries the Naphtali, one of the 'Lost Ten Tribes,' has now been found."

But whether the Indians, as Cadillac claimed, or the English, as some Britishers maintained, were the progeny of the Samaritans, the lost tribes of Israel, like Noah's ark, still exist—if not in reality, at least in the imagination of many people.

—A.A.W.

XI

Women in Judaism and Jewish Women of Special Interest

Jewish women are given barely more than a footnote in the many books depicting the part played by Jews in the American Revolution. They deserve better, for the Jewish daughters of 1776 were more than mothers and wives who lived in the shadow of their fathers, husbands, and sons.

One of the best known women during the Revolutionary era was the daughter of one of the very few Jews who remained loyal to King George III. She was the witty, flirtatious, beautiful, and light-hearted Rebecca Franks, daughter of David Franks, the only member of the Franks family who was opposed to the colonists' breakaway from England.

Rebecca found a ready entrée to Colonial society because her father, a member of the New York Provincial Legislature in 1748, was a prosperous merchant. During the French and Indian War he was the chief provisioner of the British Army. After the failure of General Braddock's campaign against the French and Indians in 1755 in western Pennsylvania, Franks raised twenty-five thousand dollars for the defense of Pennsylvania from a threatened Indian invasion. Although he signed the nonimportation resolutions in 1765, which pledged merchants not to import any goods from England until the hated Stamp Act was repealed, he refused to join the Revolution. Twice arrested during the Revolutionary War by the Americans, Franks was the chief supplier of food and clothing to the British Army during the Revolution, which ruined him.

During the British occupation of Philadelphia, Rebecca Franks became the friend of British officers, as she had been of American officers and statesmen in 1776 when the Continental Congress adopted the Declaration of Independence in Philadelphia. General Charles Lee, George Washington's rival, proposed to her. Major John André, the British spy captured in the Benedict Arnold episode, stayed at the Franks' home while he was a paroled prisoner in Philadelphia, where he spent his time making miniatures of the beautiful Rebecca.

The highest ranking British officers made the Franks' home their rendezvous. General Howe, the British commander, who was a frequent visitor, tells in his letters of the amusing remarks of the witty Rebecca. So famous was she as a satirist and punster that she was credited with being the author of an anonymous poem entitled "The Times—A Poem by Camilio Querno—Poet Laureate of Congress," which lampooned the leaders of the Revolution. Her correspondents included both

British and American officers. She married Sir Henry Johnson, a lieutenant-colonel in the British Army, who later became a general.

What Rebecca was to Philadelphia society her cousin Phila was to New York society. The daughter of the pious Jacob Franks, an officer of the Spanish-Portuguese Congregation—the first in America—she was much sought after by the gay blades of the New York aristocracy. She married Oliver De Lancey, after whose family New York's Delancey Street is named. As a bride, Phila was taken to live in a house at Pearl and Broad streets that later became famous. It was in that house, by then known as Fraunces' Tavern, that George Washington bade farewell to his officers at the close of the Revolution. Rebecca's sister, Abigail, was also a distinguished belle of her day. She became the bride of Andrew Hamilton III, grandson of the man who built Independence Hall in Philadelphia.

While these Franks women were losing their Jewish identity by marrying into prominent Christian families, two other Franks girls were achieving a fame of another kind. One of these was Rachel Franks, daughter of Moses B. Franks, a New York merchant and a cousin of Phila Franks. The other was Bilhah Abigail Franks, mother of Phila.

Rachel Franks was the wife of the famous Haym Salomon, the Polish-born patriot who helped raise funds for the struggling government. Rachel had married Salomon in 1777, a year after the Revolution began. Unlike her Philadelphia cousins, Rachel Salomon kept in the background; consequently, little is known about her. When Salomon was arrested in 1778 in New York as a British spy and jailed in a British prison ship, she was left to shift for herself among the hostile Loyalists. Not until Salomon escaped from prison and managed to reach Philadelphia was she able to join him. During the years that Salomon was expending his resources to secure American independence, Rachel lived modestly. When Salomon died in 1785 at the age of forty-five, she was left an impoverished widow with four young children.

Of all the Franks women, Bilhah Abigail was the most intensely Jewish. Although her father, Moses Levy, was accepted in Christian as well as in Jewish society because of his socially prominent business associates, Bilhah Abigail remained strictly Orthodox. It was as natural for her to marry the pious Jacob Franks as it was for Rachel Franks to be the dictator of Philadelphia society. Bilhah Abigail was a worthy mate for Jacob. It was she who organized the ladies of the Spanish-Portuguese Congregation into a fund-raising unit to get the money needed to build a synagogue. The congregation's records show that her enthusiasm was so infectious that every Jewish woman in New York contributed something. Her efforts stamped her as the spiritual mother of all synagogue sisterhoods.

Less spectacular than the women of the Franks clan was Miriam Gratz, daughter of Joseph Simon of Lancaster, Pennsylvania, who played a major part in the development of Colonial trade with the Indians. Miriam, who married Michael Gratz, her father's partner in many ventures, was the domestic type, but because her husband's business often took him away from home for months at a time, she had to familiarize herself with the business. The Simon home in Lancaster was the gathering place for traders, Indians, soldiers, and trappers, and Miriam learned much from them. In her husband's absence Miriam ruled over a commercial empire that extended as far north as Canada and as far west as the Ohio River. She could drive a bargain with the canniest trader. It was her job to keep the Simon-Gratz firm's agents in touch with each other by post. In this role she was frequently in communication with men like George Rogers Clark and soldiers from the Ohio and Tennessee valleys.

One of the most heroic Jewish women of the Revolution was Esther Hays, wife of David Hays, a patriot farmer of Bedford, in New York's Westchester County. While her husband was serving with the American forces on Long Island, the Hays home at Bedford was burned by the British and their Loyalist neighbors set fire to the house and then burned the whole village. She had refused to disclose the hideout of a party of patriots attempting to drive a small herd of cattle through the British lines to the American camp at White Plains. Among the young boys engaged in this hazardous exploit was her son, Jacob, then all of seven years old. Jacob Hays later became New York City's high constable or chief of police. The infant Hays became celebrated as Benjamin Etting Hays, who lived in Pleasantville for seventy-five years, where he was a qualified *shohet*. His grandson was Arthur Hays Sulzberger, the late publisher of the New York *Times*.

Another female patriot was Mrs. Philip Minis, whose husband not only fought with American troops in Georgia but advanced funds to the Revolutionary cause. Mrs. Minis was such an outspoken supporter of the Revolution that when the British captured Savannah, the British officers singled her out for special punishment by making her and her daughter do menial tasks for the British soldiers.

Mrs. Mordecai Sheftall's husband was so militant a rebel that the British had put a price on his head, and when they took Savannah he was thrown into prison. After her husband and son were captured, Mrs. Sheftall fled to Charleston, South Carolina, arriving just before the British besieged the city, which then had the largest Jewish community in America. At the risk of her own life, she devoted herself to nursing defenders of the city who were suffering not only from the continuous British bombardment but from a raging smallpox epidemic.

Reyna Touro, sister of Moses Michael Hays, who was related to the Westchester Hays, was the widow of Rabbi Isaac Touro of Newport, Rhode Island. She and her brother and her two young sons, Abraham and Judah, were the first permanent Jewish settlers in Boston. A man of great wealth and culture, Hays had left Newport because of a challenge to his loyalty, and that of his sister, to the American cause. In response he published a notable petition to the Rhode Island General Assembly in which he refused to sign a loyalty oath on the ground that it was unconstitutional and discriminatory. Reyna's son Judah became the famous merchant shipper and philanthropist whose generosity made possible the completion of Bunker Hill Monument in 1843.

Such were the Jewish daughters of the American Revolutionary period: the heroic Esther Hays, the tragic Rachel Salomon, the lighthearted Rebecca Franks, the patriotic Mrs. Minis, the self-sacrificing Mrs. Sheftall, the pious Bilhah Abigail Franks, the home-loving and practical Miriam Gratz, and the cultured Reyna Touro.

—B.P.

 ## Golfing with Golda and Ben-Gurion

This essay is mostly about my experiences as special golf instructor to Prime Minister Golda Meir of Israel. But the beginning of this story concerns Ben-Gurion.

In 1958, when I first became involved in the Israeli golf scene, Ben-Gurion was Prime Minister. Some of Ben-Gurion's foreign-policy advisers were under the impression that Israel was at a disadvantage in its dealings with the United States be-

cause it lacked golf capability. Eisenhower was then President of the United States. Ben-Gurion liked to bring his eminent guests to Camp David, where the official proceedings would be interrupted at least once a day for a round of golf. Some of the most fruitful discussions were held in a golf cart or in the clubhouse. The clinching argument for Ben-Gurion was that a photograph of him playing golf with Ike would confer great prestige on Israel in the community of nations.

Ben-Gurion was then told that it would be in Israel's national interest to build a golf course—not just as an international status symbol but as a tourist attraction. Israel was putting millions of dollars each year into tourist advertising, but kept bumping into complaints from travel agents who said their customers might be more interested in visiting biblical sites if they were adjacent to a golf course.

At this point my own involvement began. I received a telephone call asking me to come to Israel both to teach Ben-Gurion how to play and to help design an eighteen-hole course. The venerable Israeli leader had a large, shaggy head into which were set small eyes that shot sparks every time they twinkled. He was blunt and hearty and said he thought taking up golf was a lot of foolishness but that he would do anything to improve Israel's trade balance.

My first job, he said, was to help design a golf course, for which the government would provide land at Caesarea, famous site of the old Roman ruins. He wanted me to take as much time as required. Then I would return to Jerusalem to give him golf lessons, which would be top secret until he was ready to be put on public exhibition.

Four months later, having fulfilled my mission in Caesarea, I set about the second and more consequential part of my assignment—teaching golf to a seventy-three-year-old man who had never even touched a golf club. My first five meetings with Ben-Gurion were unforgettable. He discoursed on history, philosophy, anthropology, astronomy, biology, zoology, and architecture. He was the most energetic storyteller I ever met. One way or another he contrived, week after week, to defer his golf lessons.

Finally he let the cat out of the bag. He took me into his inner office, shut the door securely, cut off the phones, sat me down on the couch reserved for visitors of state, and shared his big secret. He had never intended, he said, to go all the way. He had agreed to the scheme because of something he alone knew. He had made up his mind six months earlier that he was going to resign at an appropriate time—certainly no later than the spring of 1959. Therefore there would be no point in his learning to play.

I asked the obvious question: Why, then, did he agree to the scheme in the first place? He threw back that beautiful, shaggy head, then his face broke wide open into the most appealing grin I had seen since I first saw a picture of Will Rogers.

"Simple," he said. "I knew that my successor would be Golda Meir. I wanted to create a precedent that would be binding on her. I would be involved in this project just long enough to commit my successor as well. And every time I think of Golda playing golf, it makes me feel good all over."

"What makes you think she'll do it?" I asked.

"She would have no way of refusing, not when all the advisers go to work on her the way they did on me. It might not even be necessary to bring in the advisers. I think I can do it all by myself."

He squinted at his watch. "It is now 10:45 A.M. I telephoned her yesterday and asked her to come to my office at 11. I want her to meet you, just so she'll know how serious I am."

A few minutes later Mrs. Meir arrived at the Prime Minister's office. Her greeting was brief, almost curt. Ben-Gurion said he intended to announce his retirement at the end of the month, and that he would throw all his weight behind her as his successor.

For maybe an hour they discussed the problems of government and the obvious need to make the transition as smooth as possible. Then, without the slightest change of inflection in his voice or expression, he said that he had accepted the advice of the top people in the government about the considerable advantage to Israel of a Prime Minister who could play golf with the American President if need be. And that was why they had brought me to Israel.

Then he sat back in his seat and, with a straight face, waited for the message to sink in. Mrs. Meir wasn't fazed.

"That makes good sense," she said after only a few seconds. Then, looking squarely at me, she asked without the slightest sign of any incredulity, "When do we start?"

An easy student she was not. At our first session she said she didn't want to do anything except hear me discourse on the theory and practice of golf. This I did for about ninety minutes, describing the dynamics of the golf swing and drawing little sketches to show her the different elements involved in hitting the ball accurately and in a way that was smooth and graceful.

At our third session she began asking questions:

"Why do you say you want me to concentrate on keeping a firm left arm, using the right arm just to steer the club?"

"Because experiences going back over many years by the world's best golfers have demonstrated that the firm left arm is the best way to transmit power to the ball and keep it from veering off line," I said.

"In that case," she countered, "I could get more power by playing with left-handed clubs and hitting the ball with a firm right arm from the right side. Since I am right-handed, I am bound to hit more accurately that way and I could probably hit it farther, too."

I made the mistake of trying to refute the argument before thinking it through, saying that it was unnatural for a right-handed player to hit the ball with the left side of his body, which was farthest away from the green.

"Nonsense!" she said. "It's no more unnatural than a right-handed tennis player turning to his left when hitting a backhand shot."

As I thought about it, I knew she had all the logic on her side, so I decided to simplify the argument.

"Very well," I said, "we will have two sets of clubs, one lefty, the other righty. I think you will find that using the right-handed clubs will be much easier."

"I don't think so," she replied. "There's no point in being extravagant. One set of clubs is enough. And if we start the correct way—that is, using clubs that I can hit with my right arm—then we'll develop good habits all the way. Now, what did you mean when you said that I had to concentrate on swinging slowly?"

"Just that there was no direct connection between a fast swing and the distance traveled by the ball," I replied.

"How can you say that," she asked, "when Arnold Palmer says in this book right on the top of my desk that you've really got to take a good cut at the ball, as he puts it?"

"Well," I said, "the professional players have been able to groove a pretty fast swing and they know how to control it."

"But that's not what you said earlier," she said abruptly. "You said there's no connection between a fast swing and distance."

"That's still correct," I said. "The important thing is the power that's transmitted to the ball at the instant of impact. That means that legs, hips, shoulders, and arms all have to be synchronized in a power flow to the ball."

"So a fast swing is not necessary?"

"No."

"Then why are the American professionals turning to lighter clubs? My assistant underlined a portion of an article for me which said that Jack Nicklaus was using very light clubs because he could generate more clubhead speed."

I pointed out that what was good for Jack Nicklaus wasn't necessarily good for beginning players.

"Oh, so you think I should use heavy clubs?" she asked.

I was beginning to get a little weary. "What I mean is," I said, "I want you to use very light clubs so that you can handle them more easily than heavier clubs."

"You haven't seen me handle any clubs. What makes you say I can't handle the heavier club?"

I decided to concede that particular point. "All I'm trying to say is that just because a professional player does things a certain way doesn't mean it's good for everyone. For example, the pros use clubs with stiff shafts. The average player uses a club with a whippy shaft."

"Why is that?"

"The whippy shaft gives the average player more distance. The stiff shaft provides more accuracy. The professional player gets plenty of distance and wants the additional accuracy."

"Forgive me, Mr. Shitewell," she said, "but I find it difficult to follow your logic."

Like most mortals, I don't like having my name mispronounced.

"The name is Sitewell," I said. "Please tell me what is so illogical about what I just said."

"What would you say is the greatest problem of the average player," she asked, "accuracy or distance?"

"Accuracy, of course."

"Then why shouldn't the average player use a stiff shaft for accuracy and leave the whippy club to the professional, who ought to know how to hit a ball straight and who can probably use the extra distance? Haven't you got the whole thing turned around?"

I suddenly felt homesick. "Mrs. Meir," I said, summoning as much courage as I could in my dispirited and depleted condition, "I really think you'll do much better without a teacher. You've thought about this game in far more basic ways than many of those who play at it for a living or who, like me, teach it and write about it. I have no doubt that whatever you do will be right for you."

"I would appreciate your resignation in writing," she said. "After all, I acquiesced to the urging of my ministers only because I wanted to do the right thing by my country. But if the person they selected to teach me thinks it is in the best interests of Israel that I give up the game, then I am in the clear, am I not?"

And that was the way it ended. Only when I was in the plane over the Atlantic did I realize that the new Prime Minister was a chip off the old Ben-Gurion block. She never had any more intention of going through with the scheme than he did. If anything, she outfoxed the wily old Ben-Gurion by putting herself in a position where she could reluctantly withdraw from the enterprise only because I gave up on it myself, thus relieving her of any charge that she was unwilling to serve her country.

Anyway, the project wasn't a total loss. At least the Israeli Tourist Bureau got a golf course out of it.

—K.J.S.

 ## Jewish Women in Remote Corners of the World

"*L'chayim*," I said as I raised my wineglass at the dinner table in a house high on a hill overlooking the harbor in Suva, capital city of the Fiji Islands, once known as the Cannibal Islands. My hosts, Doris and Claude Israel, looked at me without understanding, and I stared back at them in disbelief.

Setting out alone from New York on a spiritual odyssey to go around the world in order to meet the Jews living in the South Seas, the Pacific, and Asia, I had traveled across the Pacific to the Fiji Islands. Arriving at Nadi Airport on the west coast of Viti Levu, the main island of these 800 islands in the Fijis, I had continued another 135 miles—much of it through jungle areas, with bamboo thatched cottages inhabited by the indigenous Melanesian Fijians—till I reached Suva on the east coast of Viti Levu. Here I looked forward with great anticipation to my meeting with the first Jews in these Fiji Islands—for whom the term *l'chayim* (to life) was unknown!

The reason became clear as we talked. I had been invited for five o'clock tea, when tiny, open-faced sandwiches were served. Then, graciously, Doris Israel asked me to take "pot luck" dinner with them, a meal that included matzoh ball soup, the matzoh meal having been imported from Australia.

Claude Israel had come to the Fiji Islands sixty years ago at the invitation of his uncle, Henry Marks. He was sixteen at the time. Henry Marks was one of a group of Jewish traders, both importers and exporters, who had established themselves along the seafront now known as Victoria Parade. Some branched out into the smaller islands and built up successful chain stores. Henry Marks became the head of the largest and wealthiest mercantile establishment in the South Seas.

In 1914 Claude Israel returned to Sydney, Australia, to marry Doris Abraham. More than half a century later, when I met her, Doris Abraham Israel was an alive, alert, energetic person. She had been more than a helpmate, having worked in the business for over twelve years, and had raised two children in a country where their father had known of cannibalism when he first settled here.

Doris Israel is keenly interested in politics. During World War II she ran a canteen for the fifty thousand American soldiers stationed in the Fiji Islands. These included the U. S. Marines, who were training for their landing in Guadalcanal.

Today the Jewish community is no more. Some have left, some lie buried in the hilltop cemetery just one mile from town. Here rests Henry Marks, onetime mayor of Suva and Knight Bachelor, Commander of the Most Excellent Order of the British Empire.

And Doris and Claude Israel, separated for over half a century from the rest of world Jewry, have lost the memory of many Jewish rituals. No wonder that my toast "l'chayim" sounded strange to their ears.

From Fiji I flew 1,340 miles to bustling Auckland, where I was greeted by a luncheon arranged by a local woman with whom I had had some correspondence. Later I went on to Rotorua, where I saw the brown-skinned daughters of New Zealand's Maoris, dressed in flax and feather costumes, do a dance suggesting the hula—a reminder that the white man did not drift into New Zealand, whether as trader, settler, whaler, or missionary, until as late as the nineteenth century. I stayed for a while in windy Wellington, at the southern tip of North Island, and saw its kosher butcher shop.

I moved on to South Island's tranquil Christchurch, that most English city outside of England, with Oxford, Cambridge, Gloucester, and Worcester among the names of its streets. The Avon River flows through the town. Beautiful flowers and lawns luxuriated in the sunshine. When checking in at the Hotel Clarendon, I found an invitation to the bar mitzvah celebration of Stephen Hollander, son of Eber and Grace Hollander, who had been apprised of my coming.

On Sabbath morning I walked the short distance to the stone Christchurch synagogue on Gloucester Street, known locally as the Canterbury Hebrew Congregation, taking its name from the province in which Christchurch is located. The bar mitzvah boy did himself proud with his chanting of the complete portion of that week's reading from the sacred Scroll of the Law, in addition to his chanting of the prophetic portion of the haftarah.

Then followed an all day "at home" reception at which all the food, including the Sabbath hallah, had been prepared, not by a caterer but by the mother of the bar mitzvah boy.

But Grace Hollander was not just a housewife. She also had a full-time job as manager of a clothing manufacturing concern. In addition, she found time for community activity as well as politics.

When I met her she was the president of the Union of Jewish Women for the Dominion of New Zealand. A vital, capable person, she has more recently been chosen as president of the National Council of Women, the coordinating council of all major women's organizations in New Zealand, both Jewish and non-Jewish.

In Sydney, a 1,320 mile flight from Christchurch, I met Australia's living legend, Dr. Fanny Reading. From this gentle soul in her seventies, I heard an extraordinary story, the tale of her early childhood in Russia. Tormented by discrimination and pogroms, her father had decided to make a break for freedom. Escaping across the border, he proceeded to London, finding work there as a carpenter. His pregnant wife, fearful of making the dash for freedom, stayed on in Minsk, where Fanny was born.

When the child was three years old, her mother, now more courageous, took Fanny on a venturesome journey to search out the father and husband who by this time had proceeded to Australia. Reaching Melbourne, the mother appealed to the local rabbi for help. The husband was traced to Ballarat, and the resourceful mother and child went the seventy-five miles from Melbourne by train.

What a trip it must have been for the newcomers! When I took the same Melbourne-to-Ballarat trip some seventy years later, it was in a two-car train passing stations with such intriguing names as Moorbool, Lal lal, Cheringhap, Yendons, Warrenhelp. One place had a signpost, but no platform, to assist the descending passenger.

When her father returned that night from peddling with horse and wagon, bringing supplies to the country places surrounding the gold-rush town of Ballarat, he was told, "There's a woman and child waiting for you." The child worried as to how this handsome stranger would receive her; she had not, until that moment, met her father.

But her fears were groundless. A warm, affectionate home was established. Three sons were born in Australia. "Father thought the world of his children," Fanny Reading told me, "and hired a private teacher for us. How he managed it I can't explain. He had caught the gold fever. He opened a store and hotel up country—and was robbed." At any rate, when college years rolled round, Fanny Reading got a scholarship, studied music, and taught music for one year.

But that didn't satisfy her. She returned to the university, this time to study medicine. In 1922 she got her medical degree and joined a brother in the practice of medicine in Sydney. "But the memory of my loneliness when I first arrived in a strange country has stayed with me," Dr. Reading said.

The rest of her story I got from others. How she began to devote herself more and more to helping Australian newcomers to adjust to life in that country; and how, within a year after entering medical practice, she was already the moving force in organizing the National Council of Jewish Women of Australia. Two years later, in 1925, she was in Washington, D.C., as a delegate to a convention of the International Council of Women.

In 1935 Dr. Reading received the King George V Jubilee Medal and in 1937 the King George VI Coronation Medal. In 1961 Queen Elizabeth conferred on her the decoration of MBE—Member of the Most Excellent Order of the British Empire—in recognition of her dedication to social welfare work for all creeds and causes.

After two months in Australia, I continued on to be with the two hundred fifty Jews in Manila, the five hundred Jews living among a Chinese population in Singapore, the two families in Malaysia's capital city of Kuala Lumpur, the six families in delightful Penang, and the Jewish communities in Tokyo and Kobe.

In Hong Kong I went by Star Ferry from my hotel in Kowloon to the island of Hong Kong in order to attend Rosh Hashanah services. The Yom Kippur fast I observed in Bangkok, where the day-long service was held at the home of Farida and Isaac Djemal, there being no synagogue structure in the city then. The first evening of the Sukkot holiday I spent with the Jews in Rangoon, going on from there to Calcutta, where I crowned the Queen of Beauty chosen at the Simhat Torah Ball.

During my prolonged stay in India I came to Cochin, in the state of Kerala, near the southwestern tip of the country. One day, on a ferry plying between Ernakulam and Cochin, I met Dr. Blossom Esther Hallegua, a practicing physician who was returning after work as a gynecologist at the Ernakulam Government Hospital to her home in Jewtown, Cochin. Descending at the Mattancherry stop, she in her sari and I in Western garb, we walked together through Jewtown.

In Cochin the term "Jewtown" is not used as an anti-Semitic slur. It is merely a statement of a fact of life. In the sixteenth century, when the Jews of nearby Cranganore had to flee that community with the coming of the Portuguese, they fled southward about fifteen miles to Cochin and asked the rajah for asylum. He responded with a gift of land adjacent to his own palace. There the Jews have lived for over four hundred years.

As Dr. Blossom (as she is affectionately known) and I walked through the commercial area of Jewtown, near the waterfront, I noticed that the stores now belong to Hindus, such as the Sorabji Company, a clearing and forwarding house. Others who had bought space from previous Jewish owners also used the same legend "Jewtown, Cochin" for their address.

This was the section where Cochin's black Jews had once lived. They are all gone now, and their synagogue is locked. Farther north along Jewtown Road we came to the section where the "emancipated Jews" lived. Descended from unions of former slaves with their white masters, these people were acknowledged as Jews and were finally fully accepted into the faith.

Still farther north, where the business section gives way to the residential area, is the white Jews' section. These are the more affluent people: merchants, professionals, and government civil servants.

Here we came to Dr. Blossom's house. Except for its brass nameplate, it was similar to all the others lining both sides of narrow Jewtown Road. Two-storied and cream-colored, they have sloping red roofs and small shuttered and barred windows. On the ground floor are the kitchen and servants' quarters; on the second floor the family living quarters. These are sparsely furnished with canopied beds and brass-studded chairs and chests, a reminder that Portuguese and Dutch once were sovereign here.

As we sat on the wide window seat overlooking Jewtown Road, I asked Dr. Blossom who took care of her children while she was at the hospital. "Oh, we're nearly all one family here," came the reply. "There's always someone around to look after the children while I'm away working."

After India I came to Teheran, capital of the Land of the Peacock Throne. The throne itself, and the rest of the crown jewels, gleam in splendor in the vault at the Melli Bank.

The first Jew I met in Teheran was Shamsi Moradpour Hekmat, who as a young woman joined nine other young women in 1947, determined to "wash off the rust of ignorance, disease, and poverty from the innocent faces of the children of the *mahalleh* [ghetto]." To that end they had organized the Jewish Ladies' Organization of Iran.

I went through these *mahallehs* in Teheran and Isfahan. Unpaved streets were so narrow that I felt I could touch the mud-brick walls lining the streets by merely stretching out my arms. Opening a door in one of these walls, I found myself in a compound—a bare, stone-floored yard encircled by "apartments," one windowless room to a family, the floor raised somewhat from the yard level. In the plastered walls were a few niches holding a lamp, a kerosene cooking stove, a tea kettle, and a few dishes. Worn rugs on the stone floors and some blankets piled in a corner made up the rest of the household possessions. A few tiny holes above the wooden doors provided the only ventilation.

The *mahallehs* are what remain of an ancient Jewish community dating back more than twenty-five hundred years. In the sixteenth century the Shiites of the Safavid dynasty, through the tenet of ritual uncleanness, made anything touched by an unbeliever ritually unclean for the Shiites. The result was that Jews were confined to life in the ghettos. Life became humiliating and degrading, with hunger and squalor following. Culture declined and superstition grew.

Not until 1925, under the benevolent rule of Mohammed Reza Shah, were reforms instituted, the country secularized, and Jews permitted to leave the ghettos. But when I came to Iran most of them still remained behind the walls of the *mahallehs*.

Shamsi Hekmat and her cofounders set up day care centers for children of needy families. A nurses' training school was opened, as well as training courses for nursery school teachers. Then came literacy classes for the women to help them break out of the old mold. The programs grew and branches were opened in a number of cities.

A graduate of Teheran's Sage College and principal of the Hekmat International School, Shamsi Hekmat soon saw the need for another field of activity, a need unique to the Iranian Jewish community, namely, for a woman's right to inherit from a husband or father.

In the biblical era, property consisted of the fields owned by a family. When a daughter married, usually at a very early age, she joined her husband's tribe and had little to do with her own family. The family possessions remained with her brothers, who tilled the land. As time went on, customs changed and the "law of the land" in which Jews found themselves, particularly in the West, was accepted by them.

But in Iran the old biblical law of inheritance continued to be observed. A wife was entitled only to maintenance as long as she remained a widow, and a daughter to maintenance and a dowry upon marriage. But by the twentieth century possessions were counted in terms of money, not in land ownership. Shamsi Hekmat and the Jewish Ladies' Organization of Iran determined to bring their Jewish religious leaders into the twentieth century on the question of inheritance.

It was a long struggle. Not until 1966, when Israeli Sephardi Chief Rabbi Nissim came to Iran for discussions with the local religious leaders, was the fight on the way to being won. Now Iranian Jewish women can inherit from husband and father.

Nearing the end of my trip, I reached Istanbul, the meeting place of Asia and Europe. There I met Sarah Geron, who traces her lineage back to tenth-century Hasdai Ibn Shaprut, a physician, scholar, and diplomat at the court of Abd al Rahman in Cordova, Spain.

Born in Edirne, one of the Turkish cities where many Spanish Jews had, some centuries ago, found a haven of religious freedom from persecution in Spain, her family moved to Istanbul for better educational opportunities for the children. Sarah attended the Notre Dame de Sion School, a Christian missionary school for girls.

Among the first Jewish women to enter a Turkish university (1933), Sarah Geron received her degree in law some years later, after her marriage. Now a practicing lawyer, her office is in Istanbul's old Karakoy, her home in the newer enclave of Nisantas.

She is active in the Bar Association, the Women's Lawyers Group, the Association of University Women, the Turkish-French Cultural Association, the National Council of Women, the Soroptimist Club, the Union of Turkish Women, as well as all Jewish cultural circles.

A writer on social and cultural matters, Sarah Geron's articles have appeared in such eminent papers as the *Journal d'Orient* and the daily *Milliyet*. She also lectures on matters of law, the protection of working women, and adult education.

—I.G.C.

 ## The Lady Physicist Who Dug Her Own Grave

There are not many women nuclear physicists in the world, but Dr. Aviva Gileadi, of the University of Puerto Rico, is one of them. If that isn't enough of a distinction, this remarkable, courageous woman is a scientist with a world-renowned reputation, a citizen of Israel who spent many years teaching future physicists at the Technion, Israel's famed institution of higher learning in the engineering and scientific world—and an easygoing, always laughing person who has erased from her mind an event that took place when she was a young girl and could well have become another cipher in the Holocaust's aggregate of six million.

Aviva was born and raised in Hungary. Like all Jews in that Balkan country, she and her family watched the growing might of the Nazi regime in Germany with increasing apprehension. When the Nazis took over Austria, and then Czechoslovakia, and then, by armed might, neighboring countries in the eastern and western sections of Europe, the sense of foreboding of the large Jewish community in Hungary—a country never famous for its democratic ways—grew ever greater.

Nazi-inspired restrictions, attacks, harassment, and imprisonment became the pattern for the Jewish community. Some escaped abroad, some went into hiding in distant sections of the countryside, and some waited, hoped, and prayed—and did not know what to expect.

And then one day a group of Hungarian fascists, militiamen with a strong sense of empathy with Nazi Germany, rounded up all the Jews in the small town where Aviva lived and brought them to a nearby forest area. The Jews, ever hopeful that this was just some evil prank, went along with little protest. Each person in the group, including Aviva, now a teenager, was handed a shovel and told to dig a large, joint ditch. They were not told by the armed militiamen what the purpose was and probably assumed that they were being conscripted for forced labor and were digging a drainage or sewage ditch.

They set to work, carefully supervised by their guards, many of whom were on horseback. Aviva remembers that she, too, worked with her shovel, but a black thought kept entering her mind: this was no drainage or sewage ditch they were creating; something monstrously horrible was about to take place. She continued to work, trying to think, when suddenly one of the men on horseback approached her and she stopped digging and looked up.

Through the beads of sweat that poured down her face, obscuring her vision, she saw that the uniformed, armed horseman was a young man she had gone to school with. For a moment she hesitated, not knowing whether to speak or cry out or ask for an explanation. With a small nod he tapped her with his rifle butt and whispered, "Go, run into the forest—just keep away from here."

Her mind was a blank, she didn't understand, nor did she know if she should do what he urged. Many of the people in the group were her neighbors and friends, but she noticed that none had dared to look up from their work. Maybe it's a trap, she thought, but then she remembered that this particular young man had been an easygoing, usually gentle person in the classes they attended. She dropped her shovel into the ditch, looked at her fellow diggers one last time, and headed for the forest as fast as she could. She doesn't remember how long she ran, nor how far, but at some point she collapsed from sheer exhaustion and, alone in a dark forest, weary and frightened, she broke down and sobbed.

For the next few years she remained in hiding—in peasant huts, in far-off rustic cabins, with friends in various cities—under a disguised name. She worried only about having enough to eat and evading any contact with Nazis or their Hungarian sympathizers. Her life in hiding finally came to an end when the war was over, and the Nazis and their allies were toppled from power.

She learned then what she had always feared to learn: the ditch diggers on that fateful day had been preparing their own graves. Ordered to stand alongside the long ditch, they were shot down in cold blood, falling into their common grave.

Aviva left Hungary as quickly as possible, heading for Palestine. When Israel proclaimed its independence, she made up her mind to use all of her talents and skills to help the new state. Always an excellent student, she soon became a physicist, completing her training in nuclear physics in the United States. She became a professor at Technion, married, had two children, and continued to expand her knowledge of one of the world's newest areas of scientific knowledge.

A few years ago the Government of Puerto Rico invited her to set up a nuclear physics department at the university in Santurce. She accepted, knowing that after a few years she will return to Israel, where her children will continue their studies and her husband can work in his own field, music.

One wonders, though, what thoughts enter this lady's head on those soft Caribbean nights, when she rests from her academic chores. What a strange hegira has been hers—from Hungary to Israel to Puerto Rico, and eventually back to Israel —and all because a former classmate nodded to her and told her to flee for her life.

—D.C.G.

A Sister's Daring Rescued Young Boy from Czarist Conscription

In czarist Russia in the nineteenth century, the autocratic regime that ruled that vast region enforced a conscription law that took young boys into the armed forces for periods of twenty-five years.

For the Jewish population compulsory service in the czarist armies was a disaster, for any youngster caught up in the giant net would never return the same as he had been.

Every town and village was given a quota for draftees that had to be filled, and if it was not filled, the local authorities were held accountable. No Jew wanted to serve in the czarist forces, for not only was the draft of twenty-five years' duration, but it was common knowledge that the Jews in the Russian Army were brutally discriminated against, and a concerted effort was constantly under way to forcibly convert the young draftees. In many cases a young yeshiva boy caught up in the draft was subjected to forced feeding of pork, in a determined effort to break his will and turn him into a servile soldier ready to do the czar's bidding.

Many a young Jewish man deliberately maimed himself in order to be declared ineligible for the draft. This self-maiming consisted of cutting off fingers and even blinding oneself in one eye. Sometimes even these maimed boys were conscripted. The Jewish boys were drafted as young as twelve, and if in a particular town the quota was short, the authorities would grab a boy of ten and change his records to read that he was twelve. Sadly, there were even some Jews who joined in the conscription program and literally stole young boys for the army. They were cursed by their fellow Jews and shunned and feared by the community at large. They were known collectively as *chappers* (grabbers), for often they would simply sweep down on a school or a home and grab a boy, forcibly hauling him off to become cannon fodder for the czar.

On one cruel, wintry night a youngster in a *shtetl* failed to return home from *heder,* the traditional Jewish school attended by all the boys in the village. Frantic, his sister and parents ran into the street to find out what had happened. They feared the worst—and their fears were confirmed by the boy's classmates: a *chapper* had indeed waited in ambush, and when the boys came out of school several of them were rounded up, with the help of local militia, and spirited away to a nearby army camp to begin their twenty-five-year servitude.

The parents practically sat *shiva* for the child, not believing that there was anything they could do. But the sister was determined to try to save him. She did not permit herself to mourn. Somehow she learned that he was only a few miles from her home village and would remain there for the next six months, after which he was scheduled to be shipped out to a Siberian outpost.

She went around to the rabbi, the teacher, the local communal leader, and to others, asking for advice and help, but no one knew what could be done. The boy had been swept out of their lives and they were all prepared to give him up. But the sister remained adamant.

For weeks she sat and pondered. Finally an idea occurred to her. In a week's time the festival of Simhat Torah would take place, and she banked on the fact that if she tried she might be allowed to bring her brother some holiday food.

Without confiding in her parents, armed with a bundle full of food, and with a bottle of vodka that she planned to give to the sentries, she set off alone on the morning of the day when Simhat Torah eve would be celebrated. She made a brief stop at the synagogue, approached the Holy Ark, opened it, touched the scrolls of the Torah, kissed them, and then set off by wagon for the army camp, arriving early in the afternoon. She had to walk more than two miles to the camp. When she approached, her courage nearly left her, but she took a deep breath, determined to save her younger brother.

At the sentry box she extracted her bottle of vodka, curtsied politely, handed the gift to the soldier on duty, and said she was the sister of one of the recruits, explaining that it was a holiday and she would appreciate it if she could be permitted to bring her sibling some holiday food. The sentry hesitated, so she quickly handed him a freshly baked honey cake. He agreed, warning her not to stay more than a half hour.

Fearful of the sea of uniformed soldiers who surrounded her, she made her way into the base and almost miraculously stumbled across her younger brother, who was sitting in a barrack, dressed in a uniform that was at least five sizes too big for him. She found him looking despondent, his eyes red and swollen, as though he had just completed a crying spell.

The boy's name was Velvel. Trying hard to act tough and stern, she said to him: "Velvele, don't cry. I have come to help you. Here in this bag you will find cake and other food. At the bottom is a dress, a girl's hat, and shoes. Go to the latrine—anywhere where you can be alone for a few minutes—put everything on, and ten minutes after I leave just walk out of the camp. The dress is just like the one that I'm wearing. The sentry will think it is me. I'm going to leave right now, and I'll do it so that he won't see me. He'll think you're me. Just walk out and I'll wait for you on the road to the village, outside the camp. Don't be afraid. It'll work."

And work it did. The sister waited until the sentry was occupied elsewhere and left the camp. In a half hour her brother arrived, still clad as a girl. Together the two "sisters" traveled home and arrived in time for the Simhat Torah celebrations. They kissed the Torahs fervently as they were carried around the synagogue, and each Simhat Torah they remember the event as though it happened yesterday.

The whole family left Russia, smuggling themselves across the border the next night, and eventually settled in the United States. The story of the escape became part of the family's heritage.

—D.C.G.

 ## The Middle Ages:
A Time of Growth and Education for Jewish Women

Compared to their Christian counterparts, Jewish women in the Middle Ages were emancipated. They conducted independent businesses and used the money at their own discretion. More than a few of the charitable contributions and funds for the printing of books and the maintenance of synagogues were the direct result of the generosity of individual women.

This was also a period when women, reared in a society where Jewish Law was central and esteemed, demanded many of the privileges of that Law. They sought to exercise the right to observe positive commandments—something traditionally limited to men—and even demanded to be called to the Torah. These demands were well received and women were granted many honors heretofore denied them.

One woman who was held in high esteem in the Middle Ages was a noted teacher at the talmudic academy in Baghdad, where her father, Samuel, was the *gaon* (lit. "the genius," the Jewish spiritual leader). During the twelfth century Samuel ben Ali, a contemporary and rival of Maimonides, ran the academy and ruled over the surrounding Jewish communities. His views on women's participation in Jewish life were much more liberal than those of his more famous colleague. While Maimonides disapproved of women participating in most aspects of religious life, ben Ali believed the opposite. His daughter, referred to only as Bat HaLevi (daughter of the Levite), had been educated by him in Bible and Talmud. She was known for her beauty as well as her scholarship. For this reason she lectured the students at the Baghdad academy either from behind a screen or from an adjoining room, so that the young men would not be distracted from the Law by her lovely appearance.

A traveller of the twelfth century passing through Baghdad wrote of Bat HaLevi:

> She is expert in Scripture and Talmud. She gives instruction in Scripture to young men through a window. She herself is within the building, whilst the disciples are below outside and do not see her.

Other noted women scholars of the same period were Miriam Shapira Luria, who lectured in rabbinics and Talmud in Italy in the thirteenth century, and Dulcie of Worms. Dulcie was known to have held public discourses on the Sabbath. Hardworking and the sole support of her husband and children, she died a martyr's death with her two daughters in 1213. Some say the three were killed by two knights of the Cross. She was mourned as

> *a singer of hymns and prayers, a speaker of supplications, a declarer of "Pittum HaKetoret" and the Ten Commandments.*

Dulcie may have been one of the first of a group of women known in the Yiddish-speaking world as the *firzogerins*, or prayer leaders. These women led the women's congregation in the balcony of the synagogue while the men prayed down below. They had to be learned enough to read aloud and to translate the prayers from the Hebrew into the vernacular for those congregants who did not know Hebrew. Many of them wrote their own prayers or supplications (called *techinot*) for the women's congregation. These were written in Yiddish and usually concerned themselves with personal feelings and prayers for families or communities. Such prayers often were addressed specifically to the Mothers of Israel: Sarah, Rebecca, Leah, and Rachel.

The better known of these women prayer leaders were famous for their beautiful *techinot*. Marat Guta, daughter of Rabbi Nathan, is said to have "prayed for the women in her lovely prayers." Rebecca Tiktiner was one of the most learned of the *firzogerins*. She lived in the first half of the sixteenth century (died 1550) and was famous as a woman preacher.

The family of Rashi, the famous biblical commentator who lived in France (1040–1105), was blessed with many daughters and granddaughters. Rashi's three daughters, Yocheved, Miriam, and Rachel, were all learned. Rachel (also known as Bellejeune) was credited with having written a responsum on a question of talmudic law when her father was sick. It was a reply to Rabbi Abraham Cohen of Mayence.

Rashi's daughters, it was said, put on *tefillin* (phylacteries) every morning in accordance with the commandment (Deut. 6:4–9). His granddaughters, Alwina, Hannah, and Miriam, were reputed authorities on dietary laws. This line of French-Jewish scholarship unfortunately ended with the expulsion of the Jews from France.

England was not known as a center of Jewish scholarship, but until the expulsion of the Jews in 1290, women and men thrived in the business world. Documents exist showing that many women were active as moneylenders, among them Belia of Bedford, Mirabel of Gloucester (who was a partner with her daughter and granddaughter), Henne of York, Avigay of London, and Belassez of Oxford.

One of the most powerful of these English businesswomen was Licoricia of Winchester. She enjoyed a good relationship with King Henry III and his court, probably because they depended on her for loans. She handled large sums, regularly made loans to the royal family and their associates, and at times dealt with the largest Jewish banks of the day. The protection of the king helped her avoid heavy fines, and even imprisonment, for some of her more complicated business transactions.

Jewish women in medieval England fared better, in general, than their Christian sisters. In comparison to the Gentile world, where a married woman was considered the ward of her husband, Jewish women in England (and elsewhere) owned property in their own names and acted independently in business. They also dealt with the Jewish rabbinical court wherever that body held jurisdiction over English Jews. In all these areas they were continuing the tradition of freedom (within the limits of Jewish Law) and participating in the economic life that existed in many communities where Jews lived and prospered.

Poland and the area east of the Rhine River was slowly becoming a place of prosperity since the time of King Boleslav's invitation to the Jews in 1164. Despite ghettos, special taxes, and restrictions on owning land, Jews found ways to live and to succeed.

The ancient cities of Prague and Cracow had become Jewish printing centers by the late 1500s. Rebecca Tiktiner's book was printed in both of these cities in 1609 and 1618, respectively. It is the first book ever printed that was written in Yiddish by a woman.

Following in Rebecca's footsteps were many other learned women. Some published their works, while others remained unknown outside their immediate circle. Some had enough distinction to have their names preserved in a footnote or included in a list—we have thus been able to trace them. Names like Sarah, Serlin, and Hebel, included in lists of women doctors from the Middle Ages, suggest that Jewish women also played a role in the science of the day. Still other doctors included in license records are listed as Jewish women, but without mention of their names. One woman referred to only as Maria Hebrea, about whom little is known save that she was Jewish, stands out in the area of science and medicine for having discovered hydrochloric acid.

In the field of Jewish letters there were also women such as Hannah Ashkenazi of Cracow (1593), who was a writer on moral subjects, and historians Bella Hurwitz and Edel Mendels.

Lita of Regensburg, an elusive author whose origins remain a mystery, wrote a translation of the Book of Samuel in Yiddish verse, called the *Schmuel Buch*. The first record of it appeared in 1544, when it was printed by Chaim Schwartz. The inscription in the Hamburg, Germany, manuscript reads:

> *This book I wrote with my hand, Liva (Lita) of Regensburgh is my name. My dear* generin's *[patroness'] name is Breidlen, may she use and read it in joy. This I desire.*

Because of the vagueness of the inscription, male historians felt that the book was merely copied, or that it was by a man. They reasoned that no woman was capable of actually composing such an exceptional work. However, Johann Christoph Wolf, a noted bibliographer of Jewish books, believed that the actual author was a woman, Lita, and other sources attribute the work to her as well.

Another woman scholar was Hava Bacharach, also known as Hava of Prague. She lived from 1580 to 1651. Eva was descended from a learned family and produced learned children, all dedicated to Judaism. Her father was Rabbi Samson and her mother's name was Vogele Cohen. Her son was elected Rabbi of Moravia, and her grandson, Jair Bacharach, wrote and published 238 responsa, which he named in honor of Eva, his erudite grandmother from Prague. The collection was called *Havat Jair*, or Jair's Eva.

Eva, however, did not depend on her illustrious family for her personal fame. She was an expert in rabbinical and biblical writings and her opinions were sought on obscure passages. Later in life she journeyed to Palestine in the hope of fulfilling a long-held wish to see the Holy Land. She died on her way there before reaching her goal.

The Middle Ages was a time of spiritual darkness for much of European and Asian civilization. For some Jewish women, however, it was also a time of growth, as they became more educated and more committed to Jewish life and learning. All over the world, from England to Byzantium, from Poland to Kurdistan and beyond, Jewish women were accomplishing, building, and working to create the next generation of learned and dedicated Jews—this against all odds and adversities. Jewish women suffered the same tribulations as Jewish men in the medieval world: special Jewish badges and hats, special taxes, persecution, instability, and periodic expulsions. In addition, they experienced the special prejudices that Jewish men often felt toward them and their "accepted" role. Still, they managed to overcome many of their difficulties.

—S.He. and E.T.

 ## The *Agunah* and the Devoted Sister

As the following letters will show, not all women who lived during the Middle Ages were as educated and secure as Rebecca Tiktiner and other women scholars and writers of this period. The first moving letter was written sometime during the thirteenth century by Donna Sarah, an Italian Jewess. The letter was sent to her husband, Rabbi Solomon the Scribe, who had left their hometown in Italy and had journeyed to Egypt in order to obtain relief from paying certain taxes. We will never know whether Rabbi Solomon ever received the letter or if he did return home. The document was found among the Hebrew letters of the Cairo *geniza*. Even though it was written so long ago, Donna Sarah's longing for her husband, her indignation at his absence, and her need for support and help are familiar feelings now, as they must have been then.

Yet Donna Sarah's plea has a deeper meaning. According to Jewish law, the *agunah* (deserted woman) holds a unique and lonely place in the Jewish community. Should Rabbi Solomon have failed to return, Donna Sarah would have been left without the possibility of remarrying for the rest of her life. Lacking a witness necessary to prove his death, she could not have claimed status as a widow. And since the Jewish woman herself is not able to initiate a divorce, and the court is unable to grant her one without the husband's ultimate consent, Donna Sarah would have been doomed to a lonely life.

Even though the problem of the *agunah* still exists for many observant Jews, the desperate urgency of this dilemma in Donna Sarah's time cannot be fully appreciated today, when Jews have access to civil law and Jewish courts are not legally binding. As a member of the Jewish community of Italy, Donna Sarah was legally bound by rabbinic law and had no recourse to appeal to any other authority even if she had wished to. These facts bring to her words ("I swear to the Lord, if you do this, you must not speak with us anymore; and if you do this, [it] will make the world despise us . . .") a poignancy that would not otherwise be apparent.

Donna Sarah to her husband Solomon:

> *May ample peace and welfare be with my master and ruler, the light of my eyes, the crown of my head, my master and husband, the learned Rabbi Solomon, the Scribe, may he live long. May ample peace be bestowed upon you by the Master of peace and from Donna Sarah your wife, your daughters Reina and Rachel, from R. Moses, your son-in-law, and Rebecca.*

We are all longing to see your sweet face, as one longs after the face of God, and we are wondering that you have not answered the numerous letters we have sent you. We have written you often, begging you to return, but—no answer at all. If you can manage with the help of the esteemed physician Rabbi Solomon—may he live long—to obtain a release from taxes, it will be greatly to your profit, and this kindness will exceed all benefits which he has conferred on you. May the Lord grant him a rich reward in this world and the world to come, and may he educate his son for Torah, marriage, and good works.

And now let us return to the previous subject. We are all assembled—your wife, your daughters, and your son-in-law, Moses—to implore you from the bottom of our hearts not to go farther, either by sea or by land, because we have heard that you have the intention of leaving for Turkey. I swear to the Lord that if you do this you must not speak with us anymore; and if you do this—which will make the world despise us and cause a quarrel between your son-in-law and your daughter, who is in certain circumstances—you will inflict pain upon your daughter and perhaps she will suffer a miscarriage. And you will also endanger the happiness of your daughter Rachel, who has grown up and has become a beautiful and modest maiden.

People will talk scandal and say, "Here is a respectable old scribe who left his wife and daughters and has been missing for many years. Perhaps he is mad. For he went to a distant country and you know what the verse says: 'The eyes of a fool are in the ends of the earth.'" Beg the physician, Rabbi Solomon, therefore, to provide you with a confirmation about the release from the taxes; otherwise come home [in the name of] the Blessed One! . . . Do nothing else. And Peace!

Lady Maliha lived in Byzantium, generally known as the Eastern Roman Empire. Her letter to her brothers shows the closeness of family ties in this period and hints at some of the events and practices of the time.

There is no place name on the letter, nor any address, but since it was found in the Cairo *geniza* it was probably addressed to her brothers in Egypt. It is not known specifically where Lady Mahila was living, but because the letter reminds her brothers that "many Jews are being fetched in Byzantium," it might be reasonable to assume that she was living in or near Constantinople, the Byzantine capital. The Jewish quarter in this city had been sacked and burned by Latin Crusaders in 1204 after the Fourth Crusade. The area was in a general state of turmoil. Lady Maliha may well have wanted to leave this situation and return to the comparative stability of Egypt.

Another interesting point mentioned in the letter is Maliha's use of the Torah as an omen. ("I consulted a Torah scroll . . . and obtained a disappointing answer that boded no good . . .") The concept of using a Torah scroll as a Jewish "crystal ball" is strange to modern thinking and was most certainly frowned on by rabbis even in the eleventh and twelfth centuries. However, looking for omens was an old superstition that dated back to biblical times. King Saul consulted the high priest for an omen before deciding whether to go to battle against the Philistines.

Maliha decided that the omen was not auspicious enough for her to take a trip at that time. This apparently did not preclude her brothers' coming to take her. The risk was in her traveling alone.

Why does Maliha appeal to her brothers and not her husband for protection?

Indeed, why is she alone in Byzantium with her daughter while her family is else-where? Is her "our Master, the fourth" referred to in the letter their father, her husband, or someone else? These questions must remain unanswered.

Maliha's letter, originally written in Hebrew and full of references to Bible stories, shows her as a learned woman. She gives us a brief glimpse into a little-known world where one crisis followed another, where traveling and even communication were fraught with danger, and long separations were common. In such an atmosphere family ties and responsibilities, bolstered by the structure of Jewish law, could mean the difference between life and death for women like Lady Maliha. Understanding this makes her loving appeal to her brothers much clearer and more logical.

Lady Maliha's letter [to her brothers?]:

May this letter be delivered in gladness to my excellent brothers, Abu Said and Solomon, from your sister Maliha. May peace from Heaven, like the drops of water from above [and abundant] like the fishes in the depths [of the sea], be bestowed upon you and strength, vigor, favor, mercy and pity, and a long life like his who became father of the people [Abraham], or his who was bound as a victim on a high mountain [Isaac], or of Jacob the plain man, or of him who dreamed [Joseph], or of him who sprinkled the blood on the altar seven times [Aaron]. May all blessings come and be gathered and accumulated upon the heads of my brothers, Solomon and Abu Said, gentle and most beloved brothers, from your sister Maliha. And heartiest greetings from my little daughter Zoe.

We are in good health and trust in the Rock of your welfare that you, too, are well and safe, prosperous and free, in good heart, without trouble and sorrows. But I, while wishing you good, am not myself in good humor, for when I think of you my heart sinks, my knees quiver, my limbs tremble, my strength dwindles, because I have been separated from you for many years and am desirous of seeing your faces. I should like to run to you like a lion, nay, to fly! Oh for the wings of a dove, that I could fly and join my brothers, and also our Master, the fourth. I am, however, not able to come, as the hour is not favorable. I was ready to go with this man [the bearer of the letter], but I consulted a Torah scroll [using the passage that turned up for an omen] and obtained a disappointing answer that boded no good for myself. Thus I could not join them.

And for heaven's sake, do you not see that many Jews are being fetched from Byzantium by their relatives? Why does not one of you make up his mind to come over here in order to bring me back? You will understand that I am reluctant to engage strange people. If I should go alone, may God not deprive me of luck, but if anything evil should befall me during the voyage, it might be fatal to me and I should die. For I have been devoted to you since your infancy.

—S.He. and E.T.

 Life on a Fence

Twelve years ago I married out of my faith. It's a happy marriage. I neither condone nor condemn intermarriage. It is something that happens. It is up to the individuals involved to make it work. Make no mistake, though—you live on a fence.

My name is Ianniello. I am a Jew. I live in a religiously mixed neighborhood in a suburban town. What casual acquaintances could possibly think I am a Jew unless I say so?

I have Jewish friends and Christian friends. My Jewish friends recommended me to a local doctor. I noticed a diploma in his office from the medical college of the same university I had attended.

Because I knew he was originally from the South I said, "Oh, you went to New York University too."

The doctor, respected in my community as a professional man and a worthwhile person, laughed until he shook. He recalled his college days and what he and his friends used to do to "all the kike interns."

That doctor was the sharpest picket in my fence. He hurt the most. I never went back to him, and for the first time in my life I deliberately sought a doctor with a Jewish-sounding name. (After four years and two babies I discovered that my Jewish doctor, who was married to a Christian, was a converted Episcopalian! He has his pickets too.)

A pipe broke under the sink in my kitchen and I called a plumber. Two hours and a lot of water later, the pipe was replaced.

"Sorry I made such a mess," the plumber said. "Give me a rag and I'll clean the floor."

I watched him, down on his knees, slowly moving the muddy dirt around in a circle until it dried. While he worked he told me about replacing all the pipes in a big house on the other side of town.

"That was really a mess," he said. "I never even cleaned it up. I do lots of work for Hebes, but I sure as hell don't clean *their* floor."

I looked down at my Jew-hating plumber as he happily tried to clean my floor. The picket hurt.

What do you do when your black day worker stops vacuuming your floor to ask, "Do you like Jews?"

You think, here it comes again. What did we do now?

"I quit my Tuesday job," she said. "That lady spent all my lunchtime talking about Jews moving near her. She can't stand Jews no how."

I looked at her. She had been working since she was ten. She wrote messages in an illegible scrawl. She read newspaper headlines and looked at pictures. She cleaned a house a day and staggered with fatigue back to her cubicle in a crowded boarding house. What was she going to say?

"I quit that lady. I figure if she can't stand Jews that much . . . she must really hate me!"

The vacuum hummed again this time. I did too.

A delivery man rang my bell to hand me a package. It was an August day and he fanned himself with his hat. I live a few miles from a beach resort that is almost 90 percent Jewish.

"Whew," he said, "sure is hot. I wish I had the Jewtown route."

Another picket. Not too pointed.

A friend of a friend enthusiastically discussed his last fishing trip. It was great. He had a marvelous time.

"And then those kikes had to show up."

"How could you tell what they were?" I asked.

"Are you kidding? I can spot a kike a mile away," he shouted in my face.

It was the last hour of a series of driving lessons and my instructor suddenly laughed and slapped his thigh. I was still crawling along at fifteen miles an hour, so it couldn't have been anything I had done.

"Look at theat 'mutsa crista,' " it sounded like he said.

All I saw was a heavyset man wearing Bermuda shorts.

"What's that?" I asked.

"Don't you talk Italian? That's what I call them—Christ killers."

How do you keep from exploding? a Jewish friend of mine wants to know.

I've never "exploded." I hope I never do. When I answer, it's slowly, quietly. I am fascinated by the faces of these haters of my people.

The doctor dropped his stethoscope and actually stuttered.

"But you don't look Jewish. You're a finer type."

"Then all my family and friends are finer types too," I said.

The plumber held his rag in midair, too paralyzed to move.

"Gee, I was just kidding," he finally said. "I figure people want me to talk like that. Gee—most of my customers are Jewish people."

Not "Hebes" this time, mind you. He said "Jewish people."

The cleaning woman didn't even hear me over the noise of the vacuum cleaner.

The delivery man probably went on envying his buddies who worked in the next town.

The fisherman was a joy to behold. His jaw dropped open. When he got it back into position again, he made no apology.

"All my life I thought I could tell a Jew a mile away," he said. "All my life I said that . . ."

The driving instructor posed a different problem. That lesson was paid for and I intended getting the most out of it. But when it was over, and when he had wished me well and I was out of his car and on my own sidewalk, I could no longer remain silent.

"There's one thing you ought to know," I said casually. "We didn't kill Christ. The Romans did."

Poor man. He certainly should have known that you don't start a car in reverse.

I sit on my fence and look about me. I see a rash of swastikas dirtying the American scene. And then I read statements made by religious leaders, statesmen, and responsible citizens all over the world. From Roman Catholic pope to Methodist neighbor, the comment is the same.

"Anti-Semitism is anti-Christian heresy."

"Prejudice and discrimination affect not only Jews but the entire democratic way of life."

I watch and listen to the political campaigns. I rejoice that both parties have seen fit to include strong civil rights issues in their planks.

Legal action, education, hard work by such groups as the Anti-Defamation League and other forces fighting for civil rights and liberties have shown results. The baby steps have become giant steps.

My black day worker, who must feel the hurt of prejudice many times, voiced it so simply. If they hate you, they hate me too.

We will unite as people. All the pickets on that fence of mine cannot fall at once. They go slowly, one here, one there, now a few at a time.

The fence is getting weaker. It rocks and sways. It will fall.

—L.I.

 ## A Wedding in Cochin

Love? In Cochin that comes after marriage, not before, I learned as I sat talking to Ruth and her husband, David, in the sparsely furnished second story of their home, with its chairs of Dutch-Portuguese design, large, brass-trimmed wooden chests, and wide window seats overlooking Cochin's Jewtown Road.

David's father had settled on Ruth as a proper mate for his son after considering the family, her health, and her reputation. He then broached the subject with her father. Ruth's father accepted the proposal, and a betrothal party was held at which the bride-to-be received gifts of gold jewelry.

I had come to Cochin, the "Queen of the Arabian Sea," near land's end in the state of Kerala, in southwestern India, to be with its White Jews, its Black Jews, and its brown-skinned Emancipated group living in Cochin's Jewtown.

Here the term "Jewtown" carries no overtones of anti-Semitism, no stigma. It is merely a statement of a fact of life. When Jews found it necessary, in the sixteenth century, to flee Cranganore, fifteen miles to the north, they came to Cochin and asked for asylum. The rajah responded with a gift of land adjacent to his own palace. There Jewtown was built, and there most of Cochin's remaining Jews still live.

That morning I had crossed, by small ferryboat, from Willingdon Island, where I was staying at the Malabar Hotel, to Mattancherry, where Jewtown is located.

One is lulled by the beauty of the lagoons and canals, the calm waters of this safe, landlocked harbor, with small *valloms* (tiny cargo boats) plying back and forth, transporting their wares to the ocean steamers moored in the deep waters of the harbor. As I handed my ticket to the brown-skinned, khaki-clad, barefoot ticket collector, he smilingly informed me he was a Jew bearing the name Saul, "like the first Jewish king."

Arriving in Mattancherry, I turned down the services of a rickshaw driver in favor of walking. Small shops lined both sides of narrow Jewtown Road. There was Sorabji Company's Ahura House, a shipping, clearing, and forwarding house. Morris & Sons, whose address also is Jewtown, Cochin, were ship chandlers and commission agents. Store nameplates bore the legend "Jewtown" even where Hindus had taken over from previous Jewish owners.

As I walked through the commercial section of Jewtown Road, there was an air of busyness, of activity, of people coming and going. This was the area where the Black Jews once lived. They had been the petty traders, selling eggs, vegetables, and bananas. Some had been oil pressers, carpenters, and fishermen using the Chinese fishing nets so typical of Cochin. Here still stands the Kadavumbhagam Synagogue, now shuttered, its former congregants having migrated to Israel.

Farther north was the quarter of the Emancipated group, descendants of unions of former slaves with their Jewish masters, who had been acknowledged and accepted into the Jewish faith. Many of them were clerks and bookbinders.

As I continued north through Jewtown, I noted shops giving way to residences, and a greater calm prevailing. Here was the section where the White Jews lived. They were the more affluent—the professionals, the government officials, the merchants. Homes were two-storied, with sloping, tiled roofs, cream-colored walls, and small barred and shuttered windows. The architecture was a reminder that the Portuguese and the Dutch had once ruled here. It was in this northern sector of Jewtown that I sat talking with Ruth and David.

Soon after the announcement of their betrothal, preparations had begun for the wedding. This was to be held, according to local custom, on a Tuesday, a day believed to be one of good augury.

On the Thursday preceding the wedding a tailor began making the groom's white wedding suit, and the women busied themselves decorating the nuptial bed with a special canopy. For all of the first week after their marriage, David and Ruth would stay indoors, to protect themselves from evil spirits, who, out of jealousy of the bliss of bride and groom, would be lurking outdoors to do them harm. Seated on this canopied bed, they would receive guests all through that week.

On the Friday before the wedding the groom gave a dinner party for his best men. On the Sabbath, when he was host to all members of the small community, the bride was the guest of honor. And on Monday she was hostess for dinner at her home to all in the community.

And now the lucky day, Tuesday, arrived. At three in the morning women assembled in Ruth's home. Seated on benches arranged against two sides of the ground-floor corridor, they sang old love songs to the bride in the Malayalam tongue, the native Indian dialect. Then, preceded by a drum and brass band, the women next moved down the length of streamer-decorated Jewtown Road, making public announcements of the marriage.

Wearing a white, gold-embroidered dress draped to one side, with jewels in her hair and around her neck, her bridesmaid holding a silk parasol over her head, as had been the custom for maharajahs on ceremonial occasions, Ruth left home to perform the important rite of immersing herself in the *mikveh* (ritual bath).

Following that ritual, Ruth, still accompanied by the women, continued on to the synagogue, where she was greeted with the words "O beautiful as the moon comes the dove from her cote." The Scroll of the Law was opened to the Ten Commandments, and with hands over her eyes Ruth kissed the scroll seven times. She was hailed with biblical verses referring to Sarah and Rebecca and with blessings such as "May you merit long life with sons and daughters engaged in works of the Law."

Then, moving along Jewtown Road, she entered each home and symbolically "kissed the knee" of her elders (an act of humility), touching their knees with her hand, then raising her hand to her lips.

Meanwhile, the groom, dressed in white festive attire, with a *tallit* (fringed prayer shawl) and the usual Indian garland of flowers, left for the synagogue. As he stepped out of the house, his mother circled her head three times with some coins and then threw the coins into the street. This was done to make sure that good luck would always follow her son. Attended by his best men and preceded by musicians and people carrying four lighted wax candles, he proceeded to the synagogue.

At the far northern end of Jewtown Road we reached the Paradesi Synagogue. Only a fence and a gate separated it and the rest of Jewtown from the former rajah's palace and Hindu temple a mere thirty yards away. Betel nuts were drying in the compound. The dials of the synagogue clock, a landmark, face different directions. The numerals on each face are inscribed differently—one in Arabic, one in Hebrew, and one in the native Malayalam.

Forty feet long, the Paradesi Synagogue has two rows of crystal chandeliers and hanging silver lamps. Brass pillars support an upper gallery to which the Scroll of the Law, with its golden crown (a gift of a rajah), is brought from the carved Ark for ceremonial reading on the Sabbath. Behind this gallery and separated from it by latticework is the women's balcony. Paradesi worshipers face west toward the holy city of Jerusalem. A striking feature of the synagogue is the floor made of tiles, in a willow pattern, imported from China.

We walked down the length of the synagogue and David sat on the steps leading to the Holy Ark, where, after *mincha* and *maariv* (afternoon and evening services), he had awaited the coming of his bride on their wedding day.

Escorted by a male member of her family and a band, and followed by many companions, Ruth walked to the Paradesi. Her father met her at the entrance and escorted her into the place of worship. She was seated on an elevated chair, her head and face completely hidden behind a heavy veil.

The groom requested the assembly's permission to begin the wedding ceremony. Permission having been granted, he chanted the blessings over the wine and to the bride he said:

You are betrothed and sanctified unto me—by means of this cup and this ring, by the silver, you enter my jurisdiction in the presence of witnesses according to the Law of Moses and Israel.

He removed the ring from the cup of wine, and after each person had sipped the wine he placed the ring on her finger with the words "This is your sanctification."

Then came the reading of the *ketubah,* the formal marriage contract. Following this the *kinyan,* the solemn affirmation, took place. David and the *hazzan* faced one another. Joining hands, each one holding the fringes of his *tallit,* they repeated the following three times:

Hazzan: By the command of the Holy and Sanctified, by the Mighty One who revealed the Law at Sinai. Her support, her clothing and her conjugal rights he shall not diminish.
Groom: Her support, her clothing, and her conjugal rights I will not diminish.
Hazzan: Dost thou undertake this?
Groom: I undertake this.
Hazzan: An affirmation before Heaven and earth?
Groom: An affirmation before Heaven and earth.

David now signed the *ketubah,* as did two witnesses. It was rolled up and handed to the groom, who transferred it to his bride with the words "Here is thy *ketubah.* By virtue of all that is written therein, you enter my jurisdiction in the presence of these witnesses, according to the Law of Moses and Israel."

At this point the bride was unveiled and all exclaimed, "O beautiful as the moon!" Now followed the "Sevenfold Benediction." With final blessings and an invocation for "Life and Peace," all started out for the wedding feast, led in procession with torchbearers and fireworks.

We stepped out into the warm sunshine of Jewtown Road once more, but, alas, no torchbearers or fireworks preceded us on the route home. Along the way I learned that the wedding feast was repeated night after night for an entire week. This was the week in which they had stayed indoors to keep themselves safe from any evil spirits that might be waiting outdoors to do them harm.

A special exception to this rule was on the Sabbath morning following the wedding, when David attended worship services at the synagogue. He was honored with an *aliya,* being called up to the reading of the Torah.

The closing feast, on the seventh night after their wedding, was a particularly gay evening. Again the bride was greeted with "O beautiful as the moon," and the men danced before the groom. Heard that evening was the Song of Songs, as well as a "Song of Wine," and a melody with the chorus "A good omen, a good omen." The week's festivities were brought to a close that night with the final invocation:

> *May he bless you sevenfold*
> *You shall have length of days*
> *And years of life*
> *May peace be added to you*

—I.G.C.

 ## How a Mother Superior Defied the Church and Saved the Jews

Overlooking the ancient Polish-Lithuanian city of Vilna from a hill a few miles east of the Viliya River, a sprawling monastery, built by the Dominican Order in the thirteenth century, straddles the gentle slope and the grassy hilltop.

German soldiers patrolling the narrow village road below threw up clouds of biting white dust as their motorcycle-sidecar combinations, with mounted machine guns and grenade launchers, climbed the hill en route to the nearby Ponary Forest, where thousands of Jews, anti-Nazi suspects, Gypsies, Russians, and prisoners of war were executed daily by Adolf Eichmann's Einsatz-Gruppen special extermination commandos.

The steel-helmeted Nazi storm troopers and the local Polish, Lithuanian, and Russian traitors who joined the Nazi-organized police paid no attention to a group of some forty white-robed nuns toiling in the fruit orchards and vegetable gardens along the monastery walls.

But only twelve of the nuns were bona fide denizens of the Catholic cloister. The remaining robes hid about thirty Jewish women, and even Jewish men, masquerading as nuns. This group of Jewish underground members was hidden and saved by the convent's mother superior, Anna Borkowska.

When the first massacres of Vilna Jews in 1941 filled the antitank ditches in the Ponary Forest with thousands of writhing bodies, Mother Superior Anna Borkowska requested permission from her superiors to hide Jewish fugitives behind the monastery walls. Permission was denied. The local Catholic hierarchy commiserated with the Jews but pointed out that the monastery and its nuns could not be jeopardized, for the Nazis would surely burn down the convent and all of its nuns if even one Jew were found hiding inside.

Anna Borkowska did not take no for an answer. She went directly to the heads of the Dominican Order in Poland, bypassing the local church hierarchy, and repeated her request, adding that since it was the Dominican Order that had killed thousands of Spanish and Portuguese Jews in the name of the Holy Inquisition five hundred years ago, it was only fitting that Dominican monks and nuns should risk their lives to save Jews now.

Again the official answer was no. The mother superior was told she had no right to endanger the monastery's existence and the lives of her nuns, and that the Jews had brought all this suffering on themselves for rejecting Jesus Christ.

"This is anti-Semitic Nazi ideology, and you ought to be ashamed to repeat it!" the elderly mother superior told the startled priest, and returned to Vilna to defy her own superiors and the entire church leadership in a gallant bid to save doomed Jews.

She collected Jewish fugitives, fed them, clothed them in white robes, and hid them in the ancient monastery's cloistered cells, crypts, vaults, and cellars. Her own nuns organized a rebellion against their mother superior. "We do not wish to risk our lives for infidel Jews," a delegation of nuns told her. "If they would at least accept our true faith we would feel the risk is worthwhile."

Anna Borkowska told the nuns that no Jew's conversion would be solicited or accepted by her because it would not be a genuine conversion. "We do not need conversions out of gratitude or under pressure," she stressed. Threatening any nun who objected to the Jews' presence with immediate expulsion and excommunication (although she had no authority to do so), the mother superior defied the Germans, her own superiors, and the nuns in a gallant bid to save as many Jews as possible.

When the fugitives became aware of the opposition to their presence behind the monastery walls, they decided to go back to the doomed ghetto and organize armed Jewish resistance behind its barbed-wire barricades. Anna Borkowska pleaded with them to stay in their sanctuary, or at least leave the women behind. Her pleas were to no avail. "We must go back to fight," the Jews told her firmly.

She begged them to leave at least one Jewish youngster with her to tell the world after the war what had happened to the Vilna Jews. But the entire Jewish group left the monastery, crept back into the ghetto, and organized the famed Jewish fighting resistance movement. The mother superior contacted the Polish nationalist armia krajowa (AK) military underground. She pleaded with the Polish commanders to help the Jewish resistance fighters with arms, ammunition, and safe hiding places. The local commander contacted AK headquarters in Warsaw and the answer was negative.

"We can't help the Jews because most of them are pro-Communist," Polish officers told the mother superior. "Aren't you ashamed?" she raged. "First the Russians refuse to help them because they are Zionist and bourgeois, now you turn them down because, in your opinion, they are pro-Communist. My own Church cold-shoulders them because a group of Jews in old Jerusalem allegedly denounced Christ to the Romans. But Jesus Christ himself was a Jew! And what about the thousands of innocent Jewish children, women, and babies who are mercilessly slaughtered by the Nazis? Aren't you going to help them?"

The Polish general shrugged his shoulders. "We have enough troubles of our own. Why don't you stick to your own business—praying?"

Anna Borkowska rushed towards the ghetto entrance and demanded of startled police guards to let her in. "I want to die together with the Jews! Shoot me now or later, I don't care. There is only one God, and He is in the ghetto. I want to be where God is," she screamed.

The police captain phoned Gestapo headquarters to come and arrest the mother superior on charges of pro-Jewish propaganda. She faced horrible tortures and execution. But the Jews whom she tried to save rescued her. Members of the Jewish underground who noticed the commotion near the ghetto gates set up a diversionary action; while the attention of the police was distracted, two Jewish women grabbed the mother superior and hid her among the ruins of a burned out house.

She was persuaded to return to her monastery. But in a week Anna Borkowska was back in the ghetto. This time she brought three hand grenades in a pocket of her voluminous robes. She handed them over to Abba Kovner, commander of the underground organization in the Vilna ghetto.

This symbolic act encouraged Jewish resistance in the ghetto. Anna Borkowska's monastery became the lifesaving transit station along the final escape route when the ghetto was liquidated by the Nazis. The few survivors fled to the woods to organize Jewish guerrilla companies and partisan outfits. The convent gates were always open to them and the mother superior gave them peasant clothes and food and hid them until it was safe to cross the open fields to the dense and dark forest. She also enlisted local peasant guides to transport the Jews in their carts and hayrack wagons to a partisan base in the woods.

She never forgave her superiors for refusing to help Jews. When the war was over, she left the monastery to compile a written record of Jewish suffering. Although all nuns who leave their monastery without permission are excommunicated by the Church, Anna Borkowska was not. Albeit belatedly, her case came up for consideration at the Vatican. The Pope granted her wish to seek God outside the convent walls and create a written monument to Jewish suffering.

—L.H.

 ## The Bride Was Fourteen: Sephardic Weddings of Yesterday

In olden times Sephardic Jews in the Balkan states and Turkey were married very young. The girl was fourteen or younger, the husband eighteen or twenty. It was considered a great humiliation for the parents if their children were still unmarried after that age.

The young people were not allowed to voice their inclinations or aversions in the choice of a partner. That was strictly the parents' concern. Any opinion voiced by the girl or boy was considered a gross lack of respect. The parents also settled the details connected with the dowry and trousseau. The couple did not know each other until they were engaged. Even after the engagement they were permitted to see each other only on Passover and Succoth, an interval of six months. The young man came to visit his bride accompanied by his father. This was the only opportunity for him to risk a glance at her. Sometimes they would not see each other at all until their wedding day.

Rich families preferred to have their children marry into families of rabbis who, although poor, were considered intellectuals and were highly esteemed. Wealthy families and those of the highest social spheres considered it a great honor to have a *chacham* (scholar) for a son-in-law. The young rabbi, adored by the whole family, was encouraged to continue his studies as long as he chose.

The engagement usually lasted one year. This time was necessary for the bride and her family to prepare the trousseau. The bride was to provide complete bedding, including the mattress. The day on which the wool for the mattress was bought and washed became a family celebration. Relatives, girl friends, and women neighbors all came to help clean and bleach the wool.

The series of celebrations culminating in the wedding itself began with the *almosamma* (a word of Arabic origin, not properly traced). It took place at the bride's house on the Saturday night preceding the week of the wedding. Friends and relatives of the bride came to sing and dance, often until daybreak, and eat sweets, pastries, and other refreshments. From this day on the groom was not to see the bride until the wedding.

A custom popular even today among Sephardic families was for the groom's family to bake a certain kind of pastry, called *bollitos de susan,* and send them to their relatives and to the bride's family as a symbol of *churban,* or sacrifice, to protect the newlyweds against envy and the evil eye.

The day before the wedding was a very busy day for the couple, especially for the bridegroom. His duties were to rent a hall for the ceremony, arrange all the legal aspects of the wedding, hire servants for the banquet and the orchestra, and give instructions to the man in charge of the invitations, which were extended verbally to each guest.

The *combidador* (inviter) was an especially colorful character. He was handed a double list of relatives and friends of both families. He then had to go from house to house, loudly announcing the wedding and inviting the persons on the list. When entering a patio of a dwelling, he would call the lady of the house whose name was on his list. When she appeared, the "inviter" solemnly announced the good news to her, adding that she, her husband, children, parents, relatives, and friends were invited to the wedding. Other women of the neighborhood would stand at their doors and windows, listening and commenting, full of curiosity about the young couple and their families. In the past century the office of the *combidador* was held by a man; prior to that his female counterpart, the *combidadora,* was entrusted with the invitations.

A few days before the wedding two experts, called *preciadores,* arrived at the bride's house to evaluate her trousseau, which was displayed on tables, beds, and chairs. This led to lengthy discussions between the appraisers and the groom's friends. The event usually took place on a Saturday prior to the wedding to show that the bride's family had kept all its promises. The trousseau was then sent to the groom's house with great pomp, escorted by musicians playing Turkish music. In exchange, the groom gave the musicians a silk-wrapped package for the bride containing perfumes, ointments, and other accessories for the Turkish bath she was to take before the wedding. He also included a purse with a few gold pieces.

The ritual bath of the bride was a solemn event for the girl, but little by little it degenerated into a noisy ceremony of merrymaking, jumping and dancing, songs, and music. The morning of the wedding the bride visited the *hammam* (Turkish bath), escorted by musicians and female relatives, carrying the gift the groom had sent her for this occasion. She wore a splendid dress and was covered with jewelry.

The excess of noise and luxury in an act meant to be an intimate ceremony induced the rabbinical authorities of the eighteenth century to prohibit music on the way to or from the bathhouse. The bride was not to wear jewelry other than a string of pearls and was not to drink wine or other fermented drinks. During the ritual of the bath she immersed herself three times in a tub. Then, anointed and perfumed, in the midst of singing, dancing, and the jangling of tambourines, she returned home.

The bride was dressed in the afternoon, while the groom, his father, his father-in-law, relatives, and friends spent the afternoon at special services in the synagogue. The rabbi called upon the young man to swear a solemn oath to keep all the clauses stipulated in the *ketubah* (marriage contract).

After the services the groom and his party left for the hall where the wedding was to take place. The bride had already arrived and was seated between the two mothers. Up to the eighteenth century every woman seated next to the bride covered her face with a black veil. This custom, originating in a cabbalistic doctrine, arose from the fact that since the bride was very young and was not yet too attractive, it was feared that the beauty of her mother or mother-in-law would attract more attention.

The blessing was given to the couple while standing underneath a *tallith* held over their heads by four men. It was followed by the reading of the *ketubah* and the breaking of the traditional wine glass.

The wedding lasted four or five hours. Gay music was played and women danced half-Turkish, half-Spanish dances. In the evening the guests began to leave. Only the more intimate friends and relatives remained for the banquet given by the bridegroom in his new apartment. During the dessert, wine made by Jewish hands was served and the music, songs, and dances began once more.

Once again a rabbinical order intervened against the excess of merrymaking. The men were forbidden to play musical instruments in the presence of women, and the women were forbidden to invite men to dance and to dance with the musicians.

Around midnight all the guests had left and only the groom's mother or eldest female relative remained, along with the parents with whom the young couple were to live for the time being. The bride was led to the bridal chamber by her mother, who gave her blessing, encouraging her with good advice for the great event to come. In the meantime the groom was receiving the same kind of instructions from his relatives. The tradition was that the groom's mother stood vigil outside their door, available, should the need arise, in view of the extreme youth of the newlyweds.

The morning after the wedding the bride appeared dressed in her new clothes, suitable for a married woman, which she would wear from now on. She would bend before her father-in-law and kiss his hand, receiving his blessing, together with a gift of jewelry. It was also a tradition that the bride's family distribute sweets and confections in the neighborhood on the morning after the wedding as a sign of rejoicing that the bride was found chaste and pure.

The seven days after the wedding were a continuous holiday for the newlyweds. The groom did not leave his apartment the whole week. Friends visited throughout the day. The groom's mother was in charge of feeding the visitors and practically did not leave the kitchen. The Saturday after the wedding was a very festive day. The groom finally left the house to visit the synagogue together with his father, father-in-law, and friends, where certain passages of the Torah were read in his honor. Otherwise it was another day for visits. In the morning the groom's friends and relatives arrived. The afternoon was dedicated to women and children. Good wishes were expressed with the traditional Hebrew words *B'siman Tov* (for good luck), which are still used at today's Sephardic weddings. A servant would then pass and sprinkle the guests with rose water from a silver flask. Sweets and confections were served. As was usual on all occasions of Jewish social life, the poor were not forgotten. The parents of the young couple solemnly invited them for a distribution of wine and rice.

The last day of the wedding week was called "the Day of the Fish." In the morning the young husband went to the market for his first purchase as head of a family and bought a good fish. At home the fish was painted, adorned with flowers, and put in a dish on the floor. In the presence of relatives and neighbors the bride stepped three times over the fish, a symbol of fecundity.

Another festive meal served to the intimate members of the family lasted all day and often late into the night, bringing to an end the period of celebrations, banquets, and visits that had begun with the *almosamma*. After this gay evening, the last guest left and the young couple settled down for their new life.

These simple yet picturesque and patriarchal customs were practiced until the end of the nineteenth century. The Turkish Revolution and the great fire that destroyed much of Salonika in 1917, including most of the Jewish quarter, forced the Sephardim to disperse throughout the city and put an end to the ancient traditions to which they were so deeply attached. In addition, they were even more undermined by the rapidly growing trend of assimilation and the modernization of social life. Few of the old traditions are still practiced or even known to the present generation.

—H.V.B.

 ## Remembering Mother's Day

The idea of devoting at least one day a year to honoring one's mother is certainly commendable, although in a sense it is somewhat foreign to Jewish tradition. (Mother's Day per se is really an American phemonenon). The untraditionalness of the concept among Jews stems from the Bible, for one of the Ten Commandments instructs us to honor our fathers and our mothers, every day and for all time.

Be that as it may; the fact is that Mother's Day is well-entrenched in the American lifestyle, and it sharpens children's consciousness to the point where at least for that one day, they will make a concerted effort to pay homage to their mothers. Granted, the day has been commercialized and its meaning attenuated. Granted also, there are a number of popular writers and performers who have continued to make a (good) living out of poking fun of their mothers, sometimes good humoredly (a la Sam Levenson), and sometimes bitterly, like some others.

The fact is that for the overwhelming majority of people, one's mother is a beloved, inspiring, treasured, incomparable personality, whose influence begins at childbirth and remains constant throughout the child's life. Certainly, there are pushy mothers, and even selfish mothers. But most mothers are compassionate, loving, dedicated, caring—ready to give their all for their children.

It is not possible to pay tribute to all mothers in this space, of course. But perhaps by honoring the memory of one mother, readers will see a glint of recognition in recalling their own mothers, both those living and those who have passed on.

She was more or less typical of her times: born in Czarist Russia into a traditional, cohesive family, surrounded by loving sisters, brothers, cousins, enjoying the discovery of what life had to offer. . .and then, the dark days: bloodshed and revolution, upheavals. . .two sisters depart for Palestine, burning with Zionist zeal, while others and her mother make their way to Argentina, which at the time was hungry for immigrants (the father was already dead). . .she marries, and the young couple flees, together with nearly everybody else in the town. . .difficult months in Poland, and then on towards the United States (where the young husband's family lives), and a detour in Belgium. . .the latter, because the ships filled with Jews fleeing eastern Europe have filled and overfilled the quotas of the time. . .the couple remains in Belgium, earning a living as owners of a modest eating place. . .a child is born, a son. . .there are no immediate relatives, but there are friends and neighbors. . .a *mohel* is found, and he performs his job gratis, charmed by the naturalness, honesty and forthrightness of the young mother.

A few years later, with the son now not quite four, the family is now at last in New York, stepping stone to the *goldene medinah*. . .for the husband and wife, it's a time of reunion, for they had been separated for over a year while he sought to find employment and housing. . .a modest apartment is located; without central heating, and the meager earnings barely manage to sustain the small family. . .but the mother maintains her sense of proportion and hope: she turns the drab apartment into a warm home; she cooks and bakes, and using these products, as well as her own natural ways, she makes friends. . .she is modest about English, which frightens her but secretly she begins to learn, in her own way, without help of teachers (that was to come later). . .the little boy is taken sick, and the apartment placed under rigid quarantine. . .in that cold apartment, he burns with fever. . .she wonders, this concerned mother, whether she was right in coming to America with her husband; perhaps she should have followed her sisters to Palestine or to Argentina, or even stayed behind in Russia, as one sister did. . .but the boy recovers, and she suffers with him as he too faces the onerous task of learning a new language in an atmosphere where taunting is commonplace. . .one day, while she is in her advanced pregnancy with her second child, the little boy, now six, disappears. . .she is frantic, worried that perhaps the taunting of the neighbors' children had driven him away in this strange, still alien land. . .and then he is found, unharmed, accompanied by the neighborhood's other isolated youth, who suffered from mild retardation. . .the second child is born, a little girl, weeks after the *goldene medinah* suddenly and seemingly catastrophically sinks into a profound economic depression. . .a new apartment is found, slightly bigger, and now with steam heat. . .difficult years follow, there is little money, the depression is in full force, but the mother's cheerfulness, courage and solid intuitions keep things on an even keel. . .the children grow, an the parents glow with pride and praise. . .and the mother, watching the black clouds of Nazism overspreading Europe, realizes that their being in America was perhaps the wisest, and luckiest thing that could have happened.

The children grow and are studious and ambitious. The parents, cut off from traditional Jewish life during their many years of wandering from Russia to Belgium to America, find themselves returning. . .to the synagogue, to the organized community. Mother, a little embarrassed, but very determined, goes to school, squeezing into the young students' seats to master English, and to pass the citizenship test. Now, at long last, everybody is an American, legally and formally.

There were many good years, and many hard years. She was a woman who knew that in this world, one dared not be daunted, but had to resist, fight, and at all times remain human and kind. Life was to be treasured, and lived to the full, and shared and enjoyed.

That was one mother, in a tiny retrospect. And, probably, it is most mothers, too. To all of them, honor on Mother's Day!

–D.C.G.

XII
On Learning, Language, and Literature

There's More Hebrew in English Than You Realize!

The English translation of the Hebrew Scriptures has had a profound influence on English life and thought. Its rhythms and cadences, its turns of speech, its familiar imagery, and its very words are woven into the texture of English literature. Our own familiar, everyday speech is full of biblical phrases, such as "the land of the living," "arose as one man," "lick the dust," "the stars in their courses," "a broken reed," "a still small voice," "the sweat of his brow," "black but comely," "to heap coals of fire," "a soft answer," "a word in season." Such expressions are part and parcel of the English language. This is all the more remarkable when we recall that such happy turns of speech are not original but translations from a distant Semitic tongue.

The most intimate association between English and Hebrew, however, is found in the etymological derivation of a considerable number of English words from the Hebrew. It seems to me that these words are more numerous and significant than is commonly supposed. But it should be stated that many false and unscientific claims have been made with respect to the relationship of Semitic and Indo-European languages.

These words cover a wide and varied range and are very far from being confined to religious usage. The Jewish celebration of Passover and the Christian celebration of Easter have well-known chronological and historical connections, shown by the word Paschal (the Paschal lamb), which is directly derived from the Hebrew *Pesach*.

Another religious celebration common to Jews and Christians is the Sabbath, which derives from *Shabbat*, Hebrew for the day of rest. The biblical injunction is for its observance on the seventh day of the week; hence the Jewish observance of the day is on Saturday. Although Christians observe the Lord's day on Sunday, the first day of the week, their term Sabbath (in the general sense of "day of rest") is often applied to it.

In biblical law the Sabbatical Year, with its enactments of release and freedom, was a powerful influence for social justice. A recent extension of it is the sabbatical year, which provides a rest for university professors and others.

Still more important was the completion of seven Sabbatical Years, with the fiftieth as the year of jubilee. The word jubilee derives from the Hebrew *yovel*, so named from the blast on the ram's horn that proclaimed the jubilee's advent. In English the word jubilee is no longer strictly limited to a fiftieth anniversary. It can denote any season of rejoicing.

The Hebrew alphabet, or a Semitic one closely akin to it, served as a basis, through the medium of the Phoenicians and Greeks, of all European alphabets. The word alphabet itself, from the first two letters of the Greek alphabet, has still earlier origins in the first two letters of the Hebrew alphabet, *aleph* and *beth*. Delta is, of course, cognate with *dalet*.

The connection between the Greek and Hebrew alphabets is illustrated in the phrase "jot or title" in the English translation of the Sermon on the Mount from the Greek New Testament. The word jot represents *iota*, the smallest letter in the Greek alphabet, which in turn corresponds with *yod*, the smallest letter in the Hebrew alphabet.

The biblical story of how Jephthah used the pronunciation of shibboleth (meaning "ear of corn" or "rustling stream") to distinguish between friend and foe has given us the English expression for "password," "catchphrase" or "obsolete slogan."

Bethlehem is a place of hallowed associations, but the Bethlehem hospital in London, which became a lunatic asylum, gave rise to the word bedlam. Another Hebrew word in English denoting a "scene of uproar" is *shemozzle* (or *shlemozzle*). This word has a remarkable history with its underlying meaning of "ill luck." It is composed of three elements: *shel*— "of," *lo*— "not," and *mazzal*— "luck." Originally, *mazzal* meant "planet," "planetary influence," "a constellation of the zodiac bringing luck." *Shemozzle* is an example of a number of Hebrew words that have come into English through the medium of Yiddish. Two others are *meshugga* ("crazy" or "insane") and *chutzpa* ("cheek" or "impudence").

Amen (meaning "certainly," "truly," "so be it") is one of the most frequently used words by Jews, Christians, and Muslims alike. It is curious that *amen* seems to be etymologically a cognate word of *mammon*, both derived from the same Hebrew letters *mem* and *nun*, with the literal meaning of "trust," "deposit." *Mammon* signifies "wealth" or "riches" when regarded as an idol or evil influence. It has sometimes been personified as a demon.

Another demon is Satan, meaning "enemy" or "adversary," the personification of the evil temptations. No one can fail to recall Blake's vision of the Jerusalem that can be built even amid England's "dark Satanic Mills."

Baal or Bel, Beelzebub, Belial, Moloch were names of pagan gods who, because of the evil practices connected with their worship, have become synonymous with wickedness. Gehenna, derived from the Valley of Hinnom, near Jerusalem, where children were sacrificed to Moloch, became a synonym for "hell."

By way of contrast, there are the regions of supreme bliss and happiness: Eden ("a place of delight") and Paradise ("park" or "garden"), from *pardes*, a Persian loan-word in biblical Hebrew. And we have two lovely words of celestial beings: cherub and seraph. The biblical cherub is an angel with large wings, combining human and animal features. New light on the mysterious nature of the cherubim is found in the Dead Sea Scrolls. However, the English word cherub can also denote something very different, namely, the winged head of a beautiful, innocent child representing Cupid. Seraph is derived from a Hebrew root meaning "to burn." It denotes an angel endowed with love, light, ardor, and purity.

The Bible describes the universe before creation as being *tohu-vavohu*. The words have long been used in English in the sense of "confusion and chaos." The poet Browning describes

> *this tohu-bohu—hopes which dive,*
> *And fears which soar.*

A contemporary economist writes of "the need to bring order out of tohu-bohu of human relations."

It is paradoxical that a number of specifically Jewish terms used in English are not of Hebrew origin. Among these may be mentioned "synagogue," which is a Greek translation of the Hebrew *knesset* ("assembly") or *beth knesset* ("house of assembly"). It is only very recently that *knesset* has entered the English language as the designation of the Parliament of the State of Israel.

Another historic Jewish assembly is represented by the word *sanhedrin*, which, although of Greek origin, became naturalized in Hebrew before it reached English.

Still another kind of Israeli "assembly" has introduced a new word into the

English language: kibbutz (a collective agricultural settlement), which has aroused worldwide interest among social reformers.

Another recently coined word that has already found its way into English is *sabra*, a native-born Israeli (named after a cactus that is said to be prickly outside and sweet within). A Rumanian loan-word in modern Hebrew, the *hora* is a dance that, together with its name, has spread from Israel throughout the world.

The modern revival of Hebrew will undoubtedly lead to the incorporation into English of many more Hebrew words, both old and new.

The medieval *Star Chamber* derived its name from being the depository of Jewish financial documents known as stars, derived from the Hebrew *shetar* ("bond" or "contract"). These medieval records are of much historical interest; some of them are exhibited at the Public Record Office and elsewhere.

The Jewish mystical doctrines known as the Cabbala were originally transmitted by "oral tradition," the original meaning of the word in the sense of "teachings received." These doctrines exerted a widespread influence, not least upon Christian thought in England from the sixteenth century onwards. An English derivative of this word is cabal, a secret intrigue, clique, or faction.

Adullamite was the nickname given in 1866 to a group of MPs who seceded from the Liberal Party. It was made current by a speech in which John Bright likened them to the discontented who rallied round David in the Cave of Adullam.

The site of the medieval Jewish quarter in the city of London is still known as Old Jewry. It was not until later that the word ghetto (which is of Italian derivation) came into use. Recently ghetto has come to designate not only a restricted Jewish quarter but any district for segregation of a minority group.

In the wilderness manna was miraculously supplied as food from heaven. The biblical narrative gives an early instance of what philologists call folk-etymology, for the word is explained by the Israelites asking, when they saw the heavenly bread, *"Man hu?"* ("What is it?") The word naturally lends itself in English, no less than in Hebrew, to a wide variety of uses. These range from spiritual nourishment to an unexpected treasure, like a windfall, or to medical and pharmaceutical products.

Milton says of the fallen angel Belial that

> *his tongue*
> *Dropt manna, and could make the worse appear*
> *The better reason.*

In the Bible kosher means simply "fit" or "proper." Only in postbiblical Hebrew was it applied in particular to the purity of food. It is also familiar in modern English as a colloquial "O.K."

Another food is matza. It is becoming quite familiar in English as an everyday dietary item useful for slimming.

Shechar is a comprehensive term for intoxicating liquors other than wine. It is generally translated as "strong drink." In Talmudic language it often means beer or mead. Wycliffe's translation of the Bible in the fourteenth century rendered it by an English derivative of the original Hebrew: cider. This popular English beverage therefore remains a convivial link with biblical times.

Other items on the English menu also unite us with the "land flowing with milk and honey." From the city of Ashkelon, famous in biblical times and now rebuilt, come the names of two onions: shallot and scallion. And from Jaffa, which formerly never knew the orange, now comes the succulent Jaffa.

The Jerusalem artichoke, however, has nothing to do with the Holy City except in folk-etymology. In this case "Jerusalem" is a popular corruption of the Italian *girasole* ("turning to the sun"), the name of a species of sunflower with edible roots.

Jordan almond is another example of folk-etymology. Jordan really derives from the French *jardin* ("garden").

There are many biblical references to sweet spices with delectable names that have happily been preserved in English. The quantities required were determined by weight, and the most important weight was the *shekel*. But *shekel*, which has the literal meaning of "weight," also denoted a coin or amount of silver of a certain weight. It is in the sense of "money" that *shekel* is used colloquially in modern English. Another word of economic origin is *earnest* (derived from the Hebrew *eravon*), meaning "pledge" or "surety."

One of the loveliest Bible stories is that of Joseph and his brethren. When there was famine everywhere but sufficient corn in Egypt, they went with their sacks to buy food and had two meals with Joseph that led to unexpected and exciting consequences. The sack played a leading part in the development of the plot. This Hebrew word has traveled no less widely than the story of Joseph. *Sack* is found not only in English but in most European languages. Its remarkable universality has been explained by folklore as having been the last word uttered at the Tower of Babel before the languages were scrambled.

Connected with sack are such words as satchel, sachet, cul-de-sac, sacking, haversack, knapsack, rucksack, and so forth. Of particular Hebraic interest is sackcloth, used as a token of mourning or penitence. Tunic, too, is a word of Hebrew and Semitic origin, being derived from *kuttonet*—shirt.

A large number of botanical words stem from Hebrew. They include such trees as tamarisk, sycamore, and ebony.

Sweet spices and perfumes, which are also of medical interest, include aloe, balm, balsam, cassia, cinnamon, cumin, galbanum, henna, hyssop, myrrh, and nard.

"Rose of Sharon" and "balm in Gilead" are proverbial expressions in English. What a wealth of Hebraic imagery is conveyed in the use of the balm in Shakespeare's *Richard II:*

> *Not all the water in the rough rude sea*
> *Can wash the balm from an anointed king*
>
> . . . .
>
> *With mine own tears I wash away my balm . . .*

Associated with balm are balmy and embalm, as well as balsam.

Cane, canna, and *cannabis* derive from the Hebrew word for cane or reed. The many derivatives from cane also include: canister (originally a wicker basket); canasta (a card game also called basket rummy); cannon (literally a tube); canyon (a gorge resembling a pipe or tube); canal and channel. Canon, canonical, canonize, and so forth, derive from the idea of a measuring rod or rule. From cannabis (hemp) are derived canvas and canvass.

Another probable derivative is can, meaning a vessel or receptacle, with a multitude of modern uses ranging from canned food and drinks to canned recordings for radio and television. You may have canned Jaffas and canned hallelujahs.

Among animals the camel (Hebrew *gamal*) has had a foremost place in the biblical scene since the time of Abraham. Its importance as an animal domesticated in the service of man was paramount, and a person's wealth could be assessed by the number of camels he owned. The same term is found in Hebrew and other ancient languages. Although a stranger to Britain, the camel has secured a firm place in English literature as the "ship of the desert."

Two gigantic monsters, described in the Book of Job and elsewhere, have entered the English language under their original Hebrew names: behemoth and leviathan. Behemoth may signify the hippopotamus and leviathan the crocodile, but both words are also used figuratively.

A semihuman monster is a golem, meaning a robot or automaton. The word occurs only once in the Bible, denoting "unformed substance" or "embryo." Later, in Jewish legend, it came to mean an artificial, mechanical man. In medieval folklore there arose the belief in the possibility of infusing life into a clay or wooden human figure. The best known golem was that believed to have been created by the famous Rabbi Loew of Prague at the end of the sixteenth century. The story of this golem is not only famous as folklore. Computers, of course, are golems of a fashion and are referred to as such.

Hebrew has also contributed to the names of minerals. Examples are nitre, jasper, and sapphire.

Biblical Hebrew attached special significance to the names of persons and places:

Aaron: Aaron's beard, Aaron's rod (names of plants).

Adam: mankind; human nature or frailty; Adam's apple (forbidden fruit supposed to have stuck in Adam's throat); Adam's ale or wine (for water).

Ariel: This lovely word has had a fascinating history. It is of uncertain meaning, perhaps "lion of God," "light of God," or "hearth of God." In the Bible it is not only the proper name of a person but also a beautiful, poetic name for Jerusalem and is commented upon in rabbinic literature. In English literature Ariel appears in *The Tempest,* where Shakespeare, using poetic imagination and not scientific accuracy, explains the name as signifying "an airy spirit" able to assume any shape or even to become invisible. He certainly lives up to this reputation not only in *The Tempest* but also elsewhere in English literature. In Milton's *Paradise Lost* he is one of the rebel angels; and in Pope's *Rape of the Lock* he became a sylph who is the personification of fashionable life.

Balaam: disappointing prophet; in journalistic slang, worthless or neglected copy.

Benjamin: youngest child; darling.

David and *Jonathan:* devoted friends. David was saved from death many times by Jonathan.

Delilah: false or wily woman.

Eve: daughter of Eve, with alleged feminine frailties such as curiosity.

Goliath: brutish giant.

Ichabod: inglorious, the glory is departed; used in the sense of "alas!"

Ishmael: outcast, one at war with society.

Jehu: a fast or skillful driver; applied not only to the driver of a chariot but to a taxi driver.

Jeremiah: doleful prophet; hence, jeremiad, lamentation.

Jeroboam: a very large wine bottle of eight to ten times normal size; an allusion to King Jeroboam, "a mighty man . . . who made Israel to sin."

Jezebel: impudent or abandoned woman; a woman who paints her face.

Job: patience of Job; Job's tears; Job's comforter.

Jonah: bringer of bad luck.

Joram: brought to King David "vessels of silver . . . gold, and . . . brass." A jorum is a large drinking bowl for punch or other liquid refreshment.

Joseph: applied to various names of brightly colored garments, flowers, and fishes, after Joseph's coat.

Maccabees: heroes, heroic. Macabre, meaning grim or gruesome, originated from a death dance representing the Maccabean martyrs.

Methuselah: symbol of longevity.

Moses: leader or lawgiver; a Moses' cradle is a basket for carrying a baby.

Naboth: Naboth's vineyard is a possession that one will stop at nothing to secure.

Nimrod: great hunter.

Noah: Noah's Ark.

Pharaoh: a symbol of tyranny and oppression.

Samson: a person of extraordinary strength; Samson's post is the strong post passing through the decks of a ship.

Solomon: personification of wisdom; Solomon's seal is the name of a plant thought to resemble the mystic symbol of the six-pointed star, more familiar as the Shield of David, or Magen David.

Let us consider a few of the original Hebrew place names:

Armageddon: derived from Mount Megiddo.

Babylon, Sodom, Gomorrah: wicked cities.

Bethel: Hebrew for house of God; today, a hallowed spot, chapel, or church.

Gaza: produced *gauze.*

Jericho: city doomed to destruction; hence, "go to Jericho."

Mizpah: a token, remembrance.

Philistine: uncouth, uncultured person.

Pisgah: Mountain from which Moses had distant view of Promised Land; can signify a scientist's hunch vis-à-vis outcome of experiments.

Babel: noisy assembly.

Zion, Jerusalem: Ideal city of God.

The Hebrew *shalom,* peace, is related to the Arabic *salaam* and *Islam.* The Malay Peninsula natives pronounced the word *salang;* British soldiers brought the word back to England, and changed it to "so long."

The Salvation Army women members shout "hallelujah" to the accompaniment of their tambourines. *Abbot,* which derives from a Hebrew word meaning "father," is close to *abbé,* a title of respect for a clergyman.

—H.H.

 # A Forgotten Heritage: A Language Called Ladino

Yitzhak Navon, Israel's first Sephardic president, is both proud of and well versed in his mother tongue, Ladino. This has rekindled interest in an all-but-forgotten language and encouraged research in general on the cultural heritage of Sephardic and Oriental Jewry.

Ladino, or Judeo-Spanish, as it is sometimes called, is a Hispanic language that developed after the Jews were expelled from Spain in 1492. Forced to flee from their homes and settled in strange lands, the Jews naturally took comfort in preserving for generations the Spanish that had been spoken in the fourteenth and fifteenth centuries. Because of this, hundreds of archaic words, most of which have completely disappeared from modern Spanish, are still part of Ladino.

The Sephardic communities that flourished in more advanced parts of the world soon abandoned this language. Jews in Amsterdam and London, for example, kept up with modern Spanish as it developed. Other well-off Jews forgot the language entirely in an attempt to fully integrate with their new homelands. One such group of Sephardim were the first Jews to settle in the New World. Although they founded the first Jewish congregation there in 1654, Ladino was and remains peripheral in the United States.

Finding themselves in countries of limited cultural development, Sephardim longed to retain the knowledge of their previously rich Jewish life in Spain. The use of Ladino enabled them, for some time, to resist influences of the less-developed surroundings in which they found themselves.

Ladino borrowed and absorbed words wherever it was spoken, passing under the influences of Greek, Turkish, and Arabic. When Jews began immigrating to *Eretz Yisrael,* the language incorporated Hebrew, and even Yiddish, words. (One common example of a Hebrew word found in Ladino is *mazal,* luck. A lucky person is described as *mazalado.*)

At various times Ladino has been spoken in North Africa, Egypt, Greece, Turkey, Yugoslavia, Bulgaria, Rumania, and France. Today Israel is the country with the largest number of Ladino speakers, estimated at some two hundred thousand. A much smaller number know how to read and write Ladino.

Linguists began taking an interest in Ladino in the late nineteenth century, but it was only in the twentieth century that serious research was undertaken. By that time the Nazis had exterminated many communities in which Judeo-Spanish had been the principal means of communication. There had been 256 publications in Ladino between 1845 and the advent of World War II. A survey in the 1960s revealed hardly any regular Ladino press existing, except for two weeklies in Israel and one written partly in Ladino in Turkey.

While Ladino literature includes a rich collection of adapted and original works —covering mysticism, poetry, biblical exegesis, history, medicine, and ethics—it is the popular *romancero* that appeals to most scholars today. These are largely a continuation and adaptation of fourteenth- and fifteenth-century ballads, representing an oral treasure of poetry, folktales, and proverbs. They are often sung at weddings, bar mitzvahs, and other festive gatherings. Some are lullabies and still others are dirges.

Since Ladino *romanceros* have only recently acquired a written form, they vary quite a bit from community to community. One ongoing study has already recorded over 230 different musical themes. President Navon himself is well known for his own *Romancero Sephardi,* a concert presentation of secular and sacred songs that he wrote and edited in 1968.

The first international congress on Sephardic and Oriental Jewry, held at the Hebrew University of Jerusalem, dealt with the urgent issue that Ladino (as well as dozens of Jewish-Arabic dialects) is no longer taught and is in danger of disappearing. Various Sephardic organizations are trying to influence Israel's universities to offer courses in the language, as well as in the history of Sephardic Jewish communities.

—D.Li.

Books for the "People of the Book"

Books are so much a part of our daily existence and are so much taken for granted that it is hard for us to imagine what the invention of printing must have meant for people living in the middle of the fifteenth century. How did they receive the device that "writes with several pens at once without the aid of miracles"? We can only conceive of the impact of this innovation upon people in those days if we reflect upon what the invention of the airplane and radio meant to the last generation, and of television, supersonic travel, and nuclear fission to our own. Printing, in fact, opened up a new era in the history of human culture. It paved the way to universal education. Many of the new inventions produced since then are in some way connected with it. Indeed, if, in the course of time, books have become the close friend of man and his companion on his travels, it is due to the invention of printing.

Writing itself is the outcome of a lengthy process. It developed from various signs and symbols into letters. As it became simplified, its use grew more widespread. Writing materials, too, underwent considerable development. Stones, clay tablets, and other primitive materials gave way to parchment, papyrus and, finally, paper. Unwieldy scrolls were transformed into compact books. As the demand for books grew, enterprising men conceived the idea of having a book read aloud while copyists, sitting in rows, transcribed it from dictation. This was the beginning of the book publishing trade. The use of seals with pictures, short inscriptions, and the like is also very old—indeed, the identity of the inventor is not known. All we do know is that the Babylonians employed engraved pieces of wood to imprint signs and short texts upon bricks. In ancient times use was also made of letters engraved upon tin for making impressions, in ink or color, on suitable material, either for decoration, for marking objects, or for teaching the art of writing.

The first to apply the idea of seals and engravings to the printing of books so as to make them available to a wider public were the Chinese. It was during the fourth century that they invented printing by means of engraved wooden blocks. In this manner they printed the writings of Kungtse (Confucius), which are the first examples of printing known to us. In the year 1041 a Chinese called Pi Sheng invented movable type, which is the basis of modern printing. It is generally assumed that this type was made of earthenware and set in an iron chase. Owing, however, to the vast number of signs used in Chinese writing, the invention did not develop any further and fell into disuse. In 1314 the Chinese geographer Wang Chen printed his own work, *The Book of Farming*, with movable wooden type. In Korea, too, we learn that earthenware type was used in ancient times. Since, however, it was fragile and did not last long, in 1403 the emperor ordered type to be cast in bronze.

In Europe early in the fifteenth century, pictures of the saints and of playing cards began to be printed from engraved wooden blocks, sometimes with the addition of lettering. The letters, however, formed part of the block and could not be broken up; only single pages could be printed. The invention of modern printing as we know it goes to the credit of Johann Gensfleisch (1397–1468), better known as Gutenberg, of Mainz, Germany. After a series of experiments, he devised a way of casting movable metal type. He also invented a printing press. In this manner he launched the art of printing as it has subsequently developed. He achieved speed in printing and devised a method of printing on both sides of a folio. It is generally agreed that Gutenberg began to practice the art of printing at Strasbourg in 1440. The type that he cast was modeled on the cursive script then in use (it was, of course, given an artistic form), and the printing was done in colored ink on parchment or paper.

About 1445 Gutenberg printed, at Mainz, some tables of the alphabet and a shortened version of Donatus' Latin grammar textbook, *Ars Grammatica*. During the same period he printed several other small works, some of which have been lost while others have come down to us only in fragments or in single copies. When he felt he had acquired sufficient skill to embark upon more ambitious projects, Gutenberg printed the Vulgate (Latin Bible) between the years 1450 and 1455. This book, which contains 42 lines per page, is a beautiful specimen of the printer's art and testifies to Gutenberg's personality and to his wonderful talent for printing. In all probability the Gutenberg Bible was printed in an edition of 165 copies on paper and another 35 on parchment. Forty-five copies of it are known to exist today, only 18 of them complete. This is the rarest book in the world; in 1926 a parchment copy of it fetched $250,000.

The first book bearing a date is a Latin Psaltery (Mainz, 1457) printed by Fust and Schoeffer, Gutenberg's rivals, who won a lawsuit against him and took over his printing press. Gutenberg was dogged by misfortune since his youth and never achieved commercial success. He lost his fortune; quarrels with moneylenders, partners, and assistants made his life miserable. But his life's work, the art of printing, developed to an extent he could never have dreamed of.

The introduction of printing resulted in a lowering of the price of books, both handwritten and printed, from year to year. This, indeed, had been Gutenberg's intention from the outset. Although editions were small and books were therefore still far from cheap, many more people were now able to acquire them. The first edition of the Bible cost 1,350 guilders to print. It is estimated that a copy on paper sold for 40 guilders and a parchment copy for 50. The proportionate cost of a handwritten to a printed book was probably four or five to one, that is, if a handwritten book cost 200 guilders, the same book when printed cost 40 or 50. Both Gutenberg and his successors were idealists, not businessmen eager for profit. Their aim in making books available to all was not to enrich themselves but to spread the knowledge of God's word. At first the printers guarded the secret of their art; their assistants and everyone else concerned had to take a solemn oath not to divulge it. But despite this safeguard the new invention spread rapidly across the face of the continent, and the number of printers and printing presses grew yearly. During the first half century of printing, that is, up to 1500, a total of about 35,000 books were printed in different countries. Books printed up to this date are known as incunabula (derived from the Latin *cunae*, cradle)—in other words, books produced while the printer's art was in its infancy.

Jews have always been lovers and buyers of books. True, the expression "People of the Book" specifically denotes the Bible, but it can be taken to indicate the Jews' love of books in general. The Jewish sages of olden times regarded the book as being invested with a potency as great as that of the sword, as is illustrated by a saying in the Midrashic book of Sifrei: "The book and the sword came down from Heaven." An ancient legend relates the following: "When Adam was driven forth from the Garden of Eden, his body was bowed down and his soul was sorrowful. God, looking upon him, pitied him and said, 'The Tree of Knowledge did not make Man wise, nor did he eat his fill of the Tree of Life. What shall be his fate?' And God created the book and said unto it, 'Go forth and accompany Man into a Land of Nod. Be a friend and companion to him; comfort him, teach him, and gladden his heart.'" Hai Gaon, who lived in Babylonia in the eleventh century, commands, "At all seasons let thy book be in thy bosom." The poet Shmuel Hanagid, who lived in Spain at approximately the same time, writes:

> *The wise of heart forsakes the ease of pleasure;*
> *In reading books he finds of rest full measure.*

Elsewhere he writes:

> *A book thy friend upon the road shall be,*
> *And in thy home be it with thee alway.*
> *To toil the hours of light do thou assign,*
> *And to thy book thy night, till it be day.*

Emmanuel of Rome (1270–1330) writes:

> *For precious books thy silver give,*
> *And by the gold of wisdom live.*

Rabbi Isaac of Canpanton said, "Man's wisdom reaches only to the point to which his books extend."

As long as books were published in manuscript form, they were difficult to obtain. In one of his responsa, R. Meir of Rothenburg writes, "We have no book from which to learn and gain wisdom." R. Abraham ben R. Isaac of Narbonne complains, "There are no books of the Mishna of the Order of Zera'im for me to consult." R. Judah ibn Tibbon's testament to his son contains the following: "Most students wander from city to city in search of a book and do not find it." It is recorded that at R. Israel Isserlein Ashkenazi's yeshiva at Regensburg, those students who possessed books of their own studied from them by day, while those who had none borrowed them and used them at night.

The lending of books was accounted a great virtue in ancient times. The Talmud, commenting upon the verse "Wealth and riches shall be in his house, and his righteousness endureth forever," (Psalms, CXII, 3), states that it refers to one "who writes books and lends them to others." It was said in praise of R. Shmuel Hanagid that he had scribes sitting in his house copying books of the Mishna and Talmud, and that he used to give the books to students who lacked the means to procure their own.

There were no bookshops. Booksellers used to go from place to place to sell their wares. Booklovers used to welcome such visitors since they could learn from them what was happening in the world of scholarship. From itinerant booksellers they would receive greetings from friends and news of scholars near and far and of their latest interpretations of the Law. Lists of booksellers are known to have existed in the Middle Ages.

Needless to say, when printing became known and its vast potentialities began to be apparent, Jews also turned their attention to it. Their concern with the new art was not confined to printing and publishing; they seem also to have engaged in designing and casting type. In some countries, Spain, for instance, the Jews were the first to practice printing. It is interesting to note that the first mention of Hebrew metal type comes to us from Avignon. In 1444 a goldsmith from Prague, Procop Valdfoghel, taught a Jew of that city named Davinus (David) von Carderouse to cut Hebrew type and promised to let him have twenty-seven letters (the twenty-two letters of the Hebrew alphabet together with the five final forms) in consideration of having been taught the art of painting on cloth. The Jew, however, failed to carry out his part of the bargain and was ordered by the court two years later to return the forty-eight metal letters in his possession and to undertake not to reveal anything about the art of printing. We do not, however, know anything about a printer of that name; nor, indeed, is there any more information extant about the man. During the second half of the fifteenth century Hebrew books were published in Italy, Spain, and Portugal, the printers in all cases being Jews.

What was the first Hebrew book to appear in print and when was it printed? The general consensus of opinion is that it was Rashi's commentary on the Torah, printed by Abraham ben Isaac ben Garton at Reggio di Calabria in 1475. Since it was the first book to be printed in cursive script, the fount used became known as "Rashi type." If, however, we carefully examine another book published at the same time, R. Jacob ben R. Asher's *Arba'a Turim*, (1475), we find that it shows evidence of considerable skill in the printer's art. So well is it produced, and with such good taste, that we have good reason to wonder whether Hebrew printing does indeed date from that year, or whether it did not, in fact, begin several years earlier. We shall probably be somewhere near the truth, then, if we assign the beginning of Hebrew printing to the year 1470. It is, of course, possible that the books known as the "Rome printings," generally assumed to have been published before 1480, such as Rashi's commentary on the Torah, were actually the first Hebrew books to appear in print. On the other hand, it is equally possible that the Conat printings, which are undated and contain no indication where they were printed, were first. Apparently the new printed books were not universally welcomed and encountered opposition in some quarters, as has been the case with every innovation to this day. The preface to one of the early Hebrew printed books (Nachmanides' commentary on the Torah, Naples, 1490) contains the following admonition: "Those who disparage this craft must bear their guilt."

The new industry was also opposed by the professional copyists, who believed—not without reason—that it offered serious competition in their field. Only a few were clever enough to change their occupation and take up printing. One of them was Abraham Conat, a physician, who later became a copyist and finally a printer. The fount used at his press was of a special design and was cut from letters designed by him. As was the custom of the time, the printer was assisted in his trade by his wife, a lady named Estellina. In the preface to *Iggeret Bechinat Olam*, by R. Yeda'ya Hapenini Bedarshi (Mantua, 1477), she says, "I, Estellina, wife of my honored lord, R. Abraham Conat—may he behold numerous progeny and enjoy length of days, amen—have written this book, *Iggeret Bechinat Olam*, with the help of the young man Ya'acov Levy of Tarascon in the land of Provence, may he live, amen." At that time there were as yet no generally accepted technical terms for the processes of printing, not even the word "print," which explains why Estellina speaks of "writing."

The omission in many of the early printed books of the place and date of publication may have been intentional, so that purchasers should not immediately realize that what they were buying was not a book written by hand in the traditional manner. Even Gutenberg omitted these particulars from his early volumes. Indeed, some years elapsed before printers began to insert them. In addition to their wives, printers used to enlist the aid of all the members of their household, though they did not mention the fact in the books they printed.

Apart from compositors and printers, there were also proofreaders. Publishers considered themselves fortunate when they were able to secure the services of experts in this field. The edition of the *Historical Books of the Bible*, published in Soncino in 1486, contains a note that it was

carefully proofread by men familiar with books and conversant with scholarship, and we do not believe it contains a fault of error . . . Indeed, the only kind of error possible is the substitution of one letter for another, e.g., hé for chet, bét for kaf (in either case distinguishable from one another only by a serif). This may have happened occasionally owing to the proofreader's preoccupation with the exact sense of the text and with whole words, so that he failed to notice the distinguishing marks of the aforementioned letters, which so closely resemble each other, and the like. Similarly, he may have omitted a letter from a word. But even such errors can only be few in number.

It seems that as a rule the proofreader read three proofs. In addition, printers often used to hang galley proofs on a board outside the press, promising a reward to any member of the public who found an error.

Special care was devoted to the quality of the paper and ink used for printing and to the standard of the printing itself. No effort was spared by the early printers to beautify and embellish their books.

The printers usually sold their own books, some of which they had bound by professional bookbinders. They were wont to travel about the country, and also to attend fairs, in order to sell their merchandise. A typical dialogue between a bookseller and his customer is recorded in the *Concordance to the Vulgate* (Basel, 1525), the work of the famous printer Johann Frobenius of Basel (1469–1527).

The dialogue, which refers to the earlier period of the incunabula, runs as follows:

Buyer: *So, Master Johann Frobenius, what book do you offer us?*
Frobenius: *A book whose sale and purchase will be of benefit to us both.*
B: *It is a new book then?*
F: *Neither new nor old, but both together.*
B: *Pray tell me the secret of your riddle.*
F: *It is a key to Holy Writ, known as a Concordance to the Sacred Scriptures.*
B: *But this book has already been published several times.*
F: *What of it? If it has again been published, it must be because it is for the good of us all. Does not the sun appear day after day, and is it not always the same sun? This book, which I have only now brought out, is superior to anything I have published hitherto.*
B: *It is indeed a most worthy thing when a man thus praises himself . . .*
F: *It is my hope that my exertions in this, my latest book will be rewarded with a double crown of praise.*
B: *Great artists always think that their most recent creation, the product of their greatest exertions, is their crowning glory.*
F: *True. Yet Apelles left his Anadymene unfinished, whereas I have completed my work.*
B: *Do you really consider it complete?*
F: *You know full well that in a book of this description it is impossible to prevent a few errors from creeping in among the many characters it contains. Yet by dint of my exertions I have triumphed here as well, though the difficulties involved were of an unusual kind. Apart from this, the present volume contains additional material not to be found in the previous editions.*

B: *I offer you my congratulations. But unfortunately such labors do not bring much honor.*

F: *It is a privilege for me to meet a man like you who appreciates these matters.*

B: *Are you not afraid that your exertions in plying such a craft will cause you to age prematurely?*

F: *What shall I do? This is my mission and my destiny. If it brings the onset of old age, and the weakness and disease that accompany it, it lies within your power to preserve me from them.*

B: *How so?*

F: *By quickly purchasing this book from me. You will assuredly be grateful for what I bring you.*

B: *Are you not ashamed to hand over the children of your creation to strangers like myself?*

F: *Heaven forbid! It is for you that I created them, not for myself.*

B: *What price are you asking for the book?*

F: *Incline your ear towards me, and I shall whisper it to you . . .*

B: *Alack! It is very dear.*

F: *Take it and examine it at your leisure. If you should then regret your purchase, return it to me and I will give you back your money.*

B: *Idle words!*

F: *Say not so. Frobenius does more than he promises.*

B: *Here is good coin for you.*

F: *And here is good, fair merchandise for you. May we both prosper in this transaction.*

Early printed books, like ancient manuscripts, contain no title pages. Since the first page of an unbound book is more exposed to the ravages of time than any other page and is thus liable to become lost or badly damaged, the practice was adopted of taking everything we now say on the title page and putting it in the colophon (Gr. *kolophon,* summit), which, as the last page, remained in a better state of preservation. In place of the title page one or two blank pages were added in order to protect the first page of the text. Only one book, printed toward the end of the period, contains some semblance of a title page.

In the early printed books the sheets were not numbered either, and only occasionally does one find markers to guide the binders and prevent them from putting the sheets in the wrong order. Joshua Solomon Soncino, first of the printers of that name, introduced the practice of numbering the sheets, and the other printers followed suit. Numbered pages are to be found in only one book of the incunabula period, a Bible printed in Naples in 1492, where the pages as well as the sheets are numbered—but only on the second side of every folio. The Hebrew vowel points were introduced for the first time in Volume I of the Book of Psalms, with R. David Kimche's commentary (Bologna, 1477). The Pentateuch printed at Bologna in 1482 was fully vowelled.

Unlike Gutenberg, the early Hebrew printers did not begin with the Bible. There were several reasons for this. First, Bibles were common in Jewish homes and it was the aim of the printers to make the commentaries on the Bible, text-books, the books of the Talmud, and also a few works of purely literary interest— all of which were scarce—more readily available to the public. Second, there was probably a reluctance to reproduce the Holy Scriptures by means of a purely secular device, though after a time printing also became known as a "sacred craft."

Once printed books became more generally accepted and their novelty wore off, the Bible was printed first in parts and then in its entirety.

The first part of the Bible to be printed in Hebrew was the Book of Psalms, with the commentary of R. David Kimche (Bologna, 1477), but here it was the commentary, rather than the text, that was the main feature. The first complete Hebrew Bible (without commentary) appeared at Soncino in 1488, and a pocket edition was printed at Brescia in 1494. The first of these was the work of Joshua Solomon Soncino. The second was the work of his nephew Gershon Soncino, the only Hebrew printer to bridge the period from the incunabula well into the sixteenth century. He printed books in various parts of Italy and Turkey until 1534, the year of his death. He was the greatest Jewish printer of his own and succeeding generations. He printed books in Hebrew, Greek, Latin, and Italian, and was one of the first and most notable publishers of the works of Petrarch. In his last Hebrew work (R. David Kimche's *Mikkol*, Constantinople, 1532–34), he gives the following account of his genealogy and activities:

> *Gershon of Soncino, son of the learned R. Moses, son of the illustrious scholar R. Israel Nathan, son of Samuel, son of R. Moses of blessed memory. He fought in the city of Fürth against the wicked Juan de Capistrano and drove him out of there with all his men. He was five generations descended from R. Moses of Speier, who is mentioned in the Tosafot of Touch . . . May Almighty God help men and provide for my old age, and remember the good I did in providing for the Marranos of Spain, and especially of Portugal. I gladly risked my life in order to rescue them from persecution and guide them to shelter under the shadow of the Almighty and to rest under His wing to this day.*

From this we see that Gershon Soncino was not only a man of books but also a public figure and a Jew seeking his people's welfare. In modern-day Germany a society of booklovers was founded in tribute to him, and the well-known Anglo-Jewish firm of Soncino bears his name. Members of the Soncino family were the first to print tractates of the Talmud. It was Gershon Soncino who printed Hebrew secular works for the first time, such as *Meshal Hakadmoni*, by R. Isaac ibn Sahula (Brescia, 1491?), which appeared with numerous illustrations (a second edition appeared about 1497), and *Machberot Immanuel*, by Emmanuel of Rome (Brescia, 1491).

The last Hebrew book to be printed in the fifteenth century appeared in 1498, after which there was a gap until 1503. We do not know of any definite reason to account for this suspension of Hebrew printing activity, but it may be attributed to the misfortunes that befell the Jewish people at the close of the fifteenth century.

Some books were produced with a rapidity attesting to a considerable degree of competence and expertness in the art of printing. For example, R. Joseph Albo's *Sefer Ha-Ikkarim*, consisting of 108 folios, was printed at Soncino in 1486 in just under two months. On the other hand, the Rome *Machzor* (prayer book for festivals, Soncino-Casal Maggiore, 1485–86), comprising 320 folios, took a whole year to print. Of the larger books printed in the period of the incunabula, mention should be made of *Biurei Hatorah*, by R. Levi ben Gershon (Mantua, c.1477), comprising 410 folios, and Avicenna's *Canon* (Naples, 1492), comprising 478 folios.

The early printers at first printed two pages at a time and then four. They could produce a thousand pages a day (according to the printer's note in the *Tur Orach*

Chayim, Mantua, 1476). They sometimes left the front pages blank so as to provide an opportunity for an artist to display his skill in lettering or decorative drawing. Use was sometimes made of ornamental frames and initial letters engraved on wooden blocks.

In some of the books printed in Portugal we find a printer's crest in the form of a lion in a red or black shield or else without a shield. In the *Tur Orah Chayim* (printed in Portugal, 1495), we find a ram with the inscription *Maayan Gannim.* We have already mentioned the illustrations to *Meshal Hakadmoni.* Small illustrations are also to be found in *Machberot Immanuel* (Brescia, 1491). An illustration with the caption "Picture of a rabbi teaching his pupils" appeared in *Tur Orach Chayim* (Soncino, c.1497). A number of other books contain geometrical designs.

An edition consisted of 250 to 300 copies. Over a period of about twenty-seven years, seventeen Hebrew printing presses were at work in the following towns: Ixar, Lisbon, Bologna, Brescia, Barco, Guadalajara, Leiria, Mantua, Naples, Zamora, Faro, Pieve del Sacco, Constantinople, Casal Maggiore, Rome, Reggio di Calabria, and Soncino. During this time a total of some 250 books of all descriptions were printed, including a number of reprints. For instance, the Pentateuch was printed eight times; the *Sefer Haturim,* by R. Jacob ben R. Asher, and the Book of Psalms were each printed six times; Rashi's commentary on the Torah, five; the Book of Proverbs, four; Maimonides' *Mishneh Torah,* Nachmanides' commentary on the Torah, R. David Kimche's *Sefer Hashorashim,* the *Historical Books of the Bible,* the Prayer Book and the complete Bible, three times each. About 35 tractates of the Talmud were printed in Italy and Portugal during the same period.

—A.M.H.

 How "Kibbutz" Got Its Name

The quest for a traditional language among chalutzim of the second and third aliyot (waves of immigration) derived from a conscious desire to build a bridge to the world of the past. Symbolic of this is the source for the name "kibbutz," which was adopted by members of Hashomer Hatzair at the beginning of the third aliyah, following a suggestion by Yehuda Ya'ari.

In those days it was announced in the camp that we were about to settle in the Jezreel Valley. We asked ourselves by what name we wished to be called. The communal groups that existed in the country at the time were known by the name *kvutza;* if the group was somewhat larger than a conventional *kvutza* it was called *chavura.* For the *Gdud Ha'avoda* (labor brigade) the name *pluga* prevailed; and in discussions within the *kvutza* about its extension and the change in its character, the term "big *kvutza*" emerged.

Our camp was called the *gdud* (corps) of Hashomer Hatzair. Even though we were used to it from the days of our youth in the movement (where there were *kvutzot, gdudim,* and *plugot*), the name "corps" didn't work for us anymore. During a discussion, one of the members who had just returned from a trip to Jerusalem got up and started to speak, not of the future but of the past. He said

that while in Jerusalem he had fallen in with a group of *Bratslaver Chasidim,* and for him the encounter had been a deep experience. He spoke enthusiastically, because the *Bratslaver* were a kind of revelation for him. In Galicia, from which he came, nothing was known of this group. Only those of us who had read Martin Buber's book, *The Tales of Rabbi Nachman* [of Bratslav], knew about them, and he had not read Buber.

He spent several days in their company. He related to us a story of honest and righteous people who live on the modest earnings they derive from manual labor, about their conversations with him and with each other, and about the Rebbe's tales. At the end he said that the Bratslaver Chasidim assemble regularly once a year at Rosh Hashanah (New Year) for prayer and for study of the books of their teacher, Rabbi Nachman of Bratslav. Before the first World War they used to assemble in the town of Uman, which is in the Ukraine, where Rabbi Nachman is buried, and now they get together in Jerusalem and in other places around the world. That gathering on Rosh Hashanah the Bratslaver Chasidim call by the name "kibbutz."

Why shouldn't we also call our camp kibbutz? he asked. Our people decided to accept the suggestion of that *chaver,* and since then our camp was called Kibbutz Hashomer Hatzair.

Before long all of the *chavurot, gdudim, plugot,* and the *big kvutzot* changed their name to kibbutz.

—Y.Y.

 ## The Case of the Hidden Talmud

There is today a set of the Talmud, more than one hundred years old, leatherbound, scattered among libraries in Washington, D.C., Long Island, and Netanya, Israel, that binds one family together as no other heirloom possibly can.

At the beginning of the Hitler era there was a Jewish family living in a German community that was noted for its piety and Judaic scholarship. The family head, a pious and committed Jew, had earned rabbinic ordination but chose to earn his livelihood as a lawyer. Daily he enjoyed taking down his precious set of the Talmud, handed down to him by his father, a noted rabbi, and studying the traditional *blatt gemarah,* a page of a Talmudic tome.

He was a thoughtful man, and early during the Nazi era he concluded that Hitler-led Germany was no place for Jews. He took his wife, infant son, and the

Talmud and moved to Paris. Until he mastered French, life was difficult. He had had some engineering training, and soon he landed a job and resumed his lifelong practice of Talmud study.

A second son was born in Paris. When the war broke out in 1939 and the German forces turned their military assaults in the direction of France in 1940, the family quickly realized that their future was in great jeopardy.

There was a circuitous way to try to escape—via Portugal, North Africa, and then to the United States. But one had to travel light and swiftly, for the Nazis were not far behind. Mr. F., the family head, made a decision; he spent the better part of one night cutting a large hole in the floor of their living room, doing it as carefully as possible so that there would be little evidence of a secret hiding place. He wrapped his precious set of the Talmud carefully, placed it reverently into the secret cache, replaced the cut floorboards, and returned the carpet to its original place.

The next morning he wrote a letter to his French employer, a Christian with whom he had established friendly relations. He said that with the impending arrival of the Nazis it was not safe for his family to remain in France. He explained that they were all fleeing for their lives and told him of the set of the Talmud and the secret hiding place, begging him to tell no one. If they would all survive the fearful period into which they were heading, he would appreciate his help in retrieving the holy books.

He mailed the letter, and then the family set off on a journey that took them across France, into Spain, Portugal, and North Africa and, late in 1940, across the seas to the United States and safety. Mr. F. once again set about learning a new language. He found employment as a patent attorney, first in Iowa and later in Washington, D.C. He enrolled his sons in a local yeshiva; on a number of occasions he officiated as the rabbi of a small congregation in Iowa during the High Holy Days.

As soon as possible after the war ended in 1945, he wrote to his former employer in Paris, not knowing whether he was alive or if anything had happened to the secreted volumes of the Talmud. When a reply arrived, his fingers trembled as he tore open the letter.

His French friend survived the war, and the house in which the books of Mr. F.'s father were hidden had remained intact. He, the French friend, was delighted to learn that the F. family was well and in America, and he would now proceed to secure the release of the holy books and ship them to their new home in Washington, D.C.

In the course of a few months the carefully packed crates of books arrived. Once again Mr. F. could spend his evenings studying the Talmud and recalling that these were the very same pages that his late father's hands had also touched. The tomes came through the war in perfect, sound condition.

The years rolled on. One son entered the rabbinate and another became a lawyer. Both learned to pore over the same set of the Talmud just as they saw their father doing. The lawyer joined an Orthodox synagogue in Washington, D.C., and the rabbi, after serving as a U. S. Air Force chaplain in Alaska, became the spiritual leader of a Long Island congregation.

About three years ago Mr. F. decided to retire and go on *aliyah*. He was now in his sixties, he had a pension coming to him, he had been a lifelong Zionist, and although he loved his new home in America, he felt his place, at that point in his life, was in Israel.

The usual poignant times of departure were difficult enough for the F. family, but Mr. F.'s decision on how to divide his Talmud set was a major problem. He finally presented a few volumes from one tractate to his Washingtonian son, a few volumes to his Long Island son, and took the balance of the set with him to Netanya, Israel.

The air letters fly between the United States and Israel, and among them are numerous communications among the F. family members. Mr. F. has described to his sons the great joy he has in seeing his father's books in Israel and studying them there. He is also happy to hear that his number one son has already shared some of the Talmud study with his own son in the shadow of the U. S. Capitol, while the rabbi, perusing his few volumes, waits patiently for his children to reach the age of Talmud study.

In Netanya Mr. F. studies and waits—he has written that he is convinced that one day both his sons will settle in Israel and bring with them the remaining volumes of the family Talmud set, making it complete. When that happens, Mr. F. says, he will feel content in the knowledge that the set of the Talmud bequeathed to him by his father, saved from the Nazis, and studied in the United States will then be studied and guarded in Israel.

—D.C.G.

 ## Hebrew Literary Treasures in the U.S.S.R.

Since 1947 scholars and students of the Bible have been excited about the discovery of the Dead Sea Scrolls. Yet no matter how historic and priceless these scrolls are, they do not eclipse in importance the discovery of the treasure troves of the Cairo *genizah*—the great mass of documents, letters, and literary remains preserved through the centuries by the Jewish community of El Fostat (Old Cairo), Egypt, in an old synagogue.

After 616 c.e., when the building was transformed from a church into a synagogue, successive generations deposited sacred and secular materials in a concealed chamber. The carefully sealed room was kept a secret until the nineteenth century.

The term *genizah* comes from the Hebrew *ganaz* (store away or hide). When applied to Jewish literary works, it symbolizes the creativity of the Jewish centers of learning and the impact they made upon Judaism and the world at large.

With the Jewish zeal for learning, the pages containing the knowledge became sacred and cherished. Thus, when a book could no longer be used, the people reacted to the battered pages as they would to a human corpse. The pages were protected from defilement by being hidden. Happily for scholarship, the *genizah* encompassed any disqualified or disgraced book. In addition to the sacred or semisacred books, the *genizah* material proved a refuge for a class of nonreligious writings that never aspired to the dignity of real books but are of tremendous value today for Jewish history.

The use of the sacred tongue was, among the Jews, not confined to sacred literature. To the preservers of these treasures Hebrew was a living tongue. They used Hebrew for personal letters, for keeping accounts, and for composing love songs and wine songs. All legal documents such as leases, contracts, marriage settlements, bills of divorce, and court decisions were drawn up in Hebrew, or at least written in Hebrew letters. "As the Jews attached a certain sacredness to everything resembling the Scriptures, either in matter or in form," writes Professor

Solomon Schechter (1850–1915), "they were loathe to treat even these secular documents as mere refuse, and when they were overtaken by old age, they disposed of them by ordering them to the *genizah,* in which they found a resting-place for centuries. The *genizah* of the old Jewish community thus represents a combination of sacred slumber rooms and [a] secular record office."

Thus Professor Schechter described the Cairo *genizah* contents when he returned from Cairo after spending a year there in 1896–97. The priceless treasures that Schechter succeeded in bringing with him were presented to Cambridge University, whose teaching staff he adorned. When he later came to the United States to head the Jewish Theological Seminary of America, Schechter brought with him a vast number of these fragments.

There is hardly a branch of Jewish learning that has not been enriched by the discovery of the Cairo and other *genizah* treasures. Professor Schechter published several classic volumes of the *genizah* material, but the bulk of it is still waiting to be deciphered, organized, edited, and published in order to be made accessible to the scholarly world.

Now dispersed throughout many libraries, the letters and documents found in the *genizah* can only be made to yield their rich information in full when they are again placed together in systematic order. Many of them are incomplete and full of puzzles, since we frequently find allusions to facts entirely unknown to us. A complete corpus of these texts will immensely increase our knowledge of conditions during the period, when the center of Judaism gradually shifted from East to West. The noted scholar, Professor S. D. Goitein, is working on a comprehensive publication of this material.

Descriptive catalogs that would indicate the extent of *genizah* material in the world today are unavailable. The only printed catalogs are in the Bodleian Library (Oxford); B. Halper (Dropsie College); E. N. Adler Collection (Jewish Theological Seminary of America); R. Gotheil (Freer Collection in New York); David Kaufmann Collection (Budapest), and the catalog of the Antonin Collection in Leningrad by A. I. Katsh.

Cairo *genizah* fragments number over two hundred thousand. It is estimated that one hundred thousand fragments are in the library of Cambridge University (England); twenty thousand are in the Bodleian Library (Oxford); ten thousand in the British Museum (London); ten thousand in the Jewish Theological Seminary of America; six thousand in the Oriental Institute of the Hungarian Academy of Science (Budapest); four thousand in the Moseri Collection (Cairo); and twelve hundred in the Antonin Collection (Leningrad).

The remainder of the material is in the Saltykov-Schedrin Public Library, Leningrad, the Oriental Library of the Academy of Science (Budapest); Dropsie College (Philadelphia); the French Academy (Paris); in Strasbourg (France), and in scattered private, public, and university libraries.

The *genizah* material deals with the Bible, biblical commentaries, Targum, Hebrew grammar, Midrashim, Mishna, Babylonian and Palestinian Talmudim, Geonica-Hebrew poetry of the Middle Ages, Halakhic and Karaitic literature, liturgy, historical documents and related material in Hebrew, Arabic, Judeo-Arabic, Judeo-Persian, and other cognate languages, as well as philosophy, medicine, and mysticism.

Prior to Dr. Schechter's trip to Egypt, the ancient synagogue of old Cairo was visited by Jacob Saphir in 1864, by E. N. Adler in 1888 and 1896, and by Abraham Firkowitch in 1865. As a result of Firkowitch's travels, the Saltykov-Schedrin Library in Leningrad possesses choice material of *genizah* and biblical literature.

Firkowitch (1785–1874) was a Russian Jew who settled in the Crimean Peninsula. In his endeavor to prove that the Karaites were descendants of the Ten Lost Tribes of Israel who had settled in the Crimea in the sixth century B.C.E., he traveled to Cairo, Palestine, and Constantinople and succeeded in bringing together the largest collection of Hebrew, Samaritan, and early Karaitic manuscripts in the world. Firkowitch's efforts contributed greatly to the exemption of the Karaites from the religious persecution that the Russian Jews suffered. The Karaites, a Jewish sect, originated in Persia in the eighth century and later spread to the Middle East and Russia. They rejected the Oral Law and challenged the authority of the Talmudists. The first part of the Firkowitch Collection was purchased by the Imperial Library of Leningrad in 1867, and the second Firkowitch Collection was acquired by the Leningrad Library in 1876 after his death.

The latter collection contains 553 rabbinic and 277 Karaitic works, as well as some 159 scrolls on parchment and leather, about 1,000 Hebrew manuscripts, and over 2,000 Arabic manuscripts. It also includes over 1,500 manuscripts of the Hebrew Bible and biblical fragments. At least 14 of these, dating from the ninth to the twelfth centuries, are, for the most part, the text as fixed by Aaron Ben Asher, the great Masoretic authority, who lived in the first half of the tenth century.

Many of the manuscripts in the second Firkowitch Collection came from the Cairo *genizah*. The Firkowitch Collection has the only complete illuminated Bible Codex in the world. It was written in Egypt and the colophon date is 1009/10. No other library in the world bears comparison with the wealth of early biblical material amassed by Firkowitch.

The Leningrad Public Library also houses the Antonin Collection, consisting of about 1,200 fragments of the Cairo *genizah* brought together by Antonin Kapustin, a Russian archimandrite who lived in Jerusalem from 1865 until his death in 1894. While in Jerusalem Antonin was engaged mostly in archaeology. When he heard about the discoveries in Cairo of a great quantity of Hebrew manuscripts, he decided to have a share in it. One of the first on the scene, he was also successful in making a choice selection of the material. Except for a privileged few, the Russian collections have been inaccessible to Western scholars.

As a result of four visits to Soviet Russia in 1956, 1958, 1959, and 1960, as well as to Poland and Hungary, with grants from the Rockefeller Foundation and the American Council of Learned Societies, I microfilmed several thousand items of the rare fragments and manuscripts of the Russian collections and established a cultural relationship with the Russian academicians for the acquisition of additional material. Much of this has now been made available for the first time to Western scholars. Over sixty scholars, representing twelve countries, are now benefiting from these treasures. Three catalogs were also published by this writer to aid scholars engaged in their own research. The microfilm collection also includes material from the Friedliana Collection in the Institute of Asiatic Peoples in Leningrad, and from the Kaufmann Collection in Budapest.

I have recently published an unknown poem by Yudah Halevi (1075–1141) from a thirteenth-century manuscript I discovered in the Guenzburg Collection. Written in Barcelona in 1265, a critical Hebrew edition of the unpublished poems in this manuscript will soon appear in Israel. Mosad Harav Kook in Jerusalem is also publishing this year a commentary on Genesis by David ha-Nagid, a thirteenth-century rabbinical leader in Egypt who was a grandson of Maimonides. My translation of this work from Arabic into Hebrew is appended by copious notes and introductions.

In the Leningrad Academy I met a number of distinguished scholars of Hebrew and Islamic studies who not only train other specialists but devote much of their time and energy to the publication of vital information from their literary treasures. The Institute for Asiatic Peoples publishes annually a scholarly magazine, *Palestinsky Sbornik*, in which research is described and recorded. Recent issues contain unpublished letters of the famous Hebrew poet Yudah Halevi, newly discovered historical information on the book *Yosippon*, new data on the life of Ali ben Suleiman, the Karaite lexicographer who lived in Jerusalem at the end of the eleventh and the beginning of the twelfth century, as well as installments of a *Concordance and Dictionary of Talmud Yerushalmi*.

The Leningrad Institute of Asiatic Peoples (formerly the Oriental Institute) houses a number of collections of Hebrew manuscripts and rare books, among them the Friedliana Collection. The latter is named for the Jewish philanthropist Aryeh Lieb Friedland, who assembled a large collection of Hebraica and presented it in 1890 to the Asiatic Museum of the Leningrad Imperial Academy of Science. The collection then contained four hundred volumes of manuscripts, most of them on parchment, and over ten thousand rare printed books.

The manuscript collection in the Institute is rich in Bible, biblical commentaries, linguistic material, extensive Karaitic literature, Kabbalah, and documents pertaining to the history of Russian and Oriental Jewish communities. Among the rare items is a manuscript of the later prophets with the signature of the owner, Sai'd, who writes that he sold it in the year A.M. 4607 (847 C.E.). From this statement it would appear that the scroll itself is of a much earlier date.

The Soviet Hebraic collections represent Hebrew work in all fields and periods of learning, including ancient, medieval, and modern. Neither the Guenzburg Collection nor the Friedliana is limited to certain preferred subjects. Hence they can be regarded, to some degree, as national Hebraica libraries, where every contribution of all generations is represented, ancient as well as recent. The magnitude of these collections can be seen from the Guenzburg Collection alone. It consists of 250 volumes, Bible and biblical literature (these are divided into texts, translations, and commentaries), 300 treatises on Mishna and Talmud, 160 liturgical books and commentaries on them, several hundred manuscripts dealing with poetry (liturgical and secular)—many of them unpublished poems of the Golden Age of Spain by such scholars as Yudah Halevi, Solomon Ibn Gabirol, Joseph Ibn Abitur, and Ibn Ezra. The collection also contains several hundred treatises on philosophy and related subjects, including works by Aristotle, Averroes, Al-Ghazali, Maimonides, and Solomon Ibn Gabirol, representative works by early astronomers, mathematicians, as well as works on medicine and mysticism.

We also find in the Guenzburg Collection manuscripts of works by nineteenth-century authors, which are usually ignored by the librarians of other, older libraries. The majority of the unpublished works of the great Hebrew scholars of the eighteenth and nineteenth centuries were lost to us for lack of interest in them by older libraries.

There is hardly a subject that is not included in the Russian collections. The whole gamut of Jewish learning, covering every country in the world in a variety of tongues, from Near Eastern to European languages, is represented. These treasures show that there was no period of "dark" ages in Jewish literary creativity. Many are illuminated manuscripts.

One illuminated manuscript in my personal library contains the Pentateuch, accompanied by the Aramaic translation (Targum Onkelos); the five Megillahs; scrolls (Book of Ruth, Song of Songs, etc.); the Book of Job; Haphtarah (the Sabbath readings from the Prophets), and an additional portion for the person who ordered the writing of the illuminated codes. Exodus and Deuteronomy have a frontispiece executed in gold and various colors. All the other books except Job (which merely has fine drawings) have the first word of the book in large gold letters enclosed in ornamental borders. Because of the content of the Book of Lamentations, as a rule no gold letters would be applied. This Codex however, though omitting the illumination in Job, includes colors for Lamentations. As a rule it would take between twenty and twenty-five years to write and illuminate such a Bible codex. Since the colophon is given, the date the writing began would be around 1290. Such illuminated books negate the popular fallacy that Jews abstained from art because painting would violate one of the commandments.

—A.I.K.

 ## "Operation Parchment": The Dead Sea Scrolls

For the reporter operating in the Jewish field, June usually heralds a period of comparative ease. Thus it was that about ten o'clock on the morning of June 1, 1954, I had begun to take things in an appropriately leisurely fashion when a local newspaperman phoned and asked if I could pick up a copy of the *Wall Street Journal*. He mentioned that there was some advertisement in it about some scrolls. It did not seem to warrant any undue exertion, but nevertheless I went out and bought a copy of the paper. I skimmed it till I came to page fourteen, the greater part of which was devoted to classified advertising. I searched on, coming to the subheading "Miscellaneous for Sale," directly beneath which, in a single-column, one-and-a-half-inch space was this announcement:

THE FOUR DEAD SEA SCROLLS

Biblical manuscripts dating back to at least 200 B.C. are for sale. This would be an ideal gift to a religious or educational institution by an individual or group. Box 206.

The Dead Sea Scrolls! Someone wanting to get rid of them? Could these be *the* Dead Sea Scrolls? It didn't seem possible that a set of manuscripts whose discovery in 1947 had created a sensation all over the world could be so casually advertised.

There was only one way to find out if these were the real Dead Sea Scrolls—contact the advertiser. In the office of the *Journal* the executive editor admitted that he hadn't noticed the advertisement and, in any case, it didn't mean very

much to him. Not wanting to give the *Journal* a chance to scoop me, I remarked that it looked rather unusual but was not really anything "hot."

I remembered a man who would be able to throw light on the matter. General Yigael Yadin, Israel's soldier-archaeologist and the son of the late Professor E. L. Sukenik, who had managed to acquire three of the original seven Dead Sea Scrolls for the Hebrew University, had come to the United States with his wife for a summer swing through a number of major cities on behalf of the United Jewish Appeal. I reached the Yadins the next morning at the St. Moritz Hotel.

Mrs. Yadin answered the telephone. I told her I wanted to discuss with General Yadin the significance of an advertisement I had seen about the Dead Sea Scrolls.

There was a sudden, startling urgency in Mrs. Yadin's voice. After I repeated the whole thing, she said she was sure her husband would be interested and, if I would wait a moment, she would interrupt his shower to tell him about my call. Then she returned to the phone. "General Yadin is very interested," she exclaimed. "Can you come here now for breakfast?" We made an appointment for 11 A.M. in the hotel.

Looking cool and smart in a gray cord suit, Yadin was most cordial as he ushered me into his room. For a few minutes we reminisced about previous meetings in Israel. Then I unfolded my copy of the *Wall Street Journal* and spread page fourteen out on a coffee table.

Yadin read the advertisement to himself and then read it aloud; a broad, satisfied grin appeared on his face. "This is the most wonderful coincidence," he said. He went on to explain that with three of the seven original scrolls safely in the possession of the Hebrew University, he had often wondered about the possibility of acquiring the others—the four advertised—and returning them to Israel.

Yadin related how early in the spring of 1947, a year before the partition of Palestine, some ragged Bedouin shepherds of the Ta'amira tribe were dozing in one of their rock-sheltered haunts. Their flocks of goats slithered and scrambled among the rocks on the northwestern shore of the Dead Sea. One animal, scorning the dry, sparse vegetation, set out on a lone search for better food. Climbing up a tricky slope, his surefootedness momentarily deserted him and he tumbled into a cave. Trapped, the goat bleated out a distress signal that carried across the wild land and aroused one of the shepherds, who set off across the rocks in the direction of the bleating. As his eyes became accustomed to the dim light of the cave in which the goat was imprisoned, the shepherd noticed fragments of shattered pottery strewn over the floor of the cave. He began poking around. Among the debris and rubbish he came across a few intact earthenware jars covered with lids that resembled inverted bowls. The jars contained longish objects that, when their cloth wrappings had been ripped away, turned out to be parchment scrolls. The famous Dead Sea Scrolls, the oldest Hebrew manuscripts in existence, had been found.

Completely unaware of the historical value of the find, the shepherd and his companions went to Bethlehem and disposed of the scrolls by leaving them with an Arab storekeeper, who arranged for three of the scrolls to be sold to General Yadin's father. The Hebrew University archaeologist wanted to acquire the entire batch, but he could not make contact with anyone willing to finance the deal.

There was another interested party in the field—His Eminence Mar Athanasius Yeshue Samuel, Syrian Archbishop-Metropolitan of Jerusalem and the Hashemite Jerusalem, who subsequently bought the rest of the manuscripts and escaped with them to the United States as the Arab-Israeli battle flared up and entered its decisive phase.

The three scrolls that Sukenik acquired included two Hebrew books unknown until that time. One he called "The War of the Sons of Light Against the Sons of Darkness," which details a conflict between the ancient Israelites and the Moabites, Philistines, and Ammonites, and the second was a book of hymns. The third scroll was an incomplete copy of Isaiah. But one of the best preserved of all the manuscripts is another volume of Isaiah that, with the exception of a few small omissions, contains the full text of the biblical book. This scroll was one of the four purchased by Archbishop Samuel.

For six years General Yadin had dreamed of buying the four scrolls from the Syrian archbishop and taking them to Jerusalem to complete the Hebrew University collection. He knew how delighted his father would have been. There were a number of obstacles in the way, one of them financial. The general had heard that the price might be somewhere in the region of $2 million. Then there was a political consideration. Even if the archbishop wanted to dispose of the scrolls, the Syrian priest was not likely to entertain any negotiations with Israel, certainly not with the man who led the Israeli forces in the 1948–49 battles.

With the *Wall Street Journal* spread before him, Yadin made two phone calls. One was to a well-known American archaeologist who expressed the view that the scrolls might be available for $250,000. The second call was to a trusted friend in New York, a respectable businessman whose interest in purchasing the scrolls would not be likely to arouse the suspicion that the ancient documents were really intended for Israel. Yadin also fired off a terse cable to the Israeli Government. Their enthusiastic reaction to his plan was all that he needed. Realizing that he must remain a shadowy figure in the negotiations, Yadin busied himself in an effort to round up the needed $250,000. (The scrolls have been formally named the Gottesman collection in recognition of the financial contributions of Samuel Gottesman of New York.)

The month between the appearance of the ad in the *Wall Street Journal* and the completion of the purchase was as tense a period as any General Yadin had known in his years of command. While his agents carried out their negotiations with the archbishop's representatives, the general attended to a host of details. He had to ascertain that customs clearance would be assured when the scrolls were shipped to Israel. He had to make sure that once the precious parchments were in his possession, any attempt to upset the deal, by legal or other means, would be warded off. A civilian-garbed general in "remote control" of Operation Parchment, Yadin showed remarkable restraint in the closing days of the transaction.

The financial aspects had been agreed upon, but one last detail had to be taken care of: The scrolls had to be examined by a competent authority who could vouch for their authenticity. No one was more able, or more eager, than Yadin himself, but it was too great a risk. A reputable American Bible scholar, Dr. Harry Orlinsky, examined the scrolls, and on his word the transaction was finally closed.

Three of the scrolls—Isaiah, a manual of discipline for a Jewish sect, and a commentary on the prophecies of Habakkuk—were locked in a big black trunk whose front had been cut away and reattached with hinges so that it dropped forward to enable the scrolls, reposing in three tightly wrapped plastic drawers, to be withdrawn one at a time. Treated with chemicals to soften the brittle parchment that had survived two thousand years of cave life, the three scrolls had been given strengthening backings and were on rolls to permit them to be read with comparative ease.

The scribes who had written the Isaiah Scroll's fifty-four columns of beautifully preserved Hebrew used seventeen sheets of coarse parchment sewn with linen thread that, in one or two places, had been reinforced with a pitchlike gluey substance. The other two scrolls in the trunk were smaller but were apparently almost as well preserved.

Lying beside the trunk was a brown paper package, about the size of a bottle of whiskey. Gently Yadin eased the string off, unwrapped the paper to reveal a plain white wooden box bulging with cotton padding. In the midst of the packing lay a fat yellowish-brown roll, like an outsize Churchillian cigar. It was the Scroll of Lamech, an Aramaic document. Even as Yadin fondled this scroll, a tiny fragment of brown parchment broke away; fortunately it was caught in the wrappings.

The tedious work of decipherment began soon after.

—M.J.

 ## Four-letter Words in Jewish Literature

Each epoch has its own rules for literature. There was a time, for example, when the word dog could not be used in English poetry because it was not sufficiently poetic. Such words as bedbug, louse, and syphilis were taboo in many literatures. One of the arguments in favor of censoring these words was that books were read by young girls, and their pure souls must not be exposed to such "indecent" expressions. There are still mothers and fathers who would, if they had their way, establish a strict censorship and purge literature of everything they consider to be vulgar or dirty.

Such guardians of morality would even willingly censor the Bible itself. Yet, strangely enough, the women who were brought up on the Hebrew Bible, our grandmothers and great-grandmothers, were virtuous women. It did not corrupt them.

Indeed, the Bible is full of indecent stories. Take, for instance, the story of Lot's daughters, who got their father drunk and took turns cohabiting with him. Or the story of how Jacob was deceived at night and given Leah instead of Rachel. Or the story of the rape of Dinah, Jacob's daughter, and the revenge of her two brothers, who laid waste to the city of Shechem while its men were disabled after circumcision. Or the story of King David, who saw Bathsheba washing herself on the roof and sent her husband into battle in order to take away his wife. Or the story of how Amnon ravished his half-sister Tamar. Or, again, the story of how Judah mistook his daughter-in-law for a harlot and left her his pledge.

How did the Talmud exercise special care to avoid naming things by their names? Often enough the Talmud attributed sexual meanings to words in the Bible that seemed altogether innocent. What is true of the Talmud is also true of the Midrash and the Kabbalah. Indeed, many critics have raised the hue and cry that the Kabbalah books are full of obscenities.

Many advocates of secular enlightenment among the Jews bitterly criticized religious Jews for allowing their children to study such a book as the Ketubot tractate. They complained that the minds of the children were being poisoned with tales about sex. Yet neither the Bible nor the *gemara*, the Midrash nor the Kabbalah corrupted Jewish souls.

Our grandfathers and great-grandfathers had the right instinct and tradition in bringing up their children. It never occurred to them to publish a "cleaned up"

Bible for children, as is done today. At the tender age of six or seven our fore-bears were already studying the laws concerning sex, perversions, murder, leprosy, and other plagues. Our great-grandmothers married at the age of nine or ten. The famous philosopher Solomon Maimon recalls in his memoirs that his wife, who was nine years old at the time of their marriage, knew more about sex than he did —and he was eleven at the time and was well versed in Talmudic studies.

The Jews of old were not afraid of reality, yet they produced saintly genera-tions. On the contrary, licentiousness came to Jews with the Haskalah and its in-nocuous and flowery children's books. It was the boys and girls who attended the gymnasiums, where they were fed tales of bees and flowers, who were often cor-rupted.

Despite all the censors and puritans, world literature has never been "pure." Shakespeare, Goethe, Jean Jacques Rousseau, Balzac, Pushkin, Flaubert, Zola, Maupassant, Strindberg—none of them censored their masterpieces. If sex and murder were to be removed from literature, there would be little literature left. Did Dostoyevsky avoid murder and sex? True, some writers have been less prone to depictions of sex and murder than others. But no serious writer would attempt to shackle his talent.

In Jewish literature, for example, Sholom Aleichem did not write about sex. He was a good, middle-class man, a devoted husband and father, and he probably knew little of the "darker" aspects of life and sex. The same was true of Bialik. Sholem Asch, on the other hand, laid the scene of his play *The God of Vengeance* in a brothel. Similar themes are found in his novels *Uncle Moses, Motke the Thief, God's Captives,* and other works. Nor did Zalman Shneour, I. J. Singer, A. M. Fuchs, Ozer Warshavsky, or Afroim Kaganovsky hesitate to describe crude scenes in their works. *Jerusalem in the Shadow of the Sword,* a book by the old Jewish writer A. Reuveni (the brother of the late President of Israel, Ben Zvi), abounds in scenes of sex and even pederasty—and in Jerusalem at that.

In recent years French, Italian, and American writers have used words that men of an older generation cannot easily accept. Once and for all everything has been declared permissible, including expressions used at the lowest rungs of society by thieves, pimps, and prostitutes. I myself find it difficult to read the books of cer-tain modern writers (including women writers). I cannot get accustomed to the so-called four-letter words and would never use them.

But, at the same time, I understand the reasons for the change, brought about by changes in life itself. Even schoolchildren use such words at every step. It is impossible to write about soldiers, sailors, artists, or almost any other group of modern society and falsify their speech. The writer cannot set himself up as the censor of the language of his characters.

Modern psychology, specifically psychoanalysis, has shown the important role of sex in life, thought, creative activity, and in virtually every other area of exist-ence. It is impossible today to write about the relationship between a man and a woman and ignore their sexual compatibility or incompatibility, or the problems connected with their sexual behavior. All these matters are openly discussed. Lit-erature cannot wrap itself in a prayer shawl and play the saint.

Some people still maintain that literature must drink only from "pure springs." But where are the latter to be found? Not in our consciousness, and certainly not in dreams. Whether we pore over the Bible or the Talmud, the Midrash or Kabbalah, whether we study physiology or psychology, history, anatomy, or sociology—in none of these can we escape the phenomenon of evil.

The man who studies the writings of the sages (which constitute the Torah in its broadest sense) must constantly encounter the problems of sex, murder, robbery, and every kind of brutality. The purest sources themselves are full of these dark elements.

Modern man no longer tries to insulate his children from the knowledge of the truth of life. Some believe earnestly that in an artistic depiction of sin there can be more light and exaltation than in the chatter of those who babble of religion without having the slightest intimation of what it means. Science came to the same conclusion as did the Kabbalists: Man cannot learn to know God without confronting Satan.

The Ten Commandments do not speak in veiled and censored words; they are not camouflaged with delicate flowers. I know of a pedagogue who attempted to censor the Ten Commandments for children. He feared that "Thou shalt not commit adultery" might corrupt their pure souls. He brooded on the dangers of the various commandments so long that he was finally left with a single one: "Honor thy father and thy mother."

Censorship of words and phrases never existed among religious Jews. Our holy books used the most unholy expressions for the most exalted purposes.

From a Jewish religious point of view, worldly literature was taboo even at the time when writers avoided the so-called "dirty" words. It was the elements of mockery, calumny, frivolity, and blasphemy that worried religious Jews. Our sages called the books of Aristotle and Plato *seforim hitzonim*—forbidden books. The Vatican proscribed such books as Spinoza's *Ethics*. The Church has been, and still is, more lenient toward indecent language than toward heresy.

This is also true of Judaism. If the traditional rabbis, like other clergy, had had to choose between the spicy tales of Boccaccio and the questions of faith raised by Spinoza, they would certainly have preferred the former—and with good reason.

—I.B.S.

 ## "Yeshivah of the Air": Hams Study Judaism Nightly

There is a contingent of Kosher Hams in Baltimore.

However, the individuals involved are not in the meat business. Rather, their interests lie in the study of Torah. They, and their ham radio colleagues, tune in on frequency 3825 kilocycles every evening from nine to ten-thirty, except Fridays and holidays, to participate in a *shiur* (study session).

The idea to have a *shiur* through the airwaves was conceived about two years ago at a wedding in New York, where a few guests discovered they had two things in common: They were ham radio operators and they yearned for partners to study Torah on a daily basis. Their conversation led to the name of Rabbi Yitzchak Sokol of Lakewood, New Jersey, himself a ham operator. They contacted him and discussed the possibility of having a *shiur* through the radio. They tried it and had an exhilarating experience on August 31, 1977, when they first made contact for that purpose.

Since then the network has grown. Participants in the *Mesivta D'Rake'ah* (Yeshivah of the Air) reside in Baltimore, Potomac, Harrisburg, Toronto, Lakewood, Monsey, Cleveland, Amherst, Rochester, St. Louis, Kansas City, Chicago, Orlando, Brooklyn, Passaic, and other localities. In addition, there are unknown numbers of shortwave enthusiasts who tune in. Although they can listen, they are not licensed to transmit; consequently, they cannot participate in the discussions.

The Kosher Hams, as the group prefers to be called, must comply with the Federal Communications Commission (FCC) regulations, the same as other hams. They cannot broadcast music or news. Their communications must be between two or more individuals. They are required to maintain a log. They must identify themselves every ten minutes by the call-designation assigned by the FCC.

The participating group each evening ranges from several to many persons, depending on each individual's circumstances. During the sessions some may ask questions while others might offer answers, state references, or express contradictions. Many have come to recognize each other's voices. They address each other by first name or by call-designation.

If they get stumped on a particular passage, they can consult another authority on the spot by phone. The leader can call a scholar, or Rosh Yeshivah, for his opinion. He will respond on his own telephone and his voice will be transmitted and received by all those tuned in. On occasion they arrange for a guest to deliver a talk.

The Kosher Hams in Baltimore, Mr. and Mrs. Louis Shnidman, were licensed by the FCC to operate their ham radio about twenty-five years ago. They could receive and transmit Morse code and were knowledgeable about electronics theory as it pertains to radio. Mr. Shnidman came to Baltimore about nine years ago after he retired as Chief Chemist and Laboratory Director of the Rochester Gas and Electric Company. He edited an elaborate volume, *Gaseous Fuels,* for the American Gas Association and has contributed technical articles to various books and periodicals. He brought his 1000-watt, 2400-volt set with him. Mr. Shnidman's licensed call is W3HGP. Mrs. Shnidman's is W3HYA.

The Shnidman's two sons, Reuven and Daniel, are also Kosher Hams. Both are ordained rabbis. Each is pursuing a career in the fields of physics and electronics, respectively. They, too, participate in the Yeshivah of the Air.

Several months ago a Kosher Ham invited his study partners to a bar mitzvah. The Shnidmans went. They met personally for the first time some of the people they had known by voice only. One enthusiast moved to a distant place in upper Canada for health reasons. For him the Yeshivah of the Air has special meaning. It will be one of his few links with something Jewish.

After almost two years of participation, Mrs. Shnidman is still in awe of the Kosher Hams. "Think of it," she marvels. "Now Torah is being brought right into people's homes through the airwaves."

—H.Sp.

**Isolated from Mainstream of Jewry,
Kurdistan Jews Produced Unique Literature**

Kurdistan, the country of the Kurds, is not an independent political entity but a vast territory divided among Iraq, Syria, Soviet Armenia, Turkey, and Iran and inhabited mainly by Kurdish tribes. It is one of the most rugged, mountainous parts of western Asia, split up by ravines, gorges, and swollen rivers; nature herself seems to have determined to render it an inaccessible and impregnable fortress.

In this area, amid magnificent, majestic scenery stretching from Mosul on the Tigris across to Persian Azerbaijan, people of great racial, ethnic, religious, and linguistic diversity live—all remnants of the past. They include Circassians, Turkomen, and Persian tribesmen; Oriental-Christian groups of many denominations (Nestorians, Assyrians, Jacobites, Armenians); Yezidis (so-called Devil Worshipers) and Mandaeans—in short, a throbbing ethnological museum, a rich field for the historian, linguist, and ethnologist.

Within this web of ancient races, sects, and creeds, Jews also lived "since time immemorial," scattered over hundreds of small settlements, isolated from each other and exposed to the ravages of nature and of man.

The origin of the Kurdish Jews is shrouded in obscurity. Tradition regards them as descendants of the exiles from Samaria whom Salmanassar (722 B.C.E.) carried to "Hala, Chabor, and to the cities of Media." The Targumin of Onkelos and Jonathan, the Peshitta, and some Talmudic references identify Kardu with Kurdistan, the land of the Kardini, and with the territory of Mount Ararat, on which, according to biblical tradition, the ark of Noah rested after the deluge.

Nothing was known to the outside world about this *galut Kurd*, the dispersion of the Jews in Kurdistan, until they leaped into prominence with the appearance in central Iraqi Kurdistan (c.1147) of the pseudomessiah, David Alroy of Amadiya, the first and only Kurdish Jew ever to enter recorded history. He attracted many followers among the Jewish communities even in Persian Kurdistan, in Maragha, Urmiya, Salmas, Tabriz, and Khoy, as reported by Samuel b. Yahya al-Maghribi (1174 C.E.).

Benjamin of Tudela, the twelfth-century Jewish traveler, referred to a net of "more than one hundred Jewish congregations in the mountains of Hafton (Kurdistan) extending to the frontiers of Media," and estimated the Jewish population of Amadiya at about twenty-five thousand.

The veil of obscurity hanging over these "remnants of Israel" was lifted six centuries after Benjamin of Tudela's description, when enterprising and courageous Western travelers and scholars dared to penetrate this region.

The most comprehensive and authentic account of the Kurdish diaspora stems from the Jewish traveler Rabbi David d'Beth Hillel, whose *Travels* (1828–32) provided for posterity a vivid description of the Jewish settlements of Kurdistan. His survey of the Jewish communities in the Turkish, Iraqi, and Persian parts of Kurdistan illuminated a hitherto hidden corner on the Jewish map of Asia and bridged a long-standing gap in our knowledge.

The Kurds have a highly developed tribal consciousness; the whole Kurdish population is organized on a tribal, feudal basis. Every Kurd is first and foremost not an Iraqi, a Turki, or an Irani but a member of his tribe and adheres to its laws and customs. The shape, color, or form of the headgear and dress for men and women is, in most cases, an external sign of tribal affiliation. The Kurd's authority is the feudal lord, or *agha*, the head of the tribe, to whom he subordinates himself. In such a tribally organized society Jews could not participate, due to their differences in religion, language, and habits, and were regarded as outcasts or pariahs, and were degraded and despised.

Although they lived within an agricultural society, a majority of Jews were active as artisans, dyers, weavers, porters, and engaged in all kinds of physical labor; others engaged in agricultural pursuits. Some villages were completely inhabited by Jewish farmers who tended their soil, their vineyards, their fields, and orchards.

It could hardly have been expected that Jews at this social-economic level in the Kurdish diaspora, steadily exposed to intertribal feuds, could have developed a cultural life and literary values of their own. Yet letters written in Hebrew from the sixteenth century on, found in the *geniza* and made available by Jewish scholars (J. Mann, S. Assaf, I. Ben Zvi, M. Benayahu, W. J. Fischel), shed some light on the communal, religious, and social conditions of the Jewish communities in Amadiya, Sandor, Zakho, Nirva, Dehok, and elsewhere. They indicated that there were *Hakhamim* (sages), among whom Rabbi Samuel Barzani Adoni and his family figure most prominently. He had established yeshivas in various communities in Barazan, Mosul, Amadiya, and Akra, among others, and maintained close connections with the Jewish centers in Baghdad, Aleppo, and the Holy Land, especially Safed.

These letters, which are only a remnant of a much more extensive and voluminous "correspondence literature," served as the only means of communication among the various communities within Kurdistan and elsewhere.

Their extensive letter writing in Hebrew was only one aspect of their literary activities. They copied treatises on *shehitah* (ritual slaughter), the Sabbath, Passover, and other aspects of the *halakhah*—to which, as rabbinical Jews, they strictly adhered—as well as *midrashim* and homiletic expositions. They composed *piyyutim, pizmonim,* and *azharot* for all festive religious occasions and for all secular events. Proverbs were particularly popular among them. The names of some thirty Jewish authors of sacred and secular poetry have been uncovered from over 150 poems of the seventeenth and eighteenth centuries written in Hebrew and Aramaic (sometimes bilingual), with a great mixture of Arabic, Persian, Turkish, and Kurdish linguistic elements. Besides these, they had their cabalistic treatises, portions of the Zohar, *kameot, goralot,* talismans, amulets, and dream books—all reflecting a world deeply immersed in superstition, beliefs in demons, evil eyes, and magic.

The most characteristic feature of their literary activities was their use of a dialect of their own, Aramaic. The twelfth-century Jewish traveler Benjamin of Tudela drew attention to this linguistic oddity, as did the Jewish traveler Rabbi David d'Beth Hillel almost seven centuries later. Like Benjamin of Tudela and Petahya of Ratisbon, he was struck by this singular feature in the life of the Kurdish Jews, namely, their employment, along with Hebrew, of a Judeo-Aramaic dialect variously designated by the Kurdish Jews and their neighbors as *lashon ha-Targum, lishna Yahudiya, lashon ha-Galut,* or *Jabali* (the mountain language), which is also called New-Aramaic or New-Syriac in modern times. This dialect was divided, according to the geographical locale, into subdialects of Amadiya, Sakho, Rovandus, Arbil, Mosul, Urmiya, Salmas, and others.

While the march of Islam and the advance of the Arabic language in the seventh century swept away Aramaic and other languages in the Near and Middle

East, it seems that in the remote corner of Kurdistan, Aramaic could withstand the pressure of Arabization and halt the linguistic conquest of Arabic. Apart from some Christian Nestorian communities in this region, the Kurdish Jews are the only Jewish group in the Oriental diaspora who have preserved Aramaic to this day as a viable language.

Have the Kurdish Jews used this peculiar language as a medium of literary expression and have they created with it a literature of their own *galut* Kurd? Indeed they did! They created a Targum literature that comprised commentaries to various biblical books (Esther, Ruth, Proverbs, Song of Songs, Job), as well as various postbiblical treatises, *Pirke Avot,* the *Haggadah* of Passover, and sermons on various portions of the Torah.

This Targum literature also encompassed a great amount of folk prose and folk poetry, as well as tales for entertainment whose predominant themes dealt with love, war, and hero worship. They included stories about Adam and Eve, Jacob and his sons, Moses and the Pharaoh, Israel and Amalek, David and Goliath, Sisra and Yael, Elijah, Solomon and the Queen of Sheba, and the like—all based on biblical, rabbinic, and midrashic sources (Targum, Talmud, Ayn Jacob, Yalkut Shimoni, among others). In these compositions are embedded such religious themes as the hope for redemption, the longing for the return to Zion—for the end of *galut* Kurd.

Special attention was directed to the alleged burial places of the biblical prophets: Nahum in Alkosh; Jonah near Nineveh; Ezekiel near Hilla; the sepulchre of Daniel and his three companions near Kirkuk; Ezra near Kurna—all elevated to the status of national sanctuaries to which the Kurdish Jews make their annual pilgrimages.

It must be emphasized that most of these literary treasures that the Kurdish Jews produced in Aramaic have not been fixed in a written form. They were maintained in an oral tradition that was transmitted from generation to generation. In the last century Western scholars and Christian missionaries visiting or residing in this region began to explore their Aramaic dialect. By reducing some texts to writing, they succeeded in transferring this orally transmitted literary output into written literature.

Efforts towards a *Verschreiburg* have been accelerated in recent decades by Jewish scholars in Jerusalem. They have gathered portions of the Kurdish Jews' literary-cultural tradition as a basis for a proper understanding of this intriguing type of literature. Special credit should be accorded Abraham Z. Idelsohn, who collected tales in the Aramaic dialect of Kurdish Jews residing in Jerusalem and, as a famous musicologist, also assembled their songs. The Targum literature was enhanced by the work of the late J. J. Rivlin, of the Hebrew University, who chronicled the oral Bible version of the Kurdish Jews from the lips of *hakhamim.* He has published in his *Shirat Yehudei Targum* hitherto unknown Judeo-Aramaic texts of the Kurdish Jews; this work was supplemented by A. Ben Jacob's *Kehillat Yehudei Kurdistan.*

The Kurdish Jews' love for Zion had brought many of them to the Holy Land several decades ago, before their complete transfer to Israel was achieved. This transfer from Iraqi-Kurdistan to Israel and their rapid assimilation to their Hebrew-speaking environment may lead to the loss of this century-long "oral" Aramaic literature. To rescue from oblivion the still unexplored literary heritage of these "remnants of Israel" in the land of Israel is a cultural challenge to be met in our day.

—W.J.F.

Does More Education Mean Less Anti-Semitism?

Opinion surveys are used to measure the relation between anti-Semitic utterances and such factors as education, economic status, and age. For many years the findings have shown, by and large, that more old people than young ones and more women than men voice hostility to Jews. They also have shown that the more education people have and, up to a certain point, the more money they make the less they express anti-Semitism.

When we examine these correlations, education appears to be the common factor. Poorer people, older people, and women frequently are less educated than richer people, younger people, and men. But why this is so, why prejudice in our society apparently decreases as education increases, is not clear. This correlation has not always and everywhere held true. Thus, in the Germany of the kaisers (1871–1918), according to most observers, the more educated elements were more anti-Semitic.

One possible explanation is that the more education Americans have, the more contact they have with the American creed, which cannot be reconciled with racial or religious discrimination. Does this mean that education has little or no effect on anti-Semitic feelings, that it merely teaches people that it is improper to express them? Perhaps, but it is not easy to believe that large numbers of people will go on saying one thing and believe another for long. In the American environment education may have deeper effects than some of us think. Besides making people more cautious about speaking their minds to strangers via questionnaires, it conceivably does change some people's views about Jews.

It is probable that education reduces prejudice not—or not only—by the simple process of correcting misconceptions with facts but also in more personal ways. The emotional benefits, such as increased self-confidence, that many people derive from education may have as much of an effect as factual learning. For that matter, as a recent study points out, perhaps it is not education itself that accounts for the absence of prejudice but some other characteristic or combination of characteristics common among people who prize education. They may be more intelligent or more liberal minded than others in the first place, or they may have come from backgrounds that predisposed them toward openmindedness, such as families interested in public affairs or communities in which personal contact with Jews was frequent.

Personal contact does seem to make a difference, according to the surveys. The interviewers asked people whether they had any kind of association with Jews, such as working together, mingling socially, or living in the same neighborhood. Those with some such association seemed less anti-Semitic than those without it. Childhood friendships in particular seemed important. Respondents who recalled having Jewish friends when they were young were much less likely to express anti-Semitic sentiments than those who remembered having had no Jewish playmates.

Here again both "optimistic" and "pessimistic" conclusions can be drawn. We may conclude that people who have contact with Jews discover that the latter are "human," and thus change their prejudicial views. Acting on this theory, we will naturally place great emphasis on doing away with residential segregation between Jews and Christians, whether imposed by deeds and covenants or created voluntarily by individual action. Residential segregation not only prevents Jews and Christians from coming to know each other as neighbors but also can mean segregation of children into public schools predominantly Jewish or Christian in composition.

On the other hand, we might conclude that it is not association with Jews that reduces prejudice but rather the absence of prejudice that induces association. There is some warrant for believing that people who welcome Jewish friends had no strong feelings of anti-Semitism to begin with, and that these unprejudiced people remembered their social relationships with Jews more easily.

To sum up, perhaps the answer is roughly as follows: Jews in this country are, in general, members of the middle class. Thus, the Christian merchant, white-collar worker, and professional person tend to have the most frequent personal contact with Jews. People in these categories also tend to have more education.

On the basis of these studies, then, we see two factors that apparently are linked to less anti-Semitism in the large middle class: education and association. Which of these two is the more important we cannot yet say. Studies also suggest that economic security is a third major factor.

XIII
Choosing Judaism:
Converts and Penitents

 **Why I Became a Jew**

I'm a Jew and proud of it!

I'd like very much to get the record straight! I became a Jew because it gave me an inner strength and was the answer to a curiosity that stalked me for many years.

I started out in the backstage of a vaudeville theater in the lower drawer of a dresser. My first birthday was celebrated in a specially contrived crib made up of suitcases in a dressing room at the old Hippodrome Theater in New York City.

My mother, the former Elvita Sanchez, is a Catholic and my dad is a Baptist. Both gave me religious encouragement, although you wouldn't call us a churchgoing family.

God must have put his arms around me that horrible day in 1954 when I was in a severe accident while driving from Las Vegas to Hollywood.

Maybe it was in the hospital after the accident when it happened. Or maybe it was beginning to work before then, but the frustration of looking for that something meaningful in life began to work on me.

As I lay on the stark white hospital bed, friends came and tried to give me encouragement. I remember the Jewish chaplain in the hospital stopping at my bed one morning and asking me how I felt.

I guess I started talking to him about what I was looking for in life. I was confused and admitted it. I was looking for something morally tangible. I had everything a fellow could want—all the material things in life, that is.

Lying in that hospital bed, I began thinking out loud. I must have asked him a million questions about the miracle of my coming out of the accident alive. He listened intently, didn't give answers, but gave me a philosophy where I might find those answers. This chaplain was strong and gave me part of that strength.

As soon as I was well enough to move around, I began asking the nurses about this chaplain. I told them how easy he was to understand. The head nurse smiled and commented, "Maybe that's why you'll never find a rabbi suffering from ulcers." We joked about it, but as I came to understand more and more about Judaism, that kidding remark made me think.

I was at the Fairmont Hotel in San Francisco a few years later, at a children's charity party. I love to entertain kids. After my act, I was seated at a table with a young man in his early thirties. I thought he was an entertainer and started to kid about my working benefits. He smiled warmly and commented, "I do this almost every day of the year."

"Gee," I said, "are things that bad?"

He chuckled good-naturedly and introduced himself. He was Rabbi Alvin I. Fine of Congregation Emanu-El. He pointed out that he had spent the best part of his life working with various organizations throughout California raising funds for needy groups.

He was like the rabbi I had met in the hospital. Everything he said had meaning, not just idle conversation. He spoke so convincingly that I told him he should be on the stage. He joked that he was, in a sense, and performed 365 days a year. "Could any actor match that?" he quipped.

Our casual conversation began to develop into a deep soul-searching experience. Once more my curiosity about Judaism was set aflame. I told him about the rabbi I had met in the hospital and how I was interested in learning more about Judaism. "But," I added, "I honestly haven't the time to sit down and read half a dozen books."

He adjusted the dark-framed eyeglasses he wore with dignity and said, "Years ago another man had a similar problem. He asked the great Rabbi Hillel how he could learn as much as possible about Judaism as quickly as possible. Standing on one foot for a split second, Hillel recited eleven words which gave the stranger the complete philosophy of Judaism.

"Those eleven words were what we know today as the Golden Rule: 'Do unto others as you would have others do unto you.' "

With those words he smiled warmly, shook my hand, adding, "And here are the names of a few books you may read that will explain those words." He told me that I could reach him at his office anytime I was in San Francisco.

It was all too simple I thought. And, despite the fact that I barely have enough time to sleep, I made it my business to get some of the books he put on that list. After checking with most of the libraries around Hollywood, all I could pick up were two volumes. I wrote to a friend in New York and told him what I was doing. He sent me two more books from his personal collection.

At first, reading those books confused me. I would read a few pages, close the book, and try to figure out what the writer was saying. Little by little I began to understand. That uncertain feeling that gnawed at my bones began to relax. Something was coming through and I wasn't confused anymore.

I began to understand not only religion but everything and everybody around me. I had a pretty well-rounded knowledge of other religions, for, after all, I was brought up as a Catholic and had contact with almost every faith in show business.

I had an opportunity to visit many churches in New York and on the road. The services of each had a special beauty, mysticism, and certainly great dignity. But none gave me the feeling I had when I read a single passage from just one of the books I began to collect.

No matter where I performed, somehow or other I came in contact with the local rabbi. My idea of a rabbi with a long beard and silk frock—a crazy picture that must have stayed with me from the time I was a kid on the streets of Harlem —was so wrong. I met one once at a swimming pool in a bathing suit and swore he must have been the swimming instructor. I met another one at one of the top hotels in California and was ready to stake my life on the fact that he was the bandleader. He was sitting at the piano when I came into rehearsal and offered to accompany me until my pianist arrived. I was so embarrassed later on when the bandleader arrived and introduced me formally. He was the leader's brother and was the rabbi of one of the major temples in Ohio.

On my next trip to San Francisco I got in touch with Rabbi Fine again. I told him I had read every single one of the books he had suggested and had studied them until I was blue in the face. He chuckled and said,

"Now you know more than half of my congregation does; come over and deliver the sermon this *Shabbos*."

I almost called his bluff but couldn't make it that Saturday. I did go to his temple a few days later. It was the very first time I had really ever been in a reform temple. As I looked around I saw the basic simplicity of everything in the auditorium.

I walked toward the rostrum and saw the simple wood cabinet covered with dark red velvet. Embroidered on the velvet was a replica of the tablets Moses carried down from Mount Sinai.

My friend walked behind me and, noticing my curiosity about the cabinet, pressed a light switch, pulled the velvet curtain gently, and revealed the contents.

Inside I saw four satin-covered scrolls, with silver crownlike ornaments on top of each, resting against a board covered with plain blue velvet. It was one of the most majestic sights I have ever seen. Even the lighting was perfect.

Rabbi Fine told me that within those scrolls lay the writings of the sages of old, the history of the Jewish people, and the laws and customs by which they live.

He explained how only a small section of the scroll is read each week at services so that everyone can relive history and gain a greater appreciation of life today.

"It is a guidepost, a ruler, a staff from which we learn," he told me. "Men have spent a lifetime studying the Torah, and when they drew their last breath they confessed their only regret was that they could not finish their work."

He turned out the light, drew the velvet curtain, and asked if I had any questions. I smiled back and told him I didn't have a one. He took me into his office.

As I saw the hundreds of books in the bookcases lining the wall, I hesitantly asked, "You really don't have to read all of those books to understand Judaism, do you?"

"Remember, Hillel did it on one foot," the rabbi reminded me as he poured a cup of coffee from a pot resting on a small electric stove near his desk.

He leaned back in his huge leather chair and stared. He was waiting for me to start the conversation. I opened my mouth to talk, but nothing came out. Realizing my uneasiness, he leaned over and clutched my hand firmly.

When he began to speak, confidence flowed back into my veins. Everything this man said had meaning. We talked about show business. He was thrilled when I told him the big names who were my personal friends. He sounded like a typical fan and even asked if I could get their autographs, assuring me they were for his daughter, who was an ardent fan.

It was one of the most wonderful afternoons I had ever spent talking to one person. As I walked back to my hotel room, I still had in my mind the picture of a small framed saying in the rabbi's office. It was a commentary from Goethe and read: "The one and only real and profound thing of the world and of human history is the conflict between belief and unbelief."

Goethe said it in words far better than I ever could hope to find. I knew that there was more to reality than the material world, and giving of oneself to a world that included faith and belief in God was the first step toward becoming a human being.

When I tripped to Los Angeles a few weeks later, I looked up another rabbi in Hollywood. Rabbi Fine had said he was one person I should meet in my quest for more knowledge about Judaism.

Meeting this busy and famous man was like meeting someone from another world. His warmth burst through and made me feel as if we were friends for years. Each word he spoke sounded as if it could have been uttered by Moses on the Mount.

My many meetings with him and the books he suggested I read opened up a completely new world for me. Then the time came for my decision. I had as much information and knowledge of Judaism as I could possibly absorb. Should I become a member of the Jewish faith?

"You're crazy," one of my close Jewish friends commented. "You have two strikes against you now. We Jews have been oppressed for more than five thousand years and all of a sudden why do you want to get into the act? Quit while you're ahead."

He was right. I was a Negro and proud of my birthright. But this was different. I found something here that gave me a feeling of refreshing simplicity. It was an understanding of life all around me. It was an honesty you just can't explain because it's part of you deep inside.

A number of my close friends are Jewish. I confided in each one. Some gave me encouragement and others talked to me like a Dutch uncle, telling me that many people would misinterpret it as a publicity stunt. "It will hurt you in more ways than one," one friend told me. "Don't do it, Sammy, I love you like a brother and you'll be sorry," another said.

I argued back, knowing that every argument they raised was a valid one. I was all mixed up. I was looking for something but really didn't know what. I wanted something, something morally intangible, and I wasn't going to give up now.

Then, all of a sudden, it came to me. I knew what I was looking for. I went back to the rabbi and told him that I wanted to become a Jew.

"Why?" he asked sternly.

I began floundering for words. I thought I had the answer, but it suddenly escaped from my head. I couldn't speak.

He looked at me like my father would whenever I did something wrong. He rose from his shiny leather chair, walked to my side, and put his arm on my shoulder. We sat and talked out my problem for several hours.

"Come back in a year and then give me your answer," he concluded.

A few months before I appeared on Eddie Cantor's television show, I visited him in his dressing room one evening and noticed a *mezuzah* lying on his makeup shelf. When I expressed admiration for Eddie's *mezuzah*, he immediately gave it to me. I was happy and grateful to receive this beautiful religious item and told Eddie that I would wear it at all times around my neck. Each time we met I proudly showed Eddie the *mezuzah* around my neck.

After that automobile accident, in which I lost an eye, I was convalescing in a hospital in San Bernardino, California, when Eddie came to see me. He asked me about the *mezuzah* and wanted to know if I was still wearing it. I told him that I had worn the *mezuzah* night and day since that evening when he had given it to me, but the first time I failed to wear it was on the night of the accident, when I was unable to find it.

I spoke with my mother and dad and told them what I had planned to do and asked their guidance. Each told me the same thing: I was raised to think independently and whatever I wanted to give me happiness was their desire as well. After that I felt a little better.

The year came to an end and I returned to the rabbi. I gave him my answer— and *not* on *one* foot. I told him I wanted to be a Jew because I wanted to become part of a five-thousand-year history and hold on to something not just material that would give me that inner strength to turn the other cheek.

Jews have become strong over their thousands of years of oppression and I wanted to become part of that strength. As a Negro I felt emotionally tied to Judaism. Certainly, the background of my people and their history cannot be compared to that of Judaism, but the same oppression and obstacles thrown in our way were overcome by a greater force than mere tenacity.

I wanted to become a Jew because it gave me a great strength.

I wanted to become a Jew because I felt it gave me the answer to an inner peace in life.

I wanted to become a Jew because Judaism held an honesty and spiritual peace that was lacking in my personal makeup.

I wanted to become a Jew because the customs of Judaism hold a cleanliness that no other philosophy on this earth can offer.

I wanted to become a Jew because it was the answer to a life filled with confusion and uncertainty. Judaism gave me security and understanding.

I wanted to become a Jew because I wanted to share something with my fellow man, who has been sharing with me. I have been lucky and I am certain that luck is more than lip service. As I said in the beginning, God is on our side.

It was probably the greatest thrill of my life the day I walked out of that temple as a Jew. I became a Jew because I was ready and willing to understand the plight of a people who fought for thousands of years for a homeland, giving their lives and bodies, and finally gaining that homeland.

A few weeks after that eventful day I was working on *Porgy and Bess* and we were on location in northern California, near Stockton, for the picnic scene. The following day was Yom Kippur. When we quit that afternoon, I notified the director that I would not work the next day. He turned pale and called Sam Goldwyn in Hollywood. Goldwyn called me right back and said,

"What's this I hear, Sammy, you won't be on the set tomorrow?"

I told him that I was following the tenets of Judaism and would not work on Yom Kippur. There was a pause at the other end of the line. Then I heard Goldwyn mumble, "bless you," and he hung up.

Either there was somebody on the other end of the line who sneezed or maybe Sam did say it. Nevertheless the production was held up for one day at a cost of thirty thousand dollars.

To answer the question of why I became a Jew and how it feels to be a Jew several years later, let me try to answer it like Rabbi Hillel did, on one foot.

"It's me, that's all, just me and the way I see life and enjoy living."

I leave you with *Shalom*, meaning "peace be unto you," as it is with me.

—S.Da. as told to T.B.F.

 ## "A Pool Hall Yeshiva"

The normal yeshiva student does not usually have a prison record, a history of drug abuse, or a pair of hands trained to hot-wire a car or lift a man's wallet. Yet in the Beit Yisrael district of Jerusalem there is a yeshiva whose entire program is geared to society's losers. Unemployed youth, chronic lawbreakers, compulsive gamblers, and restless teenagers who previously had thrown beer bottles at passing cars now sit for hours in a classroom studying Torah.

Yeshivat Or HaChaim was conceived by Reuven Elbaz several years after his 1966 rabbinical appointment to the Bukharian quarter of Jerusalem. The area, occupied primarily by Oriental Jews, is riddled with cultural and economic tensions, for the North African and Yemenite communities that arrived in Israel in the 1950s were shattered on arrival. The complexity and secularity of Israeli society hit them hard, demolishing traditional values along with entire family units. The young took to the streets and the old languished in the squalid apartments of the Bukharian quarter.

Rabbi Elbaz, who came to Israel from Morocco at the age of eleven, began his program like a one-man commando unit. Dissatisfied with the state's social-welfare activities in the district, he went into the streets himself. Wearing a dark suit and a hat and tie, he started his search-and-recovery operations among drug users and pool hall and discotheque crowds.

"I was in an insane asylum for a while," one of the students told me. "Before that I got kicked out of a Christian school for choking someone." Another said: "I left school at sixteen and got heavily into drugs. I got busted a few times, then spent two years in prison."

"Most of the boys who come to the yeshiva turn their lives around," said Rabbi Elbaz. "We have a very high success rate. The self-discipline and social behavior that Judaism demands of a practicing Jew are, at first glance, far above the capabilities of a finger-snapping street punk."

"This place runs on love," said a former gambler who came because his friends talked him into it. There is a sense of warmth in the yeshiva—the kind one feels in a locker room full of athletes after a tough game. Their newly found Judaism is, for many, a tightrope act all the way, sustained only by their comrades and their rabbi. In addition, the atmosphere in the yeshiva is relaxed. In the dining room they listen to a rabbi explain a passage from the Talmud as they finish their soup.

On Thursday nights Rabbi Elbaz runs a program of songs and lectures. "At first I came because they had this far-out music," said a seventeen-year-old veteran of police stations and law courts. "Then I heard the rabbi speak. It wasn't a bore the way I thought it'd be. Pretty soon I just came to hear the rabbi."

Standing in the center of the hall during one of Rabbi Elbaz's lectures, one is struck by the incongruity of it all: hundreds of male faces, like a cast of extras from *Blackboard Jungle*, complete with faded dungarees and slicked-back hair, their jaws working wads of chewing gum or blowing smoke rings into the air. Yet on each head sits a yarmulka, and before them the black-suited rabbi quotes biblical passages. In the balcony the girls lean over the railing, most of them wearing heavy makeup and skin-tight pants.

The biggest problem the yeshiva faces at the moment is economic. Constantly skirting the edges of bankruptcy, Or HaChaim survives primarily through nickel-and-dime contributions.

"There's so much that can be done to rehabilitate these people," said an ex-shoplifter. "All the money that's wasted on prisons and mechanized welfare programs could be used so much more effectively here."

Perhaps the primary ingredient in the successful human regeneration is Rabbi Elbaz's humanity. Neither compromising nor patronizing, he has rejuvenated the crippled Oriental culture and used it to displace the landscape of the pool hall. The Sephardic flavor of the synagogue, the Sephardic music, and the ancient tradition of Torah learning suddenly become vital tools enabling a leather-jacketed loser to retrieve his self-respect and create solid relationships. But perhaps most important, it enables him to finally discover the significance of his own life.

—M.H.

The Making and Unmaking of a Jewish Moonie

Gail Goldsmith (a pseudonym) once came across a *Time* magazine report on the Moonies and tossed it into the wastebasket, disgusted that a news magazine would waste space on kooks. Less than a year later Gail became a member of the Unification Church—a Moonie.

For up to twenty hours a day she sold flowers and candy for the cult on street corners and in bars. She recruited other young people. She knelt regularly before a picture of the Reverend Sun Myung Moon and prayed to him as the messiah. Once she stood in a clenched-fist salute with four hundred other Moonies and declared her willingness to fight and die to defend Moon's homeland, South Korea. On another occasion she announced that all the persecution the Jews have endured—the Inquisition, the pogroms, the Holocaust—were richly deserved, and that Jews ought to suffer even more.

What transformed a nice Jewish girl—whom a Hillel rabbi has described as topnotch intellectually—into a cultist?

In May 1975 Gail, twenty-one, experienced what she now calls "one of the little dips in life." The year before, as a junior at a college in Ohio, she had transferred to the University of Wisconsin "to find a firmer sense of direction."

She was restless and unfocused. Still, her parents and friends were surprised when she suddenly announced that she was going to leave school for a while "to figure things out."

First she went home and worked at two jobs she disliked: photographing children at a shopping mall and operating a keypunch at night. After five months she moved to California, attracted by its reputation for excitement. While she looked for a job, she lived with a friend in Oakland and then moved to a YWCA.

She was running out of money. After two discouraging weeks, during which she was harassed by other boarders at the Y, she decided to swallow her pride and go back home. She bought a plane ticket and called her parents to tell them she'd be home in ten days. She felt defeated but relieved that she had made a decision.

Out for a walk the next day, she saw, ahead of her, a neatly dressed young woman playing the guitar who was hailing passersby. Gail ignored her, but the young woman called, "Hey! Hello! Wait a minute!" At first Gail didn't turn around; then she felt she had been too inhibited. She had always wished nice people could just walk up to each other on the street and talk. She turned around.

"Very soon she had me talking about myself," Gail remembers. Jennifer began by admiring a star sapphire ring Gail was wearing. "I later learned that this was one of the Moonies' basic techniques—to get a person talking about herself, admire her, make her feel great."

It didn't take long for Gail to admit that she had dropped out of school. "As soon as Jennifer heard that, I'm sure bells rang in her mind. She asked if I had ever heard of the Creative Community Project in San Francisco. She mentioned that there were lots of Jewish people in the group and then invited me for dinner there. It sounded interesting, but I'm not the kind of person who normally would go to dinner with a bunch of strangers, so I put her off. But I did give her my telephone number at the Y."

Later that day Jennifer telephoned. She wanted to thank Gail for their earlier conversation. "You were the nicest person I met all day," Jennifer said. "I was so interested in what you had to say. Do you always affect people this way?"

Gail says her ego "soared right up to the ozone."

When Jennifer called again, Gail had an excuse all prepared, but she was assured she would be driven back to the Y if she came that night. Gail thought, "Well, what do I have to lose?" So she went to dinner that night—just five days before she planned to go home.

A good-looking young man she just knew was Jewish met her at the door. The men, in ties and jackets, and the women, most of them in dresses—all in their twenties—were singing "No Man Is an Island" when Gail arrived. It was a song she had loved at B'nai B'rith Girls meetings. Jennifer jumped up and greeted Gail warmly.

Jennifer gave the lecture that evening. Gail was charmed by the brightly colored stick-figure illustrations and Jennifer's acting out of anecdotes such as the parable of the six blind men and the elephant.

The lecture asked, What is life?—a question Gail had been asking herself for two years—and, What is the purpose of life? The answer was: The purpose of life is joy. Jennifer discussed individual uniqueness and the potential with which God endowed each person. Joy was defined as reaching that potential.

The group members seemed to be independent, articulate, well-educated and attractive people who talked seriously and sincerely about their ideals. These were people of conscience. They felt they could make a difference in the world and were willing to devote all their time and energy to it.

A likable young Jewish man drove Gail home. She felt wonderful. She was too excited to sleep that night. "I felt that there had been something there that was the most important thing in my life. It frightened me. Something in me was holding back, yet another part of me was saying, 'You really should find out what this is all about.'"

Not sure if she wanted to go back to the Creative Community Project, as the group had suggested, she called Jennifer just two days before she planned to go home and thanked her for dinner. Jennifer sounded thrilled to hear from her and urged her to give the group another chance.

That night Gail heard the second standard indoctrination lecture on God and evolution. She was skeptical only when the lecturer, another handsome young Jew, concluded that the orderly progress of evolution proved the existence of God. She went back to the Y thinking the Project members were a little misguided but nice people. When she returned to the Project the next day, only the lecturer was there. They discussed her feelings about his talk. He said that her resistance was normal and she shouldn't worry about it but should go home instead, think it over, and have a nice night. It was the most reassuring line he could have taken, she recalls.

That night Gail woke up suddenly and sat up as if a force had pulled her. "It was as if I had stuck my finger into an electrical socket. I felt the energy surging through my entire body. The last part of the lecture—the part that had bothered me—clicked into place just like that. The entire message. And I thought, this must be God."

Gail called her mother to say she would not be coming home. She was going for a weekend in the country at a seven-hundred-acre farm two and a half hours north of San Francisco. But she planned to go home after the weekend.

Gail was surrounded by "older" members on the ride to the farm—the group always arranged it that way. She remembers being pressured to join in all the songs and games as they were driving. As for the upcoming weekend, they told her that she was not simply going to enjoy the countryside, she was going to discover the meaning of life.

On the dirt road leading up to the gate, Gail was momentarily alarmed. The farm was surrounded by barbed wire. Coasting on a spiritual "high," she dismissed her qualms.

The men and women separated and piled into two trailers. About fifty women slept in sleeping bags, so tightly packed that Gail couldn't turn over. They were allowed five hours of sleep. She slept fitfully. In the city, group members functioned on three or four hours of sleep, she learned.

During breakfast—the group never ate breakfast in the city, but over weekends at the farm they had granola bars or oatmeal because of the new recruits—they learned the rules: no drugs, no alcohol, no cigarettes, and new people were forbidden to talk to one another. This was to be a "growing experience" and "you can't grow with someone who's on the same level as you, you can only grow with people who have been around longer."

She noticed that the men and women slept separately, but she did not learn until much later that sex was forbidden, and even married members were forbidden to cohabit for their first three years.

Gail was assigned to a group of older members who were to be her "family" for the weekend. Gail's "family" went everywhere with her, even for drinks of water and to the bathroom.

They followed a rigid schedule. Every moment was occupied. There were many lectures, evaluation sessions with the group, organized games that were given religious significance, and songfests in which each "family" wrote words to popular melodies incorporating Unification Church doctrine. Gail was bothered by one particular ritual activity: Everyone—and there were over a hundred and fifty people that weekend—linked hands and walked together up a steep hill. They then all ran or were pulled down as quickly as possible while still clasping hands. It was a test of faith in which it was accepted that people sometimes fell and injured themselves. She never got used to it, even after months in the group.

Neither Sun Myung Moon nor the Unification Church was mentioned that weekend. Gail noticed that they prayed at all meals, but she could not recognize any particular religious thrust. She was reassured by the fact that many of the lecturers, the song leaders, and the game leaders were Jewish.

She didn't notice until four or five days after that weekend that she had never been left alone for a moment to think over all that she was hearing. By then she was already committed.

At the outset it was suggested that all values and beliefs had been transmitted by parents, read in books, or heard in school. Nothing really came from inside. The lecturer asked, "What if way back when those values were transmitted there were flaws and mistakes?" Already skeptical, Gail questioned all she had ever believed in.

She decided to stay on. They arranged to move her out of the Y and into their San Francisco house. From then on she depended on the group for food, lodging, clothing—everything. When the envelope with the $147 that she had obtained by cashing in her plane ticket was missing, she was ashamed of herself for thinking that one of her "brothers" or "sisters" might have taken it.

She came to believe that every person should seek perfection. She remembers one lecture that convinced her that she could reconcile Christianity with her own Jewish viewpoint—something she had never been able to do even though she had tried to see some validity in Christianity. The group told her that Christianity, Judaism, Islam, Buddhism and all the other great religions were partially right and partially wrong.

"I walked out of that lecture in tears because I was so relieved. There could be a synthesis. After all the religious conflicts in history, I was so relieved to hear about something greater that could bind them all together." Members of the group saw themselves as a vanguard striving for union with God—the "unification" in the movement's name.

It was not until she had been in the group for six weeks that Gail heard Moon's name and his demands. She was told that Moon is the first man since Christ to have reached the stage of perfection at which he is at one with God—that he had raised his wife to this same state of grace and they had produced perfect children.

She learned about Moon's doctrine of "indemnity," which, she says, must lead to anti-Semitism. Moon teaches that all suffering and grief come from man's inability to fight off Satan and accept God. His lectures on the life of Jesus Christ don't blame Jews for killing Christ but for rejecting him. If the Jews had accepted Jesus, Moon's predecessor, the heavenly kingdom would already have come to earth, and mankind would have been spared two thousand years of suffering. Jews' special trials represent repayment—"indemnity"—for the debt they owe.

After having searched for an understanding of the Holocaust, Gail finally felt that she had found an acceptable explanation for the unexplainable.

The day she was moved to make her declaration condemning the Jews, there had been competition among the group members to outdo one another with testaments of faith. She had been suffering from severe bronchitis for a month. The group interpreted her illness as both a personal indemnity and a special indemnity she owed as a Jew. Taking medicine would have nullified the indemnification.

Members often set harsh prayer and fasting requirements for themselves as part of their indemnity payment. One woman, a much-admired fund raiser, would run around the house barefoot in the winter for forty-five minutes. Any lapse of faith was treated by going up to the farm and "fighting it out with Satan" through punitive indemnities.

When Gail saw Moon in person for the first time, as she pledged her loyalty to him in a Nazi-like salute she experienced a single doubtful moment and immediately felt guilty for it.

After five months Gail's parents concluded that their daughter was a Moonie. Up to then she had lied to them deftly. Her father asked her to see a rabbi or a psychiatrist. She refused.

Two weeks after being permitted to go home for a wedding, her father telephoned her to meet him. Her cult superiors were out when she took the call. The person she consulted had only seven months more seniority than she and thought the outing would be all right because there had been no trouble with Gail's previous visit.

Her father picked her up in a rented car for a drive and lunch in the country. Her uncle and her brawny cousin unexpectedly piled in too. They were going to come along for lunch. It took her a half hour to realize that she was being kidnapped.

When she understood, she became frantic. De-programming meant persecution for the messiah. It would condemn her and her ancestors and her descendants to thousands of years of suffering. She had been told she would be raped, starved, beaten, forbidden to use the bathroom, and denied sleep.

Wedged between her father and her uncle in the front seat, she considered pushing her uncle, whom she had always thought of as a second father, out of the moving car. "My uncle was sixty-seven," she says. "He has a bad back. He has bad knees. The car was going forty miles an hour. You might know someone who could survive a fall like that, but I don't."

Shocked by her own thoughts, she decided to stop fighting. Secure in her faith, she would outsmart the de-programmer.

When she met him in an Akron, Ohio, motel room, the de-programmer told her he had worked with more than six hundred cultists and had never failed. She thought, "Well, today you've met your match."

The de-programmer and his aides pointed out discrepancies in Moon's doctrine and contrasted it with his sumptuous life-style. At the end of the second day they compared the Unification Church to a communist dictatorship. She thought, "If I say it out loud and it sounds okay, then it must be right. And if I say it out loud and it sounds horrible, then I'll be wrong."

She told the de-programmer she had begun to think that Moon ran his group like a communist dictator, except that he has really set himself up as God. "As soon as I said it, I knew it was right. I started to cry a hell of a lot, and everyone in the room cried with me. My father came in and he started to cry too. All I kept saying, over and over again, was 'Daddy, I'm so sorry.' "

For months afterward she felt guilty for the pain she had given her family, the people who loved her most. "It wasn't a little mistake, it was a big whopper.

"But I was left with nothing, absolutely nothing. Just a big emptiness. I didn't know whom to trust anymore. They had captured me so effectively that I was just arms and legs that could walk down the street and carry flowers, and a mouth that could ask for money." She hadn't read a book, a newspaper, or seen a film in seven months. She only knew about Moonies and the weather.

One day she opened the family Bible and read, "Put your trust in God and He will take care of you."

"At that moment that was all I needed to know. I just said, 'Okay, I really want to be part of things again and I'm anxious to get things straightened out. I can't be impatient. I'll just have to let things run their course.' "

She went back to college and completed her degree in microbiology. She took two courses in Jewish studies and read Martin Buber and Judah ha-Levi. Later she went to work for B'nai B'rith because she knew she needed something "good and Jewish to hold on to." She has helped to de-program cult members and has spoken to B'nai B'rith audiences. Colleagues describe her as thoughtful, bright, lively, and likable. Today it is hard to believe Gail was a Moonie.

—E.A.S.

 # From Italian Playboy to Committed Jew

There is in Italy a respected Jewish family by the name of Mayer. Not a very Italian-sounding name, perhaps, but that is best explained by the fact that the family originally came from Austria and settled in Milan, in northern Italy.

Today the family is known and respected for its massive support of Israel and Jewish educational and religious programs. The name of Mayer will be found interwoven with a number of Israeli industrial firms, and marks the sites of schools, clinics, and synagogues in Israel. The fact that the Lubavich Hassidic movement has established a center in Milan can mean only one thing: The Mayer family has been supporting that cause too.

And yet, Dr. Astore Mayer, who died a few years ago, was not always the committed, activist Jew that he was to become later in life.

The Mayer family was so rich and so powerful in Milan that their name was often equated with that of Rothschild. The father owned and managed a huge paper plant that turned out paper products for Italy and other countries, growing larger and more successful year by year. The number of employees numbered in the thousands.

The Italian Government officials, local as well as national, went out of their way to aid the Mayer enterprises because of their importance to the country's economy. The Mayer family, for its part, was generous with its gifts to local museums, schools, hospitals, and other institutions.

Young Astore Mayer received the best education that was obtainable. He was an intelligent, culture-oriented young man, and although he knew that he was Jewish—for his father tried from time to time to instill a stronger religious and cultural awareness in his son—it meant very little to him. Life in Italy was full and exciting, and fun and games were abundant; being a Jew meant very little to Astore.

Despite the fascism that overtook Italy, and in the face of Mussolini's accord with Hitler, nothing seemed to change in the life of the Mayer family. But then, suddenly, things did change: The German military forces began to enter Italy; Jews began to be arrested; and, finally, the Mayer family was warned by friendly Italian officials that it would be best for them to leave Italy, at least until the climate of the country—now fully in partnership with Germany in an all-out war—changed.

Mayer senior was a realist and understood that the time had come to rescue his family. With the help of trusted friends and employees, the Mayer family left Italy, heading north for the safety of nearby Switzerland. The procession that constituted the departure of the Mayer family from Italy was one to behold: Several dozen vehicles, large and small, laden with valuable art treasures and family heirlooms, with great amounts of clothes and other personal articles, moved in a steady stream north to the Swiss border. There were no barriers, and the entire group soon found a safe, if temporary, haven in Switzerland.

The Mayer family lived in neutral Switzerland, waiting for the day the war would end, with the Nazis defeated, so that they could resume their earlier life. They did not really know what was happening with their paper company, but they hoped things would turn out for the best.

The member of the family who was hit hardest by the experience of enforced exile was young Astore. He found it difficult to believe that this outrage, this virtual booting out of his family from their home in Italy, had actually happened. But he came to terms with the reality of the situation and made a decision: If, indeed, he was a Jew, and if the only reason he had been subjected to the indignity of exile was because he was a Jew, then he would really be a Jew!

While the war was still raging, Astore began to obtain a sound background in Judaism. He read, studied, turned away from forbidden foods and ate only kosher foodstuffs, and became a Sabbath observer. Gradually the former happy-go-lucky man-about-town was transformed into a serious, committed, religious Jew. His father was delighted.

The war ended finally, and with much trepidation the Mayers returned to Italy, not knowing what to expect. When they reached the site of the plant, they were astounded: The original facilities had doubled in size! The factories were in sound condition, turning out paper round the clock.

Their former employees wept with joy when they saw them, for the Mayers were well regarded. What had happened while they were in exile, the staff people told the Mayers, was that the Nazis who had taken over the plant needed paper desperately, and so went ahead and made sure it continued to operate smoothly and efficiently. It could be said that the Nazis had inadvertently doubled the size of the Mayers' plant—and therefore their wealth.

The Mayer family took possession of their factory and went back to business as usual, but with a marked difference: The need to help the displaced persons who had survived the Nazi death camps was crucial, as vital as the need to aid those who now tried to reach Palestine on so-called illegal vessels in spite of the British Government's ban. And then, when the magical news came, in May of 1948, of Israel's establishment, the needs were greater than ever. In all cases the Mayers were the most generous, the most active, and the most involved individuals.

Astore Mayer, in the course of time, took over the management of the family firm. But he took a great deal more interest in every single effort that affected the Jewish community in Milan, in Israel, and everywhere else.

When Astore Mayer died, he left behind a reputation for nobility of character and dedication to the welfare of the Jewish people that will be difficult to match. And if anyone wishes to say that the Nazis, by forcibly exiling him and his family, turned Astore Mayer into a good Jew, it would be no more than the truth.

—D.C.G.

 ## From Priest to Orthodox Jew

Twelve years ago I was a very devout and devoted Roman Catholic priest. Now I am an equally devout and devoted Jew.

However, it is not as simple as that. To relate the hazards of the journey from Rome to Jerusalem in a thousand words is asking for a miracle.

I began, after seven years in the priesthood, to doubt seriously and painfully the cornerstone dogma of orthodox Christianity, in particular, the divinity of Jesus. Naturally, had there been no other problems I should simply have become a single-minded Unitarian.

At about the time when I agonized about the very basic teachings of Christianity, I came across the works of Professor Josef Klausner. This very erudite and masterful writer, in his book *From Jesus to Paul,* related, in a compelling manner, the early origins of Christianity and demonstrated how the teachings of a simple Jewish "rabbi" had evolved or developed into a dogmatic system within the framework of a vast Caesar-like organization.

As a result of this and many other writings of a similar nature, as well as a complete review of history, I regretfully came to the firm conclusion that the real founder of Christianity as we know it was not Jesus but Saul of Tarsus, who was later to become the great missionary Paul.

This genius desired to take religion to the Gentile world. He was the greatest missionary in history. Moreover, in his brilliance he realized that the Gentile world could not embrace monotheistic Judaism. So he blended it with Hellenistic forms and ideas, rendering it palatable to a world unaccustomed to pure religion.

This led me to examine the source from which Christianity and, later, Islam sprang, namely, the mother faith—Judaism.

Here I found not a creed or system of beliefs but a way of life. Here were no dogmas of mystery to swallow, but a simple yet profound revelation from God himself to a people chosen by him to be the bearers, for all time, of his vital message. Every department of daily life, from morn till eve, was related to, identified with, and saturated by this way-of-life religion.

Finally I decided that I wished to become identified with this true revelation and God-given way of life. But this was the trouble. Judaism does not want proselytes. This is even more true in British Jewry than in America. The London Beth Din is the strictest in the world. It would require a special article to relate the difficulties encountered in my dealings with this formidable body. In a word, it took five years to batter my way through the doors of the Anglo-Jewish Ecclesiastical Court of Rabbis.

Meanwhile, my conscience would not permit me to continue in the priesthood. I could not preach to large congregations what I no longer believed, nor could I celebrate the Mass.

So I walked out. I had no security—no promises, no job, no income. All I had was faith in God. I found a post in an Episcopalian boarding (private) school. Here I ate only vegetables and tried to keep *Shabbat*, although as yet I was not obliged by any *mitzvoth*.

Eventually the Beth Din accepted me and I went to teach at the great Anglo-Jewish school, Carmel College, near Oxford. Here I taught English and Latin and prepared for my reception into Judaism. My eight years at Carmel College were inspiring and rewarding.

At the end of eight years I felt an urge to work in Israel, the land that the God of our fathers had miraculously restored to us. So once again I packed my bags and set off on this new stage of my spiritual journey. I taught at the Reali High School in Haifa and found the very lively sabras true friends and excellent pupils. I loved Israel, but my health failed. Acting upon medical advice, I returned to England, where I regained my health.

I was invited to visit America and lost no time in fulfilling an ambition of many years. I fell in love with America and recognized in this fortress of democracy a most desirable land.

In the course of my lecturing I became acquainted with many great institutions, both Jewish and non-Jewish. I should like to give some idea of the questions put to me, as well as my answers.

My main concern with American-Jewish life is the youth. Here is the weakest link in the communal chain. With energy and vision it could become its strongest pillar. Above all, the student body needs urgent attention. On the campuses I found hundreds of students in a complete spiritual fog. They simply have no idea of Judaism or even of Jewishness. Our grand traditions have no meaning for them, and they are marching quickly from apathy to apostasy.

Intermarriage will mean the loss of their children to any form of Jewishness. The B'nai B'rith Hillel foundations are doing magnificent work, but they need powerful allies if they are to become effective in more than the social sphere. I respectfully suggest that for the next decade a very substantial portion of the material and moral reserves of the American-Jewish community should be invested in its youth. No project is as vital; none will pay richer dividends.

Of the hundreds of questions posed during my most rewarding tour, three or four constantly recurred. I must limit myself to these in this brief article.

Question: What is your attitude now towards the Catholic Church?

Answer: My attitude is one of great respect and admiration. During the twelve years of separation from my former co-religionists, I have never uttered a word of attack against the Church. On the contrary, I have often removed misunderstandings as to her teaching, for example, the false notion that Catholics pay to have their sins forgiven, and so forth.

Question: How can we convert Jews to Judaism?

Answer: The first step is to restore to nonattached or assimilated Jews a sense of pride in Jewishness. The State of Israel is a powerful instrument in this regard. No longer need a Jew feel himself a spiritual or moral outcast. By God's mercy, we have once again our universal center. Young Americans must be encouraged to visit their traditional home and witness for themselves the great renaissance of Jewish history.

Second, Jewish schools must be given full support and a new generation prepared that will know, cherish, and practice the great way of life handed down by our fathers.

Question: Should we try to convert non-Jews?

Answer: I am opposed to Jewish missionary activities. First, we Jews believe that all righteous men, of whatever faith they may be, will be saved. Second, I am too well aware of the serious responsibilities of Judaism to encourage others to undertake them lightly. Whereas in other religions an act of faith is sufficient, nothing less than 100 percent conviction will suffice in Judaism. Let us concentrate upon "should-be Jews" before we concern ourselves with "would-be Jews."

In conclusion, I believe that if all our resources are mobilized in the cause of youth, we shall save American Jewry for the future. That is what matters!

—A.C.

 ## Some of the Best Jews Are Proselytes!

Who would have imagined, when we sat down to the seder table, that the special recitations for Soviet Jewry, and the untouched cup of wine set aside for them, as well as the empty chair symbolizing their inability to celebrate Passover in the USSR, would be answered, if only partially, so dramatically and so soon?

The news photographs of Jewish dissidents from the Soviet Union being greeted at the airport outside Tel Aviv and being warmly received by Prime Minister Menahem Begin must have sent chills up the spines of thousands of Jews in all parts of the world.

One of the "Prisoners of Zion," Edward Kuznetsov, whose wife, Silva Zalmanson, has been campaigning for his release for more than a decade, stopped briefly in New York and then, within a matter of hours, boarded an El Al airliner en route to Israel. Like Dymshitz and the others, he, too, was embraced by Begin and was warmly welcomed to Israel.

What is not widely known is that Kuznetsov is not technically, *halachically,* a Jew, that is, although his father was Jewish, his mother was not, and Jewish law stipulates that a child's religion is based on that of the mother, unless he or she undergoes a formal conversion procedure. However, Kuznetsov chose to be a Jew, to share the anguish of Soviet Jewry, to make his new home and new life in Israel —and in doing so he recalls the long roster of many non-Jews who opted to join the Jewish community, to share its trials and tribulations, its joys and glories.

Some proselytes are well known, others are not. In Israel today there is a *moshav* made up of former Yugoslav Jews, men whose wives and children were murdered during World War II by the Nazis while, in most cases, they themselves were fighting as partisans under the leadership of Tito. When the war ended, and the Jewish partisans returned to find total destruction, many chose to remarry, choosing mates from among the local non-Jewish population of women who had been raised as Christians but who quickly agreed to convert to Judaism. You can see them in Israel today—mostly they are blond, with Slavic features, almost always wearing prominent Stars of David around their necks, and in almost all cases meticulous in their observance of Jewish law and tradition—often to the dismay of their husbands, who are generally more secular in their approach to Jewish life.

History records a distinguished group of proselytes: Ruth, Naomi's daughter-in-law, who was destined to become the great-grandmother of King David; Onkelos, the insightful and still widely studied biblical commentator whose explanations of the Torah are taught to most yeshiva students; and, during the time of Rome's leadership, Flavius Clemens and Fulvia, wife of a leading Roman senator.

Josephus wrote of early Hellenists who at first became Jews but later reconverted and numbered among the Jewish religion's worst slanderers. The rabbis, to this day, have taught that proselytes who decide to enter Judaism out of a sense of conviction rather than because of an impending marriage to a Jew, or "because of a dream or because they wished to dine at the royal table," should be regarded with compassion and warmth. Cases abound in the United States today of non-Jewish spouses who join the Jewish community out of a desire to have the same faith as that of their husband or wife (generally the former), and then go on to become exemplary Jews, often shaming their own spouses into a stronger sense of identification with the Jewish people.

One thinks of an outstanding woman living in Jerusalem more than a quarter century, the wife of a rabbi who is also a scholar of world prominence. A former Catholic whose immediate family includes a priest and a nun, she is today an exemplary Israeli Jewish woman, contributing to Israel's advancement and well-being.

In one of the major national Jewish women's organizations there is a remarkable woman whose ancestors belonged to the German aristocracy and who is entitled to be known as baroness. She met, fell in love with, and married an American Jewish captain soon after World War I. Because he, a leading attorney, was an activist Jew and a committed Zionist, and because of her own strong convictions, she has become one of the principal figures in support of Israel; now a widow in her later years, she has continued to work for every Israeli program for more than three decades, undoubtedly with even more zeal and effectiveness than even large numbers of Jewish women who numbered their parents and grandparents as Jews for as long as they could remember.

Then there is the case of a former British actress, a Christian woman, who met and fell in love with a Zionist who was destined to become a leading Israeli figure until his untimely death. She is now a member of the Israeli consular staff and has spoken on behalf of Israel to thousands of people, urging support, calling for *Aliyah*, displaying a loyalty and devotion to Israel and the Jewish people that are beyond compare.

The phenomenon of the proselyte is not new in Jewish life. Nearly a millennium ago, in the days of Maimonides, a proselyte who became an outstanding scholar of the Talmud, Obadiah, wrote to the famed Jewish leader and scholar and received the following reply:

Master and teacher, the intelligent and enlightened Obadiah, the righteous proselyte: You are a great scholar and possess the understanding mind, for you have understood the issues and known the right way.

Maimonides, who fully supported the proselyte who came to the Jewish community out of conviction, went on to say:

> As every native Israelite prays and recites blessings, anyone who becomes a proselyte throughout the generations, and anyone who unifies the Name of the Holy One, as it is written in the Torah, is a pupil of our father Abraham and all of them are members of his household.

There is a former Catholic priest, now an ardent, practicing Jew, who has been a member of the faculty of a leading Brooklyn yeshiva for many years . . . On the campus of the Technion, in Haifa, there is a rabbi who serves the spiritual needs of the nine thousand students who was himself born a German Christian and whose father is said to have been a Nazi sympathizer . . . In the United States, during the period of slavery, there were cases of Jewish slave owners who converted their slaves to Judaism; a number of the Black Jewish congregations extant in the United States today stem from those converts . . . In the middle of the nineteenth century there was an American Quaker who was appointed consul in Jerusalem, and who converted to Judaism, married a local Jewish woman, and was buried on the Mount of Olives . . . The late anti-Zionist, Rabbi Amram Blau, who led the fanatic Neturei Karta sect in Jerusalem for many years, married a former French Catholic woman who carries on his work to this day . . . In West Virginia and Michigan there are small congregations of former proselytes, and a recent survey indicated that somewhere between three thousand and five thousand converts to Judaism in America join the Jewish community annually.

It is obvious that when Begin embraced Edward Kuznetsov, welcoming him to Israel and into the fold of the Jewish people, he knew that the former Soviet dissident follows a path of very special people whose devotion to Jewry can serve as a model for many Jews, inside and outside Israel, who were born Jewish but who fail to appreciate the glory of the Jewish heritage.

—D.C.G.

 ## The Western Wall: A Catalyst for Returnees to Judaism

Some four years ago a twenty-four-year-old New Yorker, brought up in a liberal, secularist Jewish home and planning a career in journalism, was passing through Jerusalem on the way home after a long trip that had taken him through Asia and the Himalayas. He made the customary tourist visit to the Western Wall and there something funny happened. He wound up stopping over at an Orthodox yeshiva for a couple of days.

A few weeks later he wrote to his sister, "I've had my lack of faith shaken." More letters followed, lengthy ones about his discovery of Judaism, particularly his discovery that Jewish philosophy was logical and that the Torah made sense. His sister, Ellen Willis, a noted journalist, wrote back, trying to puncture all his arguments. Finally Ellen went to visit him to talk more and see for herself. Her brother, Michael, finally convinced her that he knew what he was doing and had found his own direction. She could not follow him, but she wrote a powerful article about him and his return to Judaism in *Rolling Stone*, the leading magazine of popular culture.

Today Michael is an Orthodox rabbi and a guide to many other young people at a St. Louis yeshiva. The rabbi who was largely responsible for Michael's becoming a *baal tshuva* (returnee to Judaism) believes there are thousands of potential Michael Willises wandering over the face of the globe, looking for something and not knowing they can find it in their own heritage.

"Look, we have so much to offer—heritage of thirty-five hundred years," said Rabbi Noach Weinberg, glowing with enthusiasm. "We have power! We have what it takes. We're asking only one thing of the kids: Check out your own religion."

The rabbi, who heads the yeshiva at Aish Ha Torah, the last of three he has set up in Israel, said that some twelve thousand young people have passed through the yeshiva in the past five years. Some come for only a few hours, some for a few days, and others for years—long enough to become rabbis like Michael.

Rabbi Weinberg said that he has been concerned about the problem of Jewish youth turning from their own heritage ever since his own youth. "I saw this happen when I was still a kid in New York. At that time it wasn't cults, it was communism they ran to—kids from Orthodox homes like my own. I couldn't understand it. But I felt if we could just reason together, it would change their minds. I did reason with my friends and sometimes I was successful. Not always."

Today young people are more interested in feelings than in reason, according to the rabbi. He is ready to meet them on that ground too. "I say to them, 'Do you realize that happiness is an obligation? It is what God wants for His children.' From there we go on to how to achieve this happiness. What we are is a Torah institute for living."

Yeshiva representatives encounter likely prospects for Torah study at the Western Wall. "We figure if they come to the Wall they are already, well, at least interested. From there we can ask, 'Would you like to know more about this heritage?' And many, many are ready."

The rabbi said that the institute does not proselytize Christians and is not set up to deprogram Jewish young people who have joined cults. "What we say is that if they are willing to talk about it, they are welcome to come in."

The rabbi reported that one young man of Jewish background was working as an assistant Protestant minister when he turned up at the yeshiva. He embarked on a course of study that carried him through two and a half years and brought him back to his own faith. The young man, Dov Heller, wrote a pamphlet refuting the Christian missionaries.

Rabbi Weinberg noted that some Jewish young people manage to find their own way out of cults simply because they have a questioning turn of mind.

"When they asked too many questions of a cult leader they got thrown out. When they ask questions, we invite them to ask more questions," said the rabbi.

Since he had been so successful in turning American young people back to their religion, I was curious whether the rabbi felt concern for the Israelis, a great number of whom seem to feel that living in Israel affords total Jewish fulfillment. One Israeli told me, "You Americans need religion because it is your only way of having a Jewish identity. We don't need it!"

Rabbi Weinberg nodded. Yes, that attitude was common, but he hopes for changes. The yeshiva offers no special programs for Israelis. However, not long ago Uri Zohar, a noted Israeli actor, producer, and TV star, had come to the yeshiva in the course of working on a television feature and it changed his life. He has become an Orthodox Jew who spends most of his time in Torah study. The rabbi believes his influence will have an impact on Israeli young people.

Rabbi Weinberg said that originally he had gotten government funding for the yeshivot he founded, but after the Six Day War the government had been forced to curtail such subsidies. Now he is dependent upon private contributions. He has started similar programs in St. Louis and Los Angeles.

"These kids come in not knowing what Yom Kippur is," reported the rabbi. "We take them through whatever they are ready for—the Bible, the proofs of God's existence, what the commandments are, the prophets, the Ethics of the Fathers, Talmud. They don't all become Talmud scholars or rabbis, but at least they leave with some knowledge, a sense of identity, of pride. One young man who studied with us for a while said, 'I'm still an atheist, but you know what you've done for me? You've given me my people.' Oh, we're so powerful, so beautiful. Why shouldn't our young people enjoy this?"

What about women? Aren't they important in this picture? The rabbi agreed that they were and said they are welcome in the yeshiva and that his wife gives some special classes to women. One of the alumnae of those classes, Alison Karpel, a writer, reported that *rebetzin* Weinberg is a beautiful, charismatic woman, a mother of twelve children. She has a substantial, devoted following.

"These women have very full lives," said Mrs. Karpel. "They feel their main job is raising their kids, but they spend every minute they can grab in study and they jump at the opportunity to do something for someone else. There is nothing shallow about them or their lives. They don't feel they are being deprived of anything if they don't go to the yeshiva with the men.

—E.L.

 **From Ashram to Yeshiva:
Getting Your Head Together**

On New Year's Day 1978, in Jerusalem's ultrareligious Kiryat Zanz quarter, Hanna Horowitz, nineteen, shot to death her twenty-three-year-old sister, Esther. Hanna then turned her army pistol on herself and pulled the trigger. Police deduced from the note the girls left that it had been a suicide pact; a quotation from a poem by Oscar Wilde indicated that the sisters were "seeking a happier life."

To ultra-Orthodox Jews such as the Horowitz family New Year's Day is not in January but at Rosh Hashanah. Poems by Oscar Wilde and other secular writers whose works were found in the girls' room are an utter anomaly in Kiryat Zanz. And girls from religious families generally are exempt from army service in Israel. Hanna had been serving without her parents' knowledge, changing into her uniform at the base each morning and back into her modest, long-sleeved dress before she came home each afternoon. Her parents believed she had been working at a clerical job in the city.

Israelis were baffled by this tragic case. Many people at both ends of Israel's religious-secular society immediately thought of one man who might have been able to save the Horowitz girls—Rabbi Ze'ev Chaim Lifschitz.

When the state broadcasting authority sought an explanation for the suicide pact, it, too, thought of the rabbi and invited him to an interview. He declared that the sisters had been unable to reconcile the religious and secular worlds. When such people dabble in "forbidden knowledge," he said, "they swallow Shakespeare, Ayn Rand, and James Bond all of a piece. They lack all discrimination and have no defenses against the poisons circulating in the permissive world. They become utterly lost and confused."

Later I asked the rabbi if he indeed believed he could have saved the girls' lives. "I don't know," he said, "but I have dealt successfully with numerous potential suicides. I wish," he added sadly, "I do wish they had come to me."

During the past decade some six thousand troubled persons have come to the rabbi for help. Most are young religious Jews, but he has also advised numerous male secularists, including doctors, lawyers, professors, and other professionals. He has even counseled psychologists and psychiatrists—and other rabbis. Just recently Lifschitz has begun to counsel "a few women, mostly students at the new women's yeshivot on referral from their teachers, and wives of yeshiva students." The common denominator among these people is that they are all deeply engaged in intellectual activities and all have problems.

Why do they turn to a rabbi? Chaim Lifschitz is not solely a rabbi. A native Israeli with a yeshiva background, he holds an M.A. in clinical psychology from the University of Geneva, where he spent six years as an assistant to Jean Piaget, the renowned psychologist and teacher. He is intimately versed in Piaget's theories of cognitive development and the need for intellectual adaptation to environment.

As an educator Chaim Lifschitz quickly became attuned to the psychological stresses that can develop in a classroom. Before long he was alert to such problems outside the classroom as well.

Still, why would a troubled person turn to a psychologist whose area, essentially, is education? Chaim Lifschitz maintains that this relates to his being a rabbi.

"I happen to be a strictly observant Jew," he says, "which means I carry with me a fully developed system of values. This is precisely what a typical social scientist lacks. For them, I'm sorry to say, morality is a gray area, behavior is judged according to fashionable theories, and just getting a person to 'cope' or to 'function' is considered an accomplishment. Even the so-called humanists such as Abraham Maslow and Rollo May and R. D. Laing, while they are well intentioned, really don't have the moral means to help a person go beyond mere 'adjustment' to grow and develop fully."

Rabbi Lifschitz never intended to become a therapist. When he returned from Switzerland in September 1964, he took up teaching in an Israeli religious school. Soon he developed a reputation for a sympathetic ear and quick intuition as to what might be troubling people. Before long students—and their teachers—were lining up at his door for advice.

In the rather tight-knit world of the yeshiva he was respected for his "outside knowledge" of psychology. Today he is one of a handful of men and women who are highly regarded in both religious circles and secular academies in Israel.

In recent years Rabbi Lifschitz has had to devote almost all his time to counseling. Now forty-three, married, and the father of twelve children, he directs Sad-nat Enosh, the Human Workshop and Torah Center for Spiritual Guidance in Jerusalem. He doesn't charge for his services; friends raise funds for him. Dozens of assistants whom he trained aid him and serve in Human Workshop branches in New York, London, and Johannesburg. His wife, Chava, screens applicants and sets up appointments. The demands on his time are so great that hundreds must be sent elsewhere. Unusual in bureaucratized Israel, the Human Workshop has no connection with any government agency, political party, or religious group.

All sorts of people come to the rabbi. A young Hasidic scholar finds he can't get along with the bride his family selected for him. A lecturer at Tel Aviv University discovers in mid-career that his life is meaningless. A kibbutznik says angels are invading his dreams and urging him to commit murder. A secular youth has found religion and now believes he is the Messiah.

Often, the rabbi says, his visitors—he avoids the word "patients"—only need someone to talk to for an hour or two. When he detects a very serious psychological problem, he refers the person to a professional practitioner. But in many cases he finds that the problem is a troubled soul whose intellect is caught between the pincers of reason and spiritual yearning. Or he may be confronted with a mind buffeted by concurrent religious and secular winds, as was the problem with the Horowitz sisters. He takes on such cases. His counseling is not limited to fifty-minute sessions; often he spends an entire day or more with a visitor.

"Counseling may go on for months, but rarely more than a year," he notes. "I don't indulge in the archaeology of a person's past, as a psychiatrist does. These people have problems in the here and now; that's what I concentrate on. With older people, people with complex lives, counseling may take considerable time. Younger people, I'm happy to say, often find their direction in a session or two."

Fully half the rabbi's work these days involves *baalei teshuva*, people who have "returned" to their Jewish roots from the secular world. Most of them are Americans, post-Vietnam dropouts from colleges, universities, and the counterculture. Many had searched for spiritual fulfillment and had tried a variety of religions. Some, on their way to Indian ashrams, had stopped off in Jerusalem for a look at the Western Wall.

This activity parallels the phenomenal growth in Israel of *baalei teshuva* yeshivas, which began springing up after the Six Day War of 1967. Today one can see rabbis from these yeshivas "fishing" at the Wall, offering young backpackers a meal, a place to sleep, and the challenge of a lesson in Torah. Thousands have taken up the offer, and hundreds have stayed on to become full-time yeshiva students.

"Generally these people are very bright," says Rabbi Lifschitz. "They've been to the finest universities. But in the rigors of yeshiva life they find something they've never experienced at Harvard or Columbia.

"People from the secular world have fragmented values resulting in an ill-defined self. When they're swept up in the yeshiva system, which envelops the entire emotional, intellectual, and social spheres of life, they become overwhelmed. Without an integrated personality to begin with, they lose their natural reaction—even their common sense. At least 10 to 15 percent develop troublesome dreams and fantasies. In an effort to measure up, they often become compulsive or physically and mentally blocked. That's how they are when they come to see me."

In addition, Rabbi Lifschitz points out, many of the yeshivas engage in *musar*, originally solely a discussion of ethical texts but now a kind of encounter session where students confess their failings. "*Musar* can be a deadly, dangerous thing," he says, "especially when conducted in a crude and amateurish way and applied to confused and self-doubting youngsters. Similar things are done by this Reverend Moon and by other fad religions. It can be terribly damaging."

Like other yeshivas that developed over the centuries, the *baalei teshuva* yeshiva is a unique academy of Jewish studies. Sometimes called the "Original Free School," it shares certain characteristics with open experimental classrooms. Students prepare for a weekly lecture by the head rabbi, generally studying in pairs, to be able to engage in Socratic exchanges. Research is done in the yeshiva's Talmudic library. Student pairs study in a central hall with others, learning at their own rates and levels; the levels are never fixed. There are no examinations or grades. The term of study is open-ended; there is no graduation date. Studies can go on for a lifetime.

All of this suggests a cheerful informality. Indeed, when one looks into a yeshiva study hall, the impression is one of academic anarchy. Students declaim at the tops of their voices; people come and go; no pedagogue commands the situation from behind a desk. Competition is keen, for each student is driven to perform well at his rabbi's lecture. Everyone studies at least eight hours a day, attends special classes in Judaic law and ritual, prepares for the Sabbath and holidays, and participates in thrice-daily prayer services. Newcomers also study Hebrew. For someone new to such a regimen, pressures can build up.

Sid is twenty-eight, a graduate of the University of Chicago and Harvard Law School. He passed the bar examination in Massachusetts, but instead of going into practice he decided "to see a bit of the world."

"The fact is, I was spiritually undernourished," Sid says. "I wanted to take on the world as my supermarket. I was passing through Israel and there was this sign in a bus station: IF YOU'VE BEEN TO ISRAEL AND HAVEN'T BEEN TO A YESHIVA, YOU HAVEN'T BEEN TO ISRAEL. So, okay, I asked around, and there I was in a yeshiva in the Old City of Jerusalem. I was getting into Hebrew lessons, Bible, Talmud, ritual—it was the most exciting educational experience of my life. And at the end of three months I felt I was the most ignorant man on earth. I wanted to go on learning—and living—but didn't know if I could. I think I started to crack up. Fortunately, some of the students steered me to Rabbi Lifschitz."

The rabbi says Sid's case is not uncommon. "These people come from an environment which is poisoned. Let's face it, the secular world is sick—and I mean both the worlds of Western materialism and the soulless socialist states. Sidney's exposure to the yeshiva made him realize how empty his secular world had been. But if he had never gone there, he would have found out sooner or later. Because he's bright, he would have become one of those big attorneys in the United States, successful to all appearances, yet burning up inside at middle age with the knowledge that his life was lacking something essential."

The rabbi's remark about socialist states was not offhand, for he tends to rail against the "artificially imposed egalitarianism" of Eastern Europe as much as he does about the "decadence of opulence" of the West. He speaks from experience because he deals with a good many immigrants from the Soviet Union. One of them is Miron, who is thirty, married, with one son. Miron came to Israel from Kiev in 1972, learned Hebrew, and adjusted well enough to resume his career as a high school science teacher.

"I couldn't have been happier," he told me. "Working in my profession and being exposed to the religious life-style I'd always been denied. Of course I felt inadequate in the latter respect, so I started studying. Finally I took a semester off and entered a yeshiva. Then—the *musar*. The constant self-examination. We were talking about things like our imperfections. Hell and damnation. Even the principles of science were under attack. Things started to go to pieces. My wife was saying she wished we'd stayed in Russia. Rabbi Lifschitz saved me, my marriage, everything."

John Morgenstern, an American working on an M.A. in clinical psychology at the Hebrew University and one of Rabbi Lifschitz's assistant counselors, describes his methods in this way:

"The rabbi has a visitor fill out a registration form, write a bit of autobiography, and do a drawing. The person doesn't know it, but he's taking a test. The rabbi is an expert graphologist." Morgenstern pauses. "I know Americans usually think graphology is akin to palmistry. But it's much more respected in the French academic tradition, where the rabbi was trained.

"The same with the drawing. The rabbi can look at the kind of tree a person makes and tell a great deal about him. There's no magic involved. This is a simple projective test, like a Rorschach, but much more individualized and therefore more precise.

"Well, maybe this is where magic does come in. The rabbi has astounding intuitive powers. After an in-depth, no-nonsense interview he wins the cooperation of 90 percent of his patients in the first visit. Any therapist will tell you that's an amazing accomplishment. From then on the rabbi can generally tell rather quickly what a person's problem is and what he should do."

The propensity for telling people what to do is one of the two points I heard raised against the rabbi. (The other came from a Hasidic Jew who asked, "What does he need all that *goyishe* Piaget stuff for?") The fact is that Chaim Lifschitz is an authoritarian, though benevolent, figure, and he does press for results. And, not surprisingly, many who come to him do want to be told what to do.

"The problem with most of these people," the rabbi says, "is that they are extremely bright. Such intellectuals tend to be terribly sensitive, which means they simply may see and feel too much." Morgenstern mentions a name and the rabbi smiles. "A perfect example. This young man had done nothing but study all his life. When he started having problems, I suggested he go to work on a kibbutz for a while to get a feel of the concrete world. So they had him sorting apples—you know, by color, size, and so on. Simple work. And at first he couldn't do it! He would pick up an apple and contemplate it: 'In this respect it's Quality A, but in that respect it's B, although the bruise argues for C,' and so on. He intellectualized himself out of making a simple decision. But he was forced to; the apples were piling up on the conveyor. The experience did him good."

Rabbi Lifschitz believes that the problems of the very bright have been too long ignored. He is planning an educational village for boys that will combine a superelite academy of Jewish studies ("the Eton of the yeshiva world," he says), a research center, workshops, an arts project, a publishing house (he is currently working on no less than ten books, three of which—on parenthood, philosophy, and existential interpretations of the weekly Torah portions—have already been published) and a retreat hotel for frazzled intellectuals. How does he handle all this? His *minyan*, counseling, writing, and teaching all take place in two adjoining apartments in Jerusalem. He has numerous assistants and a serene wife. "Otherwise," said an observer, "how he manages everything is beyond me."

His concept took a long step toward realization last spring when a secular Israeli industrialist donated a thirty-five-acre tract on a hill overlooking the Vale of Elah—where David and Goliath clashed—eighteen miles west of Jerusalem. Called Beitaynu (Our Home), the place already has an infrastructure and several buildings, and the rabbi is bubbling with plans.

"The students will be housed with their teachers' families and will have the full psychological nurture such prodigies require; also the good, healthy atmosphere of a rural village; and the stimulation of constant visitors, the best minds in Jewish scholarship, social sciences, education. We hope that our seminars and symposia will bring together the right kind of people, so that we can stimulate more attention around the world to the educational and psychological needs of the gifted. Ours is a Jewish framework, of course, but we're hardly parochial in our efforts to deal with what is, after all, a universal problem," he says.

"Society has finally become alert to the needs of the retarded and the mentally ill. But it's only starting to wake up to the problems of intellectuals. Psychology is geared to the normative, with a good deal of work on the abnormal. But what of the supernormal? These people—often sensitive, talented, and lost—must not be neglected."

He sighs. "I've seen so many of them, intelligent, eager, and in conflict. What a waste when the gifted can't use their gifts! What a tragedy when an inquiring mind can't distinguish the values in the bombardment of ideas it's subjected to! We simply try to help a person see what his needs are and the values he's lacking to fulfill those needs. We do this by using some of the keys to the development of intelligence which Piaget discovered—and he was very interested in the development of moral judgment—and the development of Jewish philosophy over the ages.

"Now, I'm neither a psychiatrist nor a missionary. But if I can help a mind integrate itself into finding its own direction—well, we simply can't afford tragedies like the Horowitz sisters, or the daily breakdowns and disintegrations of our bright young people. Society throughout the world desperately needs every bright person it can get—whole, healthy, and alive."

—M.N.

 ## "With a Tallis I Can Die"

"How in the world do you expect to make contact with the Orthodox community in Russia?" asked the New York rabbi to whom I had come for advice. "You don't look Jewish, you don't act Jewish, you don't talk Jewish—and, besides, you're a woman. For that reason alone Orthodox men won't have anything to do with you." I agreed it was probably hopeless. Then the rabbi had an idea. "Take some *talleisim,* the shawls Jews wear when they pray; they are priceless in Russia.

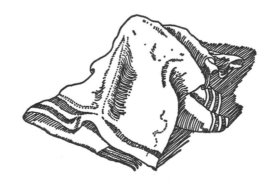

Present them to the rabbis in the synagogues. They will probably have a few words with you then."

Three days later I landed at Moscow's Unukovo Airport carrying a parcel that greatly puzzled a customs official. *"Komu eto nuzhno?* Who needs that?" he asked, fingering a dozen identical black and white woolen shawls. "I do!" I answered, hugging myself and shivering. "I'm cold-blooded. What miserable weather in Moscow!" He concurred about the weather; it was fifteen degrees below zero. I got through with my shawls.

During the next six weeks I left the *talleisim* locked in a suitcase in my hotel room while I went about other business. I had come to Russia to write a series of articles on various religious faiths. Knowing the susceptibility of Soviet officials on the Jewish question, I decided to start with Christians. I reasoned that if I were to tangle with the authorities, it would be best to do so toward the end of my assignment.

Then one Saturday morning I attended the first Jewish Orthodox service of my life in one of Moscow's two synagogues. This was a small, ramshackle wooden structure in the center of a muddy courtyard. I climbed upstairs at once to the gallery, where women are kept separated from men by ritual law. Here some twenty middle-aged and elderly women crowded around me; when I told them I was an American Jew, they squeezed and petted me. My ignorance of Yiddish did not bother them a bit. "Our young people don't know it either," said one, stroking my hair. They questioned me in Russian. By chance did I know their relatives in Brooklyn, in the Bronx, in Chicago? Anyway, would I get in touch with them and tell them they were alive and safe? Was there as much anti-Semitism in America as in Russia? Would there be war? Had Dulles been a Jew? My astonishment at this last question was matched by their disappointment at my answer. How they had trusted in him! Some form of the word "Dulles," it seemed, means "poverty" in Yiddish. When they asked for confirmation of Eisenhower's, Rockefeller's, and Harriman's Jewishness, I did not have the heart to deny it. They had personal questions for me too. What did my father do? Where was I staying in Moscow? Was I married? My reply to this last question provoked a chorus of horrified *"Oi!* And why not?"

Downstairs in the men's part of the synagogue the atmosphere was not nearly so heartening. A score of bearded, weary-looking old men sat huddled in their overcoats. A few wore tattered remnants of *talleisim.* Some were reading from oilcloth-bound prayerbooks that, I later noted, dated from the last century. Instead of the traditional black yarmulkas, they wore scruffy fur hats or brightly patterned Central Asian skullcaps that cost only a few rubles at any Moscow department store. They sat on wooden benches, swaying in prayer.

After the service I made my way downstairs. Here I was greeted with looks of unconcealed hostility. As a woman I knew I was not welcome in the synagogue proper. As a plainly identifiable foreigner I evidently spelled trouble for the congregation. Nevertheless I approached the rabbi, who was rocking back and forth in his pulpit under a bare light bulb. "What do you want?" he asked loudly. I said that I wanted nothing. I was a Jewish woman from New York who had brought him a present, a *tallis.* I held the package out to him. "If you are a Jewish woman from New York, you should know that you cannot carry packages on the Sabbath. Besides," his voice rose to a shout, "we want for nothing in the Soviet Union. We have everything we need. Everything, you understand, everything!"

I retreated, appalled by this demonstration of fear. Then the rabbi called me back, softly now. "Since you have brought me a *tallis,* it would be absurd to take it away," he reasoned with fine Talmudic logic. "Please put it on the bench beside you and leave us alone."

Early in the evening of the same Sabbath I sat at my dressing table in my hotel room, putting polish on my fingernails. Thoroughly unsettled by the morning's events, I was concentrating on the evening ahead: a dinner party and dance at the British embassy. A knock on the door roused me from these diversions, I hobbled to the door in my short sheath skirt, waving my hands to dry my nails.

On the threshold stood a tiny bearded old man wearing an ankle-length brown leather coat. From under his outsize black felt hat flowed luxuriant white earlocks. Standing waist high to me in my spike heels, this astonishing person addressed me in a torrent of Yiddish. I caught one word: *tallis*. Some of my women friends in the synagogue had evidently told him where I was staying, and he had come to plead for one of the shawls in which Orthodox Jews have for centuries wrapped themselves at the time of prayer and at the time of death. For this he had braved the cordon of militiamen and secret police around my Intourist hotel, and had allowed himself to be observed by one of the floor matrons who take note of all comings and goings. And he was fated to leave the hotel empty-handed. I could not risk his being searched at the door; we might both be arrested for black-marketeering in religious articles. How would I be able to prove I had not sold him a shawl?

Yet there was nothing to do but invite the old man in. He refused to take off his coat and hat, but when I offered him some scotch he poured himself a glass and drank it in one shot, like vodka, the sweat coursing down the creases of his face. His eyes were lowered as he repeated, in Russian, his request for a *tallis*. In answer I pointed to the ventilator in the ceiling, where I suspected a bugging apparatus might be concealed, and then cupped my hands over my ears.

"Are you telling me this place is full of spies?" he yelled. "Don't you suppose I know all about it? What can they do to me? I'm seventy-four years old. I'm retired; I've no job to be fired from. My whole family was killed by the Germans. With a *tallis* I can die." I fetched a piece of paper on which I fixed a rendezvous with him elsewhere. He would have a shawl, I wrote.

Content with this promise, the old man wanted to chat. He told me that his granddaughter would have been about my age now had she lived. Wouldn't I like to come home with him and have a nice Jewish dinner? Gefilte fish and *tsimmes*? This very night even! I refused gently, sorrowfully, whispering that we would undoubtedly be followed. And, indeed, some people were already taking an interest in our encounter. During the next half hour certain members of the hotel staff, unbidden and without knocking, entered my room with master keys. The maid exchanged one set of clean towels for another; the waiter made the same maneuver with glasses; the bellboy brought me a copy of *Evening Moscow;* the plumber, to whom I had vainly appealed for two days, appeared with a plunger and began draining the bathtub in long, sickening gurgitations.

At last he rose and gave me a warm, reassuring smile and a not so reassuring farewell: "Don't worry, little lady," he said, "I'll come back."

He came—and so did, at my reckoning, ten others, all on the same mission. Some missed me. In the evenings when I returned to the hotel after dinner, the floor matron would often greet me with a deadpan, "Another Jew was here to see you tonight." All those I met got their *talleisim* in one way or another and then dropped out of sight. Only my first visitor was faithful. He appeared again and again at my door, usually around midnight, with gifts: a small jar of chicken fat, a bag of sugar-coated cranberries, a can of herring, and, during Passover, great boxes of hard-to-get matzos that I kept, uneaten, on the top shelf of my closet. "Why are you so thin?" he would scold. "Eat! Does your mother realize that you're running around all over the world by yourself, not eating enough to keep a nightingale alive?"

Friends by now, the old man and I grew philosophical about our troubles. He had been questioned by the police and then released. As for me, after his first visit I had been continually tailed by plainclothesmen in cars and on foot. Moreover, the authorities were being unusually uncooperative about granting me permission to travel or to visit places not on the Moscow tourist circuit.

"Nu," mused the old man, "so maybe you've entered the Pale?"

On my last night in Russia the old man came to say good-bye, carrying a package somewhat larger than usual. He unwrapped it and presented me with a pair of enormous gray felt carpet slippers. "Here," he said, "when you return to New York marry a nice Jewish boy. Make a good home for him. These slippers will be more comfortable in the kitchen than those," and he pointed at a pile of high-heeled shoes I had been packing.

I leaned over and hugged him. "*Moya dochka*, my daughter," he whispered, "I shall miss you." I felt the whole of his frail little person sobbing against me. "But I'll come back to Russia soon," I said consolingly. "You'll see, we'll meet again."

He broke from my embrace and, throwing his head back, uttered a single aching wail. "No! No!" he shouted. Then for a moment my gentle gnome loomed before me like a formidable patriarch. "Give me your father's address," he commanded. I obeyed. "I shall write your father and tell him to forbid you to return to Russia." He strode to the door. "*Shalom aleichem*, peace be with you," he said, and without a backward look let himself out.

—P.B.

 ## A Sefer Torah Bequeathed to a Nurse in Nebraska Is Now in Use in Tiny Pennsylvania Congregation

Somewhere in inaccessible corners of Europe—in caves, private homes, and other hiding places—there are still to this day Scrolls of the Law, Sifrei Torah, that date back to the Nazi era of plunder and destruction. Some were carted off by the Nazis themselves, who planned to organize a museum of Judaica in which they would display "relics of the dead Jews." In London there is a cache of hundreds of recovered scrolls, many of them damaged, which were found after the war ended and are gradually being repaired and put to use again.

When people attend services, rising in tribute to the Torah when the scrolls are paraded around the synagogue prior to and immediately after the weekly reading of the Torah portion, seldom do they think of the origins or history of each Torah. In many cases the history of the scrolls found in most American synagogues is probably not terribly dramatic; but that is not true in all cases.

There is, for example, a Torah that was sequestered for some four decades in the heart of the Soviet Union, soon after the rise of the communist regime, and was not put to use for fear it would be destroyed, and which only very recently made its way out of Russia, via a still secret route, and wound up in a synagogue in New York, where it is today used on all suitable occasions.

Then there is the Torah in the southwestern part of the United States that a noted scholar has declared originated in China several hundred years ago and somehow made its way across the seas to a new, safe haven in America.

There is a deeply ingrained awe, respect, and love for the Sefer Torah among all Jews, religious or not, knowledgeable or otherwise. It contains, after all, the Five Books of Moses, the Pentateuch, the very foundation of Judaism, and was composed by a *sofer* (scribe) who copied it from an older version, letter by painstaking letter, omitting all vowels, all punctuation, and doing so in strict accordance with certain definite rules and regulations.

And when a young man or woman is called to the Torah for a bar mitzvah or bat mitzvah; or when a young man is honored at the Torah at the *aufruf* prior to his wedding; or when a father names his child; or, *l'havdil*, when a memorial prayer is recited at the morning service on the *yahrzeit* of a beloved parent, it is always at the Torah, reverently, lovingly, even mystically.

All of which leads up to a most unusual story about a particular Sefer Torah that probably could happen only in America.

Some years ago a recently married young couple moved into a small town in Pennsylvania. The husband, a liberal, progressive kind of person, had purchased the town's local weekly and was gradually transforming it from a rather staid, reactionary publication into an exciting paper with a far more liberal slant.

As every small-town publisher knows, his biggest advertising accounts are the local merchants, and in that particular town there was a group of a dozen or so Jewish families who owned large- and medium-size retail stores. The Gentile publisher and the Jewish storekeepers became friendly.

Once, in a relaxed moment, one of the storekeepers mentioned to the newcomer that the Jews would like to celebrate Rosh Hashanah and Yom Kippur properly but did not have a Sefer Torah. At which point the young publisher grinned and said, "Your problem is solved. I'll give you mine."

Naturally the retailer scoffed. Where would this non-Jewish young man have access to a Sefer Torah? Did he even know what it was?

The publisher, noticing the reaction of the Jew, smiled and said he realized that his offer must seem strange, and therefore insisted that they proceed at once to his home to see the Scroll of the Law. No sooner said than done.

When they reached the publisher's home, his wife greeted them. The reason for the visit was explained, and the skepticism of the visitor was understood. While her husband went to the attic to retrieve the Torah, the publisher's wife told the retailer how it all came about.

"I am Jewish, although my husband is not, as you know. I am a registered nurse and before we came here to Pennsylvania I worked in a hospital in Lincoln, Nebraska. There was a Jewish patient, an old, gentle, sweet man, and, as I learned after a while, a deeply religious man. The entire hospital staff came to love him for his kind and gentle ways. A very short time before he died he called me to his bedside and said, 'Before I go away, I want you to have something, a memento of my thanks for your taking such good care of me.' That gift was a Sefer Torah, one that he, a trained *sofer*, had spent years of labor on and that he hoped to bring personally to Israel.

"He asked me to name my first child for him; his name was Baruch. Now, if you will use the Torah in your little congregation here, at least I will be able to rest easily, knowing that the scroll has at last found a suitable home. I will be able to bring my children with me to services and point out the Torah that I helped bring to your synagogue."

From the young woman's brown eyes tears flowed, and a small smile played on her lips.

That Sefer Torah, lovingly created by a devout scribe, handed to a Jewish nurse married to a Gentile, transported across the country to a small town in Pennsylvania, is today in full use in a tiny congregation, all of whose members know the origins of the Torah that they unfurl and read with great care and love on every suitable occasion.

Who knows? Perhaps some day that Torah may, in accordance with the wishes of the scribe, wend its way to Israel after all.

—D.C.G.

 ## Study Torah—and Get Free Karate Lesson

Concern for the problems of juvenile delinquency, drug abuse, and alcoholism found among immigrant populations in northern Israeli development towns has spurred one rabbi to action.

He is Rabbi Yitzchak David Grossman, a fifth-generation Israeli who left his native Jerusalem seven years ago to assume the position of chief rabbi in Migdal Haemek, a town with a population of over fifteen thousand people, mostly immigrants from Romania, Russia, and North African countries.

In 1972 Grossman, his wife and children, and thirty other rabbinical couples from Jerusalem and Bnai Brak, a religious suburb of Tel Aviv, relocated to Migdal Haemek, in the lower Galilee, in an effort to bring its citizens closer to traditional Judaism.

"Just because Migdal is many miles from Jerusalem, the Western Wall, and the center of Judaism does not mean that Judaism cannot thrive there," Grossman explained. "There is no shortage of rabbis in Jerusalem, so we decided that our services could be best used in a town such as Migdal Haemek."

Affectionately called "Israel's disco rabbi" by many Migdal Haemek residents, Grossman's concern for the town's troubled youth has prompted him to frequent local bars, cafes, and discotheques, where he talks to teenagers and tries to encourage them to study Torah.

Initially, according to Grossman, the residents of Migdal Haemek were puzzled by his unconventional methods of appealing to youngsters. His long beard, curly *peot* (sidelocks), and black Hassidic garb evoked suspicion. Eventually Grossman's sincerity and devotion to Judaism succeeded in dispelling these apprehensions; teenagers began to flock to his classes at Migdal Ohr, a local yeshiva founded by him.

Grossman's efforts to help the young residents of this development town, many of whom come from broken and destitute homes, yielded much success. Hundreds began attending his afternoon Torah classes, held in individual homes throughout the town, while others enrolled in Migdal Ohr.

"My goal is to instill a love of *Yiddishkeit* into these troubled youngsters," Grossman explained. "I would like to replace their dependence on drugs and alcohol with a love for Judaism and all it offers."

Presently more than two hundred youngsters attend elementary and secondary school classes at Migdal Ohr. There are limited dormitory facilities and the rabbi is constantly engaged in fund-raising projects to enable additional students to attend his yeshiva.

Grossman's work with troubled youngsters in Israel's development towns has earned widespread acclaim throughout Israel and the United States. Since his arrival in Migdal Haemek, the rabbi has expanded his activities for youth to other development towns, including Maalot, Kiryat Shemona, Bet Shean and, most recently, Jaffa.

The rabbi revealed how he recruited a group of tough teenagers from Jaffa to join his study group. Anxious to find out who was the leader of the local gang of teenagers, Grossman spoke to the young people in Jaffa in the streets. He was informed that Yosef, a local karate instructor, was "boss." Grossman met with Yosef and asked for his cooperation to encourage the local youth to join the community center and study Torah.

As Grossman recalled, "I said to Yosef that until now he was taking care of the physical health of the youth in Jaffa. 'Now I want to do something for their spiritual welfare.'"

After several hours of serious discussion with the rabbi, Yosef agreed to move his karate classes from the street to the local community center. The rabbi announced that all those who register for his Torah classes would receive free karate training from Yosef.

Grossman's plan met with overwhelming success and the Jaffa youth began registering en masse for the combination Torah-karate classes.

—A.Mi.

XIV

Some Points of Interest
Around the World

The Secret Jews of Iran

Although the spotlight of world events remains fixed on the Middle East, the focus has sometimes shifted away from Iran, an ancient land where Jews lived for more than two thousand years and where the overthrow of the Shah and the coming to power of the Ayatollah Khomeini created great concern for the Jewish community there. Of the estimated sixty thousand Jews living in Iran in 1977, some twenty thousand are believed to have managed to leave; the fate of the remaining forty thousand Jews is not really known, inasmuch as the press is sharply censored.

One does not have to be a great seer to imagine what life must be like for the Jews of Iran today when one remembers that Iran severed all relations with Israel, cut the vital supply of oil to the Jewish State, turned over the former Israel mission building to the PLO, and openly proclaimed its undying support for Arafat and his gang.

Prior to the Shah's flight from Iran, there had been an overall impression that life for the Jews of Iran had been reasonably good for more than two millennia. But now the noted historian Reuven Kashani has thrown light on a virtually unknown chapter in the history of that ancient community.

The term Marranos, or secret Jews, has come to be fairly well known. It refers, of course, to those Jews in Spain and Portugal—and, to some extent, their descendants—who chose to remain in those countries at the time of the Inquisition in the late fifteenth century, proclaiming themselves Catholics but living secretly as Jews until such time as they could practice their faith openly and in freedom. According to Kashani, a similar situation overtook the Jews of Iran, only this time it was the fanatic Shi'ite sect of the Moslems that declared war on Judaism and demanded conversion to Islam or death. In the city of Meshed thousands converted to Islam, fearing the worst, but maintained their links to Judaism and the Jewish people in secret.

The Shi'ites consider the city of Meshed a holy city and forbade the Jews to live there for many centuries. In the early part of the eighteenth century the city was captured by the Shah Nadar, who made it his capital and drove out the Turks. He revoked all previous decrees banning Jews and bade them welcome. There is a story among the Persian Jews that the Shah, after hearing statements by Christian, Moslem, and Jewish religious leaders about their respective holy texts, announced that the Jewish Bible was truly the "Book of God" since it begins with the Creation. During his reign the Jews prospered, constructing synagogues where the community enjoyed a full Jewish life.

By 1839, however, after the Shah's demise, the Shi'ite fanatics continued their interrupted attacks on the Jews, concentrating their efforts in the sacred city of Meshed. In that same year they denounced the Jews, claiming that they used human blood for the production of Passover matzos. The mobs in the city became incensed, thirty-two Jews were murdered, and looting of all the Jewish homes followed. The Shi'ites then offered the Jews a choice: conversion to Islam or a cruel death.

Some four hundred Jews in Meshed agreed to become Moslems, but virtually all of them resolved simultaneously to maintain their Jewish identity in secret. When they would enter the mosque, they would utter Hebrew prayers silently;

surreptitiously they would face Jerusalem, as in the Jewish tradition. Although the children of these secret Jews bore Moslem names, they also were secretly given Hebrew names.

One of the children of the Iranian secret Jews who immigrated to Israel and was able to practice the tenets of Judaism freely recalled that his father would, from time to time, take him into a secret room in their home and say, "Know, my son, that we are Jews and we worship the God of Israel. Now, be careful, reveal this to no Persian—because if it becomes known that we observe the *mitzvot* of our people, we will be killed." Occasionally, the same Iranian recalled, he would accompany his father to the same secret room where he was taught Hebrew and the Torah.

The secret Jews of Meshed lived in constant terror. Every time they celebrated a Jewish holiday or observed a rite or ritual they feared for their lives. The Moslem holy men would keep a keen eye on these "new Moslems" to ascertain that they were not "backsliding." The Meshed Jews, ostensibly Moslems, concocted all kinds of schemes in order to be able to carry out a Jewish circumcision, a wedding, or to obtain kosher food.

On the High Holy Days services were conducted stealthily in cellars and secret rooms. No shofar was sounded for fear it would give them away. They fasted on Yom Kippur, recited the blessings on Lulav and Etrog on Sukkot, kindled the Hanukkah lights, read the Purim Megillah. Passover was a special challenge, but somehow the Jews managed. They began to store matza weeks in advance and continued to buy bread, which they either gave to the Moslem poor or kept until after the holiday.

Many of the Meshed Jews eventually escaped from that city and in most cases immediately resumed their lives as free and open Jews. A large number of them reached Palestine at the beginning of this century and established their own synagogues in Jerusalem. Seven years after the establishment of Israel practically all of the Meshed Jews—some three thousand souls—had arrived in Israel and had discarded their secret practices.

One cannot help but wonder if the present community of Iranian Jews may also face the same fate as the Jews of Meshed a century ago, or whether they will manage to leave that unhappy country.

—D.C.G.

 # The Little Tailors' Synagogue

The conversion of old synagogues into movie theaters or "cultural centers" is nothing new in Rumania. This one has emerged as a museum, the site of a brilliant and heartrending exhibit of two thousand years of Jewish history.

It is the Synagogue Mare a Croitorilor, the Great Synagogue of the Little Tailors, in the heart of Vacaresti, the city's once-thriving Jewish quarter. Here, before the Nazi occupation, tailors and tradesmen, butchers and bakers lived and worked, each group with its own special house of worship. There were more than seventy in this one neighborhood.

On Fridays there would be the special bustle of Sabbath preparations: children going home from *heder;* last-minute shopping on Goldfaden Street (named for the great Yiddish playwright); queues of housewives at the local butcher shops, firmly clutching the live chickens that would be slaughtered and cleaned for the evening meal, the feast of the week, which was certain to include (along with fresh *halla,* soup, and meat) *mamaliga,* the golden grains of boiled cornmeal without which no Sabbath repast is complete.

Few Jews remain in Vacaresti, or in any other Rumanian community, for that matter. Of the country's prewar Jewish population of 800,000, almost half were destroyed by Hitler and more than 300,000 have migrated to Israel in the past thirty years. Only 42,000 Jews still live in Rumania. Of that number, 25,000 are past the age of sixty. One kosher butcher shop in Bucharest (directly across the street from the museum) suffices for the local population.

Strong indeed is the will to sustain and memorialize the Jewish presence in Rumania, and the permanent display in the Great Synagogue of the Little Tailors is its most powerful expression. Inspired by a suggestion from Chief Rabbi Moses David Rosen, a volunteer group of Jewish scholars, headed by Professor Alexander Vianu of the history department of Bucharest University, has put together the best organized and most comprehensive exhibit of Jewish history I have seen in all of Europe.

The great central hall of the synagogue has been cleared of the benches and pews. In their stead a series of platforms of varying levels serves as the base for a collection of hundreds of religious artifacts created over the centuries by Jewish craftsmen: silver Torah crowns and *havdala* boxes, Passover plates, circumcision knives, and brass menoras (one in the shape of the Lion of Judah).

Flanking the entrance to the museum are two wooden grave markers (many families were too poor to pay for marble or granite tombstones) that were salvaged from the Sevastopol Street Cemetery, which was destroyed by the German Army in 1941. Along the left- and right-hand walls, from the entrance at the back to the Holy Ark at the front of the synagogue, glass cases arranged in chronological sequence trace the development and decline of Rumanian Jewry from pre-Christian times to the present.

Greek writing established the fact that Jews had settled in the Greek colonies along the Rumanian Black Sea coast as early as the fifth century B.C.E. Here, too, cut into stone blocks are the names of Taemas and Bar Simeon, Jewish centurions who led companies of legionnaires; the latter were professional Jewish soldiers who had been conscripted in Judea after the armies of Rome finally crushed the Jewish kingdom in 73 C.E.

The year was now 106 C.E. and Emperor Trajan was completing his conquest of Dacia (ancient Rumania) and imposing upon the native tribes the language, culture, and even the very name of Rome. His army included, in addition to its core of loyal, battle-scarred Roman soldiers, contingents from all the Mediterranean lands that comprised the Empire: Gauls, Iberians, Greeks, and Jews.

In the next display case are the reports of Benjamin of Tudela, that Jewish Marco Polo of the twelfth century who spent fourteen years traveling throughout the then-known world and gathering information on Jewish life in every country he visited. Benjamin crossed the Carpathian Mountains into the Rumanian province of Wallachia and wrote of Jewish life and customs there.

The third case recounts the exploits of one Isaac Beg, a Jewish physician attached to the royal court of Persia and dispatched by the Shah to the Rumanian prince Stephen the Great of Moldavia in order to negotiate an alliance between Persia and Moldavia against their common enemy, Mohammed II, Sultan of Turkey. The year was 1476, and chronicles of the period document the names of Jews who participated as doctors, intelligence agents (they were skilled linguists), and soldiers in the struggle against Turkish domination—centuries of unending conflict and conspiracy that did not cease until 1877, when Rumania finally expelled the Turks.

At the front of the synagogue, to the left and right of the raised *bima* and the Holy Ark, are the documents, photographs, letters, and insignia marking Jewish participation in the 1876–77 War of Independence and in World War I, justifying the assertion I heard repeatedly from Abram Zilberstayn, curator of the museum, and from other community officials that the Jews have been an integral and involved element in Rumanian life for two millennia. As elsewhere in conquered Europe, the Jew was viewed as an alien creature to be exterminated; and in Rumania the Germans found willing collaborators in the extermination process.

The highlight of the museum—located at the very front of the old Synagogue of the Little Tailors, on the raised *bima* and in front of the Holy Ark—is the grim remembrance of that extermination. The display here is a miniature Yad Vashem, the terrible evidence of the fate of four hundred thousand Rumanian Jews.

Its dominant feature is the lectern upon which the Torah scroll would be placed and opened for the Sabbath reading of the week. Six tall white candles now glow upon the lectern. They are set in black wrought-iron candlesticks whose spiraled, twisted shapes are artistically and emotionally appropriate for the object on the lectern that the candles serve to illuminate.

That object is a shallow, rectangular box encased in black velvet upon which are embroidered the letters R.I.P. (*requiescat in pace*, rest in peace). Inside the box a dozen small bars of yellow soap have been carefully placed. If you look closely you will see that each bar has been stamped with a number cut into the waxy surface—0031, 0172, 0178. A simple message typed on a piece of white cardboard tells the rest: *Reines Jüdisches Fett*—pure Jewish fat. This is the soap with which the thrifty Germans provided their soldiers. The numbers designate the source of the manufacture: 0031, Treblinka; 0172, Birkenau; 0178, Auschwitz.

On the *bima* itself are three showcases filled with the sad artifacts of the years 1940–44: the armbands, the special money issued in the camps, the identity cards, the ration (or, rather, nonration) books. Here, too, are the five thick volumes documenting the major pogroms in Rumania during that period—at Iassi, Bucharest, and other locations.

The women's galleries on the second and third floors of the building carry displays that further amplify the role of the Jew in Rumanian history in the centuries before the Holocaust. They contain the works of such painters as Constantin Daniel Rosenthal, a national hero who died in the 1848 revolution while fighting to liberate his country from the Turks; photographs of the Malbim, the great Talmudic scholar of the nineteenth century; copies of the first newspapers in Yiddish, in *mamaloshen*, the mother tongue, reporting on the migration of "the Walkers," who crossed Europe on foot from Bucharest to Hamburg to escape anti-Semitism at home and sailed to America.

Down the street and around the corner from the Synagogue of the Little Tailors is another kind of museum, a living museum. It is the Teatrul Evreiscu de Stat Bucaresti, the Jewish State Theater of Bucharest. Two years ago the highly professional acting company produced a festival of plays in the Rumanian town of Iassi to commemorate the hundredth anniversary of the creation of the world Jewish theater by Abraham Goldfaden. Among the productions were Goldfaden's own works, Anski's *The Dybbuk*, and Sholom Aleichem's *Tevye the Dairyman*.

As the houselights dimmed and the curtain rose to reveal stage settings of East European *shtetlakh*, and as the men and women of the cast spoke and sang their lines in a fragrant, classical Yiddish, the audience was transported to a world now gone, a world of rueful laughter and tears, of *mamaliga* and *mamaloshen*, the world of their grandparents.

—G.L.

 ## Visiting Spanish Jewry: Site of Past Glories

More than twelve centuries have passed since Tariq Ibn Ziyad and his Moslem army crossed the western straits of the Mediterranean and camped on the cliffs facing North Africa.

This act marked the beginning of seven hundred years of Arab occupation in Spain and one of the most fruitful periods in Semitic history. In the Iberian Peninsula Arabs and Jews reached the zenith of their respective civilizations and enjoyed a golden age of cooperation.

Under the House of Umayyah proud Jews walked the streets of Granada, Cordoba, and Seville, enjoying life, loyal to their religion, in close contact with their Arab neighbors in almost every field.

The age of Maimonides, Ben Labrat, Hanagid, and Even Shoshan was also the period when Arabic poetry, astronomy, and medicine reached unprecedented heights. Under the liberal rule of Abdul Rahman, el-Hakam, and el-Mansour, the royal courts became centers of knowledge.

Arab architecture and ornamental art reached their peak. At the same time Jewish theology, literature, and poetry flowered. Yehuda Halevi wrote his songs of love, while in the tenth century the Jewish "president" Hasdai Ibn Shaprut practiced medicine in Cordoba as a member of the Royal Medical Association.

All this left an imprint that was felt even after Granada fell into Christian hands in the late fifteenth century. It lingers still among the cross-encrusted synagogues, Catholic shrines, and bell towers that grace the ruined Jewish quarters of modern-day Andalusia.

For the visiting Israeli the gateway to Spain is Portugal. In the absence of diplomatic relations with Spain, El Al Israel Airlines has introduced a direct flight to Lisbon, where an international travel company called Melia handles the bulk of Israeli traffic to Andalusia.

Growing numbers of Portuguese pilgrims, farmers, and technicians have begun visiting Israel, taking a warm view of this exchange between "two peoples who have much affection for each other."

A day's bus ride away from Lisbon, Seville is the site of one of the greatest schools of Judaism in the past. Many of Seville's public buildings are in the famous "Mudejar" (Andalusian) style, a blend of Gothic and Renaissance architecture retaining Moslem features. But not a trace remains of the former Jewish quarter. Razed in the fifteenth century and called the Barrio de Santa Cruz today, the area still has a few streets and gates with Jewish names. But no visible signs exist to evoke the city's past greatness as a Jewish center, where Jews were viziers, royal accountants, and high-ranking officials.

The situation is slightly different in Cordoba, a city of 250,000 inhabitants and an easy three hours' drive from Seville. Here, where our forefathers established a

Jewish "capital" long before the Moslem occupation, little of the Jewish quarter remains.

Hasdai Ibn Shaprut practiced medicine here, and thanks to his influence Moshe Ben Hanoch was able to open his famous Beit Midrash, where he and his pupils studied the Talmud in the tenth century. Here also Maimonides wrote his philosophical and medical works.

Entering the Jewish quarter through the Bab el Joz (the "Nut Gate"), the visitor walks through the "lane of the kissing balconies"—so named because the facing houses are so close they almost touch. Breathtakingly beautiful patios, marble fountains, and multicolored geranium pots adorn what remains of this ancient Jewish center.

Of twenty-three synagogues, the ruins of only one survive. A few walls retain Hebrew inscriptions, but, as in other Spanish towns, this Jewish holy place was converted into a church in the fourteenth century and Christian symbols cover most of its walls.

Today the site is a national Spanish monument, as is the adjacent Maimonides Plaza, where there is a bronze statue of the philosopher holding a book in his right hand.

Passing historic markers along the streets, the visitor sees where Jewish poets taught and then comes to the great mosque, completed in 796, with its magnificent tenth-century "mihrab"—one of the most beautiful Moslem monuments in Spain today. Occupied by the Moslems in 717, Cordoba was the city where Islamic culture reached its peak.

Moslem edifices are even more dominant in Granada, which was also a celebrated center of Spanish Jewry. In Granada some old Jewish families claimed descent from the House of David. The eleventh-century leader Shmuel Hanagid lived and worked here until the massacre of 1066 put an end to the Jewish community. Today tour guides point out the former Jewish quarter situated to the north, just across the Darro River. But they dwell more on Alhambra, the fabulous winter palace. Here one testament to Jewish craftsmanship in the Golden Age remains. Mohammed IV had twelve lions set up around the courtyard in his palace. Said to represent the twelve tribes of Israel and to have been the work of a Jewish artist, the lions still stand.

But for the Jewish traveler Toledo is the most melancholic city. Surrounded on three sides by the Tajo River, this city of 55,000 was once called the Jerusalem of Spain because of its ancient walls and high gates, inside which lived a vigorous Jewish community. Here Shmuel Halevi attained so high a position that Peter the Cruel was afraid of him. (In 1360 Toledo's Christian ruler assassinated Halevi.)

Moslem rule in Toledo lasted 154 years, from 932 to 1085. In 1250 the city's main synagogue was burned down, rebuilt, and converted to a Christian shrine. The exquisite white columns of another former temple, renamed Santa Maria la Blanca, impress visitors with their beauty and the way they are dominated by the crosses and bell towers of a later faith.

The nearby Jewish museum arouses similar feelings. Its three small rooms are a sad and silent witness to the glorious heritage of the Jews of Toledo. The museum houses some samples of calligraphic art, ornamented colored Bibles and Torah scrolls, tombstones with Hebrew inscriptions, and a few traditional Spanish-Jewish dresses. This tiny place is the last remnant in Spain of the Iberian Peninsula's magnificent Jewish culture.

—G.W.

Journey to the Kingdom of Morocco

"This is called the Casbah de Juifs—the Fortress of Jews," a ten-year-old boy said, pointing to a huddle of massive rectangular structures built of sun-dried red mud—thirty, forty, even fifty feet high, with infrequent tiny windows. He volunteered to lead us through narrow, labyrinthine alleys to what he called "the Jewish mosque," a building indistinguishable from its neighbors, its padlocked door of rough cedar boards. It might have been a hundred years old, or five hundred.

Our little barefoot guide said that he and his friends had never been inside but they knew that the owner, an Arab merchant, had bought it from the Jews and then kept it, unused, "for good luck."

"There were once hundreds of Jews in this village," he recited in schoolboy French. "It's a pity they all left. They made the best daggers, and they were clever merchants and honest folk. They lived here as long as my people, the Berbers. There was even a Jewish kingdom in this region, but the last Jewish king was killed about a thousand years ago in a war against Moslems and Christians. The Christians converted to Islam, but not the Jews."

The boy did not know we were Jewish. To outsiders armed with cameras and notebooks he offered what he learned from the elders in Amazrou, his village.

Scholars find this oral tradition surprisingly accurate. They have also confirmed the legend of entire Jewish tribes among Berbers, the original inhabitants of Morocco. To this day, Berber tribes carry the names of Jacob, Isaac, and other biblical figures. In Tazrourt, another Berber village, a Muslim warlord's abandoned casbah abuts on the old Jewish quarter.

The family living in the rabbi's house had the key to the synagogue, a room measuring fifteen by twenty feet, with built-in benches all around, the whitewash of the walls giving way to the red adobe underneath. The central *bima* was removed long ago, and the sagging ceiling has developed a gaping hole. The synagogue is empty save for a broken chair, which was probably used for circumcisions, and a carved *aron kodesh* with its treasure gone.

The Jewish cemetery is just outside the village wall. Slabs of granite are sunk in the ground, some with Hebrew inscriptions, some without, often with mortar poured over the sides as anchor. Fragments of marble with still legible Hebrew letters lie next to amethyst and cobalt rocks. "Grave robbers look for money and other valuables Jews and Muslims sometimes bury in a grave," a local authority explained, "but all pious men respect the sanctity of the dead."

Halfway up a slope, cemented to a giant boulder, is a small whitewashed structure. A middle-aged villager in a tattered Arab robe whispered respectfully: "It is the grave of Rabbi Sidna Yakub, a Jewish holy man beloved while alive and responsible for many miracles since his death some two hundred years ago. Many people used to come here on pilgrimages, but since the Jews left few people come, mostly Muslims. Rabbi Yakub helps everybody."

Inside the vaulted building are two tiny rooms, one for the grave, which is covered with a linen cloth (perhaps a *tallit*), and another where pilgrims spend the night.

Meir Hazzan, one of the few Jews in Morocco's deep south, knows people Rabbi Yakub has cured: barren women who bore children and retarded youngsters who caught up with their peers.

Hazzan, in his sixties, trades sheep and cattle. He wears a threadbare *jellaba*, the traditional ankle-length robe of Morocco, and a black skullcap that identifies him as a Jew.

From a distance the villages look like lunar castles. The high walls, often six feet thick, were built to resist raids by nomads from the Sahara and attacks by an army that might have belonged to a neighboring chieftain or to the sultan, who was always on the move, subduing tribes and collecting taxes. The majority of Moroccan Jews originated in these Berber villages flanking the three rivers that flow in the valleys of the Atlas Mountains and vanish in the sands of the Sahara. Each settlement had a Jewish quarter, the *mellah*, sometimes larger than the Muslim square, the *medina*.

With the advent of the French protectorate just before World War I, Jews began a migration to the cities of the north. There was also a trickle of *aliya*. In the early 1950s, Israeli emissaries went to the south, looking for farmers to join *moshavim*. By the time Morocco gained its independence in 1956, some three hundred thousand Jews had left. From the rural south the vast majority went to Israel, but from the cities many thousands immigrated to France, Canada, and the United States. Emigration continued throughout the 1960s. Today twenty thousand Jews are left in the kingdom—the largest Jewish community in the Arab world. In Israel Jews of Moroccan descent number perhaps as many as five hundred thousand and constitute the largest single immigrant group.

In both the north and south Jews thrived as farmers, merchants, warriors, craftsmen, ambassadors, scholars in the Jewish tradition, and advisers to Muslim potentates. Streets and neighborhoods were named after Jews. What is astonishing, and usually unexplained, is the fact that rivers, mountains, and caves are called *Yehudi* (Jew). The Jewish presence is ubiquitous, as if Morocco had been a spiritual turf of Jewry, a surrogate land of Israel.

The greatest rabbi claimed by Morocco was Maimonides, Moses ben Maimon. For seven years he lived in the heart of the old imperial city of Fez in a house facing the Karaouine mosque and university, the most famous medieval center of medical science and Islamic learning.

The guide who led us through the resplendent mosque showed us the house where "the illustrious Moroccan Jewish physician and philosopher Maimonides lived." The twelfth-century structure is no longer in use. But the cedar beams from the Atlas Mountains are still in place and the blue roof tiles of Fez have not lost their gloss.

Our guide, Mohammed Benjelloun, who lives nearby, says, "Don't be misled by the dirt and poverty. There are mansions in every *medina* and *mellah*—marble courtyards, priceless collections of art. And great men in the seclusion of tiny rooms, guarding their secrets."

Benjelloun is a name borne by many Jewish converts to Islam. But our guide knows nothing about that. He says he is "100 percent Muslim."

When a fanatic Almohad sultan gave the Jews the choice between conversion and death, Maimonides declared that it was not necessary to choose martyrdom. He confirmed the ruling—originally made by his father, the rabbinical judge of Cordoba, and later accepted as the law among Jews in Muslim countries—that proclaimed Islam free from the personification of deity and, as such, not idolatrous. He declared that feigned conversion was acceptable and a later return to Judaism possible. He condemned those who condemned converts and stressed the *mitzva* of observing Judaism in secret; in his opinion, even a recitation of the *amida* in Arabic sufficed.

Maimonides concluded, however, that a Jew should not remain in a land of forced conversions. He fled Fez in 1165, as he had fled his birthplace of Cordoba. He went to Jerusalem, then to Cairo, where he became court physician and wrote his *Guide of the Perplexed* and other books, which earned him acclaim as "the light of the East and West, and unique master and marvel of the generation."

Many of the Jews who converted at the time remained Muslim, particularly rich Jews afraid of being dispossessed. Their descendants are identifiable today by names such as El-Cohen. Lineage can never be entirely concealed in a traditional society. Their ranks have included Morocco's elite—theologians, merchants, political leaders, and scholars. Some of them are proud of their Jewish ancestry, and there are families that contract marriages only with other converts.

A unique event in Moroccan Jewish life is the *Hilloula,* an Aramaic word meaning "festivity." It is a celebration at the grave of a great rabbi on the anniversary of his death, or Lag Báomer.

Near the Rif mountain village of Wazzen our group participated in a three-day *Hilloula* for the venerated Rabbi Amram ben Diwan, who had raised funds for the *yishuv* in Palestine in the mid-eighteenth century.

To an Ashkenazi sensibility the *Hilloula* is alien, a rite of Northern Africa: a *simcha* in a graveyard. There is dancing and singing of songs both sacred and popular. To feast and sleep in tents near the rabbi's grave is considered a privilege, a *mitzva.*

The *Hilloula* is a sacred picnic, a communion of the dead and the living, a family holiday, a time for hospitality and generosity, for friendship and courtship.

In Tetuan, a city thirty miles from the Strait of Gibraltar, a Jew with the appearance and manners of an upper-class Spaniard showed us three cemeteries: one for the exiles from Aragon, another for those from Castile (both dating from the sixteenth century), and a third for the descendants of the two groups, which began to intermarry after three generations.

"But in Tetuan, we Spanish Jews never mixed with the indigenous Jews. Never! Moroccan Jews have a different mentality. They are Arabs, Berbers. We are Europeans.

"When the Spaniards came here in the nineteenth century they were astonished to find us speaking classical Castilian. We composed their letters, even their documents. Most of them were illiterate peasants conscripted into a Christian army that took over token parts of this Muslim kingdom.

"The Spanish officials were a miserable, bigoted lot. They thought we Jews had tails. They hated Muslims. They feared and distrusted Jews.

"The French were better *colons.* They established hospitals, roads, administration. But they exploited the country ruthlessly, and when they left they abandoned and betrayed those Moroccans who had helped them, among them some Jews."

In 1951 there were 7,500 Jews in Tetuan; now there are 500. They have three active synagogues, and their *mellah,* built in 1808 in the Spanish style, is the only *mellah* in Morocco still inhabited by Jews.

Tetuan Jews speak Spanish, a mixture of Spanish, Hebrew, and Arabic they call *Hakitia,* and, of course, French. Their melodies are Spanish. They sing of governors cruel or gracious, duennas strict or compassionate, and girls rich, beautiful, and inaccessible.

"I love Tetuan," my dapper friend exclaimed as he pointed at the view from the spacious Jewish community center called the Casino. "People are gentle here, and life has a sweetness I could never find in Europe or Israel.

"But there is no future for Jews here. The young do not want to stay. They find this city and this country confining. So we hold on, grow old, and learn to live without our children and grandchildren. And we pray to the Most High that this benevolent monarchy does not succumb to assassins and agitators.

"All my children live abroad. They come back to visit, and some of them are willing to get married here. I can visit them whenever I want. The authorities know I go to Israel every year; I don't advertise the fact and they don't raise any questions.

"But I will not leave Tetuan. I expect to be buried next to my parents and near my ancestors in that hillside cemetery overlooking the blue mountains."

—C.F.

 ## Jews in the Emerald Isle

Irish Jews, like the Irish generally, just refuse to take themselves too seriously— not even the very real prospect that within two or three decades those who are left will all be in the cemetery, which, with unusual foresight, has enough room for almost every one of them who will want to be buried there.

Already the grass grows high over the gravestones in Limerick's near-forgotten cemetery. Waterford, a place that boasted a Jewish community twice revived, is a gray town without Jews. Cork, despite the year in office just concluded of a flamboyantly Zionist-Revisionist Jewish lord mayor, has fewer than twenty Jewish families and prays—if it can muster a *minyan*—three times a year. Only Dublin in the republic has a Jewish community, despite the proud boastfulness of an office entitled "Chief Rabbinate of Ireland."

There is indeed a chief rabbi, but he is not the first among equals. He is the only resident bearer of rabbinic title. Keeping him in the style that the representative nature of the office calls for is proving an ever more worrisome problem for a community that—such is the nature of the Jew—maintains six synagogues for scarcely more than two thousand Jews. Not that all agree that this is the true number of Jewish souls. Dr. Isaac Cohen, the chief rabbi, hotly disputes a head count conducted by two of the community's most respected lay leaders, a husband-and-wife team by the name of Gerald and Jenny Z. Gilbert. Dr. Cohen prefers a figure nearer three thousand. Even this is less than half the total in the immediate prewar years.

The community will continue to decline. The reasons are familiar to those living in small communities in Britain: emigration for social or economic reasons; the difficulty of finding marriage partners or maintaining Jewish observance in an increasingly less observant society; the claustrophobic feeling experienced by some young people who describe themselves as hemmed in and limited by the lack of professional (and other) opportunities available to them in Dublin. (For most Jews Ireland is Dublin.) Almost every one of last year's graduates has gone or is going. The same thing will happen this year. With some frequency the parents who can afford it follow them or are contemplating a retirement home in Israel.

But none of this should leave the impression of a community already donning shrouds and awaiting the Great Reaper. There is a buzz, a hubbub of activity, although some, admittedly, is contumelious. The notion of Dublin as a metropolitan Jewish community is almost universally sustained. The Irish-Jewish Year Book lists, apart from synagogues, fourteen communal, religious, and educational institutions, eight charitable ones, two professional organizations (clergy-with-teachers and just teachers), seventeen Zionist groups, four friendly societies, nine vaguely classified as "general," and seven youth organizations.

There are communities ten times Dublin's size that don't have half this number of organizations, although closer examination reveals shadowy areas among the claims to substance. Dublin Maccabi, for example, has impressively busy facilities, whether in the expanding clubhouse or out on its playing fields. It also has a kosher restaurant, which chimes nicely with the typically Irish compromise of allowing sports on a Sabbath afternoon provided the main gates are kept closed so that no one can drive in to enjoy them. If some of the rugby team's members appear a little more Celtic than Jewish, then it is just an acknowledgement of one of the facets of Irish-Jewish life. It is less and less self-sustaining.

Much the same is to be found at Edmonstown Golf Club, a magnificent and valuable piece of real estate rolling over some of the most beautiful green acres of the Dublin outskirts. It could not be financially viable without non-Jewish guest players, who are allowed to use its greens and clubhouse (where the catering is "kosher-style"). Here, on a Sunday morning, you will meet many of the lawyers, estate agents, and medical men that Dublin Jewry seems to proliferate and whose chatter is as lively as their capacity for a "drop of the hard stuff" is impressive. In deference to the predominantly traditional ethic of Irish Jewry, the club is closed three days a year, on Rosh Hashana and Yom Kippur, a fact that is proudly advertised in the Irish national press. Should it ever become necessary to dispose of this desirable property, its assets will accrue to the community.

One of the two major Jewish day schools, Zion Schools, had to admit non-Jewish children—about forty in a school of just over one hundred pupils—in order to maintain its Department of Education grant. Plans to combine this school with a private institution, Stratford College, which has an all-Jewish student body, had been discussed off and on for a long time. At very long last a compromise was finally agreed upon, putting both schools under unified control. This, however, does not obscure the fact that a large proportion of Jewish children go to neither Jewish school and receive what Hebrew instruction they do get either through *heder* classes or from private tutors.

Because Dublin is a small community with many interfamilial relationships and associations—in many instances reaching back to the same small area of Lithuania from which the founding fathers of modern Irish Jewry came—"opting out" of Jewish life is neither as easy nor as common as in other big cities of the West. There is indeed a sense of kinship unusual in its intensity—and an equally intense degree of heat when there is a quarrel in the family.

To the outsider there is a curious lack of contact between the Jews of Dublin and the even smaller and physically troubled congregation in the northern capital of Belfast. According to the first and almost certainly the last Jewish lord mayor of Cork, Gerald Goldberg, a keen scholar of Irish-Jewish history, the border which in 1922 separated Irishman from Irishman did far more harm to the Jewish communities of Ireland than to any other group. While it did not separate the northern Roman Catholic from the southern (there is only one hierarchy for the two), nor divide the Protestant Church (which similarly maintains one hierarchy), it did separate the Jewish communities of Northern Ireland from those in the republic.

According to Goldberg, it did more.

It resulted in the introduction of Irish politics as a way of life into the lives of Ireland's Jews. It resulted, also, in Northern Ireland's Jews severing and cutting themselves apart from a united Irish religious and ecclesiastical juris-

diction under an Irish Chief Rabbi. It resulted in their turning outwards from rather than inwards and towards their fellow Irish Jews. It resulted, inevitably, in a retrogression in the religious development of Ireland's Jews as a single, united religious community and, while they are on friendly terms and in communication with each other, there has been no common council, no common educational policy or program, no sharing of communal or religious problems, no attempt to coordinate or rationalize institutions or activities, an incalculable loss to Ireland's Jews and, indeed, to the country at large.

Whether Belfast has lost all that much by being "in communion" with London rather than Dublin is arguable and would undoubtedly be disputed by leaders of Belfast Jewry. What is a fact is that Ireland's most famous Jewish sons came primarily from the south and are more readily associated with the republic than with Northern Ireland. Dublin has to grant that it was from Belfast that Isaac Herzog was brought to be chief rabbi, but it is with Dublin that his sons, Yaacov and Chaim, were associated when they went into the service of Israel, and it was Dublin that, after Jerusalem, stood at the forefront of their father's affection.

The name of Robert Briscoe, too, will always be associated with Dublin, of which he was lord mayor and in whose republican cause he spent almost a lifetime. One of his sons, Ben, is a member of the Irish Parliament, sitting on the Government benches and, like his father, as avowedly proud of his Jewish as of his Irish origins. Another Dublin Jew, Mervyn Taylor (son-in-law of Lord Fisher of Camden) is a senior member of the Dublin County Council and has just served as its chairman for a year. Ben Briscoe is a member of this council, too. The two are on opposite sides of the political spectrum.

In the academic and artistic life of the city Jews are also prominent. Trinity College recently renamed its Museum of Biblical Antiquities in honor of Professor Jacob Weingreen, professor of Hebrew at Trinity for many years, a bulwark of the community and familiar figure to generations of Dublin Jewry. A Jew, Serge Philipson, is director of the National Gallery, Louis Marcus is recognized as Ireland's leading film producer, and Gerald Davis is quickly coming to the front rank of Irish painting. Davis's near-obsession with James Joyce's Ulyssean Jew, Leopold Bloom, figures consistently in his work. Harriet Cooke, the art critic, wrote of him: "Gerald Davis is an Irish Jew, combining the vision of the Celt, the romanticism of Yeats, the wit of Joyce with a sense of fatalism, an irony that can only be Jewish." And Wolf Mankowitz, now living in Ireland, has remarked that "Davis remains, in the amazing light of Ireland, indelibly Jewish . . ."

Which is as good a way as any of summing up this distinctive troubled community, living out its time in the amazing light of Ireland, which has enabled it to flourish, illuminates it even as it contemplates its depletion, yet remains, for all that, incredibly and delightfully Jewish.

—G.P.

 Jews in the Land of the Incas

One of the first English poems I knew, and one I long seemed to enjoy more than many others, was W. J. Turner's "Romance":

When I was but 13 or so
I went into a golden land:
Chimborazo, Cotopaxi
Took me by the hand.
The houses, people, traffic seemed
Thin fading dreams by day:
Chimborazo, Cotopaxi
They had stolen my soul away.

I often wondered why these lines kept bobbing up in my mind until I realized that I myself, though then rather older than thirteen or so, was sometimes straying into golden land, not even too far away from Chimborazo, Cotopaxi, a land I heard about in my childhood because members of the family had immigrated there from our little place in Posen to, well, yes, Peru, the land of the Incas, on the west coast of South America, which to me sounded as legendary as, perhaps, the other side of the moon, which, come to think of it, seemed nearer and more familiar.

In the year 1865, at the age of sixteen, Gustav Badt, a step-brother of my grandmother's, set off for Lima, where he joined an older brother, Michaelis. How they came to choose that far-off city I never knew. Tradition has it that news was received from an enterprising and successful railway constructor of American-German (Jewish?) extraction who told the folks back home in Posen about great opportunities available in Peru. Some no doubt pricked up their ears; some were also attracted by visions of a golden land, the stories current about the gold mines of Hancavelica.

All I know for certain is that my forebears were not then the only Jews to venture overseas. There were scores, in fact, so many that as early as 1854 the *Allgemeine Zeitung des Judentums* reported from Bremen not an emigration but a veritable migration of the peoples (*Völkerwanderung*)—Jews from southern Germany and from Posen especially—and not all were moving for material reasons. The Jewish paper wistfully remarked, "We cannot really say we are sorry to see them go. Unfair discrimination, humiliation, and the denial of solemnly granted civil rights can be given no better answer than—emigration."

Among the forty-odd thousand Jews who left the province of Posen between 1830 and 1870, a small number settled in Peru. Soon afterwards, as a result of the Franco-Prussian War, a handful of fellow Jews arrived from Alsace-Lorraine. By 1872 there were upwards of twenty families plus thirty to forty eligible young men; actually there were a good many more, but they frequently intermarried and so disappeared from Jewish life. Today hardly a trace of them is left; their descendants occasionally emerge as faithful Christians (e.g., Ambassador Berkmeyer, a grandson of Berko Meyer, from Posen).

Though Peru at that time, like other South American republics, enjoyed political liberty to the point of political license, in religious matters the Roman Catholic Church made sure there were no other gods. Any public worship other than Roman Catholicism was forbidden, so when the emigrants from Germany founded, in 1870, the first Peruvian Jewish congregation, the Sociedad de Beneficiencia Israelita—the first of its kind in Latin America—it was a strictly private body. The spiritual head was Moises Moses, from Inowraclav, and the lay leaders were J. Herzberg (president), Michael Badt (vice-president), A. Gosdinsky (secretary), and F. Lowy (treasurer). They built a synagogue in 1874, and the earliest grave in a Lima Jewish cemetery is that of Minna Rosenberg, aged 42, born in Bromberg in 1833.

By profession most of the immigrants were businessmen, especially wool and cotton traders, jewelers, and exporters and importers; also heading for Hancavelica, were geologists and mining engineers. The brothers Sigismund and Eduard Jacoby, while acting as Rothschild's agents, were the first to open a foreign exchange in Lima. Paul Ascher, legal adviser to the Sociedad, established the Commercial Bank of Peru. Though it was some time before Jews were able to acquire Peruvian nationality, the government never failed to demonstrate its goodwill towards aliens and citizens alike.

Gustav Badt seems to have begun his career in business, but apparently only for the purpose of making sufficient money to devote himself to his true interest, which was farming. He bought two estates near (now inside) Lima, which he developed by way of agricultural experiments. He specialized in the breeding of silkworms and the production of raw silk; on his two haciendas he planted fourteen thousand mulberry trees for this purpose. The extent of the enterprise as well as the new methods he introduced soon brought his name to public notice; in fact, this "distinguished German citizen" was recognized as "the first to establish the entirely new industry of sericulture," which was felt to have a bright future in Peru.

Badt enlarged his operations when he joined forces with a native whose more technological mind had devised modern machinery. Financial help by Badt enabled Señor Julio Chocano to order the necessary plant from Europe. When the suitably named La Germanica silk factory was opened in 1907, the much publicized ceremony was attended by Badt's personal friend, the German minister in Lima, Count von Hake.

The new industry, which helped substantially to promote Peru's economy, was seen as a credit to the prominent part played in it by Badt, "one of that liberal-minded band of foreigners who have come to our country not only to gain a livelihood for themselves but above all to make a solid and effective contribution to the nation's moral and material advance."

Don Gustavo, as Badt was called, proved himself, in fact, an ardent patriot in peculiar circumstances. During the War of the Pacific between Chile and Peru, which began in 1879, he raised a special military unit made up of his circle of friends and the laborers he employed. He himself served as captain, setting what one of the Lima papers called "a noble example of civic virtue and love of country which we can only wish would often be emulated." In this war (which Peru lost) the brothers Jacoby practically went bankrupt as a result of the loans they lavished on the government.

Though actively associated with the Sociedad from the start, uncle Gustav never achieved greater congregational distinction than that of burial secretary. He was not much of a *macher*, but he served his adopted country well, and the widely read magazine *El Peru Moderno* had ample cause to declare: "Those who, like Señor Gustavo Badt, have put at the disposal of their second fatherland, Peru, all their labor, their fortune, and the most precious gift of all, a lifetime of devotion, deserve the gratitude of the nation."

—C.C.A.

Jews in China: A Flourishing Community —in the Twelfth Century

The United States's decision to establish formal relations with China has wide potential repercussions for many countries on many different levels: political, military, economic, cultural, social, and scientific. As President Carter correctly noted, China has a population equal to nearly one-fourth of the world's population, and it is certainly logical and sensible to enter into relations with her.

For Jews the new development is of special interest. Of all the large countries in the world, China today is virtually *Judenrein,* this despite the fact that not so long ago—before and during World War II—under the previous government the Japanese occupation forces helped save thousands of Jews by making Shanghai an open city. At one time it had a sizable Jewish population, with thriving synagogues, schools, and organizations, and served as a transit station for Jewish refugees from Nazi Europe and, to a lesser extent, from Communist Russia en route to Israel, the United States, Australia, and other havens.

Actually, there is a longtime connection between China and the Jewish people. In central China, in the province of Honan, there is a town called Kaifeng in which Jews settled in the twelfth century. Most historians believe they came from Persia. They brought with them skills in manufacturing cotton garments, as well as the know-how in dyeing fabric and even printing patterns on cotton fabric. Early records indicate that a synagogue was established in Kaifeng in 1163 and restored in 1279, following a cataclysmic flood. In 1653 the synagogue, which apparently had been badly damaged again, was rebuilt thanks to the efforts of a Jewish mandarin named Chao Ying-ch'en.

From the middle of the seventeenth century until the middle of the nineteenth century the small Jewish community began to shrink in size; commitment to Judaism and knowledge of even the most rudimentary rituals and customs of Jewish life attenuated. The synagogue was permitted to deteriorate and gradually became an abandoned ruin. Sketches show that it was constructed in typically oriental style.

Christian missionaries who journeyed through the interior of China in the 1800s brought back ancient Hebrew books, including an illuminated manuscript of the Book of Esther replete with typically Chinese art. According to genealogical records, the small Jewish community gradually intermarried, adopted Chinese names and customs, and were lost to the Jewish people. At the time of World War II, there were an estimated two hundred descendants of the Jews of Kaifeng.

Imaginative novelists speculated that the Chinese Jews were descendants of the Lost Ten Tribes, but this was never taken seriously. Early travelers to China found documentary evidence that individual Jews had journeyed to China even before the eighth century. One such piece of evidence was a Jewish prayer, inscribed in square Hebrew letters, found on a single sheet of paper, apparently in the possession of an adventurous explorer who had carried the prayer with him.

When Marco Polo made his famous expedition to China toward the end of the thirteenth century, he reported that Jews, Christians, and Moslems were debating the respective advantages of their religions before the Mongol leaders and their aides. A Mongol decree of the fourteenth century specified that equal taxation should be levied on "Jews, Christians, and Moslems." A decade later another decree was issued by the Mongols that outlawed the ancient levirate custom of marriage practiced by Jews and Moslems, which the Chinese described as an abomination. And in the year 1354 another Mongol decree said that all wealthy Jews and Moslems were to serve in the army. The evidence of the existence of a sizable Jewish community in China many centuries ago is thus quite strong.

There have been Jewish residents in Hong Kong for many years, and the vast majority of them are British subjects. One estimate said that in 1937 there were as many as ten thousand Jews in China, most of them in Shanghai, Tientsin, and Harbin. Many of the old-timers who lived in then Japanese-occupied Manchurian cities were refugees who had fled Russia after the 1917 Bolshevik Revolution. A sizable number of Russian-born Jews were forced to return to the Soviet Union at the end of World War II.

After the establishment of the People's Republic of China, Israel announced its recognition of the new Chinese Government in 1950, which resulted in the severing of relations between her and Taiwan. The Chinese Government in Peking at first showed a serious interest in establishing relations with the Jewish State. In 1955 an Israeli delegation, led by David Hacohen, a veteran diplomat, paid a month-long visit to China. The Israelis hoped to establish diplomatic and trade relations with the new government. An invitation to the Chinese to pay a return visit to Israel was extended but was never acted upon. The anti-Israeli Bandung Conference of 1955, comprised of African and Asian leaders, persuaded the Chinese to cut all ties with Israel. By 1956, soon after the Sinai campaign, the Chinese were broadcasting virulent anti-Israeli propaganda, and making their pro-Arab position crystal clear.

After the Six Day War the Chinese established close ties with representatives of the PLO. In 1970 Yasir Arafat paid a formal visit to Peking and was received with full diplomatic honors. During the past decade the anti-American tone of Chinese propaganda has generally included Israel among the "imperialist" states that it saw fit to condemn.

Whether or not the Chinese attitude toward Israel will now change, in view of its radical change of attitude towards the United States, remains to be seen. Israel has always sought to establish friendly relations with China, but it has accepted the reality of the larger number of potential friends that the Chinese viewed in the Arab world as a geopolitical fact of life.

In recent years American tourists have begun to visit China, and among them have been American Jews. To date, none of them have been able to throw any light on the fate of the ancient Jewish community of Kaifeng.

Some years ago an ancient Sefer Torah that had made its way to a synagogue in New Mexico was discovered to be a scroll that had originally been used by the Jews of China. The expert who attested to that fact cited, among other things, the threads that were used to bind together the various parchment sheets. (They were silken threads used only by the Chinese.)

Examples of ancient Chinese Judaica can be seen in the Hebrew Union College in Cincinnati and in the Royal Ontario Museum in Toronto.

Perhaps another miracle will occur and the hand of friendship that Israel extended to China more than a quarter of a century ago will be accepted. Israel could certainly use a new customer of nine hundred million consumers for its exports.

**An Oriental Jewish Mystery:
The Case of the Nagasaki Cemetery**

To Jewish personnel stationed in Japan a Jewish cemetery served as a gateway to Jewish history and an unequaled opportunity to observe the mitzvah of *Kibud Hamet,* reverence for the dead.

As a United States Air Force chaplain I was assigned to Kyushu, the south-ernmost island of Japan. One morning I received a long-distance telephone call from Nagasaki, and the first words I heard were *"Shalom Aleichem."* The caller, a Jewish physician from New York who was studying the effects of atomic radia-tion in Nagasaki, now needed assistance for the *brit milah* of his newly born son. Enroute to the island, which was one hundred miles away, I noticed for the first time Christian churches, monuments, and grave sites. Since Nagasaki was the first Japanese city open to Western traders, one could readily understand the Christian influence, but history also records a Jewish community in Nagasaki. I wondered if there were still Jews in the area. I soon learned that the Jews of Nagasaki left for Tokyo and Kobe forty years ago. A recent search for the synagogue and cemetery proved unsuccessful.

However, I frequently met Jews who were born or raised in Nagasaki but cur-rently resided in Hong Kong, Seoul, Kobe, or Tokyo. Jacob Gotlieb of Kobe, for example, remembered that the Torah and *siddurim* of the Nagasaki synagogue had been returned to the Jewish community of Shanghai. He recalled seeing pages of the Talmud stained with candle drippings. Apparently there were at one time learned Jews on the island. Robert Lurie, who was born in Nagasaki and had recently served as president of the Tokyo Jewish Community Center, recalled that the Jewish merchants used to supply food and coal to visiting ships. But where was the synagogue or cemetery? No one remembered. Even the Japanese officials had no records. All these tidbits of information whetted my curiosity, and I in-tensified my search.

On *Erev Pesach* we achieved our first breakthrough. A doctor in Nagasaki lo-cated a wood-block print of the synagogue and an artist by the name of Ken-tagawa took me to the synagogue site. It was no more! The bombings had leveled the area. A fish store now occupies that location.

I revisited the City Hall cemetery division. All the employees smiled as the *nud-nik* pursued his search. With my Japanese now more fluent, I asked for prewar maps. An old tourist map indicated a Christian cross atop a mountain. "It's a church," they claimed, but who builds a church on a mountaintop? A short taxi ride ended the search. It was a Christian cemetery with a small walled section that

promptly aroused my suspicion. Was this it? Tears came to my eyes as I saw engraved in stone the words *Bait Olam*—"home of eternity." The cemetery was filled with tombstones engraved in Hebrew, English, Russian, and Japanese. Every grave had a headstone and footstone, with the headstone always in Hebrew and the footstone in the vernacular. The cemetery overlooks a granite pillar marking the epicenter of the nuclear blast. The hill protected the graves from heat and blast effects, but since the graves had not been tended for the last fifty years, the cemetery needed immediate care.

The discovery of the cemetery proved the existence of a once flourishing Jewish community on the island of Nagasaki. I subsequently learned that Jews had first arrived there as traders in the ninth century. They also accompanied Portuguese and Dutch merchants in the fifteenth and sixteenth centuries, respectively. After Commodore Perry had opened Japan to the West in 1854, the Jews began to come in more substantial numbers. An active Jewish community dates from the 1880s. By 1904 about a hundred Jewish families lived on the island. The use of Hebrew inscriptions on the tombstones and conformity to traditional *halacha*, for the most part in regard to burial practices, showed that these Jews were quite aware of their heritage. I was informed, moreover, that in the absence of a *mohel* parents would take their children by sea to Shanghai for circumcision, a distance of over five hundred miles. Apparently, despite their isolation the Jews of Nagasaki remained conscious of their way of life and dedicated themselves to its preservation.

News of the cemetery's existence inspired the Jewish soldiers at Kyushu to labor indefatigably in order to put it into proper shape. The men carefully cleaned and scrubbed the stones; pruned, cut, and plowed away the underbrush; and did everything necessary to refurbish the graves of an extinct community. All desired to demonstrate their reverence and give final tribute to this community of the past.

Though the immediate puzzle of the whereabouts of the Jewish community was solved, we were confronted with a series of finds that only increased our puzzlement.

As one entered the cemetery, the largest and most conspicuous tombstone bore the inscription of the life and death of the community's leader, Frederic David Lessner. Born in Rumania, he moved to Istanbul and finally settled in Nagasaki. Having prospered economically and socially, he left as a legacy a bust bearing his likeness, which was mounted atop the gravestone. This strange parallel, namely, the grand style of the Hebrew eulogy inscribed on the gravestone and the graven image atop the stone, which was so contrary to Jewish practice, perplexed everyone. A reading of the inscriptions seemed to imply a highly educated Jewish community, but the presence of a graven image of the departed involved a baffling and incomprehensible deviation from Jewish law.

The next puzzle was even more confounding. While cleaning the cemetery, Morris A. Goldberg, a career naval officer and keen student of Jewish history, wandered about and discovered a totally incredible and cryptic scene. Completely removed from the perimeter of the Jewish graves and surrounded by tall weeds in a remote area was a tombstone inscribed in Hebrew and Russian. Why, we wondered, was this Jew buried outside the Jewish cemetery? After consulting Rabbi Jair Adler of the Tokyo Jewish Community Center, it was decided to move the remains to the Jewish section. However, we soon discovered that the remains were in an eighteen-inch earthenware vase, suggesting cremation, another practice alien to the Jewish people. The stone above the grave (translated by a Japanese professor of Russian) revealed a tale of love, a modern Romeo and Juliet tragedy. The vase contained the remains of a young girl, aged twenty-one, who was plucked away from the side of her beloved when she died of the Black Death. The couple had been betrothed and planned to wed when the plague struck. All this was told in a Russian poem by the young man she loved. Presumably the cremation had been effected to halt the progress of the contagion, but the subsequent burial outside the confines of the Jewish boundary remains a mystery.

—M.T.

 ## The Hidden Synagogue of the Azores

"There are only four Jews left here. Our synagogue is seldom used. Twice a year, on Rosh Hashanah and Yom Kippur, we enter the sanctuary, sit in our designated seats, which once belonged to our fathers, grandfathers and great-grandfathers, and their great-grandfathers before them, and recite our prayers alone."

These were the words of two aged sisters, both in their nineties, garbed in black from head to toe, in the rear of whose dilapidated but sparklingly clean flat I found the hidden synagogue of the Azores.

As a Jewish chaplain in the U. S. Air Force assigned to Westover Air Force Base in Massachusetts, I had been temporarily assigned to the Azores to conduct Rosh Hashanah and Yom Kippur services for the isolated American Jewish military and civilian personnel stationed at the Lajes Air Force Base. This U. S. Air Force outpost is on Terceira, one of the nine Azores islands, a 924-square-mile group in the Atlantic owned by Portugal. An important station on the Atlantic air routes, the Azores, located 875 miles from the coast of Portugal, has had U.S. bases since World War II.

Before I came to the Azores I knew something of its almost forgotten place in Jewish history. Jews had first reached the Azores as refugees from the Portuguese Inquisition in 1497 when the islands were a Dutch possession. When the Portuguese conquered the Azores, the Inquisition followed. In the early 1500s many Portuguese Jews were sent to the Azores as captives and slaves. Over the centuries they established a tenuous community, erected a synagogue at Ponta Delgada (on the island of San Miguel), and opened cemeteries at Ponta Delgada, Horta (on the island of Faial), and at Angra de Heroismo (on Terceira). On the outskirts of Angra there is an ancient port still known as Porto Judaeo, probably because this is where the refugees of 1497 first landed.

By the early 1900s only a handful of practicing Jews remained, together with an unknown number of Marranos. On the eve of World War II visitors to the Azores counted forty Jews on the islands: thirty in Ponta Delgada, four at Horta, and six at Angra. Most of the Jews were in the export business and the old Sephardic families of Portuguese ancestry had become mixed with Jews from Morocco. In 1961 another Jewish Air Force chaplain, Rabbi Paul S. Laderman, who came to conduct Passover services at Lajes Air Force Base, found only two Jews on the island of Terceira, both in their eighties.

When I arrived in 1965, Solomon Levy, the last of these Jewish natives of Terceira, had been dead for two years. The only Jews living on Terceira now were those serving with the U. S. Air Force. The leader of the Jewish community was a civilian, Robert Richman, housing and billeting officer at Lajes Air Force Base, who had been there for a number of years with his wife and three children. Except for Passover and the High Holy Days, when a Jewish chaplain or civilian rabbi was flown in from the United States, Richman conducted Friday evening services.

Between Rosh Hashanah and Yom Kippur I explored the main islands of the Azores. At Ponta Delgada I set out to investigate a report that there was a synagogue in the poorer and oldest section of the city. No one seemed to know about it, nor had anyone actually seen it. The U.S. consul in Ponta Delgada, Perry Hallam, was eager to be of help, but all inquiries proved fruitless. A chance conversation with a Portuguese laborer who had once been the gardener of a Dr. Freedman, a Jewish physician who had since moved to Lisbon, proved to be the key to the mystery. The laborer remembered Dr. Freedman as the only doctor on the Azores who would care for the poor for nominal fees. Other physicians confined their practice to the rich. Mr. Hallam, it turned out, was living in the mansion that had once belonged to Dr. Freedman.

It was this gardener who told me about the Jewish community that had once existed in Ponta Delgada, and about the four remaining Jews on the island. Consul Hallam generously offered me his chauffeur and interpreter and we went in search of the four Jews. We drove to a narrow, cobblestoned street, Rua do Brum, where there were only shabby and ancient-looking houses. At Number 16 we halted and began to climb the stairs of a rickety building.

On the way up we were met by two elderly ladies, dressed entirely in black, who greeted us with a smile and welcomed us cordially. These were two of the surviving Jews, both in their nineties. At first they doubted I was a rabbi, owing to the absence of a beard.

When I asked them where the synagogue was and who its rabbi was, they explained softly that the rabbi on the island was their late father, and that since his death years earlier they had cared for the synagogue. They led me to the rear of their apartment and quietly opened a set of sliding doors.

There before me was a splendid synagogue that dated from the sixteenth century. It was distinctly Spanish in architecture. The Torah scrolls were obviously of museum quality, symbolically wrapped around with *wimples*. I had never seen more clearly written Torahs. The parchment was brown, instead of the customary white, and each letter and every word were works of art. The *Yad, Rimmonin,* and *Keter* had the look of relics and the aura of grandeur.

When I offered to buy some of these appurtenances, the women quickly informed me that they and the synagogue were their last links with Jewish life. Their mere presence gave them a feeling of warmth and inspiration with which they did not wish to part. When I offered to provide transportation for the two ladies and the other two Jews on the island to Lajes so they could join their American co-religionists for Yom Kippur services, they politely declined. They told me Yom Kippur was one of the two days on which all four Jews entered the sanctuary, took their hereditary seats, and prayed in solitary grandeur. Before leaving I gave the ladies a case of kosher wine, a supply of matzoh, and some cans of gefilte fish—part of the supplies furnished me by the Jewish Welfare Board Commission on Jewish Chaplaincy. The gefilte fish puzzled them because they had never seen any before.

As we left the building, the ladies asked if I would like to see the old Jewish cemetery. It was hidden behind brick walls. The tombstones, which were all flat per the old Sephardic custom, included some dating back to the fifteenth century. The synagogue is also said to have been erected in the late sixteenth or early seventeenth century. The most recent grave was that of the father of one of the

Jews from another island, Elias Sebag, who had accompanied us on the tour. He asked me to say a special prayer, and as I recited the *El Moleh Rachamim* for his father and others who were buried in the cemetery, tears rolled down his face. He was close to seventy and had spent most of his life in Portugal, far from a Jewish community.

Before I left the Azores I encouraged the Jewish personnel at Lajes Air Force Base to build a *sukkah*, the first ever erected there. Thus the light of Jewishness shone once again where a long-forgotten and vanished Jewish community once existed.

—B.D.S.

 ## Jews in the Frozen North

Thule is called the "Roof of the World." This northern district of Greenland was discovered by the Danish explorer Knud Rasmussen, who visited the Eskimo tribes many times and lived among the Karnaks for long stretches of time. A few of his native friends still live there, but the whole colony has been relocated at a point about fifty miles away. The seal, the only source of their income, was promptly frightened away by the hustle and roar of the new American Air Force base, which interrupted its peaceful existence.

A trip to the Thule base is almost an expedition in itself. From Greenland's capital, Godthaab, a small ship brought us, after forty-eight hours, to the tiny town of Holsteinsborg, almost crippled by an epidemic. Of the twelve hundred residents, five hundred were sick. We continued our journey on a Danish patrol boat through one of the most beautiful fjords in the world. After another twenty-hour journey we were received by a Danish liaison officer and two American officers. We had reached the base of Søndre Strømfjord and spent the night at the one and only hotel on the largest island in the world.

Thule is a gigantic technical adventure. Encircled by icebergs and under the steady menace of a hostile climate, a modern city arose there, equipped with the latest technical perfections that brave even the Arctic winter blizzards. It has its own radio and television stations.

We had heard that Jewish personnel were assigned to the base and were anxious to find out about their life there, so far away and completely cut off from the rest of the Jewish world. A pleasant surprise awaited us. We were invited to hear a

routine report by the base commander, Colonel Rohr, who laid special emphasis upon the approaching Jewish High Holy Days.

Religious services were announced for Rosh Hashanah and Yom Kippur at the base's joint chapel. Jewish personnel were relieved from duty so that they could participate in these services. Later I was introduced to Lieutenant Maurice Burk, who told me the strange story of his small flock, which had the honor of being the northernmost *minyan* on earth.

One of the interested friends was Captain Robert Holt, theologian and Christian Scientist. His knowledge of Hebrew was excellent and many of the members did not suspect that he belonged to another religion. Chaplain Graydon E. Terbuch, in charge of religious activities at the base, was really the organizing spark in developing Jewish activities. Since his arrival, the bulletin board of the joint chapel bears the inscription "Jewish Services Friday 1900 hours."

After the departure of the Christian Scientist, a Jewish flyer took over for a short time, followed by Lieutenant Burk. Services have been conducted ever since, and the occasional *minyan* had developed into a steady attendance of at least fifteen persons.

Several Gentile guests were invited to Seder services: a few officers, the head of religious activities, and the Danish liaison officer. The Jewish Welfare Board [JWB] shipped Passover supplies, including a traditional dinner of gefilte fish, soup with matzoh balls, matzohs, *chrane,* and *haroset.*

Lieutenant Burk, a lawyer by profession, worked in the Judge Advocate Section of the Air Force but dedicated all his free time to Jewish matters. Born in New Orleans, son of an immigrant from Pinsk, Russia, who was said to be as learned as a rabbi, Burk had a strictly Orthodox education and went to a *Cheder.*

In telling us of Jewish life in Thule, he assured us that the Air Force and the JWB do whatever is possible to make the life of Jewish soldiers more comfortable. As an example, he told us of a twenty-two-year-old boy from New York by the name of Kleinmann who was excused from duty on Saturdays. Then, after Chaplain Terbuch wrote to the JWB, the soldier received kosher food, which was specially flown in for him.

We met a few of the members of the community. There were not two who had the same background or origin. One, a language wizard from Casablanca, spoke Arabic, French, Spanish, Italian, English, and German. Another, a young Sephardic Jew from Istanbul, Turkey, still knew Ladino, the old Spanish-Jewish dialect spoken by his family.

Berlin was represented by a twenty-four-year-old sergeant and radio operator, Louis Helish, an ex-deportee to Theresienstadt. He survived and managed to immigrate to the United States. In 1949 Helish joined the Army and returned to Berlin as an American soldier. He was married by a field rabbi in Berlin to a childhood sweetheart.

Another German Jew had served with the British Army in Palestine and in the Near East and had been seriously wounded. America has become his second home. He is currently employed as a civil engineer building new army bases. Most of the civil employees brave the harsh working conditions because of the high pay, but many try to return home before the cold and dark Arctic night closes in.

The services for Rosh Hashanah took place in the festively decorated chapel. The sermon was delivered by Chaplain Kalman L. Levitan, of the U. S. Air Force, sent for assigned duty. The Jewish chaplain—one of hundreds recruited and served by the JWB Commission on Jewish Chaplaincy—said that sacrifice has within it a potential for individual growth if it is understood and properly applied.

There are fifty-three Jews registered at the base, but sixty-eight attended the services. A few men from several small sites in the vicinity of Thule Air Force Base came in for the holidays.

As I looked over this group—each individual with a different background, bound only by one common factor, their Jewishness—I knew that the same binding and driving forces that have kept the Jewish people together over the centuries were at work in the far North.

—A.J.Fi.

XV
Mishmash:
A Little of This
and a Little of That

A Christian Diplomat Offers
Unique Interpretation of *Kashruth*

The eminent historian Will Durant wrote: "The Jews, . . . without any political structure, without any legal compulsion to social unity, without even a common language—this wonderful people has maintained itself in body and soul, has preserved its racial and cultural integrity, has guarded with jealous love its oldest rituals and traditions . . . has emerged greater than ever before, renowned in every field for the contributions of its geniuses, and triumphantly restored after two thousand years of wandering to its ancient and unforgotten home."

"Rituals and traditions"—an apt description, but not really. To an observant Jew the rituals, customs, traditions, and mores of Jewish religious life are life itself. Judaism is suffused with rules and regulations for every day, secular or holy; for every age, from early childhood to advanced years; for every aspect of the daily routines of life—rules about eating, sleeping, resting, study, work; regulations concerning births, marital relations, bar mitzvahs, weddings, and times of mourning.

The observant Jew feels—and the not-so-observant Jew senses—that by performing all or a major portion of the *mitzvahs,* he is absorbing into his life-style the wisdom, serenity, and fulfillment of some four thousand years of continuous Jewish life—and that in so doing he will come closer to a happier life, a life lived on a higher plane than would otherwise be the case.

These thoughts result from reading a provocative, insightful, and remarkable article on "The Dietary Prohibitions of the Hebrews," written by a former French diplomat, Jean Soler, stationed in Tel Aviv, who decided to probe until he understood with all his being the meaning behind the ancient laws of *kashruth,* of which he had become aware for the first time in his life. (The article appeared in the June 14, 1979, issue of *The New York Review of Books.*)

Soler disdains the oft-used explanations of defenders of *kashruth* that the rules are good for one's health and ensure better hygiene. He takes a totally different approach that leads him to certain fascinating conclusions. "The dietary laws of the Hebrews," he writes, "have been laid down in the Book—a set of writings composed of texts from various eras over a wide span of time . . . They have been sewn together and coexist in the consciousness of a people." The Bible stipulates: "I have given you every plant-yielding seed which is upon the face of all the earth, and every tree with seed in its fruit; you shall have them for your food."

Thus, the eating of meat (as enunciated in Genesis) is excluded. The idyllic Garden of Eden is totally vegetarian. The "major prohibition of the Bible is killing," the author writes. "If man freely uses it for his own ends, he encroaches on God's domain . . . From this it follows that meat eating is impossible. For in order to eat an animal one must first kill it, but animals, like man, belong to the category of beings that have within them a living soul."

A change came about, however, after the Flood; it was, in a sense, a new Creation. A new dietary law was promulgated in Genesis: "Every living thing that lives shall be food for you; as I gave you the green plants, I give you everything." It would thus appear that God has given man the right to include meat in his diet. However, it must be noted that the new law allowing man to eat meat follows an earlier verse that talks of the evil that lurks in man. The permission granted, it would seem, is therefore a grudging, reluctant dispensation.

At this point in biblical history there is still no differentiation between clean and unclean animals. These new rules do not appear until after Moses sets foot on the stage of history.

A covenant between God and the Hebrews has been concluded. God explains that "I have separated you from the peoples. You shall therefore make a distinction between the clean beasts and the unclean, between the unclean bird and the clean." Soler writes that the new distinction of the Hebrews is visible in three signs involving a cut:

> a cut on the male organ, analagous to an offering which in return will bring God's blessing upon the organ that ensures the transmission of life and thereby the survival of the Hebrew people;
>
> a cut in the regular course of the days—one day in seven is set apart so that the sacrificed day will desacralize the others and bring God's blessings on their work;
>
> a cut in the continuum of the created animals, applying to each animal, between flesh and blood, and later to be strengthened by an additional cut within each species decreed to be clean between the first-born, which are God's, and the others.

When the Israelites of the Exodus rebelled against Moses in the wilderness and demanded meat, he relented but stipulated that blood must not be consumed and certain animals were forbidden. Among the many fascinating observations made by the French scholar-diplomat are:

> * Animals only with a cloven foot or a hoofed foot, and if they chew the cud, may be eaten. This is because carnivorous animals, which are not acceptable, have the means to seize a prey; eating them would be doubly sinful. The permissible animals are non-meat eating.
>
> * The Passover feast is a "sacrifice of renewal," in which the participants consume the food of the Origins.
>
> * The concept of clean animals conforms to the "plan of Creation." God "created three elements: the firmament, the water and the earth; then He created three kinds of animals out of each of these elements. Each animal is thus tied to one element, and one only.
>
> * A man is a man. A human being is either a man or a woman, not both. Homosexuality is outlawed; the prohibition even extends to clothes (the exchange of clothing between the sexes is banned).

The author concludes:

> The Mosaic logic is remarkable for its rigor, indeed its rigidity . . . Christianity could only be born by breaking with the strictures that separated the Hebrews from the other peoples.
>
> Whatever variations the Mosaic system may have undergone in the course of history, they do not seem to have shaken its fundamental strictures. This logic, which lives by the rule of refusing all that is hybrid, mixed or arrived at by synthesis and compromise, can be seen in action to this day in Israel, and not only in its cuisine.

—D.C.G.

Jewish First Names Through the Ages

For Jews first names are inevitably something more than convenient labels for identification. They take on a highly charged symbolic value, as the feverish name coinings and Hebraizations of old names in Israel in the past few years tell us, or our own searchings for a "suitable" name for a newborn infant. So it is that Jewish names can serve as clues for deciphering the cultural patterns of Jewish history. Names also reveal something about the changing political and economic orientations of Jews through the centuries.

It is a strong tradition among American Jews to name their children after departed relatives. And yet we find no trace of this custom in the Bible. In ancient days the name a Jew gave his child was generally connected with some event that had happened at his birth. The name usually took on a symbolic meaning, denoting a wish for the newborn infant's good fortune, expressing thanks to God, and so forth. In remote antiquity the custom was to name a male infant immediately at the time of birth (a practice still followed by the Arabs today); later on a boy received his official name at the ceremony of circumcision.

In the early biblical period first names were the exclusive possession of the person upon whom they were first conferred. Every child bore a name uniquely his, coined on the occasion of his birth; no one would ever use that name again.

Over a period of two thousand years we find no recurrence of the names Abraham, Isaac, Jacob, Moses, David, Solomon, and so forth. Even in the royal family no names were repeated. Not one of the twenty-one kings of Judah was named after David, first of the dynasty.

In the later biblical period, however, names begin to be repeated. Later still we find the Talmud (tractate Yoma 38b) prohibiting the use of the name of a wicked person. But Jews, it would seem, never abided by this prohibition. Even rabbis in the Talmudic period disregarded it. Thus we find several high priests and *tannaim* who bore the name of Ishmael. (In the Bible Ishmael is classed among the wicked, and in rabbinic literature he is a symbol of impiety, though some rabbis considered him to have turned penitent at the end of his life.)

Menachem, which was the name of a king of Israel, is found only once in the Bible: "And he did that which was evil in the sight of the Lord; he departed not all his days from the sins of Jeroboam." Yet many *tannaim* and *amoraim* (ancient rabbinical scholars) were named Menachem, and it is very common even today. On the other hand, the names of such pious figures as the prophets Habakkuk, Zephaniah, Malachi, and others completely disappeared among Jews after the biblical era. If there are special reasons why some names have withstood the test of time, scholars have not been able to discover them.

In the early biblical period Jewish names are Hebrew names. But in the period following the destruction of the First Temple and the carrying off of the Jews into the Babylonian Captivity, foreign names and modifications begin to make their appearance. From this period date many of the traditional modes of Jewish name-giving, as well as that process of admixture and combination that has resulted in the bizarre assortment of names borne by Jews today.

During this sojourn by the waters of Babylon, and even in the first generation of the Return, the Jews displayed two contrary tendencies, one nationalist and the other assimilationist. One group of exiles was full of a fierce, patriotic fervor, as evidenced by their loyal devotion to the Hebrew language and the pure biblical names they bestowed on their children. Throughout the later books of the Bible the old Hebrew names of the patriarchal era (Joseph, Benjamin, Simeon) reappear.

This devotion to Judaism was not only a looking back to the glorious past. For in addition to reviving the old, disused names, which had been half forgotten or never popular, the Jewish patriots of the period created Hebrew names that do not appear in the earlier books of the Bible. These names (Nehemiah, Chasadiah, Pedaiah, Melatiah, and so forth) express the sentiments of the people in an era of transition, sentiments of hope, consolation, thanksgiving, joy, and trust in the Almighty.

Side by side with this patriotic emphasis on Hebrew tradition there was an opposite tendency to imitate and assimilate foreign forms. We find many names in Ezra, Nehemiah, and Chronicles with the Aramaic ending *ai*. Even names that have a Hebrew root are converted into an Aramaic form, as, for example, Piltai (from Pelatiah), Shammai (from Shemaiah), Atlai (from Ataliah), and a name that has been much in the public eye, Adlai (from Adaliah).

We also come across names entirely and directly Aramaic, as well as names borrowed by the Jews from neighboring peoples. Persian-Babylonian names, brought back from the Exile, make their first appearance at this time. Two names in this last category, Mordecai and Shabbetai, have remained popular to this day despite their pagan origin.

During the period of Alexander's rule new Hebrew names continued to be invented. Examples of these are Shatach, Admon, and Perachiah. But most of the Jewish names of the time were Aramaic, with the members of the aristocracy beginning to use Greek ones. Even the first scholar of the Mishnah bore the purely Greek name of Antigonos.

In the Hasmonean period, when Hellenistic culture dominated the Western world, we already find widespread use of Greek names among the Jews. Jews even bore the name of their fiercest persecutor, Antiochus, against whom the Maccabees had successfully rebelled.

Greek names were employed by the Jews for many centuries after the destruction of the Second Temple by the Roman Titus in 70 C.E.; in the Mishnah and Talmudic literatures we find many *tannaim* and *amoraim* with such Greek names as Alexander, Theodorus, Dosa, Nanos, Nakdimon, Polemo, Pappos, Patros, Symmachos, Tarfon, and so forth.

Following the Roman conquest of Palestine, a strong Latin influence made itself felt, though it was never so extensive as the Greek. In the Mishnaic and Talmudic literatures (especially the Palestinian Talmud) we encounter many rabbis with such Latin names as Drusus, Marinus, Valens, Romanus, Justus—and, *mirabile dictu*, in several places in the Palestinian Talmud mention is made of a Rabbi Titus! There were Jews who even bore the names of the pagan Roman gods Apollo and Castor. However, the Persian-Aramaic names of previous times continued to predominate in the Talmudic period.

The custom of using a non-Jewish name as a companion and addition to one's Hebrew name originated several centuries before the destruction of the Second Temple. In the later books of the Bible we encounter such double names as Hadassah Esther and Daniel Belshazzar; Channaniah, Michael, and Azariah are also called Shedrach, Mishech, and Abed Nego.

During the period of Greek influence it became customary to have two Hebrew names (a practice still followed today). We find such combinations as Mahalalel Judah, Sarah Miriam, and Yochanan Joseph. Sometimes a Hebrew and an

Aramaic name were used together. During this period, too, the linking of a Jewish with a non-Jewish name became more the fashion. Beginning among the Hellenizing Jewish assimilationists, it gradually spread to the traditionalists. All the Hasmonean kings had a dual Hebrew-Greek name: Yochanan-Hyrcanos; Yannai-Alexander; Judah-Aristobolos; Shlomis-Alexandra.

At first the non-Jewish names were used only in relations with non-Jews. One's Greek name was a direct translation of one's Hebrew name, with Tuvia becoming Ariston, Ezra being metamorphosed into Boethus, Zadok into Justus, Yedidiah into Philo, Nathaniel into Theodorus, and so forth. Gradually, however, the non-Jewish name became the more important name and, finally, the only name. (The same process is taking place today.)

Some names of the Talmudic era were authentic Hebrew names and were readily recognizable as such, but they were Hellenized in form or spelling: Joseph appears in the form of Jose, Levi as Levites, Yitzchak as Isak; Shimon as Simon, and so forth.

A small percentage of feminine proper names were Hebrew; many were Aramaic (e.g., Uman, Martha, and Yalta, a shortened version of Ayalta, which is the Aramaic form of the Hebrew Ayala). Some feminine Latin and Greek names were used: Alexandra, Berenice, Doris, Beruria (the Aramaized form of Veluria). Women were, for the most part, excluded from political and economic life, so that there was less need for Hellenizing or Romanizing their names.

In the Talmudic period the strong influence of Graeco-Roman culture acted to reduce the number of Hebrew names, though there was never any danger, of course, of their being extinguished. We find obscure biblical names suddenly growing popular because of the distinction won by certain of their bearers, as in the case of Hillel and Gamliel. New Hebrew names not found in the Bible, such as Akabiah, Akashiah, Akiba, Meir, and Nachman, came to the fore at this time.

The custom of naming a child after a deceased relative seems to have begun in the time of the Hasmoneans. At first the practice was confined to the royal family and aristocracy. Among the Hasmoneans we find a recurrence of the names of Judah, Yochanan, and Jonathan; among the Patriarchs of Judea we find two Hillels, three Judahs, six Gamliels, and four Simeons. Gradually the custom spread among the people; it has been followed to this day. The practice was well established by the first century of the Common Era, as we can see from Luke 1:59–61, where a departure from it occasions surprise.

Early in the Middle Ages the Jews began to give their children biblical names that had not been used for eight hundred years: Abraham, Moses, Aaron, David, Solomon, Isaiah, Ammon, Elchanon, Baruch, Noah.

At this time, too, the new practice arose of enlisting abstract terms to serve as proper names: Emunah (faith), Nissim (miracles), and so forth. Also, special names were given to children born on certain days or during certain holidays. This custom was already prevalent in the Christian community: boys born on Sunday were called Dominic; during Easter, Pasquale; girls born on Christmas were called Natalie.

In like manner, boys born on Saturday were called Sabbetai by Jewish parents; children born in the Purim season were called Mordecai or Esther; Yom Tov was conferred on children born during a festival; boys born on the Passover were called Pesach. There is even a record of one boy of the Middle Ages named Chanukah!

Until the twelfth century the Jews of Babylonia continued to use Aramaic and Persian names. A roster of the names of the *gaonim* of the academies of Sura and

Pumbedita shows that new Aramaic and Persian names were continually being added. Since Babylonia was then under Islamic rule and influence, pure Arabic names also occur. Thus, one of the exilarchs is named Josiah Hassan.

In Christian lands the Jews very early began to give their children Christian names. There was, for example, Rabbi Peter, the brilliant young tosafist who died a martyr's death in France during the Second Crusade. Many of these Christian names were mere additional names or translations of the Hebrew; but others were the only names their bearers possessed. Some of these are still used by Jews today, and men are called up to read the Torah by means of them, so accepted is their Jewish status now.

From the twelfth century onward, so widespread was the use of non-Jewish names that the rabbis decreed that every Jewish boy must be given a purely Jewish name at his circumcision. Thus the use of two names became the custom: a religious name by which a Jew was called up to read the Torah and which was employed in documents of a religious nature, and a non-Jewish name for civil and business purposes. In the category of religious names were included not only old and new Hebrew names but also all the Aramaic and Greek names that had been sanctified, as it were, by constant usage in the Jewish community. This rabbinic statute is valid to this day.

The Ashkenazic (German, Alsatian, Polish, Austrian, Russian) Jews were more lavish in their use of non-Jewish names for extracommunity purposes than any other group. When they used their Hebrew names, they were so garbled in pronunciation as to be virtually unrecognizable. There are two reasons for this process of corruption: the peculiar dialects of the German language; and the tendency for the nicknames and diminutives conferred on children by doting parents to be retained in mature years and handed down to the next generation in place of the original Hebrew names, which were soon forgotten.

Thus, the Hebrew name Yoseph (Joseph) was corrupted into Yosel, Jesselman, and other forms; Jacob (Yaakov) became Yekel, Yankel; Kopel, Kopelman; Samuel (Schmuel) became Shmulik; Sanvill became Zavill, Zangwill; Isaac (Yitzchak) became Eisnik, Itzik, Itzl, Zekl, and so forth.

The Jewish names that the Ashkenazim adopted were related in a variety of ways to their non-Jewish names:

1. In many cases they were a direct translation into Hebrew of the German names. The German Baer, for example, was translated by Dov, so that a Jew of this name became Dov Ber, or, in its syncopated form, Duber. The popular German name Hirsch was translated by Zvi, which yielded the dual form Zvi Hirsch. Gottlieb became Yedidiah Gottlieb. Bendit (a form of Benedict) became Baruch, in its dual form Baruch Bendit. Phoebus (the Greek god of light) was translated by the Aramaic Shraga or Hebrew Uri, becoming Uri Phoebus and Shraga Phoebus, which in turn changed into Uri Feivish or Uri Feivel. A popular diminutive of the German Gottfried was Gotze; this was corrupted into Goetzl or Getzel, which was translated as Eliakim, and many Jews were called Eliakim Getz or Getzl.

2. A second way of inventing Jewish names called into play the skill in casuistry that Jews had developed through study of the Talmud. In the Bible certain names are found in association with certain terms. For example, Judah is called *gur aryeh*, a lion. A Jew called Loeb (lion in Yiddish) would therefore adopt as his Hebrew name Judah or Aryeh; this gave him as his full name Judah Layb or Aryeh Layb. Hertz (hart) became Naphtali Hertz, for in blessing Naphtali the patriarch Jacob calls him a swift-footed hart. In the same way, Wolff

became Benjamin Wolff. And because Jacob said to Ephraim that his seed would multiply as the fish in the sea, the popular German name Fischlin became Ephraim Fischel.

3. Finally, mere similarity of sound with one's German name was a sufficient warrant for adopting a Hebrew name. The French *bon homme* was popular as a name among the German Jews in the form of Bunim. Phonetically it was related to Benjamin; therefore a German Jew whose non-Jewish name was Bunim took Benjamin as his religious name, his name becoming Benjamin Bunim. The old German name Mann, whose diminutive is Mannish or Mendel, was associated with the Hebrew Menachem, the result of which was Menachem Mendel. The Germanic Anselm was adopted in the corrupted form of Anschel and linked with the Hebrew Asher to become Asher Anschel. In many instances, however, a Hebrew name was conjoined with a non-Jewish name in a purely arbitrary fashion, without any logical or phonetic warrant.

While only a few of the many Italian and French names that Jews have used have come down to us, almost all the German names are with us in one form or another, in large part because the Yiddish language came to us from German Jewry.

One of the chief factors that preserved the Hebrew character of Jewish names was the rabbinical requirement of a Hebrew name for synagogue and other religious purposes; but since women did not participate in religious activities and were not called up to read the Torah, it is no surprise to discover that the feminine names of this era were predominantly non-Jewish.

If one looks at lists of feminine Jewish names one finds the strangest conglomeration of corruptions and diminutives, borrowings and mutations. They present a weird cacophony of sounds to modern ears if we are ignorant of their provenance and of the metamorphoses they have undergone. Among these names are: Trestel (from the German *Troest,* consolation, used for the Hebrew name Nechama, which also means consolation); Kreindel (from the German *Krone,* crown); Breindel (from the German *Braune,* brunette); Treindel (from Trina, the diminutive of Katarina); Dvoshke (corrupted form of Devora); Tzirel (from Sarah); Rayzel (from Rosa); Mindel (from Minne, the diminutive of Wilhelmina).

In all fairness to our forefathers, however, it must be stated that even in the Middle Ages Jews coined new Hebrew names—even for their daughters. This was truer of the Italian Jews and other Sephardic communities than for the Ashkenazim, who allowed accident and circumstance to distort their names out of all recognition.

Names brought by Jewish immigrants from one country to another were changed to suit the tastes and fancy of the Jews among whom they settled. In this way the Jews in Germany took over the names of the French and English Jews who passed their way in the later Middle Ages and altered both their sound and spelling. Polish Jews "improved" on Italian and German names. This went on from one generation to the next until hardly a trace of the original name remained. For this reason it is difficult today to determine the origins of many names.

Who would ever guess that Shprinzel is a Polish Jewish "improvement" on Esperanza, brought east by Italian Jews? It was a regular practice for the Jews of Italy to translate the Hebrew Tikvah into Esperanza. Or how can one discover that the name Feitel is a German Jewish corruption of the Italian Vital, itself a translation of the Hebrew Chayim? The popular Yiddish Zelde is the old German name Salida; Gimpel comes from Gumprecht; Yente had an exotic origin in Juanita; Yachne is the biblical Yocheved. These metamorphoses can be recounted by the hundreds. But for every name we can trace back there are dozens whose origins are lost.

On the American scene today, we follow many of the practices established by our forefathers long ago. We still translate and assimilate names. In the United States it is common to give a child an English name whose initial letter is the same as that of his Hebrew name. Thus a boy who inherits the Hebrew name of Abraham from his grandfather will have Allen, Arthur, or Avery for his English name; a girl named Shaindel after her grandmother is called Susan, Sandra, or Shirley in English.

In Israel, Jewish patriotism expresses itself in much the same way as it did in the days of the first Return under Ezra. Names are devised or changed in Israel according to certain definite procedures that can be summed up as follows:

1. Elimination of Diaspora influences and admixtures. Jewish names are purged of all the "foreign" accretions that were acquired while living in the Dispersion. The original Hebrew component, if missing, is restored; if present, it is left standing alone. Thus Mendel disappears and Menachem remains; Feivel is dropped and Uri is reinstated; Judeo-Polish Zlate and German Golde are changed to Zahava; Gitel becomes Tova; Shaindel becomes Yaffa, and so forth.

2. Ransacking of the Bible and Hebrew literary sources for names for children. So strong is this reverence for biblical names that no attention is paid to whether they are pre-patriarchal or post-patriarchal, Hebrew or heathen. Even ancient Hebrew names for things and objects are made use of. The only criteria are euphony, simplicity, and brevity. Some of these new names are Alon, Aran, Aviv, Ofra, and Kochevet.

3. Coinages. New names are being created in every walk of life. These names express the sentiments, hopes, and impulses of a people restored to the land of their forefathers, and recall the era of the Return following the Babylonian Captivity. Some of these names are: Yigal (he will redeem), Geula (redemption), Ron (he sings), Zimra (song), Shira (song), and Aviva (spring).

It looks as though our present increasing desire to identify ourselves as Jewish will lead us to adopt more traditional Jewish first names in the future. But the choice will necessarily be limited by what English-speaking people happen to find euphonious. Whether we can expand that notion of euphony in naming our children remains to be seen.

—B.C.K.

 # How the Mezuzah Got in the Church Compound

Isaac Cohen, a burly forty-six-year-old Jerusalem shoemaker, is an observant Jew. He lives in a small two-room flat in a compound surrounding the Church of Notre Dame de France. The building is owned by the church. Cohen's hole-in-the-wall shop is in the same building.

He used to live in the Old City of Jerusalem, where he was born, but when the Arabs captured the city during the 1948 War of Independence Cohen fled. Homeless and destitute, he moved his family into the shell-battered Church of Notre Dame, then situated in the no-man's-land between Arab and Jewish front lines. Snipers of both armies used the building, which suffered heavy damage.

After Israel became independent, the Church of Notre Dame remained in Israeli territory. The priests and monks who repaired the church could have evicted Cohen and his family as illegal squatters, but they let them stay. "You are refugees made homeless by war, and it is our duty to help you," Father Fabian told Cohen.

Cohen moved out of the church proper into a nearby building in the church compound. He has been there now for sixteen years. He pays only nominal rent. His only problem was how to affix a mezuzah to his door. As a pious Jew he should not live in an apartment without a mezuzah. But how could he hang up a mezuzah on the doorpost of a building that belonged to the Catholic Church? He went to see Father Fabian about the problem and was told, "Go ahead, hang up your mezuzah. After all, Jesus had a mezuzah on his door too. We never forget that."

When Pope Paul arrived in the Old City of Jerusalem in January 1965, the bells of the Church of Notre Dame, which is close by the Mandelbaum Gate frontier between Israel and Jordan, began to toll. Father Fabian and his assistant, Brother Theo, were pulling on the bell ropes. "Father Fabian is no longer young," Cohen said, "and I saw he was beginning to tire after pulling the ropes for nearly an hour, so I asked his permission to help. That's how I, Isaac Cohen, an Orthodox Jew, became the first Jew to have rung the bells of a Catholic Church for the arrival of a Pope in Jerusalem. I rang them for fifty-five minutes."

—L.H.

 **King Hezekiah's Tunnel:
A Mystery to This Day**

The choice of the southeastern hill as the site on which to found Jerusalem at the beginning of the Bronze Age was dictated by the presence of a nearby source of water, the Gihon Spring.

Some of Jerusalem's most interesting ancient water-supply engineering projects involve this spring. The oldest was discovered about a hundred years ago by the English explorer Charles Warren. It consisted of underground galleries and a shaft, cut into bedrock, which allowed the inhabitants to get water from the fountain without going outside the city walls. Some scholars believe this is the *tzinor* mentioned in connection with King David's conquest of Jerusalem (2 Sam. 5:8) around 1000 B.C.E., and that the shaft served as a hidden approach to the city.

By far the most sophisticated engineering project connected with the Gihon Spring is the celebrated Tunnel of Hezekiah. The Bible speaks about it as one of the most important achievements of King Hezekiah (2 Chron. 32:30). The underground tunnel, discovered in the last century, follows an S-shaped path as it carries the waters of the Gihon Spring from the eastern side of the city to the Tyropoeon Valley on the western side of the hill.

It is clear that the tunnel was cut by two groups of workmen who began working at opposite ends and then met in the middle. Just how this engineering feat was accomplished more than twenty-five hundred years ago remains an unsolved riddle.

During the Second Temple period, the city's population increased and, as a consequence, the problem of Jerusalem's water supply became even more pressing. Additional public pools were now erected in the new areas of the city: the "Pool of the Towers" (near the present Jaffa Gate) and the "Snake Pool" collected water from the western side of the city. The "Sheep Pool" gathered water from north of the city, while the "Pool of Siloam" continued to collect the water from Hezekiah's Tunnel.

A major problem of city life was posed by the water supply required by the Temple and its surroundings. Thousands of pilgrims arrived at the Temple mount three times a year to sacrifice and pray. The gathering of thousands of people at one time obviously required enormous quantities of water. The problem was solved by building a long-distance aqueduct—a technique in widespread use throughout the Hellenistic and Roman world at the time. The Talmud refers to an aqueduct that brought water to the Temple from "Etam," a place mentioned in the Bible as a city located in the vicinity of Bethlehem. This "low-level aqueduct" supplied water to the Temple. The Talmud says that its waters were used by the high priest for ritual bathing. The southern part was probably the aqueduct mentioned by the Jewish historian Josephus Flavius as having been built by the Roman Procurator Pontius Pilate, who used the Temple treasures to finance the project, arousing the antagonism of the indignant Jewish population.

An additional carrier known as the "high-level aqueduct" was built by the Tenth Roman Legion during the second century B.C.E. Part of it passes through a huge conduit made of stone pipe segments carefully fitted together.

While use of this "high-level aqueduct" was discontinued after the Roman period, the "low-level aqueduct" continued to serve the city until the beginning of this century. It was kept in repair by the succession of Byzantine, Arab, Mameluke, and Ottoman regimes that ruled Jerusalem.

Towards the end of the last century Jerusalem's water-supply situation became critical. The private cisterns and public pools were in bad condition. Descriptions of the period tell us how water was brought to the city from far away by train or donkey and then sold locally at fancy prices.

When the British conquered the city in 1917, one of the urgent major problems they had to solve without delay was that of Jerusalem's water supply. Knowing about the aqueducts from nineteenth-century research, they had recourse to the old sources in the "Springs of Arrub" and "King Solomon's Pools," restored the pools themselves, built pumping stations and iron pipelines, so that for a few years the ancient springs once again became the major water source for the city. In 1924 another pumping station was built at Ein Fara, a capacious fountain north of Jerusalem.

A decade later a pipeline was built to carry water to the city from the springs of Rosh Ha'ayin, the major source of the Yarkon River, east of Tel Aviv. This pipeline finally solved the problem of Jerusalem's water supply and still meets the current requirements of the nation's now vastly more populous capital city. However, in time of war the conduit was in danger. During the Arab siege of Jerusalem in Israel's War of Independence in 1948, the pipe was cut and the Jewish population found itself without an external source of water. During those critical months only the continued existence of cisterns in the courtyards of many buildings saved the population from disaster. In other words, the private cisterns—Jerusalem's most ancient method of collecting water—had once again provided the only feasible solution during a time of siege.

—A.M.

Origins of Some Jewish Philanthropic Practices

The Middle Ages, so far as the Jewish people are concerned, cover the period that falls, roughly speaking, between the years 700 and 1700 of the Christian era. This happens to be a period the understanding of whose Jewish philanthropy requires not a little recourse to the imagination. The records, though precise and reliable, are singularly devoid of color and concreteness.

Among the striking features of this period, especially in the later centuries, is the high degree of philanthropic specialization and diversity. We hear of societies for visiting the sick, for burying the indigent dead, for providing the poor with candles needed on the Sabbath and the holidays, for supplying Passover and other holiday victuals, for furnishing poor girls with dowries, for ransoming captives, and for the outfitting of needy women and children with clothes, shoes, undergarments, mattresses, and blankets. There were societies for the relief of prisoners, of widows, and of the aged, as well as societies that looked after maternity needs and circumcision arrangements.

I. *Hospitality:* The custom of welcoming needy strangers to the family table, especially on the Sabbath and on holidays, is one of the best known forms of Jewish philanthropy. These strangers were sometimes men of learning who were obliged to seek their livelihood by traveling from community to community. Not rarely were they refugees from wars and persecutions. A famous Jewish traveler observed this form of benevolence around the year 1170 even among the Jews of distant Persia.

When the Jews were expelled from Spain in 1492, the refugees were signally cared for by their co-religionists in Pisa, Corfu, Candia, and Turkey. About the year 1652, when Cossack uprisings sent homeless Jews swarming into Lithuania, the resident Jewish householders were required by their own communal officers to accept their respective quotas of refugees for temporary shelter. Large-scale relief for the unfortunates was planned in the Jewish synodal statutes of the time.

In the fifteenth century in Treviso, the president of the congregation would draw from the urn the tickets by which poor wayfarers were assigned to the homes that would entertain them. A noted rabbi of the time ruled against those congregants who, aiming to keep transients away, sought to impose upon them the embarrassment of having to draw their own tickets.

Mention is frequently made of "hospitals" maintained by Jews in various European centers for the lodging of needy co-religionists. Christian reference to one of these Jewish "hospitals" occurs as early as the year 1210, although both Jewish and Christian writings several centuries earlier speak of communal lodges for wayfarers as an extremely ancient Jewish institution. It must be understood that these "hospitals" were originally hospitals only in the Latin sense of inns, taverns, and lodges.

A rare exception in which "hospital" is almost used in its modern sense is a hospital for Jewish lepers mentioned in the year 1349 as existing in Heidelberg. Otherwise, facilities for the sick (primarily for sick strangers) were a later development connected with these wayfarers' lodges, from which facilities the Jewish hospital in its modern form evolved.

The Hebrew term for such public taverns and shelters for the sick was *Hekdesh,* that is, a "holy object," a word that in ancient Hebrew was applied to any object deemed to be sacred and dedicated to the divine. "Sometimes," says Israel Abrahams, "the ordinary Jewish innkeepers were paid from the communal funds, and tramps or wandering mendicants were freely entertained on the ground floor while the more respectable paying guests occupied the upper story of the inn."

II. *Higher Education:* Jewish education in its philanthropic aspects coincides with hospitality at various points. Poor students would receive, aside from small allowances from benevolent funds, meals or lodging in the homes of the Jewish community in which their academy was situated. A student would usually dine with a number of families in rotation.

Benevolence toward poor students is reported to have been practiced among the Jews of France as well as those of far-off Arabia as early as the year 1170. In 1662 the communities of Lithuania adopted regulations for distributing students among their respective members. It was later ordained that each congregation should care for at least nine poor students. Still later, regulations were adopted for the assistance of students stranded in academy towns during vacation periods between sessions. A Polish community of fifty householders once supported about thirty students.

The providing of books was also a philanthropic venture supported both by communal regulation, as in Lithuania, or by private benevolence. When philanthropic individuals devoted certain sums for books to be loaned to impecunious students, that fact had to be recorded on the flyleaves to prevent the heirs from mistaking such books for personal property.

III. *Children:* Educational programs and relief programs overlapped in the care of orphans. The first Jewish orphan asylum was founded in London in 1831. Prior to that time, orphans would be reared privately, a plan to which modern social workers are reverting.

A Lithuanian synod of the seventeenth century had to adopt measures for the shelter and the training of numerous destitute refugee children. An extremely interesting provision of this period required the registration of refugee children to prevent inadvertent marriage of brothers and sisters. We find these seventeenth-century Lithuanian synods particularly concerned about the vocational training of boys. In sixteenth-century Avignon a sum for free education had to be contributed from every marriage portion.

IV. *Women:* Outstanding among the provisions for orphaned girls was that of dowries supplied either from communal funds or by special associations within the community. Poor girls, even if not orphaned, were eligible to receive this bounty.

In sixteenth-century Avignon the customary sum for a philanthropic dowry was one florin (approximately sixteen dollars). In Lithuania it was twenty shok (a shok was approximately equal to a dollar and a half), which relatives might raise to sixty shok or, according to a later ruling, to four hundred shok, but which they could not be required to raise above one hundred shok. In Rome in 1618 the sum was fixed at two hundred scudi (a scudo was equal to about ninety-seven cents). When applicants for dowries exceeded the resources, the recipients were chosen by lot, an inevitable arrangement where, as in Rome in 1618, the number of dowries had to be limited to twelve a year. The Lithuanian synod of a somewhat later period stipulated the following annual choice of dowry recipients by lot: twelve at Brisk; ten at Horodna; and eight at Pinsk. Three judges representing the community were to conduct the selection.

Women are mentioned in the Lithuanian protocols among the refugees who were to receive special attention. In Rome in 1617 there was a society of women for helping women, while in 1682 there existed in Rome special organizations that supplied needy women with clothes, shoes, mattresses, and blankets. Widows and lying-in women were particular objects of solicitude. Noticeable among the special benevolences for women are those concerned with ritual requirements such as oil for Sabbath and Hanukkah lights, ritual baths, and so forth.

V. *Ritual:* A large phase of the medieval Jewish philanthropic program involved the aiding of poor persons to fulfil their ritual obligations. We hear of double allowance granted the poor before each festival in sixteenth-century Avignon and of special bounties for the Sabbath and for the several holidays, such as wine and unleavened bread for Passover and the necessities of Purim and Hoshana Rabba.

VI. *The Sick:* Visiting the sick is an extremely venerable form of Jewish benevolence. The medieval custom was to call upon the sick immediately after the Sabbath morning service. A communal usage in Avignon provided an allowance of three sous a week for any bedridden poor person. Care of the sick is also mentioned by an early seventeenth-century Italian writer.

Sometimes the visiting of the sick, except in periods of pestilence, was enforced by the imposition of fines. Such fines existed, for instance, among the shoemakers who formed a guild of mutual aid in Saragossa, Spain, in 1336. In Avignon visitors to the sick were chosen by lot and were subject to fine for noncompliance. A special society for sick relief was founded in Rome in the pestilence year of 1657. There was also a society in Rome that looked especially after the needs of those who were extremely ill.

A Jewish physician in Frankfurt in 1394 gave free medical treatment to the inmates of the Jewish communal inn. In Rome there was an organization that maintained a physician for the free treatment of indigent co-religionists. At the end of the fourteenth century there was in Algiers a Jewish physician who gave charitable assistance and free treatment to the Jewish and Mohammedan poor alike.

VII. *Prisoners and Captives:* The same regulation of sixteenth-century Avignon that allotted three sous a week to every indigent sick person allowed one sou a week to Jewish prisoners. There was in Rome in 1615 a society whose object it was to improve the detention quarters of Jewish prisoners. The question of securing clemency for Jewish prisoners through communal action was occasionally considered. Cases are on record in which rabbis favored such action and other cases in which they opposed it.

Rabbi Meir of Rothenburg languished in prison for seven years and died there in 1293, declining to avail himself of the ransom that was being raised by his people. The rabbi feared that the payment of the ransom would only encourage further extortions from the Emperor Rudolph, whose object in imprisoning the rabbi was manifestly that of exacting money from the Jews.

Much less qualified was the readiness of the Jews to ransom those of their own flock who had been taken captive in the vicissitudes of war or travel. Owing to the inordinate hardships and perils of captivity, the ransoming of captives was, from the earliest times, deemed a philanthropy par excellence. All of the charity codes of the period contain provisions for the ransoming of captives.

The founder of Jewish scholarship in Spain, Moses ben Hanoch, had himself been brought to Cordova as a captive (about 945) and had been ransomed by the local community. The average cost per ransom in eleventh-century Egypt was the equivalent of two hundred and fifty dollars. To raise ransom money for their co-religionists at the time of the expulsion from Spain, the Jews of Corfu and Candia sold their gold synagogue ornaments.

Moses Kapsali, a noted Turkish rabbi of the time, levied a tax and traveled from town to town soliciting money for ransoms. The Jews of Constantinople ransomed three thousand Jews from Podolia in the year 1648. In 1656 Leghorn Jews gave one fourth of their income for the ransoming and assisting of Jewish refugees from Poland.

Since antiquity the rule had existed to decline to pay exorbitant ransoms so as to avoid encouraging high ransom charges. Emergencies were common, however, and this rule had to be set aside. It was also forbidden to assist captives to escape for fear of reprisals and increased severities.

Lithuanian agreements of 1649 look to the sharing of the heavy ransom costs among several communities, with due regard for promptness, on the one hand, and the consent of the assessed communities, on the other. Communities would federate and cooperate for this purpose sooner than for any other. Sometimes the communities would function merely as sureties to the captors for the ransom that the captive would himself eventually pay. Frequently communities were reimbursed by captives or by the kinsmen of the captives.

VIII. *The Dead:* Like the visiting of the sick, the burial of the dead was a philanthropic activity only in certain instances. There was an early Lithuanian provision allowing for recourse to the charity fund for funeral costs.

As a rule, the same burial societies that served the rich also functioned for the poor. The ancient law requiring inexpensive habiliments and appurtenances at the funerals of rich and poor alike was observed throughout the centuries. Financial assistance would, when needed, be accorded the survivors, especially in cases of sudden death.

IX. *Palestine:* One of the benevolences that a twelfth-century Jewish traveler found among the Jews of distant Khaibar in Arabia was that of remittances to the "mourners of Zion." Donations for Palestine are commonly mentioned in the philanthropic literature of this epoch. In Rome there was a special society concerned with collecting alms for Palestine.

As early as the thirteenth century a rabbi named Jacob, formerly of Paris, went from Jerusalem to solicit aid for his scholarly colleagues residing in the Holy City. This Rabbi Jacob was the first in a long series of emissaries (*meshullachim*) who went abroad seeking aid for needy Palestinians, although the first to be sent officially as a representative of the community began his activities in 1441.

The still-familiar Halukkah box for Palestinian benevolence was introduced in the seventeenth century. Halukkah means "distribution" and refers to the apportionment of the money among the several needy groups or individuals.

X. *Modes of Financing:* One source of philanthropic income was the custom whereby a person made donations when honored with the privilege of participating in certain synagogue rituals. Thus we hear that in seventeenth-century Rome people called up to the reading of the Law would pledge sums for the providing of dowries, the ransoming of captives, and the relief of the needy. Occasionally a sum would be donated whose interest would go to charity.

In Barbary, whenever money was needed for charity the synagogue scroll of the Law would be sold to the highest bidder, who would thereupon donate the scroll back to the synagogue, contenting himself with the honor of affixing his name as having been the onetime owner.

Special donations would be made on occasions of joy, such as marriages and circumcisions, or on occasions of sorrow, where a bereavement or the anniversary of a bereavement would prompt memorial offerings. Hanukkah, Purim, and fast days were held to be particularly suitable as times for remembering the needy. One man on record directed his heirs to give alms to the poor annually on Hanukkah. We also hear of a Jewish butcher "who weighed his children three times a year and gave their weight in meat to the poor."

A highly munificent source of income was the custom of making charitable bequests. Records tell of a certain Roman Jew who bequeathed, among other things, four thousand Florentine scudi for the ransoming of captives and eighteen thousand for the dowering of needy brides.

There was also house-to-house canvassing or synagogal solicitation by duly accredited officials or representatives of the community. In seventeenth-century Rome the prominent philanthropic leaders would make collections in the synagogue every Purim and at every recurrence of the fast day of Ab (*Tisha b'Ab*).

At times and places where the community could assess its members, that prerogative would, among other things, be exercised in behalf of charitable needs. The Lithuanian communities were assessed for the support of poor students and for dowries, ransoms, and the relief of refugees. In Avignon every marriage settlement would be taxed in the interests of the free education fund.

In 1469 a prominent rabbi at Bamberg required the members of the community to donate to charity one fortieth of their profits. All of the Jewish law codes vest the Jewish communal authorities with the right to compel just contributions. Everybody, even recipients of alms, had to give something.

Occasionally we hear of the tithing system. Our twelfth-century Jewish traveler found it prevalent among the Jews of Khaibar in Arabia. Other sources tell us of a fifteenth-century Jew who laid down for himself meticulous rules about computing the tenth of his income that he had dedicated to benevolence. We also learn of the practice existing in Germany and in Spain. In fact, the Jewish law codes of the period specify one tenth as characterizing the average Jew and less than one tenth as marking the stingy one.

Not a little unique and curious was the widespread Jewish practice of diverting to charity the fines incurred for various derelictions. Thus we find a Florentine regulation of 1428 stating that under certain conditions a Jew who, by using a Gentile intermediary, evades the law forbidding a Jew to take interest from a Jew, must pay that ill-gotten interest to the charity fund.

A law adopted in Frankfurt in 1603 required that a fine be paid to the charity fund by any Jew who took to a Gentile court a case against another Jew. A 1432 ruling in Valladolid, Spain, punished repeated failure to obey the summons of a Jewish court with the requirement that the offender pay one gold piece to the charity fund for the first offense, three for the second, and ten for the third; similarly, a Jew or a Jewess who defamed a co-religionist would be fined one hundred maravedos (about three dollars), one half of which would go to charity.

In sixteenth-century Avignon part of the fine imposed for failure to attend the Sabbath service went to charity. Similarly, in seventeenth-century Lithuania the charity fund received the fines imposed for violation of the communal statute forbidding certain excesses of ornamentation in the attire of women.

The sixteenth-century law code ruled that fines destined for charity must go to charity even if, by virtue of some other settlement of the difficulty, the fines were eventually remitted. Highly interesting is the case of a Jew who, fining himself, gave to charity a gold piece for every glass of wine he drank, every meal he ate, and every costly garment he acquired in excess of certain self-imposed limits; nor does he seem to have been chary about transgressing those limits.

There were, finally, various miscellaneous ways of aiding the poor. Thus we find a Lithuanian regulation stating that there shall be one or two poor persons in every group of ten invited to any sacred festivity. Certain indigent classes, again, would be exempt from wedding charges, just as they had been in sixteenth-century Avignon; indigent widows and octogenarians paid no *capage* and poor orphans no *taille* (forms of taxation).

There were also in seventeenth-century Lithuania certain generous relaxations of trade barriers permitting refugees and other needy outsiders to trade at certain seasons and within certain areas where the privilege was not normally theirs. A Hebrew devotional book of the eleventh century commends the act of selling food to the poor at low prices in times of scarcity and high prices.

There is noticeable in Jewish philanthropy a tendency to put charity on an official basis, under the supervision of reputable and responsible persons. The law codes abound in rules to this effect. Maimonides, in the twelfth century, knew of no Jewish community that was devoid of some type of philanthropic organization.

In Lithuania the solicitors and disbursers of charity were commonly the rabbi and the congregational officials or boards on which the community is represented. According to Israel Abrahams, "By the 13th century, philanthropic societies for various purposes made themselves apparent, but several centuries elapsed before the synagogue finally delegated most of its benevolent functions to semi-independent bodies."

In seventeenth-century Rome the official upon whom devolved the task of making collections was, under penalty of a fine, obligated to carry the collection box personally. The elimination of uncontrolled begging was always among Jewish philanthropic objectives. House-to-house canvassing was permitted in the Roman ghetto only on Fridays and on the middle days of festivals. Begging could not occur at all on the streets or in front of the synagogue.

A person under necessity of leaving home in search of maintenance as a scholar or in need of assistance in raising his daughter's dowry or ransoming or burying a relative would obtain from his local rabbi a certificate vouching for his probity.

This certificate had to be endorsed by a rabbi or by some high communal official in every locality in which solicitation was to be made. In Avignon six sous a day would be granted a transient having such a certificate.

Often the communal officials would do the collecting for the bearer of the certificate, thus obviating direct solicitation on his part. It appears that these certificates did not always prevent imposture.

We also find drastic measures for the deportation of beggars in the Lithuanian protocols of 1623. The Lithuanian synod of 1639 ruled that all beggars coming from Poland be peremptorily returned. The following year the ruling appeared that the entire district bear the costs of such deportation. Supplying mendicants with transportation rendered one liable to a fine.

Three communal representatives had to investigate a girl's eligibility for a communal dowry. Such girls had to be at least fifteen years of age. They had to be thrifty enough to renounce the wearing of silk garments. One regulation contains the requirement that candidates for communal dowries perform domestic service for three years prior to marriage, that is, from the age of twelve to the age of fifteen, and that they pay the surplus of their earnings to one of the communal representatives.

By 1618 in Rome the dowry privilege had been so abused by fathers who made sumptuous promises to suitors and then came to the society for help that a rule was passed rendering ineligible for help any father who had promised more than two hundred scudi.

Students in Lithuania who received communal stipends had to reciprocate by tutoring pupils younger than themselves; these pupils were to be examined periodically by the charity administrators with a view to testing the caliber of the student's pedagogy. Something is also said about the obligations of refugees to the communities that befriend them, such as contributing to the maintenance of the communal institutions as soon as circumstances permit.

Nor is it likely that practice departed very far from the law against too ready and too frequent ransoming of persons who would repeatedly sell themselves into captivity, especially as a means of satisfying their creditors. Similar was the law excluding from philanthropic benefits those who were guilty of extreme departures from ethical and ritual usages.

While the rendering of aid to non-Jews was a regular part of Jewish law and practice, the taking of aid from non-Jews was discountenanced.

On the whole, when a non-Jewish Englishman wrote, in 1676, regarding the contemporary Jews of Barbary, that they live "in a more mutual charity of alms than either Moor or Christian," his words were equally applicable to other countries and other centuries of Jewish life.

—A.C.

 ## Tracking Down the Yarmulke

It is strange that the word "yarmulke"—describing as it does the distinctive religious head covering of the Jew—should have such uncertain origin.

Polish and Russian sources trace it back for four centuries. The term occurs in early Hassidic literature, that is, in the eighteenth century, and it may also occur earlier. It was used in Eastern European countries, in the Ukraine, Lithuania, and Poland; but Dr. Shlomo Noble, research director of the Yiddish Scientific Institute (YIVO), states that he has heard it as far west as Frankfurt-am-Main.

Some believe that it is of Slavic origin, possibly Russian or Osman (Turkish). Other explanations trace it to Hebrew or German. The alleged Hebrew source is said to be *yere melakhim*, which means "fearing kings." For a possible German origin the word *Jahrmarkt* is adduced. This word—often dropping the final "t"—is used in Polish and Russian to describe a county fair. It has been suggested that the distinctive headgear of the Jew was called *yarmokke* or *yarmolke* because of its wearers' frequent attendance at fairs.

While etymology cannot rule out any of these explanations, it is evident that all of them suffer from one or another serious defect. The explanations that trace the word to Slavic tongues leave it without specific relation to Jews. We must keep in mind that the cap that finally was called yarmulke was not merely a head cover but a cap particularly connected with religious worship, and whose usage distinguished Jews from their neighbors.

The explanation using the German *Jahrmarkt*, while having a possible Jewish connection, has no religious connotation. The assumption that the Hebrew *yere*

melakhim is at the basis of its origin is labored and ill-founded. *Yere melakhim* would never refer to God and is not the type of term that, through frequent usage, might give rise to a popular derivative. It is a late and etymologically unsound use of unrelated terms, which is always striking at first sight but erroneous nonetheless. It reminds one of the "obvious" derivation of the Yiddish *davenen* from the English dawn.

A clue to the mystery is provided when we examine the distinctive headgear of the Jews, particularly that which was imposed upon them since the days of Pope Innocent III and Charles V, the Holy Roman Emperor. These caps, which often were connected to a cowl-like cape, were variously called *capucium, Judenhut, Gugelhut,* or *Kappe.* The term *Gugeln (cuclya)* was especially popular in Hungary, which, like Czechoslovakia, was an area where various languages met and where West and East traditionally influenced each other.

Occasionally the special Jewish headgear is also referred to as *bireta*, which is the common term for the small clerical hat. This is particularly significant, for it emphasizes the fact that probably the Jewish head covering was at times called by a term derived from Christian church usage.

All available pictures of Jewish headgear during the sixteenth and seventeenth centuries show a striking relation to one particular cap that had its origin among the clergy. This was the *amice* (or *almuce*), which covered head and shoulder and was worn by the priest until he arrived at the altar. The Latin word for *amice* was *almucia,* and most scholars agree that the German *Mütze* is derived from *almucia* or its related forms, *aumucia* and *armutia.*

The earliest German forms were *almutz* and *aremutz;* and there is also an interesting Portuguese variation, *mursa.* Since these forms go back to the thirteenth century, it is likely that they recall the original shape of the *almuce,* namely, a cap separate from the hood. At first only the clergy wore this garment, but in time it was taken over by the laity. It was then that *Mütze* in Germany, *mursa* in Portugal, and *mutch* in Scotland came into greater use.

The word *almucia* had a diminutive form, *almucella* or *amucella.* It should be borne in mind that the Latin pronunciation of the "c" varied considerably and was quite often consistently pronounced as a "k." It is suggested, therefore, that "the small *amice,*" or *armucella,* gave rise to the use of the word yarmulke. The transposition of the "l" and "c" is a common phenomenon in linguistic derivation. It appears plausible to assume that *almucia* was an oft-used term in medieval Germany; hence its adoption into everyday language, later taking the form of *Mütze.* This same process then gave rise to calling the small Jewish cap by this term; and the Jews who took their medieval German with them to Eastern lands probably also took the word *armucella* along. With them it traveled as far east as Turkey. We suggest that the Osman term came from the West, either through the mediation of the Jew or more directly in some similar way. It is entirely possible that the ultimate adoption of the word in its present popular form was hastened by a "re-inoculation" from Slavic or other languages; and it is equally possible that the word yarmulke came into prominence among the Jews because their neighbors used it to describe the Jewish cap.

We suggest, therefore, that the word yarmulke was derived from *armucella.* Not only is the etymology suggestive, but the original pictures lead us to the same conclusion. The *armucella* (or *almucia*) that gave rise to the German *Mütze,* the Portuguese *mursa,* and the Scottish *mutch* was thus also the source for the Jewish *yarmulke,* the Slavic *yermolka,* and probably also the Osman *yarmuluk.*

—W.G.P.

The Torah That Was Rescued by a Chandelier

In the black years of World War II, when synagogues in scattered parts of Europe were torched by the Nazis and their willing cohorts, Jews lost their lives while springing into blazing buildings to rescue the holy Scrolls of the Law—and, in doing so, they died *al kiddush ha-Shem.*

We will never know how many such events took place and who the martyrs were. Only a few of the incidents have come down to us from those evil days, as witnessed by survivors of the Holocaust.

There is, however, a happier side of the coin. In the large basement of a synagogue in England there are stored today hundreds of Sifrei Torah, rescued from the Nazi era and brought to safety in England. Most of them have been badly damaged, and a painstaking effort is under way to restore them, to make them kosher again so that they can be used in synagogues in various parts of the world where the Torah is read, studied, and loved.

One Viennese Jew, anticipating the infamous *Kristallnacht* in November 1938, when thousands of synagogues and Jewish communal buildings and privately owned stores were attacked and razed by the Nazis in Germany and Austria, succeeded in smuggling four Scrolls of the Law out of the synagogue, hiding them, and bringing them out to the refuge of America. These four scrolls are now read at weekly services in synagogues located in the United States and Israel.

Perhaps one of the most remarkable stories of a Sefer Torah rescued from the Nazi abominations has been told by Chief Rabbi Moses Rosen of Romania. During a visit to Israel, accompanying a whole group of Scrolls of the Law that the Romanian Government had permitted to be brought to Israel, Rabbi Rosen spoke at a dedication ceremony for a small synagogue to which one of the Torahs had been brought.

Facing the packed synagogue, Rabbi Rosen, his hand on the Sefer Torah that rested on the lectern of the *bimah,* recalled the life of that particular scroll.

"It was during the darkest days," he remembered. "Romanian disciples of Hitler had run wild in the streets of Bucharest, attacking Jews, Jewish-owned shops, synagogues, and Jewish communal buildings. Terror filled the streets and blood flowed in the gutters. A mob had entered one of the largest synagogues in Bucharest and had begun to ransack and destroy everything in sight, including the Sifrei Torah.

"Several hoodlums had thrown open the Holy Ark and had thrown the holy

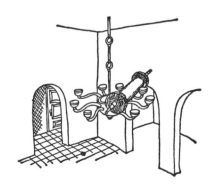

scrolls to the floor, ripping the sacred parchment, stomping on the Torahs, shouting obscenities. But the Torahs were strong; they were not easily destroyed. In a frenzy one rioter picked up a scroll and hurled it high into the air, confident that when it would fall to the floor of the building it would be smashed to smithereens.

"And that is when a miracle took place, for the Torah was caught in the arms of a large chandelier that dominated the room. As though it were a live thing, the chandelier would not let go of its precious cargo, and the hoodlum, gazing upward, perhaps felt that this was an omen. Instead of trying to climb to the chandelier and shake the Torah loose so that it would fall and be smashed, he retreated and let the Torah remain where it was, ensnared on the chandelier.

"And that is how the Torah in question remained for several days, until the madness died down. Synagogue members made their way to the desecrated building cautiously and began to restore what they could, to pick up the torn prayer books and the ripped *taleisim,* and that is when they saw the Torah on high, resting comfortably in the grip of the overhead chandelier.

"Working carefully and quietly, a ladder was brought to the sanctuary. While men held the ladder below to steady it, one Jew ascended and, with his heart beating fast, he cautiously untangled the Sefer Torah from the chandelier and brought it down safely. Their eyes brimming with tears, the congregants lovingly rerolled the Sefer, kissed it, and replaced it in the Holy Ark, marking it as a very special scroll that had been rescued from a wild pack.

"Years passed, conditions in Romania improved, and the Torah in question became a favorite of the congregation. But when permission was granted by the authorities to ship several hundred Sifrei Torah from the destroyed synagogues of Romania to the hundreds of new synagogues sprouting up all over Israel, the congregation decided to include that particular Sefer in the shipment.

"They felt that it had been saved for a purpose, and the purpose was to be used regularly, to be read from, to receive the love and devotion of new generations of Jews, and that is why it was shipped to Israel."

His voice faltering, Rabbi Rosen picked up the Torah, held it aloft, and proclaimed to a deeply moved congregation, "This is the same Torah that was brought down from the chandelier, and this is the same Torah that will now serve this congregation in Israel, now and for evermore."

In all, Rabbi Rosen succeeded in transferring from Romania's defunct and depopulated synagogues some three thousand Sifrei Torah to Israel. Visitors can find them in regular use in thousands of synagogues in towns and villages, in army camps and kibbutzim, through the length and breadth of Israel.

If the scrolls could talk, they might say, "We were accustomed to being read in the Ashkenazic Hebrew, but now we are being recited aloud in the beautiful modern Sephardic Hebrew. Our readers used to be Romanian Jews. Now some of our readers are Jews from Yemen or Kurdistan, some are uniformed chaplains in the Israeli Army, and others are new emigrants from Argentina, Russia, or America. It does not matter. Here in Israel the message that we have to give is being read aloud and with no fear, and that is what makes us so happy in our new home."

—D.C.G.

New York Once Had a Hebrew Daily

July 1979 marked the seventieth anniversary of the birth of *HaYom* (*Today*), the first Hebrew daily newspaper published in the United States, whose short-lived existence has seemingly been forgotten—except for a professor of Hebrew literature at the Jewish Theological Seminary who is doing his best to preserve its memory.

"My students are surprised to hear that such a vital newspaper existed here. In trying to show the way Jewish life developed in America, this source has been neglected entirely," said Prof. Zvulun Ravid recently in his Morningside Heights apartment as he pored over a bound volume containing yellowing, flaking copies of *HaYom.*

HaYom, named for a pioneering Hebrew newspaper from St. Petersburg, Russia, was founded by Moses Goldman, a Pinsk-born Hebraist and journalist who had immigrated to the United States in 1890. The first issue, selling for two cents, was published on July 18, 1909, from the paper's offices at 58 Canal Street.

HaYom's circulation was one thousand readers, Ravid said, but for financial reasons it ceased publication on November 5, 1909, after ninety issues. Goldman revived *HaYom* in 1913, but the paper folded again, this time after four months. Goldman died in 1918 and, according to Ravid, "very few people knew about his death . . . they didn't understand or appreciate his efforts at keeping the Hebrew language alive.

"*HaYom* offered guidelines on how to live in America and also fought for Jews who were living outside America," explained the gray-haired professor as he carefully flipped the well-worn copies of the four-page newspaper.

Among the issues in which *HaYom* became involved were championing the establishment of a *Kehillah* in New York and opposing immigration restrictions and the assimilationist tendencies of Jewish students at City College. Another time *HaYom* denounced as a "moral pogrom" an article in *McClure's* magazine that had accused one quarter of all Jewish women in New York of being prostitutes.

At the time Hebrew was spoken primarily by scholars, while Yiddish was the language of the Jewish masses. In fact, an international conference had been held in 1908 in Czernowitz at which Yiddish was proposed as the national language of the Jewish people. "Thus the creation of *HaYom* a year later was a slap in the face to all those who had proclaimed that Hebrew was dead," Ravid said.

"Goldman was constantly asked to raise the price of the newspaper to five cents so it would survive, but he refused because he felt it would have been too much money for the readers, who were mostly scholars and *yeshiva bocherim,*" Ravid related.

The crumbling bound volume in Ravid's possession was loaned to him by the Seminary. Ravid said he believed the only other copies of the newspaper in existence were in the New York Public Library and were "in even worse condition."

—A.E.

When Jews Quarrel

A cantor in New York sues a congregation for allegedly failing to pay him for services rendered during the High Holy Days. After the case has been partly tried, the justice of the city court recommends to the litigants that they take their controversy before the Jewish Conciliation Board of America, where the merits of both claims would be better understood.

A seventy-year-old woman complains that a plot that she purchased from a fraternal organization has been sold, and that someone else was buried on the coveted site. The case is heard by the Jewish Conciliation Board.

An eighty-year-old resident of Israel complains that a rabbi living in New York refuses to return a Torah scroll that he entrusted to him when the Nazis overran the town in Rumania in which they lived. The case is heard by the Board.

A young man, married just before he went into the army, returns after two years of combat to find that his wife and he are comparative strangers and are unable to assume the responsibilities of marriage. They turn to the Board.

These are but a few of the all-too-human cases and problems that come before the Jewish Conciliation Board of America, which for more than five decades has sought, without fanfare and with dignity and understanding, to resolve disputes and misunderstandings that arise in the Jewish community.

The Board was organized in 1920 when a serious problem of congestion existed in the courts of New York City, as in many other American communities, due to an accumulation of cases that followed the end of the First World War.

To help remedy these conditions, and because many Jewish problems were being aired in the public courts, a number of public-spirited Jewish residents of New York City banded together to form what is now the Jewish Conciliation Board.

This group felt that there were disputes in the Jewish community of such a nature that they should not come before the courts because they involved details of Jewish religious customs that a non-Jewish judge or jury could hardly understand and appreciate. Often the litigants were aged Jews who were unacclimated to the American environment; they therefore found the civil court a trying and embarrassing experience. Sometimes there were disputes affecting Jewish communal institutions that did not have to be aired in public courts.

The Board, in short, was organized to carry out the Jewish ideal of justice without the encumbrances of complicated legal procedure. It is interesting to observe that the movement for the adjudication of claims by agencies outside the civil courts has made tremendous strides in this country because it is founded upon real needs.

Our court procedures are expensive and take a long time. The procedure of the Jewish Conciliation Board is simple and direct. The complaint is registered with the executive secretary of the Board. Thereupon it is arranged to have both parties to the dispute appear with their respective witnesses at a fixed session of the Board. There is no fee or expense of any kind to the litigants.

At every session there are three judges: a rabbi, a businessman, and a jurist. Every case thus receives thorough consideration from several viewpoints. The litigants must sign an agreement to abide by the decision of the judges. This agreement is binding, pursuant to the Arbitration Laws of the State of New York.

The case is then heard. The litigants are permitted to present their stories in person, either in English or Yiddish. There are no lawyers to argue for them, no technical rules of procedure. The aim of the court is to adjudicate the disputes in the spirit of peace and mediation. Within a single afternoon it is possible to dispose of as many cases as would ordinarily take a week in the legal courts. The decision of the Board has the full sanction of the law, and a judgment may be entered thereon.

The bulk of the Board's work has been concerned with conflicts within benevolent, fraternal, and charitable organizations; claims for sick and endowment benefits; cantors, sextons, and Hebrew teachers asking for compensation; and disputes over cemetery graves and excessive charges for funerals.

Recently two distinct types of cases have gained prominence, namely, problems arising in the family unit, a result of emotional strains and tensions, and problems arising from the dissolution of old societies that have ceased functioning but have money and property that require just distribution.

The first of these problems is becoming increasingly difficult and challenging. Formerly it was a comparatively simple task to determine how much each child should contribute towards the support of aged parents or how much a husband should pay to his wife and children. But the problems that may confront the Board are not so easily adjudicated.

The financial problem is generally no longer the crux of the family dispute. It is, rather, the emotional problems among members of the family that cause the greatest concern. The Board has been able to grapple with these problems through increased social work. These services begin before these cases are brought to a hearing and continue long afterwards.

Many persons applying for help request that their cases not be called for a hearing, but rather that the matter be handled by a social worker, who is called upon to act as friend, adviser, teacher, and guide. Thus, many cases that ordinarily would have been heard at the Board's sessions are now heard and settled in the privacy of an office.

Cases settled in this manner seem to bring more lasting peace to the persons involved than a formal hearing. The Board has come a long way from its original conception of its responsibilities. It evinces today a deeper understanding of the emotional problems involved in disputes and the modern resources available for their amelioration.

The second type of case, relating to defunct societies and the distribution of their funds, is becoming increasingly frequent. In some instances many thousands of dollars are involved; sometimes a few Torahs or cemetery plots are the subject of controversy. In almost every instance no meetings have been held for many years and the funds are in the hands of one or two self-appointed trustees. Usually the Board sees to it that provision is made for the remaining members and families to receive proper interment at the time of their death, that the remaining assets should be converted into cash and distributed among worthy relief and other organizations, and that the holy articles be sent to Israel.

In twenty years the Board adjudicated and conciliated more than forty-two hundred cases. Six hundred leading rabbis, lawyers, jurists, and businessmen have served on its panels. It has probably saved the City and State of New York hundreds of thousands of dollars. The clientele of the Board has comprised chiefly an economically deprived portion of the Jewish population consisting of immigrants and as yet "un-Americanized" elements that have welcomed a tribunal where they could speak in Yiddish or German, and where they would be spared the emotional strain of appearing in a courtroom.

In measuring the value of the Board's work, one incidental aspect should not be overlooked. An examination of the cases that have come before the Board and a study of the decisions that have been rendered forms an instructive basis for determining the high ideals and traditions incorporated in the Jewish sense of justice.

—L.R.

 ## The Dinghy Comes Home

The amazing story began in August 1847 when Captain T. M. C. Symonds (later Admiral Symonds) of the H.M.S. *Spartan,* lying in Acre port, conceived the idea of tracing the course of the Jordan River to the Dead Sea. Lieutenant Thomas Howard Molyneux and three crew members volunteered for the expedition, and on August 20 the four men set off for Lake Tiberias, fifty kilometers away. Whoever they encountered en route must have blinked in amazement at the travelers, for strapped securely to the back of the camel that accompanied them was a stout little dinghy.

Unloading their boat on the lake, the crew sailed south. Often they had to drag their vessel along the riverbanks in places where the Jordan was impassable. A number of times they fought for their lives against bands of hostile Arabs. More dangerous than their human foes were the deadly anopheles mosquitos that bred in the dank swamps of the Jordan Valley. Molyneux came down with malaria.

The men finally reached the Dead Sea on September 3. (They little knew that an American expedition led by a Lieutenant Flint had preceded them by almost twenty years.) Molyneux and his men sailed about for two days on that steaming, lifeless body of water, taking soundings of up to 225 fathoms. The heat reached 130 degrees Fahrenheit as the men rowed across the great salt lake, 1,300 feet below sea level, the lowest point in the world.

Although he managed to return to the *Spartan,* Molyneux died of his fever one month later. Captain Symonds, grieving for the young lieutenant whom he had unwittingly sent to his death, took the dinghy home with him as a private memorial to the young officer. On the boat he inscribed: "This boat was built in 1836, visited Acre, Cana of Galilee, Lake Tiberias, Dead Sea, Jerusalem, Jaffa—1847." After his death one of his descendants turned it into the roof of a summer cottage.

The mystery writer Agatha Christie heard of the incident. In one of her novels, set in southern England, she alluded to the quaint old summer house

roofed by a dinghy that was once used by the British Navy to explore the Jordan River and the Dead Sea.

One of Miss Christie's fans wrote to Dr. Ze'ev Vilnay, a well-known Jerusalem authority on Holy Land lore, who in turn passed the information on to Avraham Ben-Eli, director of the National Maritime Museum in Haifa. Stirred by the possibility of locating the dinghy, Ben-Eli left for England, where he contacted septuagenarian Jonathan Bunt, a Christian Zionist, who served as the honorary secretary of the Devon and Cornwall districts of the British Zionist Federation. Bunt, who lived not far from Torquay, scoured the area and finally located the boat on the property of an elderly widow.

There was the dinghy, serving as the roof of a small house. The vessel had been neglected and was almost falling apart. A local boatbuilder agreed to repair it, and after much persuasion the widow was induced to part with it.

Ben-Eli enlisted the help of General Mordechai Makleff, former Chief of Staff, who later served as managing director of the Dead Sea Works. Ben-Eli proposed to Makleff that the dinghy become the central exhibit of the museum that the Dead Sea Works intended to build in Sodom. Makleff agreed to finance the purchase, repair, and transport of the dinghy to its former port of call.

The little boat has now arrived in Israel and is housed temporarily in the Haifa National Maritime Museum until its final berth is completed. A trim little vessel, it conjures up memories of one of the most colorful, although almost totally unknown, expeditions in the history of the British Navy.

But had it not been for Agatha Christie, the dinghy would have rotted away unremembered, serving as the roof in a forgotten village in southern England.

—E.W.

 The Mizrah: Compass of the Heart

"From the rising of the sun unto the going down thereof, the name of the Lord is to be praised" (Psalms, 113:3).

When a Jew prays, said our sages of blessed memory, he should face towards Jerusalem. "And if a worshiper is unable to face towards Jerusalem, let him concentrate mentally on the Holy of Holies" (*Mishna, Berakhot, 4.5*). A worshiper should "turn in his mind to the Holy of Holies. Thus will all Jews turn their hearts towards one place." For the pious Jew whose sense of direction may be weak, even though his soul yearns for Jerusalem three times a day, the *mizrah* (east) plaque hung on the eastern walls of synagogues and homes is a compass of the heart, always pointing to Zion.

The *mizrah* has developed into a colorful and imaginative branch of Jewish folk art. Sometimes the *mizrah* was the most beautiful art object in the Jewish home. Jewish craftsmen made use of standard Jewish symbols, although non-Jewish influences can be seen in many *mizrahs*.

Roaring lions and a freemason's compass, the prophet Jeremiah among the ruins, roosters with bright red combs, Moses and his brother, Aaron, and secular figures, European art styles and traditional Jewish designs, motifs from church architecture and imagined pictures of the Temple in Jerusalem—these have all been incorporated into the fanciful folk art of the *mizrah*.

In biblical times the Hebrew word *mizrah* signified the "rising of the sun." Its connotation changed significantly, however, with the destruction of the Jerusalem Temple and the subsequent dispersion of the exiles.

Recalling the biblical custom of facing toward the Temple during prayer (Solomon's prayer in I Kings 8:34,44, and the prayer of Daniel in Daniel 6:11), the rabbis of the Talmud decreed that Jews living in the diaspora should direct their prayers to Eretz Yisrael; if in Israel, to Jerusalem; and if in Jerusalem, to the site of the Temple.

For those living west of Jerusalem the term *mizrah* thenceforth indicated not merely a direction of a compass point but, more importantly, the very location of the once flourishing and now longed-for Temple.

The architecture of most early synagogues anticipated the function of the *mizrah* plaque. Synagogues situated east of Jerusalem, such as the third-century c.e. chapel at Dura-Europos, placed the Torah niche in the west wall of the building so that congregants facing the Ark would automatically face Jerusalem. Likewise, synagogues constructed in the Galilee were built on a north-south axis. The sixth-century c.e. synagogue at Beth Alpha was entered on the north side precisely so that worshipers, passing through the portal, would literally approach the Torah at the south wall and metaphorically approach Jerusalem and the Temple site.

Placed on the east wall of the home, the *mizrah* plaque serves to orient the Jewish home on a symbolic axis towards Jerusalem. In European homes where a plaque was not affordable, the same effect was sometimes achieved by skipping a brick or leaving a small portion of the east wall unplastered.

A form analogous to the *mizrah*, the *shivti*, developed in synagogue art during the eighteenth century. Bearing a quotation from Psalms 16:8, whence its name is derived (*Shivti Adonai lenegdi tamid*—I have set the Lord always before me), the *shivti* was usually hung over the cantor's reading stand on the east wall of the synagogue near the Ark.

In North Africa yet another form of the *mizrah-shivti* evolved, called simply menorah for the obvious reason that its dominant motif was a seven-branched candelabrum. The design of the North African menorah-*mizrah* usually took the form of a parchment cutout laid over a metallic paper backing. Often the entire text of Psalm 67 would be inked in microscript inside the narrow branches of the menorah.

The form of the European *mizrah* quite often played upon the etymology of the word itself. Very often the plaque would bear the verse from Psalm 113:3, or a portion of it, which reinforces the association of the *mizrah* to prayer while recalling the original meaning of the word itself. Sometimes a verse was included as well that made the word *mizrah* an acronym for *mitzad ze ruah haim*—from this direction (the east) is the spirit of life.

Since the origins of the *mizrah* are traced to a remembrance of the Jerusalem Temple, it is not surprising that the design elements of these plaques often include visual references to the Temple building, Temple implements, the city of Jerusalem, and prominent figures in Jewish history.

A *mizrah-shivti* from nineteenth-century Germany, for example, includes in its iconography the dominant figures of Moses and Aaron, whose priestly descendants served in the Temple; symbols for the Twelve Tribes; the seven-branched Temple menorah; and the Ark of the Covenant flanked, in traditional manner, by the image of the Western Wall, the only remaining portion of the original Temple.

The architecture of the Temple is often featured in the traditional *mizrah*. A paper cutout *shivti* crafted by artist Phillip Cohen in 1861 depicts a portal flanked by two freestanding pillars. Apart from the charming assertion of Americana embodied in the American flags that sit atop the pillars, these columns clearly recall the two pillars, "Yakhin" and "Boaz," that stood outside the edifice of Solomon's Temple. The suggestion of the Temple is further strengthened by the inscription within the portal itself. In translation it reads: "This is the gateway to the Lord."

A most remarkable *mizrah* made in Cincinnati, Ohio, around 1850 repeats many of the motifs previously described and adds some surprising elements. Here are Temple implements (menorah, Ark, incense, altar); Moses and Aaron; even an American eagle! Among the multitude of items that seem to float through the design are a *mezuza,* a pair of *tefillin,* a *lulav* branch, a Torah scroll—all decidedly Jewish objects—and then a compass, a level, a plumb line, and a trowel! These last items, the symbols of the fraternal order of Freemasons, are not at all inconsistent with the iconography of the *mizrah.* Presumably the artist was a Mason; in any event, the symbols themselves reflect upon the Masonic tradition that Jerusalem was the birthplace of the order and that arcane Masonic rituals descended from the building of the Solomonic Temple.

While the *mizrah* is primarily a focusing lens, directing one's prayers eastward, it has also served multiple purposes in Jewish ritual life. One *mizrah* in the Hebrew Union College Skirball Museum collection in Los Angeles doubles as an *omer* counter for use during the seven weeks between Passover and Shavuot. The *mizrah* was often hung in the *sukkah* during Sukkot to give a feeling of domesticity to the temporary structure. A watercolor *shivti* in Vienna shows seven huts for each day of Sukkot and bears prayers specific to the holiday.

Both *mizrah* and *shivti* forms have doubled as amulets to ward off evil spirits. Seen as protective devices for the home and synagogue, such plaques usually contain cabbalistic phrases and standard protective devices from the Bible. When originating in North Africa, they often bear the image of the *hamsa* or hand, which is thought, among Oriental Jews, to protect one from the evil eye.

The *mizrah* as a Jewish art form is rich in symbolism, abundant in historical and traditional references, and diverse in character, style, and place of origin. It has graced the walls of Jewish homes and synagogues in Holland, France, Germany, Italy, Poland, Russia, North Africa, and the United States. The *shivti* form, too, not limited to an easterly placement, has evolved in many Oriental Jewish communities, including those of Persia and India.

Mizrah plaques were made with a wide range of materials: lithographed or engraved in the great European printing centers of Holland and Germany; paper cutouts as a folk art in the Jewish communities of Eastern Europe, where the craft of paper filigree was familiar to the general populace; embroidered in colorful threads on perforated cardboard canvases; and elegantly painted with the formal symmetry of a neoclassical style.

An unusual Viennese *mizrah* in triptych form has been painted directly on carved wood, while a more modern *mizrah* by Ludwig Wolpert takes the form of an enameled plate bearing only the brass letters for the Hebrew word meaning east.

The *mizrah,* in its infinite variety, is a perfect example of *hiddur mitzvah*—the Talmudic dictum to observe the commandments in the most beautiful way possible. The sages of the Talmud urged us to "make a beautiful *sukkah,* a beautiful *lulav,* a beautiful *shofar,* beautiful *tzitzit,* and a beautiful Scroll of the Law." Psalm 29 puts it even more succinctly when it tells us to "worship the Lord in the beauty of holiness."

The *mizrah* is the compass of the heart, giving direction to thought; its beauty and the ingenuity of its design affirm the creative resources and spiritual vitality of a tradition rich in allusion and self-interpretation.

—A.M.G.

 ## The Case of the Stolen Torah

Naive popular beliefs and practices hallowed by their antiquity are at times reflected in the modern courtroom, often in unexpected ways. Thus, a judge may be faced with a case that, superficially, is quite simple, calling only for an application of the law to the facts, but suddenly, out of the confused legal argument, there emerges a revelation of the human heart that throws an entirely new light on the case and on the individuals involved.

An old woman was brought to court on a charge of theft. This is a fairly common charge and rarely arouses any special interest. But this case was different. Here, in fact, was an unusual situation: a pious old woman had transgressed against a clearcut legal and religious prohibition. In the depth of night she had stolen a Torah out of the Holy Ark in a synagogue. Has such a thing ever been heard of? She did not even deny the charge that with a few pennies she had bribed a poor Jew to enter the synagogue after the *Ma'ariv* service, remove the Torah from the Ark, and give it to her. But what had brought her to this strange crime? The following was her story.

"My husband and I spent most of our lives in the Diaspora. We had no children, but we lived together in peace and contentment. Our one wish was to go to the Holy Land. All our lives we saved every penny and at last, in our old age, when we had accumulated a modest sum, we gathered our belongings and came here. We did not have to worry about a livelihood, thank God, and hoped to spend our last days peacefully and quietly in the land of our fathers. But we did want to leave behind some memorial to our name. So we decided to engage an expert *sofer* (scribe) to write two Torah scrolls for us, one in my husband's name and one in mine. Our names were inscribed on the silver plates that decorate the scrolls and were also embroidered on their velvet mantles. Joyfully we donated our scrolls to a synagogue, and every Sabbath and holiday we went there to hear the Reading of the Law from our Torah. This was my only pleasure. Then suddenly some evil spirit overtook my husband. I do not know why or how such a great misfortune befell me. All at once he began to come to me with all sorts of complaints and grievances, scolding me for every little thing, annoying and harassing me constantly. In short, I had lost favor in his eyes. One day he left the house, took all his belongings with him, and went to live somewhere else."

Here the old woman could no longer control her tears. Weeping, she continued. "We two no longer live under one roof, and now I don't want my scroll to stand alongside his scroll. I had to take it out of the synagogue secretly because the synagogue officials have been influenced by him and refused to return it to me. With God's help I shall give my scroll to another synagogue."

There was no doubt that in the eyes of the law she had committed a crime. But what is the dead letter of the law against the loneliness of an old woman who has nothing left but a scroll that she guards with jealous love, like an only child? No, it is not easy to measure this crime against paragraph such and such of the criminal code.

—S.Z.C.

 Jew, Go Home!

This editorial was written following a rash of swastika and other anti-Semitic defilements of Jewish public buildings in the United States that stirred public opinion.

"Jew, go home!"

Well, now, this is nothing new. Never in the past have you ever taken this gentle suggestion to move on.

But suppose just this once you thought that this expression of a few sick people actually expressed the conviction of all the people in this wonderful land of ours, and all of you started to pack your bags and leave for parts unknown.

Just before you leave, would you do me a favor? Would you leave your formula to the Salk vaccine with me before you leave? You wouldn't be so heartless as to let my children contract polio.

And would you please leave your knack for government, and politics, and persuasion, and literature, and good food, and fun and love, and all those things? And would you please leave with me the secret to your drive to succeed, to make money? I need more.

And please have pity on us, please show us the secret of how to develop such geniuses as Einstein, Steinmetz, and oh so many others who have helped us all. After all, we owe you most of the A-bomb, most of our rocket research, and perhaps the fact that we are alive today instead of looking up from our chains and from our graves to see an aging, happy Hitler drive slowly by in one of our Cadillacs.

On your way out, Jews, will you do me just one more favor? Will you please drive by my house and pick me up, too?

I'm just not sure I could live too well in a land where you weren't around to give as much as you have given us.

If you ever have to leave, love goes with you, democracy goes with you, everything I and all my buddies fought for in World War II goes with you, and God goes with you.

Just pull up in front of my house, slow down and honk, because, so help me, I'm going with you, too.

—W.A.

The Rabbi and the Wafer

The chaplain in the armed forces of the United States bears a heavy burden. He counsels. He is available to men of all faiths. He conducts religious services for the men of his denomination, but in the event that there are no chaplains to lead those of other persuasions, he is duty-bound to arrange for such services. He is, in the last analysis, spiritual leader to all men and women regardless of race, color, or creed. All these facts are stated and implied in the various manuals of the armed forces. He symbolizes the democratic ideal of unity in diversity in the American way of life.

Sometimes this spirit of ecumenism can create theological, psychological, moral, and even gastronomic problems for the chaplain. A Catholic or Protestant chaplain does not compromise his religious philosophy if, for example, he arranges for a Passover Seder and eats the matzoh. Nor does he break with the traditions of his faith if he recites the *Shema* or reads from the Psalms, which are found in abundance in the prayer books at a service for Jewish servicemen. After all, Judaism is the mother religion and all that is basic in the Jewish faith should create no moral problem for the Christian. It is somewhat different with the Jew, as a true experience in the chaplaincy would indicate.

It was 1943. The month escapes me, since seasons of the year become blurred into one succession of rains, williwaws (winds whose velocity is as high as most tropical hurricanes), sleet, slush, and muddy tundra. So it could have been spring or autumn—or even summer or winter. There was a group of men in one of the islands of the Aleutian chain. It probably was either Amchitka or Attu. These men, all Lutherans, were temporarily without the services of their chaplain. Some units were being shipped out at that time and their chaplains were moving with them. This left the Protestant chaplaincy depleted. An officer among the Lutherans stationed near the field artillery battalion to which I was attached, a good friend and son of a Lutheran minister, came to see me in my subterranean habitat. "Padre," he said, "you've got to help us. I will assist you in getting the men together. I will do the communion service since I've seen my father do it on occasion. We need your assistance in arranging for the service." This was a legitimate request of any chaplain.

It was a miserable Sunday morning—bleak, cold, windy. But here I was at a Lutheran service. The portable organ issued by the government was placed in front of the improvised chapel. In my desire to be of assistance I volunteered to play the hymns. Here was I, sitting at the organ, pedaling my feet in perpetual motion (no motion, no sound), and my officer friend was leading the singing and reciting the prayers.

Then the trauma of my life occurred! He began to serve the little cups of grape juice, a sacred symbol in Christian theology. Since I was playing the organ with both hands, he figured he would not offer the "wine" to me. So he passed me by. A moment or two later, however, he distributed the wafers representing the body of the founder of Christianity. He walked over and, in the sight of the GIs, he pushed a wafer into my mouth.

What to do? I was playing with my hands, pedaling with my feet, but my heart sank, as did my intestines. How is a rabbi, who is doing his duty as a chaplain and is facing the most challenging experience of his spiritual life, to react? Thousands of years of Jewish history, most of it tragic, flashed through my mind. I did not know as yet what Buber had written about religions as "receptacles into which the spirit of man is fitted. Each of them has its origin in a separate revelation . . . with myths and rites." My lips were the "receptacles" and what was being "fitted" was a wafer. I swallowed the wafer.

It appears that I survived psychologically and physically. There are, no doubt, psychoneurotic tendencies on my part that are not unrelated to this experience. On occasion I have relived the shock in dreams. Above all, there remains the memory of the mystical representation of the body of the founder of another religion being forced into the mouth of a rabbi who was the son of rabbis.

—E.T.S.

The Man Who Brought Hope and Love

Everyone who knew him loved him. He had about him an aura of warmth, love, goodness, openness seldom encountered in our fast-paced, often superficial, society. In a world of double-talk, he spoke plainly and honestly. In his own life, he was a huge success, for every person with whom he ever came into contact was touched by him, and thought of him affectionately. When he died the world lost a very rare human being.

In his own life, he was a one-man lesson in contemporary Jewish history. And his story is worthy of telling, for he added to his life those basic precepts of Jewish teaching that so few people attain. Without ever really knowing about the legendary *lamed vavniks*—those 36 righteous men for whose sake the world continues to exist—he was, throughout his lifetime, one of those righteous people.

Sam, as everyone called him, was born in Czarist Russia. Unlike so many of his fellow Jews, he was not raised in the traditional *shtetl*, but was brought up in Moscow, with servants and governesses in attendance. Russian, not Yiddish, was his mother tongue.

When the Bolshevik revolution erupted, Jews fled, and Sam fled too, arriving in Cuba, and finding work as a storekeeper. Still a young man, separated from his parents, sisters, a large family of cousins, he made the best of things. He learned Spanish, and made friends. He always made friends, for he was born with an innate love for God's creatures.

After a few years, when he realized that his sisters and parents would not be able to leave the Soviet Union and join him, he decided to come to America, to rejoin the many cousins he knew had taken up residence in the New York area. The immigration laws were tough, and he had no entry visa to the U.S. So, one day he simply boarded a United States-bound vessel, landed at New Orleans, bluffed his way past the authorities, and, without a word of English (or Yiddish), made his way north, to New York, in search of family.

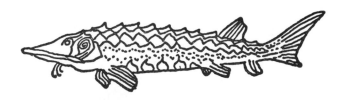

His cousins greeted him warmly, and set about helping him establish himself. One cousin set about teaching him Yiddish, without which it was felt he could not survive in New York; another went out in search of a suitable bride. Soon enough, he married, and his father-in-law helped him get started as the owner of a grocery store. The marriage bloomed, and soon a daughter was born and was named for his father, and later, another daughter. His customers became his friends, and everyone knew that in Sam they had a friend.

Time moved along. Sam was a happy man. He had a family, a business, and many friends. He tried to maintain correspondence with his sisters in the U.S.S.R., but they discouraged him; they were fearful of the authorities, who frowned on anyone with an American connection.

When his father-in-law died, Sam moved to the Brownsville section of Brooklyn, then a major center of Jewish life, and took over his store. His elder daughter, now grown, met and married a fine young man, and in the course of time gave birth to a daughter of her own. Sam's life was good: a loving family, and a first grandchild. He made a living, never complaining of the long hours. He had mastered Yiddish well enough to read the Yiddish daily, and now bought himself a *tallis* and a *siddur*, and began to learn the rudiments of Jewish religious life. He legalized his status and became a citizen.

And then, his world collapsed. The neighborhood changed; crime became rampant, and he could not remain as storekeeper. His elder daughter, in giving birth to a second child, died in the delivery room. He mourned and grieved, but would not let life beat him down. At the age of 65, he found work as a messenger-mail clerk in the office of an American Jewish organization supporting the Technion-Israel Institute of Technology. Before stepping into that office, it is doubtful that he had ever seen a typewriter, or a postage meter, or a mimeograph machine. But he learned swiftly, and became a hard-working, dedicated staff member, making friends all the time.

It took him a little time to understand the full nature of the organization that he worked for, but when he fully comprehended that he was involved in a program that provided Israel with future generations of engineers and scientists, a whole new dimension of life opened up for him. He seemed to live life on a higher plane, cognizant of the fact that his work in the mailroom helped to contribute to Israel's security and survival. That knowledge gave him an added measure of self-esteem, and a feeling that he was helping to improve the lot of the Jewish people.

Every day of his life he seemed to go forth with a desire to be helpful to another person. If someone needed a few dollars for a few days, Sam was there; if he knew of an eligible young man and an eligible young lady, he set about seeking to make an introduction between them; he received from a Soviet immigrant news that his sisters were well, and that bolstered him.

His younger daughter married, and he and his son-in-law became like father and son. Whatever pain he lived with because of the passing of his elder daughter, it never showed. He showered his younger daughter, and the two children of his deceased daughter, and his son-in-law, and his ex-son-in-law, and those who came into contact with him with love. His closest friends knew that he was a rare person.

At a seventy-fifth birthday party, his innumerable friends and relatives celebrated and sang his praises. The Technion organization, in honor of his 10th year of service, voted to send him to Israel, to see for himself what he had helped achieve.

But he never went. He fell ill, and his illness persisted for nearly two years. And when visitors came to the hospital to see him, he was always smiling, trying to make it easy for them. The nurses and his fellow patients loved him, for he brought a ray of hope and love into their lives.

He died in his seventy-seventh year, and will be remembered always. Like Moses, he never made it to the Promised Land. His life was a page of living Jewish history of our time.

—D.C.G.

JUDAICA * JUDAICA * JUDAICA * JUDAICA * JUDAICA * JUDAICA

FROM HIPPOCRENE

1,201 QUESTIONS
AND ANSWERS
ABOUT JUDAISM

David C. Gross

Now in its third edition, this book has distinguished itself as one of our bestselling Judaica books of all times and was a Book-of-the-Month Club selection. Filled with fun and fascinating facts, the former two editions received rave reviews.
328 pages
0-7818-0050-1 $11.95 pb

"Ideal for busy people seeking ready answers on the basic questions....the amount of information packed into this one volume is amazing..."
—Rabbi Alexander Shindler, Pres., Union of Hebrew Congregations

"A kaleidoscopic vision of the rich heritage of Judaism."
—Rabbi Norman Lamm, Pres., Yeshiva University

All prices subject to change.
Order directly from HIPPOCRENE BOOKS by sending a check or money order for the price of the book, plus $4.00 shipping and handling for the first book, and $.50 for each additional book to: HIPPOCRENE BOOKS, 171 MADISON AVE., NEW YORK, NY 10016.

NEW FROM HIPPOCRENE
*A POWERFUL WORK ADDRESSING THE MOST COMPELLING
ISSUES OF CONTEMPORARY JUDAISM*

WHY REMAIN JEWISH?
David C. Gross

One of America's premier Jewish authors tackles the number one issue facing the American Jewish community—the large number of young Jewish people, teens and young adults, who are abandoning Judaism and the Jewish community. The high rate of intermarriage—now exceeding 50% of all marriages involving American Jews—along with the significant number of Jews who convert to another religion, missionary sect or cult, has caused a widespread feeling of dismay and sorrow throughout the Jewish community as a result of these losses.

Why Remain Jewish presents a wide range of arguments, facts and figures, and historical and contemporary insights designed to reverse the current trend. The book shows young people that Judaism is a religion and a way of life that brings fulfillment and serenity to its practitioners, and adds a meaningful dimension to their lives; and that being Jewish is a glorious, lifelong commitment to intellectual growth and ethical insight.

244 pages
0-7818-0216-4 $9.95 pb

All prices subject to change.

Order directly from HIPPOCRENE BOOKS by sending a check or mail order for the price of the book, plus $4.00 shipping and handling for the first book, and $.50 for each additional book to: HIPPOCRENE BOOKS, 171 MADISON AVE., NEW YORK, NY 10016